Praise for the Unabridged Edition of

The Hidden History of the Human Race

by Michael A. Cremo and Richard L. Thompson

"The book is a detective novel as much as a scholarly *tour de force*. But the murderer is not the butler. Neither is the victim a rich old man with many heirs. The victim is Man himself, and the role of the assassin is played by numerous scientists. The book takes the case to court, and asks the reader to judge for himself."

—Dr. Mikael Rothstein, University of Copenhagen, Denmark

"A remarkably complete review of all the evidence concerning human origins, including the evidence that has been ignored because it does not fit the dominant paradigm."

—Dr. Phillip E. Johnson, University of California at Berkeley,
author of *Darwin on Trial*

"If it stimulates professional reinvestigation of reports not fitting the current paradigm on human evolution, this book will have contributed to the advancement of knowledge of the history of mankind."

—Dr. Siegfried Scherer, Biologist,
Technical University of Munich, Germany

"A weighty, eye-opening exposé of scientific cover-ups . . . documents the real evidence about human origins, with a researcher and scientist joining forces to examine how inherent prejudice has affected the research establishing evolution. The authors gather a wealth of arguments and facts to help readers rethink human origins and history: they probe the key moments of archaeological discovery and how these finds were regarded. Over eight years of researching results in a controversial challenge in conventional thinking, making for an impressive, scholarly work."

—Diane C. Donovan, *The Midwest Book Review*

"What an eye-opener! I didn't realize how many sites and how much data are out there that don't fit modern concepts of human evolution. . . . I predict the book will become an underground classic."

—Dr. Virginia Steen-McIntyre, Geologist

"Michael Cremo and Richard Thompson are to be congratulated on spending eight years producing the only definitive, precise, exhaustive and complete record of practically all the fossil finds of man, regardless of whether they fit the established scientific theories or not. To say that the research is painstaking is a wild understatement. No other book of this magnitude and caliber exists. It should be compulsory reading for every first year biology, archeology, and anthropology student—and many others too! The book is entertaining and scholarly—a rare combination. . . . This book deserves to provoke discussion and controversy. It should not be swept aside or ignored."

—John H. Davidson, in *International Journal
of Alternative and Complementary Medicine*

"A new book penetrates the murky establishment tunnel. Primarily it explains and denounces the vicious efforts of the academic establishment to protect its outmoded *status quo*. It exposes the outrageous methods— and intense efforts to bury (literally and figuratively) evidence. . . . fascinating, though depressing tales of academic misdeed."

—Col. W.R. Anderson, President, Leif Ericson Society

"A teeth-rattling new hypothesis has been proposed in *The Hidden History of the Human Race* . . . what you have done is to prove the case by giving 'chapter and verse'; the rest of us—those who have tried to use the scientific method with existing archeological reports—knew what had been happening, but none of us had proved it on the massive scale that you have."

—Jean Hunt, President, Louisiana Mounds Society

"Cremo and Thompson have launched a startling attack on our whole picture of human origins and the way that we've arrived at that picture; not only is the evidence impugned, but also the scientific method of handling it . . . It might be thought that detailed material on anomalously dated flint tools, broken bones, and fragmentary skeletons might not make the most absorbing reading, but by providing the human controversies as well, the authors tell a gripping story."

—Steve Moore, *Fortean Times*

"If we imagine the history of humanity as a giant museum, containing all knowledge on this topic, then we shall find that several of the rooms of this museum have been locked. Scientists have locked away the facts that contradict the generally accepted picture of history. Michael A. Cremo and Richard L. Thompson have, however, opened many of the locked doors and allowed laymen as well as scientists to see inside. Even scientists have been influenced, and rightly so. *The Hidden History of the Human Race* compels the world of science to enter new territories and calls into question many revered theories about humanity and human history."

—Walter J. Langbein, *PARA* magazine, Austria

"I have recently completed reading a copy of Michael Cremo & Richard Thompson's fascinating book, and found it to be comprehensive and above all, intellectually stimulating. Their in-depth research efforts are impressive. Having conducted nearly 30 years of intensive research work on this very subject myself, I can say without hesitation that this encyclopedic collection of 'misfit' anthropologic discoveries is about the most convincing I have ever digested."

—Ron C. Calais, Archivist of Evidence for Human Antiquity

"I find the entire gamut of human origins and prehistory has been brought out in one single comprehensive volume, a task few people can achieve. I congratulate you for writing this excellent reference book, which will act as a catalyst for further research on a subject of immense interest, not only to scholars and students but also laymen."

—Dr. K. N. Prasad, Former Director of the Geological Survey of India and former President of the Archeological Society of India.

"This is a careful piece of scholarship about a fascinating subject, and I am confident that it will become a classic, in print for many years."

—Dr. Jean Burns, Physicist

"A work of thoroughgoing scholarship and intellectual adventure. It ascends and descends into the realms of the human construction of scientific 'fact' and theory: postmodern territories that historians, philosophers, and sociologists of scientific knowledge are investigating with increasing frequency . . . With exacting research into the history of paleoanthropological discovery, Cremo and Thompson zoom in on the epistemological crisis of the human fossil record, the process of disciplinary suppression, and the situated scientific handling of 'anomalous evidence' to build persuasive theory and local institutions of knowledge and power."

—Dr. Pierce Flynn, Sociologist,
California State University, San Marcos

"I enjoyed your iconoclastic presentation . . . Best wishes for your bold reinterpretive enterprise."

—Dr. Roger Wescott, President, International Society
for the Comparative Study of Civilizations

"I recently finished reading the book and would like to congratulate you and thank you for writing it. . . . I am particularly grateful to you for bringing out the misinformation which comes across from the establishment."

—Thomas A. Dorman, M.D., Member Royal College of Physicians (UK)

"You have done a marvelous job, and I congratulate you. Thanks for this magnificent source book."

—Dr. George Carter, Archeologist

"Written for the nonspecialist and specialist alike, it is bound to become a landmark in the literature on human evolution. Scrupulously researched . . . it is expertly crafted in a flowing style that invites readers onward in their exploration of 'the hidden history of the human race.'"

—Lori Erbs, Biological Librarian, U.S. Forestry Service,
Forestry Sciences Laboratory, Juneau, Alaska

"It is truly wonderful and provocative. Congratulations on such an excellent piece of work!"

—Dr. Benetta Jules-Rosette, Professor of Sociology,
University of California at San Diego

"I view this book as a challenging and encouraging piece of work. I believe the authors reveal the interdisciplinary nature of the inquiry into the history of the human race. To solve the issues it raises, we need the integrated efforts of archeologists, historians, sociologists, philosophers, scholars of religion, and others. Many of us, scholars who inquire into those issues, develop severe cases of hardening of the categories. *Hidden History* reminds us that we oversimplify or forget the conceptual complexity that lies behind terms like 'fact' or 'datum.'"

—Gene C. Sager, Professor of Philosophy, Palomar College, California

"All the reasons and evidence why modern humans are not rather recent, but most ancient."

—Cyprian Broodbank, in *Antiquity*

Adverse Criticism from Establishment Scientists

"Your book is pure humbug and does not deserve to be taken seriously by anyone but a fool. Sadly, there are some, but that's a part of selection and there is nothing that can be done."

—Richard Leakey, Anthropologist

"A must for anyone interested in keeping up with goofy, popular anthropology; it is a veritable cornucopia of dreck."

—Jonathan Marks, *American Journal of Physical Anthropology*

"To have modern human beings . . . appearing a great deal earlier, in fact at a time when even simple primates did not exist as possible ancestors, would be devastating not only to the accepted pattern. It would be devastating to the whole theory of evolution."

—W. W. Howells, Physical Anthropologist

THE
HIDDEN
HISTORY
OF THE
HUMAN
RACE

THE
HIDDEN
HISTORY
OF THE
HUMAN
RACE

Michael A. Cremo
—AND—
Richard L. Thompson

BHAKTIVEDANTA
BOOK PUBLISHING
LOS ANGELES

Permission credits:

Figure 2.2, "Patterns of grooves and ridges produced by a serrated shark tooth moving along the serface of a whale bone," is from *Journal of Paleontology* (1982, 56:6). Used with permission.

Figure 5.9, "A Folsom blade embedded in the lower surface of a travertine crust from Sandia Cave, New Mexico," is reprinted by permission of the Smithsonian Institution Press from *Smithsonian Miscellaneous Collections*; Vol. 99, no. 23. © Smithsonian Institution, Washington, D. C. October 15, 1941. plate 7.

Figures 3.3 and 4.7, the drawings of stone tools from Olduvai Gorge, Tanzania, are from *Olduvai Gorge* by Mary Leakey (1971) and are reprinted by permission of the Cambridge University Press.

Figures 5.5–7, the drawings of stone tools from Sheguiandah, Canada, are from *The Canadian Field-Naturalist* (1957, vol. 71). Used with permission.

Readers interested in the subject matter of this book are invited to correspond with the authors at:

Bhaktivedanta Book Publishing, Inc.
3764 Watseka Avenue
Los Angeles, CA 90034
Or visit www.mcremo.com

Printing history (softbound edition):
First printing, 1999
Second printing, 1999
Third printing, 2001
Fourth printing, 2002
Fifth printing, 2005
Sixth printing, 2007

Published simultaneously in the United States of America and Canada by Bhaktivedanta Book Publishing, Inc.

Distributed exclusively by Torchlight Publishing, Inc.
P. O. Box 52, Badger, CA 93603
www.torchlight.com

Cataloging-in-Publication Data
Cremo, Michael A., 1948–
    The Hidden History of the Human Race: Major Scientific Coverup Exposed
    Michael A. Cremo, Richard L. Thompson. — 1st ed.
        p.   cm.
    Popular condensed version of: Forbidden Archeology.
    Includes bibliographical references and index.
    ISBN 0-89213-325-2 (S/cover): $15.95
    1. Anthropology, Prehistoric. 2. Human evolution. I. Thompson, Richard L.
II. Cremo, Michael A. 1948–Forbidden Archeology. III. Title.
GN743.C84   1994   94-15720
573.2--dc20   CIP

Dedicated to

His Divine Grace
A.C. Bhaktivedanta Swami Prabhupāda

oṁ ajñāna-timirāndhasya jñānāñjana-śalākayā
cakṣur unmīlitaṁ yena tasmai śrī-gurave namaḥ

Contents

Foreword

by Graham Hancock

(Author of *Fingerprints of the Gods*)

It is my great pleasure and honor to introduce this abridged edition of *Forbidden Archeology*. Let me say at the outset that I believe this book to be one of the landmark intellectual achievements of the late twentieth century. It will take more conservative scholars a long while, probably many years, to come to terms with the revelations it contains. Nevertheless, Michael Cremo and Richard Thompson have put the revelations out there and the clock cannot now be turned back. Sooner or later, whether we like it or not, our species is going to have to come to terms with the facts that are so impressively documented in the pages that follow, and these facts are stunning.

Cremo and Thompson's central proposition is that the model of human prehistory, carefully built-up by scholars over the past two centuries, is sadly and completely wrong. Moreover, the authors are not proposing that it can be put right with minor tinkering and adjustments. What is needed is for the existing model to be thrown out the window and for us to start again with open minds and with absolutely no preconceptions at all.

This is a position that is close to my own heart; indeed it forms the basis of my book *Fingerprints of the Gods*. There, however, my focus was exclusively on the last 20,000 years and on the possibility that an advanced global civilization may have flourished more than 12,000 years ago only to be wiped out and forgotten in the great cataclysm that brought the last Ice Age to an end.

In *The Hidden History of the Human Race* Cremo and Thompson go much further, pushing back the horizons of our amnesia not just 12,000 or 20,000 years, but millions of years into the past, and showing that almost everything we have been taught to believe about the origins and evolution of our species rests on the shaky foundation of academic opinion, and on a highly selective sampling of research results. The two authors then set about putting the record straight by showing all the other research results that have been edited out of the record during the past two centuries, not because there was anything wrong or bogus about the results themselves, but simply because they did not fit with prevailing academic opinion.

Anomalous and out-of-place discoveries reported by Cremo and Thompson in *The Hidden History of the Human Race* include convincing evidence that anatomically modern humans may have been present on the Earth not just for 100,000 years or less (the orthodox view), but for millions of years, and that metal objects of advanced design may have been in use at equally early periods. Moreover, although sensational claims have been made before about out-of-place artifacts, they have never been supported by such overwhelming and utterly convincing documentation as Cremo and Thompson provide.

In the final analysis, it is the meticulous scholarship of the authors, and the cumulative weight of the facts presented in *The Hidden History of the Human Race,* that really convince. The book is, I believe, in harmony with the mood of the public at large in the world today, a mood which no longer unquestioningly accepts the pronouncements of established authorities, and is willing to listen with an open mind to heretics who make their case reasonably and rationally.

Never before has the case for a complete re-evaluation of the human story been made more reasonably and rationally than it is in these pages.

Graham Hancock
Devon, England
January, 1998

Preface

The unabridged edition of *Forbidden Archeology* is 952 pages long. It thus presents quite a challenge to many readers. Richard L. Thompson and I therefore decided to bring out *The Hidden History of the Human Race*—a shorter, more readable, and more affordable version of *Forbidden Archeology*.

The Hidden History of the Human Race does, however, contain almost all of the cases discussed in *Forbidden Archeology*. Missing are the bibliographic citations in the text and detailed discussions of the geological and anatomical aspects of many of the cases. For example, in *The Hidden History of the Human Race* we might simply state that a site is considered to be Late Pliocene in age. In *Forbidden Archeology*, we would have given a detailed discussion of why this is so, providing many references to past and present technical geological reports. Readers who desire such detail can acquire *Forbidden Archeology* by using the order form printed in the back of this book.

Michael A. Cremo
Pacific Beach, California
March 26, 1994

Introduction and Acknowledgements

In 1979, researchers at the Laetoli, Tanzania, site in East Africa discovered footprints in volcanic ash deposits over 3.6 million years old. Mary Leakey and others said the prints were indistinguishable from those of modern humans. To these scientists, this meant only that the human ancestors of 3.6 million years ago had remarkably modern feet. But according to other scientists, such as physical anthropologist R. H. Tuttle of the University of Chicago, fossil foot bones of the known australopithecines of 3.6 million years ago show they had feet that were distinctly apelike. Hence they were incompatible with the Laetoli prints. In an article in the March 1990 issue of *Natural History,* Tuttle confessed that "we are left with somewhat of a mystery." It seems permissible, therefore, to consider a possibility neither Tuttle nor Leakey mentioned—that creatures with anatomically modern human bodies to match their anatomically modern human feet existed some 3.6 million years ago in East Africa. Perhaps, as suggested in the illustration on the opposite page, they coexisted with more apelike creatures. As intriguing as this archeological possibility may be, current ideas about human evolution forbid it.

But from 1984 to 1992, Richard Thompson and I, with the assistance of our researcher Stephen Bernath, amassed an extensive body of evidence that calls into question current theories of human evolution. Some of this evidence, like the Laetoli footprints, is fairly recent. But much of it was reported by scientists in the nineteenth and early twentieth centuries.

Without even looking at this older body of evidence, some will assume that there must be something wrong with it—that it was properly disposed of by scientists long ago, for very good reasons. Richard and I have looked rather deeply into that possibility. We have concluded, however, that the quality of this controversial evidence is no better or worse than the supposedly noncontroversial evidence usually cited in favor of current views about human evolution.

In Part I of *The Hidden History of the Human Race,* we look closely at the vast amount of controversial evidence that contradicts current ideas about human evolution. We recount in detail how this evidence has been systematically suppressed, ignored, or forgotten, even though it is qualitatively (and quantitatively) equivalent to the evidence favoring currently accepted views on human origins. When we speak of suppression of evidence, we are not referring to scientific conspirators carrying out a satanic plot to deceive the public. Instead, we are talking about an ongoing social process of knowledge filtration that appears quite innocuous but has a substantial cumulative effect. Certain categories of evidence simply disappear from view, in our opinion unjustifiably.

This pattern of data suppression has been going on for a long time. In 1880, J. D. Whitney, the state geologist of California, published a lengthy review of advanced stone tools found in California gold mines. The implements, including spear points and stone mortars and pestles, were found deep in mine shafts, underneath thick, undisturbed layers of lava, in formations ranging from 9 million to over 55 million years old. W. H. Holmes of the Smithsonian Institution, one of the most vocal critics of the California finds, wrote: "Perhaps if Professor Whitney had fully appreciated the story of human evolution as it is understood today, he would have hesitated to announce the conclusions formulated [that humans existed in very ancient times in North America], notwithstanding the imposing array of testimony with which he was confronted." In other words, if the facts do not agree with the favored theory, then such facts, even an imposing array of them, must be discarded.

This supports the primary point we are trying to make in *The Hidden History of the Human Race,* namely, that there exists in the scientific community a knowledge filter that screens out unwelcome evidence. This process of knowledge filtration has been going on for well over a century and continues to the present day.

In addition to the general process of knowledge filtration, there also appear to be cases of more direct suppression.

In the early 1950s, Thomas E. Lee of the National Museum of Canada found advanced stone tools in glacial deposits at Sheguiandah, on Manitoulin Island in northern Lake Huron. Geologist John Sanford of Wayne State University argued that the oldest Sheguiandah tools were at least 65,000 years old and might be as much as 125,000 years old. For those adhering to standard views on North American prehistory, such ages were unacceptable. Humans supposedly first entered North America from Siberia about 12,000 years ago.

Thomas E. Lee complained: "The site's discoverer [Lee] was hounded from his Civil Service position into prolonged unemployment; publication outlets were cut off; the evidence was misrepresented by several prominent authors . . . ; the tons of artifacts vanished into storage bins of the National Museum of Canada; for refusing to fire the discoverer, the Director of the National Museum, who had proposed having a monograph on the site published, was himself fired and driven into exile; official positions of prestige and power were exercised in an effort to gain control over just six Sheguiandah specimens that had not gone under cover; and the site has been turned into a tourist resort. . . . Sheguiandah would have forced embarrassing admissions that the Brahmins did not know everything. It would have forced the rewriting of almost every book in the business. It had to be killed. It was killed."

In Part II of *The Hidden History of the Human Race,* we survey the body of accepted evidence that is generally used to support the now-dominant ideas about human evolution. We especially examine the status of *Australopithecus.* Most anthropologists say *Australopithecus* was a human ancestor with an apelike head, a humanlike body, and a humanlike bipedal stance and gait. But other researchers make a convincing case for a radically different view of *Australopithecus*. According to these researchers, the australopithecines were very apelike, partly tree-dwelling creatures with no direct connection to the human evolutionary lineage.

In Part II we also consider the possible coexistence of primitive hominids and anatomically modern humans not only in the distant past but in the present. Over the past century, scientists have accumulated evidence suggesting that humanlike creatures resembling *Gigantopithecus, Australopithecus, Homo erectus,* and the Neanderthals are living in various wilderness areas of the world. In North America, these creatures are known as Sasquatch. In Central Asia, they are called Almas. In Africa, China, Southeast Asia, Central America, and South America, they are known by other names. Some researchers use the general term "wildmen" to include them all. Scientists and physicians have reported seeing live wildmen, dead wildmen, and footprints. They have also catalogued thousands of reports from ordinary people who have seen wildmen, as well as similar reports from historical records.

Some might question why we would put together a book like *The Hidden History of the Human Race,* unless we had some underlying purpose. Indeed, there is some underlying purpose.

Richard Thompson and I are members of the Bhaktivedanta Institute, a branch of the International Society for Krishna Consciousness that studies the relationship between modern science and the world view expressed in the Vedic literature of India. From the Vedic literature, we derive the idea that the human race is of great antiquity. For the purpose of conducting systematic research into the existing scientific literature on human antiquity, we expressed the Vedic idea in the form of a theory that various humanlike and apelike beings have coexisted for long periods of time.

That our theoretical outlook is derived from the Vedic literature should not disqualify it. Theory selection can come from many sources—a private inspiration, previous theories, a suggestion from a friend, a movie, and so on. What really matters is not a theory's source but its ability to account for observations.

Because of space considerations, we were not able to develop in this volume our ideas about an alternative to current theories of human origins. We are therefore planning a second volume relating our extensive research results in this area to our Vedic source material.

At this point, I would like to say something about my collaboration with Richard Thompson. Richard is a scientist by training, a mathematician who has published refereed articles and books in the fields of mathematical biology, remote sensing from satellites, geology, and physics. I am not a scientist by training. Since 1977, I have been a writer and editor for books and magazines published by the Bhaktivedanta Book Trust.

In 1984, Richard asked his assistant Stephen Bernath to begin collecting material on human origins and antiquity. In 1986, Richard asked me to take that material and organize it into a book.

As I reviewed the material provided to me by Stephen, I was struck by the very small number of reports from 1859, when Darwin published *The Origin of Species,* until 1894, when Dubois published his report on Java man. Curious about this, I asked Stephen to obtain some anthropology books from the late nineteenth and early twentieth centuries. In these books, including an early edition of Marcellin Boule's *Fossil Men,* I found highly negative reviews of numerous reports from the period in question. By tracing out footnotes, we dug up a few samples of these reports. Most of them, by nineteenth-century scientists, described incised bones, stone tools, and anatomically modern skeletal remains encountered in unexpectedly old geological contexts. The reports were of high quality, answering many possible objections. This encouraged me to make a more systematic search.

Digging up this buried literary evidence required another three years. Stephen Bernath and I obtained rare conference volumes and journals from around the world, and together we translated the material into English. Writing the manuscript from the assembled material took another couple of years. Throughout the entire period of research and writing, I had almost daily discussions with Richard about the significance of the material and how best to present it.

Stephen obtained much of the material in Chapter 6 from Ron Calais, who kindly sent us many xeroxes of original reports from his archives. Virginia Steen-McIntyre was kind enough to supply us with her correspondence on the dating of the Hueyatlaco, Mexico, site. We also had useful discussions about stone tools with Ruth D. Simpson of the San Bernardino County Museum and about shark teeth marks on bone with Thomas A. Deméré of the San Diego Natural History Museum.

This book could not have been completed without the varied services of Christopher Beetle, a computer science graduate of Brown University, who came to the Bhaktivedanta Institute in San Diego in 1988.

For overseeing the design and layout of this abridged edition, Richard and I thank Alister Taylor. The jacket design is the work of Yamarāja dāsa. The illustrations opposite the first page of the introduction and in Figure 12.8 are the much-appreciated work of Miles Triplett. Beverly Symes, David Smith, Sigalit Binyaminy, Susan Fritz, Barbara Cantatore, Joseph Franklin, and Michael Best also helped in the production of this book.

Richard and I would especially like to thank the international trustees of the Bhaktivedanta Book Trust, past and present, for their generous support for the research, writing, and publication of this book.

Finally, we encourage readers to bring to our attention any additional evidence that may be of interest to us, especially for inclusion in future editions of this book. Correspondence may be addressed to us at Govardhan Hill Publishing, P. O. Box 52, Badger, CA 93603.

Michael A. Cremo
Pacific Beach, California
March 26, 1994

Part I

ANOMALOUS EVIDENCE

1

The Song of the Red Lion:
Darwin and Human Evolution

One evening in 1871, an association of learned British gentlemen, the Red Lions, gathered in Edinburgh, Scotland, to feed happily together and entertain each other with humorous songs and speeches. Lord Neaves, known well for his witty lyrics, stood up before the assembled Lions and sang twelve stanzas he had composed on "The Origin of Species a la Darwin." Among them:

> *An Ape with a pliable thumb and big brain,*
> *When the gift of gab he had managed to gain,*
> *As Lord of Creation established his reign*
> *Which Nobody can Deny!*

His listeners responded, as customary among the Red Lions, by gently roaring and wagging their coattails.

Just a dozen years after Charles Darwin published *The Origin of Species* in 1859, growing numbers of scientists and other educated persons considered it impossible, indeed laughable, to suppose that humans were anything other than the modified descendants of an ancestral line of apelike creatures. In *The Origin of Species* itself, Darwin touched but briefly on the question of human beginnings, noting in the final pages only that "Light will be thrown on the origin of man and his history." Yet despite Darwin's caution, it was clear that he did not see humanity as an exception to his theory that one species evolves from another.

DARWIN SPEAKS

It was not until 1871 that Darwin came out with a book (*Descent of Man*) expressing his detailed views on human evolution. Explaining his delay, Darwin wrote: "During many years I collected notes on the origin or descent of

3

man, without any intention of publishing on the subject, but rather with the determination not to publish, as I thought that I should thus only add to the prejudices against my views. It seemed to me sufficient to indicate, in the first edition of my 'Origin of Species,' that by this work 'light would be thrown on the origin of man and his history;' and this implies that man must be included with other organic beings in any general conclusion respecting his manner of appearance on this earth."

In *Descent of Man*, Darwin explicitly denied any special status for the human species. "We thus learn," he said, "that man is descended from a hairy, tailed quadruped, probably arboreal in its habits, and an inhabitant of the Old World." It was a bold statement, yet one lacking the most convincing kind of proof— fossils of species transitional between the ancient apes and modern humans.

Aside from two poorly dated Neanderthal skulls from Germany and Gibraltar, and a few other little-reported finds of modern morphology, there were no discoveries of hominid fossil remains. This fact soon became ammunition to those who were revolted by Darwin's suggestion that humans had apelike ancestors. Where, they asked, were the fossils to prove it?

Today, however, almost without exception, modern paleoanthropologists believe that they have fulfilled the expectations of Darwin by positive discoveries of fossil human ancestors in Africa, Asia, and elsewhere.

APPEARANCE OF THE HOMINIDS

In this book, we take the modern system of geological ages (Table 1.1) for granted. We use it as a fixed frame of reference for our study of the history of ancient humans and near humans. This is for convenience. We acknowledge that our findings might require serious reconsideration of the geological time scale.

According to modern views, the first apelike beings appeared in the Oligocene period, which began about 38 million years ago. The first apes thought to be on the line to humans appeared in the Miocene, which extends from 5 to 25 million years ago. These include *Dryopithecus*.

Then came the Pliocene period. During the Pliocene, the first hominids, or erect-walking humanlike primates, are said to appear in the fossil record. The earliest known hominid is *Australopithecus,* the southern ape, and is dated back as far as 4 million years, in the Pliocene.

This near human, say scientists, stood between 4 and 5 feet tall and had a cranial capacity of between 300 and 600 cubic centimeters (cc). From the neck down, *Australopithecus* is said to have been very similar to modern humans, whereas the head displayed some apelike and some human features.

One branch of *Australopithecus* is thought to have given rise to *Homo habilis* around 2 million years ago, at the beginning of the Pleistocene period. *Homo habilis* appears similar to *Australopithecus* except that his cranial capacity is said to have been larger, between 600 and 750 cc.

Homo habilis is thought to have given rise to *Homo erectus* (the species that includes Java man and Beijing man) around 1.5 million years ago. *Homo erectus* is said to have stood between 5 and 6 feet tall and had a cranial capacity varying between 700 and 1,300 cc. Most paleoanthropologists now believe that from the neck down, *Homo erectus* was, like *Australopithecus* and *Homo habilis,* almost the same as modern humans. The forehead, however, sloped back from behind massive brow ridges, the jaws and teeth were large, and the lower jaw lacked a chin. It is believed that *Homo erectus* lived in Africa, Asia, and Europe until about 200,000 years ago.

Paleoanthropologists believe that anatomically modern humans (*Homo sapiens sapiens*) emerged gradually from *Homo erectus*. Somewhere around

TABLE 1.1

Geological Eras and Periods

Era	Period	Start in Millions of Years Ago
Cenozoic	Holocene	.01
	Pleistocene	2
	Pliocene	5
	Miocene	25
	Oligocene	38
	Eocene	55
	Paleocene	65
Mesozoic	Cretaceous	144
	Jurassic	213
	Triassic	248
Paleozoic	Permian	286
	Carboniferous	360
	Devonian	408
	Silurian	438
	Ordovician	505
	Cambrian	590

300,000 or 400,000 years ago, the first early *Homo sapiens* or archaic *Homo sapiens* are said to have appeared. They are described as having a cranial capacity almost as large as that of modern humans, yet still manifesting to a lesser degree some of the characteristics of *Homo erectus,* such as the thick skull, receding forehead, and large brow ridges. Examples of this category are the finds from Swanscombe in England, Steinheim in Germany, and Fontechevade and Arago in France. Because these skulls also possess, to some degree, Neanderthal characteristics, they are also classified as pre-Neanderthal types. Most authorities now postulate that both anatomically modern humans and the classic Western European Neanderthals evolved from the pre-Neanderthal or early *Homo sapiens* types of hominids.

In the early part of the twentieth century, some scientists advocated the view that the Neanderthals of the last glacial period, known as the classic Western European Neanderthals, were the direct ancestors of modern human beings. They had brains larger than those of *Homo sapiens sapiens.* Their faces and jaws were much larger, and their foreheads were lower, sloping back from behind large brow ridges. Neanderthal remains are found in Pleistocene deposits ranging from 30,000 to 150,000 years old. However, the discovery of early *Homo sapiens* in deposits far older than 150,000 years effectively removed the classic Western European Neanderthals from the direct line of descent leading from *Homo erectus* to modern humans.

The type of human known as Cro-Magnon appeared in Europe approximately 30,000 years ago, and they were anatomically modern. Scientists used to say that anatomically modern *Homo sapiens sapiens* first appeared around 40,000 years ago, but now many authorities, in light of discoveries in South Africa and elsewhere, say that they appeared 100,000 or more years ago.

The cranial capacity of modern humans varies from 1,000 cc to 2,000 cc, the average being around 1,350 cc. As can be readily observed today among modern humans, there is no correlation between brain size and intelligence. There are highly intelligent people with 1,000 cc brains and morons with 2,000 cc brains.

Exactly where, when, or how *Australopithecus* gave rise to *Homo habilis,* or *Homo habilis* gave rise to *Homo erectus,* or *Homo erectus* gave rise to modern humans is not explained in present accounts of human origins. However, most paleoanthropologists agree that only anatomically modern humans came to the New World. The earlier stages of evolution, from *Australopithecus* on up, are all said to have taken place in the Old World. The first arrival of human beings in the New World is generally said to have occurred some 12,000 years ago, with some scientists willing to grant a Late Pleistocene date of 25,000 years.

Even today there are many gaps in the presumed record of human descent. For example, there is an almost total absence of fossils linking the Miocene apes such as *Dryopithecus* with the Pliocene ancestors of modern apes and humans, especially within the span of time between 4 and 8 million years ago.

Perhaps it is true that fossils will someday be found that fill in the gaps. Yet, and this is extremely important, there is no reason to suppose that the fossils that turn up will be supportive of evolutionary theory. What if, for example, fossils of anatomically modern humans turned up in strata older than those in which *Dryopithecus* were found? Even if anatomically modern humans were found to have lived a million years ago, 4 million years after the Late Miocene disappearance of *Dryopithecus*, that would be enough to throw out the current accounts of the origin of humankind.

In fact, such evidence has already been found, but it has since been suppressed or conveniently forgotten. Much of it came to light in the decades immediately after Darwin published *The Origin of Species*, before which there had been no notable finds except Neanderthal man. In the first years of Darwinism, there was no clearly established story of human descent to be defended, and professional scientists made and reported many discoveries that now would never make it into the pages of any journal more academically respectable than the *National Enquirer*.

Most of these fossils and artifacts were unearthed before the discovery by Eugene Dubois of Java man, the first protohuman hominid between *Dryopithecus* and modern humans. Java man was found in Middle Pleistocene deposits generally given an age of 800,000 years. The discovery became a benchmark. Henceforth, scientists would not expect to find fossils or artifacts of anatomically modern humans in deposits of equal or greater age. If they did, they (or someone wiser) concluded that this was impossible and found some way to discredit the find as a mistake, an illusion, or a hoax. Before Java man, however, reputable nineteenth-century scientists found a number of examples of anatomically modern human skeletal remains in very ancient strata. And they also found large numbers of stone tools of various types, as well as animal bones bearing signs of human action.

SOME PRINCIPLES OF EPISTEMOLOGY

Before beginning our survey of rejected and accepted paleoanthropological evidence, we shall outline a few epistemological rules that we have tried to follow. Epistemology is defined in *Webster's New World Dictionary* as "the study or theory of the origin, nature, methods, and limits of knowledge." When engaged in the study of scientific evidence, it is important to keep the nature, methods, and limits of knowledge in mind; otherwise one is prone to fall into illusion.

Paleoanthropological evidence has certain key limitations that should be pointed out. First, the observations that go into paleoanthropological facts tend to involve rare discoveries that cannot be duplicated at will. For example, some scientists in this field have built great reputations on the basis of a few famous discoveries, and others, the vast majority, have spent their whole careers without making a single significant find.

Second, once a discovery is made, key elements of the evidence are destroyed, and knowledge of these elements depends solely on the testimony of the discoverers. For example, one of the most important aspects of a fossil is its stratigraphic position. However, once the fossil is removed from the earth, the direct evidence indicating its position is destroyed, and we simply have to depend on the excavator's testimony as to where he or she found it. Of course, one may argue that chemical or other features of the fossil may indicate its place of origin. This is true in some cases but not in others. And in making such judgements, we also have to depend on reports concerning the chemical and other physical properties of the strata in which the fossil was allegedly found.

Persons making important discoveries sometimes cannot find their way back to the sites of those discoveries. After a few years, the sites are almost inevitably destroyed, perhaps by erosion, by complete paleoanthropological excavation, or by commercial developments (involving quarrying, building construction, and so forth). Even modern excavations involving meticulous recording of details destroy the very evidence they are recording, leaving one with nothing but written testimony to back up many key assertions. And many important discoveries, even today, involve very scanty recording of key details.

Thus a person desiring to verify paleoanthropological reports will find it very difficult to gain access to the real facts, even if he or she is able to travel to the site of a discovery. And, of course, limitations of time and money make it impossible to personally examine more than a small percentage of the totality of important paleoanthropological sites.

A third problem is that the facts of paleoanthropology are seldom (if ever) simple. A scientist may testify that the fossils were clearly weathering out of a certain Early Pleistocene layer. But this apparently simple statement may depend on many observations and arguments involving geological faulting, the possibility of slumping, the presence or absence of a layer of hillwash, the presence of a refilled gully, and so on. If one consults the testimony of another person present at the site, one may find that he or she discusses many important details not mentioned by the first witness.

Different observers sometimes contradict one another, and their senses and memories are imperfect. Thus, an observer at a given site may see certain things, but miss other important things. Some of these things might be seen by other observers, but this could turn out to be impossible because the site has become inaccessible.

Then there is the problem of cheating. This can occur on the level of systematic fraud, as in the Piltdown case. As we shall see, to get to the bottom of this kind of cheating one requires the investigative abilities of a super Sherlock Holmes plus all the facilities of a modern forensic laboratory. Unfortunately, there are always strong motives for deliberate or unconscious fraud, since fame and glory await the person who succeeds in finding a human ancestor.

Cheating can also occur on the level of simply omitting to report observations that do not agree with one's desired conclusions. As we will see in the course of this book, investigators have sometimes observed artifacts in certain strata, but never reported this because they did not believe the artifacts could possibly be of that age. It is very difficult to avoid this, because our senses are imperfect, and if we see something that seems impossible, then it is natural to suppose that we may be mistaken. Indeed, this may very well be the case. Cheating by neglecting to mention important observations is simply a limitation of human nature that, unfortunately, can have a deleterious impact on the empirical process.

The drawbacks of paleoanthropological facts are not limited to excavations of objects. Similar drawbacks are also found in modern chemical or radiometric dating studies. For example, a carbon 14 date might seem to involve a straightforward procedure that reliably yields a number—the age of an object. But actual dating studies often turn out to involve complex considerations regarding the identity of samples, and their history and possible contamination. They may involve the rejection of some preliminary calculated dates and the acceptance of others on the basis of complex arguments that are seldom explicitly published. Here also the facts can be complex, incomplete, and largely inaccessible.

The conclusion we draw from these limitations of paleoanthropological facts is that in this field of study we are largely limited to the comparative study of reports. Although hard evidence does exist in the form of fossils and artifacts in museums, most of the key evidence that gives importance to these objects exists only in written form.

Since the information conveyed by paleoanthropological reports tends to be incomplete, and since even the simplest paleoanthropological facts tend to involve complex, unresolvable issues, it is difficult to arrive at solid conclusions about reality in this field. What then can we do? We suggest that one important thing we can do is compare the quality of different reports. Although we do not have access to the real facts, we can directly study different reports and objectively compare them.

A collection of reports dealing with certain discoveries can be evaluated on the basis of the thoroughness of the reported investigation and the logic and consistency of the arguments presented. One can consider whether or not various skeptical counterarguments to a given theory have been raised and answered. Since reported observations must always be taken on faith in some respect, one can also inquire into the qualifications of the observers.

We propose that if two collections of reports appear to be equally reliable on the basis of these criteria, then they should be treated equally. Both sets might be accepted, both might be rejected, or both might be regarded as having an uncertain status. It would be wrong, however, to accept one set of reports while rejecting the other, and it would be especially wrong to accept one set as proof of a given theory while suppressing the other set, and thus rendering it inaccessible to future students.

We apply this approach to two particular sets of reports. The first set consists of reports of anomalously old artifacts and human skeletal remains, most of which were discovered in the late nineteenth and early twentieth centuries. These reports are discussed in Part I of this book. The second set consists of reports of artifacts and skeletal remains that are accepted as evidence in support of current theories of human evolution. These reports range in date from the late nineteenth century to the 1980s, and they are discussed in Part II. Due to the natural interconnections between different discoveries, some anomalous discoveries are also discussed in Part II.

Our thesis is that in spite of the various advances in paleoanthropological science in the twentieth century there is an essential equivalence in quality between these two sets of reports. We therefore suggest that it is not appropriate to accept one set and reject the other. This has serious implications for the modern theory of human evolution. If we reject the first set of reports (the anomalies) and, to be consistent, also reject the second set (evidence currently accepted), then the theory of human evolution is deprived of a good part of its observational foundation. But if we accept the first set of reports, then we must accept the existence of intelligent, toolmaking beings in geological periods as remote as the Miocene, or even the Eocene. If we accept the skeletal evidence presented in these reports, we must go further and accept the existence of anatomically modern human beings in these remote periods. This not only contradicts the modern theory of human evolution, but it also casts grave doubt on our whole picture of the evolution of mammalian life in the Cenozoic era.

2

Incised and Broken Bones:
The Dawn of Deception

Intentionally cut and broken bones of animals comprise a substantial part of the evidence for human antiquity. They came under serious study in the middle of the nineteenth century and have remained the object of extensive research and analysis up to the present.

In the decades following the publication of Darwin's *The Origin of Species,* many scientists found incised and broken bones indicating a human presence in the Pliocene, Miocene, and earlier periods. Opponents suggested that the marks and breaks observed on the fossil bones were caused by the action of carnivores, sharks, or geological pressure. But supporters of the discoveries offered impressive counterarguments. For example, stone tools were sometimes found along with incised bones, and experiments with these implements produced marks on fresh bone exactly resembling those found on the fossils. Scientists also employed microscopes in order to distinguish the cuts on fossil bones from those that might be made by animal or shark teeth. In many instances, the marks were located in places on the bone appropriate for specific butchering operations.

Nonetheless, reports of incised and broken bones indicating a human presence in the Pliocene and earlier are absent from the currently accepted stock of evidence. This exclusion may not, however, be warranted. From the incomplete evidence now under active consideration, scientists have concluded that humans of the modern type appeared fairly recently. But in light of the evidence covered in this chapter, it appears they may be deceiving themselves.

ST. PREST, FRANCE

In April of 1863, Jules Desnoyers, of the French National Museum, came to St. Prest, in northwestern France, to gather fossils. From the sandy gravels, he recovered part of a rhinoceros tibia. He noticed on the bone a series of narrow grooves. To Desnoyers, some of the grooves appeared to have been produced by a sharp knife or blade of flint. He also observed small circular marks that could well have been made by a pointed implement. Later, Desnoyers examined collections of St. Prest fossils at the museums of Chartres and the School of Mines in Paris and saw they bore the same types of marks. He then reported his findings to the French Academy of Sciences.

Some modern scientists have said that the St. Prest site belongs to the Late Pliocene. If Desnoyers concluded correctly that the marks on many of the bones had been made by flint implements, then it would appear that human beings had been present in France during that time. One might ask, "What's wrong with that?" In terms of our modern understanding of paleoanthropology, quite a bit is wrong. The presence at that time in Europe of beings using stone tools in a sophisticated manner would seem almost impossible. It is believed that at the end of the Pliocene, about 2 million years ago, the modern human species had not yet come into being. Only in Africa should one find primitive human ancestors, and these were limited to *Australopithecus* and *Homo habilis,* the latter considered the first toolmaker. According to reports by other scientists, the St. Prest site might be more recent than the Pliocene—perhaps as little as 1.2–1.6 million years old. But the incised bones would still be anomalous.

Even in the nineteenth century, Desnoyers's discoveries of incised bones at St. Prest provoked controversy. Opponents argued that the marks were made by the tools of the workmen who excavated them. But Desnoyers showed that the cut marks were covered with mineral deposits just like the other surfaces of the fossil bones. The prominent British geologist Sir Charles Lyell suggested the marks were made by rodents' teeth, but French prehistorian Gabriel de Mortillet said the marks could not have been made by animals. He instead suggested that they were made by sharp stones moved by geological pressure across the bones. To this, Desnoyers replied: "Many of the incisions have been worn by later rubbing, resulting from transport or movement of the bones in the midst of the sands and gravels. The resulting markings are of an essentially different character than the original marks and striations."

So who was right, Desnoyers or de Mortillet? Some authorities believed the question could be settled if it could be shown that the gravels of St. Prest contained flint tools that were definitely of human manufacture. Louis Bourgeois, a clergyman who had also earned a reputation as a distinguished paleontologist, carefully searched the strata at St. Prest for such evidence. By his patient research he eventually found a number of flints that he believed were genuine tools and made them the subject of a report to the Academy of Sciences in January, 1867. The famous French anthropologist Armand de Quatrefages said the tools included scrapers, borers, and lance points.

Even this did not satisfy de Mortillet, who said the flints discovered by Bourgeois at St. Prest had been chipped by geological pressure. It appears that in our attempt to answer one question, the nature of cut marks on bones, we have stumbled upon another, the question of how to recognize human workmanship on flints and other stone objects. This latter question shall be fully treated in the next chapter. For now we shall simply note that judgements about what constitutes a stone tool are a matter of considerable controversy even to this day. It is, therefore, quite definitely possible to find reasons to question de Mortillet's rejection of the flints found by Bourgeois. In 1910, the famous American paleontologist Henry Fairfield Osborn made these interesting remarks in connection with the presence of stone tools at St. Prest: "the earliest traces of man in beds of this age were the incised bones discovered by Desnoyers at St. Prest near Chartres in 1863. Doubt as to the artificial character of these incisions has been removed by the recent explorations of Laville and Rutot, which resulted in the discovery of eolithic flints, fully confirming the discoveries of the Abbé Bourgeois in these deposits in 1867."

So as far as the discoveries at St. Prest are concerned, it should now be apparent that we are dealing with paleontological problems that cannot be quickly or easily resolved. Certainly, there is not sufficient reason to categorically reject these bones as evidence for a human presence in the Pliocene. This might lead one to wonder why the St. Prest fossils, and others like them, are almost never mentioned in textbooks on human evolution, except in rare cases of brief mocking footnotes of dismissal. Is it really because the evidence is clearly inadmissible? Or is, perhaps, the omission or summary rejection more related to the fact that the potential Late Pliocene antiquity of the objects is so much at odds with the standard account of human origins?

Along these lines, Armand de Quatrefages, a member of the French Academy of Sciences and a professor at the Museum of Natural History in Paris, wrote in his book *Hommes Fossiles et Hommes Sauvages* (1884): "The objections made to the existence of humans in the Pliocene and Miocene periods seem to habitually be more related to theoretical considerations than to direct observation."

A MODERN EXAMPLE: OLD CROW RIVER, CANADA

Before moving on to further examples of nineteenth-century discoveries that challenge modern ideas about human origins, let us consider a more recent investigation of intentionally modified bones. One of the most controversial questions confronting New World paleoanthropology is determining the time at which humans entered North America. The standard view is that bands of Asian hunter-gatherers crossed over the Bering land bridge about 12,000 years ago. Some authorities are willing to extend the date to about 30,000 years ago, while an increasing minority are reporting evidence for a human presence in the Americas at far earlier dates in the Pleistocene. We shall examine this question in greater detail in coming chapters. For now, however, we want only to consider the fossil bones uncovered at Old Crow River in the northern Yukon territory as a contemporary example of the type of evidence dealt with in this chapter.

In the 1970s, Richard E. Morlan of the Archeological Survey of Canada and the Canadian National Museum of Man, conducted studies of modified bones from the Old Crow River sites. Morlan concluded that many bones and antlers exhibited signs of intentional human work executed before the bones had become fossilized. The bones, which had undergone river transport, were recovered from an Early Wisconsin glacial floodplain dated at 80,000 years B.P. (before present). This greatly challenged current ideas about the peopling of the New World.

But in 1984 R. M. Thorson and R. D. Guthrie published a study showing that the action of river ice could have caused the alterations that suggested human work to Morlan. Afterwards, Morlan backed away from his assertions that all the bones he had collected had been modified by human agency. He admitted 30 out of 34 could have been marked by river ice or other natural causes.

Even so, he still believed the other four specimens bore definite signs of human work. In a published report, he said: "The cuts and scrapes . . . are indistinguishable from those made by stone tools during butchering and defleshing of an animal carcass."

Morlan sent two of the bones to Dr. Pat Shipman of Johns Hopkins University, an expert on cut bones. Shipman examined the marks on the bones under an electron scanning microscope and compared them with more than 1,000 documented marks on bone. Shipman said the marks on one of the bones were inconclusive. But in her opinion the other bone had a definite tool mark on it. Morlan noted that stone implements have been found in the Old Crow River area and in nearby uplands, but not in direct association with bones.

What this all means is that the bones of St. Prest, and others like them, cannot be easily dismissed. Evidence of the same type is still considered important today, and the methods of analysis are almost identical to those practiced in the nineteenth century. Scientists of those days may not have had electron microscopes, but optical microscopes were, and still are, good enough for this kind of work.

ANZA-BORREGO DESERT, CALIFORNIA

Another recent example of incised bones like those found at St. Prest is a discovery made by George Miller, curator of the Imperial Valley College Museum in El Centro, California. Miller, who died in 1989, reported that six mammoth bones excavated from the Anza-Borrego Desert bear scratches of the kind produced by stone tools. Uranium isotope dating carried out by the U.S. Geological Survey indicated that the bones are at least 300,000 years old, and paleomagnetic dating and volcanic ash samples indicated an age of some 750,000 years.

One established scholar said that Miller's claim is "as reasonable as the Loch Ness Monster or a living mammoth in Siberia," while Miller countered that "these people don't want to see man here because their careers would go down the drain." The incised mammoth bones from the Anza-Borrego Desert came up in a conversation we had with Thomas Deméré, a paleontologist at the San Diego Natural History Museum (May 31, 1990). Deméré said he was by nature skeptical of claims such as those made by Miller. He called into question the professionalism with which the bones had been excavated, and pointed out that no stone tools had been found along with the fossils. Furthermore, Deméré suggested that it was very unlikely that anything about the find would ever be published in a scientific journal, because the referees who review articles probably would not pass it. We later learned from Julie Parks, the curator of George Miller's specimens, that Deméré had never inspected the fossils or visited the site of discovery, although he had been invited to do so.

Parks said that one incision apparently continues from one of the fossil bones to another bone that would have been located next to it when the mammoth skeleton was intact. This is suggestive of a butchering mark. Accidental marks resulting from movement of the bones in the earth after the skeleton had broken up probably would not continue from one bone to another in this fashion.

INCISED BONES FROM ITALIAN SITES

Specimens incised in a manner similar to those of St. Prest were found by J. Desnoyers in a collection of bones gathered from the valley of the Arno River (Val d'Arno) in Italy. The grooved bones were from the same types of animals found at St. Prest—including *Elephas meridionalis* and *Rhinoceros etruscus*. They were attributed to the Pliocene stage called the Astian. This would yield a date of 3–4 million years. But it is possible that the bones could be as little as 1.3 million years old, which is when *Elephas meriodionalis* became extinct in Europe.

Grooved bones also were discovered in other parts of Italy. On September 20, 1865, at the meeting of the Italian Society of Natural Sciences at Spezzia, Professor Ramorino presented bones of extinct species of red deer and rhinoceros bearing what he believed were human incisions. These specimens were found at San Giovanni, in the vicinity of Siena, and like the Val d' Arno bones were said to be from the Astian stage of the Pliocene period. De Mortillet, not deviating from his standard negative opinion, stated that he thought the marks were most probably made by the tools of the workers who extracted the bones.

RHINOCEROS OF BILLY, FRANCE

On April 13, 1868, A. Laussedat informed the French Academy of Sciences that P. Bertrand had sent him two fragments of a lower jaw of a rhinoceros. They were from a pit near Billy, France. One of the fragments had four very deep grooves on it. These short grooves, situated on the lower part of the bone, were approximately parallel. According to Laussedat, the cut marks appeared in cross section like those made by a hatchet on a piece of hard wood. And so he thought the marks had been made in the same way, that is, with a handheld stone chopping instrument, when the bone was fresh. That indicated to Laussedat that humans had been contemporary with the fossil rhino in a geologically remote time. Just how remote is shown by the fact that the jawbone was found in a Middle Miocene formation, about 15 million years old.

Were the marks on the bone really produced by human beings? De Mortillet thought not. After ruling out gnawing by carnivores, he wrote, "They are simply geological impressions." Although de Mortillet may be right, he offered insufficient evidence to justify his view.

A highly regarded modern authority on cut bones is Lewis R. Binford, an anthropologist from the University of New Mexico at Albuquerque. In his book *Bones: Ancient Men and Modern Myths,* Binford said: "Marks from stone tools tend to be short, occurring in groups of parallel marks." The marks described by Laussedat conform to this description.

COLLINE DE SANSAN, FRANCE

The April 1868 proceedings of the French Academy of Sciences contain this report by F. Garrigou and H. Filhol: "We now have sufficient evidence to permit us to suppose that the contemporaneity of human beings and Miocene mammals is demonstrated." This evidence was a collection of mammalian bones, apparently intentionally broken, from Sansan, France. Especially noteworthy were broken bones of the small deer *Dicrocerus elegans.* Modern scientists consider the bone beds of Sansan to be Middle Miocene. One may consider the devastating effect that the presence of human beings about 15 million years ago would have on current evolutionary doctrines.

De Mortillet, in his usual fashion, said that some of the Sansan bones were broken by natural forces at the time of fossilization, perhaps by desiccation, and others afterward by movement of the strata.

Garrigou, however, maintained his conviction that the bones of Sansan had been broken by humans, in the course of extracting marrow. He made his case in 1871 at the meeting in Bologna, Italy, of the International Congress of Prehistoric Anthropology and Archeology. Garrigou first presented to the Congress a series of recent bones with undisputed marks of butchering and breaking. For comparison, he then presented bones of the small deer (*Dicrocerus elegans*) collected from Sansan. The markings on these bones matched the modern bones.

Garrigou also showed that many of the bone fragments had very fine scrape marks such as found on broken marrow bones of the Late Pleistocene. According to Binford, the first step in processing marrow bones is to remove the layer of tissue from the bone surface by scraping with a stone tool.

PIKERMI, GREECE

At a place called Pikermi, near the plain of Marathon in Greece, there is a fossil-rich stratum of Late Miocene (Tortonian) age, explored and described by the prominent French scientist Albert Gaudry. During the meeting in 1872 at Brussels of the International Congress of Prehistoric Anthropology and Archeology, Baron von Dücker reported that broken bones from Pikermi proved the existence of humans in the Miocene. Modern authorities still place the Pikermi site in the Late Miocene, which would make the bones at least 5 million years old.

Von Dücker first examined numerous bones from the Pikermi site in the Museum of Athens. He found 34 jaw parts of *Hipparion* (an extinct three-toed horse) and antelope as well as 19 fragments of tibia and 22 other fragments of bones from large mammals such as rhinoceros. All showed traces of methodical fracturing for the purpose of extracting marrow. According to von Dücker, they all bore "more or less distinct traces of blows from hard objects." He also noted many hundreds of bone flakes broken in the same manner.

In addition, von Dücker observed many dozens of crania of *Hipparion* and antelope showing methodical removal of the upper jaw in order to extract the brain. The edges of the fractures were very sharp, which may generally be taken as a sign of human breakage, rather than breakage by gnawing carnivores or geological pressures.

Von Dücker then journeyed to the Pikermi site itself to continue his investigation. During the course of his first excavation, he found dozens of bone fragments of *Hipparion* and antelope and reported that about one quarter of them bore signs of intentional breakage. In this regard, one may keep in mind Binford's finding that in assemblages of bones broken in the course of human marrow extraction about 14–17 percent have signs of impact notches. "I also found," stated von Dücker, "among the bones a stone of a size that could readily be held in the hand. It is pointed on one side and is perfectly adapted to making the kinds of marks observed on the bones."

PIERCED SHARK TEETH FROM THE RED CRAG, ENGLAND

At a meeting of the Royal Anthropological Institute of Great Britain and Ireland, held on April 8, 1872, Edward Charlesworth, a Fellow of the Geological Society, showed many specimens of shark (*Carcharodon*) teeth, each with a hole bored through the center, as is done by South Seas islanders for the purpose of making weapons and necklaces. The teeth were recovered from eastern England's Red Crag formation, indicating an age of approximately 2.0–2.5 million years.

Charlesworth gave convincing arguments why marine animals such as boring molluscs could not have made the holes. During the discussion, one scientist suggested tooth decay as the cause, but sharks are not known to have that problem. Another suggested parasites, but admitted that no parasites are known to reside in the teeth of fishes.

At that point Dr. Collyer gave his opinion in favor of human action. The record of the meeting stated: "He had carefully examined by aid of a powerful magnifying glass the perforated shark's teeth. . . . The perforations, to his mind, were the work of man." Among his reasons were "the bevelled conditions of the edges of the perforations," "the central position of the holes in the teeth," and "the marks of artificial means employed in making the borings."

CARVED BONE FROM THE DARDANELLES, TURKEY

In 1874, Frank Calvert found in a Miocene formation in Turkey (along the Dardanelles) a *Deinotherium* bone with carved figures of animals upon it. Calvert noted: "I have found in different parts of the same cliff, not far from the site of the engraved bone, a flint flake and some bones of animals, fractured longitudinally, obviously by the hand of man for the purpose of extracting the marrow, according to the practice of all primitive races."

The elephantlike *Deinotherium* is said by modern authorities to have existed from the Late Pliocene to the Early Miocene in Europe. It is thus quite possible that Calvert's dating of the Dardanelles site as Miocene was correct. The Miocene is now said to extend from 5 to 25 million years before the present. According to the current dominant view, only exceedingly apelike hominids are supposed to have existed during that period. Even a Late Pliocene date of 2–3 million years for the Dardanelles site would be far too early for the kind of artifacts found there. Carvings of the kind found on the *Deinotherium* bone are said to be the work of anatomically modern humans of the last 40,000 years.

In *Le Préhistorique,* de Mortillet did not dispute the age of the Dardanelles formation. Instead he commented that the simultaneous presence of a carved bone, intentionally broken bones, and a flint flake tool was almost too perfect, so perfect as to raise doubts about the finds. This is quite remarkable. In the case of the incised bones of St. Prest, de Mortillet complained that no stone tools or other signs of a human presence were to be found at the site. But here, with the requisite items discovered along with the carved bone, de Mortillet said the ensemble was "too perfect," hinting at cheating by Calvert.

But David A. Traill, a professor of classics at the University of California at Davis, gives this information about him: "Calvert was the most distinguished of a family of British expatriates that was prominent in the Dardanelles. . . . he had a good knowledge of geology and paleontology." Calvert conducted several important excavations in the Dardanelles region, and played a role in the discovery of Troy. Traill noted: "Calvert was, as far as I have been able to determine from extensive reading of his correspondence, scrupulously truthful."

BALAENOTUS OF MONTE APERTO, ITALY

During the latter part of the nineteenth century, fossil whale bones bearing cut marks turned up in Italy. On November 25, 1875, G. Capellini, professor of geology at the University of Bologna, reported that the marks had been made when the bone was fresh, apparently by flint tools. Many other European scientists agreed with Capellini's interpretation. The bones bearing the marks were from an extinct Pliocene whale of the genus *Balaenotus*. Some of the bones were from museum collections, and others were excavated personally by Capellini from Pliocene formations around Siena, at places such as Poggiarone.

The cut marks on the bones were found in places appropriate for butchering operations, such as the external surfaces of the ribs. On a nearly complete whale skeleton excavated by Capellini, the cut marks were found only on bones from one side of the whale. "I am convinced that the animal ran aground in the sand and rested on its left side and that the right side was thus exposed to the direct attack of humans, as is demonstrated by the places in which marks are found on the bones," said Capellini. That only the bones on one side of the whale were marked tends to rule out any purely geological explanation as well as the action of sharks in deep water. Furthermore, the cut marks on the fossil whale bones exactly resembled cut marks found on modern whale bones.

Capellini reported to the International Congress of Prehistoric Anthropology and Archeology: "In the vicinity of the remains of the *Balaenotus* of Poggiarone, I collected some flint blades, lost in the actual beach deposits." He added: "With those same flint implements I was able to reproduce on fresh cetacean bones the exact same marks found on the fossil whale bones." He also noted that human skeletal remains had been found in the same part of Italy, at Savona (see Chapter 7).

After Capellini's report, the members of the Congress engaged in discussion. Some, such as Sir John Evans, raised objections. Others, such as Paul Broca, secretary general of the Anthropological Sociey in Paris, agreed with Capellini that the marks on the whale bones were made by humans. He particularly ruled out the hypothesis that the marks were made by sharks and said the marks gave every sign of having been made by a sharp blade. Broca was one of the foremost authorities on bone physiology of his time.

Armand de Quatrefages was among the scientists accepting the Monte Aperto *Balaenotus* bones as being cut by sharp flint instruments held by a human hand.

He wrote in 1884: "However one may try, using various methods and implements of other materials, one will fail to duplicate the marks. Only a sharp flint instrument, moved at an angle and with a lot of pressure, could do it."

The whole issue was nicely summarized in English by S. Laing, who wrote in 1893: "The cuts are in regular curves, and sometimes almost semi-circular, such as the sweep of the hand could alone have caused, and they invariably show a clean cut surface on the outer or convex side, to which the pressure of a sharp edge was applied, with a rough or abraided surface on the inner side of the cut. Microscopic examination of the cuts confirms this conclusion, and leaves no doubt that they must have been made by such an instrument as a flint knife, held obliquely and pressed against the bone while in a fresh state, with considerable force, just as a savage would do in hacking the flesh off a stranded whale. Cuts exactly similar can now be made on fresh bone by such flint knives, and in no other known or conceivable way. It seems, therefore, more like obstinate prepossession, than scientific skepticism, to deny the existence of Tertiary man, if it rested only on this single instance."

A modern authority, Binford, stated: "There is little chance that an observer of modified bone would confuse cut marks inflicted during dismembering or filleting by man using tools with the action of animals."

But the teeth of sharks (Figure 2.1) are sharper than those of terrestrial mammalian carnivores such as wolves and might produce marks on bone that more closely resemble those that might be made by cutting implements. After inspecting fossil whale bones in the paleontology collection of the San Diego Natural History Museum, we concluded that shark's teeth can in fact make marks closely resembling those that might be made by implements.

The bones we saw were from a small Pliocene species of baleen whale. We examined cuts on the bone through a magnifying glass. We saw evenly spaced parallel longitudinal striations on both surfaces of the cuts. These are just the kind of marks one would expect from the serrated edge of a shark's

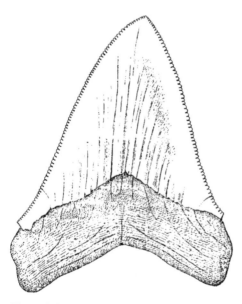

Figure 2.1. Tooth of *Carcharodon megalodon,* a Pliocene great white shark.

tooth. We also saw scrape marks on the bone (Figure 2.2). These could have been produced by a glancing blow, with the edge of the tooth scraping along the surface of the bone rather than cutting into it.

With this knowledge, it should be possible to reexamine the Pliocene whale bones of Italy and arrive at some fairly definite conclusions as to whether or not the marks on them were made by shark teeth. Patterns of parallel ridges and grooves on the surfaces of the fossils would be an almost certain sign of shark predation or scavenging. And

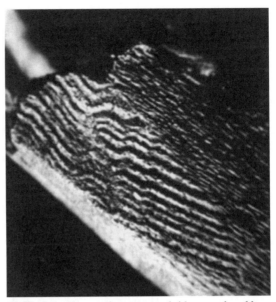

Figure 2.2. Pattern of grooves and ridges produced by a serrated shark tooth moving across the surface of a whale bone.

if close examination of deep V-shaped cuts also revealed evenly spaced, parallel longitudinal striations, that, too, would have to be taken as evidence that shark teeth made the cuts. One would not expect the surfaces of marks made by flint blades to display evenly spaced striations.

HALITHERIUM OF POUANCÉ, FRANCE

In 1867, L. Bourgeois caused a great sensation when he presented to the members of the International Congress of Prehistoric Anthropology and Archeology, meeting in Paris, a *Halitherium* bone bearing marks that appeared to be human incisions. *Halitherium* is a kind of extinct sea cow, an aquatic marine mammal of the order Sirenia (Figure 2.3).

The fossilized bones of *Halitherium* had been discovered by the Abbé Delaunay in the shell beds at Barriére, near Pouancé in northwestern France. Delaunay

Figure 2.3. Cut marks on *Halitherium* bone from the Miocene at Pouancé, France.

was surprised to see on a fragment of the humerus, a bone from the upper forelimb, a number of cut marks. The surfaces of the cuts were of the same appearance as the rest of the bone and were easily distinguished from recent breaks, indicating that the cuts were quite ancient. The bone itself, which was fossilized, was firmly situated in an undisturbed stratum, making it clear that the marks on the bone were of the same geological age. Furthermore, the depth and sharpness of the incisions showed that they had been made before the bone had fossilized. Some of the incisions appeared to have been made by two separate intersecting strokes.

Even de Mortillet admitted that they did not appear to be the products of subterranean scraping or compression. But he would not admit they could be the product of human work, mainly because of the Miocene age of the stratum in which the bones were found. De Mortillet wrote in 1883, "This is much too old for man." Here again, we have a clear case of theoretical preconceptions dictating how one will interpret a set of facts.

SAN VALENTINO, ITALY

In 1876, at a meeting of the Geological Committee of Italy, M. A. Ferretti showed a fossil animal bone bearing "traces of work of the hand of man, so evident as to exclude all doubt to the contrary." This bone, of elephant or rhinoceros, was found firmly in place in Astian (Late Pliocene) strata in San Valentino (Reggio d'Emilie), Italy. Of special interest is the fact that the fossil bone has an almost perfectly round hole at the place of its greatest width. According to Ferretti, the hole in the bone was not the work of molluscs or crustaceans. The next year Ferretti showed to the Committee another bone bearing traces of human work. It was found in blue Pliocene clay, of Astian age, at San Ruffino. This bone appeared to have been partially sawn through at one end, and then broken.

At a scientific conference held in 1880, G. Bellucci, of the Italian Society for Anthropology and Geography, called attention to new discoveries in San Valentino and Castello delle Forme, near Perugia. These included animal bones bearing cuts and impact marks from stones implements, carbonized bones, and flint flakes. All were recovered from lacustrine Pliocene clays, characterized by a fauna like that of the classic Val d'Arno. According to Bellucci, these objects proved the existence of man in the Pliocene.

CLERMONT-FERRAND, FRANCE

In the late nineteenth century, the museum of natural history at Clermont-Ferrand acquired a femur of *Rhinoceros paradoxus* with grooves on its surface. The specimen was found in a freshwater limestone at Gannat, which contained fossils of animals typical of the Middle Miocene. Some suggested the grooves on the bone were caused by animal teeth. But Gabriel de Mortillet disagreed, offering his usual explanation—the bone had been marked by stones moving under geological pressure.

But de Mortillet's own description of the markings on the bone leaves this interpretation open to question. The cut marks were located near the end of the femur, near the joint surfaces. According to Louis Binford, a modern expert on cut bones, this is where butchering marks would normally be found. De Mortillet also said that the marks were "parallel grooves, somewhat irregular, transverse to the axis of the bone." Binford's studies revealed: "Cut marks from stone tools are most commonly made with a sawing motion resulting in short and frequently multiple but roughly parallel marks."

CARVED SHELL FROM THE RED CRAG, ENGLAND

In a report delivered to the British Association for the Advancement of Science in 1881, H. Stopes, F.G.S. (Fellow of the Geological Society), described a shell, the surface of which bore a carving of a crude but unmistakably human face. The carved shell was found in the stratified deposits of the Red Crag, which is between 2.0 and 2.5 million years old.

Marie C. Stopes, the discoverer's daughter, argued in an article in *The Geological Magazine* (1912) that the carved shell could not have been a forgery: "It should be noted that the excavated features are as deeply coloured red-brown as the rest of the surface. This is an important point, because when the surface of Red Crag shells are scratched they show white below the colour. It should also be noticed that the shell is so delicate that any attempt to carve it would merely shatter it." One should keep in mind that in terms of conventional paleoanthropological opinion, one does not encounter such works of art until the time of fully modern Cro-Magnon man in the Late Pleistocene, about 30,000 years ago.

BONE IMPLEMENTS FROM BELOW THE RED CRAG, ENGLAND

In the early twentieth century, J. Reid Moir, the discoverer of many anomalously old flint implements (see Chapter 3), described "a series of mineralised bone implements of a primitive type from below the base of the Red and Coralline Crags of Suffolk." The top of the Red Crag in East Anglia is now considered to mark the boundary of the Pliocene and Pleistocene, and would thus date back about 2.0–2.5 million years. The older Coralline Crag is Late Pliocene and would thus be at least 2.5–3.0 million years old. The beds below the Red and Coralline Crags, the detritus beds, contain materials ranging from Pliocene to Eocene in age. Objects found there could thus be anywhere from 2 million to 55 million years old.

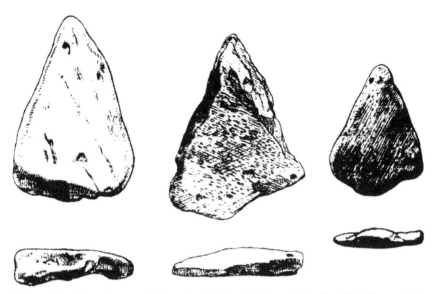

Figure 2.4. Three bone tools from the detritus bed beneath the Coralline Crag, which contains materials ranging from Pliocene to Eocene in age. These implements could thus be anywhere from 2 to 55 million years old.

One group of Moir's specimens is of triangular shape (Figure 2.4). In his report, Moir stated: "These have all been formed from wide, flat, thin pieces of bone, probably portions of large ribs, which have been so fractured as to now present a definite form. This triangular form has, in every case, been produced by fractures across the natural 'grain' of the bone." Moir conducted experiments on bone and came to the conclusion that his specimens were "undoubted works of man." According to Moir, the triangular pieces of fossilized whale bone discovered in the strata below the Coralline Crag might have once been used as spear points. Moir also found whale ribs that had been worked into pointed implements.

Moir and others also found incised bones and bone implements in various levels of the Cromer Forest Bed, from the youngest to the oldest. The youngest levels of the Cromer Forest Bed are about .4 million years old; the oldest are at least .8 million years old, and, according to some modern authorities, might be as much as 1.75 million years old.

In addition, Moir described a bone discovered by a Mr. Whincopp, of Woodbridge in Suffolk, who had in his private collection a "piece of fossil rib partially sawn across at both ends." This object came from the detritus bed below the Red Crag and was, said Moir, "regarded by both the discoverer and the late Rev. Osmond Fisher as affording evidence of human handiwork." Indications of sawing would be quite unexpected on a fossil bone of this age.

A piece of sawn wood was recovered by S. A. Notcutt from the Cromer Forest Bed at Mundesley. Most of the Mundesley strata are about .4 –.5 million years old.

In the course of his comments about the piece of cut wood, Moir made these observations: "The flat end appears to have been produced by sawing with a sharp flint, and at one spot it seems that the line of cutting has been corrected (Figure 2.5), as is often necessary when starting to cut wood with a modern steel saw." Moir further noted: "The pointed end is somewhat blackened as if by fire, and it is possible that the specimen represents a primitive digging stick used for grubbing up roots."

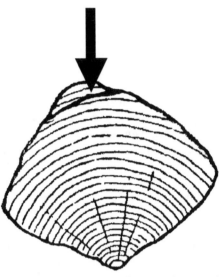

Figure 2.5. Cross section of a piece of cut wood from the Cromer Forest Bed. The arrow indicates a groove, possibly from an initial cut by a sawing implement.

While there is an outside chance that beings of the *Homo erectus* type might have been present in England during the time of the Cromer Forest Bed, the level of technological sophistication implied by this sawn wood tool is suggestive of *sapiens*-like capabilities. In fact, it is hard to see how this kind of sawing could have been produced even by stone implements. Small flint chips mounted in a wooden holder, for example, would not have produced the clean cut evident on the specimen because the wooden holder would have been wider than the flint teeth. Hence one could not have cut a narrow groove with such a device. A saw blade made only of stone would have been extremely brittle and would not have lasted long enough to perform the operation. Furthermore, it would have been quite an accomplishment to make such a stone blade. Thus it seems that only a metal saw could produce the observed sawing. Of course, a metal saw at .4–.5 million years is quite anomalous.

It is remarkable that the incised bones, bone implements, and other artifacts from the Red Crag and Cromer Forest Beds are hardly mentioned at all in today's standard textbooks and references. This is especially remarkable in the case of the Cromer Forest Bed finds, most of which are, in terms of their age, bordering on the acceptable, in terms of the modern paleoanthropological sequence of events.

DEWLISH ELEPHANT TRENCH, ENGLAND

Osmond Fisher, a fellow the Geological Society, discovered an interesting feature in the landscape of Dorsetshire—the elephant trench at Dewlish. Fisher said in *The Geological Magazine* (1912): "This trench was excavated in chalk and was 12 feet deep, and of such a width that a man could just pass along it. It is not on the line of any natural fracture, and the beds of flint on each side correspond. The bottom was of undisturbed chalk, and one end, like the sides, was vertical. At the other end it opened diagonally on to the steep side of a valley. It has yielded substantial remains of *Elephas meridionalis,* but no other fossils. . . . This trench, in my opinion, was excavated by man in the later Pliocene age as a pitfall to catch elephants." *Elephas meridionalis,* or "southern elephant," was in existence in Europe from 1.2 to 3.5 million years ago. Thus, while the bones found in the trench at Dewlish could conceivably be Early Pleistocene in age, they might also date to the Late Pliocene.

Photographs show the vertical walls of the trench were carefully chipped as if with a large chisel. And Fisher referred to reports showing that primitive hunters of modern times made use of similar trenches.

But further excavation of the trench by the Dorset Field Club, as reported in a brief note in *Nature* (October 16, 1914), revealed that "instead of ending below in a definite floor it divides downward into a chain of deep narrow pipes in the chalk." However, it is not unlikely that ancient humans might have made use of small fissures to open a larger trench in the chalk. It would be worthwhile to examine the elephant bones found in the trench for signs of cut marks.

Fisher made another interesting discovery. In his 1912 review, he wrote: "When digging for fossils in the Eocene of Barton Cliff I found a piece of jet-like substance about $9^{1}/_{2}$ inches square and $2^{1}/_{4}$ inches thick. . . . It bore on at least one side what seemed to me marks of the chopping which had formed it into its accurately square shape. The specimen is now in the Sedgwick Museum, Cambridge." Jet is a compact velvety-black coal that takes a good polish and is often used as jewelry. The Eocene period dates back about 38–55 million years from the present.

CONCLUDING WORDS ABOUT
INTENTIONALLY MODIFIED BONE

It is really quite curious that so many serious scientific investigators in the nineteenth century and early twentieth century independently and repeatedly reported that marks on bones and shells from Miocene, Pliocene, and Early Pleistocene formations were indicative of human work. Among the researchers making such claims were Desnoyers, de Quatrefages, Ramorino, Bourgeois, Delaunay, Bertrand, Laussedat, Garrigou, Filhol, von Dücker, Owen, Collyer,

Calvert, Capellini, Broca, Ferretti, Bellucci, Stopes, Moir, Fisher, and Keith.

Were these scientists deluded? Perhaps so. But cut marks on fossil bones are an odd thing about which to develop delusions—hardly romantic or inspiring. Were the above-mentioned researchers victims of a unique mental aberration of the last century and the early part of this one? Or does evidence of primitive hunters really abound in the faunal remains of the Pliocene and earlier periods?

Assuming such evidence is there, one might ask why it is not being found today. One very good reason is that no one is looking for it. Evidence for intentional human work on bone might easily escape the attention of a scientist not actively searching for it. If a paleoanthropologist is convinced that toolmaking human beings did not exist in the Middle Pliocene, he is not likely to give much thought to the exact nature of markings on fossil bones from that period.

3

Eoliths: Stones of Contention

Nineteenth-century scientists found many stone tools and weapons in Early Pleistocene, Pliocene, Miocene, and older strata. They were reported in standard scientific journals, and they were discussed at scientific congresses. But today hardly anyone has heard of them. Whole categories of facts have disappeared from view.

We have, however, managed to recover a vast hoard of such "buried" evidence, and our review of it shall take us from the hills of Kent in England to the valley of the Irrawady in Burma. Researchers of the late twentieth century have also discovered anomalously old stone tool industries.

The anomalous stone tool industries we shall consider fall into three basic divisions: (1) eoliths, (2) crude paleoliths, and (3) advanced paleoliths and neoliths.

According to some authorities, eoliths (or dawn stones) are stones with edges naturally suited for certain kinds of uses. These, it was said, were selected by humans and used as tools with little or no further modification. To the untrained eye, Eolithic stone implements are often indistinguishable from ordinary broken rocks, but specialists developed criteria for identifying upon them signs of human modification and usage. At the very least, unmistakable marks of usage should be present in order for a specimen to qualify as an eolith.

In the case of more sophisticated stone tools, called crude paleoliths, the signs of human manufacture are more obvious, involving an attempt to form the whole of the stone into a recognizable tool shape. Questions about such implements center mainly upon the determination of their correct age.

Our third division, advanced paleoliths and neoliths, refers to anomalously old stone tools that resemble the very finely chipped or smoothly polished stone industries of the standard Late Paleolithic and Neolithic periods.

For most researchers, eoliths would be the oldest implements, followed in turn by the paleoliths and neoliths. But we will use these terms mainly to indicate degrees of workmanship. It is impossible to assign ages to stone tools simply on the basis of their form.

29

EOLITHS OF THE KENT PLATEAU, ENGLAND

The small town of Ightham, in Kent, is situated about twenty-seven miles southeast of London. During the Victorian era, Benjamin Harrison kept a grocery shop in Ightham. On holidays he roamed the nearby hills and valleys, collecting flint implements which, though now long forgotten, were for decades the center of protracted controversy in the scientific community.

Harrison did much of his work in close consultation with Sir John Prestwich, the famous English geologist, who lived in the vicinity. Harrison also corresponded regularly with other scientists involved in paleoanthropological research and carefully catalogued and mapped his finds, according to standard procedures.

Harrison's first finds were polished stone artifacts of the Neolithic type. According to modern opinion, Neolithic cultures date back only about 10,000 years, and are associated with agriculture and pottery. Harrison found neoliths scattered over the present land surfaces around Ightham.

Later, he began to find paleoliths in ancient river gravels. These Paleolithic implements, although cruder than Neolithic implements, are still easily recognized as objects of human manufacture.

How old were the these Paleolithic tools? Prestwich and Harrison considered some of the stone implements found near Ightham to be Pliocene in age. Twentieth-century geologists, such as Francis H. Edmunds of the Geological Survey of Great Britain, have also said that the gravels in which many of the implements were found are Pliocene. Hugo Obermaier, a leading paleoanthropologist of the early twentieth century, stated that the flint implements collected by Harrison from the Kent Plateau belong to the Middle Pliocene. A Late or Middle Pliocene date for the implements of the Kent Plateau would give them an age of 2–4 million years. Modern paleoanthropologists attribute the Paleolithic implements of the Somme region of France to *Homo erectus,* and date them at just .5–.7 million years ago. The oldest currently recognized implements in England are about .4 million years old.

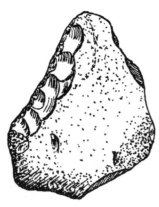

Figure 3.1. An eolith from the Kent Plateau.

Among the Paleolithic implements collected by Benjamin Harrison from the Kent Plateau were some that appeared to belong to an even more primitive level of culture. These were the eoliths, or dawn stones (Figure 3.1). The Paleolithic implements discovered by Harrison, although somewhat crude in appearance, had been extensively worked in order to bring them into definite tool and weapon shapes (Figure 3.2).

 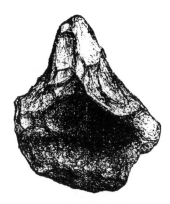

Figure 3.2. These implements from the Kent Chalk Plateau were characterized as paleoliths by Sir John Prestwich. Prestwich called the one on the left, from Bower Lane, a roughly made implement of the spear-head type.

The Eolithic implements, however, were natural flint flakes displaying only retouching along the edges. Such tools are still employed today by primitive tribal people in various parts of the world, who pick up a stone flake, chip one of the edges, and then use it for a scraper or cutter.

Critics claimed Harrison's eoliths were just figments of his imagination— merely broken pieces of flint. But Leland W. Patterson, a modern authority on stone tools, believes it is possible to distinguish even very crude intentional work from natural action. "It would be difficult," said Patterson, "to visualize how random applications of force could create uniform, unidirectional retouch along a significant length of a flake edge."

Unifacial tools, with regular chipping confined to one side of a surface, formed a large part of the eoliths gathered by Harrison. According to Patterson's criterion, these would have to be accepted as objects of human manufacture. On September 18, 1889, A. M. Bell, a Fellow of the Geological Society, wrote to Harrison: "There seems to be something more in the uniform though rude chipping than mere accidental attrition would have produced. . . . having made my conclusion, I hold it with all firmness."

On November 2, 1891, Alfred Russell Wallace, one of the most famous scientists of his time, paid an unannounced visit to Benjamin Harrison at his grocery shop in Ightham. Harrison showed Wallace his collection of stone tools and took him to some of the sites. Wallace accepted the tools as genuine and asked Harrison to write a thorough report on them.

Sir John Prestwich, one of England's foremost authorities on stone tools, also accepted Harrison's find as genuine. Answering the charge that the eoliths were perhaps naturefacts rather than artifacts, Prestwich stated in 1895: "Challenged to

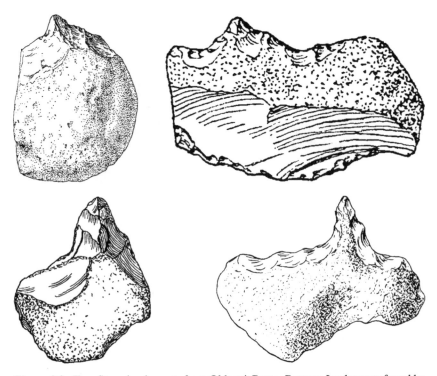

Figure 3.3. Top: Stone implements from Olduvai Gorge. Bottom: Implements found by Benjamin Harrison on the Kent Plateau, England.

show any such natural specimens, those who have made the assertion have been unable, although nearly three years have elapsed since the challenge was given, to bring forward a single such specimen. . . . So far from running water having this constructive power, the tendency of it is to wear off all angles, and reduce the flint to a more or less rounded pebble."

In another article, published in 1892, Prestwich made this important observation: "Even modern savage work, such as exhibited for example by the stone implements of the Australian natives, show, when divested of their mounting, an amount of work no greater or more distinct, than do these early palaeolithic specimens."

Therefore, we need not attribute the Plateau eoliths to a primitive race of apemen. Since the eoliths are practically identical to stone tools made by *Homo sapiens sapiens,* it is possible that the eoliths (and the paleoliths) may have been made by humans of the fully modern type in England during the Middle or Late Pliocene. As we shall see in Chapter 7, scientists of the nineteenth century made several discoveries of skeletal remains of anatomically modern human beings in strata of Pliocene age.

Interestingly, modern experts accept tools exactly resembling Harrison's eoliths as genuine human artifacts. For example, the cobble and flake tools of the lower levels of Olduvai Gorge (Figure 3.3) are extremely crude. But scientists have not challenged their status as intentionally manufactured objects.

Some critics thought that even if Harrison's tools were made by humans, they might not be of Pliocene age. They might have been dropped in the Pliocene gravels during fairly recent times.

In order to resolve the controversy over the age of the eoliths, the British Association, a prestigious scientific society, financed excavations in the high-level Plateau gravels and other localities in close proximity to Ightham. The purpose was to show definitively that eoliths were to be found not only on the surface but *in situ*, deep within the Pliocene preglacial gravels. Harrison had already found some eoliths *in situ* (such as some from post holes), but this excavation, financed by the respected British Association, would be more conclusive. The British Association selected Harrison himself to supervise the Plateau excavations, under the direction of a committee of scientists. Harrison recorded in his notebooks that he found many examples of eoliths *in situ,* including "thirty convincers."

In 1895, Harrison was invited to exhibit his eoliths at a meeting of the Royal Society. Some of the scientists remained skeptical. Others, however, were quite impressed. Among them was E. T. Newton, a Fellow of the Royal Society and member of the Geological Survey of Great Britain, who wrote to Harrison on December 24, 1895 about the implements: "Some of them, to say the least, show human work. . . . they have been done intentionally, and, therefore, by the only intellectual being we know of, *Man*."

In 1896, Prestwich died, but Harrison, in his prominent patron's absence, continued with the Plateau excavations and answered the doubters. Ray E. Lankester, who was a director of the British Museum (Natural History), became a supporter of Harrison's Kent Plateau eoliths.

One may question the necessity of giving such a detailed treatment of the Harrison eoliths. One reason is to show that evidence of this kind was not always of a marginal, crackpot nature. Rather anomalous evidence was quite often the center of serious, longstanding controversy within the very heart of elite scientific circles, with advocates holding scientific credentials and positions just as prestigious as those of the opponents. By presenting detailed accounts of the interplay of conflicting opinion, we hope to give the reader a chance to answer for himself or herself the crucial question—was the evidence actually rejected on purely objective grounds, or was it dropped from consideration and forgotten simply because it did not lie within the parameters of certain circumscribed theories?

Harrison died in 1921, and his body was buried on the grounds of the parish church, St. Peter's, in Ightham. A memorial tablet, set in the north wall of St. Peter's on July 10, 1926, bears this inscription: "IN MEMORIAM.—Benjamin Harrison of Ightham, 1837–1921, the village grocer and archaeologist whose discoveries of eolithic flint implements around Ightham opened a fruitful field of scientific investigation into the greater antiquity of man."

But the fruitful field of scientific investigation into the greater antiquity of man opened by the eoliths of the Kent Plateau was buried along with Harrison. Here is what appears to have taken place. In the 1890s, Eugene Dubois discovered and promoted the famous, yet dubious, Java ape-man (Chapter 8). Many scientists accepted Java man, found unaccompanied by stone tools, as a genuine human ancestor. But because Java man was found in Middle Pleistocene strata, the extensive evidence for toolmaking hominids in the far earlier Pliocene and Miocene periods no longer received much serious attention. How could such toolmaking hominids have appeared long before their supposed ape-man ancestors? Such a thing would be impossible; so better to ignore and forget any discoveries that fell outside the bounds of theoretical expectations.

DISCOVERIES BY J. REID MOIR IN EAST ANGLIA

Our journey of exploration now takes us to the southeast coast of England and the discoveries of J. Reid Moir, a fellow of the Royal Anthropological Institute and president of the Prehistoric Society of East Anglia. Starting in 1909, Moir found flint implements in and beneath the Red and Coralline Crags.

The Red Crag formation, in which Moir made some of his most significant discoveries, is composed of the shelly sands of a sea that once washed the shores of East Anglia. At some places beneath the Red Crag is found a similar formation called the Coralline Crag.

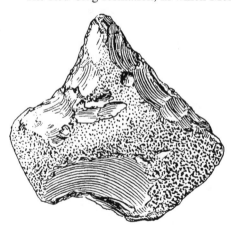

After studying modern geological reports, we have arrived at an age of at least 2.0–2.5 million years for the Red Crag. The Coralline Crag would thus be older. Below the Red and Coralline Crags of East Anglia there are detritus beds, sometimes called bone beds. These are composed of a mixture of materials—sands, gravels, shells, and bones derived from a variety of older

Figure 3.4. Pointed implement from below the Red Crag. This specimen is over 2.5 million years old.

formations, including the Eocene London Clay.

J. Reid Moir found in the sub-Crag detritus beds stone tools, showing varying degrees of intentional work (Figure 3.4). Having concluded that the cruder tools were from as far back as the Eocene, Moir said "it becomes necessary to recognize a much higher antiquity for the human race than has hitherto been supposed."

At the very least, Moir's implements are Late Pliocene in age. But according to present evolutionary theory one should not expect to find signs of toolmaking humans in England at 2–3 million years ago.

Moir thought that the makers of his oldest and crudest tools must "represent an early and brutal stage in human evolution." But even

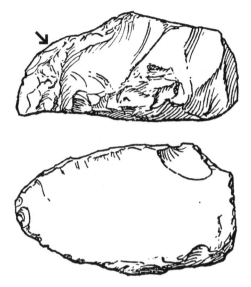

Figure 3.5. The Norwich test specimen. J. Reid Moir said it was found beneath the Red Crag at Whitlingham, England. The beak (arrow) forms the working portion of the implement, which, if from below the Red Crag, would be over 2.5 million years old.

today, modern tribal people are known to manufacture very primitive stone tools. It is thus possible that beings very much like *Homo sapiens sapiens* could have made even the crudest of the implements recovered by Moir from below the Red Crag.

The implements themselves were a matter of extreme controversy. Many scientists thought them to be products of natural forces rather than of human work. Nevertheless, Moir had many influential supporters. These included Henri Breuil, who personally investigated the sites. He found in Moir's collection an apparent sling stone from below the Red Crag. Another supporter was Archibald Geikie, a respected geologist and president of the Royal Society. Yet another was Sir Ray Lankester, a director of the British Museum. Lankester identified from among Moir's specimens a representative type of implement he named rostro-carinate. This word calls attention to two prominent characteristics of the tools. "Rostro" refers to the beaklike shape of the working portion of the implements, and "carinate" refers to the sharp keellike prominence running along part of their dorsal surface.

Lankester presented a detailed analysis of what he called "the Norwich test specimen" (Figure 3.5). A particularly good example of the rostro-carinate type

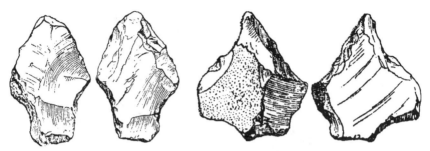

Figure 3.6. Front and rear views of two stone tools from the Red Crag at Foxhall, England. They are Late Pliocene in age. Henry Fairfield Osborn said of the tool on the left: "Two views of pointed flint implement flaked on the upper and lower surfaces and with a constricted base, from sixteen-foot level of Foxhall pit. Primitive arrowhead type, which may have been used in the chase." Of the implement on the right, Osborn wrote: "Borer (*perçoir*) from sixteen-foot level of Foxhall."

of implement, it was discovered beneath the Red Crag at Whitlingham, near Norwich. If the Norwich test specimen is from below the Red Crag, it would be over 2.5 million years old. The Norwich test specimen combined a good demonstration of intentional work with clear stratigraphic position. Lankester wrote in a Royal Anthropological Institute report in 1914: "It is not possible for anyone acquainted with flint-workmanship and also with the non-human fracture of flint to maintain that it is even in a remote degree possible that the sculpturing of this Norwich test flint was produced by other than human agency." Lankester thought tools of this type might be of Miocene age.

An important set of discoveries by Moir occurred at Foxhall, where he found stone tools (Figure 3.6) in the middle of the Late Pliocene Red Crag formation. The Foxhall implements would thus be over 2.0 million years old. Moir wrote in 1927: "The finds consisted of the debris of a flint workshop, and included hammer-stones, cores from which flakes had been struck, finished implements, numerous flakes, and several calcined stones showing that fires had been lighted at this spot. . . . if the famous Foxhall human jaw-bone, which was apparently not very primitive in form, was, indeed, derived from the old land surface now buried deep beneath the Crag and a great thickness of Glacial Gravel, we can form the definite opinion that these ancient people were not very unlike ourselves in bodily characteristics."

The jaw spoken of by Moir has an interesting history (see Chapter 7). Some scientists who examined it considered it like that of a modern human being. It is unfortunate that the Foxhall jaw is not available for further study, for it might offer additional confirmation that the flint implements from Foxhall were of human manufacture. But even without the jaw, the tools themselves point strongly to a human presence in England during the Late Pliocene, perhaps 2.0–2.5 million years ago.

In 1921, the American paleontologist Henry Fairfield Osborn came out strongly in favor of the implements and argued for a Pliocene date. He said that proofs of humans in the Pliocene "now rest on the firm foundation of the Foxhall flints in which human handiwork cannot be challenged." According to Osborn, the Foxhall specimens included borers, arrowheadlike pointed implements, scrapers, and side scrapers.

Osborn backed not only the Foxhall flints but the rest of Moir's work as well: "The discoveries of J. Reid Moir of evidences of the existence of Pliocene man in East Anglia open a new epoch in archaeology. . . they bring indubitable evidence of the existence of man in southeast Britain, man of sufficient intelligence to fashion flints and to build a fire, before the close of the Pliocene time and before the advent of the First Glaciation."

Another scientist won over by the Foxhall finds was Hugo Obermaier, previously a consistent and vocal opponent of Eolithic discoveries. Obermaier was one of those scientists who believed that eoliths were produced by natural forces similar to the forces operating in cement and chalk mills. But Obermaier wrote in 1924: "This discovery of Foxhall is the first evidence we have of the existence of Tertiary man." The Tertiary epoch extends from the Eocene through the Pliocene.

Moir also made discoveries in the more recent Cromer Forest Bed of Norfolk. These tools would be about .4 million years to about .8 million years old. Some estimates for the age of the lower part of the Cromer Forest Bed formation go up to 1.75 million years.

But many scientists continued to refuse to accept Moir's specimens as genuine tools. They argued that the objects had been produced by purely natural forces. For example, S. Hazzledine Warren said they were produced by geological pressure that crushed pieces of flint against hard beds of chalk. As proof, he referred to some specimens of chipped stone from the Bullhead Bed, an Eocene site in England. About one such object (Figure 3.7), Warren said in a 1920 report to the Geological Society of London: "This, a good example of a trimmed-flake point, is the most

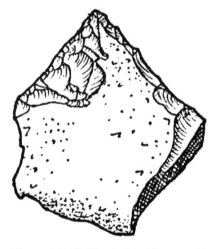

Figure 3.7. S. Hazzledine Warren said that this object, which he believed to be the product of natural pressure flaking, almost exactly resembled a Mousterian trimmed point implement. But although found in an Eocene formation, it could in fact be of human manufacture.

remarkable specimen of the group. If considered by itself, upon its own apparent merits, and away from its associates and the circumstances of its discovery, its Mousterian affinities could scarcely be questioned." The Mousterian is an accepted stone tool industry of the later Pleistocene. Warren thought it impossible that one could find tools in Eocene strata. But those free from such prejudices might wonder whether Warren had actually discovered, in the Eocene strata of Essex, a genuine implement.

In the discussion following Warren's report to the Geological Society, one of the scientists present pointed out that in some cases the Moir's tools were found in the middle of Tertiary sedimentary beds and not directly on the hard chalk. This would rule out the particular pressure explanation given by Warren.

At this point, the controversy over Moir's discoveries was submitted to an international commission of scientists for resolution. The commission, formed at the request of the International Institute of Anthropology, was composed of eight prominent European and American anthropologists, geologists, and archeologists. This group supported Moir's conclusions. They concluded that the flints from the base of the Red Crag near Ipswich were in undisturbed strata, at least Pliocene in age. Furthermore, the flaking on the flints was undoubtedly of human origin. Members of the commission also carried out four excavations into the detritus bed below the Red Crag and themselves found five typical specimens. These tools would be at least 2.5 million years old. And because the detritus bed contains materials from ancient Eocene land surfaces, the tools might be up to 55 million years old.

Commission member Louis Capitan stated: "There exist at the base of the Crag, in undisturbed strata, worked flints (we have observed them ourselves). These are not made by anything other than a human or hominid which existed in the Tertiary epoch. This fact is found by us prehistorians to be absolutely demonstrated."

Surprisingly, even after the commission report, Moir's opponents, such as Warren, persisted in attempting to show that the flint implements were the product of natural pressure flaking. Warren said that the flints may have been crushed by icebergs against the ocean bottom along the coast. But to our knowledge no one has shown that icebergs can produce the numerous bulbs of percussion and elaborate retouching reported on Moir's implements. Furthermore, many of the Red Crag specimens are lying in the middle of sediments and not on hard rock surfaces against which an iceberg might have crushed them. In addition, J. M. Coles, an English archeologist, reported that at Foxhall implements occur in layers of sediment that appear to represent land surfaces and not beach deposits. This would also rule out the iceberg action imagined by Warren.

After Warren put forward his iceberg explanation, the controversy faded. Coles wrote in 1968: "That . . . the scientific world did not see fit to accept either side without considerable uncertainty must account for the quite remarkable inattention that this East Anglian problem has received since the days of active controversy." This may be in part true, but there is another possible explanation— that elements of the scientific community decided silence was a better way to bury Moir's discoveries than active and vocal dissent. By the 1950s, scientific opinion was lining up solidly behind an Early Pleistocene African center for human evolution. Therefore, there would have been little point, and perhaps some embarrassment and harm, in continually trying to disprove evidence for a theoretically impossible Pliocene habitation of England. That would have kept both sides of the controversy too much alive. The policy of silence, deliberate or not, did in fact prove highly successful in removing Moir's evidence from view. There was no need to defeat something that was beneath notice, and little to gain from defending or supporting it either.

Coles provides an exception to the usual instinctive rejection of Moir's discoveries (or complete silence about them). He felt it "unjust to dismiss all this material without some consideration" and in a 1968 report hesitantly accepted some of the implements as genuine.

Although most modern authorities do not even mention Moir's discoveries, a rare notice of dismissal may be found in *The Ice Age in Britain,* by B. W. Sparks and R. G. West: "Early in this century many flints from the Lower Pleistocene Crags were described as being artifacts, such as the flints, some flaked bifacially, in the Red Crag near Ipswich, and the so-called rostrocarinates from the base of the Norwich Crag near Norwich. All are now thought to be natural products. They do not satisfy the requirements for identification as a tool, namely, that the object conforms to a set and regular pattern, that it is found in a geologically possible habitation site, preferably with other signs of man's activities (e.g. chipping, killing, or burial site), and that it shows signs of flaking from two or three directions at right angles." Sparks and West, of Cambridge University, are experts on the Pleistocene in Britain.

Briefly responding to Sparks and West, we may note that Moir and other authorities, such as Osborn and Capitan, were able to classify the Crag specimens into definite tool types (handaxes, borers, scrapers, etc.) comparable to those included in accepted Paleolithic industries, including the Mousterian. The Foxhall site, with the Foxhall jaw, was taken by many authorities to represent a geologically possible habitation site. Moir considered it to be a workshop area and noted signs of fire having been used there. As far as flaking from several directions at right angles is concerned, this is not the only criterion that might be applied for judging human workmanship upon stone objects. Even so, M. C. Burkitt of Cambridge did find flaking from several different directions at right angles on some of the implements collected by J. Reid Moir.

Burkitt, who served on the international commission that examined Moir's implements in the 1920s, gave favorable treatment to them in his book *The Old Stone Age,* published in 1956.

Burkitt was particularly impressed with the site at Thorington Hall, 2 miles south of Ipswich, where flint implements had been collected from the Crag deposits. "At Thorington Hall bivalve shells with the hinges still intact have been collected from just above the artifacts . . . no subsequent differential movement of the gravel, such as might have caused fracturing of the contained flints, can have taken place, since it would certainly have led to the smashing of the delicate hinges of these shells."

Burkitt then delivered a striking conclusion about the implements discovered in and below the Red Crag: "The eoliths themselves are mostly much older than the late pliocene deposits in which they were found. Some of them might actually date back to pre-pliocene times." In other words, he was prepared to accept the existence of intelligent toolmaking hominids in England over 5 million years ago. Because there is much evidence, including skeletal remains, that humans of the fully modern type existed in pre-Pliocene times, there is no reason to rule out the possibility that Moir's implements from the below the Crag formations were made by *Homo sapiens* over 5 million years ago.

Another supporter of Moir's finds was Louis Leakey, who wrote in 1960: "It is more than likely that primitive humans were present in Europe during the Lower Pleistocene, just as they were in Africa, and certainly a proportion of the specimens from the sub-crag deposits appear to be humanly flaked and cannot be regarded merely as the result of natural forces. Implements from below the Crags would, however, be not Early (Lower) Pleistocene but at least Late Pliocene in age."

TWO FAMOUS DEBUNKERS OF EOLITHS

In paleoanthropology, we sometimes encounter the definitive debunking report—one that is used again and again to invalidate certain evidence. In the case of European eoliths, there are two good examples of definitive debunking reports. These are H. Breuil's paper claiming that pseudoeoliths were formed by geological pressure in the French Eocene formations at Clermont (Oise), and A. S. Barnes's paper claiming to demonstrate, by statistical analysis of platform striking angles, the natural origin of Eolithic industries.

In 1910, Henri Breuil conducted investigations he thought would put an end to the eolith controversy. In his often cited report, he said he found flints resembling stone tools in the Thanetian formation at Belle-Assise, near Clermont, France. This formation is Early Eocene, making the flints about 50–55 million years old. But Breuil could not imagine human beings existed in the Eocene. How, then, had the flint objects been produced? During his excavations, Breuil found a few pieces of flint with detached flakes lying nearby. Some of these detached flakes had bulbs of percussion. Others had some flaking on them that resembled retouching. The cause of these effects, according to Breuil, was simply geological pressure.

Can geological pressure really create the effects observed by Breuil? Leland W. Patterson, a modern authority on stone tools, says that pressure flaking very rarely produces clearly marked bulbs of percussion. It usually takes an intentionally directed blow.

Breuil probably selected for illustration his best examples of flakes found in contact with the parent block of flint (Figures 3.8). But the flaking and retouching on them is far cruder than on the cores and flakes selected by Breuil as examples of pseudoeoliths (Figure 3.9). Breuil said all the effects

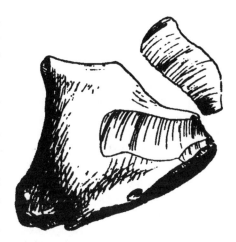

Figure 3.8. Henri Breuil found examples of flakes removed from parent blocks of flint by geological pressure in an Eocene formation in Clermont (Oise), France. Such specimens, he believed, showed that eoliths were not made by human beings.

resulted from natural geological pressure flaking. But he would have been justified in making such a statement only if he had found the flakes from better looking eoliths in contact with their parent blocks of flint. And this he did not do.

The unsatisfactory nature of Breuil's geological pressure hypothesis becomes even clearer when we consider what Breuil called "two truly exceptional objects,

Figure 3.9. These objects, from an Eocene formation at Clermont (Oise), France, were characterized by H. Breuil as "pseudoeoliths."

of which the site of discovery, in the interior of the beds, is absolutely certain."

Breuil said the first object (Figure 3.10) was virtually indistinguishable from an Azilio-Tardenoisian *grattoir,* or end scraper. Scientists generally attribute Azilio-Tardenoisian stone implements to *Homo sapiens sapiens* in the Late Pleistocene of Europe. In describing the second exceptional object (Figure 3.11), Breuil compared it to tools found at Les Eyzies, a Late Pleistocene site in France. Geological pressure flaking does not seem adequate to explain these two tools, which are over 50 million years old.

Breuil's paper is still cited as proof that eoliths are natural rather than artificial productions. This kind of citing is a very effective propaganda technique. After all, how many people will bother to dig up Breuil's original article and see for themselves if what he had to say really made sense?

Breuil's definitive 1910 report came before most of J. Reid Moir's discoveries in East Anglia. Eventually, when Moir's finds began to attract attention, Breuil went to England to conduct firsthand evaluations. Surprisingly, Breuil backed Moir. He accepted the implements from the Pliocene Red Crag at Foxhall as genuine and also said that some of the implements from the beds below the Red Crag were "absolutely indistinguishable from classic flint implements." The sub-Crag formations could be anywhere from 2 to 55 million years old. Breuil apparently became noncommittal later on. The 1965 edition of his book *Men of the Old Stone Age,* published after his death, stated only that "a certain number of flakes might be accepted, though their angle of cut is generally against it." One wonders why there is no mention of the objects Breuil previously said were "not simply eoliths but are absolutely indistinguishable from classic flint implements."

Another important element in the eolith controversy was the platform angle test, promoted by Alfred S. Barnes. Barnes, who defended Moir in the 1920s, later became opposed. In 1939, he delivered what many authorities still regard as the death blow to Moir's English eoliths. But Barnes did not limit his attention to Moir. In his study, titled "The Differences Between Natural and Human Flaking on Prehistoric Flint Implements," Barnes also considered stone tool industries from France, Portugal, Belgium, and Argentina.

Supporters of eoliths generally argued that natural forces could not produce the kinds of chipping observed on the objects in question. Barnes looked for some measurable way to demonstrate whether or not this was so. For this purpose, Barnes chose what he called the angle platform-scar. "The angle platform-scar," he said, "is the angle between the platform or surface on which the blow was struck or the pressure was applied which detached the flake, and the scar left on the tool where the flake has been detached." In genuine human work, the angle would be acute. Natural fractures would, he said, yield obtuse angles.

We find Barnes's description of the angle to be measured somewhat ambiguous. We have spoken with experts on stone tools at California's San Bernardino

Figure 3.10. This flint object was found by H. Breuil and Obermaier in an Eocene formation at Clermont (Oise), France. Breuil said it was identical in form to certain Late Pleistocene implements, but he nevertheless considered it the product of natural geological pressure.

County Museum, including Ruth D. Simpson, and they have also been unable to specify exactly what angle Barnes was measuring. In any case, in the angle platform-scar, Barnes believed he had found the objectively measurable feature by which one could distinguish natural chipping from human work.

To be effective, the measurement had to be applied not to a single specimen, but to a large sample of specimens from the industry in question. Barnes stated that a sample "may be considered of human origin if less than 25% of the angles platform-scar are obtuse (90 degrees and over)." Having established this, Barnes delivered a devastating conclusion: none of the eoliths he examined, including those of Moir, were of human origin. Interestingly enough, it appears that Moir himself was aware of the Barnes criterion and believed his specimens were within the required range. But for Barnes, and almost everyone else in the scientific community, the controversy was over.

In fact, in mainstream circles the controversy about the eoliths and other Tertiary stone tool industries had long since ceased to be a burning issue. With the discoveries of Java man and Beijing man, the scientific community had become increasingly convinced that the key transition from apelike precursors to toolmaking humans (or protohumans) had taken place in the Early to Middle Pleistocene. This made the presumed stone tools of humans in the Pliocene and earlier a sideshow topic of little

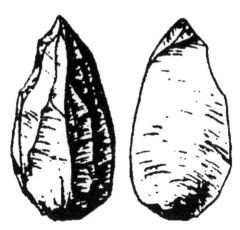

Figure 3.11. A flint object found in an Eocene formation at Clermont (Oise), France. Although H. Breuil said it resembled a Late Pleistocene pointed tool, he claimed it was formed by geological pressure.

concern. Barnes, however, performed the valuable, if menial task, of sweeping away some useless remnants of irrelevant evidence. Thereafter, whenever the topic of very old stone tool industries happened to come up, as it still does from time to time, scientists could conveniently cite Barnes's report. Even today scientists studying stone tools apply the Barnes method.

But on close examination, it appears that Barnes's definitive debunking report may be in need of some debunking itself. Alan Lyle Bryan, a Canadian anthropologist, wrote in 1986: "The question of how to distinguish naturefacts from artifacts is far from being resolved and demands more research. The way the problem was resolved in England, by application of the Barnes' statistical method of measuring the angles of platform scar, is not generally applicable to all problems of differentiating naturefacts from artifacts." During a phone conversation with one of us on May 28, 1987, Bryan also expressed a cautious belief that Barnes may have gone too far in trying to eliminate all of the anomalous European stone tool industries. Giving attention to more recent discoveries, Bryan said that there are Late Pleistocene Australian tools that do not conform to Barnes's specifications.

Another example of an industry that apparently does not conform to the Barnes criterion is the Oldowan, from the lower levels of the Olduvai Gorge. Considering the extremely crude nature of the objects, which Louis Leakey said were comparable to Moir's implements, it is remarkable that they have never been challenged by the scientific community. This is probably because the Oldowan industry offers support to the African evolution hypothesis of human origins, which is accepted as dogma.

In light of the views presented by Bryan and others, it is clear that wholesale rejection of the Eolithic and other early stone tool industries by application of the Barnes criterion is unwarranted.

RECENT EXAMPLES OF EOLITHIC IMPLEMENTS
FROM THE AMERICAS

Despite the best efforts of Barnes and Breuil, the eolith question continues to haunt archeologists. Several anomalously old crude stone tool industries of Eolithic type have been discovered in the Americas.

Most archeologists say Siberian hunters crossed into Alaska on a land bridge that existed when the last glaciation lowered sea levels. During this period, the Canadian ice sheet blocked southward migration until about 12,000 years ago, when the first American immigrants followed an ice free passage to what is now the United States. These people were the so-called Clovis hunters, famous for their characteristic spearpoints. These correspond to the highly evolved stone implements of the later Paleolithic in Europe.

Nevertheless, many sites, excavated with modern archeological methods, have yielded dates as great as 30,000 years for humans in America. These sites include El Cedral in northern Mexico, Santa Barbara Island off California, and the rock-shelter of Boquierão do Sitio da Pedra Furada in northern Brazil. Other controversial sites are far older than 30,000 years.

GEORGE CARTER AND THE TEXAS STREET SITE

A good example of a controversial American early stone tool industry reminiscent of the European eoliths is the one discovered by George Carter in the 1950s at the Texas Street excavation in San Diego. At this site, Carter claimed to have found hearths and crude stone tools at levels corresponding to the last interglacial period, some 80,000–90,000 years ago. Critics scoffed at these claims, referring to Carter's alleged tools as products of nature, or "cartifacts,"and Carter was later publicly defamed in a Harvard course on "Fantastic Archeology." However, Carter gave clear criteria for distinguishing between his tools and naturally broken rocks, and lithic experts such as John Witthoft have endorsed his claims.

In 1973, Carter conducted more extensive excavations at Texas Street and invited numerous archeologists to come and view the site firsthand. Almost none responded. Carter stated: "San Diego State University adamantly refused to look at work in its own backyard."

In 1960, an editor of *Science,* the journal of the American Academy for the Advancement of Science, asked Carter to submit an article about early humans in America. Carter did so, but when the editor sent the article out to two scholars for review, they rejected it.

Upon being informed of this by the editor, Carter replied in a letter, dated February 2, 1960: "I must assume now that you had no idea of the intensity of feeling that reigns in the field. It is nearly hopeless to try to convey some idea of the status of the field of Early Man in America at the moment. But just for fun: I have a correspondent whose name I cannot use, for though he thinks that I am right, he could lose his job for saying so. I have another anonymous correspondent who as a graduate student found evidence that would tend to prove me right. He and his fellow student buried the evidence. They were certain that to bring it in would cost them their chance for their Ph.D's. At a meeting, a young professional approached me to say, 'I hope you really pour it on them. I would say it if I dared, but it would cost me my job.' At another meeting, a young man sidled up to say, 'In dig *x* they found core tools like yours at the bottom but just didn't publish them.'"

The inhibiting effect of negative propaganda on the evaluation of Carter's discoveries is described by archeologist Brian Reeves, who wrote with his co–authors in 1986: "Were actual artifacts uncovered at Texas Street, and is the site really Last Interglacial in age? . . . Because of the weight of critical 'evidence' presented by established archaeologists, the senior author [Reeves], like most other archaeologists, accepted the position of the skeptics uncritically, dismissing the sites and the objects as natural phenomena." But when he took the trouble to look at the evidence himself, Reeves changed his mind. He concluded that the objects were clearly tools of human manufacture and that the Texas Street site was as old as Carter had claimed.

LOUIS LEAKEY AND THE CALICO SITE

Early in his career, Louis Leakey, who later became famous for his discoveries at Olduvai Gorge in Africa, began to have radical ideas about the antiquity of humans in America. At that time, scientists thought the entry date for the Siberian hunters was no greater than 5,000 years ago.

Leakey recalled: "Back in 1929–1930 when I was teaching students at the University of Cambridge . . . I began to tell my students that man must have been in the New World at least 15,000 years. I shall never forget when Ales Hrdlicka, that great man from the Smithsonian Institution, happened to be at Cambridge, and he was told by my professor (I was only a student supervisor) that Dr. Leakey was telling students that man must have been in America 15,000 or more years ago. He burst into my rooms—he didn't even wait to shake hands."

Hrdlicka said, "Leakey, what's this I hear? Are you preaching heresy?"

"No, Sir!" said Leakey.

Hrdlicka replied, "You are! You are telling students that man was in America 15,000 years ago. What evidence have you?"

Leakey answered, "No positive evidence. Purely circumstantial evidence. But with man from Alaska to Cape Horn, with many different languages and at least two civilizations, it is not possible that he was present only the few thousands of years that you at present allow."

Figure 3.12. A beaked graver—a stone tool from Calico in southern California, dated at about 200,000 years.

Leakey continued to harbor unorthodox views on this matter, and in 1964 he made an effort to collect some definite evidence at the Calico site in the Mojave Desert of California. This site is situated near the shore of now-vanished Pleistocene Lake Manix. Over a period of eighteen years of excavation under the direction of Ruth D. Simpson, 11,400 eolithlike artifacts were recovered from a number of levels. The oldest artifact-bearing level has been given an age of 200,000 years by the uranium series method.

However, as happened with Texas Street, mainstream archeologists rejected the artifacts discovered at Calico as products of nature, and the Calico site is passed over in silence in popular accounts of archeology. Leakey's biographer Sonia Cole said, "For many colleagues who felt admiration and affection for Louis and his family, the Calico years were an embarrassment and a sadness."

Yet the artifacts of Calico also have their defenders, who give elaborate arguments showing that they were human artifacts, not geofacts resulting from natural processes. Phillip Tobias, the well-known associate of Raymond Dart, discoverer of *Australopithecus,* declared in 1979: "When Dr. Leakey first showed me a small collection of pieces from Calico . . . I was at once convinced that some, though not all, of the small samples showed unequivocal signs of human authorship."

Ruth D. Simpson stated in 1986: "It would be difficult for nature to produce many specimens resembling man-made unifacial tools, with completely unidirectional edge retouch done in a uniform, directed manner. The Calico site has yielded many completely unifacial stone tools with uniform edge retouch. These include end scrapers, side scrapers, and gravers." Flake tools with unifacial, unidirectional chipping, like those found at Calico, are typical of the European eoliths. Examples are also found among the Oldowan industries of East Africa. Among the best tools that turned up at Calico was an excellent beaked graver (Figure 3.12). Bola stones have also been reported.

In general, however, the Calico discoveries have met with silence, ridicule, and opposition in the ranks of mainstream paleoanthropology. Ruth Simpson nevertheless stated: "The data base for very early man in the New World is growing rapidly, and can no longer simply be ignored, because it does not fit current models of prehistory in the New World. . . . there is a need for flexibility in thinking to assure unbiased peer reviews."

TOCA DA ESPERANÇA, BRAZIL

Support for the authenticity of the Calico tools has come from a find in Brazil. In 1982, Maria Beltrao found a series of caves with wall paintings in the state of Bahia. In 1985, a trench was cut in the Toca da Esperança (Cave of Hope), and excavations in 1986 and 1987 yielded crude stone tools associated with Pleistocene mammals. When the bones were tested by the uranium series method, ages in excess of 200,000 years were obtained. The maximum age was 295,000 years.

The discovery was reported to the scientific world by Henry de Lumley, a famous French archeologist.

The tools were fashioned from quartz pebbles and were somewhat like those from Olduvai Gorge. The nearest source of quartz pebbles is about 10 kilometers from the cave site.

De Lumley and his coworkers said in their report: "The evidence seems to indicate that Early Man entered into the American continent much before previously thought." They went on to say: "In light of the discoveries at the Toca da Esperança, it is much easier to interpret the lithic industry of the Calico site, in the Mojave Desert, near Yermo, San Bernardino County, California, which is dated at between 150,000 and 200,000 years."

According to de Lumley and his associates, humans and human ancestors entered the Americas from northern Asia several times during the Pleistocene. The early migrants, who manufactured the tools in the Brazilian cave, were, they said, *Homo erectus*. While this view is in harmony with the consensus on human evolution, there is no reason why the tools in the Toca da Esperança could not have been made by anatomically modern humans. As we have several times mentioned, such tools are still being manufactured by humans in various parts of the world.

MONTE VERDE, CHILE

Another archeological site that has bearing on the evaluation of crude stone tools is the Monte Verde site in south central Chile. According to a report in *Mammoth Trumpet* (1984), this site was first surveyed by archeologist Tom Dillehay in 1976. Although the age of 12,500 to 13,500 years for the site is not highly anomalous, the archeological finds uncovered there challenge the standard Clovis hunter theory. The culture of the Monte Verde people was completely distinct from that of the Clovis hunters. Although the Monte Verde people made some advanced bifacial implements, they mostly made minimally modified pebble tools. Indeed, to a large extent, they obtained stone tools by selecting naturally occurring split pebbles. Some of these show signs of nothing more than usage; others show signs of deliberate retouching of a working edge. This is strongly reminiscent of the descriptions of the European eoliths.

In this case, the vexing question of artifacts versus naturefacts was resolved by a fortunate circumstance: the site is located in a boggy area in which perishable plant and animal matter has been preserved. Thus two pebble tools were found hafted to wooden handles. Twelve architectural foundations were found, made of cut wooden planks and small tree trunks staked in place. There were large communal hearths, as well as small charcoal ovens lined with clay. Some of the stored clay bore the footprint of a child 8 to 10 years old. Three crude wooden mortars were also found, held in place by wooden stakes. Grinding stones (metates) were uncovered, along with the remains of wild potatoes, medicinal plants, and sea coast plants with a high salt content. All in all, the Monte Verde site sheds an interesting light on the kind of creatures who might have made and used crude pebble tools during the Pliocene and Miocene in Europe or at the Plio-Pleistocene boundary in Africa. In this case, the culture was well equipped with domestic amenities made from perishable materials. Far from being subhuman, the cultural level was what we might expect of anatomically modern humans in a simple village setting even today.

By an accident of preservation, we thus see at Monte Verde artifacts representing an advanced culture accompanying the crudest kinds of stone tools. At sites millions of years older, we see only the stone tools, although perishable artifacts of the kind found at Monte Verde may have once accompanied them.

RECENT PAKISTAN FINDS

Eolithlike implements that do not fit into standard ideas of human evolution continue to be found in parts of the world outside the Americas. Some fairly recent finds by British archeologists in Pakistan provide an example. These crude chopping tools are about 2 million years old. But according to the dominant African homeland idea, the human ancestor of that time period, *Homo habilis,* should have been confined to Africa.

Some scientists considering the Pakistan tools tried to discredit the discovery. Anthropologist Sally McBrearty complained in a *New York Times* report that the discoverers "have not supplied enough evidence that the specimens are that old and that they are of human manufacture." Our review of anomalous stone implements should make us suspicious of this sort of charge. Scientists typically demand higher levels of proof for anomalous finds than for evidence that fits within the established ideas about human evolution.

A 1987 report from the British journal *New Scientist* suggests that McBrearty was being overly skeptical. Concerning doubts expressed about the stratigraphical context and age of the stone tools, the *New Scientist* stated: "Such doubts do not apply in the case of the stone pieces from the Soan Valley southeast of Rawalpindi, argues Robin Dennell, the field director of the Paleolithic Project of the British Archaeological Mission and the University of Sheffield. He and his colleague Helen Rendell, a geologist at the University of Sussex, report that the stone pieces, all of quartzite, were so firmly embedded in a deposit of conglomerate and gritstone called the Upper Siwalik series, that they had to chisel them out." According to the *New Scientist,* the dating was accomplished using a combination of paleomagnetic and stratigraphic studies.

What about McBrearty's suggestion that the stone objects were not made by humans? The *New Scientist* gave a more balanced view: "Of the pieces that they extracted, eight, Dennell believes are 'definite artefacts.' In Dennell's view, the least equivocal artefact is a piece of quartzite that a hominid individual supposedly struck in three directions with a hammer stone, removing seven flakes from it [Figure 3.13]. This multifaceted flaking together with the fresh appearance of the scars left on the remaining 'core' make a 'very convincing' case for human involvement."

So what is going on with the find in Pakistan? Scientists holding the view that *Homo erectus* was the first representative of the *Homo* line to leave Africa, and did so about a million years ago, were apparently quite determined to discredit stone tools found in Pakistan, about 2 million years old, rather than modify their ideas. We can just imagine how such scientists would react to stone tools found in Miocene contexts.

SIBERIA AND INDIA

Many other discoveries of stone implements around 2 million years old have been made at other Asian sites, in Siberia and northwestern India.

In 1961, hundreds of crude pebble tools were found near Gorno-Altaisk, on the Ulalinka river in Siberia. According to a 1984 report by Russian scientists A. P. Okladinov and L. A. Ragozin, the tools were found in layers 1.5–2.5 million years old.

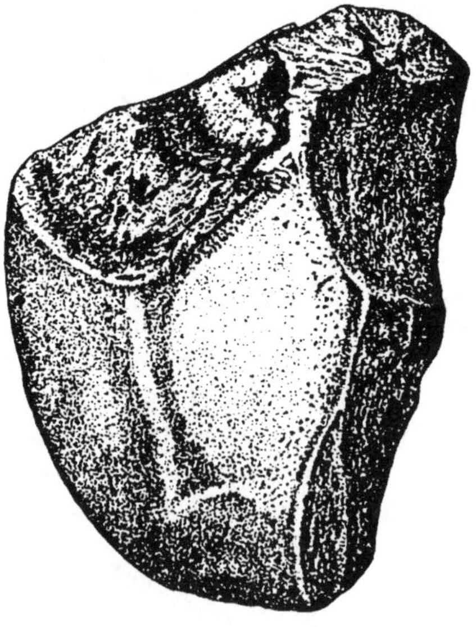

Figure 3.13. A stone tool discovered in the Upper Siwalik formation in Pakistan. British scientists estimated its age at about 2 million years.

Another Russian scientist, Yuri Mochanov, discovered stone tools resembling the European eoliths at a site overlooking the Lena River at Diring Yurlakh, Siberia. The formations from which these implements were recovered were dated by potassium-argon and magnetic methods to 1.8 million years before the present. Recent evidence from India also takes us back about 2 million years. Many discoveries of stone tools have been made in the Siwalik Hills region of northwestern India. The Siwaliks derive their name from the demigod Shiva (Sanskrit Śiva), the lord of the forces of universal destruction. In 1981, Anek Ram Sankhyan, of the Anthropological Survey of India, found a stone tool near Haritalyangar village, in the late Pliocene Tatrot

Formation, which is over 2 million years old. Other tools were recovered from the same formation.

The above-mentioned Siberian and Indian discoveries, at 1.5–2.5 million years old, do not agree very well with the standard view that *Homo erectus* was the first representative of the *Homo* line to emigrate from Africa, doing so about a million years ago. Here is an example from an even more remote time. In 1982, K. N. Prasad of the Geological Survey of India reported the discovery of a "crude unifacial hand-axe pebble tool" in the Miocene Nagri formation near Haritalyangar, in the Himalayan foothills of northwest India. Prasad stated in his report: "The implement was recovered *in situ,* during remeasuring of the geological succession to assess the thickness of the beds. Care was taken to confirm the exact provenance of the material, in order to rule out any possibility of its derivation from younger horizons."

Prasad thought the tool had been manufactured by a very apelike creature called *Ramapithecus.* "The occurrence of this pebble tool in such ancient sediments," said Prasad, "indicates that early hominids such as *Ramapithecus* fashioned tools, were bipedal with erect posture, and probably utilized the implements for hunting." But today most scientists regard *Ramapithecus* not as a human ancestor but as the ancestor of the living orangutans. This newly defined *Ramapithecus* was definitely not a maker of stone tools.

So who made the Miocene tool reported by Prasad? The makers could very well have been anatomically modern humans living in the Miocene. Even if we were to propose that some primitive creature like *Homo habilis* made the Miocene tool, that would still raise big questions. According to current ideas, the first tool makers arose in Africa about 2 million years ago.

WHO MADE THE EOLITHIC IMPLEMENTS?

Even after having heard all of the arguments for eoliths being of human manufacture, arguments which will certainly prove convincing to many, some might still legitimately maintain a degree of doubt. Could such a person, it might be asked, be forgiven for not accepting the eoliths? The answer to that question is a qualified yes. The qualification is that one should then reject other stone tool industries of a similar nature. This would mean rejecting many accepted industries, including the Oldowan industries of East Africa, discovered by Louis and Mary Leakey. When illustrations of the eoliths found on the Kent Plateau and in East Anglia are set alongside those of tools from Olduvai Gorge (Figure 3.3, p. 32) we do not notice much of a difference in workmanship.

The most reasonable conclusion is that both the European eoliths and the Oldowan tools of East Africa were intentionally manufactured. But by whom? Scientists accept practically without question that the Oldowan implements were made by *Homo habilis,* a primitive hominid species. It should not, therefore, be completely unthinkable for scientists to entertain the possibility that a creature like *Homo habilis* might also have made the eoliths from East Anglia and the Kent Plateau, some of which are roughly comparable in age to the Oldowan tools.

But there is another possibility. Mary Leakey said this in her book about the Oldowan stone tools: "An interesting present-day example of unretouched flakes used as cutting tools has recently been recorded in South-West Africa and may be mentioned briefly. An expedition from the State Museum, Windhoek, discovered two stone-using groups of the Ova Tjimba people who not only make choppers for breaking open bones and for other heavy work, but also employ simple flakes, un-retouched and un-hafted, for cutting and skinning." Nothing, therefore, prevents one from entertaining the possibility that anatomically modern humans might have been responsible for even the crudest stone tools found at Olduvai Gorge and the European eolith sites.

The standard reply will be that there are no fossils showing that humans of the fully modern type were around then, in the Early Pleistocene or Late Pliocene, roughly 1–2 million years ago, whereas there are fossils of *Homo habilis*. But *Homo sapiens* fossils are quite rare even at Late Pleistocene sites where there are lots of stone tools and other signs of human habitation.

Furthermore, as described in Chapters 7 and 12, fossil skeletal remains of human beings of the fully modern type have been discovered by scientists in strata at least as old as the lower levels of Olduvai Gorge, Tanzania. Among them may be numbered the fossil human skeleton discovered in 1913 by Dr. Hans Reck, in Bed II of Olduvai Gorge, and some fossil human femurs discovered by Richard Leakey at Lake Turkana, Kenya, in a formation slightly older than Bed I at Olduvai.

It is, therefore, not correct to say that there is no fossil evidence whatsoever for a fully human presence in the lower levels of Olduvai Gorge. In addition to fossil evidence, we have a report from Mary Leakey about a controversial circular formation of stones at the DK site in lower Bed I. She suggested that "they may have been placed as supports for branches or poles stuck into the ground to form a windbreak or rough shelter."

"In general appearance," she wrote, "the circle resembles temporary structures often made by present-day nomadic peoples who build a low stone wall round their dwellings to serve either as a windbreak or as a base to support upright branches which are bent over and covered with either skins or grass." For illustration, Mary Leakey provided a photograph of such a temporary shelter made by the Okombambi tribe of SouthWest Africa (now Namibia).

Not everyone agreed with Leakey's interpretation of the stone circle. But accepting Leakey's version, the obvious question may be raised: if she believed the structure resembled those made by present-day nomadic peoples like the

Okombambi, then why could she not assume that anatomically modern humans made the Olduvai stone circle 1.75 million years ago?

Interestingly enough, there is evidence that some of the tools from Olduvai Gorge were quite advanced. J. Desmond Clark wrote in his foreword to the 1971 study by Mary Leakey: "Here are artefacts that conventional usage associates typologically with much later times (the late Paleolithic or even later)—diminutive scraper forms, awls, burins . . . and a grooved and pecked cobble." We note, however, that tools of the type found in "the late Paleolithic and even later" are considered by modern scientists to be specifically the work of *Homo sapiens* rather than *Homo erectus* or *Homo habilis*. Advanced stone tools also turn up in the European eolith assemblages. We might thus entertain the possibility that anatomically modern humans were responsible for some if not all of the Oldowan and Eolithic tools.

Louis and Mary Leakey also found in Bed I of Olduvai Gorge bola stones and an apparent leather-working tool that might have been used to fashion leather cords for the bolas. Using bola stones to capture game would seem to require a degree of intelligence and dexterity beyond that possessed by *Homo habilis*. This concern is heightened by the recent discovery of a relatively complete skeleton of *Homo habilis,* which shows this hominid to have been far more apelike than scientists previously imagined.

So where does this leave us? In today's world, we find that humans manufacture stone tools of various levels of sophistication, from primitive to advanced. And as described in this chapter and the next two chapters, we also find evidence of the same variety of tools in the Pleistocene, Pliocene, Miocene, and even as far back as the Eocene. The simplest explanation is that anatomically modern humans, who make such a spectrum of tools today, also made them in the past. One could also imagine that such humans coexisted with other more primitive humanlike creatures who also made stone tools.

4

Crude Paleoliths

Crude paleoliths represent an advance over the eoliths. Eoliths are naturally broken pieces of stone that are used as tools with little or no further modification. A working edge might be slightly retouched or it might simply show signs of wear. Paleoliths, however, are often deliberately flaked from stone cores and are more extensively modified.

THE FINDS OF CARLOS RIBEIRO IN PORTUGAL

The first hint of Carlos Ribeiro's discoveries came to our attention quite accidentally. While going through the writings of the nineteenth-century American geologist J. D. Whitney, we encountered a sentence or two about Ribeiro having discovered flint implements in Miocene formations near Lisbon, Portugal.

We found more brief mentions in the works of S. Laing, a popular English science writer of the late nineteenth century. Curious, we searched libraries, but turned up no works under Ribeiro's name and found ourselves at a dead end. Sometime later, Ribeiro's name turned up again, this time in the 1957 English edition of *Fossil Men* by Boule and Vallois, who rather curtly dismissed the work of the nineteenth-century Portuguese geologist. We were, however, led by Boule and Vallois to the 1883 edition of *Le Préhistorique,* by Gabriel de Mortillet, who gave a favorable report of Ribeiro's discoveries, in French. By tracing out the references mentioned in de Mortillet's footnotes, we gradually uncovered a wealth of remarkably convincing original reports in French journals of archeology and anthropology from the latter part of the nineteenth century.

The search for this buried evidence was illuminating, demonstrating how the scientific establishment treats reports of facts that no longer conform to accepted views. Keep in mind that for most current students of paleoanthropology, Ribeiro and his discoveries simply do not exist. You have to go back to textbooks printed over 30 years ago to find even a mention of him.

In 1857, Carlos Ribeiro was named to head the Geological Survey of Portugal, and he would also be elected to the Portuguese Academy of Sciences. During the

55

years 1860–63, he conducted studies of stone implements found in Portugal's Quaternary strata. Nineteenth-century geologists generally divided the geological periods into four main groups: (1) the Primary, encompassing the periods from the Precambrian through the Permian; (2) the Secondary, encompassing the periods from the Triassic through the Cretaceous; (3) the Tertiary, encompassing the periods from the Paleocene through the Pliocene; and (4) the Quaternary, encompassing the Pleistocene and Recent periods. During the course of his investigations, Ribeiro learned that flints bearing signs of human work were being found in Tertiary beds between Canergado and Alemquer, two villages in the basin of the Tagus River northeast of Lisbon.

Ribeiro immediately began his own investigations, and in many localities found flakes of worked flint and quartzite in Tertiary beds. But Ribeiro felt he must submit to the prevailing scientific dogma, still current, that human beings were not older than the Quaternary.

In 1866, on the official geological maps of Portugal, Ribeiro reluctantly assigned Quaternary ages to certain of the implement-bearing strata. Upon seeing the maps, the French geologist Edouard de Verneuil took issue with Ribeiro's judgement, pointing out that the so-called Quaternary beds were certainly Pliocene or Miocene. Meanwhile, in France, the Abbé Louis Bourgeois, a reputable investigator, had reported finding stone implements in Tertiary beds. Influenced by de Verneuil's criticism and the discoveries of Bourgeois, Ribeiro began openly reporting that human implements were being found in Pliocene and Miocene formations in Portugal.

In 1871, Ribeiro presented to the Portuguese Academy of Science at Lisbon a collection of flint and quartzite implements, including some gathered from the Tertiary formations of the Tagus valley. In 1872, at the International Congress of Prehistoric Anthropology and Archeology meeting in Brussels, Ribeiro displayed more specimens, mostly pointed flakes. Scientific opinion was divided.

At the Paris Exposition of 1878, Ribeiro displayed 95 specimens of Tertiary flint tools. Gabriel de Mortillet, the influential French anthropologist, visited Ribeiro's exhibit and declared that 22 specimens had undoubted signs of human work. Along with his friend and colleague Emile Cartailhac, de Mortillet brought other scientists to see Ribeiro's specimens, and they were all of the same opinion—a good many of the flints were definitely made by humans.

De Mortillet wrote: "The intentional work is very well established, not only by the general shape, which can be deceptive, but much more conclusively by the presence of clearly evident striking platforms and strongly developed bulbs of percussion." The bulbs of percussion also sometimes had eraillures, small chips removed by the force of impact. Some of Ribeiro's specimens also had several long, vertical flakes removed in parallel, something not likely to occur in the course of random battering by the forces of nature.

Leland W. Patterson, a modern expert on stone tools, holds that the bulb of percussion is the most important sign of intentional work on a flint flake. If the flake also shows the remnants of a striking platform, then one can be even more certain that one is confronted with a flake struck deliberately from a flint core and not a piece of naturally broken flint resembling a tool or weapon.

Figure 4.1 shows one of Ribeiro's Miocene tools from Portugal and for comparison an accepted stone tool from the Mousterian cultural stage of the European Late Pleistocene. They share the typical features of intentional human work on stone: the striking platform, bulb of percussion, eraillure, and parallel removal of flakes.

De Mortillet further observed: "Many of the specimens, on the same side as the bulb of percussion, have hollows with traces and fragments of sandstone adhering to them, a fact which establishes their original position in the strata." But some scientists were still doubtful. At the 1880 meeting of the International Congress of Prehistoric Anthropology and Archeology, held in Lisbon, Portugal, Ribeiro displayed more specimens from Miocene beds. In his report, Ribeiro stated: "(1) They were found as integral parts of the beds themselves. (2) They had sharp, well-preserved edges, showing that they had not been subject to transport for any great distance. (3) They had a patina similar in color to the rocks in the strata of which they formed a part."

The second point is especially important. Some geologists claimed that Pleistocene flint implements had been washed into fissures in Miocene beds by floods and torrents. But if the flints had been subjected to such transport, then the

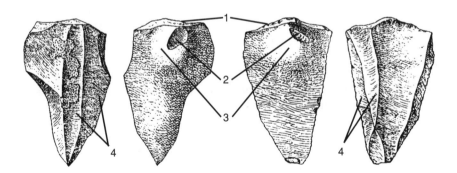

Figure 4.1. Left: Front and back views of a stone tool recovered from a Tertiary formation in Portugal. It would be over 2 million years old. Right: An accepted stone tool, less than 100,000 years old, from the Mousterian cultural stage of the European Late Pleistocene. Both implements clearly display the following features of intentional human work: (1) striking platforms, (2) eraillures, (3) bulbs of percussion, and (4) parallel flake removal.

sharp edges would
most probably have
been damaged, and
this was not the case.
The Congress as-
signed a special com-
mission to inspect the
the implements and
the sites. On Septem-
ber 22, 1880, the com-
mission members
boarded a train and
proceeded north from
Lisbon. During the
journey, they gazed at
the old forts topping
the hilltops, and
pointed out to each

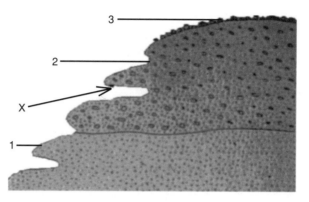

Figure 4.2. Stratigraphy of the site at the base of Monte Redondo hill in Otta, Portugal, where G. Bellucci found an implement: (1) sandstone; (2) Miocene sandstone conglomerate with flints; (3) surface deposit of eroded flints. The arrow marked 'X' indicates the position of the implement.

other the Jurassic, Cretaceous, and Tertiary terrains as they moved through the valley of the Tagus River. They stepped off the train at Carregado. They then proceeded to nearby Otta and two kilometers (just over a mile) from Otta arrived at the hill of Monte Redondo. At that point, the scientists dispersed into various ravines in search of flints.

In his book *Le Préhistorique,* Gabriel de Mortillet gave an informative account of the events that took place at Monte Redondo: "The members of the Congress arrived at Otta, in the middle of a great freshwater formation. It was the bottom of an ancient lake, with sand and clay in the center, and sand and rocks on the edges. It is on the shores that intelligent beings would have left their tools, and it is on the shores of the lake that once bathed Monte Redondo that the search was made. It was crowned with success. The able investigator of Umbria [Italy], Mr. Bellucci, discovered *in situ* a flint bearing incontestable signs of intentional work. Before detaching it, he showed it to a number of his colleagues. The flint was strongly encased in the rock. He had to use a hammer to extract it. It is definitely of the same age as the deposit. Instead of lying flat on a surface onto which it could have been secondarily recemented at a much later date, it was found firmly in place on the under side of a ledge extending over a region removed by erosion [Figure 4.2]. It is impossible to desire a more complete demonstration attesting to a flint's position in its strata." Some modern authorities consider the Otta conglomerates to be Early Miocene, about 15–20 million years old. Altogether, there seems little reason why Ribeiro's discoveries should not be receiving some serious attention, even today.

THE FINDS OF L. BOURGEOIS AT THENAY, FRANCE

On August 19, 1867, in Paris, L. Bourgeois presented to the International Congress for Prehistoric Anthropology and Archeology a report on flint implements he had found in Early Miocene beds (15–20 million years old) at Thenay, in north central France. Bourgeois said they resembled the types of Quaternary implements (scrapers, borers, blades, etc.) he had found on the surface in the same region. He found on almost all of the Miocene specimens the standard indications of human work: fine retouching, symmetrical chipping, and traces of use.

At the Paris congress, only a few scientists admitted they were actual artifacts. Undeterred, Bourgeois continued finding more specimens and convincing individual paleontologists and geologists they were the result of intentional work. Gabriel de Mortillet was one of the first to be so convinced.

Some scientists questioned the stratigraphic position in which the flints had been found. The first specimens collected by Bourgeois came from rocky debris along the sides of a small valley cutting through the plateau at Thenay. Geologists such as Sir John Prestwich objected that these were essentially surface finds. In response, Bourgeois dug a trench in the valley and found flints showing the same signs of human work.

Still unsatisfied, critics proposed that the flints found in the trench had come to their positions through fissures leading from the top of the plateau, where Pleistocene implements were often found. To meet this objection, Bourgeois, in 1869, sank a pit into the top of the plateau. During the excavation, he came to a layer of limestone one foot thick, with no fissures through which Pleistocene stone tools might have slipped to lower levels.

Deeper in his pit, at a depth of about 14 feet in Early Miocene strata, Bourgeois discovered many flint tools. De Mortillet stated in *Le Préhistorique:* "There was no further doubt about their antiquity or their geological position."

Despite this clear demonstration, many scientists retained their unreasonable doubts. A showdown came in Brussels, at the 1872 meeting of the International Congress of Prehistoric Anthropology and Archeology.

Bourgeois presented many specimens, figures of which were included in the published proceedings of the Congress. Describing a pointed implement (Figure 4.3), Bourgeois stated: "Here is an awllike specimen, on a broad base. The point in the middle has been obtained by regular retouching. This is a type

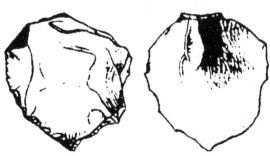

Figure 4.3. A pointed implement from a Miocene formation at Thenay, France.

common to all epochs. On the opposite side is a bulb of percussion."

Bourgeois described another
implement, which he characterized
as a knife or cutting tool: "The edges
have regular retouching, and the
opposite side presents a bulb of percussion." On many of his specimens, noted Bourgeois, the edges
on the part of the tool that might be
grasped by the hand remained un-
worn, while those on the cutting
surfaces showed extensive wear and
polishing.

Another specimen (Figure 4.4),
was characterized by Bourgeois as
a projectile point or an awl. He
noted the presence of retouching on
the edges, obviously intended to
make a sharp point. Bourgeois also
saw among the objects he collected
a core with the two extremities re-

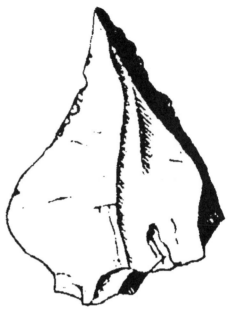

Figure 4.4. A pointed artifact from Miocene
strata at Thenay, France, with retouching near
the point.

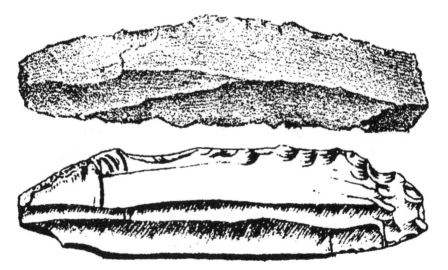

Figure 4.5. Top: A Late Pleistocene flint implement. Bottom: An implement from Early
Miocene strata at Thenay, France.

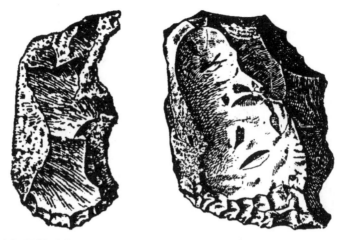

Figure 4.6. Unifacially retouched implements from the Early Miocene at Thenay, France.

touched with the aim of being utilized for some purpose. He observed: "The most prominent edge has been chipped down by a series of artificial blows, probably to prevent discomfort to the hand grasping the implement. The other edges remain sharp, which shows this flaking is not due to rolling action." Figure 4.5 shows the implement from the Early Miocene of Thenay alongside a similar accepted implement from the Late Pleistocene.

In order to resolve any controversy, the Congress of Prehistoric Anthropology and Archeology nominated a fifteen-member commission to judge the discoveries of Bourgeois. A majority of eight members voted that the flints were of human manufacture. Only five of the fifteen found no trace of human work in the specimens from Thenay. One member expressed no opinion and another supported Bourgeois with some reservations.

Bulbs of percussion were rare on the Early Miocene flints of Thenay, but most of the flints displayed fine retouching of the edges. The retouching tended to be concentrated on just one side of an edge, while the other side remained untouched; this is called unifacial flaking. De Mortillet, like modern authorities, believed that in almost all cases unifacial flaking is not the result of chance impacts but of deliberate work. In his book *Musée Préhistorique,* de Mortillet included reproductions of some Thenay flints that displayed very regular unifacial retouching (Figure 4.6).

Some of the critics of Bourgeois commented that among all the Early Miocene flint pieces he collected at Thenay, there were only a very few good specimens, about thirty. But de Mortillet stated: "Even one incontestable specimen would be enough, and they have thirty!"

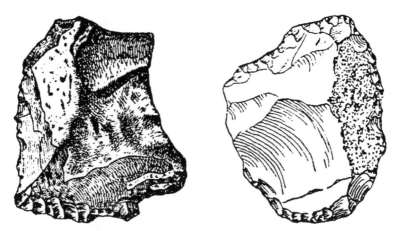

Figure 4.7. Left: A flint implement from an Early Miocene formation at Thenay, France. Right: An accepted implement from the lower middle part of Bed II, Olduvai Gorge, Africa. The lower edges of both specimens show roughly parallel flake scars, satisfying requirements for recognition as objects of human manufacture.

Modern authorities on stone stools, such as L. W. Patterson, say that parallel flake scars of approximately the same size are good indications of human work. Illustrations of the flints from the Early Miocene of Thenay show such flake scars. Figure 4.7 shows a unifacial implement from Thenay along with a similar accepted unifacial implement from Olduvai Gorge.

Many of the flints of Thenay have finely cracked surfaces indicating exposure to fire. De Mortillet concluded that humans had used fire to fracture large pieces of flint. The resulting flakes were then made into tools.

Through the writings of S. Laing, knowledge of the Thenay tools from the Early Miocene reached the intelligent reading public of the English-speaking countries. Laing stated: "The human origin of these implements has been greatly confirmed by the discovery that the Mincopics of the Andaman Islands manufacture whet-stones or scrapers almost identical with those of Thenay, and by the same process of using fire to split the stones into the requisite size and shape. . . . On the whole, the evidence for these Miocene implements seems to be very conclusive, and the objections to have hardly any other ground than the reluctance to admit the great antiquity of man."

Who made the flint implements of Thenay? Some thought they had been made by primitive, apelike human ancestors. But in 1894, S. Laing said of the flints of Thenay: "Their type continues, with no change except that of slight successive improvements, through the Pliocene, Quaternary, and even down to the present day. The scraper of the Esquimaux and the Andaman islanders is but an enlarged and improved edition of the Miocene scraper." If humans make such scrapers today, it is certainly possible that identical beings made similar scrapers back in the Miocene. And, as we shall see in coming chapters, scientists did in fact uncover skeletal remains of human beings indistinguishable from *Homo sapiens* in the Tertiary.

It thus becomes clearer why we no longer hear of the flints of Thenay. At one point in the history of paleoanthropology, several scientists who believed in evolution actually accepted the Thenay Miocene tools, but attributed them to a precursor of the human type. Evolutionary theory convinced them such a precursor existed, but no fossils had been found. When the expected fossils were found in 1891, in Java, they occurred in a formation now regarded as Middle Pleistocene. That certainly placed any supporters of Miocene ape-men in a dilemma. The human precursor, the creature transitional between fossil apes and modern humans, had been found not in the Early Miocene, 20 million years ago by current estimate, but in the Middle Pleistocene, less than 1 million years ago. Therefore, the flints of Thenay, and all the other evidences for the existence of Tertiary humans (or toolmaking Tertiary ape-men), were quietly, and apparently quite thoroughly, removed from active consideration and then forgotten.

The extensive evidence for the presence of toolmaking hominids in the Tertiary was in fact buried, and the stability of the entire edifice of modern paleoanthropology depends upon it remaining buried. If even one single piece of evidence for the existence of toolmakers in the Miocene or Early Pliocene were to be accepted, the whole picture of human evolution, built up so carefully in this century, would disintegrate.

IMPLEMENTS FROM AURILLAC, FRANCE

In 1870, Anatole Roujou reported that geologist Charles Tardy had removed a flint knife (Figure 4.8) from the exposed surface of a Late Miocene conglomerate at Aurillac, in southern France. To describe the removal, Roujou used the word *arraché,* which means the flint had to be extracted with some force. De Mortillet believed Tardy's flint tool had only recently been cemented onto the surface of the Late Miocene conglomerate and therefore chose to assign it a Pleistocene date.

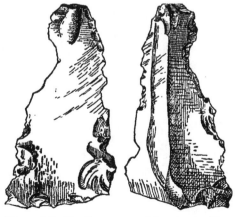

Figure 4.8. The first stone tool found at Aurillac, France.

The French geologist J. B. Rames doubted that the object found by Tardy was actually of human manufacture. But in 1877 Rames made his own discoveries of flint implements in the same region, at Puy Courny, a site near Aurillac. These implements were taken from sediments lying between layers of volcanic materials laid down in the Late Miocene, about 7–9 million years ago.

In 1894, S. Laing gave a detailed description of the signs of human manufacture that Rames had observed on the flints: "The specimens consist of several well-known palaeolithic types, celts, scrapers, arrow-heads, and flakes, only ruder and smaller than those of later periods. They were found at three different localities in the same stratum of gravel, and comply with all the tests by which the genuineness of Quaternary implements is ascertained, such as bulbs of percussion, conchoidal fractures, and above all, intentional chipping in a determinate direction." According to Laing, French anthropologist Armand de Quatrefages noted fine parallel scratches on the chipped edges of many specimens, indicating usage. These use marks were not present on other unchipped edges. The flint implements of Puy Courny were accepted as genuine at a congress of scientists in Grenoble, France.

Laing also said about the tools: "The gravelly deposit in which they are found contains five different varieties of flints, and of these all that look like human implements are confined to one particular variety, which from its nature is peculiarly adapted for human use. As Quatrefages says, no torrents or other natural causes could have exercised such a discrimination, which could only have been made by an intelligent being, selecting the stones best adapted for his tools and weapons."

Max Verworn, of the University of Göttingen in Germany, was initially doubtful of reports of stone tools from the Pliocene and earlier. So in 1905 he went to Aurillac to conduct his own investigations of the stone tools found there.

Verworn remained at Aurillac for six days, making excavations at a site called Puy de Boudieu, not far from Puy Courny. Describing the results of his first day's work, he wrote: "I had the luck to come upon a place where I found a great number of flint objects, whose indisputable implemental nature immediately staggered me. I had not expected this. Only slowly could I accustom myself to the thought that I had in my hand the tools of a human being that had lived in Tertiary times. I raised all the objections of which I could think. I questioned the geological age of the site, I questioned the implemental nature of the specimens, until I reluctantly admitted that all possible objections were not sufficient to explain away the facts."

The sharp-edged, chipped flint objects, apparently tools, were found in small groups, among stones that were very much rolled and worn. This meant that the flint objects had not been subjected to much movement since their deposition and that the flaking upon them was therefore of human rather than geological origin. The fact that the sharp-edged implemental flints were found in groups also suggested the presence of workshop sites.

Verworn then discussed at length various ways to identify human work on a flint object. He divided evidence of such work into three groups: (1) signs of percussion resulting from the primary blow that detached the flake from a flint core; (2) signs of percussion resulting from secondary edge chipping on the flake itself; (3) signs of use on the working edges.

Considering all the various characteristics of percussion and use, Verworn suggested that none of them are in themselves conclusive. "The critical analysis of a given combination of symptoms is the only thing that will put us in a position to make decisions," he stated.

This is the same methodology suggested by L. W. Patterson, a modern expert on stone tools. Patterson does, however, give more weight than Verworn to bulbs of percussion and unidirectional flaking along single edges of flakes, especially when numerous specimens are found at a site. Patterson's studies showed that natural forces almost never produce these effects in significant quantities.

Verworn then provided an example to illustrate how his method of analysis might be applied: "Suppose I find in an interglacial stone bed a flint object that bears a clear bulb of percussion, but no other symptom of intentional work. In that case, I would be doubtful as to whether or not I had before me an object of human manufacture. But suppose I find there a flint which on one side shows all the typical signs of percussion, and which on the other side shows the negative impressions of two, three, four, or more flakes removed by blows in the same direction. Furthermore, let us suppose one edge of the piece shows numerous, successive parallel small flakes removed, all running in the same direction, and all, without exception, are located on the same side of the edge. Let us suppose that all the other edges are sharp, without a trace of impact or rolling. Then I can say with complete certainty—it is an implement of human manufacture."

Verworn, after conducting a number of excavations at sites near Aurillac, analyzed the many flint implements he found, employing the rigorously scientific methodology described above. He then came to the following conclusion: "With my own hands, I have personally extracted from the undisturbed strata at Puy de Boudieu many such unquestionable artifacts. That is unshakable proof for the existence of a flintworking being at the end of the Miocene."

Most of the implements found by Verworn in the Miocene beds of Aurillac were scrapers of various kinds. "Some scrapers," he wrote, "show only use marks on the scraping edge, while the other edges on the same piece are quite sharp and unmarked. On other specimens the scraping edge displays a number of chips intentionally removed in the same direction. This chipping displays quite clearly all the usual signs of percussion. Even today the edges of the impact marks of previous blows on the upper part of some implements are perfectly sharp. The goal of the work on the edges is clearly and without doubt recognizable as the removal of cortex or the giving of a definite form. On many pieces there are clearly visible handgrip areas, fashioned by the removal of sharp edges and points from places where they would injure or interfere."

About another object, Verworn said: "The flake scars on the scraper blade lie so regularly next to each other in parallel fashion that one is reminded of Paleolithic or even Neolithic examples." In the accepted sequence, Paleolithic and Neolithic tools are assigned to the later Pleistocene.

Verworn also found many pointed scrapers (Figure 4.9): "Among all the flint objects, these show most clearly the intentional fashioning of definite tool shapes, at least in the area of the working edges. In fact, the points are generally made in such a way that one can speak of genuine care and attention in the technique. The edges have been worked by many unidirectional blows in such a way as to make the intention of fashioning a point unequivocal."

Also found at Aurillac were notched scrapers (Figure 4.10), with rounded concave openings on the working edge suitable for scraping cylindrical objects like bones or spear shafts. Verworn observed: "In most cases the notched scrapers are made by chipping out one of the edges in a curved shape by unidirectional blows."

Verworn also uncovered several tools adapted for hammering, hacking, and digging. Describing one such tool, Verworn wrote: "A large pointed tool for chopping or digging. It is formed from a natural slab of flint by the working of a point. One sees on the surfaces of the piece the cortex of the flint and at the top a point made from numerous flakes, mostly removed in the same direction." About another pointed tool, Verworn stated: "This tool has on the side directly below the point a handgrip made by removing the sharp, cutting edges. It might have been a primitive handaxe used for hammering or chopping." Verworn also found tools he thought were adapted for stabbing, boring, and engraving.

Verworn concluded: "At the end of the Miocene there was here a culture, which was, as we can see from its flint tools, not in the very beginning phases but had already proceeded through a long period of development. . . . this Miocene population of Cantal knew how to flake and work flint."

Verworn went on to say: "The size of the implements points toward a being with a hand of the same size and shape as our own, and therefore a similar body. The existence of large scrapers and choppers that fill our own hands, and above all the perfect adaptation to the hand found in almost all the tools, seems to verify this conclusion in the highest degree. Tools of the most different sizes, which show with perfect clarity useful edges, use marks, and handgrips, lie for the most part so naturally and comfort-

Figure 4.9. A pointed flint tool from the Late Miocene at Aurillac, France.

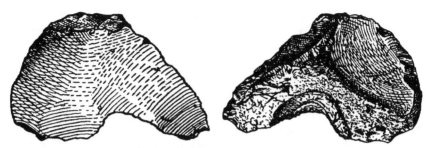

Figure 4.10. Left: Ventral surface of a notched scraper from the Late Miocene of Aurillac, France. Right: Dorsal surface, showing the curved working edge, upon which Verworn observed tiny use marks.

ably in our hands, with the original sharp points and edges intentionally removed from the places where a hand would grasp, that one would think the tools were made directly for our hands."

Verworn then said about the makers of the tools: "While it is possible that this Tertiary form might possibly have stood closer to the animal ancestors of modern humans than do modern humans themselves, who can say to us that they were not already of the same basic physical character as modern humans, that the development of specifically human features did not extend back into the Late Miocene?"

As we explain in Chapter 7, fossil skeletal remains indistinguishable from those of fully modern humans have been found in the Pliocene, Miocene, Eocene and even earlier. When we also consider that humans living today make implements not much different from those taken from Miocene beds in France and elsewhere, then the validity of the standard sequence of human evolution begins to seem tenuous. In fact, the standard sequence only makes sense when a lot of very good evidence is ignored. When all the available evidence, implemental and skeletal, is considered, it is quite difficult to construct any kind of evolutionary sequence. What we are left with is the supposition that there have been various types of human and humanlike beings, living at the same time and manufacturing stone tools of various levels of sophistication, for tens of millions of years into the past.

As late as 1924, George Grant MacCurdy, director of the American School of Prehistoric Research in Europe, reported positively in *Natural History* about the flint implements of Aurillac. Similar tools had been found in England by J. Reid Moir. Some critics argued that natural forces, such as movements of the earth, had fractured flints by pressure, thus creating stone objects resembling tools. But scientists showed that in the particular locations where Moir's flint tools were found, the geological evidence did not suggest the operation of such natural causes.

MacCurdy wrote: "Conditions favoring the play of natural forces do not exist in certain Pliocene deposits of East Anglia, where J. Reid Moir has found worked flints. . . . Can the same be said of the chipped flints from Upper Miocene deposits near Aurillac (Cantal)? Sollas and Capitan have both recently answered in the affirmative. Capitan finds not only flint chips that suggest utilization but true types of instruments which would be considered as characteristic of certain Palaeolithic horizons. These not only occur but reoccur: punches, bulbed flakes, carefully retouched to form points and scrapers of the Mousterian type, disks with borders retouched in a regular manner, scratchers of various forms, and, finally, picks. He concludes that there is a complete similitude between many of the chipped flints from Cantal and the classic specimens from the best-known Palaeolithic sites." William Sollas held the Chair of Geology at Oxford, and Louis Capitan, a highly respected French anthropologist, was professor at the College of France.

DISCOVERIES BY A. RUTOT IN BELGIUM

In Belgium, A. Rutot, conservator of the Royal Museum of Natural History in Brussels, made a series of discoveries that brought anomalous stone tool industries into new prominence during the early twentieth century. Most of the industries identified by Rutot dated to the Early Pleistocene. But in 1907, Rutot's ongoing research resulted in more startling finds in sandpits near Boncelles, in the Ardennes region of Belgium. The tool-bearing layers were were Oligocene, which means they were from 25 to 38 million years old.

Describing the tools, Georg Schweinfurth wrote in the *Zeitschrift für Ethnologie*: "Among them were choppers, anvil stones, knives, scrapers, borers, and throwing stones, all displaying clear signs of intentional work that produced forms exquisitely adapted for use by the human hand. . . . the fortunate discoverer had the pleasure to show the sites to 34 Belgian geologists and students of prehistory. They all agreed that there could be no doubt about the position of the finds."

Rutot's complete report on the Boncelles finds appeared in the bulletin of the Belgian Society for Geology, Paleontology, and Hydrology. Rutot also said that stone tools like those of Boncelles had been found in Oligocene contexts at Baraque Michel and the cavern at Bay Bonnet. At Rosart, on the left bank of the Meuse, stone tools had also been found in a Middle Pliocene context.

"Now it appears," wrote Rutot, "that the notion of the existence of humanity in the Oligocene . . . has been affirmed with such force and precision that one cannot detect the slightest fault." Rutot noted that the Oligocene tools from Boncelles almost exactly resembled tools made within the past few centuries by the native inhabitants of Tasmania (Figures 4.11 and 4.12).

Rutot then described in detail the various types of tools from the Oligocene of Boncelles, beginning with *percuteurs* (or choppers). These included: plain choppers, sharpened choppers, pointed choppers, and retouchers, which were used to

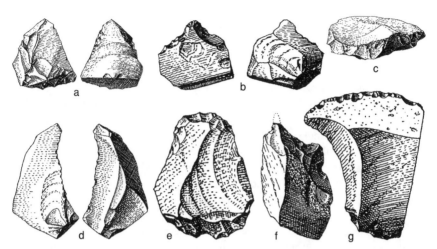

Figure 4.11. Implements manufactured by native Tasmanians in recent historical times. Rutot said they resembled almost exactly the tools from the Oligocene period at Boncelles, Belgium. (a) Side scraper (*racloir*), compare Figure 4.12a. (b) Pointed implement (*perçoir*), compare Figure 4.12b. (c) Anvil (*enclume*), compare Figure 4.12c. (d) Stone knife (*couteau*), compare Figure 4.12d. (e) Double end scraper (*grattoir double*), compare Figure 4.12e. (f) Awl (*perçoir*), compare Figure 4.12f. (g) End scraper (*grattoir*), compare Figure 4.12g.

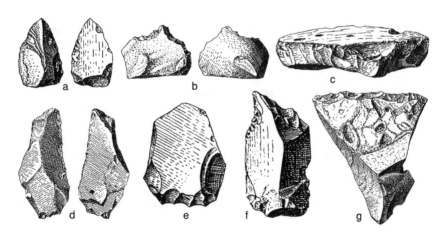

Figure 4.12. Stone tools from below the Late Oligocene sands at Boncelles, Belgium: (a) Side scraper resembling a Mousterian point from the Late Pleistocene of Europe. (b) Pointed implement with a well-developed bulb of percussion. (c) Anvil with signs of percussion. (d) Stone knife with use marks on the cutting edge. (e) End scraper. (f) Awl. (g) Large end scraper.

resharpen the working edges of other stone implements. All categories of *percuteurs* displayed chipping to make the implements easier to hold in the hand and signs of usage on the working edge.

Also found at the Boncelles sites were several anvil stones characterized by a large flat surface showing definite signs of percussion.

Rutot then described some implements he called *couteaux,* best translated as cutters. "One can see," he wrote, "that *couteaux* are made from relatively long flakes of flint, blunt on one side and sharp on the other."

Another type of implement was the *racloir,* or side scraper. The *racloir* was ordinarily made from an oval flake, with one of the edges blunt and the opposite edge sharp. After retouching for a suitable grip, the blunt edge was held in the palm of the hand, and the sharp edge of the implement was moved along the length of the object to be scraped. During this operation, small splinters were detached from the cutting edge of the implement and these use marks could be seen on many specimens.

Rutot then described other types of *racloirs:* the notched *racloir,* probably used for scraping long, round objects, and the double *racloir* with two sharp edges. Some of the double *racloirs* resembled Mousterian pointed implements from the Late Pleistocene.

Rutot also described a special category of tools, which he called mixed implements, because they looked as if they could have been employed in more than one fashion. Rutot stated: "They tend to have on the sharp edge a point formed by the intersection of two straight edges, or more frequently, two notches, made by retouching."

The next type of implement discussed by Rutot was the *grattoir,* another category of scraper. He also described *perçoirs,* which might be called awls or borers. Rutot also noted the presence at Boncelles of objects that appeared to be throwing stones or sling stones. Finally, Rutot suggested that certain flint objects bearing traces of repeated impacts may have been used by the ancient inhabitants of Boncelles to make fire. Such stones are found in Late Pleistocene tool collections.

"We find ourselves," Rutot said, "confronted with a grave problem—the existence in the Oligocene of beings intelligent enough to manufacture and use definite and variegated types of implements." Today scientists do not give any consideration at all to the possibility of a human—or even protohuman—presence in the Oligocene. We believe there are two reasons for this—unfamiliarity with evidence such as Rutot's and unquestioning faith in currently held views on human origin and antiquity.

DISCOVERIES BY FREUDENBERG NEAR ANTWERP

In February and March of 1918, Wilhelm Freudenberg, a geologist attached to the German army, was conducting test borings for military purposes in Tertiary formations west of Antwerp, Belgium. In clay pits at Hol, near St. Gillis, and at other locations, Freudenberg discovered flint objects he believed to be implements, along with cut bones and shells. Most of the objects came from sedimentary deposits of the Scaldisian marine stage. The Scaldisian spans the Early Pliocene and Late Miocene and is thus 4–7 million years old. Freudenberg suggested that the objects he discovered may have dated to the period just before the

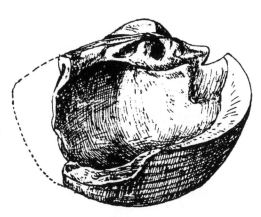

Figure 4.13. A shell from a Scaldisian formation (Early Pliocene to Late Miocene) near Antwerp, Belgium, with a cut mark to the right of the hinge.

Scaldisian marine transgression, which, if true, would give them an age of at least 7 million years.

Freudenberg believed some of the flint implements he found had been used to open shells. Many of these were found along with cut shells and burned flints, which Freudenberg took as evidence that intelligent beings had used fire during the Tertiary in Belgium. Concerning the cut shells (Figure 4.13), Freudenberg stated: "I found many intentional incisions, mostly on the rear part of the shells, quite near the hinge." He said the incisions were "such as could only have been made with a sharp instrument." Some of the shells also bore puncture marks. In addition to cut shells, Freudenberg also found bones of marine mammals bearing what he thought were cut marks. He carefully considered and rejected alternative hypotheses such as chemical corrosion or geological abrasion. He also found bones bearing deep impact marks that could have been made by stone hammers.

Further confirmation of a human presence came in the form of partial footprints, apparently made when humanlike feet compressed pieces of clay. From a clay pit at Hol, Freudenberg recovered one impression of the ball of a foot and four impressions of toes. According to Freudenberg, patterns of ridges and pores matched those of human feet and were distinct from those of apes.

Freudenberg was an evolutionist and believed that his Tertiary man must have been a small hominid, displaying, in addition to its humanlike feet, a combination of apelike and human features. Altogether, Freudenberg's description of his Flemish Tertiary man seems reminiscent of *Australopithecus*. But one would not, according to current paleoanthropological doctrine, expect to find any australopithecines in Belgium during the Late Miocene, over 7 million years ago. The oldest australopithecines date back only about 4 million years in Africa.

Then who made the footprints discovered by Freudenberg? There are today, in Africa and the Phillipines, pygmy tribes, with adult males standing less than five feet tall and females even shorter. The proposal that a small human being rather than an australopithecine made the footprints is more consistent with the whole spectrum of evidence—stone tools, incised bones, isolated signs of fire, and artificially opened shells. Australopithecines are not known to have manufactured stone tools or used fire.

CENTRAL ITALY

In 1871, Professor G. Ponzi presented to the meeting in Bologna of the International Congress of Prehistoric Anthropology and Archeology a report about evidence for Tertiary humans in central Italy. The evidence consisted of pointed flint implements recovered by geologists from deposits of breccia from the Pliocene Acquatraversan erosional phase (over 2 million years old). A breccia is a deposit composed of rock fragments in a fine-grained matrix of hardened sand or clay.

STONE TOOLS FROM BURMA

In 1894 and 1895, scientific journals announced the discovery of worked flints in Miocene formations in Burma, then part of the British India. The implements were reported by Fritz Noetling, a paleontologist who directed the Geological Survey of India in the region of Yenangyaung, Burma.

While collecting fossils, Noetling noticed a rectangular flint object (Figure 4.14). He said its implementlike form was "difficult to explain by natural causes." Noetling noted, "The shape of this specimen reminds me very much of the chipped

flint described in Volume I of the Records, Geological Survey of India, and discovered in the Pleistocene of the Nerbudda river, the artificial origin of which nobody seems to have ever doubted." Noetling searched further and found about a dozen more chipped pieces of flint.

How certain was the stratigraphic position of Noetling's flints? Noetling offered this account: "The exact spot where the flints were found . . . is situated on the steep eastern slope of a ravine, high above its bottom, but be-

Figure 4.14. Two sides of a flint implement from the Miocene Yenangyaung formation in Burma.

low the edge in such a position that it is inconceivable how the flints should have been brought there by any foreign agency. There is no room for any dwelling place in this narrow gorge, nor was there ever any; it is further impossible from the way in which the flints were found that they could have been brought to that place by a flood. If I weigh all the evidence, quite apart from the fact that I actually dug them out of the bed, it is my strong belief that they were *in situ* when found."

In conclusion, Noetling said: "If flints of this shape can be produced by natural causes, a good many chipped flints hitherto considered as undoubtedly artificial [i.e., human] products are open to grave doubts as to their origin."

TOOLS FROM BLACK'S FORK RIVER, WYOMING

In 1932, Edison Lohr and Harold Dunning, two amateur archeologists, found many stone tools on the high terraces of the Black's Fork River in Wyoming, U.S.A. The implements appeared to be of Middle Pleistocene age, which would be anomalous for North America.

Lohr and Dunning showed the tools they collected to E. B. Renaud, a professor of anthropology at the University of Denver. Renaud, who was also director of the Archaeological Survey of the High Western Plains, then organized an expedition to the region where the tools were found. During the summer of 1933, Renaud's party collected specimens from the ancient river terraces between the towns of Granger and Lyman.

Among the specimens were crude handaxes and other flaked implements of a kind frequently attributed to *Homo erectus,* who is said to have inhabited Europe during the Middle Pleistocene.

The reaction from anthropologists in America was negative. Renaud wrote in 1938 that his report had been "harshly criticized by one of the irreconcilable opponents of the antiquity of man in America, who had seen neither the sites nor the specimens."

In response, Renaud mounted three more expeditions, collecting more tools. Although many experts from outside America agreed with him that the tools represented a genuine industry, American scientists have continued their opposition to the present day.

The most common reaction is to say the crude specimens are blanks (unworked flakes) dropped fairly recently by Indian toolmakers. But Herbert L. Minshall, a collector of stone tools, stated in 1989 that the tools show heavy stream abrasion even though they are fixed in desert pavements on ancient flood plain surfaces that could not have had streams for over 150,000 years.

If found at a site of similar age in Africa or Europe or China, stone tools like those found by Renaud would not be a source of controversy. But their presence in Wyoming is certainly very much unexpected at 150,000 or more years ago. The view now dominant is that humans entered North America not earlier than about 30,000 years ago at most. And before that there was no migration of any other hominid.

Some suggested that the abrasion on the implements was the result of wind-blown sand rather than water. In reply Minshall observed: "The specimens were abraded on all sides, top and bottom, ventral and dorsal surfaces equally. That is extremely unlikely for windblown dust to achieve on heavy stone tools lying in heavy gravel but expectable on objects subjected to surf or heavy stream action."

Minshall also noted that the tools were covered with a thick mineral coating of desert varnish. This varnish, which takes a long time to accumulate, was thicker than that on tools found on lower, and hence more recent, terraces in the same region.

The cumulative evidence appears to rule out the suggestion that the implements discovered by Renaud were blanks dropped fairly recently on the high desert floodplain terraces. But Minshall noted: "The reaction of American scientists to Renaud's interpretation of the Black's Fork collections as evidences of great antiquity was, and has continued to be for over half a century, one of general skepticism and disbelief, even though probably not one in a thousand archaeologists has visited the site nor seen the artifacts."

According to Minshall, the tools found by Renaud were the work of *Homo erectus,* who may have entered North America during a time of lowered sea levels in the Middle Pleistocene. Minshall believed this was also true of stone tools found at other locations of similar age, such as Calico and his own excavation at Buchanan Canyon, both in southern California.

Minshall was, however, skeptical of another Middle Pleistocene site. In January 1990, Minshall told one of us (Thompson) that he was not inclined to accept as genuine the technologically advanced stone tools found at Hueyatlaco in Mexico (Chapter 5). The advanced stone tools found at Hueyatlaco were characteristic of *Homo sapiens sapiens* and were thus not easy to attribute to *Homo erectus.* Minshall's response to Hueyatlaco was to suggest, without supporting evidence, that the stratigraphy had been misinterpreted and that the animal bones used to date the site, as well as the sophisticated stone artifacts, had been washed onto the site from different sources. This shows that researchers who accept some anomalies may rule out others using the double standard method.

5

Advanced Paleoliths and Neoliths

Advanced paleoliths are more finely worked than the crude paleoliths. But industries containing advanced paleoliths may also contain cruder tools. We shall first discuss the discoveries of Florentino Ameghino, as well as the attacks upon them by Ales Hrdlicka and W. H. Holmes. Next we shall consider the finds of Carlos Ameghino, which provide some of the most solid and convincing evidence for a fully human presence in the Pliocene. We shall then proceed to anomalous finds made at sites in North America, including Hueyatlaco, Mexico; Sandia Cave, New Mexico; Sheguiandah, Ontario; Lewisville, Texas; and Timlin, New York. We shall conclude with the Neolithic finds from the Tertiary gold-bearing gravels of the California gold rush country.

DISCOVERIES OF FLORENTINO AMEGHINO IN ARGENTINA

During the late nineteenth century, Florentino Ameghino thoroughly investigated the geology and fossils of the coastal provinces of Argentina, thereby gaining an international reputation. Ameghino's controversial discoveries of stone implements, carved bones, and other signs of a human presence in Argentina during the Pliocene, Miocene, and earlier periods served to increase his worldwide fame.

In 1887, Florentino Ameghino made some significant discoveries at Monte Hermoso, on the coast of Argentina about 37 miles northeast of Bahia Blanca. Summarizing the Monte Hermoso evidence, F. Ameghino said: "The presence of man, or rather his precursor, at this ancient site, is demonstrated by the presence of crudely worked flints, like those of the Miocene of Portugal, carved bones, burned bones, and burned earth proceeding from ancient fireplaces." The layers containing this evidence are in the Pliocene Monte Hermosan formation, which is about 3.5 million years old.

Among the fossils recovered from Monte Hermoso was a hominid atlas (the first bone of the spinal column, at the base of the skull). Ameghino thought it displayed primitive features, but A. Hrdlicka judged it to be fully human. This

75

strongly suggests that beings of the modern human type were responsible for the artifacts and signs of fire discovered in the Montehermosan formation.

Ameghino's discoveries at Monte Hermoso and elsewhere in the Tertiary formations of Argentina attracted the interest of several European scientists. Ales Hrdlicka, an anthropologist at the Smithsonian Institution in Washington, D. C., also took great, though unsympathetic, interest in Ameghino's discoveries. Hrdlicka found the degree of support they enjoyed among professional scientists, particularly in Europe, dismaying. In addition to being opposed to the existence of Tertiary humans, Hrdlicka was also extremely hostile to any reports of a human presence in the Americas earlier than a few thousand years before the present. After building an immense reputation by discrediting, with questionable arguments, all such reports from North America, Hrdlicka then turned his attention to the much-discussed South American discoveries of Florentino Ameghino. In 1910, Hrdlicka visited Argentina, and Florentino Ameghino himself accompanied him to Monte Hermoso. Hrdlicka took an interesting approach to the discoveries that were made at that site. In his book *Early Man in South America* (1912), Hrdlicka briefly mentioned the stone implements and other signs of human occupation uncovered by Ameghino in the Montehermosan formation. Strangely, he did not directly dispute them. Instead, he devoted dozens of pages to casting doubt on subsequent, and less convincing, discoveries that he and Ameghino made in the Puelchean, a more recent formation overlying the Pliocene Montehermosan at Monte Hermoso. The Puelchean formation is about 1–2 million years old.

Apparently, Hrdlicka believed his lengthy refutation of the finds from the Puelchean formation was sufficient to discredit the finds in the far older Montehermosan formation at the same site. This tactic is often used to cast doubt on anomalous discoveries—criticize the weakest evidence in detail and ignore the strongest evidence as much as possible. Nevertheless, there is much evidence to suggest that the Puelchean finds, as well as the Montehermosan finds, were genuine.

Most of the tools discovered by Hrdlicka and Ameghino during their joint expedition were roughly chipped from quartzite pebbles. Hrdlicka did not dispute the human manufacture of even the crudest specimens. Instead, he questioned their age. He suggested that the layer containing them was recent. In making this judgement, Hrdlicka relied heavily in the testimony of Bailey Willis, the American geologist who accompanied him.

The layer containing the tools was at the top of the Puelchean formation. With some hesitation, Willis accepted the Puelchean as being at least Pliocene in age. He said it consisted of "stratified, slightly indurated, gray sands or sandstone . . . marked by very striking cross stratification and uniformity of gray color and grain." Willis described the topmost layer, apparently included by

Ameghino in the Puelchean formation, as a band about 6 to 16 inches thick, "composed of gray sand, angular pieces of gray sandstone and pebbles, some fractured by man."

Willis remarked that the top layer of gray implement-bearing sand is "identical in constitution" to the lower layers of the Puelchean but is separated from them by "an unconformity by erosion." An unconformity is a lack of continuity in deposition between strata in contact with each other, corresponding to a period of nondeposition, weathering, or, as in this case, erosion. For judging how much time might have passed between the deposition of the formations lying above and below the line of unconformity, the surest indicator is animal fossils. Willis, however, did not mention any. It is thus unclear how much time might be represented by the unconformity. It could have been very short, making the layers above and below the uncomformity roughly the same age—about 1–2 million years old.

Attempting to eliminate this alternative, Willis wrote "hand-chipped stones associated with the sands would mark them as recent." Willis assumed that any stone tools had to be recent and that the layer in which they were found therefore also had to be recent. It would appear, however, that the implement-bearing gray gravelly sand may actually belong to the Puelchean formation, as Ameghino believed, and that the stone implements found there could be as much as 2 million years old.

Ameghino also found stone tools, along with cut bones and signs of fire, in the Santacrucian and Entrerrean formations in Argentina. The Santacrucian formation is of Early and Middle Miocene age, making the tools found therein about 15–25 million years old. We have not encountered any mention of the Entrerrean in the current literature we have examined, but since this formation comes before the Monte Hermosan, it would be at least Late Miocene, over 5 million years old.

In many places, Ameghino found evidence of fires much hotter than campfires or grass fires. This evidence included large, thick pieces of hard, burned clay and slag. It is possible these may represent the remains of primitive foundries or kilns used by the Pliocene inhabitants of Argentina.

TOOLS FOUND BY CARLOS AMEGHINO
AT MIRAMAR, ARGENTINA

After Ales Hrdlicka's attack on the discoveries of Florentino Ameghino, Ameghino's brother Carlos launched a new series of investigations on the Argentine coast south of Buenos Aires. From 1912 to 1914, Carlos Ameghino and his associates, working on behalf of the natural history museums of Buenos Aires and La Plata, discovered stone tools in the Pliocene Chapadmalalan formation at the base of a *barranca,* or cliff, extending along the seaside at Miramar.

In order to confirm the age of the implements, Carlos Ameghino invited a commission of four geologists to give their opinion. These were Santiago Roth, director of the Bureau of Geology and Mines for the province of Buenos Aires; Lutz Witte, a geologist of the Bureau of Geology and Mines for the province of Buenos Aires; Walther Schiller, chief of the mineralogy section of the Museum of La Plata and consultant to the National Bureau of Geology and Mines; and Moises Kantor, chief of the geology section of the Museum of La Plata.

After carefully investigating the site, the commission unanimously concluded that the implements had been found in undisturbed Chapadmalalan sediments. The implements would thus be 2–3 million years old.

While present at the site, the commission members witnessed the extraction of a stone ball and a flint knife from the Pliocene formation. They were thus able to confirm the genuineness of the discoveries. Pieces of burned earth and slag were found nearby. The commission members also reported: "Digging with a pick at the same spot where the bola and knife were found, someone discovered in the presence of the commission other flat stones, of the type that the Indians use to make fire." Further discoveries of stone implements were made at the same site. All of this suggests that humans, capable of manufacturing tools and using fire, lived in Argentina about 2–3 million years ago in the Late Pliocene.

After the commission left for Buenos Aires, Carlos Ameghino remained at Miramar conducting further excavations. From the top of the Late Pliocene Chapadmalalan layers, Ameghino extracted the femur of a toxodon, an extinct South American hoofed mammal, resembling a furry, short-legged, hornless rhinoceros. Ameghino discovered embedded in the toxodon femur a stone arrowhead or lance point (Figure 5.1), giving evidence for culturally advanced humans 2–3 million years ago in Argentina.

Is it possible the toxodon femur with the arrowhead was a recent bone that had worked itself down from the above? Carlos Ameghino pointed out that the femur was found attached to all the other bones of the toxodon's rear leg. This indicated that the femur was not a loose bone that had somehow slipped into the Pliocene Chapadmalalan formation but was part of an animal that had

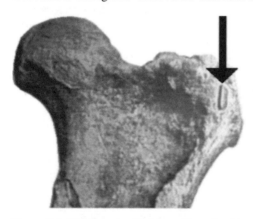

Figure 5.1. This toxodon thighbone (femur), with a stone projectile point embedded in it, was discovered in a Pliocene formation at Miramar, Argentina.

died when this formation was being laid down. Ameghino noted: "The bones are of a dirty whitish color, characteristic of this stratum, and not blackish, from the magnesium oxides in the Ensenadan." He added that some of the hollow parts of the leg bones were filled with the Chapadmalalan loess. Of course, even if the bones had worked there way in from the overlying Ensenadan formation, they would still be anomalously old. The Ensenadan is from 0.4 – 1.5 million years old.

Those who want to dispute the great age attributed to the toxodon femur will point out that the toxodon survived until just a few thousand years ago in South America. But Carlos Ameghino reported that the toxodon he found at Miramar, an adult specimen, was smaller than those in the upper, more recent levels of the Argentine stratigraphic sequence. This indicated it was a distinct, older species. Carlos Ameghino believed his Miramar toxodon was of the Chapadmalalan species *Toxodon chapalmalensis,* first identified by F. Ameghino, and characterized by its small size.

Furthermore, Carlos Ameghino directly compared his Chapadmalalan toxodon femur with femurs of toxodon species from more recent formations and observed: "The femur of Miramar is on the whole smaller and more slender." Ameghino then reported more details showing how the femur he found in the Late Pliocene Chapadmalalan of Miramar differed from that of *Toxodon burmeisteri* of more recent Pampean levels.

Carlos Ameghino then described the stone point found embedded in the femur: "This is a flake of quartzite obtained by percussion, a single blow, and retouched along its lateral edges, but only on one surface, and afterward pointed at its two extremities by the same process of retouch, giving it a form approximating a willow leaf, therefore resembling the double points of the Solutrean type, which have been designated *feuille de saule*. . . . by all these details we can recognize that we are confronted with a point of the Mousterian type of the European Paleolithic period." That such a point should be found in a formation dating back as much as 3 million years provokes serious questions about the version of human evolution presented by the modern scientific establishment, which holds that 3 million years ago we should find only the most primitive australopithecines at the vanguard of the hominid line.

In December of 1914, Carlos Ameghino, with Carlos Bruch, Luis Maria Torres, and Santiago Roth, visited Miramar to mark and photograph the exact location where the toxodon femur had been found. Carlos Ameghino stated: "When we arrived at the spot of the latest discoveries and continued the excavations, we uncovered more and more intentionally worked stones, convincing us we had come upon a veritable workshop of that distant epoch." The many implements included anvils and hammer stones. Stone tools were also found in the Ensenadan formation, which overlies the Chapmalalan at Miramar.

ATTEMPTS TO DISCREDIT CARLOS AMEGHINO

Carlos Ameghino's views about the antiquity of humans in Argentina were challenged by Antonio Romero. In his 1918 paper, Romero made many combative remarks, and after reading them one might expect to find some cogent geological arguments to back them up. Instead one finds little more than some unique and fanciful views of the geological history of the Miramar coastal region. Romero claimed all the formations in the *barranca* at Miramar were recent. "If you find the fossils of distinct epochs in different levels of the *barranca*," he wrote, "that does not signify a succession of epochs there, because water may have elsewhere eroded very ancient fossil-bearing deposits of previous epochs, depositing the older fossils at the base of the *barranca*."

Significantly, these same formations at Miramar had been extensively studied on several occasions by different professional geologists and paleontologists, none of whom viewed them in the manner suggested by Romero. The incorrectness of Romero's interpretation of the stratigraphy at Miramar is confirmed by modern researchers, who identify the formation at the base of the cliff as Chapadmalalan and assign it to the Late Pliocene, making it 2–3 million years old.

Romero also suggested that there had been massive resorting and shifting of the beds in the *barranca,* making it possible that implements and animal bones from surface layers had become mixed into the lower levels of the cliff. But the only facts that he could bring forward to support this conclusion were two extremely minor dislocations of strata.

Some distance to the left of the spot where the commission of geologists extracted a bola stone from the Chapadmalalan level of the *barranca,* there is a place where a section of a layer of stones in the formation departs slightly from the horizontal. This dislocation occurs near the place where the *barranca* is interrupted by a large gully. As might be expected, part of the *barranca* slopes down to the left at this point, but at the place where the bola stone was extracted, the horizontal stratigraphy remained intact. At another place in the *barranca,* a small portion of a layer of stones departed only 16 degrees from the horizontal.

On the basis of these two relatively inconsequential observations, Romero suggested that all the strata exposed in the barranca had been subjected to extreme dislocations. This would have allowed the intrusion into the lower levels of stone tools from relatively recent Indian settlements that might have existed above the cliffs. But from photographs and the observations of many other geologists, including Willis, it appears that the normal sequence of beds in the *barranca* at Miramar was intact in locations where discoveries were made.

In the 1957 edition of *Fossil Men,* Marcellin Boule said that after the original discovery of the toxodon femur, Carlos Ameghino found in the Chapadmalalan at Miramar an intact section of a toxodon's vertebral column, in which two stone projectile points were embedded. Boule stated: "These discoveries were disputed. Reliable geologists affirmed that the objects came from the upper beds, which formed the site of a *paradero* or ancient Indian settlement, and that they were found today in the Tertiary bed only as a consequence of disturbances and resortings which that bed had suffered." Here Boule footnoted as a reference only the 1918 report by Romero! Boule did not mention the commission of four highly qualified geologists who reached a conclusion exactly opposite that of Romero, perhaps because they were, in his opinion, not reliable. However, having closely studied Romero's geological conclusions, particularly in light of those of Bailey Willis and modern researchers, we are mystified that Romero should be characterized as reliable.

Boule added: "The archaeological data support this conclusion, for the same Tertiary bed yielded dressed and polished stones, *bolas* and *boladeras,* identical with those used as missiles by the Indians." Boule said that Eric Boman, an "excellent enthnographer," had documented these facts.

Could human beings have lived continuously in Argentina since the Tertiary and not changed their technology? Why not, especially if, as certified by a commission of geologists, implements were found *in situ* in beds of Pliocene antiquity? The fact that these implements were identical to those used by more recent inhabitants of the same region poses no barrier to acceptance of their Tertiary age. Modern tribal people in various parts of the world fashion stone implements indistinguishable from those recognized as having been manufactured 2 million years ago. Furthermore, in 1921 a fully human fossil jaw was found in the Chapadmalalan at Miramar (see Chapter 7).

In his statements about the Miramar finds, Boule provides a classic case of prejudice and preconception masquerading as scientific objectivity. In Boule's book, all evidence for a human presence in the Tertiary formations of Argentina was dismissed on theoretical grounds and by ignoring crucial observations by competent scientists who happened to hold forbidden views. For example, Boule said nothing at all about the above-mentioned discovery of a human jaw in the Chapadmalalan at Miramar. We should thus be extremely careful in accepting the statements one finds in famous textbooks as the final word in paleoanthropology.

Scientists who disagree with controversial evidence commonly take the same approach as Boule. One mentions an exceptional discovery, one states that it was disputed for some time, and then one cites an authority (such as Romero) who supposedly settled the matter, once and for all. But when one takes the time to dig up the report that, like Romero's, supposedly delivered the coup de grace, it often fails to make a convincing case.

What was true of Romero's report is also true of Boman's. Boule, we have seen, advertised Boman as an excellent ethnographer. But in examining Boman's report, the reason for Boule's favorable judgement becomes apparent. Throughout his paper, which attacked Florentino Ameghino's theories and Carlos Ameghino's discoveries at Miramar, Boman, taking the role of a dutiful disciple, regularly cited Boule as an authority. As might be expected, Boman also quoted extensively from Hrdlicka's lengthy negative critique of Florentino Ameghino's work. Nevertheless, Boman, despite his negative attitude, inadvertently managed to give some of the best possible evidence for a human presence in Argentina during the Pliocene.

Boman suspected fraud on the part of Lorenzo Parodi, a museum collector who worked for Carlos Ameghino. But Boman had no proof. Boman himself said: "I had no right to express any suspicions about him, because Carlos Ameghino had spoken highly of him, assuring me that he was as honest and trustworthy a man as could be found." But Boman noted: "Concerning the question of where it is possible to obtain objects for fraudulent introduction into the Chapadmalalan strata, that is a problem easily resolved. A couple of miles from the discoveries exists a *paradero,* an abandoned Indian settlement, exposed on the surface and relatively modern—about four or five hundred years old—where there exist many objects identical to those found in the Chapadmalalan strata."

a   b   c

Figure 5.2. These stone bolas were extracted from the Late Pliocene Chapadmalalan formation at Miramar, Argentina, in the presence of ethnographer Eric Boman.

Boman went on to describe his own visit to the Miramar site on November 22, 1920: "Parodi had given a report of a stone ball, uncovered by the surf and still encrusted in the *barranca.* Carlos Ameghino invited various persons to witness its extraction, and I went there along with Dr. Estanislao S. Zeballos, ex-minister of foreign affairs; Dr. H. von Ihering, ex-director of the Museum of São Paulo in Brazil; and Dr. R. Lehmann-Nitsche, the well known anthropologist." At the Miramar *barranca,* Boman convinced himself that the geological information earlier reported by Carlos Ameghino was essentially correct. Boman's admission confirms our assessment that the contrary views of Romero are not to be given much credibility. This also discredits Boule, who relied solely upon Romero in his own attempt to dismiss the discovery at Miramar of the toxodon femur and vertebral column, both with stone arrowheads embedded in them.

"When we arrived at the final point of our journey," wrote Boman, "Parodi showed us a stone object encrusted in a perpendicular section of the *barranca,* where there was a slight concavity, apparently produced by the action of waves. This object presented a visible surface only 2 centimeters [just under an inch] in diameter. Parodi proceeded to remove some of the surrounding earth so it could be photographed, and at that time it could be seen that the object was a stone ball with an equatorial groove of the kind found on bola stones. Photographs were taken of the ball *in situ,* the *barranca,* and the persons present, and then the bola stone was extracted. It was so firmly situated in the hard earth that it was necessary to use sufficient force with cutting tools in order to break it out little by little."

Boman then confirmed the position of the bola stone (Figure 5.2a), which was found in the *barranca* about 3 feet above the beach sand. Boman stated: "The *barranca* consists of Ensenadan above and Chapadmalalan below. The boundary between the two levels is undoubtedly a little confused. . . . Be that as it may, it appears to me that there is no doubt that the bola stone was found in the Chapadmalalan layers, which were compact and homogeneous."

Boman then told of another discovery: "Later, at my direction, Parodi continued to attack the *barranca* with a pick at the same point where the bola stone was discovered, when suddenly and unexpectedly, there appeared a second ball 10 centimeters lower than the first. . . . It is more like a grinding stone than a bola. This tool [Figure 5.2b] was found at a depth of 10 centimeters [4 inches] in the face of the cliff." Boman said it was worn by use. Still later Boman and Parodi discovered another stone ball (Figure 5.2c), 200 meters from the first ones, and about half a meter lower in the *barranca.* Of this last discovery at Miramar, Boman said "there is no doubt that the ball has been rounded by the hand of man."

Altogether, the circumstances of discovery greatly favored a Pliocene date for the Miramar bolas. Boman reported: "Dr. Lehmann-Nitsche has said that according to his opinion the stone balls we extracted were found *in situ,* are contemporary with the Chapadmalalan terrain, and were not introduced at any later time. Dr. von Ihering is less categorical in this regard. Concerning myself, I can declare that I did not observe any sign that indicated a later introduction. The bolas were firmly in place in the very hard terrain that enclosed them, and there was no sign of there having been any disturbance of the earth that covered them."

Boman then artfully raised the suspicion of cheating. He suggested different ways that Parodi could have planted the stone balls. And he pounded a stone arrowhead into a toxodon femur, just to show how Parodi might have accomplished a forgery. But in the end, Boman himself said: "In the final analysis there undoubtedly exists no conclusive proof of fraud. On the contrary many of the circumstances speak strongly in favor of their authenticity."

It is difficult to see why Boman should have been so skeptical of Parodi. One could argue that Parodi would not have wanted to jeopardize his secure and longstanding employment as a museum collector by manufacturing fake discoveries. In any case, the museum professionals insisted that Parodi leave any objects of human industry in place so they could be photographed, examined, and removed by experts. This procedure is superior to that employed by scientists involved in many famous discoveries that are used to uphold the currently accepted scenario of human evolution. For example, most of the *Homo erectus*

Figure 5.3. A sling stone from the detritus bed beneath the Red Crag at Bramford, England. At least Pliocene in age, the sling stone could be as old as the Eocene.

discoveries reported by von Koenigswald in Java were made by native diggers, who, unlike Parodi, did not leave the fossils *in situ* but sent them in crates to von Koenigswald, who often stayed in places far from the sites. Furthermore, the famous Venus of Willendorf, a Neolithic statuette from Europe, was discovered by a road workman. It is obvious that if one were to apply Boman's extreme skepticism across the board one could raise suspicions of fraud about almost every paleoanthropological discovery ever made.

Ironically, Boman's testimony provides, even for skeptics, very strong evidence for the presence of toolmaking human beings in Argentina as much as 3 million years ago. Even if, for the sake of argument, one admits that the first bola stone recovered during Boman's visit to Miramar was planted by the collector Parodi, how can one explain the second and third finds? These were instigated not by the collector Parodi but by Boman himself, on the spot and without any warning. Significantly, they were completely hidden from view, and Parodi did not even hint at their existence.

Altogether, it appears that Boule, Romero, and Boman have offered little to discredit the discoveries of Carlos Ameghino and others at the Miramar site. In fact, Boman gave first-class evidence for the existence of bola makers there in the Pliocene period.

MORE BOLAS AND SIMILAR OBJECTS

The bolas of Miramar are significant in that they point to the existence of human beings of a high level of culture during the Pliocene, and perhaps even earlier, in South America. Similar implements have been found in Africa and Europe in formations of Pliocene age.

In 1926, John Baxter, one of J. Reid Moir's assistants uncovered a particularly interesting object (Figure 5.3) from below the Pliocene Red Crag at Bramford, near Ipswich, England.

Moir did not carefully examine the object. But three years later, it attracted the attention of Henri Breuil, who wrote: "While I was staying in Ipswich with my friend J. Reid Moir, we were examining together a drawer of objects from the base of the Red Crag at Bramford, when J. Reid Moir showed me a singular egg-shaped object, which had been picked up on account of its unusual shape. Even at first sight it appeared to me to present artificial striations and facets, and I therefore examined it more closely with a mineralogist's lens [Figure 5.4]. This examination showed me that my first impression was fully justified, and that the object had been shaped by the hand of man." Breuil compared the object to the "sling stones of New Caledonia." According to Moir, several other archeologists agreed with Breuil. Sling stones and bola stones represent a level of technological sophistication universally associated with modern *Homo sapiens*. It may be recalled that the detritus bed below the Red Crag contains fossils and sediments from habitable land surfaces ranging from Pliocene to Eocene in age. Therefore the Bramford sling stone could be anywhere from 2 to 55 million years old.

In 1956, G. H. R. von Koenigswald described some human artifacts from the lower levels of the Olduvai Gorge site in Tanzania, Africa. These included "numbers of stones that have been chipped until they were roughly spherical." Von Koenigswald wrote: "They are believed to be an extremely primitive form of throwing ball. Stone balls of this type, known to them as *bolas,* are still used by native hunters in South America. They are tied in little leather bags and two or three of them are attached to a long cord. Holding one ball in his hand, the hunter whirls the other one or two around his head and then lets fly."

The objects reported by von Koenigswald, if used in the same manner as South American bolas, imply that their makers were adept not only at stoneworking but leatherworking as well.

All this becomes problematic, however, when one considers that Bed I at Olduvai, where stone balls were found, is 1.7–2.0 million years old. According to standard views on human evolution, only *Australopithecus* and *Homo habilis* should have been around at that time. At present, there is not any definite evidence that *Australopithecus* used tools, and *Homo habilis* is not generally thought to have

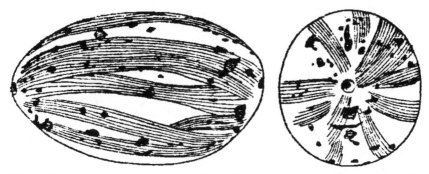

Figure 5.4. A drawing showing marks of intentional shaping on the sling stone from the detritus bed beneath the Red Crag at Bramford, England.

been capable of employing a technology as sophisticated as that represented by bola stones, if that is what the objects really are.

Once more we find ourselves confronted with a situation that calls for an obvious, but forbidden, suggestion—perhaps there were creatures of modern human capability at Olduvai during the earliest Pleistocene.

Those who find this suggestion incredible will doubtlessly respond that there is no fossil evidence to support such a conclusion. In terms of evidence currently accepted, that is certainly true. But if we widen our horizons somewhat, we encounter Reck's skeleton, fully human, recovered from upper Bed II, right at Olduvai Gorge. And not far away, at Kanam, Louis Leakey, according to a commission of scientists, discovered a fully human jaw in Early Pleistocene sediments, equivalent in age to Bed I. In more recent times, humanlike femurs have been discovered in East Africa, in Early Pleistocene contexts. These isolated femurs were originally attributed to *Homo habilis,* but the subsequent discovery of a relatively complete skeleton of a *Homo habilis* individual has shown the *Homo habilis* anatomy, including the femur, to be somewhat apelike. This opens the possibility that the humanlike femurs once attributed to *Homo habilis* might have belonged to anatomically modern human beings living in East Africa during the Early Pleistocene. If we expand the range of our search to other parts of the world, we can multiply the number of examples of fully human fossil remains from the Early Pleistocene and earlier. In this context, the bola stones of Olduvai do not seem out of place.

But perhaps the objects are not bolas. To this possibility Mary Leakey replied: "Although there is no direct evidence that spheroids were used as bolas, no alternative explanation has yet been put forward to account for the numbers of these tools and for the fact that many have been carefully and accurately shaped. If they were intended to be used merely as missiles, with little chance of recovery, it seems unlikely that so much time and care would have been spent on their manufacture." Mary Leakey added: "Their use as bola stones has been strongly supported by L. S. B. Leakey and may well be correct."

Louis Leakey claimed to have found a genuine bone tool in the same level as the bola stones. Leakey said in 1960, "This would appear to be some sort of a 'lissoir' for working leather. It postulates a more evolved way of life for the makers of the Oldowan culture than most of us would have expected."

RELATIVELY ADVANCED NORTH AMERICAN FINDS

We shall now examine relatively advanced anomalous Paleolithic implements from North America, beginning with those found at Sheguiandah, Canada, on Manitoulin Island in northern Lake Huron. Many of these North American discoveries are not particularly old, but they are nonetheless significant because they give insight into the inner workings of archeology and paleoanthropology. We have already seen how the scientific community suppresses data with uncomfortable implications for the currently dominant picture of human evolution. And now we shall encounter revelations of another aspect of this—the personal distress and bitterness experienced by scientists unfortunate enough to make anomalous discoveries.

Figure 5.5. Projectile point from Level III of the Sheguiandah site, Manitoulin Island, Ontario, Canada.

SHEGUIANDAH: ARCHEOLOGY AS A VENDETTA

Between 1951 and 1955, Thomas E. Lee, an anthropologist at the National Museum of Canada, carried out excavations at Sheguiandah, on Manitoulin Island in Lake Huron.

Figure 5.6. Bifacially chipped implement from upper glacial till (Level IV) at the Sheguiandah site.

The upper layers of the site contained, at a depth of approximately 6 inches (Level III), a variety of projectile points (Figure 5.5). Lee considered these recent.

Further excavation exposed implements (Figure 5.6) in a layer of glacial till, a deposit of stones left by receding glaciers. It thus appeared that human beings had lived in the area during or before the time of the last North American glaciation, the Wisconsin. Further study showed that there was a second layer of till, which also contained implements (Figure 5.7). Stone implements were also discovered in the layers beneath the tills.

How old were the tools? Three of the four geologists who studied the site thought the tools were from the last interglacial. This

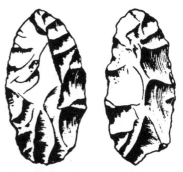

Figure 5.7. Quartzite bifaces from the lower glacial till (Level V) at Sheguiandah. Geologist John Sanford argued these tools and the one in Figure 5.6, were at least 65,000 years old.

would make them from 75,000 to 125,000 years old. Finally, in a joint statement, all four geologists compromised on a "minimum" age of 30,000 years. Lee himself continued to favor an interglacial age for his implements.

One of the original four geologists, John Sanford of Wayne State University, later came out in support of Lee. He provided extensive geological evidence and arguments suggesting the Sheguiandah site dated back to the Sangamon inter-glacial or to the St. Pierre interstadial, a warm interlude in the earliest part of the Wisconsin glaciation. But the view advocated by Lee and Sanford did not receive serious consideration from other scientists.

Lee recalled: "The site's discoverer [Lee] was hounded from his Civil Service position into prolonged unemployment; publication outlets were cut off; the evidence was misrepresented by several prominent authors among the Brahmins; the tons of artifacts vanished into storage bins of the National Museum of Canada; for refusing to fire the discoverer, the Director of the National Museum [Dr. Jacques Rousseau], who had proposed having a mono-graph on the site published, was himself fired and driven into exile; official positions of prestige and power were exercised in an effort to gain control over just six Sheguiandah specimens that had not gone under cover; and the site has been turned into a tourist resort. All of this, without the profession, in four long years, bothering to take a look, when there was still time to look. Sheguiandah would have forced embarrassing admissions that the Brahmins did not know everything. It would have forced the re-writing of almost every book in the business. It had to be killed. It was killed."

Lee experienced great difficulty in getting his reports published. Expressing his frustration, he wrote: "A nervous or timid editor, his senses acutely attuned to the smell of danger to position, security, reputation, or censure, submits copies of a suspect paper to one or two advisors whom he considers well placed to pass safe judgement. They read it, or perhaps only skim through it looking for a few choice phrases that can be challenged or used against the author (their opinions were formed long in advance, on the basis of what came over the grapevine or was picked up in the smoke-filled back rooms at conferences—little bits of gossip that would tell them that the writer was far-out, a maverick, or an untouchable). Then, with a few cutting, unchallenged, and entirely unsupported statements, they 'kill' the paper. The beauty—and the viciousness—of the system lies in the fact that they remain forever anonymous."

Most of the key reports about Sheguiandah were published in the *Anthropologi-cal Journal of Canada,* which Lee himself founded and edited. Lee died in 1982, and the journal was then edited for a short time by his son, Robert E. Lee.

Of course, it has not been possible for establishment scientists to completely avoid mentioning Sheguiandah, but when they do, they tend to downplay, ignore, or misrepresent any evidence for an unusually great age for the site.

Lee's son Robert wrote: "Sheguiandah is erroneously explained to students as an example of postglacial mudflow rather than Wisconsin glacial till."

The original reports, however, give cogent arguments against the mudflow hypothesis. The elder Lee wrote that many geologists "have stated that the deposits would definitely be called glacial till were it not for the presence of artifacts within them. This has been the reaction of almost all visiting geologists." And Sanford said: "Perhaps the best corroboration of these unsorted deposits as ice-laid till was the visit of some 40 or 50 geologists to the site in 1954 during the annual field trip of the Michigan Basin Geological Society. At that time the excavation was open and the till could be seen. The sediments were presented to this group in the field as till deposits, and there was no expressed dissension from the explanation. Certainly had there been any room for doubt as to the nature of these deposits it would have been expressed at this time."

If one approach is to deny that the unsorted tool-bearing deposits are till, another is to demand excessively high levels of proof for a human presence at the site at the designated time. James B. Griffin, an anthropologist at the University of Michigan, stated: "There are a large number of locations in North America for which considerable antiquity has been claimed as places inhabited by early Indians. Even whole books have been published on nonsites." Griffin included Sheguiandah in the category of a nonsite.

Griffin said that a proper site must possess "a clearly identifiable geologic context. . . . with no possibility of intrusion or secondary deposition." He also insisted that a proper site must be studied by several geologists expert in the particular formations present there, and that there must be substantial agreement among these experts. Furthermore, there must be "a range of tool forms and debris . . . well preserved animal remains . . . pollen studies . . . macrobotanical materials . . . human skeletal remains." Griffin also required dating by radiocarbon and other methods.

By this standard, practically none of the locations where major paleoanthropological discoveries have been made would qualify as genuine sites. For example, most of the African discoveries of *Australopithecus, Homo habilis,* and *Homo erectus* have occurred not in clearly identifiable geological contexts, but on the surface or in cave deposits, which are notoriously difficult to interpret geologically. Most of the Java *Homo erectus* finds also occurred on the surface, in poorly specified locations.

Interestingly enough, the Sheguiandah site appears to satisfy most of Griffin's stringent requirements. Implements were found in a geological context clearer than that of many accepted sites. Several geologists expert in North American glacial deposits did apparently agree on an age in excess of 30,000 years. Evidence suggested there was no secondary deposition or intrusion. A variety of tool types were found, pollen studies and radiocarbon tests were performed, and macrobotanical materials (peat) were present.

The Sheguiandah site deserves more attention than it has thus far received. Looking back to the time when it first became apparent to him that stone implements were being found in glacial till, T. E. Lee wrote: "At this point, a wiser man would have filled the trenches and crept away in the night, saying nothing. . . . Indeed, while visiting the site, one prominent anthropologist, after exclaiming in disbelief, 'You aren't finding anything down *there?*' and being told by the foreman, 'The hell we aren't! Get down in here and look for yourself!,' urged me to forget all about what was in the glacial deposits and to concentrate upon the more recent materials overlying them."

LEWISVILLE AND TIMLIN: THE VENDETTA GOES ON

In 1958, at a site near Lewisville, Texas, stone tools and burned animal bones were found in association with hearths. Later, as the excavation progressed, radiocarbon dates of at least 38,000 years were announced for charcoal from the hearths. Still later, a Clovis point was found. Herbert Alexander, who was a graduate student in archeology at the time, recalled how this sequence of finds was received. "On a number of occasions," stated Alexander, "the opinions voiced at that time were that the hearths were man-made, and the faunal associations valid. Once the dates were announced, however, some opinions were changed and after the Clovis point was found, the process of picking and ignoring began in earnest. Those who had previously accepted the hearths and/or faunal associations began to question their memories."

Finding a Clovis point in a layer 38,000 years old was disturbing, because orthodox anthropologists date the first Clovis points at 12,000 years, marking the entry of humans into North America. Some critics responded to the Lewisville find by alleging that the Clovis point had been planted as a hoax. Others have said the radiocarbon dates were wrong.

After mentioning a number of similar cases of ignored or derided discoveries, Alexander recalled a suggestion that "in order to decide issues of early man, we may soon require attorneys for advocacy." This may not be a bad idea in a field of science like archeology, where opinions determine the status of facts, and facts resolve into networks of interpretation. Attorneys and courts may aid archeologists in arriving more smoothly at the consensus among scholars that passes for the scientific truth in this field. But Alexander noted that a court system requires a jury, and the first question asked of a prospective juror is, "Have you made up your mind on the case?" Very few archeologists have not made up their minds on the date humans first entered North America.

The idea that Clovis-type projectile points represent the earliest tools in the New World is challenged by an excavation at the Timlin site in the Catskill mountains of New York State. In the mid-1970s, tools closely resembling the Upper Acheulean tools of Europe were found there. In the Old World, Acheulean tools are routinely attributed to *Homo erectus*. But such attribution is uncertain because skeletal remains are usually absent at tool sites. The Catskill tools have been given an age of 70,000 years on the basis of glacial geology.

HUEYATLACO, MEXICO

In the 1960s, sophisticated stone tools (Figure 5.8) rivaling the best work of Cro-magnon man in Europe were unearthed by Juan Armenta Camacho and Cynthia Irwin-Williams at Hueyatlaco, near Valsequillo, 75 miles southeast of Mexico City. Stone tools of a somewhat cruder nature were found at the nearby site of El Horno. At both the Hueyatlaco and El Horno sites, the stratigraphic location of the implements does not seem to be in doubt. However, these artifacts do have a very controversial feature: a team of geologists who worked for the U.S. Geological Survey gave them ages of about 250,000 years. This team, working under a grant from the National Science Foundation, consisted of Harold Malde and Virginia Steen-McIntyre, both of the U.S. Geological Survey, and the late Roald Fryxell of Washington State University.

These geologists said four different dating methods independently yielded unusually great ages for the artifacts found near Valsequillo. The dating methods used were (1) uranium series dating, (2) fission track dating, (3) tephra hydration dating, and (4) study of mineral weathering.

As might be imagined, the date of about 250,000 years obtained for Hueyatlaco by the team of geologists provoked a great deal of controversy. If accepted, it would have revolutionized not only New World anthropology but the whole picture of human origins. Human beings capable of making the sophisticated tools found at Hueyatlaco are not thought to have come into existence until about 100,000 years ago in Africa.

In attempting to get her team's conclusions published, Virginia Steen-McIntyre experienced many social pressures and obstacles. In a note to a colleague (July 10, 1976), she stated: "I had found out through backfence gossip that Hal, Roald, and I are considered opportunists and publicity seekers in some circles, because of Hueyatlaco, and I am still smarting from the blow."

The publication of a paper by Steen-McIntyre and her colleagues on Hueyatlaco was inexplicably held up for years. The paper was first presented at an anthropological conference in 1975 and was to appear in a symposium volume. Four years later, Steen-McIntyre wrote to

Figure 5.8. Stone tools found at Hueyatlaco, Mexico, a site dated at about 250,000 years by a team from the United States Geological Survey.

H. J. Fullbright of the Los Alamos Scientific Laboratory, one of the editors of the forever forthcoming book: "Our joint article on the Hueyatlaco site is a real bombshell. It would place man in the New World 10x earlier than many archaeologists would like to believe. Worse, the bifacial tools that were found *in situ* are thought by most to be a sign of *H. sapiens.* According to present theory, *H.s.* had not even evolved at that time, and certainly not in the New World."

Steen-McIntyre continued, explaining: "Archaeologists are in a considerable uproar over Hueyatlaco—they refuse even to consider it. I've learned from second-hand sources that I'm considered by various members of the profession to be 1) incompetent; 2) a news monger; 3) an opportunist; 4) dishonest; 5) a fool. Obviously, none of these opinions is helping my professional reputation! My only hope to clear my name is to get the Hueyatlaco article into print so that folks can judge the evidence for themselves." Steen-McIntyre, upon receiving no answer to this and other requests for information, withdrew the article. But her manuscript was never returned to her.

A year later, Steen-McIntyre wrote (February 8, 1980) to Steve Porter, editor of *Quaternary Research,* about having her article about Hueyatlaco printed. "The ms I'd like to submit gives the geologic evidence," she said. "It's pretty clear-cut, and if it weren't for the fact a lot of anthropology textbooks will have to be rewritten, I don't think we would have had any problems getting the archaeologists to accept it. As it is, no anthro journal will touch it with a ten foot pole."

Steve Porter wrote to Steen-McIntyre (February 25, 1980), replying that he would consider the controversial article for publication. But he said he could "well imagine that objective reviews may be a bit difficult to obtain from certain archaeologists." The usual procedure in scientific publishing is for an article to be submitted to several other scientists for anonymous peer review. It is not hard to imagine how an entrenched scientific orthodoxy could manipulate this process to keep unwanted information out of scientific journals.

On March 30, 1981, Steen-McIntyre wrote to Estella Leopold, the associate editor of *Quaternary Research:* "The problem as I see it is much bigger than Hueyatlaco. It concerns the manipulation of scientific thought through the suppression of 'Enigmatic Data,' data that challenges the prevailing mode of thinking. Hueyatlaco certainly does that! Not being an anthropologist, I didn't realize the full significance of our dates back in 1973, nor how deeply woven into our thought the current theory of human evolution had become. Our work at Hueyatlaco has been rejected by most archaeologists because it contradicts that theory, period. Their reasoning is circular. *H. sapiens sapiens* evolved *ca.* 30,000– 50,000 years ago in Eurasia. Therefore any *H.s.s.* tools 250,000 years old found in Mexico are impossible because *H.s.s.* evolved *ca* 30,000–. . . . etc. Such thinking makes for self-satisfied archaeologists but *lousy* science!"

Eventually, *Quaternary Research* (1981) published an article by Virginia Steen-McIntyre, Roald Fryxell, and Harold E. Malde. It upheld an age of 250,000 years for the Hueyatlaco site. Of course, it is always possible to raise objections to archeological dates, and Cynthia Irwin-Williams did so in a letter responding to Steen-McIntyre, Fryxell, and Malde. Her objections were answered point for point in a counter-letter by Malde and Steen-McIntyre. But Irwin-Williams did not relent. She, and the

Figure 5.9 A Folsom blade embedded in the lower surface of a travertine crust from Sandia Cave, New Mexico. The layer of travertine is said to be 250,000 years old.

American archeological community in general, have continued to reject the dating of Hueyatlaco carried out by Steen-McIntyre and her colleagues.

The anomalous findings at Hueyatlaco resulted in personal abuse and professional penalties, including withholding of funds and loss of job, facilities, and reputation for Virginia Steen-McIntyre. Her case opens a rare window into the actual social processes of data suppression in paleoanthropology, processes that involve a great deal of conflict and hurt.

A final note—we ourselves once tried to secure permission to reproduce photographs of the Hueyatlaco artifacts in a publication. We were informed that permission would be denied if we intended to mention the "lunatic fringe" date of 250,000 years.

SANDIA CAVE, NEW MEXICO

In 1975, Virginia-Steen McIntyre learned of the existence of another site with an impossibly early date for stone tools in North America—Sandia Cave, New Mexico, U.S.A., where the implements, of advanced type (Folsom points), were discovered beneath a layer of stalagmite considered to be 250,000 years old. One such tool is shown in Figure 5.9.

In a letter to Henry P. Schwartz, the Canadian geologist who had dated the stalagmite, Virginia Steen-McIntyre wrote (July 10, 1976): "I can't remember if it was you or one of your colleagues I talked to at the 1975 Penrose Conference (Mammoth Lakes, California). The fellow I spoke to as we waited in line for lunch mentioned a uranium series date on the stalagmite layer above artifacts at Sandia

Cave that was very upsetting to him—it disagreed violently with the commonly held hypothesis for the date of entry of man into the New World. When he mentioned a date of a quarter million years or thereabouts, I nearly dropped my tray. Not so much in shock at the age, but that this date agreed so well with dates we have on a controversial Early Man site in Central Mexico. . . . Needless to say, I'd be interested to learn more about your date and your feelings about it!" According to Steen-McIntyre, she did not receive an answer to this letter.

After writing to the chief archeological investigator at the Sandia site for information about the dating, Steen-McIntyre received this reply (July 2, 1976): "I hope you don't use this 'can of worms' to prove anything until after we have had a chance to evaluate it."

Steen-McIntyre sent us some reports and photos of the Sandia artifacts and said in an accompanying note: "The geochemists are sure of their date, but archaeologists have convinced them the artifacts and charcoal lenses beneath the travertine are the result of rodent activity. . . . But what about the artifacts *cemented in* the crust?"

NEOLITHIC TOOLS FROM THE CALIFORNIA GOLD COUNTRY

In 1849, gold was discovered in the gravels of ancient riverbeds on the slopes of the Sierra Nevada Mountains in central California, drawing hordes of rowdy adventurers to places like Brandy City, Last Chance, Lost Camp, You Bet, and Poker Flat. At first, solitary miners panned for flakes and nuggets in the gravels that had found their way into the present stream beds. But soon gold-mining companies brought more extensive resources into play, some sinking shafts into mountainsides, following the gravel deposits wherever they led, while others washed the auriferous (gold-bearing) gravels from hillsides with high pressure jets of water. The miners found hundreds of stone artifacts, and, more rarely, human fossils (Chapter 7). The most significant artifacts were reported to the scientific community by J. D. Whitney, then the state geologist of California.

The artifacts from surface deposits and hydraulic mining were of doubtful age, but the artifacts from deep mine shafts and tunnels could be more securely dated. J. D. Whitney thought the geological evidence indicated the auriferous gravels were at least Pliocene in age. But modern geologists think some of the gravel deposits are from the Eocene.

Many shafts were sunk at Table Mountain in Tuolumne County, going under thick layers of a basaltic volcanic material called latite before reaching the gold-bearing gravels. In some cases, the shafts extended horizontally for hundreds of feet beneath the latite cap (Figure 5.10). Discoveries from the gravels just above the bedrock could be from 33.2 to 55 million years old, but discoveries from other gravels may be anywhere from 9 to 55 million years old.

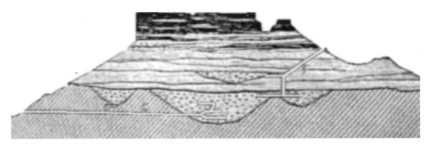

Figure 5.10. Side view of Table Mountain, Tuolumne County, California, showing mines penetrating into Tertiary gravel deposits beneath the lava cap, shown in black.

Whitney personally examined a collection of Tuolumne Table Mountain artifacts belonging to Dr. Perez Snell, of Sonora, California. Snell's collection included spearheads and other implements. There is not much information about the discoverers or original stratigraphic positions of the implements. There was, however, one exception. "This was," wrote Whitney, "a stone muller, or some kind of utensil which had apparently been used for grinding." Dr. Snell informed Whitney "that he took it with his own hands from a car-load of 'dirt' coming out from under Table Mountain." A human jaw, inspected by Whitney, was also present in the collection of Dr. Snell. The jaw was given to Dr. Snell by miners, who claimed that the jaw came from the gravels beneath the latite cap at Table Mountain in Tuolumne County.

A better-documented discovery from Tuolumne Table Mountain was made by Mr. Albert G. Walton, one of the owners of the Valentine claim. Walton found a stone mortar, 15 inches in diameter, in gold-bearing gravels 180 feet below the surface and also beneath the latite cap. Significantly, the find of the mortar occurred in a drift, a mine passageway leading horizontally from the bottom of the main vertical shaft of the Valentine mine. This tends to rule out the possibility that the mortar might have fallen in from above. A piece of a fossil human skull was also recovered from the Valentine mine.

William J. Sinclair suggested that many of the drift tunnels from other mines near the Valentine shaft were connected. So perhaps the mortar had entered through one of these other tunnels. But Sinclair admitted that when he visited the area in 1902 he was not even able to find the Valentine shaft. Sinclair simply used his unsupported suggestion to dismiss Walton's report of his discovery. Operating in this manner, one could find good reason to dismiss any paleoanthropological discovery ever made.

Another find at Tuolumne Table Mountain was reported by James Carvin in 1871: "This is to certify that I, the undersigned, did about the year 1858, dig out of some mining claims known as the Stanislaus Company, situated in Table

Mountain, Tuolumne County, opposite O'Byrn's Ferry, on the Stanislaus River, a stone hatchet. . . . The above relic was found from sixty to seventy-five feet from the surface in gravel, under the basalt, and about 300 feet from the mouth of the tunnel. There were also some mortars found, at about the same time and place."

In 1870, Oliver W. Stevens submitted the following notarized affidavit: "I, the undersigned, did about the year 1853, visit the Sonora Tunnel, situated at and in Table Mountain, about one half a mile north and west of Shaw's Flat, and at that time there was a car-load of auriferous gravel coming out of said Sonora Tunnel. And I, the undersigned, did pick out of said gravel (which came from under the basalt and out of the tunnel about two hundred feet in, at the depth of about one hundred and twenty-five feet) a mastodon tooth. . . . And at the same time I found with it some relic that resembled a large stone bead, made perhaps of alabaster." The bead, if from the gravel, is at least 9 million years old and perhaps as much as 55 million years old.

William J. Sinclair objected that the circumstances of discovery were not clear enough. But in the cases of many accepted discoveries, the circumstances of discovery are similar to that of the marble bead. For example, at Border Cave in South Africa, *Homo sapiens sapiens* fossils were taken from piles of rock excavated from mines years earlier. The fossils were then assigned dates of about 100,000 years, principally because of their association with the excavated rock. If Sinclair's strict standards were to be applied to such finds, they also should have to be rejected.

In 1870, Llewellyn Pierce gave the following written testimony: "I, the undersigned, have this day given to Mr. C. D. Voy, to be preserved in his collection of ancient stone relics, a certain stone mortar, which has evidently been made by human hands, which was dug up by me, about the year 1862, under Table Mountain, in gravel, at a depth of about 200 feet from the surface, under the basalt, which was over sixty feet deep, and about 1,800 feet in from the mouth of the tunnel. Found in the claim known as the Boston Tunnel Company." The gravels that yielded the mortar are 33–55 million years old.

William J. Sinclair objected that the mortar was made of andesite, a volcanic rock not often found in the deep gravels at Table Mountain. But modern geologists report that in the region north of Table Mountain there are four sites that are just as old as the prevolcanic auriferous gravels and contain deposits of andesite. Andesite mortars might have been a valuable trade item, and could have been transported good distances by rafts or boats, or even by foot.

According to Sinclair, Pierce found another artifact along with the mortar: "The writer was shown a small oval tablet of dark colored slate with a melon and leaf carved in bas-relief. . . . This tablet shows no signs of wear by gravel. The scratches are all recent defacements. The carving shows very evident traces of a steel knife blade and was conceived and executed by an artist of considerable ability."

Sinclair did not say exactly what led him to conclude the tablet had been carved with a steel blade. Therefore, he may have been wrong about the type of implement that was used. In any case, the slate tablet was in fact discovered, with the mortar, in prevolanic gravels deep under the latite cap of Tuolumne Table Mountain. So even if the tablet does display signs of carving by a steel blade, that does not mean it is recent. One could justifiably conclude that the carving was done by human beings of a relatively high level of cultural achievement between 33 million and 55 million years ago. Sinclair also said that the tablet showed no signs of wear by gravel. But perhaps it was not moved very far by river currents and therefore remained unabraded. Or perhaps the tablet could have been dropped into a gravel deposit of a dry channel.

On August 2, 1890, J. H. Neale signed the following statement about discoveries made by him: "In 1877 Mr. J. H. Neale was superintendent of the Montezuma Tunnel Company, and ran the Montezuma tunnel into the gravel underlying the lava of Table Mountain, Tuolumne County. . . . At a distance of between 1400 and 1500 feet from the mouth of the tunnel, or of between 200 and 300 feet beyond the edge of the solid lava, Mr. Neale saw several spear-heads, of some dark rock and nearly one foot in length. On exploring further, he himself found a small mortar three or four inches in diameter and of irregular shape. This was discovered within a foot or two of the spear-heads. He then found a large well-formed pestle, now the property of Dr. R. I. Bromley, and near by a large and very regular mortar, also at present the property of Dr. Bromley." This last mortar and pestle are shown in Figure 5.11.

Figure 5.11. This mortar and pestle were found by J. H. Neale, who removed them from a mine tunnel penetrating Tertiary deposits (33–55 million years old) under Table Mountain, Tuolumne County, California.

Neale's affidavit continued: "All of these relics were found. . . . close to the bed-rock, perhaps within a foot of it. Mr. Neale declares that it is utterly impossible that these relics can have reached the position in which they were found excepting at the time the gravel was deposited, and before the lava cap formed. There was not the slightest trace of any disturbance of the mass or of any natural fissure into it by which access could have been obtained either there or in the neighborhood." The position of the artifacts in gravel close to the bed-rock at Tuolumne Table Mountain indicates they were 33–55 million years old.

In 1898, William H. Holmes decided to interview Neale and in 1899 published the following summary of Neale's testimony: "One of the miners coming out to lunch at noon brought with him to the superintendent's office a stone mortar and a broken pestle which he said had been dug up in the deepest part of the tunnel, some 1500 feet from the mouth of the mine. Mr. Neale advised him on returning to work to look out for other utensils in the same place, and agreeable to his expectations two others were secured, a small ovoid mortar, 5 or 6 inches in diameter, and a flattish mortar or dish, 7 or 8 inches in diameter. These have since been lost to sight. On another occasion a lot of obsidian blades, or spear-heads, eleven in number and averaging 10 inches in length, were brought to him by workmen from the mine."

The accounts differ. Holmes said about Neale: "In his conversation with me he did not claim to have been in the mine when the finds were made." This might be interpreted to mean that Neale had lied in his original statement. But the just-quoted passages from Holmes are not the words of Neale but of Holmes, who said: "His [Neale's] statements, written down in my notebook during and immediately following the interview, were to the following effect." It is debatable whether one should place more confidence in Holmes's indirect summary of Neale's words than in Neale's own notarized affidavit, signed by him. Significantly, we have no confirmation from Neale himself that Holmes's version of their conversation was correct.

That Holmes may have been mistaken is certainly indicated by a subsequent interview with Neale conducted by William J. Sinclair in 1902. Summarizing Neale's remarks, Sinclair wrote: "A certain miner (Joe), working on the day shift in the Montezuma Tunnel, brought out a stone dish or platter about two inches thick. Joe was advised to look for more in the same place. . . . Mr. Neale went on the night shift and in excavating to set a timber, 'hooked up' one of the obsidian spear points. With the exception of the one brought out by Joe, all the implements were found personally by Mr. Neale, at one time, in a space about six feet in diameter on the shore of the channel. The implements were in gravel close to the bed-rock and were mixed with a substance like charcoal." When all the testimony is duly weighed, it appears that Neale himself did enter the mine and find stone implements in place in the gravel.

About the obsidian spearheads found by Neale, Holmes said: "Obsidian blades of identical pattern were now and then found with Digger Indian remains in the burial pits of the region. The inference to be drawn from these facts is that the implements brought to Mr. Neale had been obtained from one of the burial places in the vicinity by the miners." But Holmes could produce no evidence that the any miners had actually obtained the blades from burial pits.

Holmes simply stated: "How the eleven large spearheads got into the mine, or whether they came from the mine at all, are queries that I shall not assume to answer."

Using Holmes's methods, one could discredit any paleoanthropological discovery ever made: one could simply refuse to believe the evidence as reported, and put forward all kinds of vague alternative explanations, without answering legitimate questions about them.

Holmes further wrote about the obsidian implements: "That they came from the bed of a Tertiary torrent seems highly improbable; for how could a cache of eleven, slender, leaf-like implements remain unscattered under these conditions; how could fragile glass blades stand the crushing and grinding of a torrent bed; or how could so large a number of brittle blades remain unbroken under the pick of the miner working in a dark tunnel?" But one can imagine many circumstances in which a cache of implements might have remained undamaged in the bed of a Tertiary stream. Let us suppose that in Tertiary times a trading party, while crossing or navigating a stream, lost a number of obsidian blades securely wrapped in hide or cloth. The package of obsidian blades may have been rather quickly covered by gravel in a deep hole in the stream bed and remained there relatively undamaged until recovered tens of millions of years later. As to how the implements could have remained unbroken as they were being uncovered, that poses no insuperable difficulties. As soon as Neale became aware of the blades, he could have, and apparently did, exercise sufficient caution to preserve the obsidian implements intact. Maybe he even broke some of them.

In a paper read before the American Geological Society in 1891, geologist George F. Becker said: "It would have been more satisfactory to me individually if I had myself dug out these implements, but I am unable to discover any reason why Mr. Neale's statement is not exactly as good evidence to the rest of the world as my own would be. He was as competent as I to detect any fissure from the surface or any ancient workings, which the miner recognizes instantly and dreads profoundly. Some one may possibly suggest that Mr. Neale's workmen 'planted' the implements, but no one familiar with mining will entertain such a suggestion for a moment. . . . The auriferous gravel is hard picking, in large part it requires blasting, and even a very incompetent supervisor could not possibly be deceived in this way. . . . In short, there is, in my opinion, no escape from the conclusion that the implements mentioned in Mr. Neale's statement actually occurred near the bottom of the gravels, and that they were deposited where they were found at the same time with the adjoining pebbles and matrix."

Although the tools discussed so far were found by miners, there is one case of a stone tool being found in place by a scientist. In 1891, George F. Becker told the American Geological Society that in the spring of 1869, geologist Clarence King, director of the Survey of the Fortieth Parallel, was conducting research at Tuolumne Table Mountain. At that time, he found a stone pestle firmly embedded in a deposit of gold-bearing gravel lying beneath the cap of basalt, or latite. The gravel deposit had only recently been exposed by erosion. Becker stated: "Mr. King is perfectly sure this implement was in place and that it formed an original part of the gravels in which he found it. It is difficult to imagine a more satisfactory evidence than this of the occurrence of implements in the auriferous, pre-glacial, sub-basaltic gravels." From this description and the modern geological dating of the Table Mountain strata, it is apparent that the object was over 9 million years old.

Even Holmes had to admit that the King pestle, which was placed in the collection of the Smithsonian Institution, "may not be challenged with impunity." Holmes searched the site very carefully and noted the presence of some modern Indian mealing stones lying loose on the surface. He stated: "I tried to learn whether it was possible that one of these objects could have become embedded in the exposed tufa deposits in recent or comparatively recent times, for such embedding sometimes results from resetting or recementing of loose materials, but no definite result was reached." If Holmes had found the slightest definite evidence of such recementing, he would have seized the opportunity to cast suspicion upon the pestle discovered by King.

Unable, however, to find anything to discredit the report, Holmes was reduced to wondering "that Mr. King failed to publish it—that he failed to give to the world what could well claim to be the most important observation ever made by a geologist bearing upon the history of the human race, leaving it to come out through the agency of Dr. Becker, twenty-five years later." But Becker noted in his report: "I have submitted this statement of his discovery to Mr. King, who pronounces it correct."

J. D. Whitney also reported discoveries that were made under intact volcanic layers at places other than under the latite cap of Tuolumne Table Mountain. These included stone tools found in gold-bearing gravels at San Andreas in Calaveras County, Spanish Creek in El Dorado County, and Cherokee in Butte County.

EVOLUTIONARY PRECONCEPTIONS

In light of the evidence we have presented, it is hard to justify the sustained opposition to the California finds by Holmes and Sinclair. They uncovered no actual evidence of fraud, and their suggestions that Indians might have carried portable mortars and spearheads into the mines are not very believable. A modern historian, W. Turrentine Jackson of the University of California at Davis, points out: "During the gold rush era the Indians were driven from the mining region, and they seldom came into contact with the forty-niners from the mining region."

One might therefore ask why Holmes and Sinclair were so determined to discredit Whitney's evidence for the existence of Tertiary humans. The following statement by Holmes provides an essential clue: "Perhaps if Professor Whitney had fully appreciated the story of human evolution as it is understood to-day, he would have hesitated to announce the conclusions formulated, notwithstanding the imposing array of testimony with which he was confronted." In other words, if the facts do not fit the favored theory, the facts, even an imposing array of them, must go.

It is not hard to see why a supporter of the idea of human evolution, such as Holmes, would want to do everything possible to discredit information pushing the existence of humans in their present form too far into the past. Why did Holmes feel so confident about doing so? One reason was the discovery in 1891, by Eugene Dubois, of Java man (*Pithecanthropus erectus*), hailed as the much sought after missing link connecting modern humans with supposedly ancestral apelike creatures. Holmes stated that "Whitney's evidence stands absolutely alone" and that "it implies a human race older by at least one-half than *Pithecanthropus erectus* of Dubois, which may be regarded as an incipient form of human creature only." For those who accepted the controversial Java man (Chapter 8), any evidence suggesting the modern human type existed before him had to be cut down, and Holmes was one of the principal hatchet men. Holmes stated about the California finds: "It is probable that without positive reinforcement the evidence would gradually lose its hold and disappear; but science cannot afford to await this tedious process of selection, and some attempt to hasten a decision is demanded." Holmes, Sinclair, and others all did their part, using questionable tactics.

Alfred Russell Wallace, who shares with Darwin the credit for formulating the theory of evolution by natural selection, expressed dismay that evidence for anatomically modern humans existing in the Tertiary tended to be "attacked with all the weapons of doubt, accusation, and ridicule."

In a detailed survey of the evidence for the great antiquity of humans in North America, Wallace gave considerable weight to Whitney's record of the discoveries in California of human fossils and stone artifacts from the Tertiary. In light of the incredulity with which the auriferous gravel finds and others like them were received in certain quarters, Wallace advised that "the proper way to treat evidence as to man's antiquity is to place it on record, and admit it provisionally wherever it would be held adequate in the case of other animals; not, as is too often now the case, to ignore it as unworthy of acceptance or subject its discoverers to indiscriminate accusations of being impostors or the victims of impostors."

Nevertheless, in the early part of the twentieth century, the intellectual climate favored the views of Holmes and Sinclair. Tertiary stone implements just like those of modern humans? Soon it became uncomfortable to report, unfashionable to defend, and convenient to forget such things. Such views remain in force today, so much so that discoveries that even slightly challenge dominant views about human prehistory are effectively suppressed.

6

Evidence for Advanced Culture
In Distant Ages

Up to this point, most of the evidence we have considered gives the impression that even if humans did exist in the distant past, they remained at a somewhat primitive level of cultural and technological achievement. One might well ask the following question. If humans had a long time to perfect their skills, then why do we not find ancient artifacts indicative of an advancing civilization?

In 1863, Charles Lyell expressed this doubt in his book *Antiquity of Man:* "instead of the rudest pottery or flint tools. . . . we should now be finding sculptured forms, surpassing in beauty the master-pieces of Phidias or Praxiteles; lines of buried railways or electric telegraphs, from which the best engineers of our day might gain invaluable hints; astronomical instruments and microscopes of more advanced construction than any known in Europe, and other indications of perfection in the arts and sciences." The following reports do not quite measure up to this standard, but some of the objects described do give hints of unexpected accomplishments.

Not only are some of the objects decidedly more advanced than stone tools, but many also occur in geological contexts far older than we have thus far considered.

The reports of this extraordinary evidence emanate, with some exceptions, from nonscientific sources. And often the artifacts themselves, not having been preserved in standard natural history museums, are impossible to locate.

We ourselves are not sure how much importance should be given to this highly anomalous evidence. But we include it for the sake of completeness and to encourage further study.

In this chapter, we have included only a sample of the published material available to us. And given the spotty reporting and infrequent preservation of these highly anomalous discoveries, it is likely that the entire body of reports now existing represents only a small fraction of the total number of such discoveries made over the past few centuries.

ARTIFACTS FROM AIX-EN-PROVENCE, FRANCE

In his book *Mineralogy,* Count Bournon recorded an intriguing discovery that had been made by French workmen in the latter part of the eighteenth century. In his description of the details about the discovery, Bournon wrote: "During the years 1786, 1787, and 1788, they were occupied near Aix-en-Provence, in France, in quarrying stone for the rebuilding, upon a vast scale, of the Palace of Justice. The stone was a limestone of deep grey, and of that kind which are tender when they come out of the quarry, but harden by exposure to the air. The strata were separated from one another by a bed of sand mixed with clay, more or less calcareous. The first which were wrought presented no appearance of any foreign bodies, but, after the workmen had removed the ten first beds, they were astonished, when taking away the eleventh, to find its inferior surface, at the depth of forty or fifty feet, covered with shells. The stone of this bed having been removed, as they were taking away a stratum of argillaceous sand, which separated the eleventh bed from the twelfth, they found stumps of columns and fragments of stone half wrought, and the stone was exactly similar to that of the quarry: they found moreover coins, handles of hammers, and other tools or fragments of tools in wood. But that which principally commanded their attention, was a board about one inch thick and seven or eight feet long; it was broken into many pieces, of which none were missing, and it was possible to join them again one to another, and to restore to the board or plate its original form, which was that of the boards of the same kind used by the masons and quarry men: it was worn in the same manner, rounded and waving upon the edges."

Count Bournon, continuing his description, stated: "The stones which were completely or partly wrought, had not at all changed in their nature, but the fragments of the board, and the instruments, and pieces of instruments of wood, had been changed into agate, which was very fine and agreeably colored. Here then, we have the traces of a work executed by the hand of man, placed at a depth of fifty feet, and covered with eleven beds of compact limestone: every thing tended to prove that this work had been executed upon the spot where the traces existed. The presence of man had then preceded the formation of this stone, and that very considerably since he was already arrived at such a degree of civilization that the arts were known to him, and that he wrought the stone and formed columns out of it."

These passages appeared in the *American Journal of Science* in 1820; today, however, it is unlikely such a report would be found in the pages of a scientific journal. Scientists simply do not take such discoveries seriously.

LETTERS IN MARBLE BLOCK, PHILADELPHIA

In 1830, letterlike shapes were discovered within a solid block of marble from a quarry 12 miles northwest of Philadelphia. The marble block was taken from a depth of 60–70 feet. This was reported in the *American Journal of Science* in 1831. The quarry workers removed layers of gneiss, mica slate, hornblende, talcose slate, and primitive clay slate before coming to the layer from which the block containing the letterlike shapes was cut.

Figure 6.1. Raised letterlike shapes found inside a block of marble from a quarry near Philadelphia, Pennsylvania . The block of marble came from a depth of 60–70 feet.

While they were sawing through the block, the workmen happened to notice a rectangular indentation, about 1.5 inches wide by .625 inches high, displaying two raised characters (Figure 6.1). Several respectable gentlemen from nearby Norristown, Pennsylvania, were called to the scene and inspected the object. It is hard to explain the formation of the characters as products of natural physical processes. This suggests the characters were made by intelligent humans from the distant past.

NAIL IN DEVONIAN SANDSTONE, SCOTLAND

In 1844, Sir David Brewster reported that a nail had been discovered firmly embedded in a block of sandstone from the Kingoodie (Mylnfield) Quarry in Scotland. Dr. A. W. Medd of the British Geological Survey wrote to us in 1985 that this sandstone is of "Lower Old Red Sandstone age" (Devonian, between 360 and 408 million years old). Brewster was a famous Scottish physicist. He was a founder of the British Association for the Advancement of Science and made important discoveries in the field of optics.

In his report to the British Association for the Advancement of Science, Brewster stated: "The stone in Kingoodie quarry consists of alternate layers of hard stone and a soft clayey substance called 'till'; the courses of stone vary from six inches to upwards of six feet in thickness. The particular block in which the nail was found, was nine inches thick, and in proceeding to clear the rough block for dressing, the point of the nail was found projecting about half an inch (quite eaten with rust) into the 'till,' the rest of the nail lying along the surface of the stone to within an inch of the head, which went right down into the body of the stone." The fact that the head of the nail was buried in the sandstone block would seem to rule out the possibility the nail had been pounded into the block after it was quarried.

GOLD THREAD IN CARBONIFEROUS STONE, ENGLAND

On June 22, 1844, this curious report appeared in the London *Times*: "A few days ago, as some workmen were employed in quarrying a rock close to the Tweed about a quarter of a mile below Rutherford-mill, a gold thread was discovered embedded in the stone at a depth of eight feet." Dr. A. W. Medd of the British Geological Survey wrote to us in 1985 that this stone is of Early Carboniferous age (between 320 and 360 million years old).

METALLIC VASE FROM PRECAMBRIAN ROCK
AT DORCHESTER, MASSACHUSETTS

The following report, titled "A Relic of a Bygone Age," appeared in the magazine *Scientific American* (June 5, 1852): "A few days ago a powerful blast was made in the rock at Meeting House Hill, in Dorchester, a few rods south of Rev. Mr. Hall's meeting house. The blast threw out an immense mass of rock, some of the pieces weighing several tons, and scattered fragments in all directions. Among them was picked up a metallic vessel in two parts, rent asunder by the explosion. On putting the two parts together it formed a bell-shaped vessel, 4-1/2 inches high, 6-1/2 inches at the base, 2-1/2 inches at the top, and about an eighth of an inch in thickness. The body of this vessel resembles zinc in color, or a composition metal, in which there is a considerable portion of silver. On the side there are six figures or a flower, or bouquet, beautifully inlaid with pure silver, and around the lower part of the vessel a vine, or wreath, also inlaid with silver. The chasing, carving, and inlaying are exquisitely done by the art of some cunning workman. This curious and unknown vessel was blown out of the solid pudding stone, fifteen feet below the surface. It is now in the possession of Mr. John Kettell. Dr. J. V. C. Smith, who has recently travelled in the East, and examined hundreds of curious domestic utensils, and has drawings of them, has never seen anything resembling this. He has taken a drawing and accurate dimensions of it, to be submitted to the scientific. There is not doubt but that this curiosity was blown out of the rock, as above stated; but will Professor Agassiz, or some other scientific man please to tell us how it came there? The matter is worthy of investigation, as there is no deception in the case."

The editors of *Scientific American* ironically remarked: "The above is from the Boston *Transcript* and the wonder is to us, how the *Transcript* can suppose Prof. Agassiz qualified to tell how it got there any more than John Doyle, the blacksmith. This is not a question of zoology, botany, or geology, but one relating to an antique metal vessel perhaps made by Tubal Cain, the first inhabitant of Dorchester."

According to a recent U.S. Geological Survey map of the Boston-Dorchester area, the pudding stone, now called the Roxbury conglomerate, is of Precambrian age, over 600 million years old. By standard accounts, life was just beginning to form on this planet during the Precambrian. But in the Dorchester vessel we have evidence indicating the presence of artistic metal workers in North America over 600 million years before Leif Erikson.

A TERTIARY CHALK BALL FROM LAON, FRANCE

The April 1862 edition of *The Geologist* included an English translation of an intriguing report by Maximilien Melleville, the vice president of the Academic Society of Laon, France. In his report, Melleville described a round chalk ball (Figure 6.2) discovered 75 meters (about 246 feet) below the surface in early Tertiary lignite beds near Laon.

Lignite (sometimes called ash) is a soft brown coal. The lignite beds at Montaigu, near Laon, lie at the base of a hill and were mined by horizontal shafts. The main shaft ran 600 meters (about 1,969 feet) into a bed of lignite.

In August of 1861, workmen digging at the far end of the shaft, 225 feet below the surface of the hill, saw a round object fall down from the top of the excavation. The object was about 6 centimeters (2.36 inches) in diameter and weighed 310 grams (about 11 ounces).

Melleville stated: "They looked to see exactly what place in the strata it had occupied, and

Figure 6.2. This chalk ball was discovered in an Early Eocene lignite bed near Laon, France. On the basis of its stratigraphic position, it can be assigned a date of 45–55 million years ago.

they are able to state that it did not come from the interior of the 'ash,' but that it was imbedded at its point of contact with the roof of the quarry, where it had left its impression indented." The workmen carried the chalk ball to a Dr. Lejeune, who informed Melleville.

Melleville then stated: "Long before this discovery, the workmen of the quarry had told me they had many times found pieces of wood changed into stone. . . . bearing the marks of human work. I regret greatly now not having asked to see these, but I did not hitherto believe in the possibility of such a fact."

According to Melleville, there was no possibility that the chalk ball was a forgery: "It really is penetrated over four-fifths of its height by a black bituminous colour that merges toward the top into a yellow circle, and which is evidently due to the contact of the lignite in which it had been for so long a time plunged. The upper part, which was in contact with the shell bed, on the contrary has preserved its natural colour—the dull white of the chalk. . . . As to the rock in which it was found, I can affirm that it is perfectly virgin, and presents no trace whatever of any ancient exploitation. The roof of the quarry was equally intact in this place, and one could see there neither fissure nor any other cavity by which we might suppose this ball could have dropped down from above."

Regarding human manufacture of the chalk object, Melleville was cautious. He wrote: "from one fact, even so well established, I do not pretend to draw the extreme conclusion that man was contemporary with the lignites of the Paris basin. . . . My sole object in writing this notice is to make known a discovery as curious as strange, whatever may be its bearing, without pretending to any mode of explanation. I content myself with giving it to science, and I shall wait before forming an opinion in this respect, for further discoveries to furnish me with the means of appreciating the value of this at Montaigu."

Geology's editors wrote: "We consider his resolution wise in hesitating to date back the age of man to the lower Tertiary period of the Paris basin without further confirmatory evidence." In 1883, Gabriel de Mortillet suggested that a piece of white chalk was rolled in the waves of the incoming Tertiary seas and after it became round was left where it was found.

This does not, however, seem to be a likely explanation. First of all, the ball had features inconsistent with the action of waves. Melleville reported: "Three great splinters with sharp angles, announce also that it had remained during the working attached to the block of stone out of which it was made, and that it had been separated only after it was finished, by a blow, to which this kind of fracture is due." If wave action is accepted as the explanation of the general roundness of the object, this action should also have smoothed the sharp edges described by Melleville. Furthermore, it is likely that sustained exposure to waves would have disintegrated a piece of chalk.

De Mortillet stated that the ball was found in an Early Eocene stratum. If humans made the ball, they must have been in France 45–55 million years ago. As extraordinary as this might seem to those attached to the standard evolutionary views, it is in keeping with the evidence considered in this book.

OBJECTS FROM ILLINOIS WELL BORING

In 1871, William E. Dubois of the Smithsonian Institution reported on several man-made objects found at deep levels in Illinois. The first object was a copper quasi coin (Figure 6.3) from Lawn Ridge, in Marshall County, Illinois. In a letter to the Smithsonian Institution, J. W. Moffit stated that in August 1870 he was drilling a well using a "common ground auger." When Moffit brought the auger up from a depth of 125 feet, he discovered the coinlike object "on the auger."

To get down to 125 feet, Moffit drilled through the following strata: 3 feet of soil; 10 feet of yellow clay; 44 feet of blue clay; 4 feet of clay, sand, and gravel; 19 feet of purple clay; 10 feet of brown hard pan; 8.5 feet of green clay; 2 feet of vegetable mould; 2.5 feet of yellow clay; 2 feet of yellow hard pan; and 20.5 feet of mixed clay.

In 1881, A. Winchell also described the coinlike object. Winchell quoted a letter by W. H. Wilmot, who listed a sequence of strata slightly different from that given by Moffit. Wilmot reported that the quasi coin had been discovered in the well boring at a depth of 114 feet rather than 125 feet.

Using the sequence of strata given by Winchell, the Illinois State Geological Survey gave us an estimate for the age of the deposits at the 114-foot level. They would have formed during the Yarmouthian Interglacial "sometime between 200,000 and 400,000 years ago."

W. E. Dubois said that the shape of the quasi coin was "polygonal approaching to circular," and that it had crudely portrayed figures and inscriptions on both sides. The inscriptions were in a

Figure 6.3. This coinlike object, from a well boring near Lawn Ridge, Illinois, was reportedly found at a depth of about 114 feet below the surface. According to information supplied by the Illinois State Geological Survey, the deposits containing the coin are between 200,000 and 400,000 years old.

language that Dubois could not recognize, and the quasi coin's appearance differed from any known coin.

Dubois concluded that the coin must have been made in a machine shop. Noting its uniform thickness, he said the coin must have "passed through a rolling-mill; and if the ancient Indians had such a contrivance, it must have been pre-historic." Furthermore, Dubois reported that the coin must have been cut with shears or a chisel and the sharp edges filed down.

The quasi coin described above suggests the existence of a civilization at least 200,000 years ago in North America. Yet beings intelligent enough to make and use coins (*Homo sapiens sapiens*) are generally not thought to have lived much earlier than 100,000 years ago. According to standard views, metal coins were first used in Asia Minor during the eighth century B.C.

Moffit also reported that other artifacts were found in nearby Whiteside County, Illinois. At a depth of 120 feet, workmen discovered "a large copper ring or ferrule, similar to those used on ship spars at the present time. . . . They also found something fashioned like a boat-hook." Mr. Moffit added: "There are numerous instances of relics found at lesser depths. A spear-shaped hatchet, made of iron, was found imbedded in clay at 40 feet; and stone pipes and pottery have been unearthed at depths varying from 10 to 50 feet in many localities." In September 1984, the Illinois State Geological Survey wrote to us that the age of deposits at 120 feet in Whiteside County varies greatly. In some places, one would find at 120 feet deposits only 50,000 years old, while in other places one would find Silurian bedrock 410 million years old.

A CLAY IMAGE FROM NAMPA, IDAHO

A small human image, skillfully formed in clay, was found in 1889 at Nampa, Idaho (Figure 6.4). The figurine came from the 300-foot level of a well boring. In 1912, G. F. Wright wrote: "The record of the well shows that in reaching the stratum from which the image was brought up they had penetrated first about fifty feet of soil, then about fifteen feet of basalt, and afterwards passed through alternate beds of clay and quicksand. . . . down to a depth of about three hundred feet, when the sand pump began to bring up numerous clay balls, some of them more than two inches in diameter, densely coated with iron oxide. In the lower portion of this stratum there were evidences of a buried land surface, over which there had been a slight accumulation of vegetable mould. It was from this point that the image in question was brought up at a depth of three hundred and twenty feet. A few feet farther down, sand rock was reached."

As for the figurine, Wright noted: "The image in question is made of the same material as that of the clay balls mentioned, and is about an inch and a half long; and remarkable for the perfection with which it represents the human form. . . . It was a female figure, and had the lifelike lineaments in the parts which were finished that would do credit to the classic centers of art."

"Upon showing the object to Professor F. W. Putnam," wrote Wright, "he at once directed attention to the character of the incrustations of iron upon the surface as indicative of a relic of considerable antiquity. There were patches of anhydrous red oxide of iron in protected places upon it, such as could not have been formed upon any fraudulent object. In visiting the locality in 1890 I took special pains, while on the ground, to compare the discoloration of the oxide upon the image with that upon the clay balls still found among the debris which has come from the well, and ascertained it to be as nearly identical as it is possible to be. These confirmatory evidences, in connection with the very satisfactory character of the evidence furnished by the parties who made the discovery, and confirmed by Mr. G. M. Cumming, of Boston (at that time superintendent of that division of the Oregon Short Line Railroad, and who knew all the parties, and was upon the ground a day or two after the discovery) placed the genuineness of the discovery beyond reasonable doubt. To this evidence is to be added, also, the general conformity of the object to other relics of man which have been found beneath the lava deposits on the Pacific coast. In comparing the figurine one cannot help being struck with its resemblance to numerous 'Aurignacian figurines' found in prehistoric caverns in France, Belgium, and Moravia. Especially is the resemblance striking to that of 'The Venus impudica' from Laugerie-Basse." The Nampa image is also similar to the famous Willendorf Venus, thought to be about 30,000 years old (Figure 6.5).

Wright also examined the bore hole to see if the figurine could have slipped down from a higher level. He stated: "To answer objections it will be well to give the facts more fully. The well was six inches in diameter and was tubed with heavy iron tubing, which was driven down, from the top, and screwed together,

Figure 6.4. Figurine from a well at Nampa, Idaho. This object is of Plio-Pleistocene age, about 2 million years old.

Figure 6.5. The Willendorf Venus, from Europe, dated at 30,000 years old.

section by section, as progress was made. Thus it was impossible for anything to work in from the sides. The drill was not used after penetrating the lava deposit near the surface, but the tube was driven down, and the included material brought out from time to time by use of a sand pump."

Responding to our inquiries, the United States Geological Survey stated in a letter that the clay layer at a depth of over 300 feet is "probably of the Glenns Ferry Formation, upper Idaho Group, which is generally considered to be of Plio-Pleistocene age." The basalt above the Glenns Ferry formation is considered Middle Pleistocene.

Other than *Homo sapiens sapiens,* no hominid is known to have fashioned works of art like the Nampa figurine. The evidence therefore suggests that humans of the modern type were living in America around 2 million years ago, at the Plio-Pleistocene boundary.

That the Nampa figurine strongly challenges the evolutionary scenario was noted by W. H. Holmes of the Smithsonian Institution. In 1919, Holmes wrote in his *Handbook of Aboriginal American Antiquities:* "According to Emmons, the formation in which the pump was operating is of late Tertiary or early Quaternary age; and the apparent improbability of the occurrence of a well-modeled human figure in deposits of such great antiquity has led to grave doubt about its authenticity. It is interesting to note that the age of this object, supposing it to be authentic, corresponds with that of the incipient man whose bones were, in 1892, recovered by Dubois from the late Tertiary or early Quaternary formations of Java."

Here we find the Java man discovery, itself questionable, once more being used to dismiss evidence for humans of modern abilities in very ancient times. The evolutionary hypothesis was apparently so privileged that any evidence contradicting it could be almost automatically rejected. But although Holmes doubted that beings capable of making the Nampa image could have existed at the same time as the primitive Java ape-man, we find today that humans, of various levels of technological expertise, coexist in Africa with gorillas and chimpanzees.

Holmes went on to say: "Like the auriferous gravel finds of California, if taken at its face value the specimen establishes an antiquity for Neolithic culture in America so great that we hesitate to accept it without further confirmation. While it may have been brought up as reported, there remains the possibility that it was not an original inclusion under the lava. It is not impossible that an object of this character could have descended from the surface through some crevice or water course penetrating the lava beds and have been carried through deposits of creeping quicksand aided by underground waters to the spot tapped by the drill." It is instructive to note how far a scientist like Holmes will go to explain away evidence he does not favor. One should keep in mind, however, that any evidence, including evidence currently used to buttress the theory of evolution, could be explained away in this fashion.

A barrier to the supposition that the Nampa image was recently manufactured by recent Indians and somehow worked its way down from the surface may be found in this statement by Holmes: "It should be remarked, however, that forms of art closely analogous to this figure are far to seek, neither the Pacific slope on the west nor the Pueblo region on the south furnishing modeled images of the human figure of like character or of equal artistic merit."

GOLD CHAIN IN CARBONIFEROUS COAL FROM MORRISONVILLE, ILLINOIS

On June 11, 1891, *The Morrisonville Times* reported: "A curious find was brought to light by Mrs. S.W. Culp last Tuesday morning. As she was breaking a lump of coal preparatory to putting it in the scuttle, she discovered, as the lump fell apart, embedded in a circular shape a small gold chain about ten inches in length of antique and quaint workmanship. At first Mrs. Culp thought the chain had been dropped accidentally in the coal, but as she undertook to lift the chain up, the idea of its having been recently dropped was at once made fallacious, for as the lump of coal broke it separated almost in the middle, and the circular position of the chain placed the two ends near to each other, and as the lump separated, the middle of the chain became loosened while each end remained fastened to the coal. This is a study for the students of archaeology who love to puzzle their brains over the geological construction of the earth from whose ancient depth the curious is always dropping out. The lump of coal from which this chain was taken is supposed to come from the Taylorville or Pana mines [southern Illinois] and almost hushes one's breath with mystery when it is thought for how many long ages the earth has been forming strata after strata which hid the golden links from view. The chain was an eight-carat gold and weighed eight penny-weights."

In a letter to Ron Calais, Mrs. Vernon W. Lauer, recently the publisher of *The Morrisonville Times*, stated: "Mr. Culp was editor and publisher of the *Times* in 1891. Mrs. Culp, who made the discovery, moved to Taylorville after his death—remarried and her death occurred on February 3, 1959." Calais told our research assistant (Stephen Bernath) that he had information the chain was given to one of Mrs. Culp's relatives after her death, but Calais could not trace the chain further.

The Illinois State Geological Survey has said the coal in which the gold chain was found is 260–320 million years old. This raises the possibility that culturally advanced human beings were present in North America during that time.

CARVED STONE FROM LEHIGH COAL MINE
NEAR WEBSTER, IOWA

The April 2, 1897 edition of the *Daily News* of Omaha, Nebraska, carried an article titled "Carved Stone Buried in a Mine," which described an object from a mine near Webster City, Iowa. The article stated: "While mining coal today in the Lehigh coal mine, at a depth of 130 feet, one of the miners came upon a piece of rock which puzzles him and he was unable to account for its presence at the bottom of the coal mine. The stone is of a dark grey color and about two feet long, one foot wide and four inches in thickness. Over the surface of the stone, which is very hard, lines are drawn at angles forming perfect diamonds. The center of each diamond is a fairly good face of an old man having a peculiar indentation in the forehead that appears in each of the pictures, all of them being remarkably alike. Of the faces, all but two are looking to the right. How the stone reached its position under the strata of sandstone at a depth of 130 feet is a question the miners are not attempting to answer. Where the stone was found the miners are sure the earth had never before been disturbed." Inquiries to the Iowa State Historical Preservation and Office of State Archaeology at the University of Iowa revealed nothing new. The Lehigh coal is probably from the Carboniferous.

IRON CUP FROM OKLAHOMA COAL MINE

On January 10, 1949, Robert Nordling sent a photograph of an iron cup to Frank L. Marsh of Andrews University, in Berrien Springs, Michigan. Nordling wrote: "I visited a friend's museum in southern Missouri. Among his curios, he had the iron cup pictured on the enclosed snapshot."

At the private museum, the iron cup had been displayed along with the following affidavit, made by Frank J. Kenwood in Sulphur Springs, Arkansas, on November 27, 1948: "While I was working in the Municipal Electric Plant in Thomas, Okla. in 1912, I came upon a solid chunk of coal which was too large to use. I broke it with a sledge hammer. This iron pot fell from the center, leaving the impression or mould of the pot in the piece of coal. Jim Stall (an employee of the company) witnessed the breaking of the coal, and saw the pot fall out. I traced the source of the coal, and found that it came from the Wilburton, Oklahoma, Mines." According to Robert O. Fay of the Oklahoma Geological Survey, the Wilburton mine coal is about 312 million years old. In 1966, Marsh sent the photo of the cup and the correspondence relating to it to Wilbert H. Rusch, a professor of biology at Concordia College, in Ann Arbor, Michigan. Marsh stated: "Enclosed is the letter and snap sent me by Robert Nordling some 17 years ago. When I got interested enough in this 'pot' (the size of which can be gotten at somewhat by comparing it with the seat of the straight chair it is resting on) a year or two later I learned that this 'friend' of Nordling's had died and his little museum was scattered. Nordling knew nothing of the whereabouts of the iron cup. It would challenge the most alert sleuth to see if he could run it down. . . . If this cup is what it is sworn to be, it is truly a most significant artifact." It is an unfortunate fact that evidence such as this iron cup tends to get lost as it passes from hand to hand among people not fully aware of its significance.

A SHOE SOLE FROM NEVADA

On October 8, 1922, the *American Weekly* section of the *New York Sunday American* ran a prominent feature titled "Mystery of the Petrified 'Shoe Sole' 5,000,000 Years Old," by Dr. W. H. Ballou. Ballou wrote: "Some time ago, while he was prospecting for fossils in Nevada, John T. Reid, a distinguished mining engineer and geologist, stopped suddenly and looked down in utter bewilderment and amazement at a rock near his feet. For there, a part of the rock itself, was what seemed to be a human footprint! [Figure 6.6] Closer inspection showed that it was not a mark of a naked foot, but was, apparently, a shoe sole which had been turned into stone. The forepart was missing. But there was the outline of at least two-thirds of it, and around this outline ran a well-defined sewn thread which had, it appeared, attached the welt to the sole. Further on was another line of sewing, and in the center, where the foot would have rested had the object been really a shoe sole, there was an indentation, exactly such as would have been made by the

bone of the heel rubbing upon and wearing down the material of which the sole had been made. Thus was found a fossil which is the foremost mystery of science today. For the rock in which it was found is at least 5,000,000 years old."

Reid brought the specimen to New York, where he tried to bring it to the attention of other scientists. Reid reported: "On arrival at New York, I showed this fossil to Dr. James F. Kemp, geologist of Columbia University; Professors H. F. Osborn, W. D. Matthew and E. O. Hovey,

Figure 6.6. Partial shoe sole in Triassic rock from Nevada. The Triassic is dated at 213–248 million years ago.

of the American Museum of Natural History. All of these men reached the same conclusion, in effect that 'it was the most remarkable natural imitation of an artificial object they had ever seen.' These experts agreed, however, that the rock formation was Triassic, and manufacturers of shoes agreed that originally the specimen was a hand-welted sole. Dr. W. D. Matthew wrote a brief report on the find declaring that while all the semblances of a shoe were present, including the threads with which it had been sewn, it was only a remarkable imitation, a *lusus naturae,* or 'freak of nature.'" Curiously enough, an inquiry by us to the American Museum of Natural History resulted in a reply that the report by Matthew is not in their files.

Reid, despite Matthew's dismissal, nevertheless persisted: "I next got hold of a microphotographer and an analytical chemist of the Rockefeller Institute, who, on the outside, so as not to make it an institute matter, made photos and analyses of the specimen. The analyses proved up [removed] any doubt of the shoe sole having been subjected to Triassic fossilization. . . . The microphoto magnifications are twenty times larger than the specimen itself, showing the minutest detail of thread twist and warp, proving conclusively that the shoe sole is not a resemblance, but is strictly the handiwork of man. Even to the naked eye the threads can be seen distinctly, and the definitely symmetrical outlines of the shoe sole. Inside this rim and running parallel to it is a line which appears to be regularly perforated as if for stitches. I may add that at least two geologists whose names will develop some day have admitted that the shoe sole is valid, a genuine fossilization in Triassic rocks." The Triassic rock bearing the fossil shoe sole is now recognized as being far more than 5 million years old. The Triassic period is now generally dated at 213–248 million years ago.

BLOCK WALL IN AN OKLAHOMA MINE

W. W. McCormick of Abilene, Texas, reported his grandfather's account of a stone block wall that was found deep within a coal mine: "In the year 1928, I, Atlas Almon Mathis, was working in coal mine No. 5., located two miles north of Heavener, Oklahoma. This was a shaft mine, and they told us it was two miles deep. The mine was so deep that they let us down into it on an elevator. . . . They pumped air down to us, it was so deep." This report was reprinted in a book by Brad Steiger. One evening, Mathis was blasting coal loose by explosives in "room 24" of this mine. "The next morning," said Mathis, "there were several concrete blocks laying in the room. These blocks were 12-inch cubes and were so smooth and polished on the outside that all six sides could serve as mirrors. Yet they were full of gravel, because I chipped one of them open with my pick, and it was plain concrete inside." Mathis added: "As I started to timber the room up, it caved in; and I barely escaped. When I came back after the cave-in, a solid wall of these polished blocks was left exposed. About 100 to 150 yards farther down our air core, another miner struck this same wall, or one very similar." The coal in the mine was probably Carboniferous, which would mean the wall was at least 286 million years old.

According to Mathis, the mining company officers immediately pulled the men out of the mine and forbade them to speak about what they had seen. This mine was closed in the fall of 1928, and the crew went to mine number 24, near Wilburton, Oklahoma.

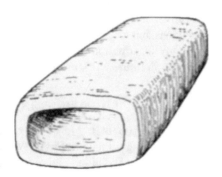

Figure 6.7. Metallic tube found at Saint-Jean de Livet, France, in a 65-million-year-old chalk bed.

Mathis said the Wilburton miners told of finding "a solid block of silver in the shape of a barrel. . . . with the prints of the staves on it." The coal from Wilburton was formed between 280 and 320 million years ago.

Admittedly, these are very bizarre stories, accompanied by very little in the way of proof. But such stories are told, and we wonder how many of them there are and if any of them are true.

In a book by M. K. Jessup, we recently ran across the following wall-in-coal-mine story: "It is. . . . reported that James Parsons, and his two sons, exhumed a slate wall in a coal mine at Hammondville, Ohio, in 1868. It was a large, smooth wall, disclosed when a great mass of coal fell away from it, and on its surface, carved in bold relief, were several lines of hieroglyphics." Of course, such stories could be tall tales, but they might also be leads for interesting research.

The foregoing sampling of discoveries indicating a relatively high level of civilization in very distant ages was compiled from reports published in the nineteenth and early twentieth centuries, but similar reports continue up to the present day. We shall now review some of them.

METALLIC TUBES FROM CHALK IN FRANCE

Y. Druet and H. Salfati announced in 1968 the discovery of semi-ovoid metallic tubes of identical shape but varying size in Cretaceous chalk (Figure 6.7). Our source is *Ancient Man: A Handbook of Puzzling Artifacts,* by William R. Corliss. The chalk bed, exposed in a quarry at Saint-Jean de Livet, France, is estimated to be least 65 million years old. Having considered and eliminated several hypotheses, Druet and Salfati concluded that intelligent beings had lived 65 million years ago.

Desiring more information, we wrote to the geomorphology laboratory at the University of Caen, to which Druet and Salfati reportedly turned over their specimens, but we have not received a reply. We invite readers to communicate to us any information they might have about this case or similar cases, for inclusion in future editions of this book.

SHOE PRINT IN SHALE FROM UTAH

In 1968, William J. Meister, a draftsman and amateur trilobite collector, reported finding a shoe print in the Wheeler Shale near Antelope Spring, Utah. This shoelike indentation (Figure 6.8) and its cast were revealed when Meister split open a block of shale. Clearly visible within the imprint were the remains of trilobites, extinct marine arthropods. The shale holding the print and the trilobite fossils is from the Cambrian, and would thus be 505 to 590 million years old.

Meister described the ancient shoelike impression in an article that appeared in the *Creation Research Society Quarterly:* "The heel print was indented in the rock about an eighth of an inch more than the sole. The footprint was clearly that of the right foot because the sandal was well worn on the right side of the heel in characteristic fashion."

Meister supplied the following important piece of additional information: "On July 4, I accompanied Dr. Clarence Coombs, Columbia Union College, Tacoma, Maryland, and Maurice Carlisle, graduate geologist, University of Colorado at Boulder, to the site of the discovery. After a couple of hours of digging, Mr. Carlisle found a mudslab, which he said convinced him that the discovery of fossil tracks in the location was a distinct possibility, since this discovery showed that the formation had at one time been at the surface."

Scientists who were made aware of the Meister discovery were sometimes contemptuous in their dismissals. This is evident from private correspondence supplied to us by George F. Howe of Los Angeles Baptist College, who requested that we quote from it anonymously. A geologist from Brigham Young University, quite familiar with the Antelope Springs region, wrote in 1981 that the track represented "an oddity of weathering which uninformed people mistakenly interpret for fossil forms."

A professor of evolutionary biology from a Michigan university stated, when asked about the Meister print: "I am not familiar with the trilobite case. . . . but I would be greatly surprised if this isn't another case of fabrication or willful misrepresentation. There is not one case where a juxtaposition of this type has ever been confirmed. So far the fossil record is one of the best tests that evolution has occurred. I put the creationists and those that believe in a flat earth in the same category. They simply do not want to believe in facts and hard evidence. There is not much you can do with such people. . . . Nothing has emerged in recent years to refute the fact that evolution has, and continues to occur, irrespective of what the self-proclaimed 'scientific' creationists claim. The ability of individuals in our society to be duped and brainwashed, either intentionally or unknowingly, by our mass media and certain leaders never ceases to amaze me."

The evolutionary biologist admitted he had not familiarized himself with the "facts and hard evidence" relating to the Meister sandal print before passing judgment. He was thus guilty of the same sin he accused the creationists of committing. We do not necessarily accept the Meister print as genuine, but we believe it should be evaluated on its own merits, rather than on the basis of inflexible preconceptions.

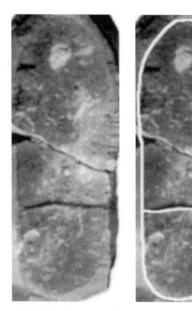

Figure 6.8. Left: Shoelike print discovered by William Meister in Cambrian shale near Antelope Spring, Utah (our photograph). If genuine, the shoe print would be over 505 million years old. Right: Outlined in white, the Meister print does not deviate from the shape of a modern shoe.

William Lee Stokes, a biologist and geologist at the University of Utah, examined the Meister print shortly after it was discovered. Stokes stated: "After seeing the specimen I explained to Mr. Meister why I could not accept it as a footprint and why geologists in general would not accept it. At the very least, we would expect a true footprint to be one of a sequence showing right and left prints somewhat evenly spaced, of the same size and progressing regularly in one direction. . . . It is most significant that no other matching prints were obtained. I know of no instance where a solitary one-of-a-kind impression has been accepted and reported in a scientific journal as a genuine footprint no matter how well-preserved it might be." But in an article that appeared in *Scientific American* in 1969, H. de Lumley reported a single humanlike footprint from the Middle Pleistocene habitation site at Terra Amata in southern France.

Stokes further stated: "A true footprint should also show displacement or squeezing aside of the soft material into which the foot was pressed. . . . From my examination of this specimen I can say that there is no evidence of squeezing or pushing aside of the matrix."

In 1984, one of us (Thompson) visited Meister in Utah. Close inspection of the print revealed no obvious reason why it could not be accepted as genuine. Concerning squeezing aside of the matrix, much depends on the consistency of the matrix and the nature of the object making the imprint. The rounded contours of a bare foot result in more pushing aside of the matrix than the sharp edges of the soles of footwear. We have observed that shoes and sandals can leave very sharp impressions in relatively compact, moist beach sand, with very little sign of pushing aside of the matrix. Shale, the rock in which the Meister print was made, is formed by the consolidation of clay, mud, or silt. One could microscopically examine the grain structure of the shale within the region of the print in order to determine whether or not there is any evidence suggesting that the print was not caused by pressure from above.

Stokes concluded that the Meister specimen was the result of spalling, a natural fracturing of the rock, and stated that the geology department of the University of Utah had in its collection several products of spalling, some resembling footprints. One would have to see these specimens to judge if they really resemble footprints to the extent the Meister specimen does. The shape of the Meister print, as shown by our visual inspection and computer analysis, almost exactly matches that of a modern shoe print.

Furthermore, spalling normally occurs on the surfaces of rocks. The Meister print, however, was found in the interior of a block of shale that was split. Significantly, the shale in the region of the print is of a rougher texture than the shale on the other parts of the split block's surface. This suggests that the rock split where it did not accidentally but because of a line of weakness along the boundary of the two textures. One could, therefore, propose that an ancient shoe caused this shoe-shaped area of weakness. Alternatively, the area of weakness might have resulted from some other unknown cause, in which case the shoelike shape is entirely coincidental. This would be a rather remarkable freak of nature, for the print does not even slightly depart from the shape of a genuine shoe.

The Meister print, as evidence for a human presence in the distant past, is ambiguous. Some scientists have dismissed the print after only cursory examination. Others have rejected it sight unseen, simply because its Cambrian age puts it outside the realm of what might be expected according to evolutionary theory. We suggest, however, that the resources of empirical investigation have not yet been exhausted and that the Meister print is worthy of further research.

GROOVED SPHERE FROM SOUTH AFRICA

Over the past several decades, South African miners have found hundreds of metallic spheres, at least one of which has three parallel grooves running around its equator (Figure 6.9). According to an article by J. Jimison, the spheres are of two types—"one of solid bluish metal with white flecks, and another which is a hollow ball filled with a white spongy center." Roelf Marx, curator of the museum of Klerksdorp, South Africa, where some of the spheres are housed, said: "The spheres are a complete mystery. They look man-made, yet at the time in Earth's history when they came to rest in this rock no intelligent life existed. They're nothing like I have ever seen before."

We wrote to Roelf Marx for further information about the spheres. He replied in a letter dated September 12, 1984: "There is nothing scientific published about the globes, but the facts are: They are found in pyrophyllite, which is mined near the little town of Ottosdal in the Western Transvaal. This pyrophyllite is a quite soft secondary mineral with a count of only 3 on the Mohs' scale and was formed by sedimentation about 2.8 billion years ago. On the other hand the globes, which have a fibrous structure on the inside with a shell around it, are very hard and cannot be scratched, even by steel." The Mohs' scale of hardness is named after Friedrich Mohs, who chose ten minerals as references points for comparative hardness, with talc the softest (1) and diamond the hardest (10).

In his letter to us, Marx said that A. Bisschoff, a professor of geology at the University of Potchefstroom, told him that the spheres were "limonite concretions." Limonite is a kind of iron ore. A concretion is a compact, rounded rock mass formed by localized cementation around a nucleus.

One problem with the hypothesis that the objects are limonite concretions concerns their hardness. As noted above, the metallic spheres cannot be scratched with a steel point, indicating they are extremely hard. But standard references on minerals state that limonite registers only 4 to 5.5 on the Mohs' scale, indicating a relatively low degree of hardness. Furthermore, limonite concretions usually occur in groups, like masses of soap bubbles stuck together. They do not, it seems, normally appear isolated and perfectly round, as is the case with the objects in question. Neither do they normally appear with parallel grooves encircling them (Figure 6.9).

For the purposes of this study, it is the sphere with three parallel

Figure 6.9. A metallic sphere from South Africa with three parallel grooves around its equator. The sphere was found in a Precambrian mineral deposit, said to be 2.8 billion years old.

grooves around its equator that most concerns us. Even if it is conceded that the sphere itself is a limonite concretion, one still must account for the three parallel grooves. In the absence of a satisfactory natural explanation, the evidence is somewhat mysterious, leaving open the possibility that the South African grooved sphere—found in a mineral deposit 2.8 billion years old—was made by an intelligent being.

7

Anomalous Human Skeletal Remains

In the nineteenth and early twentieth centuries scientists found numerous stone implements and other artifacts in extremely old formations. They also discovered anatomically modern human skeletal remains in similarly ancient geological contexts.

Although these human bones originally attracted considerable attention, they are now practically unknown. Most current literature gives one the impression that after the discovery of the first Neanderthal in the 1850s no significant skeletal finds were made until the discovery of Java man in the 1890s.

TRENTON FEMUR

On December 1, 1899, Ernest Volk, a collector working for the Peabody Museum of American Archaeology and Ethnology at Harvard University, discovered a human femur in a fresh railroad cut south of Hancock Avenue within the city limits of Trenton, New Jersey. The femur was found lying on a small ledge, 91 inches beneath the surface. Volk stated: "About four inches over or above the bone. . . . was a place about the length of the bone where it evidently had fallen out of." The human femur was photographed by Volk, who declared that the overlying strata immediately above and for some distance on either side of the find were undisturbed. Volk said that the femur was thoroughly fossilized. Two human skull fragments were taken from the same layer that yielded the femur.

In a letter dated July 30, 1987, Ron Witte of the New Jersey Geological Survey told us that the stratum containing the Trenton femur and skull fragments is from the Sangamon interglacial and is about 107,000 years old. According to standard ideas, human beings of modern type arose in southern Africa about 100,000 years ago and migrated to America at most 30,000 years ago.

On December 7, 1899, Volk returned to the railway cut. About 24 feet west of the spot where he found the fossilized femur, and in the same layer, Volk recovered two fragments of a human skull. The strata immediately overhead and for some distance on either side were said to be undisturbed.

Could the human bones have worked their way down from the upper layers? Volk pointed out that the upper layers were red and yellow. But the human bones were "white and chalky," consistent with the white sand layer in which they were found.

Because the Trenton femur was like that of modern humans, Ales Hrdlicka of the Smithsonian Institution thought it must be of recent age. He expected that a genuinely ancient human femur should display primitive features. Hrdlicka therefore said about the Trenton femur: "The antiquity of this specimen must rest on the geological evidence alone." But he was unable to point out anything wrong with the geological evidence.

During the nineteenth century and early twentieth century, several discoveries of human skeletal remains were made in Middle Pleistocene formations in Europe. These discoveries include those made at Galley Hill, Moulin Quignon, Clichy, La Denise, and Ipswich. Doubts remain as to the true age of these bones. We have nevertheless included them in our discussion for the sake of completeness. The presence of these skeletons in Middle Pleistocene strata could be attributed to recent intrusive burial, mistakes in reporting, or fraud. Nonetheless, there are reasons for thinking that the skeletons might in fact be of Middle Pleistocene age. We shall now briefly review some of the more noteworthy cases.

GALLEY HILL SKELETON

In 1888, workmen removing deposits at Galley Hill, near London, England, exposed a bed of chalk. The overlying layers of sand, loam, and gravel were about 10 or 11 feet thick. One workman, Jack Allsop, informed Robert Elliott, a collector of prehistoric items, that he had discovered a human skeleton firmly embedded in these deposits about 8 feet below the surface and about 2 feet above the chalk bed.

Allsop had removed the skull but left the rest of the skeleton in place. Elliott stated that he saw the skeleton firmly embedded in the stratum: "We carefully looked for any signs of the section being disturbed, but failed: the stratification being unbroken." Elliott then removed the skeleton and later gave it to E. T. Newton, who published a report granting it great age.

A schoolmaster named M. H. Heys observed the bones in the apparently undisturbed deposits before Elliott removed the skeleton. Heys also saw the skull just after it was exposed by a workman excavating the deposits. Heys said about the bones: "No doubt could possibly arise to the observation of an ordinary intelligent person of their deposition contemporaneously with that of the gravel. . . . This undisturbed state of the stratum was so palpable to the workman that he said, 'The man or animal was not buried by anybody.'" Numerous stone tools were also recovered from the Galley Hill site.

According to modern opinion, the Galley Hill site would date to the Holstein interglacial, which occurred about 330,000 years ago. Anatomically, the Galley Hill skeleton was judged to be of the modern human type. Most scientists now think that anatomically modern humans (*Homo sapiens sapiens*) originated in Africa around 100,000 years ago. They say that *Homo sapiens sapiens* eventually entered Europe in the form of Cro-Magnon man approximately 30,000 years ago, replacing the Neanderthals.

Just what do modern paleoanthropologists say about the Galley Hill skeleton? Despite the stratigraphic evidence reported by Heys and Elliott, K. P. Oakley and M. F. A. Montagu concluded in 1949 that the skeleton must have been recently buried in the Middle Pleistocene deposits. They considered the bones, which were not fossilized, to be only a few thousand years old. This is also the opinion of almost all anthropologists today.

The Galley Hill bones had a nitrogen content similar to that of fairly recent bones from other sites in England. Nitrogen is one of the constituent elements of protein, which normally decays with the passage of time. But there are many recorded cases of proteins being preserved in fossils for millions of years. Because the degree of nitrogen preservation may vary from site to site, one cannot say for certain that the relatively high nitrogen content of the Galley Hill bones means they are recent. The Galley Hill bones were found in loam, a clayey sediment known to preserve protein.

Oakley and Montagu found the Galley Hill human bones had a fluorine content similar to that of Late Pleistocene and Holocene (recent) bones from other sites. It is known that bones absorb fluorine from groundwater. But the fluorine content of groundwater may vary widely from place to place and this makes comparison of fluorine contents of bones from different sites an unreliable indicator of their relative ages.

Later, the British Museum Research Laboratory obtained a carbon 14 date of 3,310 years for the Galley Hill skeleton. But this test was performed using methods now considered unreliable. Also, it is highly probable that the Galley Hill bones, kept in a museum for 80 years, were contaminated with recent carbon, causing the test to give a falsely young date.

In attempting to discredit the testimony of Elliott and Heys, who said no signs of burial were evident at Galley Hill, Oakley and Montagu offered several arguments in addition to their chemical and radiometric tests.

For example, Oakley and Montagu argued that the relatively complete nature of the Galley Hill skeleton was a sure sign that it was deliberately buried. In fact, almost all of the ribs, the backbone, the forearms, hands, and feet were missing. In the case of Lucy, the most famous specimen of *Australopithecus afarensis,* more of the skeleton was preserved. And no one has yet suggested that australopithecines buried their dead. Scientists have also discovered fairly complete skeletal remains of *Homo erectus* and *Homo habilis* individuals. These cases, as all paleoanthropologists would agree, definitely do not involve deliberate burial. It is thus possible for relatively complete hominid skeletons to be preserved apart from burial.

But even if the Galley Hill skeleton was a burial, the burial may not have been recent. Sir Arthur Keith suggested in 1928: "Weighing all the evidence, we are forced to the conclusion that the Galley Hill skeleton represents a man. . . . buried when the lower gravel formed a land surface."

As can be seen, old bones point beyond themselves, quite obliquely, to events in the remote and inaccessible past. Controversy about their age is almost certain to arise, and in many cases the available evidence is insufficient to allow disputes to be definitely settled. This would appear to be true of Galley Hill. The report of Oakley and Montagu casts doubt on the testimony of Elliott and Heys. At the same time, the testimony of Elliott and Heys casts doubt on the report of Oakley and Montagu.

MOULIN QUIGNON JAW

In 1863, J. Boucher de Perthes discovered an anatomically modern human jaw in the Moulin Quignon pit at Abbeville, France. He removed it from a layer of black sand and gravel that also contained stone implements of the Acheulean type. The black layer was 16.5 feet below the surface of the pit. The Acheulean sites at Abbeville are of the same age as the Holstein interglacial and would thus be about 330,000 years old.

Upon hearing of the discovery of the Abbeville jaw and tools, a group of distinguished British geologists visited Abbeville and were at first favorably impressed. Later, however, it was alleged that some of the stone implements in Boucher de Perthes's collection were forgeries foisted on him by workmen. The British scientists then began to doubt the authenticity of the jaw. Taking a tooth found with the jaw back to England, they cut it open and were surprised at how well preserved it appeared. This enhanced their doubt, but many physical anthropologists have noted that fossil teeth of great age are often well preserved.

Also, the Moulin Quignon jaw had a coloring "which was found to be superficial" and "was easily scrubbed from one of the portions of bone." Some took this to be an indication of forgery. But British anthropologist Sir Arthur Keith later said this feature of the jaw "does not invalidate its authenticity."

In May 1863, British geologists met with their French counterparts in Paris to decide the status of the jaw. The commission jointly declared in favor of the authenticity of the jaw, despite some reservations by two of the British members. Thereafter, however, the British members continued to oppose the Moulin Quignon jaw and eventually won most scientists over to their side.

"French anthropologists," said Keith, "continued to believe in the authenticity of the jaw until between 1880 and 1890, when they ceased to include it in the list of discoveries of ancient man. At the present time opinion is almost unanimous in regarding the Moulin Quignon jaw as a worthless relic. We see that its relegation to oblivion begins when the belief became fixed that Neanderthal man represented a Pleistocene phase in the evolution of modern races. That opinion, we have seen, is no longer tenable."

In other words, scientists who believed the Neanderthals were the immediate ancestors of *Homo sapiens* could not accommodate the Moulin Quignon jaw because it would have meant that anatomically modern human beings were in existence before the Neanderthals. Today, the idea that the Neanderthals were the direct ancestors of the modern human type is out of vogue, but this in itself does not clear the way for acceptance of the Abbeville jaw, which if genuine, would be over 300,000 years old.

From the information we now have at our disposal, it is difficult to form a definite opinion about the authenticity of the Moulin Quignon jaw. Even if we accept that the jaw and the many flint implements found along with it were fakes, what does this tell us about the nature of paleoanthropological evidence? As we shall see, the Moulin Quignon jaw and tools, if they were forgeries, are not alone. Piltdown man (Chapter 9) was accepted for 40 years before being dismissed as an elaborate hoax.

MOULIN QUIGNON UPDATE

We have recently uncovered new information that gives us a better impression of the Moulin Quignon jaw. In the aftermath of the Moulin Quignon debate, Boucher des Perthes continued to maintain that his discoveries were genuine. To help prove this, he conducted several more excavations at Moulin Quignon, under very strict controls and in the presence of trained scientific observers. These excavations yielded many more anatomically modern human bones, bone fragments, and teeth. These discoveries, which received almost no attention in the English-speaking world, are significant demonstrations of a human presence in the Middle Pleistocene of Europe, over 300,000 years ago.

They also tend to strengthen the case for the authenticity of the original Moulin Quignon jaw. These important discoveries, here mentioned only briefly, are the subject of a future book by Michael A. Cremo.

CLICHY SKELETON

In 1868, Eugene Bertrand reported to the Anthropological Society of Paris that he found parts of a human skull, along with a femur, tibia, and some foot bones, in a quarry on the Avenue de Clichy. The bones were found 5.25 meters (17.3 feet) beneath the surface. Sir Arthur Keith believed the layer in which Clichy human bones were found was the same age as the one in which the Galley Hill skeleton was discovered. This would make the Clichy bones approximately 330,000 years old. The depth at which the Clichy human fossils were found (over 17 feet) argues against recent burial.

But Gabriel de Mortillet said that a workman at the quarry on the Avenue de Clichy told him that he had stashed a skeleton in the pit.

Even after hearing de Mortillet relate the workman's story about stashing the bones of the Clichy skeleton, a number of scientists remained convinced Bertrand's discovery was genuine. For example, Professor E. T. Hamy said: "Mr. Bertrand's discovery seems to me to be so much less debatable in that it is not the first of this kind at Avenue de Clichy. Indeed, our esteemed colleague, Mr. Reboux, found in that same locality, and almost at the same depth (4.20 meters), human bones that he has given me to study."

Keith reported that initially almost all authorities in France believed that the Clichy skeleton was as old as the layer in which Bertrand said it was found. Later, after accepting the Neanderthals as the Pleistocene ancestors of modern humans, French anthropologists dropped the Clichy skeleton, which predated the Neanderthals, from the list of bona fide discoveries. A representative of the modern human type should not have been existing before his supposed ancestors. The Neanderthals are thought to have existed from 30,000 to 150,000 years ago. But the Clichy skeleton would be over 300,000 years old.

In his remarks to the Anthropological Society, Bertrand provided additional evidence for the great antiquity of the Clichy skeleton. He stated that he found a human ulna in the stratum containing the other bones of the Clichy human skeleton. The ulna is the larger of the two long bones of the forearm. When Bertrand tried to extract the ulna it crumbled into dust. He offered this as proof that the Clichy human skeleton must have been native to the layer in which it was found. Apparently, Bertrand reasoned that a bone as fragile as the decayed ulna could not possibly have been removed from an upper layer of the quarry and stashed by a workman in the lower layer in which Bertrand found it—it would certainly have been destroyed in the process. This indicated that the ulna belonged to the stratum in which Bertrand found it, as did the other human bones.

LA DENISE SKULL FRAGMENTS

In the 1840s, pieces of human bone were discovered in the midst of volcanic strata at La Denise, France. Of particular interest was the frontal bone of a human skull. Sir Arthur Keith stated that the frontal "differs in no essential particular from the frontal bone of a modern skull."

The frontal was taken from sediments deposited between two layers of lava. The first lava layer was from the Pliocene and the last from the Late Pleistocene. The skull bone thus could be either a few thousand years or as many as 2 million years old. The bone was found to have about the same nitrogen and fluorine content as bones from Late Pleistocene sites elsewhere in France. But such comparisons are not of much value, because the content of nitrogen or fluorine in bones depends heavily on sediment type, temperature, and water flow, which can vary greatly from place to place.

The true age of the La Denise frontal remains unknown, but because there is reason to believe it could be as old as 2 million years, we have included it here.

IPSWICH SKELETON

In 1911, J. Reid Moir discovered an anatomically modern human skeleton beneath a layer of glacial boulder clay near the town of Ipswich, in the East Anglia region of England. Reading through various secondary accounts, we learned that J. Reid Moir later changed his mind about the skeleton, declaring it recent. We thus did not consider the Ipswich skeleton for inclusion in this book. But after further investigation, we determined that the Ipswich skeleton could be genuinely old.

The skeleton was found at a depth of 1.38 meters (about 4.5 feet), between a layer of boulder clay and some underlying glacial sands. These deposits could be as much as 400,000 years old. Moir was aware of the possibility that the skeleton might represent a recent burial. Therefore, he carefully verified the unbroken and undisturbed nature of the strata in and under which the skeleton lay. As for the condition of the bones, Sir Arthur Keith said it was similar to that of Pleistocene animal fossils found elsewhere in the glacial sands.

The discovery, however, inspired intense opposition. Keith wrote that if the skeleton had been as primitive as Neanderthal man, no one would have doubted it was as old as the boulder clay. "Under the presumption that the modern type of man is also modern in origin," he stated, "a degree of high antiquity is denied to such specimens."

Despite opposition, Moir initially stuck to his guns, holding that the Ipswich skeleton was genuinely old. What then happened to change his mind? He found nearby, at the same level, some stone tools resembling those from the Aurignacian period, considered to be about 30,000 years old. He concluded that the layer of boulder clay above the skeleton had been formed at that time from the sludgelike remnants of the original boulder clay deposit, formed hundreds of thousands of years earlier.

In Moir's statements we find nothing that compels us to accept a recent age of 30,000 years for the skeleton. Sophisticated stone tools, comparable to those of Aurignacian Europe, turn up all over the world, in very distant times. In the 1960s, such implements were discovered at Hueyatlaco, Mexico, in strata yielding a uranium series age of over 200,000 years. During the nineteenth century, very advanced stone objects turned up in the California gold mines, in gravels that might be as old as the Eocene. Therefore, we cannot agree with Moir that the discovery of tools of advanced type at the same level as the Ipswich skeleton was sufficient reason to reinterpret the site stratigraphy to bring the age of the skeleton into harmony with the supposed age of the tools.

Also, Moir gave no geological reasons whatsoever in support of his conclusion that the boulder clay was a recently deposited sludge. Therefore, the simplest hypothesis is that it really was a layer of intact glacial boulder clay, as originally reported by Moir and recorded by the British Geological Survey on its detailed map of the region.

The glacial sands in which the Ipswich skeleton was found must have been laid down between the onset of the Anglian glaciation, about 400,000 years ago, and onset of the Hoxnian interglacial, about 330,000 years ago. It would thus appear that the Ipswich skeleton is between 330,000 and 400,000 years old. Some authorities put the onset of the Mindel glaciation (equivalent to the Anglian) at about 600,000 years, which would give the Ipswich skeleton an age potentially that great. Yet human beings of modern type are not thought to have appeared in Western Europe before 30,000 years ago.

TERRA AMATA

The Terra Amata site is located on the Mediterranean coast of southern France. There, in the late 1960s, French anthropologist Henry de Lumley found oval patterns of post holes and stone circles indicating that hominids erected temporary shelters and built fires about 400,000 years ago. Also found were bone tools. Among them was one apparently used as an awl, perhaps to sew skins. Impressions found in the old land surface at the site were said to demonstrate that the hominids slept or sat on hides. Stone implements were also found, including an object described as a projectile point, made from volcanic rock obtained from the Esterel region, 30 miles away.

Significantly, no hominid fossils were found at Terra Amata. In his 1969 article about the Terra Amata discoveries published in *Scientific American,* de Lumley did, however, report the imprint of a right foot, 9.5 inches long, preserved in the sand of a dune. De Lumley did not identify the type of hominid that made the print. But judged from the available reports, the footprint is not different from that of an anatomically modern human being. This print tends to strengthen the skeletal evidence from the Middle Pleistocene sites we have just discussed.

BUENOS AIRES SKULL

A very strong case for anatomically modern humans existing in very early times comes from Argentina. In 1896, workers excavating a dry dock in Buenos Aires found a human skull (Figure 7.1). They took it from the rudder pit at the bottom of the excavation, after breaking through a layer of a hard, limestonelike substance called *tosca.* The level at which the skull was found was 11 meters (36 feet) below the bed of the river La Plata.

The workers who found the skull gave it to Mr. Junor, their supervisor, a senior member of the public works division of the Port of Buenos Aires. Information about the skull was furnished to the Argentine paleontologist Florentino Ameghino by Mr. Edward Marsh Simpson, an engineer for the company contracted to excavate the port of Buenos Aires. In the opinion of Ameghino, the skull removed from the rudder pit belonged to a Pliocene precursor of *Homo sapiens.* He called this precursor *Diprothomo platensis.* But according to Ales Hrdlicka of the Smithsonian Institution, the skull was just like that of modern humans.

The skull was found in what Ales Hrdlicka called "the upper-most portion of the

Figure 7.1. Human skull taken from an Early Pleistocene formation in Buenos Aires, Argentina.

Pre-Ensenadean stratum." According to modern geological opinion, the Pre-Ensenadan stratum should be at least 1.0–1.5 million years old. Even at 1 million years, the presence of a fully modern human skull anywhere in the world—what to speak of South America—would be unexpected. Mr. J. E. Clark, the foreman of the workers who found the skull, said he was "quite sure the skull was found at the Rudder Pit and under *tosca*."

Bailey Willis, the geologist who accompanied Hrdlicka on his expedition to Argentina, interviewed Mr. Junor and reported: "The fragment of skull was taken out of the well [i.e., the rudder pit]. And although this statement rests on the say-so of the foreman who was told so by a workman, it appears to be the one item in the early history of the find that is not open to serious doubt." Willis went on to offer some vague, unfounded speculations about how the skull could have arrived in that position.

For his part, Hrdlicka thought the fact the skull was modern in shape was enough to rule out any great age for it. Hrdlicka's prejudice is evident in the following statement from his 1912 book: "The antiquity, therefore, of any human skeletal remains which do not present marked differences from those of modern man may be regarded, on morphologic grounds, as only insignificant geologically, not reaching in time, in all probability, beyond the modern, still unfinished, geologic formations." Here we have a very clear formulation of the dubious principle of dating by morphology.

SOUTH AMERICAN HOMO ERECTUS?

Before moving on, let us consider another South American find with unsettling implications for current thinking about human evolution in general and the populating of the New World in particular.

In 1970, Canadian archeologist Alan Lyle Bryan found in a Brazilian museum a fossil skullcap with very thick walls and exceptionally heavy brow ridges, reminiscent of *Homo erectus*. This skullcap came from a cave in the Lagoa Santa region of Brazil. When Bryan showed photographs of the skullcap to several American physical anthropologists, they were unable to believe it could have come from the Americas, and proposed that it was either a fake, a cast, or possibly an Old World skullcap that had somehow been introduced into the Brazilian collection examined by Bryan.

But Bryan countered that both he and his wife, who also saw the skullcap, had abundant experience with human fossil bones. And they were both quite sure that the skullcap could not have been a fake or a cast—it was a genuine, highly fossilized human skullcap. That the Lagoa Santa calotte was not an Old World fossil, accidentally introduced into the Brazilian collection, was supported, said

Bryan, by the fact that it differed in several important measurements from known Old World skulls.

What is the significance of the Lagoa Santa calotte? The presence of hominids with *Homo erectus* features in Brazil at any time in the past is highly anomalous. Paleoanthropologists holding standard views say that only anatomically modern humans ever came to the Americas. The methodology of science allows for views to change, but the kind of change inherent in accepting the presence of *Homo erectus* in the New World would be revolutionary.

The Lagoa Santa skullcap mysteriously disappeared from the Brazilian museum after it was examined by Bryan. An important skeleton discovered by Hans Reck at Olduvai Gorge also disappeared from a museum. In the case of Bryan's and Reck's discoveries, we at least had a chance to hear about them before they disappeared. But we suspect that other fossils have escaped our attention because they were misplaced in museums or were perhaps intentionally discarded—without report.

FOXHALL JAW

In 1855, a human jaw was discovered at Foxhall, England, by workers digging in a quarry. John Taylor, the town druggist, purchased the Foxhall jaw (Figure 7.2) from a workman who wanted a glass of beer, and Taylor called it to the attention of Robert H. Collyer, an American physician then residing in London. Collyer, having acquired the fossil, visited the quarry on Mr. Law's farm. He noted that the bed from which the jaw was said to have been taken was 16 feet below the surface. The condition of the jaw, thoroughly infiltrated with iron oxide, was consistent with incorporation in this bed. Collyer said that the Foxhall jaw was "the oldest relic of the human animal in existence." The 16-foot level at Foxhall is the same from which Moir later recovered stone tools and signs of fire. Anything found at this level would be at least 2.5 million years old.

Aware that he was in the possession of a fossil of great significance, Collyer showed it to various English scientists, including Charles Lyell, George Busk, Richard Owen, Sir John Prestwich, and Thomas Huxley. All of them were skeptical of

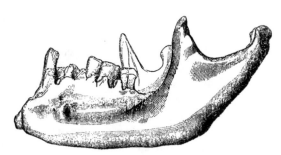

Figure 7.2. Human jaw discovered in 1855 in the Late Pliocene Red Crag formation at Foxhall, England.

its antiquity. Huxley, for example, objected that the shape of the bone "did not indicate it belonged to an extinct or aberrant race of mankind." Here again we encounter the mistaken belief that a modern-looking bone cannot be genuinely old.

American paleontologist Henry Fairfield Osborn, writing in the 1920s about Moir's finds of flint tools in the same area where the Foxhall jaw was uncovered, wondered why the above-mentioned scientists did not take the trouble to visit the site. They disbelieved, said Osborn, "probably *because the shape of the jaw was not primitive.*" Also, the bone was not completely fossilized, but this is true of many other bones of similar age.

After some time, the jaw mysteriously disappeared. It is almost never mentioned by modern authorities, and those who do mention it are invariably scornful. For example, we find in *Fossil Men,* by Marcellin Boule, this statement: "It requires a total lack of critical sense to pay any heed to such a piece of evidence as this."

But many conventionally accepted bones and artifacts have also been found by uneducated workers. For example, most of the *Homo erectus* finds from Java were made by unsupervised, paid native collectors. And the Heidelberg *Homo erectus* jaw was found by German workmen, whose foreman later turned it over to scientists. If scientists can seriously consider these discoveries, then why can they not seriously consider the Foxhall jaw as well? One might object that the Java *Homo erectus* fossils and the Heidelberg *Homo erectus* jaw are still available for inspection, while the Foxhall jaw has vanished. But the original Peking *Homo erectus* fossils disappeared from China during World War II; yet they are still accepted as evidence for human evolution.

CASTENEDOLO SKELETONS

Millions of years ago, during the Pliocene period, a warm sea washed the southern slopes of the Alps, depositing layers of coral and molluscs. Late in the summer of 1860, Professor Giuseppe Ragazzoni, a geologist at the Technical Institute of Brescia, traveled to Castenedolo, about 6 miles southeast of Brescia, to gather fossil shells in the Pliocene strata exposed in a pit at the base of a low hill, the Colle de Vento (Figure 7.3).

Ragazzoni reported: "Searching along a bank of coral for shells, there came into my hand the top portion of a cranium, completely filled with pieces of coral cemented with the blue-green clay characteristic of that formation. Astonished, I continued the search, and in addition to the top portion of the cranium I found other bones of the thorax and limbs, which quite apparently belonged to an individual of the human species."

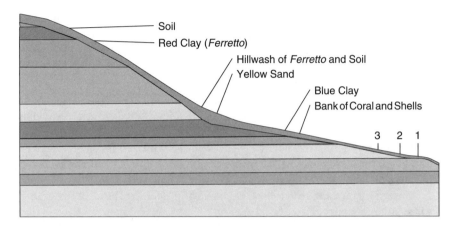

Soil
Red Clay (*Ferretto*)
Hillwash of *Ferretto* and Soil
Yellow Sand
Blue Clay
Bank of Coral and Shells

3 2 1

Figure 7.3. This section of the Colle de Vento, near Castenedolo, Italy, shows the general stratigraphic position of human skeletal remains found there. (1) The human fossils found by geologist G. Ragazzoni in 1860 lay on the bank of coral and shells, at a place where it was surmounted by Middle Pliocene blue clay, which was itself covered by red clay (*ferretto*) washed from the top of the hill. (2) On January 2 and January 25, 1880, more human fossils, representing three individuals (a man and two children), were found about 15 meters (49 feet) from the 1860 site. The bones lay on the bank of coral, and were covered by about 2 meters (7 feet) of Pliocene blue clay, surmounted by a red layer of *ferretto*. (3) On February 16, 1880, the bones of a woman were found at a depth of 1 meter (3 feet) in the blue clay, which was overlain by a layer of yellow sand and a layer of bright red *ferretto*. In all three cases, Ragazzoni looked for signs of burial and found none.

Ragazzoni took the bones to the geologists A. Stoppani and G. Curioni. According to Ragazzoni, their reaction was negative: "Not giving much credence to the circumstances of discovery, they expressed the opinion that the bones, instead of being those of a very ancient individual, were from a very recent burial in that terrain."

"I then threw the bones away," stated Ragazzoni, "not without regret, because I found them lying among the coral and marine shells, appearing, despite the views of the two able scientists, as if transported by the ocean waves and covered with coral, shells, and clay."

But that was not the end of the story. Ragazzoni could not get out of his mind the idea that the bones he had found belonged to a human being who lived during the Pliocene. "Therefore," he wrote, "I returned a little later to the same site, and was able to find some more fragments of bone in the same condition as those first discovered."

In 1875, Carlo Germani, on the advice of Ragazzoni, purchased land at Castenedolo for the purpose of selling the phosphate-rich shelly clay to local farmers for use as fertilizer. Ragazzoni stated: "I explained to Germani about the bones I had found, and strongly advised him to be vigilant while making his excavations and to show me any new human remains."

In December of 1879, Germani noticed some bones in his excavations, about 15 meters (49 feet) from the place where the first human bones were found. On January 2, 1880, Germani sent a message to Ragazzoni about the discoveries. Ragazzoni recalled: "The next day, I went there with my assistant Vincenzo Fracassi, in order to remove the bones with my own hands." The bones included pieces of the skull, some teeth, and parts of the backbone, ribs, arms, legs, and feet.

More discoveries were to follow. On January 25, Germani brought Ragazzoni some jaw fragments and teeth. These were found about 2 meters (7 feet) from the bones uncovered earlier in January. Ragazzoni returned to Castenedolo and found more fragments of skull, jaw, backbone, and ribs, as well as some loose teeth. "All of them," said Ragazzoni, "were completely covered with and penetrated by the clay and small fragments of coral and shells, which removed any suspicion that the bones were those of persons buried in graves, and on the contrary confirmed the fact of their transport by the waves of the sea."

On February 16, Germani advised Ragazzoni that a complete skeleton was discovered. Ragazzoni journeyed to the site and supervised the excavation. The skeleton, enveloped in a mass of blue green clay, turned out to be that of an anatomically modern human female.

"The complete skeleton, " said Ragazzoni, "was found in the middle of the layer of blue clay. . . . The stratum of blue clay, which is over 1 meter [3 feet] thick, has preserved its uniform stratification, and does not show any sign of disturbance." He added, "The skeleton was very likely deposited in a kind of marine mud and not buried at a later time, for in this case one would have been able to detect traces of the overlying yellow sand and the iron-red clay called *ferretto*."

In short, any burial would have certainly produced a noticeable mixing of different colored materials in the otherwise undisturbed blue clay layer, and Ragazzoni, a geologist, testified that there was no sign of such mixing. Also, the blue clay had its own stratification, which was intact.

Ragazzoni considered another possible objection to his conclusion that the human bones from Castenedolo were as old as the Pliocene layer in which they were found. Perhaps streams had stripped away the layers covering the blue clay and penetrated part way into the blue clay itself. The human bones could then have been washed into hollows, and new material could have been deposited over them. This could explain why there were no signs of burial. But Ragazzoni said that it was unlikely that the human fossils had been washed recently into the positions in which they were found: "The fossil remains discovered on January 2 and January 25 lay at a depth of approximately 2 meters. The bones were situated at the boundary between the bank of shells and coral and the overlying blue clay. They were dispersed, as if scattered by the waves of the sea among the shells. The way they were situated allows one to entirely exclude any later mixing or disturbance of the strata."

Ragazzoni further stated: "The skeleton found on the 16th of February occurred at a depth of over 1 meter in the blue clay, which appeared to have covered it in a state of slow deposition." Slow deposition of the clay, which Ragazzoni said was stratified, ruled out the hypothesis that the skeleton had recently been washed into the blue clay by a torrential stream.

Modern geologists place the blue clays at Castenedolo in the Astian stage of the Middle Pliocene, which would give the discoveries from Castenedolo an age of about 3–4 million years.

In 1883, Professor Giuseppe Sergi, an anatomist from the University of Rome, visited Ragazzoni and personally examined the human remains at the Technical Institute of Brescia. After studying the bones, he determined they represented four individuals—an adult male, an adult female, and two children.

Sergi also visited the site at Castenedolo. He wrote: "I went there accompanied by Ragazzoni, on the 14th of April. The trench that had been excavated in 1880 was still there, and the strata were clearly visible in their geological succession."

Sergi added: "If a hole had been excavated for a burial, then it would not have been refilled exactly as before. The clay from the upper surface layers, recognizable by its intense red color, would have been mixed in. Such discoloration and disturbance of the strata would not have escaped the notice of even an ordinary person what to speak of a trained geologist." Sergi also noted that, except for the almost complete female skeleton, most of the bones were dispersed among the shells and coral below the blue clay, as if across a single flat surface. This supported the view that these bodies had come to rest on the shallow sea bottom. When they decayed, their bones were scattered by the action of the water. "The almost entirely preserved female skeleton," said Sergi, "was not found in a posture indicating ordinary burial, but overturned."

Sergi was convinced that the Castenedolo skeletons were the remains of humans who lived during the Pliocene period of the Tertiary. About the negative opinions of others, he said: "The tendency to reject, by reason of theoretical preconceptions, any discoveries that can demonstrate a human presence in the Tertiary is, I believe, a kind of scientific prejudice. Natural science should be stripped of this prejudice." This prejudice was, however, not overcome, and it persists today. Sergi wrote: "By means of a despotic scientific prejudice, call it what you will, every discovery of human remains in the Pliocene has been discredited."

But Sergi was not alone in his acceptance of Ragazzoni's discoveries at Castenedolo. Armand de Quatrefages, familiar to us from our review of stone implements, also accepted them. Concerning the female skeleton uncovered at Castenedolo, he said in his book *Races Humaines:* "There exists no serious reason for doubting the discovery of M. Ragazzoni, and . . . if made in a Quaternary deposit no one would have thought of contesting its accuracy. Nothing, therefore, can be opposed to it but theoretical *a priori* objections."

In 1889, an additional human skeleton was discovered at Castenedolo. This find introduced an element of confusion about the discoveries of 1880.

Ragazzoni invited G. Sergi and A. Issel to examine the new skeleton, which had been found in an ancient oyster bed. Sergi reported that both he and Issel believed this new 1889 skeleton to be a recent intrusion into the Pliocene layers because the almost intact skeleton lay on its back in a fissure of the oyster bed and showed signs of having been buried.

But in his own paper, Issel went on to conclude that the 1880 discoveries were also recent burials. In a footnote, Issel claimed that Sergi agreed with him that none of the skeletons found at Castenedolo were of Pliocene age. For the scientific community, this apparently resolved the ongoing controversy.

But Sergi later wrote that Issel was mistaken. Despite his view that the 1889 skeleton was recent, Sergi said he had never given up his conviction that the 1880 bones were Pliocene. But the damage had been done, and Sergi was not up to fighting a new battle to rehabilitate the 1880 discoveries. Thereafter, silence or ridicule became the standard responses toward Castenedolo.

A good example of the unfair treatment given to the Castenedolo finds may be found in Professor R. A. S. Macalister's *Textbook of European Archaeology,* written in 1921. Macalister admitted that the Castenedolo finds "whatever we may think of them, have to be treated seriously." He noted that they were "unearthed by a competent geologist, Ragazzoni . . . and examined by a competent anatomist, Sergi." Still he could not accept their Pliocene age. Faced with the uncomfortable facts, Macalister claimed "there must be something wrong somewhere." First of all the bones were anatomically modern. "Now, if they really belonged to the stratum in which they were found," wrote Macalister, "this would imply an extraordinarily long standstill for evolution. It is much more likely that there is something amiss with the observations." Macalister also said: "The acceptance of a Pliocene date for the Castenedolo skeletons would create so many insoluble problems that we can hardly hesitate in choosing between the alternatives of adopting or rejecting their authenticity."

Here once more we find a scientist's preconceived ideas about evolution influencing him to reject skeletal evidence that would otherwise be considered of good quality.

Macalister cited Issel in support of his attempt to discredit all the Castenedolo finds, even though Issel's 1889 report really discredited only the 1889 skeleton. For example, Macalister, referring to all of the Castenedolo finds, wrote: "Examination of the bones and their setting, by Issel of Geneva, revealed the fact that the strata were full of marine deposits, and that everything solid within them, *except the human bones,* shewed marine incrustations." While it is true that Issel reported that the bones of the skeleton uncovered in 1889 were smooth and free of incrustations, the same cannot be said of the earlier discoveries, which both Ragazzoni and Sergi said were incrusted with blue Pliocene clay and pieces of shells and coral.

Another example of the unfair treatment given the Castenedolo discoveries is found in *Fossil Men.* In this book, Boule and Vallois stated that "it seems certain that at Castenedolo . . . we are dealing with more or less recent burials." But in *Fossil Men,* Boule and Vallois devoted only one paragraph to Castenedolo, and did not mention the undisturbed layers lying over the skeletons or the scattered and incomplete state of some of the skeletons—information that tends to rule out intrusive burial.

Boule and Vallois noted: "In 1889, the discovery of a new skeleton was the subject of an official report by Professor Issel, who then observed that the various fossils from this deposit were all impregnated with salt, with the sole exception of the human bones." Here Boule and Vallois implied that what was true of the bones found in 1889 was also true of the bones found previously. But in his 1889 report, Issel described only the bones found in 1889. In fact, Issel did not even mention the word *salt,* referring instead to "marine incrustations"—which were, as above mentioned, present on the bones found in 1860 and 1880.

Scientists have employed chemical and radiometric tests to deny a Pliocene age to the Castenedolo bones. Fresh bones contain a certain amount of nitrogen in their protein, and this tends to decrease with time. In a 1980 report, K. P. Oakley found the Castenedolo bones had a nitrogen content similar to that of bones from Late Pleistocene and Holocene Italian sites and thus concluded the Castenedolo bones were recent. But the degree of nitrogen preservation in bone can vary widely from site to site, making such comparisons unreliable as age indicators. The Castenedolo bones were found in clay, a substance known to preserve nitrogen-containing bone proteins.

Bones tend to accumulate fluorine from ground water. The Castenedolo bones had a fluorine content that Oakley considered relatively high for bones he thought were recent. Oakley explained this discrepancy by positing higher past levels of fluorine in the Castenedolo groundwater. But this was simply guesswork. The Castenedolo bones also had an unexpected high concentration of uranium, consistent with great age.

A carbon 14 test yielded an age of 958 years for some of the Castenedolo bones. But, as in the case of Galley Hill, the methods employed are now considered unreliable. And the bones themselves, which had been mouldering in a museum for almost 90 years, were very likely contaminated with recent carbon, causing the test to yield a falsely young age.

The case of Castenedolo demonstrates the shortcomings of the methodology employed by paleoanthropologists. The initial attribution of a Pliocene age to the discoveries of 1860 and 1880 appears justified. The finds were made by a trained geologist, G. Ragazzoni, who carefully observed the stratigraphy at the site. He especially searched for signs of intrusive burial, and observed none. Ragazzoni duly reported his findings to his fellow scientists in scientific journals. But because the remains were modern in morphology they came under intense negative scrutiny. As Macalister put it, there had to be something wrong.

The account of human origins now dominant in the scientific community is the product of attitudes such as Macalister's. For the last century, the idea of progressive evolution of the human type from more apelike ancestors has guided the acceptance and rejection of evidence. Evidence that contradicts the idea of human evolution is carefully screened out. Therefore, when one reads textbooks about human evolution, one may think, "Well, the idea of human evolution must be true because all the evidence supports it." But such textbook presentations are misleading, for it is the unquestioned belief that humans did in fact evolve from apelike ancestors that has determined what evidence should be included and how it should be interpreted.

SAVONA SKELETON

We now turn our attention to another Pliocene find, made at Savona, a town on the Italian Riviera, about 30 miles west of Genoa. In the 1850s, while constructing a church, workmen discovered an anatomically modern human skeleton at the bottom of a trench 3 meters (10 feet) deep. The layer containing the skeleton was 3–4 million years old.

Arthur Issel communicated details of the Savona find to the members of the International Congress of Prehistoric Anthropology and Archeology at Paris in 1867. He declared that the Savona human "was contemporary with the strata in which he was found."

De Mortillet, however, wrote in 1883 that the Pliocene layers at Savona, deposited in shallow coastal waters, contained isolated bones of land mammals while the human skeleton was largely intact. "Does this not prove," he said, "that instead of the remains of a human cadaver tossing in the waves of a Pliocene sea, we are simply in the presence of a later burial of undetermined date?"

At the International Congress of Prehistoric Anthropology and Archeology at Bologna in 1871, Father Deo Gratias, a priest who had been present at the time of the discovery of the human skeleton at Savona, gave a report indicating that it was not an intrusive burial. Deo Gratias, a student of paleontology, noted: "The body was discovered in an outstretched position, with the arms extending forward, the head slightly bent forward and down, the body very much elevated relative to the legs, like a man in the water. Can we suppose a body was buried in such a position? Is it not, on the contrary, the position of a body abandoned to the mercy of the water? The fact that the skeleton was found on the side of a rock in the bed of clay makes it probable that it was washed against this obstacle."

Deo Gratias further stated: "Had it been a burial we would expect to find the upper layers mixed with the lower. The upper layers contain white quartzite sands. The result of mixing would have been the definite lightening of a closely circumscribed region of the Pliocene clay sufficient to cause some doubts in the spectators that it was genuinely ancient, as they affirmed. The biggest and smallest cavities of the human bones are filled with compacted Pliocene clay. This could only have happened when the clay was in a muddy consistency, during Pliocene times." Deo Gratias pointed out that the clay was now hard and dry. Also, the skeleton as found at a depth of 3 meters (10 feet), rather deep for a burial.

The combination of fossils found at Savona can thus be explained as follows. The site was once covered by the shallow shoreline waters of a Pliocene sea, as shown by the presence of characteristic shells. Animals could have died on the land, and their isolated bones could have been washed into the sea and incorporated into the formation. The human bones, found in natural connection, could have come to rest in the same marine formation as a result of someone drowning there during the Pliocene, perhaps after the sinking of a boat. This accounts for the presence of a relatively complete human skeleton amid scattered animal bones, without recourse to the hypothesis of recent intrusive burial. Keep in mind that the posture of the skeleton, face down and with limbs outstretched, was like that of a drowned corpse rather than one deliberately buried.

MONTE HERMOSO VERTEBRA

In Chapter 5, we discussed the discovery of flint tools and signs of intentional use of fire at Monte Hermoso in Argentina. Now we will consider the human bone found there—an atlas, the topmost bone of the spinal column. Santiago Pozzi, an employee of the Museum of La Plata, collected it from the Early Pliocene Montehermosan formation during the 1880s. It did not attract much notice until years later. At that time, it was still covered by the characteristic yellowish-brown loess of the Montehermosan formation, which is 3–5 million years old.

That the bone lay for years in a museum before it was recognized should not disqualify it. The Gibraltar skull lay for many years in the garrison museum before it was recognized as a Neanderthal specimen. Also, several *Homo erectus* femurs from Java were shipped to Holland in boxes of bones. They went unrecognized and uncataloged for several decades but are now listed in textbooks with other accepted finds. The number of similar cases could be expanded, the point being that scientists have become aware of many fully accepted fossil finds in the same way as the Monte Hermoso atlas.

After the Pliocene loess was removed, scientists carefully studied the bone. Florentino Ameghino, accepting that it was truly Pliocene, assigned the atlas to an apelike human ancestor. In his description of the bone, he identified features he thought were primitive.

But Ales Hrdlicka convincingly demonstrated that the bone was actually modern in form. Like Ameghino, Hrdlicka believed the human form should, as we proceed back in time, become more and more primitive. According to Hrdlicka, if a bone was of the fully modern human type, then no matter what layer it was found in, it had to be of recent origin. Such a bone's presence in an ancient stratum always could be, indeed had to be, explained as some kind of intrusion.

There is, however, another possible explanation: human beings of the modern physiological type were living over 3 million years ago in Argentina. This is supported by the fact that the atlas showed signs of having been thoroughly embedded in sediments from the Montehermosan formation.

All in all, Hrdlicka felt that the Monte Hermoso atlas was worthy of being "dropped of necessity into obscurity." That is exactly what happened. Otherwise, Hrdlicka's claim that humans only recently entered the Americas would have been placed on very shaky ground. Today there are many who will insist that the Monte Hermoso atlas remain in the obscurity into which it was of necessity dropped. Evidence for a fully human presence 3 million or more years ago, in Argentina of all places, is still not welcome in mainstream paleoanthropology.

MIRAMAR JAW

In 1921, M. A. Vignati reported that a human lower jaw, with two molars, was discovered in the Late Pliocene Chapadmalalan formation at Miramar, Argentina. Previously, stone tools and a mammalian bone with an arrow head embedded in it had been discovered at this site (Chapter 5). The jaw was discovered by Lorenzo Parodi, a museum collector. E. Boman reported that Parodi found the jaw and its attached molars "embedded in the *barranca,* at great depth in the Chapadmalalan strata, at about the level of the sea." The jaw would thus be about 2–3 million years old.

Boman, however, was skeptical. He stated: "The newspapers published bombastic articles about 'the most ancient human remains in the world.' But all who examined the molars found them to be identical to the corresponding molars of modern human beings."

Boman took it for granted that the fully human nature of the Miramar jaw fragment unequivocally insured its recent date. But nothing Boman said excludes the possibility that the Miramar fossil demonstrates a fully human presence in the Pliocene of Argentina.

CALAVERAS SKULL

In Chapter 5, we discussed the numerous stone implements discovered in the auriferous gravels of the Sierra Nevada Mountains of California. Human bones were also found in these gravels, which range from 9 million to 55 million years old.

In February 1866, Mr. Mattison, the principal owner of the mine on Bald Hill, near Angels Creek in Calaveras County, removed a skull from a layer of gravel 130 feet below the surface. The gravel was near the bedrock, underneath several distinct layers of volcanic material. Volcanic eruptions began in this region during the Oligocene, continued through the Miocene, and ended in the Pliocene. Since the skull occurred near the bottom of the sequence of interspersed gravel and lava layers at Bald Hill, it would seem likely that the gravel in which the skull was found was older than the Pliocene, perhaps much older.

After finding the skull, Mattison later carried it to Mr. Scribner, an agent of Wells, Fargo and Co.'s Express at Angels. Mr. Scribner's clerk, Mr. Matthews, cleaned off part of the incrustations covering most of the fossil. Upon recognizing that it was part of a human skull, he sent it to Dr. Jones, who lived in the nearby village of Murphy's and was an enthusiastic collector of such items. Then Dr. Jones wrote to the office of the Geological Survey in San Francisco, and after receiving a reply, he forwarded the skull to this office, where it was examined by J. D. Whitney, the state geologist. Whitney at once made the journey to Murphy's and Angels, where he personally questioned Mr. Mattison, who confirmed the report that was given by Dr. Jones. Both Scribner and Jones were personally known to Whitney and were regarded by him as trustworthy.

On July 16, 1866, Whitney presented to the California Academy of Sciences a report on the Calaveras skull, affirming that it was found in Pliocene strata. The skull caused a great sensation in America.

According to Whitney, "The religious press in this country took the matter up . . . and were quite unanimous in declaring the Calaveras skull to be a 'hoax.'" Whitney noted that the hoax stories did not arise until after his discovery was publicized widely in newspapers.

Some of the hoax stories were propagated not by newspaper writers but by scientists such as William H. Holmes of the Smithsonian Institution. During a visit to Calaveras County, he gathered testimony from some people who were acquainted with Mr. Scribner and Dr. Jones, and this testimony raised the possibility that the skull examined by Whitney was not a genuine Tertiary fossil. But there is a problem with the hoax hypothesis—there are many versions. Some say religious miners planted the skull to deceive the scientist Whitney. Some say the miners planted a skull to deceive another miner. Some say a genuine skull was found by Mattison and later a different skull was given to Whitney. Some say Mattison's friends from a nearby town planted the skull as a practical joke. This contradictory testimony casts doubt on the hoax idea.

After visiting Calaveras county, Holmes examined the actual Calaveras skull at the Peabody Museum in Cambridge, Massachusetts, and concluded that "the skull was never carried and broken in a Tertiary torrent, that it never came from the old gravels in the Mattison mine, and that it does not in any way represent a Tertiary race of men." Some testimony supporting this conclusion comes from persons who examined the matrix of pebbles and earth in which the Calaveras skull had been discovered. Dr. F. W. Putnam of Harvard University's Peabody Museum of Natural History said the skull did not bear any trace of gravel from the mines. William J. Sinclair of the University of California also personally examined the skull and said the material attached to it was not gravel from the gold mine. He thought it was the kind of material one might find in a cave, where Indians sometimes placed bodies.

On the other hand, Holmes reported: "Dr. D. H. Dall states that while in San Francisco in 1866, he compared the material attached to the skull with portions of the gravel from the mine and that they were alike in all essentials." And W. O. Ayres, writing in the *American Naturalist* in 1882, stated: "I saw it and examined it carefully at the time when it first reached Professor Whitney's hands. It was not only incrusted with sand and gravel, but its cavities were crowded with the same material; and that material was of a peculiar sort, a sort which I had occasion to know thoroughly." It was, said Ayres, the gold-bearing gravel found in the mines, not a recent cave deposit.

Regarding the skull, Ayres noted: "It has been said that it is a modern skull which has been incrusted after a few years of interment. This assertion, however, is never made by anyone knowing the region. The gravel has not the slightest tendency toward an action of that sort . . . the hollows of the skull were crowded with the solidified and cemented sand, in such a way as they could have been only by its being driven into them in a semi-fluid mass, a condition the gravels have never had since they were first laid down."

Whitney, in his original description of the fossil, observed that the Calaveras skull was highly fossilized. This is certainly consistent with great age; however, as Holmes pointed out, it is also true that bones can become fossilized over the course of a few hundred or thousand years. Yet geologist George Becker reported in 1891: "I find that many good judges are fully persuaded of the authenticity of the Calaveras skull, and Messrs. Clarence King, O. C. Marsh, F. W. Putnam, and W. H. Dall have each assured me that this bone was found in place in the gravel beneath the lava." Becker added that this statement was made with the permission of the authorities named. Clarence King, as mentioned previously, was a famous geologist attached to the U.S. Geological Survey. O. C. Marsh, a paleontologist, was a pioneer dinosaur fossil hunter and served as president of the National Academy of Sciences from 1883 to 1895. But F. W. Putnam of Harvard's Peabody Museum, as we have seen, later changed his mind, saying that the matrix of the skull appeared to be a cave deposit.

Can it really be said with certainty that the Calaveras skull was either genuine or a hoax? The evidence is so contradictory and confusing that although the skull could have come from an Indian burial cave we might regard with suspicion anyone who comes forward with any kind of definite conclusion. The reader may pause to contemplate what steps one would take to make one's own determination of the true age of the Calaveras skull.

It should, however, be kept in mind that the Calaveras skull was not an isolated discovery. Great numbers of stone implements were found in nearby deposits of similar age. And, as we shall see, additional human skeletal remains were also uncovered in the same region.

In light of this, the Calaveras skull cannot be dismissed without the most careful consideration. As Sir Arthur Keith put it in 1928: "The story of the Calaveras skull . . . cannot be passed over. It is the 'bogey' which haunts the student of early man . . . taxing the powers of belief of every expert almost to the breaking point."

MORE HUMAN FOSSILS
FROM THE CALIFORNIA GOLD COUNTRY

On January 1, 1873, the president of the Boston Society of Natural History read extracts from a letter by Dr. C. F. Winslow about a discovery of human bones at Table Mountain in Tuolumne County. The find was made in 1855 or

1856, and the details were communicated to Winslow by Capt. David B. Akey, who had witnessed it. The discovery took place about 10 years before J. D. Whitney first reported on the famous Calaveras skull.

Winslow stated: "During my visit to this mining camp I have become acquainted with Capt. David B. Akey, formerly commanding officer of a California volunteer company, and well known to many persons of note in that State, and in the course of my conversation with him I learned that in 1855 and 1856 he was engaged with other miners in running drifts into Table Mountain in Tuolumne County at the depth of about two hundred feet from its brow, in search of placer gold. He states that in a tunnel run into the mountain at the distance of about fifty feet from that upon which he was employed, and at the same level, a complete human skeleton was found and taken out by miners personally known to him, but whose names he does not now recollect. He did not see the bones in place, but he saw them after they were brought down from the tunnel to a neighboring cabin. All the bones of the skeleton apparently were brought down in the arms of miners and placed in a box, and it was the opinion of those present that the skeleton must have been perfect as it laid in the drift. He does not know what became of the bones, but can affirm to the truth of this discovery, and that the bones were those of a human skeleton, in an excellent state of preservation. The skull was broken in on the right temple, where there was a small hole, as if a part of the skull was gone, but he cannot tell whether this fracture occurred before the excavation or was made by the miners. . . . He thinks that the depth from the surface at which this skeleton was found was two hundred feet, and from one hundred and eighty to two hundred feet from the opening cut or face of the tunnel. The bones were in a moist condition, found among the gravel and very near the bed rock, and water was running out of the tunnel. There was a petrified pine tree, from sixty to eighty feet in length and between two and three feet in diameter at the butt, lying near this skeleton. Mr. Akey went into the tunnel with the miners, and they pointed out to him the place where the skeleton was found. He saw the tree in place and broke specimens from it. He cannot remember the name of this tunnel, but it was about a quarter of a mile east of the Rough and Ready tunnel and opposite Turner's Flat, another well known point. He cannot tell the sex of the skeleton, but it was of medium size. The bones were altogether, and not separated, when found."

The gravel just above the bedrock at Tuolumne Table Mountain, where the skeleton was found, is said to be between 33 and 55 million years old. This must be the age of the skeleton unless it was introduced into the gravels at a later time, and we are not aware of any evidence indicating such an intrusion.

Dr. Winslow did not find any of the bones of the skeleton seen by Akey. But in another case, Winslow did collect some fossils, which he sent to museums in the eastern United States. A skull fragment, characterized by Dr. J. Wyman, a leading craniologist, as human, was dispatched by Winslow to the Museum of the Natural History Society of Boston. The fossil was labeled as follows: "From a shaft in Table Mountain, 180 feet below the surface, in gold drift, among rolled stones and near mastodon debris. Overlying strata of basaltic compactness and hardness. Found July, 1857. Given to Rev. C. F. Winslow by Hon. Paul K. Hubbs, August, 1857." Another fragment, from the same skull, and similarly labeled, was sent to the Museum of the Philadelphia Academy of Natural Sciences.

Upon learning of this discovery, J. D. Whitney began his own investigation. He learned that Hubbs was a well-known citizen of Vallejo, California, and a former State Superintendent of Education. Whitney got from Hubbs a detailed written account of the discovery, which occurred in the Valentine Shaft, south of Shaw's Flat. Whitney stated: "The essential facts are, that the Valentine Shaft was vertical, that it was boarded up to the top, so that nothing could have fallen in from the surface during the working under ground, which was carried on in the gravel channel exclusively, after the shaft had been sunk. There can be no doubt that the specimen came from the drift in the channel under Table Mountain, as affirmed by Mr. Hubbs." The skull fragment was found in a horizontal mine shaft (or drift) leading from the main vertical shaft, at a depth of 180 feet from the surface. Hubbs stated that he "saw the portion of skull immediately after its being taken out of the sluice into which it had been shoveled." Adhering to the bone was the characteristic gold-bearing gravel. A stone mortar was found in the same mine. William J. Sinclair suggested tunnels from other mines had possibly intersected those of the Valentine mine. This might explain how the skull fragment got deep below the surface. But Sinclair admitted that during his 1902 visit he was not even able to find the old Valentine shaft. This means he had no direct evidence that the Valentine mine shafts were connected to any others. His objection was simply a weak and highly speculative attempt to discredit a discovery he opposed on theoretical grounds. The gravels containing the skull fragment lay 180 feet below the surface and beneath the lava cap of Table Mountain, which is 9 million years old. The oldest gravels below the lava are 55 million years old. The skull fragment could thus be from 9 million to 55 million years old.

When examining a collection of stone artifacts belonging to Dr. Perez Snell, J. D. Whitney noted the presence of a human jaw. The jaw and artifacts all came from gold-bearing gravels beneath the lava cap of Tuolumne Table Mountain. The jaw measured 5.5 inches across from condyle to condyle, which is within the normal human range. Whitney remarked that all the human fossils uncovered in the gold-mining region, including this one, were of the anatomically modern type. The gravels from which the jaw came could be anywhere from 9 to 55 million years old.

Whitney also reported several discoveries from Placer County. In particular, he gave this account of human bones that were found in the Missouri tunnel: "In this tunnel, under the lava, two bones had been found. . . . which were pronounced by Dr. Fagan to be human. One was said to be a leg bone; of the character of the other nothing was remembered. The above information was obtained by Mr. Goodyear from Mr. Samuel Bowman, of whose intelligence and truthfulness the writer has received good accounts from a personal friend well acquainted with him. Dr. Fagan was at that time one of the best known physicians of the region." According to information provided by the California Division of Mines and Geology, the deposits from which the bones were taken are over 8.7 million years old.

In 1853, a physician named Dr. H. H. Boyce discovered human bones at Clay Hill in El Dorado County, California. In 1870, Dr. Boyce wrote to Whitney, who had requested information: "I purchased an interest in a claim on this hill, on condition that it prospected sufficiently well to warrant working it. The owner and myself accordingly proceeded to sink a shaft for the purpose of working it. It was while doing so that we discovered the bones to which you refer. Clay Hill is one of a series of elevations which constitute the water-shed between Placerville Creek and Big Cañon, and is capped with a stratum of basaltic lava, some eight feet thick. Beneath this there are some thirty feet of sand, gravel, and clay. . . . It was in this clay that we came across the bones. While emptying the tub, I saw some pieces of material which on examination I discovered were pieces of bones; and, on further search, I found the scapula, clavicle, and parts of the first, second, and third ribs of the right side of a human skeleton. They were quite firmly cemented together; but on exposure to the air began to crumble. We made no further discoveries." According to Whitney, Boyce "stated there could be no mistake about the character of the bones, and that he had made a special study of human anatomy."

William J. Sinclair persistently attempted to cast whatever doubt he could on the discovery. He said he could not locate the clay stratum because the slope was covered with rocky debris. He further stated: "The impression conveyed. . . . is that the skeleton found by Dr. Boyce was at a depth of thirty-eight feet, in undisturbed strata under eight feet of so-called basalt. There is nothing, however, in the letter to show that this was the section passed through in sinking the Boyce shaft." Because of the ambiguity about the exact location of the shaft, Sinclair thus concluded: "The skeleton may have been found in such a place and at such a depth in the clay that the possibility of recent interment would have to be considered."

The points raised by Sinclair are valid, and we agree that there are reasons to doubt the antiquity of the skeletal remains found at Clay Hill. Yet the presence of so much rocky debris that Sinclair was not able to gain access to the stratum of clay, at the base of the hill, argues against, rather than for, the possibility of a recent burial into the clay from the slope of the hill. Also, if there were a recent burial, it is peculiar that so few bones were recovered.

This brings us to the end of our review of fossil human skeletal remains from the gold-bearing gravels of California. Despite the imperfections of the evidence, one thing is certain—human bones were found in the Tertiary gravels, dating as far back as the Eocene. How the bones got there is open to question. The reports of the discoveries are sometimes vague and inconclusive, yet they are suggestive of something other than pranks by miners or recent intrusive burials by Indians. The presence of numerous stone tools, incontestably of human manufacture, in the same formations, lends additional credibility to the finds.

In an address to the American Association for the Advancement of Science, delivered in August, 1879, O. C. Marsh, president of the Association and one of America's foremost paleontologists, said about Tertiary man: "The proof offered on this point by Professor J. D. Whitney in his recent work (*Aurif. Gravels of Sierra Nevada*) is so strong, and his careful, conscientious method of investigation so well known, that his conclusions seem irresistible. . . . At present, the known facts indicate that the American beds containing human remains and works of man, are as old as the Pliocene of Europe. The existence of man in the Tertiary period seems now fairly established."

EXTREMELY OLD FINDS IN EUROPE

More evidence for human beings in the early and middle Tertiary comes from Europe. According to Gabriel de Mortillet, M. Quiquerez reported the discovery of a skeleton at Delémont in Switzerland in ferruginous clays said to be Late Eocene. About this find, de Mortillet simply said one should be suspicious of human skeletons found with the bones in natural connection. De Mortillet further stated that one should be cautious about a similarly complete skeleton found by Garrigou in Miocene strata at Midi de France.

It is possible, however, that these skeletons were from individuals buried during the Eocene or Miocene periods. A burial does not necessarily have to be recent. The truly frustrating thing about finds such as these is that we are not able to get more information about them. We find only a brief mention by an author bent on discrediting them. Because such finds seemed doubtful to scientists like de Mortillet, they went undocumented and uninvestigated, and were quickly forgotten. How many such finds have been made? We may never know. In contrast, finds which conform to accepted theories are thoroughly investigated, extensively reported, and safely enshrined in museums.

EXTREME ANOMALIES

As we have seen, some scientists believed ape-men existed as far back as the Miocene and Eocene. A few bold thinkers even proposed that fully human beings were alive during those periods. But now we are going to proceed into times still more remote. Since most scientists had trouble with Tertiary humans, we can just imagine how difficult it would have been for them to give any serious consideration to the cases we are about to discuss. We ourselves were tempted not to mention such finds as these because they seem unbelievable. But the result of such a policy would be that we discuss evidence only for things we already believe. And unless our current beliefs represent reality in total, this would not be a wise thing to do.

In December of 1862, the following brief but intriguing report appeared in a journal called *The Geologist*: "In Macoupin county, Illinois, the bones of a man were recently found on a coal-bed capped with two feet of slate rock, ninety feet below the surface of the earth. . . . The bones, when found, were covered with a crust or coating of hard glossy matter, as black as coal itself, but when scraped away left the bones white and natural." The coal in which the Macoupin County skeleton was found is at least 286 million years old and might be as much as 320 million years old.

Our final examples of anomalous pre-Tertiary evidence are not in the category of fossil human bones, but rather in the category of fossil humanlike footprints. Professor W. G. Burroughs, head of the department of geology at Berea College in Berea, Kentucky, reported in 1938: "During the beginning of the Upper Carboniferous (Coal Age) Period, creatures that walked on their two hind legs and had human-like feet, left tracks on a sand beach in Rockcastle County, Kentucky. This was the period known as the Age of Amphibians when animals moved about on four legs or more rarely hopped, and their feet did not have a human appearance. But in Rockcastle, Jackson and several other counties in Kentucky, as well as in places from Pennsylvania to Missouri inclusive, creatures that had feet strangely human in appearance and that walked on two hind legs did exist. The writer has proved the existence of these creatures in Kentucky. With the cooperation of Dr. C. W. Gilmore, Curator of Vertebrate Paleontology, Smithsonian Institution, it has been shown that similar creatures lived in Pennsylvania and Missouri."

The Upper Carboniferous (the Pennsylvanian) began about 320 million years ago. It is thought that the first animals capable of walking erect, the pseudosuchian thecodonts, appeared around 210 million years ago. These lizardlike creatures, capable of running on their hind legs, would not have left any tail marks since they carried their tails aloft. But their feet did not look at all like those of human beings; rather they resembled those of birds. Scientists say the first appearance of apelike beings was not until around 37 million years ago, and it was not until around 4 million years ago that most scientists would expect to find footprints anything like those reported by Burroughs from the Carboniferous of Kentucky.

Burroughs stated: "Each footprint has five toes and a distinct arch. The toes are spread apart like those of a human being who has never worn shoes." Giving more details about the prints, Burroughs stated: "The foot curves back like a human foot to a human appearing heel."

David L. Bushnell, an ethnologist with the Smithsonian Institution, suggested the prints were carved by Indians. In ruling out this hypothesis, Dr. Burroughs used a microscope to study the prints and noted: "The sand grains within the tracks are closer together than the sand grains of the rock just outside the tracks due to the pressure of the creatures' feet. . . . The sandstone adjacent to many of the tracks is uprolled due to the damp, loose sand having been pushed up around the foot as the foot sank into the sand." These facts led Burroughs to conclude that the humanlike footprints were formed by compression in the soft, wet sand before it consolidated into rock some 300 million years ago. Burrough's observations were confirmed by other investigators.

According to Kent Previette, Burroughs also consulted a sculptor. Previette wrote in 1953: "The sculptor said that carving in that kind of sandstone could not have been done without leaving artificial marks. Enlarged photomicrographs and enlarged infrared photographs failed to reveal any 'indications of carving or cutting of any kind.'"

Burroughs himself stopped short of claiming that the prints were made by humans, but his presentation leaves one with the strong impression that they were human. When asked about them, Burroughs said, "They look human. That is what makes them especially interesting."

Mainstream science reacted predictably to any suggestion that the prints were made by humans. Geologist Albert G. Ingalls, writing in 1940 in *Scientific American,* said: "If man, or even his ape ancestor, or even that ape ancestor's early mammalian ancestor, existed as far back as in the Carboniferous Period in any shape, then the whole science of geology is so completely wrong that all the geologists will resign their jobs and take up truck driving. Hence, for the present at least, science rejects the attractive explanation that man made these mysterious prints in the mud of the Carboniferous with his feet."

Ingalls suggested the prints were made by some as yet unknown kind of amphibian. But today's scientists do not really take the amphibian theory seriously. Human-sized Carboniferous bipedal amphibians do not fit into the accepted scheme of evolution much better than Carboniferous human beings— they wreak havoc with our ideas of early amphibians, requiring a host of evolutionary developments we now know nothing about.

Ingalls wrote: "What science does know is that, anyway, unless 2 and 2 are 7, and unless the Sumerians had airplanes and radios and listened to Amos and Andy, these prints were not made by any Carboniferous Period man."

In 1983, the *Moscow News* gave a brief but intriguing report on what appeared to be a human footprint in 150-million-year-old Jurassic rock next to a giant three-toed dinosaur footprint. The discovery occurred in the Turkmen Republic in what was then the southeastern USSR. Professor Amanniyazov, corresponding member of the Turkmen SSR Academy of Sciences, said that although the print resembled a human footprint, there was no conclusive proof that it was made by a human being. This discovery has not received much attention, but then, given the current mindset of the scientific community, such neglect is to be expected. We only know of a few cases of such extremely anomalous discoveries, but considering that many such discoveries probably go unreported we wonder how many there actually might be.

Part II
ACCEPTED EVIDENCE

8

Java Man

At the end of the nineteenth century, a consensus was building within an influential portion of the scientific community that human beings of the modern type had existed as far back as the Pliocene and Miocene periods—and perhaps even earlier.

Anthropologist Frank Spencer stated in 1984: "From accumulating skeletal evidence it appeared as if the modern human skeleton extended far back in time, an apparent fact which led many workers to either abandon or modify their views on human evolution. One such apostate was Alfred Russell Wallace (1823–1913)." Wallace shares with Darwin the credit for having discovered evolution by natural selection.

Darwin thought Wallace was committing heresy of the worst sort. But Spencer noted that Wallace's challenge to evolutionary doctrine "lost some of its potency as well as a few of its supporters when news began circulating of the discovery of a remarkable hominid fossil in Java." Considering the striking way in which the Java man fossils were employed in discrediting and suppressing evidence for the great antiquity of the modern human form, we shall now review their history.

EUGENE DUBOIS AND PITHECANTHROPUS

Past the Javanese village of Trinil, a road ends on a high bank overlooking the Solo River. Here one encounters a small stone monument, marked with an arrow pointing toward a sand pit on the opposite bank. The monument also carries a cryptic German inscription, "P.e. 175 m ONO 1891/93," indicating that *Pithecanthropus erectus* was found 175 meters east northeast from this spot, during the years 1891–1893.

The discoverer of *Pithecanthropus erectus* was Eugene Dubois, born in Eijsden, Holland, in 1858, the year before Darwin published *The Origin of Species*. Although the son of devout Dutch Catholics, he was fascinated by the idea of evolution, especially as it applied to the question of human origins.

155

Figure 8.1. *Pithecanthropus* skullcap discovered by Eugene Dubois in 1891 in Java.

After studying medicine and natural history at the University of Amsterdam, Dubois became a lecturer in anatomy at the Royal Normal School in 1886. But his real love remained evolution. Dubois knew that Darwin's opponents were constantly pointing out the almost complete lack of fossil evidence for human evolution. He carefully studied the principal evidence then available—the bones of Neanderthal specimens. These were regarded by most authorities (among them Thomas Huxley) as too close to the modern human type to be truly intermediate between fossil apes and modern humans. The German scientist Ernst Haeckel had, however, predicted that the bones of a real missing link would eventually be found. Haeckel even commissioned a painting of the creature, whom he called *Pithecanthropus* (in Greek, *pitheko* means ape, and *anthropus* means man). Influenced by Haeckel's vision of *Pithecanthropus,* Dubois resolved to someday find the apeman's bones.

Mindful of Darwin's suggestion that humanity's forbearers lived in "some warm, forest-clad land," Dubois became convinced *Pithecanthropus* would be found in Africa or the East Indies. Because he could more easily reach the East Indies, then under Dutch rule, he decided to journey there and begin his quest. He applied first to private philanthropists and the government, requesting financing for a scientific expedition, but was turned down. He then accepted an appointment as an army surgeon in Sumatra. With his friends doubting his sanity, he gave up his comfortable post as a college lecturer and with his young wife set sail for the East Indies in December 1887 on the *S. S. Princess Amalie.*

In 1888, Dubois found himself stationed at a small military hospital in the interior of Sumatra. In his spare time, and using his own funds, Dubois investigated Sumatran caves, finding fossils of rhino and elephant, and the teeth of an orangutan, but no hominid remains.

In 1890, after suffering an attack of malaria, Dubois was placed on inactive duty and transferred from Sumatra to Java, where the climate was somewhat drier and healthier. He and his wife set up housekeeping in Tulungagung, on eastern Java's southern coast.

During the dry season of 1891, Dubois conducted excavations on the bank of the Solo River in central Java, near the village of Trinil. His laborers took out many fossil animal bones. In September, they turned up a particularly interesting item—

a primate tooth, apparently a third upper right molar, or wisdom tooth. Dubois, believing he had come upon the remains of an extinct giant chimpanzee, ordered his laborers to concentrate their work around the place where the tooth had turned up. In October,

Figure 8.2. Thighbone found by Eugene Dubois at Trinil, Java. Dubois attributed it to *Pithecanthropus erectus*.

they found what appeared to be a turtle shell. But when Dubois inspected it, he saw it was actually the top part of a cranium (Figure 8.1), heavily fossilized and having the same color as the volcanic soil. The fragment's most distinctive feature was the large, protruding ridge over the eye sockets, leading Dubois to suspect the cranium had belonged to an ape. The onset of the rainy season then brought an end to the year's digging. In a report published in the government mining bulletin, Dubois made no suggestion that his fossils belonged to a creature transitional to humans.

In August 1892, Dubois returned to Trinil and found there—among bones of deer, rhinoceroses, hyenas, crocodiles, pigs, tigers, and extinct elephants—a fossilized humanlike femur (thighbone). This femur (Figure 8.2) was found about 45 feet from where the skullcap and molar were dug up. Later another molar was found about 10 feet from the skullcap. Dubois believed the molars, skull, and femur all came from the same animal, which he still considered to be an extinct giant chimpanzee.

In 1963, Richard Carrington stated in his book *A Million Years of Man*: "Dubois was at first inclined to regard his skull cap and teeth as belonging to a chimpanzee, in spite of the fact that there is no known evidence that this ape or any of its ancestors ever lived in Asia. But on refection, and after corresponding with the great Ernst Haeckel, Professor of Zoology at the University of Jena, he declared them to belong to a creature which seemed admirably suited to the role of the 'missing link.'" We have not found any correspondence Dubois may have exchanged with Haeckel, but if further research were to turn it up, it would add considerably to our knowledge of the circumstances surrounding the birth of *Pithecanthropus erectus*. Obviously, both men had a substantial emotional and intellectual stake in finding an ape-man specimen. Haeckel, on hearing from Dubois of his discovery, telegraphed this message: "From the inventor of *Pithecanthropus* to his happy discoverer!"

It was only in 1894 that Dubois finally published a complete report of his discovery. Therein he wrote: "*Pithecanthropus* is the transitional form which, in accordance with the doctrine of evolution, must have existed between man and the anthropoids." *Pithecanthropus erectus,* we should carefully note, had itself undergone an evolutionary transition within the mind of Dubois, from fossil chimpanzee to transitional anthropoid.

What factors, other than Haeckel's influence, led Dubois to consider his specimen transitional between fossil apes and modern humans? Dubois found that the volume of the *Pithecanthropus* skull was in the range of 800–1000 cubic centimeters. Modern apes average 500 cubic centimeters, while modern human skulls average 1400 cubic centimeters, thus placing the Trinil skull midway between them. To Dubois, this indicated an evolutionary relationship. But logically speaking, one could have creatures with different sizes of brains without having to posit an evolutionary progression from smaller to larger. Furthermore, in the Pleistocene many mammalian species were represented by forms much larger than today's. Thus the *Pithecanthropus* skull might belong not to a transitional anthropoid but to an exceptionally large Middle Pleistocene gibbon, with a skull bigger than that of modern gibbons.

Today, anthropologists still routinely describe an evolutionary progression of hominid skulls, increasing in size with the passage of time—from Early Pleistocene *Australopithecus* (first discovered in 1924), to Middle Pleistocene Java man (now known as *Homo erectus*), to Late Pleistocene *Homo sapiens sapiens*. But the sequence is preserved only at the cost of eliminating skulls that disrupt it. For example, the Castenedolo skull, discussed in Chapter 7, is older than that of Java man but is larger in cranial capacity. In fact, it is fully human in size and morphology. Even one such exception is sufficient to invalidate the whole proposed evolutionary sequence.

Dubois observed that although the Trinil skull was very apelike in some of its features, such as the prominent brow ridges, the thighbone was almost human. This indicated that *Pithecanthropus* had walked upright, hence the species designation *erectus*. It is important, however, to keep in mind that the femur of *Pithecanthropus erectus* was found fully 45 feet from the place where the skull was unearthed, in a stratum containing hundreds of other animal bones. This circumstance makes doubtful the claim that both the thighbone and the skull actually belonged to the same creature or even the same species.

When Dubois's reports began reaching Europe, they received much attention. Haeckel, of course, was among those celebrating *Pithecanthropus* as the strongest proof to date of human evolution. "Now the state of affairs in this great battle for truth has been radically altered by Eugene Dubois's discovery of the fossil *Pithecanthropus erectus*," proclaimed the triumphant Haeckel. "He has actually provided us with the bones of the ape-man I had postulated. This find is more important to anthropology than the much-lauded discovery of the X-ray was to physics." There is an almost religious tone of prophecy and fulfillment in Haeckel's remarks. But Haeckel had a history of overstating physiological evidence to support the doctrine of evolution. An academic court at the

University of Jena once found him guilty of falsifying drawings of embryos of various animals in order to demonstrate his particular view of the origin of species.

In 1895, Dubois decided to return to Europe to display his *Pithecanthropus* to what he was certain would be an admiring and supportive audience of scientists. Soon after arriving, he exhibited his specimens and presented reports at the Third International Congress of Zoology at Leyden, Holland. Although some of the scientists present at the Congress were, like Haeckel, anxious to support the discovery as a fossil ape-man, others thought it merely an ape, while still others challenged the idea that the bones belonged to the same individual.

Dubois exhibited his treasured bones at Paris, London, and Berlin. In December of 1895, experts from around the world gathered at the Berlin Society for Anthropology, Ethnology, and Prehistory to pass judgement on Dubois's *Pithecanthropus* specimens. The president of the Society, Dr. Virchow, refused to chair the meeting. In the controversy-ridden discussion that followed, the Swiss anatomist Kollman said the creature was an ape. Virchow himself said the femur was fully human, and further stated: "The skull has a deep suture between the low vault and the upper edge of the orbits. Such a suture is found only in apes, not in man. Thus the skull must belong to an ape. In my opinion this creature was an animal, a giant gibbon, in fact. The thigh-bone has not the slightest connection with the skull." This opinion contrasted strikingly with that of Haeckel and others, who remained convinced that Dubois's Java man was a genuine human ancestor.

THE SELENKA EXPEDITION

To resolve some of the questions surrounding the *Pithecanthropus* fossils and their discovery, Emil Selenka, professor of zoology at Munich University in Germany, prepared a full-fledged expedition to Java, but he died before it departed. His wife, Professor Lenore Selenka, took over the effort and conducted excavations at Trinil in the years 1907–1908, employing 75 laborers to hunt for more *Pithecanthropus erectus* fossils. Altogether, Selenka's team of geologists and paleontologists sent back to Europe 43 boxes of fossils, but they included not a single new fragment of *Pithecanthropus*. The expedition did, however, find in the Trinil strata signs of a human presence—splintered animal bones, charcoal, and foundations of hearths. Signs like this led Lenore Selenka to conclude that humans and *Pithecanthropus erectus* were contemporary. The implications of all this for an evolutionary interpretation of Dubois's *Pithecanthropus* specimens were, and still are, unsettling.

Furthermore, in 1924 George Grant MacCurdy, a Yale professor of anthropology, wrote in his book *Human Origins:* "The Selenka expedition of 1907–

1908 . . . secured a tooth which is said by Walkoff to be definitely human. It is a third molar from a neighboring stream bed and from deposits older (Pliocene) than those in which *Pithecanthropus erectus* was found."

DUBOIS WITHDRAWS FROM THE BATTLE

Meanwhile, the status of Dubois's ape-man remained controversial. Surveying the range of opinion about *Pithecanthropus,* Berlin zoologist Wilhelm Dames gathered statements from several scientists: three said *Pithecanthropus* was an ape, five said it was human, six said it was an ape-man, six said it was a missing link, and two said it was a link between the missing link and man.

But while many scientists maintained their doubts, others followed Haeckel in hailing Java man as stunning proof of Darwin's theory. Some used Java man to discredit evidence for a fully human presence in the Tertiary. As we learned in Chapter 5, W. H. Holmes dismissed discoveries of stone tools in the Tertiary auriferous gravels of California because "they implied a human race older by at least one-half than *Pithecanthropus erectus* of Dubois, which may be regarded as an incipient form of human creature only."

At a certain point, Dubois became completely disappointed with the mixed reception the scientific community gave to his *Pithecanthropus.* He stopped showing his specimens. Some say that he kept them for some time beneath the floorboards in his home. In any case, they remained hidden from view for some 25 years, until 1932.

During and after the period of withdrawal, the controversies concerning *Pithecanthropus* continued. Marcellin Boule, director of the Institute of Human Paleontology in Paris, reported, as had other scientists, that the layer in which the *Pithecanthropus* skullcap and femur were said to have been found contained numerous fossil bones of fish, reptiles, and mammals. Why, therefore, should anyone believe the skullcap and femur came from the same individual or even the same species? Boule, like Virchow, stated that the femur was identical to that of a modern human whereas the skullcap resembled that of an ape, possibly a large gibbon. In 1941, Dr. F. Weidenreich, director of the Cenozoic Research Laboratory at Beijing Union Medical College, also stated that there was no justification for attributing the femur and the skullcap to the same individual. The femur, Weidenreich said, was very similar to that of a modern human, and its original position in the strata was not securely established. Modern researchers have employed chemical dating techniques to determine whether or not the original *Pithecanthropus* skull and femur were both contemporary with the Middle Pleistocene Trinil fauna, but the results were inconclusive.

MORE FEMURS

The belated revelation that more femurs had been discovered in Java further complicated the issue. In 1932, Dr. Bernsen and Eugene Dubois recovered three femurs from a box of fossil mammalian bones in the Leiden Museum in the Netherlands. The box contained specimens said to have been excavated in 1900 by Dubois's assistant, Mr. Kriele, from the same Trinil deposits on the left bank of the Solo river that had yielded Dubois's first Java man finds. Dr. Bernsen died very shortly thereafter, without providing further information about the details of this museum discovery.

Dubois stated that he was not present when the femurs were taken out by Kriele. Therefore the exact location of the femurs in the excavation, which was 75 meters (246 feet) long by 6–14 meters (20–46 feet) wide, was unknown to him. According to standard paleontological procedures, this uncertainty greatly reduces the value of the bones as evidence of any sort. Nevertheless, authorities later assigned these femurs to a particular stratum without mentioning the dubious circumstances of their discovery in boxes of fossils over 30 years after they were originally excavated. In addition to the three femurs found by Kriele, two more femoral fragments turned up in the Leiden Museum.

The existence of the additional femurs has important implications for the original *Pithecanthropus* skull and femur found by Dubois in the 1890s. The apelike skull and humanlike femur were found at a great distance from each other, but Dubois assigned them to the same creature. He suggested that the bones were found separated because *Pithecanthropus* had been dismembered by a crocodile. But if you throw in more humanlike femurs, that argument loses a great deal of its force. Where were the other skulls? Were they apelike skulls, like the one found? And what about the skull that was found? Does it really go with the femur that was found 45 feet away? Or does it belong with one of the other femurs that later turned up? Or maybe with a femur of an entirely different sort?

ARE THE TRINIL FEMURS MODERN HUMAN?

In 1973, M. H. Day and T. I. Molleson concluded that "the gross anatomy, radiological [X-ray] anatomy, and microscopical anatomy of the Trinil femora does not distinguish them significantly from modern human femora." They also said that *Homo erectus* femurs from China and Africa are anatomically similar to each other, and distinct from those of Trinil.

In 1984, Richard Leakey and other scientists discovered an almost complete skeleton of *Homo erectus* in Kenya. Examining the leg bones, these scientists found that the femurs differed substantially from those of modern human beings.

About the Java discoveries, the scientists stated: "From Trinil, Indonesia, there are several fragmentary and one complete (but pathological) femora. Despite the fact that it was these specimens that led to the species name [*Pithecanthropus erectus*], there are doubts as to whether they are *H. erectus* with the most recent consensus being that they probably are not."

In summary, modern researchers say the Trinil femurs are not like those of *Homo erectus* but are instead like those of modern *Homo sapiens*. What is to be made of these revelations? The Java thighbones have traditionally been taken as evidence of an ape-man (*Pithecanthropus erectus,* now called *Homo erectus*) existing around 800,000 years ago in the Middle Pleistocene. Now it appears we can accept them as evidence for anatomically modern humans existing 800,000 years ago.

Some have said that the femurs were mixed in from higher levels. Of course, if one insists that the humanlike Trinil femurs were mixed in from higher levels, then why not the *Pithecanthropus* skull as well? That would eliminate entirely the original Java man find, long advertised as solid proof of human evolution.

Indeed, late in his life Eugene Dubois himself concluded that the skullcap of his beloved *Pithecanthropus* belonged to a large gibbon, an ape not thought by evolutionists to be closely related to humans. But the heretofore skeptical scientific community was not about to say good-bye to Java man, for by this time *Pithecanthropus* was firmly entrenched in the ancestry of modern *Homo sapiens*. Dubois's denials were dismissed as the whims of a cantankerous old man. If anything, the scientific community wanted to remove any remaining doubts about the nature and authenticity of Java man. This, it was hoped, would fortify the whole concept of Darwinian evolution, of which human evolution was the most highly publicized and controversial aspect.

Visitors to museums around the world still find models of the Trinil skullcap and femur portrayed as belonging to the same Middle Pleistocene *Homo erectus* individual. In 1984, the much-advertised *Ancestors* exhibit, at the Museum of Natural History in New York, brought together from around the world the major fossil evidence for human evolution, including prominently displayed casts of the Trinil skullcap and femur.

THE HEIDELBERG JAW

In addition to Dubois's Java man discoveries, further evidence relating to human evolution turned up in the form of the Heidelberg jaw. On October 21, 1907, Daniel Hartmann, a workman at a sand pit at Mauer, near Heidelberg, Germany, discovered a large jawbone at the bottom of the excavation, at a depth of 82 feet. The workmen were on the lookout for bones, and many other nonhuman fossils had already been found there and turned over to the geology department at the nearby University of Heidelberg. The workman then brought the jaw (Figure 8.3) over to J. Rüsch, the owner of the pit, who sent a message to Dr. Otto Schoetensack: "For twenty long years you have sought some trace of early man in my pit . . . yesterday we found it. A lower jaw belonging to early man has been found on the floor of the pit, in a very good state of preservation."

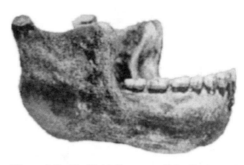

Figure 8.3. The Heidelberg mandible, discovered in 1907 at Mauer, near Heidelberg, Germany.

Professor Schoetensack designated the creature *Homo heidelbergensis,* dating it using the accompanying fossils to the Günz-Mindel interglacial period. In 1972, David Pilbeam said the Heidelberg jaw "appears to date from the Mindel glaciation, and its age is somewhere between 250,000 and 450,000 years."

The German anthropologist Johannes Ranke, an opponent of evolution, wrote in the 1920s that the Heidelberg jaw belonged to a representative of *Homo sapiens* rather than an apelike predecessor. Even today, the Heidelberg jaw remains somewhat of a morphological mystery. The thickness of the mandible and the apparent lack of a chin are features common in *Homo erectus*. But mandibles of some modern Australian aboriginals are also massive compared to jaws of modern Europeans and have chins that are less well developed.

According to Frank E. Poirier (1977), the teeth in the Heidelberg jaw are closer in size to those of modern *Homo sapiens* than those of Asian *Homo erectus* (Java man and Beijing man). T. W. Phenice of Michigan State University wrote in 1972 that "the teeth are remarkably like those of modern man in almost every respect, including size and cusp patterns." Modern opinion thus confirms Ranke, who wrote in 1922: "The teeth are typically human."

Another European fossil generally attributed to *Homo erectus* is the Vértesszöllös occipital fragment, from a Middle Pleistocene site in Hungary. The morphology of the Vértesszöllös occipital is even more puzzling than that of the Heidelberg jaw. David Pilbeam wrote in 1972: "The occipital bone does not resemble that of *H. erectus,* or even archaic man, but instead that of earliest modern man. Such forms are dated elsewhere as no older than 100,000 years." Pilbeam believed the Vértesszöllös occipital to be approximately the same age as the Heidelberg jaw, between 250,000 and 450,000 years old. If the Vértesszöllös occipital is modern in form, it helps confirm the genuineness of anatomically modern human skeletal remains of similar age found in England at Ipswich and Galley Hill (Chapter 7).

Returning to the Heidelberg jaw, we note that the circumstances of discovery were less than perfect. If an anatomically modern human jaw had been found by a workman in the same sand pit, it would have been subjected to merciless criticism and judged recent. After all, no scientists were present at the moment of discovery. But the Heidelberg jaw, because it fits, however imperfectly, within the bounds of evolutionary expectations, has been granted a dispensation.

FURTHER JAVA MAN DISCOVERIES BY VON KOENIGSWALD

In 1929, another ancient human ancestor was discovered, this time in China. Eventually, scientists would group Java man, Heidelberg man, and Beijing man together as examples of *Homo erectus,* the direct ancestor of *Homo sapiens.* But initially, the common features and evolutionary status of the Indonesian, Chinese, and German fossils were not obvious, and paleoanthropologists felt it particularly necessary to clarify the status of Java man.

In 1930, Gustav Heinrich Ralph von Koenigswald of the Geological Survey of the Netherlands East Indies was dispatched to Java. In his book *Meeting Prehistoric Man,* von Koenigswald wrote, "Despite the discovery of Pekin [Beijing] man, it remained necessary to find a further *Pithecanthropus* sufficiently complete to prove the human character of this disputed fossil."

Von Koenigswald arrived in Java in January 1931. In August of that same year, one of von Koenigswald's colleagues found some hominid fossils at Ngandong on the River Solo. Von Koenigswald classified the Solo specimens as a Javanese variety of Neanderthal, appearing later in time than *Pithecanthropus erectus.*

Gradually, the history of human ancestors in Java seemed to be clearing up, but more work was needed. In 1934, von Koenigswald journeyed to Sangiran, a site west of Trinil on the Solo River. He took with him several Javanese workers, including his trained collector, Atma, who also served as von Koenigswald's cook and laundryman in the field.

Von Koenigswald wrote: "There was great rejoicing in the *kampong* over our arrival. The men gathered all the jaws and teeth they could lay hands on and offered to sell them to us. Even the women and girls, who are generally so retiring, took part." When one considers that most of the finds attributed to von Koenigswald were actually made by local villagers or native collectors, who were paid by the piece, the scene described cannot but cause some degree of uneasiness.

At the end of 1935, in the midst of the worldwide economic depression, von Koenigswald's position with the Geological Survey in Java was terminated. Undeterred, von Koenigswald kept his servant Atma and others working at Sangiran, financing their activities with contributions from his wife and colleagues in Java.

Uncovered during this period was what appeared to be the fossilized right half of the upper jaw of an adult *Pithecanthropus erectus.* An examination of many reports by von Koenigswald has failed to turn up any description by him of exactly how this specimen was found. But in 1975 the British researcher K. P. Oakley and his associates stated that the fossil was found in 1936 on the surface of exposed lake deposits east of Kalijoso in central Java by collectors employed by von Koenigswald. Because the jaw was found on the surface, its exact age is uncertain.

An anthropologist might say that this jaw fragment exhibits the features of *Homo erectus,* as *Pithecanthropus erectus* is now known. Hence it must have been deposited at least several hundred thousand years ago, despite the fact that it was found on the surface. But what if there existed in geologically recent times, or even today, a rare species of hominid having physical features similar to those of *Homo erectus?* In that case one could not automatically assign a date to a given bone based on the physical features of that bone. In Chapter 11 can be found evidence suggesting that a creature like *Homo erectus* has lived in recent times and in fact may be alive today.

During the difficult year of 1936, in the course of which the fossil jaw discussed above was uncovered, the unemployed von Koenigswald received a remarkable visitor—Pierre Teilhard de Chardin, whom von Koenigswald himself had invited to come and inspect his discoveries in Java. Teilhard de Chardin, a world-famous archeologist and Jesuit priest, had been working in Peking (now Beijing), where he had participated in the Peking man excavations at Choukoutien (now Zhoukoudian).

During his visit to Java, Teilhard de Chardin advised von Koenigswald to write to John C. Merriam, the president of the Carnegie Institution. Von Koenigswald did so, informing Merriam that he was on the verge of making important new *Pithecanthropus* finds.

Merriam responded positively to von Koenigswald's letter, inviting him to come to Philadelphia in March 1937 to attend the Symposium on Early Man, sponsored by the Carnegie Institution. There von Koenigswald joined many of the world's leading scientists working in the field of human prehistory.

One of the central purposes of the meeting was to form an executive committee for the Carnegie Institution's financing of paleoanthropological research. Suddenly, the impoverished von Koenigswald found himself appointed a research associate of the Carnegie Institution and in possession of a large budget.

THE ROLE OF THE CARNEGIE INSTITUTION

Considering the critical role played by private foundations in the financing of research in human evolution, it might be valuable at this point to further consider the motives of the foundations and their executives. The Carnegie Institution and

John C. Merriam provide an excellent case study. In Chapter 10, we will examine the Rockefeller Foundation's role in financing the excavation of Beijing man.

The Carnegie Institution was founded in January 1902 in Washington, D.C., and a revised charter approved by Congress became effective in 1904. The Institution was governed by a board of 24 trustees, with an executive committee meeting throughout the year, and was organized into 12 departments of scientific investigation, including experimental evolution. The Institution also funded the Mt. Wilson Observatory, where the first systematic research leading to the idea that we live in an expanding universe was conducted. Thus the Carnegie Institution was actively involved in two areas, namely evolution and the big bang universe, that lie at the heart of the scientific cosmological vision that has replaced earlier religiously inspired cosmologies.

It is significant that for Andrew Carnegie and others like him, the impulse to charity, traditionally directed toward social welfare, religion, hospitals, and general education, was now being channeled into scientific research, laboratories, and observatories. This reflected the dominant position that science and its world view, including evolution, were coming to occupy in society, particularly within the minds of its wealthiest and most influential members, many of whom saw science as the best hope for human progress.

John C. Merriam, president of the Carnegie Institution, believed that science had "contributed very largely to the building of basic philosophies and beliefs," and his support for von Koenigswald's fossil-hunting expeditions in Java should be seen in this context. A foundation like the Carnegie Institution had the means to use science to influence philosophy and belief by selectively funding certain areas of research and publicizing the results. "The number of matters which might be investigated is infinite," wrote Merriam. "But it is expedient in each period to consider what questions may have largest use in furtherance of knowledge for the benefit to mankind at that particular time."

The question of human evolution satisfied this requirement. "Having spent a considerable part of my life in advancing studies on the history of life," said Merriam, "I have been thoroughly saturated with the idea that evolution, or the principle of continuing growth and development, constitutes one of the most important truths obtained from all knowledge."

By training a paleontologist, Merriam was also by faith a Christian. But his Christianity definitely took a back seat to his science. "My first contact with science," Merriam recalled in a 1931 speech, "was when I came home from grammar school to report to my mother that the teacher had talked to us for fifteen minutes about the idea that the days of creation described in Genesis were long periods of creation and not the days of twenty-four hours. My mother and I held a consultation—she being a Scotch Presbyterian—and agreed that this was rank heresy. But a seed had been sown. I have been backing away from that position through subsequent decades. I realize now that the elements of science, so far as creation is concerned, represent the uncontaminated and unmodified record of what the Creator did."

Having dispensed with scriptural accounts of creation, Merriam managed to turn Darwinian evolution into a kind of religion. At a convocation address at the George Washington University in 1924, Merriam said of evolution, "There is nothing contributing to the support of our lives in a spiritual sense that seems so clearly indispensable as that which makes us look forward to continuing growth or improvement."

He held that science would give man the opportunity to take on a godlike role in guiding that future development. "Research is the means by which man will assist in his own further evolution," said Merriam in a 1925 address to the Carnegie Institution's Board of Trustees. He went on to say: "I believe that if he [man] had open to him a choice between further evolution directed by some Being distant from us, which would merely carry him along with the current; or as an alternative could choose a situation in which that outside power would fix the laws and permit him to use them, man would say, 'I prefer to assume some responsibility in this scheme.'"

"According to the ancient story," Merriam continued, "man was driven from the Garden of Eden lest he might learn too much; he was banished so that he might become master of himself. A flaming sword was placed at the east gate, and he was ordered to work, to till the ground, until he could come to know the value of his strength. He is now learning to plough the fields about him, shaping his life in accordance with the laws of nature. In some distant age a book may be written in which it will be stated that man came at last to a stage where he returned to the Garden, and at the east gate seized the flaming sword, the sword that symbolized control, to carry it as a torch guiding him to the tree of life." Seizing the flaming sword and marching to take control of the tree of life? One wonders if there would be enough room in Eden for both God and a hard-charging scientific superachiever like Merriam.

BACK TO JAVA

Armed with Carnegie grant money, von Koenigswald returned to Java in June of 1937. Immediately upon his arrival, he hired hundreds of natives and sent them out in force to find more fossils. More fossils were found. But almost all of them were jaw and skull fragments that came from poorly specified locations on the surface near Sangiran. This makes it difficult to ascertain their correct ages.

During the course of most of the Sangiran finds, von Koenigswald remained at Bandung, about 200 miles away, although he would sometimes travel to the fossil beds after being notified of a discovery.

In the fall of 1937, one of von Koenigswald's collectors, Atma, mailed him a temporal bone that apparently belonged to a thick, fossilized, hominid cranium. This specimen was said to have been discovered near the bank of a river named the Kali Tjemoro, at the point where it breaks through the sandstone of the Kabuh formation at Sangiran.

Von Koenigswald took the night train to central Java and arrived at the site the next morning. "We mobilized the maximum number of collectors," stated von Koenigswald. "I had brought the fragment back with me, showed it round, and promised 10 cents for every additional piece belonging to the skull. That was a lot of money, for an ordinary tooth brought in only 1/2 cent or 1 cent. We had to keep the price so low because we were compelled to pay cash for every find; for when a Javanese has found three teeth he just won't collect any more until these three teeth have been sold. Consequently we were forced to buy an enormous mass of broken and worthless dental remains and throw them away in Bandung—if we had left them at Sangiran they would have been offered to us for sale again and again."

The highly motivated crew quickly turned up the desired skull fragments. Von Koenigswald would later recall: "There, on the banks of a small river, nearly dry at that season, lay the fragments of a skull, washed out of the sandstones and conglomerates that contained the Trinil fauna. With a whole bunch of excited natives, we crept up the hillside, collecting every bone fragment we could discover. I had promised the sum of ten cents for every fragment belonging to that human skull. But I had underestimated the 'big-business' ability of my brown collectors. The result was terrible! Behind my back they broke the larger fragments into pieces in order to increase the number of sales! . . . We collected about 40 fragments, of which 30 belonged to the skull. . . . They formed a fine, nearly complete *Pithecanthropus* skullcap. Now, at last, we had him!"

How did von Koenigswald know that the fragments found on the surface of a hill really belonged, as he claimed, to the Middle Pleistocene Kabuh formation? Perhaps the native collectors found a skull elsewhere and broke it apart, sending one piece to von Koenigswald and scattering the rest by the banks of the Kali Tjemoro.

Von Koenigswald constructed a skull from the 30 fragments he had collected, calling it *Pithecanthropus II*, and sent a preliminary report to Dubois. The skull was much more complete than the original skullcap found by Dubois at Trinil. Von Koenigswald had always thought that Dubois had reconstructed his *Pithecanthropus* skull with too low a profile, and believed the *Pithecanthropus* skull fragments he had just found allowed a more humanlike interpretation. Dubois, who by this time had concluded his original *Pithecanthropus* was merely a fossil ape, disagreed with von Koenigswald's reconstruction and published an accusation that he had indulged in fakery. He later retracted this indictment and said that the mistakes he saw in von

Koenigswald's reconstruction were probably not deliberate.

But von Koenigswald's position was gaining support. In 1938, Franz Weidenreich, supervisor of the Beijing man excavations at Zhoukoudian, stated in the prestigious journal *Nature* that von Koenigswald's new finds had definitely established *Pithecanthropus* as a human precursor and not a gibbon as claimed by Dubois.

In 1941, one of von Koenigswald's native collectors, at Sangiran, sent to him, at Bandung, a fragment of a gigantic lower jaw. According to von Koenigswald, it displayed the unmistakable features of a human ancestor's jaw. He named the jaw's owner *Meganthropus palaeojavanicus* (giant man of ancient Java) because the jaw was twice the size of a typical modern human jaw.

A careful search of original reports has not revealed a description of the exact location at which this jaw was found, or who discovered it. If von Koenigswald did report the exact circumstances of this find then it is a well-kept secret. He discussed *Meganthropus* in at least three reports; however, in none of these did he inform the reader of the details of the fossil's original location. All he said was that it came from the Putjangan formation, but no further information was supplied. Hence all we really know for certain is that some unnamed collector sent a jaw fragment to von Koenigswald. Its age, from a strictly scientific standpoint, remains a mystery.

Meganthropus, in the opinion of von Koenigswald, was a giant offshoot from the main line of human evolution. Von Koenigswald had also found some large humanlike fossil teeth, which he attributed to an even larger creature called *Gigantopithecus*. According to von Koenigswald, *Gigantopithecus* was a large and relatively recent ape. But Weidenreich, after examining the *Meganthropus* jaws and the *Gigantopithecus* teeth, came up with another theory. He proposed that both creatures were direct human ancestors. According to Weidenreich, *Homo sapiens* evolved from *Gigantopithecus* by way of *Meganthropus* and *Pithecanthropus*. Each species was smaller than the next. Most modern authorities, however, consider *Gigantopithecus* to be a variety of ape, living in the Middle to Early Pleistocene, and not directly related to humans. The *Meganthropus* jaws are now thought to be much more like those of Java man (*Homo erectus*) than von Koenigswald originally believed. In 1973, T. Jacob suggested that *Meganthropus* fossils might be classified as *Australopithecus*. This is intriguing, because according to standard opinion, *Australopithecus* never left its African home.

LATER DISCOVERIES IN JAVA

Meganthropus was the last major discovery reported by von Koenigswald, but the search for more bones of Java man has continued up to the present. These later finds, reported by P. Marks, T. Jacob, S. Sartono, and others, are uniformly accepted as evidence for *Homo erectus* in the Javanese Middle and Early

Pleistocene. Like the discoveries of von Koenigswald, these fossils were almost all found on the surface by native collectors or farmers.

For example, T. Jacob reported that in August 1963 an Indonesian farmer discovered fragments of a fossilized skull in the Sangiran area while working in a field. When assembled, these skull fragments formed what appeared to be a skull similar to the type that is designated as *Homo erectus*. Although Jacob asserted that this skullcap was from the Middle Pleistocene Kabuh formation, he did not state the exact position of the fragments when found. All we really know is that a farmer discovered some fossil skull fragments that were most likely on or close to the surface.

In 1973, Jacob made this interesting remark about Sangiran, where all of the later Java *Homo erectus* finds were made: "The site seems to be still promising, but presents special problems. . . . This is mainly due to the site being inhabited by people, many of whom are collectors who had been trained in identifying important fossils. Chief collectors always try to get the most out of the Primate fossils found accidentally by primary discoverers. In addition, they may not report the exact site of the find, lest they lose one potential source of income. Occasionally, they may not sell all the fragments found on the first purchase, but try to keep a few pieces to sell at a higher price at a later opportunity."

Nevertheless, the Sangiran fossils are accepted as genuine. If anomalously old human fossils were found in situations like this, they would be subjected to merciless criticism. As always, our point is that a double standard should not be employed in the evaluation of paleoanthropological evidence—an impossibly strict standard for anomalous evidence and an exceedingly lenient standard for acceptable evidence.

In order to clear up uncertainties, letters were written in 1985 to both S. Sartono and to T. Jacob for further information about discoveries reported by them from Java. No answers were received..

CHEMICAL AND RADIOMETRIC DATING OF THE JAVA FINDS

We shall now discuss issues related to the potassium-argon dating of the formations yielding hominid fossils in Java, as well as attempts to date the fossils themselves by various chemical and radiometric methods.

The Kabuh formation at Trinil, where Dubois made his original Java man finds, has been given a potassium-argon age of 800,000 years. Other finds in Java came from the Djetis beds of the Putjangan formation. According to T. Jacob, the Djetis beds of the Putjangan formation near Modjokerto yielded an Early Pleistocene potassium-argon date of about 1.9 million years. The date of 1.9 million years is significant for the following reasons. As we have seen, many *Homo erectus* fossils (previously designated *Pithecanthropus* and *Meganthropus*) have been assigned to the Djetis beds. If these fossils are given an age of 1.9 million years, this makes them older than the oldest African *Homo erectus* finds, which are about 1.6 million years old. According to standard views, *Homo erectus* evolved in Africa and did not migrate out of Africa until about 1 million years ago.

Also, some researchers have suggested that von Koenigswald's *Meganthropus* might be classified as *Australopithecus*. If one accepts this opinion, this means that Javan representatives of *Australopithecus* arrived from Africa before 1.9 million years ago or that *Australopithecus* evolved separately in Java. Both hypotheses are in conflict with standard views on human evolution.

It should be kept in mind, however, that the potassium-argon technique that gave the 1.9-million-year date is not foolproof. T. Jacob and G. Curtis, who attempted to date most of the hominid sites in Java, found it difficult to obtain meaningful dates from most samples. In other words, dates were obtained, but they deviated so greatly from what was expected that Jacob and Curtis had to attribute the unsatisfactory results to contaminants. In 1978, G. J. Bartstra reported a potassium-argon age of less than 1 million years for the Djetis beds.

We have seen that the Trinil femurs are indistinguishable from those of modern humans and distinct from those of *Homo erectus*. This has led some to suggest that the Trinil femurs do not belong with the *Pithecanthropus* skull and were perhaps mixed into the early Middle Pleistocene Trinil bone bed from higher levels. Another possibility is that anatomically modern humans were living alongside ape-man-like creatures during the early Middle Pleistocene in Java. In light of the evidence presented in this book, this would not be out of the question.

The fluorine content test has often been used to determine if bones from the same site are of the same age. Bones absorb fluorine from groundwaters, and thus if bones contain similar percentages of fluorine (relative to the bones' phosphate content) this suggests such bones have been buried for the same amount of time.

In a 1973 report, M. H. Day and T. I. Molleson analyzed the Trinil skullcap and femurs and found they contained roughly the same ratio of fluorine to phosphate. Middle Pleistocene mammalian fossils at Trinil contained a fluorine-to-phosphate ratio similar to that of the skullcap and femurs. Day and Molleson stated that their results apparently indicated the contemporaneity of the calotte and femora with the Trinil fauna.

If the Trinil femurs are distinct from those of *Homo erectus* and identical to those of *Homo sapiens sapiens,* as Day and Molleson reported, then the fluorine content of the femurs is consistent with the view that anatomically modern humans existed in Java during the early Middle Pleistocene, about 800,000 years ago.

Day and Molleson suggested that Holocene (recent) bones from the Trinil site might, like the Java man fossils, also have fluorine-to-phosphate ratios similar to those of the Middle Pleistocene animal bones, making the fluorine test useless here. K. P. Oakley, the originator of the fluorine content testing method, pointed out that the rate of fluorine absorption in volcanic areas, such as Java, tends to be quite erratic, allowing bones of widely differing ages to have similar fluorine contents. This could not be directly demonstrated at the Trinil site, because there only the Middle Pleistocene beds contain fossils.

Day and Molleson showed that Holocene and Late Pleistocene beds at other sites in Java contained bones with fluorine-to-phosphate ratios similar to those of the Trinil bones. But they admitted that the fluorine-to-phosphate ratios of bones from other sites "would not be directly comparable" with those of bones from the Trinil site. This is because the fluorine absorption rate of bone depends upon factors that can vary from site to site. Such factors include the groundwater's fluorine content, the groundwater's rate of flow, the nature of the sediments, and the type of bone.

Therefore, the fluorine content test results reported by Day and Molleson remain consistent with (but are not proof of) an early Middle Pleistocene age of about 800,000 years for the anatomically modern human Trinil femurs.

A nitrogen content test was also performed on the Trinil bones. Dubois had boiled the skullcap and the first femur in animal glue, the protein of which contains nitrogen. Day and Molleson attempted to correct for this by pre-treating the samples in order to remove soluble nitrogen before analysis. Results showed that the Trinil bones had very little nitrogen left in them. This is consistent with all of the bones being of the same early Middle Pleistocene age, although Day and Molleson did report that nitrogen in bone is lost so rapidly in Java that even Holocene bones often have no nitrogen.

MISLEADING PRESENTATIONS OF THE JAVA MAN EVIDENCE

Most books dealing with the subject of human evolution present what appears at first glance to be an impressive weight of evidence for *Homo erectus* in Java between 0.5 and 2.0 million years ago. One such book is *The Fossil Evidence for Human Evolution* (1978), by W. E. Le Gros Clark, professor of anatomy at Oxford University, and Bernard G. Campbell, adjunct professor of anthropology at the University of California at Los Angeles. An impressive table showing discoveries of *Homo erectus* is presented in their book. These discoveries (Table 8.1) have been used widely to support the belief that man has evolved from an apelike being.

T3 is the femur found by Dubois at a distance of 45 feet from the original cranium, T2. We have already discussed how unjustified it is to assign these two bones to the same individual. Yet ignoring many important facts, Le Gros Clark and Campbell stated that "the accumulation of evidence speaks so strongly for their natural association that this has become generally accepted."

TABLE 8.1

Fossil Hominids from Java

Stratigraphic Unit	Sites	Age Bracket
Trinil (Kabuh Formation)	Sangiran S2 Adult female calotte (1937) S3 Juvenile calotte (1938) S8 Right mandible (1952) S10 Adult male calotte (1963) S12 Old male calotte (1965) S15 Maxilla (1969) S17 Cranium (1969) S21 Mandible (1973) Trinil T2 Calotte (1892) = *Pithecanthropus* T3,T6,T7,T8,T9 Femora Kedung Brubus KB1 Right juvenile mandible (1890)	0.7–1.3 million years, (potassium-argon date of about .83 million years)
Djetis (Putjangan Formation)	Sangiran S1a Right maxilla (1936) S1b Right mandible (1936) S4 Adult male calvaria & maxilla (1938–39) = *P. robustus* S5 Right mandible (1939) = *P. dubius* S6 Right mandible (1941) = *Meganthropus* S9 Right mandible (1960) S22 Maxilla, mandible (1974) Modjokerto M1 Child, 7 years, calvaria (1936)	1.3–2.0 million years, (potassium-argon date of about 1.9 million years)

This table is reproduced from a standard text on human evolution. Calotte, cranium, and calvaria mean skull, mandible means lower jaw, maxilla means upper jaw, and femora means thighbones.

T6, T7, T8, and T9 are the femurs found in boxes of fossils in Holland over 30 years after they were originally excavated in Java. Le Gros Clark and Campbell apparently ignored Dubois's statement that he himself did not excavate them, and that the original location of the femurs was unknown. Furthermore, von Koenigswald stated that the femurs were from Dubois's general collection, which contained fossils from "various sites and various ages which are very inadequately distinguished because some of the labels got lost." Nevertheless, Le Gros Clark and Campbell assumed that these femurs came from the Trinil beds of the Kabuh formation. But Day and Molleson observed: "If the rigorous criteria that are demanded in modern excavations were applied to all of the Trinil material subsequent to the calotte and Femur I, it would all be rejected as of doubtful provenance and unknown stratigraphy."

Fossil M1 and fossils S1a through S6 are those discovered by Javanese native collectors employed by von Koenigswald. Only one of them (M1) was reported to have been discovered buried in the stratum to which it is assigned, and even this report is subject to question. The remaining fossils of the S series are the ones reported by Marks, Sartono, and Jacob, and the majority of these were surface finds by villagers and farmers, who sold the fossils, perhaps by way of middlemen, to the scientists. One familiar with the way these specimens were found can only wonder at the intellectual dishonesty manifest in Table 8.1, which gives the impression that the fossils were all found in strata of definite age.

Le Gros Clark and Campbell noted that the real location of many of von Koenigswald's finds was unknown. Nevertheless, they said that the fossils must have come from Middle Pleistocene Trinil beds of the Kabuh formation (0.7–1.3 million years old) or the Early Pleistocene Djetis beds of the Putjangan formation (1.3–2.0 million years old).

The ages given by Le Gros Clark and Campbell, derived from the potassium-argon dates discussed previously, refer only to the age of the volcanic soils, and not to the bones themselves. Potassium-argon dates have meaning only if the bones were found securely in place within or beneath the layers of dated volcanic material. But the vast majority of fossils listed in Table 8.1 were surface finds, rendering their assigned potassium-argon dates meaningless.

Concerning the age of 1.3–2.0 million years given by Le Gros Clark and Campbell for the Djetis beds of the Putjangan formation, we note that this is based on the potassium-argon date of 1.9 million years reported by Jacob and Curtis in 1971. But in 1978 Bartstra reported a potassium-argon age of less than 1 million years. Other researchers have reported that the fauna of the Djetis and Trinil beds are quite similar and that the bones have similar fluorine-to-phosphate ratios.

Le Gros Clark and Campbell concluded that "at this early time there existed in Java hominids with a type of femur indistinguishable from that of *Homo sapiens*, though all the cranial remains so far found emphasize the extraordinarily primitive characters of the skull and dentition." All in all, the presentation by Le Gros Clark and Campbell was quite misleading. They left the reader with the impression that cranial remains found in Java can be definitely associated with the femurs when such is not the case. Furthermore, discoveries in China and Africa have shown that *Homo erectus* femurs are different from those collected by Dubois in Java.

Judging strictly by the hominid fossil evidence from Java, all we can say is the following. As far as the surface finds are concerned, these are all cranial and dental remains, the morphology of which is primarily apelike with some humanlike features. Because their original stratigraphic position is unknown, these fossils simply indicate the presence in Java, at some unknown time in the past, of a creature with a head displaying some apelike and humanlike features.

The original *Pithecanthropus* skull (T2) and femur (T3) reported by Dubois were found *in situ,* and thus there is at least some basis for saying they are perhaps as old as the early Middle Pleistocene Trinil beds of the Kabuh formation. The original position of the other femurs is poorly documented, but they are said to have been excavated from the same Trinil beds as T2 and T3. In any case, the original femur (T3), described as fully human, was not found in close connection with the primitive skull and displays anatomical features that distinguish it from the femur of *Homo erectus.* There is, therefore, no good reason to connect the skull with the T3 femur or any of the other femurs, all of which are described as identical to those of anatomically modern humans. Consequently, the T2 skull and T3 femur can be said to indicate the presence of two kinds of hominids in Java during the early Middle Pleistocene—one with an apelike head and the other with legs like those of anatomically modern humans. Following the typical practice of giving a species identification on the basis of partial skeletal remains, we can say that the T3 femur provides evidence for the presence of *Homo sapiens sapiens* in Java around 800,000 years ago. Up to now, no creature except *Homo sapiens sapiens* is known to have possessed the kind of femur found in the early Middle Pleistocene Trinil beds of Java.

9

The Piltdown Showdown

After Eugene Dubois's discovery of Java man in the 1890s, the hunt for fossils to fill the evolutionary gaps between ancient apelike hominids and modern *Homo sapiens* intensified. It was in this era of strong anticipation that a sensational find was made in England—Piltdown man, a creature with a humanlike skull and apelike jaw.

The outlines of the Piltdown story are familiar to both the proponents and opponents of the Darwinian theory of human evolution. The fossils, the first of which were discovered by Charles Dawson in the years 1908–1911, were declared forgeries in the 1950s by scientists of the British Museum. This allowed the critics of Darwinian evolution to challenge the credibility of the scientists who for several decades had placed the Piltdown fossils in evolutionary family trees.

Scientists, on the other hand, were quick to point out that they themselves exposed the fraud. Some sought to identify the forger as Dawson, an eccentric amateur, or Pierre Teilhard de Chardin, a Catholic priest-paleontologist with mystical ideas about evolution, thus absolving the "real" scientists involved in the discovery.

In one sense, it would be possible to leave the story of Piltdown at this and go on with our survey of paleoanthropological evidence. But a deeper look at Piltdown man and the controversies surrounding him will prove worthwhile, giving us greater insight into how facts relating to human evolution are established and disestablished.

Contrary to the general impression that fossils speak with utmost certainty and conviction, the intricate network of circumstances connected with a paleoanthropological discovery can preclude any simple understanding. Such ambiguity is especially to be expected in the case of a carefully planned forgery, if that is what the Piltdown episode represents. But as a general rule, even "ordinary" paleoanthropological finds are enveloped in multiple layers of uncertainty. As we trace the detailed history of the Piltdown controversy it becomes clear that the line between fact and forgery is often indistinct.

DAWSON FINDS A SKULL

Sometime around the year 1908, Charles Dawson, a lawyer and amateur anthropologist, noticed that a country road near Piltdown, in Sussex, was being mended with flint gravel. Always on the lookout for flint tools, Dawson inquired from the workmen and learned that the flint came from a pit on a nearby estate, Barkham Manor, owned by Mr. R. Kenward, with whom Dawson was acquainted. Dawson visited the pit and asked two workers there to be on the lookout for any implements or fossils that might turn up. In 1913, Dawson wrote: "Upon one of my subsequent visits to the pit, one of the men handed to me a small portion of an unusually thick human parietal bone. I immediately made a search but could find nothing more. . . . It was not until some years later, in the autumn of 1911, on a visit to the spot, that I picked up, among the rain-washed spoil-heaps of the gravel pit, another and larger piece belonging to the frontal region of the same skull." Dawson noted that the pit contained pieces of flint much the same in color as the skull fragments.

Dawson was not a simple amateur. He had been elected a Fellow of the Geological Society and for 30 years had contributed specimens to the British Museum as an honorary collector. Furthermore, he had cultivated a close friendship with Sir Arthur Smith Woodward, keeper of the Geological Department at the British Museum and a fellow of the Royal Society. In February 1912, Dawson wrote a letter to Woodward at the British Museum, telling how he had "come across a very old Pleistocene bed . . . which I think is going to be very interesting . . . with part of a thick human skull in it . . . part of a human skull which will rival *Homo heidelbergensis.*" Altogether, Dawson had found five pieces of the skull. In order to harden them, he soaked them in a solution of potassium dichromate.

On Saturday, June 2, 1912, Woodward and Dawson, accompanied by Pierre Teilhard de Chardin, a student at a local Jesuit seminary, began excavations at Piltdown and were rewarded with some new discoveries. On the very first day, they found another piece of skull. More followed. Dawson later wrote: "Apparently the whole or greater portion of the human skull had been shattered by the workmen, who had thrown away the pieces unnoticed. Of these we recovered, from the spoil-heaps, as many fragments as possible. In a somewhat deeper depression of the undisturbed gravel I found the right half of a human mandible. So far as I could judge, guiding myself by the position of a tree 3 or 4 yards away, the spot was identical with that upon which the men were at work when the first portion of the cranium was found several years ago. Dr. Woodward also dug up a small portion of the occipital bone of the skull from within a yard of the point where the jaw was discovered, and at precisely the same level. The jaw appeared to have been broken at the symphysis and abraded, perhaps when it lay fixed in the gravel, and before its complete deposition. The fragments of the cranium show little or no sign of rolling or other abrasion, save an incision at the back of the parietal, probably caused by a workman's pick." A total of nine fossil skull pieces were found, five by Dawson alone and an additional four after Woodward joined the excavation.

In addition to the human fossils, the excavations at Piltdown yielded a variety of mammalian fossils, including teeth of elephant, mastodon, horse, and beaver. Stone tools were also found, some comparable to eoliths and others of more advanced workmanship. Some of the tools and mammalian fossils were more worn than the others. Dawson and Woodward believed that the tools and bones in better condition, including the Piltdown man fossils, dated to the Early Pleistocene, while the others had originally been part of a Pliocene formation.

In the decades that followed, many scientists agreed with Dawson and Woodward that the Piltdown man fossils belonged with the Early Pleistocene mammal fossils, contemporary with the Piltdown gravels. Others, such as Sir Arthur Keith and A. T. Hopwood, thought the Piltdown man fossils belonged with the older Late Pliocene fauna that had apparently been washed into the Piltdown gravels from an older horizon.

From the beginning, the Piltdown skull was deemed morphologically humanlike. According to Woodward, the early apelike ancestors of humans had a humanlike skull and apelike jaw, like that of Piltdown man. At a certain point, said Woodward, the evolutionary line split. One branch began to develop thick skulls with big brow ridges. This line led to to Java man and the Neanderthals, who had thick skulls with big brow ridges. Another line retained the smooth-browed skull while the jaw became more humanlike. This is the line in which anatomically modern humans appeared.

Woodward had thus come up with his own theory about human evolution, which he wanted to support by fossil evidence, however limited and fragmentary. Today, a version of Woodward's proposed lineage survives in the widely accepted idea that *Homo sapiens sapiens* and *Homo sapiens neanderthalensis* are both descendants of a species called archaic or early *Homo sapiens*. Not at all widely accepted, but quite close to Woodward's idea, is Louis Leakey's proposal that both *Homo erectus* and the Neanderthals are side branches from the main line of human evolution. But all of these proposed evolutionary lineages ignore the evidence, catalogued in this book, for the presence of anatomically modern humans in periods earlier than the Pleistocene.

Not everyone agreed with the idea that the Piltdown jaw and skull belonged to the same creature. Sir Ray Lankester of the British Museum suggested they might belong to separate creatures of different species. David Waterston, professor of anatomy at King's College, also thought the jaw did not belong to the skull. He said that connecting the jaw with the skull was akin to linking a chimpanzee's foot with a human leg. If Waterston was correct, he was confronted with a skull that appeared to be very much like that of a human and was quite possibly from the Early Pleistocene.

So right from the start, some experts were uncomfortable with the seeming incompatibility between the humanlike skull and apelike jaw of the Piltdown man (Figure 9.1). Sir Grafton Eliot Smith, an expert in brain physiology, tried to defuse this doubt. After examining a cast showing the features of the brain cavity of the Piltdown skull, Smith wrote: "We must consider this as being the most primitive and most simian human brain so far recorded; one, moreover, such as might reasonably have been expected to be associated in one and the same individual with the [apelike] mandible." But according to modern scientists, the Piltdown skull is a fairly recent *Homo sapiens sapiens* skull that was planted by a hoaxer. If we accept this, that means Smith, a renowned expert, was seeing simian features where none factually existed.

It was hoped that future discoveries would clarify the exact status of Piltdown man. The canine teeth, which are more pointed in the apes than in human beings, were missing from the Piltdown jaw. Woodward thought a canine would eventually turn up, and even made a model of how a Piltdown man canine should look.

On August 29, 1913, Teilhard de Chardin did in fact find a canine tooth in a heap of gravel at the Piltdown excavation site, near the place where the mandible had been uncovered. The point of the tooth was worn and flattened like that of a human canine. Some nose bones were also found.

By this time, Piltdown had become quite a tourist attraction. Visiting researchers were politely allowed to assist in the ongoing excavations. Motor coaches came with members of natural history societies. Dawson even had a picnic lunch at the Piltdown site for the Geological Society of London. Soon Dawson achieved celebrity status. Indeed, the scientific name for the Piltdown hominid became *Eoanthropus dawsoni,* meaning "Dawson's dawn man." But Dawson's enjoyment of his fame was short-lived; he died in 1916.

Doubts persisted that the jaw and skull of *Eoanthropus* belonged to the same creature, but these doubts weakened when Woodward reported the discovery in 1915 of a second set of fossils about 2 miles from the original Piltdown site. Found there were two pieces of human skull and a humanlike molar tooth. For many scientists, the Piltdown II discoveries helped establish that the original Piltdown skull and jaw belonged to the same individual.

But as more hominid fossils were found, the Piltdown fossil, with its *Homo sapiens* type of cranium, introduced a great deal of uncertainty into the construction of the line of human evolution. At Choukoutien (now Zhoukoudian), near Peking (now Beijing), researchers initially uncovered a primitive-looking jaw resembling that of Piltdown man. But when the first Beijing man skull was uncovered in 1929, it had the low forehead and pronounced brow ridge of *Pithecanthropus erectus* of Java, now classified with Beijing man as *Homo erectus.* In the same decade, Raymond Dart uncovered the first *Australopithecus* specimens in Africa. Other *Australopithecus* finds followed, and like Java man and Beijing man they also had low foreheads and prominent brow ridges. Most British anthropologists, however, decided that

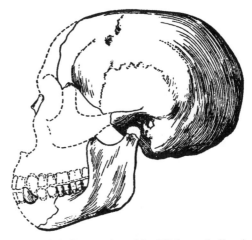

Figure 9.1. Restoration of the Piltdown skull and jaw by Dawson and Woodward.

Australopithecus was an apelike creature that was not a human ancestor.

But after World War II, new finds by Robert Broom in Africa led the British to change their minds about *Australopithecus,* accepting it as a human ancestor. So now what was to be done with Piltdown man, who was thought to be as old as the *Australopithecus* finds that had by then been made?

A FORGERY EXPOSED?

Meanwhile, an English dentist named Alvan Marston kept badgering British scientists about Piltdown man, contending that something was not quite right about the fossils. In 1935, Marston discovered a human skull at Swanscombe, accompanied by fossil bones of 26 kinds of Middle Pleistocene animals. Desiring that his discovery be hailed as "the oldest Englishman," Marston challenged the age of the Piltdown fossils.

In 1949, Marston convinced Kenneth P. Oakley of the British Museum to test both the Swanscombe and Piltdown fossils with the newly developed fluorine content method. The Swanscombe skull had the same fluorine content as the fossil animal bones found at the same site, thus confirming its Middle Pleistocene antiquity. The test results for the Piltdown specimens were more confusing.

Oakley, it should be mentioned, apparently had his own suspicions about Piltdown man. Oakley and Hoskins, coauthors of the 1950 fluorine content test report, wrote that "the anatomical features of *Eoanthropus* (assuming the material to represent one creature) are wholly contrary to what discoveries in the

Far East and in Africa have led us to expect in an early Pleistocene hominid."

Oakley tested the Piltdown fossils in order to determine whether the cranium and jaw of Piltdown man really belonged together. The fluorine content of four of the original Piltdown cranial bones ranged from 0.1 to 0.4 percent. The jaw yielded a fluorine content of 0.2 percent, suggesting it belonged with the skull. The bones from the second Piltdown locality gave similar results. Oakley concluded that the Piltdown bones were from the Riss-Würm interglacial, which would make them between 75,000 and 125,000 years old. This is quite a bit more recent than the Early Pleistocene date originally ascribed to the Piltdown fossils, but it is still anomalously old for a skull of the fully human type in England. According to current theory, *Homo sapiens sapiens* arose in Africa about 100,000 years ago and only much later migrated to Europe, at around 30,000 years ago.

Oakley's report did not entirely satisfy Marston, who was convinced the Piltdown jaw and skull were from completely different creatures. From his knowledge of medicine and dentistry, Marston concluded that the skull, with its closed sutures, was that of a mature human, while the jaw, with its incompletely developed molars, was from an immature ape. He also felt that the dark staining of the bones, taken as a sign of great antiquity, was caused by Dawson soaking them in a solution of potassium dichromate to harden them.

Marston's ongoing campaign about the Piltdown fossils eventually drew the attention of J. S. Weiner, an Oxford anthropologist. Weiner soon became convinced that something was wrong with the Piltdown fossils. He reported his suspicions to W. E. Le Gros Clark, head of the anthropology department at Oxford University, but Le Gros Clark was at first skeptical. On August 5, 1953, Weiner and Oakley met with Le Gros Clark at the British Museum, where Oakley removed the actual Piltdown specimens from a safe so they could examine the controversial relics. At this point, Weiner presented to Le Gros Clark a chimpanzee tooth he had taken from a museum collection and then filed and stained. The resemblance to the Piltdown molar was so striking that Le Gros Clark authorized a full investigation of all the Piltdown fossils.

A second fluorine content test, using new techniques, was applied to the Piltdown human fossils. Three pieces of the Piltdown skull now yielded a fluorine content of .1 percent. But the Piltdown jaw and teeth yielded a much lower fluorine content of .01–04 percent. Because fluorine content increases with the passing of time, the results indicated a much older age for the skull than for the jaw and teeth. This meant they could not belong to the same creature.

Regarding the two fluorine content tests by Oakley, we see that the first indicated both the skull and jaw were of the same age whereas the second indicated they were of different ages. It was stated that the second set of tests made use of new techniques—that happened to give a desired result. This sort of thing occurs quite often in paleoanthropology—researchers run and rerun tests, or refine their methods, until an acceptable result is achieved. Then they stop. In such cases, it seems the test is calibrated against a theoretical expectation.

Nitrogen content tests were also run on the Piltdown fossils. Examining the results, Weiner found that the skull bones contained 0.6–1.4 percent nitrogen whereas the jaw contained 3.9 percent and the dentine portion of some of the Piltdown teeth contained 4.2–5.1 percent. The test results therefore showed that the cranial fragments were of a different age than the jaw and teeth, demonstrating they were from different creatures. Modern bone contains about 4–5 percent nitrogen, and the content decreases with age. So it appeared the jaw and teeth were quite recent, while the skull was older.

The results of the fluorine and nitrogen content tests still allowed one to believe that the skull, at least, was native to the Piltdown gravels. But finally even the skull fragments came under suspicion. The British Museum report said: "Dr. G. F. Claringbull carried out an X-ray crystallographic analysis of these bones and found that their main mineral constituent, hydroxy-apatite, had been partly replaced by gypsum. Studies of the chemical conditions in the Piltdown sub-soil and ground-water showed that such an unusual alteration could not have taken place naturally in the Piltdown gravel. Dr. M. H. Hey then demonstrated that when sub-fossil bones are artificially iron-stained by soaking them in strong iron sulphate solutions this alteration does occur. Thus it is now clear that the cranial bones had been artificially stained to match the gravel, and 'planted' at the site with all the other finds."

Despite the evidence presented in the British Museum report, it can still be argued that the skull was originally from the Piltdown gravels. All of the skull pieces were darkly iron-stained throughout, while the jaw bone, also said to be a forgery, had only a surface stain. Furthermore, a chemical analysis of the first skull fragments discovered by Dawson showed that they had a very high iron content of 8 percent, compared to only 2–3 percent for the jaw. This evidence suggests that the skull fragments acquired their iron-staining (penetrating the entire bone and contributing 8 percent iron to the bones' total mineral content) from a long stay in the iron-rich gravels at Piltdown. The jaw, with simply a surface stain and much smaller iron content, appears to be of a different origin.

If the skull fragments were native to the Piltdown gravels and were not artificially stained as suggested by Weiner and his associates, then how is one to explain the gypsum (calcium sulfate) in the skull fragments? One possibility is that Dawson used sulfate compounds (along with or in addition to potassium dichromate) while chemically treating the bones to harden them after their excavation, thus converting part of the bones' hydroxy-apatite into gypsum.

Another option is that the gypsum accumulated while the skull was still in the Piltdown gravels. The British Museum scientists claimed that the concentration of sulfates at Piltdown was too low for this to have happened. But M.Bowden observed that sulfates were present in the area's groundwater at 63 parts per million and that the Piltdown gravel had a sulfate content of 3.9 milligrams per 100 grams. Admitting these concentrations were not high, Bowden said they could have been considerably higher in the past. We note that Oakley appealed to higher past concentrations of fluorine in groundwater to explain an abnormally high fluorine content for the Castenedolo human skeletons.

Significantly, the Piltdown jaw contained no gypsum. The fact that gypsum is present in all of the skull fragments but not in the jaw is consistent with the hypothesis that the skull fragments were originally from the Piltdown gravel while the jaw was not.

Chromium was present in the five skull fragments found by Dawson alone, before he was joined by Woodward. This can be explained by the known fact that Dawson dipped the fragments in potassium dichromate to harden them after they were excavated. The additional skull fragments found by Dawson and Woodward together did not contain any chromium.

The jaw did have chromium, apparently resulting from an iron-staining technique involving the use of an iron compound and potassium dichromate.

To summarize, it may be that the skull was native to the Piltdown gravels and became thoroughly impregnated with iron over the course of a long period of time. During this same period of time, some of the calcium phosphate in the bone was transformed into calcium sulfate (gypsum) by the action of sulfates in the gravel and groundwater. Some of the skull fragments were later soaked by Dawson in potassium dichromate. This would account for the presence in them of chromium. The fragments found later by Dawson and Woodward together were not soaked in potassium dichromate and hence had no chromium in them. The jaw, on the other hand, was artificially iron-stained, resulting in only a superficial coloration. The staining technique involved the use of a chromium compound, which accounts for the presence of chromium in the jaw, but the staining technique did not produce any gypsum.

Alternatively, if one accepts that the iron-staining of the skull fragments (as well as the jaw) was accomplished by forgery, then one has to assume that the forger used three different staining techniques: (1) According to the British Museum scientists, the primary staining technique involved the use of an iron sulfate solution with potassium dichromate as an oxidizer, yielding gypsum (calcium sulfate) as a byproduct. This would account for the presence of gypsum and chromium in the five iron-stained skull fragments first found by Dawson. (2) The four skull fragments found by Dawson and Woodward together contained gypsum but no chromium. So the staining technique in this case would not have employed potassium dichromate. (3) The jaw, which contained chromium but no gypsum, must have been stained by a third method that involved use of iron and chromium compounds, but which did not produce gypsum. It is hard to see why a forger would have used so many methods when one would have sufficed. We must also wonder why the forger carelessly stained the jaw to a far lesser extent than the skull, thus risking detection.

Additional evidence, in the form of eyewitness testimony, suggests that the skull was in fact originally from the Piltdown gravels. The eyewitness was Mabel Kenward, daughter of Robert Kenward, the owner of Barkham Manor. On February 23, 1955, the *Telegraph* published a letter from Miss Kenward that contained this statement: "One day when they were digging in the unmoved gravel, one of the workmen saw what he called a coconut. He broke it with his pick, kept one piece and threw the rest away." Particularly significant was the testimony that the gravel was unmoved.

Even Weiner himself wrote: "we cannot easily dismiss the story of the gravel diggers and their 'coconut' as pure invention, a plausible tale put about to furnish an acceptable history for the pieces. . . . Granting, then the probability that the workmen did find a portion of skull, it is still conceivable that what they found was not the semi-fossil *Eoanthropus* but some very recent and quite ordinary burial." Weiner suggested that the culprit, whoever he may have been, could have then substituted treated skull pieces for the ones actually found. But if the workmen were dealing with "a very recent and quite ordinary burial" then where were the rest of the bones of the corpse? In the end, Weiner suggested that an entire fake skull was planted, and the workmen found it. But Mabel Kenward testified that the surface where the workman started digging was unbroken.

Robert Essex, a science teacher personally acquainted with Dawson in the years 1912 to 1915, provided interesting testimony about the Piltdown jaw, or jaws, as it turns out. Essex wrote in 1955: "Another jaw not mentioned by Dr. Weiner came from Piltdown much more human than the ape's jaw, and therefore much more likely to belong to the Piltdown skull parts which are admittedly human. I saw and handled that jaw and know in whose bag it came to Dawson's office."

Essex then gave more details. At the time, he had been science master at a local grammar school, located near Dawson's office. Essex stated: "One day when I was passing I was beckoned in by one of the clerks whom I knew well. He had called me in to show me a fossil half-jaw much more human than an ape's and with three molars firmly fixed in it. When I asked where this object came from, the answer was 'Piltdown.' According to the clerk, it had been brought down by one of the 'diggers' who, when he called and asked for Mr. Dawson, was carrying a bag such as might be used for carrying tools. When he was told that Mr. Dawson was busy in court he said he would leave the bag and come back. When he had gone, the clerk opened the bag and saw this jaw. Seeing me passing he had called me in. I told him he had better put it back and that Mr. Dawson would be cross if he knew. I found afterwards that when the 'digger' returned, Mr. Dawson was still busy in court, so he picked up his bag and left." Essex later saw photographs of the Piltdown jaw. Noting the jaw was not the same one he had seen in Dawson's office, he communicated this information to the British Museum.

The discovery of a human jaw tends to confirm the view that the human skull found at Piltdown was native to the gravels. Even if we grant that every other bone connected with Piltdown is a forgery, if the skull was found *in situ,* we are confronted with what could be one more case of *Homo sapiens sapiens* remains from the late Middle Pleistocene or early Late Pleistocene.

IDENTIFYING THE CULPRIT

Most recent writing, totally accepting that all the Piltdown fossils and implements were fraudulent, has focused on identifying the culprit. Weiner and Oakley, among others, insinuated that Dawson, the amateur paleontologist, was to blame. Woodward, the professional scientist, was absolved.

But it appears that the Piltdown forgery demanded extensive technical knowledge and capability—beyond that seemingly possessed by Dawson, an amateur anthropologist. Keep in mind that the Piltdown man fossils were accompanied by many fossils of extinct mammals. It appears that a professional scientist, who had access to rare fossils and knew how to select them and modify them to give the impression of a genuine faunal assemblage of the proper age, had to be involved in the Piltdown episode.

Some have tried to make a case against Teilhard de Chardin, who studied at a Jesuit college near Piltdown and became acquainted with Dawson as early as 1909. A *Stegodon* tooth found at Piltdown was believed by Weiner and his associates to have come from a North African site that might have been visited by Teilhard de Chardin in the period from 1906 to 1908, during which time he was a lecturer at Cairo University.

Woodward is another suspect. He personally excavated some of the fossils. If they were planted, it seems he should have noticed something was wrong. This leads to the suspicion that he himself was involved in the plot. Also, he tightly controlled access to the original Piltdown fossils, which were stored under his care in the British Museum. This could be interpreted as an attempt to prevent evidence of forgery from being noticed by other scientists.

Ronald Millar, author of *The Piltdown Men,* suspected Grafton Eliot Smith. Having a dislike for Woodward, Smith may have decided to entrap him with an elegant deception. Smith, like Teilhard de Chardin, had spent time in Egypt, and so had access to fossils that could have been planted at Piltdown.

Frank Spencer, a professor of anthropology at Queens College of the City University of New York, has written a book that blames Sir Arthur Keith, conservator of the Hunterian Museum of the Royal College of Surgeons, for the Piltdown forgery. Keith believed that modern humans evolved earlier than other scientists could accept, and this, according to Spencer, impelled him to conspire with Dawson to plant evidence favoring his hypothesis.

Another suspect was William Sollas, a professor of geology at Cambridge. He was named in a tape-recorded message left by English geologist James Douglas, who died in 1979 at age 93. Sollas disliked Woodward, who had criticized a method developed by Sollas for making plaster casts of fossils. Douglas recalled he had sent mastodon teeth like those found at Piltdown to Sollas from Bolivia and that Sollas had also received some potassium dichromate, the chemical apparently used in staining many of the Piltdown specimens. Sollas had also "borrowed" some ape teeth from the Oxford museum collection. According to Douglas, Sollas secretly enjoyed seeing Woodward duped by the Piltdown forgeries.

But if Piltdown does represent a forgery, it is likely that something more than personal revenge was involved. Spencer said that the evidence "had been tailored to withstand scientific scrutiny and thereby promote a particular interpretation of the human fossil record."

One possible motivation for forgery by a professional scientist was the inadequacy of the evidence for human evolution that had accumulated by the beginning of the twentieth century. Darwin had published *The Origin of Species* in 1859, setting off almost immediately a search for fossil evidence connecting *Homo sapiens* with the ancient Miocene apes. Leaving aside the discoveries suggesting the presence of fully modern humans in the Pliocene and Miocene, Java man and the Heidelberg jaw were the only fossil discoveries that science had come up with. And, as we have seen in Chapter 8, Java man in particular did not enjoy unanimous support within the scientific community. Right from the start there were ominous suggestions that the apelike skull did not really belong with the humanlike thighbone found 45 feet away from it. Also, a number of scientists in England and America, such as Arthur Smith Woodward, Grafton Eliot Smith, and Sir Arthur Keith, were developing alternative views of human evolution in which the formation of a high-browed humanlike cranium preceded the formation of a humanlike jaw. Java man, however, showed a low-browed cranium like that of an ape.

Since so many modern scientists have indulged in speculation about the identity and motives of the presumed Piltdown forger, we would also like to introduce a tentative hypothesis. Consider the following scenario. Workmen at Barkham Manor actually discovered a genuine Middle Pleistocene skull, in the manner described by Mabel Kenward. Pieces of it were given to Dawson.

Dawson, who had regularly been communicating with Woodward, notified him. Woodward, who had been developing his own theory of human evolution and who was very worried about science's lack of evidence for human evolution after 50 years of research, planned and implemented the forgery. He did not act alone, but in concert with a select number of scientists connected with the British Museum, who assisted in acquiring the specimens and preparing them so as to withstand the investigations of scientists not in on the secret.

Oakley, who played a big role in the Piltdown exposé himself wrote: "The Trinil [Java man] material was tantalizingly incomplete, and for many scientists it was inadequate as confirmation of Darwin's view of human evolution. I have sometimes wondered whether it was a misguided impatience for the discovery of a more acceptable 'missing link' that formed one of the tangled skein of motives behind the Piltdown Forgery."

Weiner also admitted the possibility: "There could have been a mad desire to assist the doctrine of human evolution by furnishing the 'requisite' 'missing link.' . . . Piltdown might have offered irresistible attraction to some fanatical biologist to make good what Nature had created but omitted to preserve."

Unfortunately for the hypothetical conspirators, the discoveries that turned up over the next few decades did not support the evolutionary theory represented by the Piltdown forgery. The discoveries of new specimens of Java man and Beijing man, as well as the *Australopithecus* finds in Africa, were accepted by many scientists as proving the low-browed ape-man ancestor hypothesis, the very idea the high-browed Piltdown man was meant to discredit and replace.

Time passed, and the difficulties in constructing a viable evolutionary lineage for the fossil hominids increased. At a critical moment, the remaining insiders connected with the British Museum chose to act. Perhaps enlisting unwitting colleagues, they organized a systematic exposé of the forgery they had perpetrated earlier in the century. In the course of this exposé, perhaps some of the specimens were further modified by chemical and physical means to lend credence to the idea of forgery.

The idea of a group of conspirators operating in connection with the British Museum, perpetrating a forgery and then later exposing the same, is bound to strike many as farfetched. But it is founded upon as much, or as little, evidence as the indictments made by others. Doubt has been cast on so many British scientists individually, including some from the British Museum, that this conspiracy theory does not really enlarge the circle of possible wrongdoers.

Perhaps there were no conspirators at the British Museum. But according to many scientists, someone with scientific training, acting alone or with others, did carry out a very successful forgery.

Gavin De Beer, a director of the British Museum of Natural History, believed the methods employed in uncovering of the Piltdown hoax would "make a successful repetition of a similar type of forgery virtually impossible in the future." But a forger with knowledge of modern chemical and radiometric dating methods could manufacture a fake that would not be easily detectable. Indeed, we can hardly be certain that there is not another Piltdown-like forgery in one of the world's great museums, just waiting to be uncovered.

The impact of Piltdown remains, therefore, damaging. But incidents of this sort appear to be rare, given our present knowledge. There is, however, another more insidious and pervasive kind of cheating—the routine editing and reclassifying of data according to rigid theoretical preconceptions.

Vayson de Pradenne, of the Ecole d'Anthropologie in Paris, wrote in his book *Fraudes Archéologiques* (1925): "One often finds men of science possessed by a pre-conceived idea, who, without committing real frauds, do not hesitate to give observed facts a twist in the direction which agrees with their theories. A man may imagine, for example, that the law of progress in prehistoric industries must show itself everywhere and always in the smallest details. Seeing the simultaneous presence in a deposit of carefully finished artefacts and others of a coarser type, he decides that there must be two levels: the lower one yielding the coarser specimens. He will class his finds according to their type, not according to the stratum in which he found them. If at the base he finds a finely worked implement he will declare there has been accidental penetration and that the specimen must be re-integrated with the site of its origin by placing it with the items from the higher levels. He will end with real trickery in the stratigraphic presentation of his specimens; trickery in aid of a preconceived idea, but more or less unconsciously done by a man of good faith whom no one would call fraudulent. The case is often seen, and if I mention no names it is not because I do not know any."

This sort of thing goes on not just in the British Museum, but in all museums, universities, and other centers of paleoanthropological research the world over. Although each separate incident of knowledge filtration seems minor, the cumulative effect is overwhelming, serving to radically distort and obscure our picture of human origins and antiquity.

An abundance of facts suggests that beings quite like ourselves have been around as far back as we care to look—in the Pliocene, Miocene, Oligocene, Eocene, and beyond. Remains of apes and apelike men are also found throughout the same expanse of time. So perhaps all kinds of hominids have coexisted throughout history. If one considers all the available evidence, that is the clearest picture that emerges. It is only by eliminating a great quantity of evidence—keeping only the fossils and artifacts that conform to preconceived notions—that one can construct an evolutionary sequence. Such unwarranted elimination of evidence, evidence as solidly researched as anything now accepted, represents a kind of deception carried out by scientists desiring to maintain a certain theoretical point of view. This deception is apparently not the result of a deliberately organized plot, as with the Piltdown man forgery (if that is what Piltdown man was). It is instead the inevitable outcome of social processes of knowledge filtration operating within the scientific community.

But although there may be a lot of unconscious fraud in paleoanthropology, the case of Piltdown demonstrates that the field also has instances of deception of the most deliberate and calculating sort.

10

Beijing Man and Other Finds in China

After the discoveries of Java man and Piltdown man, ideas about human evolution remained unsettled. Dubois's *Pithecanthropus erectus* fossils did not win complete acceptance among the scientific community, and Piltdown simply complicated the matter. Scientists waited eagerly for the next important discoveries—which they hoped would clarify the evolutionary development of the Hominidae. Many thought the desired hominid fossils would be found in China.

The ancient Chinese called fossils dragon bones. Believing dragon bones to possess curative powers, Chinese druggists have for centuries powdered them for use in remedies and potions. For early Western paleontologists, Chinese drug shops therefore provided an unexpected hunting ground.

In 1900, Dr. K. A. Haberer collected mammalian fossils from Chinese druggists and sent them to the University of Munich, where they were studied and catalogued by Max Schlosser. Among the specimens, Schlosser found a tooth from the Beijing area that appeared to be a "left upper third molar, either of a man or hitherto unknown anthropoid ape." Schlosser suggested China would be a good place to search for primitive man.

ZHOUKOUDIAN

Among those who agreed with Schlosser was Gunnar Andersson, a Swedish geologist employed by the Geological Survey of China. In 1918, Andersson visited a place called Chikushan, or Chicken Bone Hill, near the village of Zhoukoudian, 25 miles southwest of Beijing. There, on the working face of an old limestone quarry, he saw a fissure of red clay containing fossil bones, indicating the presence of an ancient cave, now filled in.

In 1921, Andersson again visited the Chikushan site. He was accompanied by Otto Zdansky, an Austrian paleontologist who had been sent to assist him, and Walter M. Granger, of the American Museum of Natural History. Their first excavations were not very productive, resulting only in the discovery of some fairly recent fossils.

Then some of the local villagers told Zdansky about a nearby place with bigger dragon bones, near the small Zhoukoudian railway station. Here Zdansky found another limestone quarry, the walls of which, like the first, had fissures filled with red clay and broken bones. Andersson visited the site and discovered some broken pieces of quartz, which he thought might be very primitive tools. Quartz did not occur naturally at the site, so Andersson reasoned that the quartz pieces must have been brought there by a hominid. Zdansky, who did not get along very well with Andersson, disagreed with this interpretation.

Andersson, however, remained convinced. Looking at the limestone wall, he said, "I have a feeling that there lies here the remains of one of our ancestors and it's only a question of finding him." He asked Zdansky to keep searching the filled-in cave, saying, "Take your time and stick to it until the cave is emptied if need be."

In 1921 and 1923, Zdansky, somewhat reluctantly, conducted brief excavations. He uncovered signs of an early human precursor—two teeth, tentatively dated to the Early Pleistocene. The teeth, a lower premolar and an upper molar, were crated up with other fossils and shipped to Sweden for further study. Back in Sweden, Zdansky published a paper in 1923 on his work in China, with no mention of the teeth.

There the matter rested until 1926. In that year, the Crown Prince of Sweden, who was chairman of the Swedish China Research Committee and a patron of paleontological research, planned to visit Beijing. Professor Wiman of the University of Uppsala, asked Zdansky, his former student, if he had come across anything interesting that could be presented to the Prince. Zdansky sent Wiman a report, with photographs, about the teeth he had found at Zhoukoudian. The report was presented by J. Gunnar Andersson to a meeting in Beijing, attended by the Crown Prince. Andersson declared in regard to the teeth: "The man I predicted had been found."

DAVIDSON BLACK

Another person who thought Zdansky's teeth represented clear evidence of fossil man was Davidson Black, a young Canadian physician residing in Beijing.

Davidson Black graduated from the University of Toronto medical school in 1906. But he was far more interested in human evolution than medicine. Black believed humans had evolved in northern Asia, and he desired to go to China to find the fossil evidence to prove this theory. But the First World War delayed his plans.

In 1917, Black joined the Canadian military medical corps. Meanwhile, a friend, Dr. E. V. Cowdry, was named head of the anatomy department at the

Rockefeller Foundation's Beijing Union Medical College. Cowdry asked Dr. Simon Flexner, director of the Rockefeller Foundation, to appoint Black as his assistant. Flexner did so, and in 1919, after his release from the military, Black arrived in Beijing. At the Beijing Union Medical College, Black did everything possible to minimize his medical duties so he could concentrate on his real interest—paleoanthropology. In November 1921, he went on a brief expedition to a site in northern China, and other expeditions followed. Black's superiors were not pleased.

But gradually the Rockefeller Foundation would be won over to Black's point of view. The series of events that caused this change to take place is worth looking into.

Late in 1922, Black submitted a plan for a Thailand expedition to Dr. Henry S. Houghton, director of the medical school. Black expertly related his passion for paleoanthropology to the mission of the medical school. Houghton wrote to Roger Greene, the school's business director: "While I cannot be certain that the project which Black has in mind is severely practical in its nature, I must confess that I have been deeply impressed by . . . the valuable relationship he has been able to establish between our department of anatomy and the various institutions and expeditions which are doing important work in China in the fields which touch closely upon anthropology research. With these points in mind I recommend the granting of his request." Here can be seen the importance of the intellectual prestige factor—ordinary medicine seems quite pedestrian in comparison with the quasi-religious quest for the secret of human origins, a quest that had, since Darwin's time, fired the imaginations of scientists all over the world. Houghton was clearly influenced. The expedition took place during Black's summer vacation in 1923, but unfortunately produced no results.

In 1926, Black attended the scientific meeting at which J. Gunnar Andersson presented to the Crown Prince of Sweden the report on the molars found by Zdansky at Zhoukoudian in 1923. Excited on learning of the teeth, Black accepted a proposal by Andersson for further excavations at Zhoukoudian, to be carried out jointly by the Geological Survey of China and Black's department at the Beijing Union Medical School. Dr. Amadeus Grabau of the Geological Survey of China called the hominid for which they would search "Beijing man." Black requested funding from the Rockefeller Foundation, and to his delight he received a generous grant.

By spring 1927, work was underway at Zhoukoudian, in the midst of the Chinese civil war. During several months of painstaking excavation, there were no discoveries of any hominid remains. Finally, with the cold autumn rains beginning to fall, marking the end of the first season's digging, a single hominid tooth was uncovered. On the basis of this tooth, and the two previously reported by Zdansky (now in Black's possession), Black decided to announce the discovery of a new kind of fossil hominid. He called it *Sinanthropus*—China man.

Black was eager to show the world his discovery. In the course of his travels with his newly found tooth, Black discovered that not everyone shared his enthusiasm for *Sinanthropus*. For example, at the annual meeting of the American Association of Anatomists in 1928, some of the members heavily criticized Black for proposing a new genus on so little evidence.

Black kept making the rounds, showing the tooth to Ales Hrdlicka in the United States and then journeying to England, where he met Sir Arthur Keith and Sir Arthur Smith Woodward. At the British Museum, Black had casts made of the Beijing man molars, for distribution to other workers. This is the kind of propaganda work necessary to bring a discovery to the attention of the scientific community. Even for a scientist political skills are not unimportant.

On returning to China, Black kept in close touch with the excavations at Zhoukoudian. For months nothing turned up. But Black wrote to Keith on December 5, 1928: "It would seem that there is a certain magic about the last few days of the season's work for again two days before it ended Böhlin found the right half of the lower jaw of *Sinanthropus* with the three permanent molars *in situ*."

TRANSFORMATION OF THE ROCKEFELLER FOUNDATION

Now a financial problem loomed. The Rockefeller Foundation grant that supported the digging would run out in April of 1929. So in January Black wrote the directors, asking them to support the Zhoukoudian excavations by creating a Cenozoic Research Laboratory (the Cenozoic includes the periods from the Paleocene to the Holocene). In April, Black received the funds he desired.

Just a few years before, Rockefeller Foundation officials had actively discouraged Black from becoming too involved in paleoanthropological research. Now they were backing him to the hilt, setting up an institute specifically devoted to searching for remains of fossil human ancestors. Why had the Rockefeller Foundation so changed its attitude toward Black and his work? This question bears looking into, because the financial contribution of foundations would turn out to be vital to human evolution research carried out by scientists like Black. Foundation support would also prove important in broadcasting the news of the finds and their significance to the waiting world.

As Warren Weaver, a scientist and Rockefeller Foundation official, wrote in 1967: "In a perfect world an idea could be born, nourished, developed and made known to everyone, criticized and perfected, and put to good use without the crude fact of financial support ever entering into the process. Seldom, if ever, in the practical world in which we live, does this occur."

For Weaver, biological questions were of the highest importance. He regarded the highly publicized particle accelerators and space exploration programs as something akin to scientific fads. He added: "The opportunities not yet rigorously explored lie in the understanding of the nature of living things. It seemed clear in 1932, when the Rockefeller Foundation launched its quarter-century program in that area, that the biological and medical sciences were ready for a friendly invasion by the physical sciences. . . . the tools are now available for discovering, on the most disciplined and precise level of molecular actions, how man's central nervous system really operates, how he thinks, learns, remembers, and forgets. . . . Apart from the fascination of gaining some knowledge of the nature of the mind-brain-body relationship, the practical values in such studies are potentially enormous. Only thus may we gain information about our behavior of the sort that can lead to wise and beneficial control."

It thus becomes clear that at the same time the Rockefeller Foundation was channeling funds into human evolution research in China, it was in the process of developing an elaborate plan to fund biological research with a view to developing methods to effectively control human behavior. Black's research into Beijing man must be seen within this context in order to be properly understood.

Over the past few decades, science has developed a comprehensive cosmology that explains the origin of human beings as the culmination of a 4-billion-year process of chemical and biological evolution on this planet, which formed in the aftermath of the Big Bang, the event that marked the beginning of the universe some 16 billion years ago. The Big Bang theory of the origin of the universe, founded upon particle physics and astronomical observations suggesting we live in an expanding cosmos, is thus inextricably connected with the theory of the biochemical evolution of all life forms, including human beings. The major foundations, especially the Rockefeller Foundation, provided key funding for the initial research supporting this materialistic cosmology, which has for all practical purposes pushed God and the soul into the realm of mythology—at least in the intellectual centers of modern civilization.

All this is quite remarkable, when one considers that John D. Rockefeller's charity was initially directed toward Baptist churches and missions. Raymond D. Fosdick, an early president of the Rockefeller Foundation, said that both Rockefeller and his chief financial adviser, Baptist educator Frederick T. Gates, were "inspired by deep religious conviction."

In 1913, the present Rockefeller Foundation was organized. The trustees included Frederick T. Gates; John D. Rockefeller, Jr.; Dr. Simon Flexner, head of the Rockefeller Institute for Medical Research; Henry Pratt Judson, president of the University of Chicago; Charles William Eliot, former president of Harvard; and A. Barton Hepburn, president of the Chase National Bank. Alongside this new foundation, other Rockefeller charities continued to operate.

At first, the Rockefeller Foundation concentrated its attention on public health, medicine, agriculture, and education, avoiding anything controversial. Thus the Foundation began to distance itself from religion, particularly the Baptist Church. Exactly why this happened is difficult to say. Perhaps Rockefeller was coming to realize that his fortune was founded on exploiting the advances of modern science and technology. Perhaps it was the increasing role that science was beginning to play in the objects of traditional charitable giving—such as medicine. But whatever the reason, Rockefeller began to staff his foundation with scientists, and the giving policies reflected this change.

Even Gates, the former Baptist educator, seemed to be changing his tune. He wanted to create a nonsectarian university in China. But he noted that the "missionary bodies at home and abroad were distinctly and openly, even threateningly hostile to it as tending to infidelity." Furthermore, the Chinese government wanted control, an idea that the Foundation could not support.

Charles W. Eliot, who had overseen the Harvard Medical School in Shanghai, proposed a solution: a medical college, which would serve as an opening to the rest of Western science. Here mechanistic science shows itself a quiet but nevertheless militant ideology, skillfully promoted by the combined effort of scientists, educators, and wealthy industrialists, with a view towards establishing worldwide intellectual dominance.

The medical college strategy outlined by Eliot worked. The Chinese government approved establishment of the Beijing Union Medical College under Foundation auspices. Meanwhile, Dr. Wallace Buttrick, director of Rockefeller's newly created China Medical Board, negotiated with the Protestant mission hospitals already in China. He agreed to provide financial support for these hospitals, in effect bribing them.

In 1928, the Rockefeller Foundation and other Rockefeller charities underwent changes to reflect the growing importance of scientific research. All programs "relating to the advance of human knowledge" were shifted to the Rockefeller Foundation, which was reorganized into five divisions: international health, medical sciences, natural sciences, social sciences, and the humanities.

The change reached right to the top, with Dr. Max Mason, a scientist himself, taking over as president. Mason, a mathematical physicist, was formerly president of the University of Chicago. According to Raymond D. Fosdick, Mason "emphasized the structural unity involved in the new orientation of program. It was not to be five programs, each represented by a division of the Foundation; it was to be essentially one program, directed to the general problem of human behavior, with the aim of control through understanding." Black's Beijing man research therefore took place within the larger framework of the explicitly stated goal of the Rockefeller Foundation, which reflected the implicit goal of big science—control, by scientists, of human behavior.

AN HISTORIC FIND AND A COLD-BLOODED CAMPAIGN

With the financial backing of the Rockefeller Foundation for the Cenozoic Research Laboratory secure, Black resumed his travels for the purpose of promoting Beijing man. He then returned to China, where work was proceeding slowly at Zhoukodian, with no new major *Sinanthropus* finds reported. Enthusiasm seemed to be waning among the workers.

But then on the first of December, at the very end of the season, Pei Wenzhong made an historic find. Pei later wrote: "I encountered the almost complete skull of *Sinanthropus*. The specimen was imbedded partly in loose sands and partly in a hard matrix so that it was possible to extricate it with relative ease." Pei then rode 25 miles on a bicycle to the Cenozoic Research Laboratory, where he presented the skull to Black.

The discovery made Black a media sensation. In September of 1930, Sir Grafton Elliot Smith arrived in Beijing to inspect the site of the discovery and examine the fossils. During Smith's stay, Black primed him for a propaganda blitz in America on behalf of Beijing man. Smith then departed and apparently did his job well. In December, Black wrote an extremely candid letter to Dr. Henry Houghton, director of the Beijing medical school, who was vacationing in America: "If I blushed every time I thought of the cold-blooded advertising campaign I thought of and G. E. S. has carried through, I'd be permanently purple."

Black's newly won fame insured continued access to Rockefeller Foundation funds. Black wrote to Sir Arthur Keith: "We had a cable from Elliot Smith yesterday so he is evidently safe home after his strenuous trip. He characteristically has not spared himself in serving the interests of the Survey and the Cenozoic Laboratory and after his popularizing *Sinanthropus* for us in America I should have a relatively easy task before me a year from now when I will have to ask for more money from the powers that be."

Beijing man had come at just the right moment for advocates of human evolution. A few years previously, in one of the most famous trials in the world's history, a Tennessee court had found John T. Scopes guilty of teaching evolution in violation of state law. Scientists wanted to fight back hard. Thus any new evidence bearing on the question of human evolution was highly welcome.

Then there had been the matter of *Hesperopithecus,* a highly publicized prehistoric ape-man constructed in the minds of paleoanthropologists from a single humanlike tooth found in Nebraska. To the embarrassment of the scientists who had promoted this human ancestor, the humanlike tooth had turned out to be that of a fossil pig.

Meanwhile, the lingering doubts and continuing controversy about Dubois's *Pithecanthropus erectus* also needed to be resolved. In short, scientists in favor of evolutionary ideas, reacting to external threat and internal disarray, were in need of a good discovery to rally their cause.

FIRE AND TOOLS AT ZHOUKOUDIAN

It was in 1931 that reports showing extensive use of fire and the presence of well-developed stone and bone tools at Zhoukoudian were first published. What is quite unusual about these announcements is that systematic excavations had been conducted at Zhoukoudian by competent investigators since 1927, with no mention of either fire or stone tools. For example, Black wrote in 1929: "Though thousands of cubic meters of material from this deposit have been examined, no artifacts of any nature have yet been encountered nor has any trace of the usage of fire been observed." But only a a couple of years later, other researchers, such as Henri Breuil, were reporting thick beds of ash and were finding hundreds of stone tools in the exact same locations.

In 1931, Black and others, apparently embarrassed by the new revelations about fire and tools from Zhoukoudian, sought to explain how such important evidence had for several years escaped their attention. They said they had noticed signs of fire and tools but they had been so uncertain about them they did not mention them in their reports.

Concerning the failure of Teilhard de Chardin, Black, Pei, and others to report abundant tools and signs of fire at Zhoukoudian, there are two possible explanations. The first is the one they themselves gave—they simply over-looked the evidence or had so many doubts about it that they did not feel justified in reporting it. The second possibility is that they were very much aware of the signs of fire and stone tools, before Breuil reported them, but deliberately withheld this information.

But why? At the time the discoveries were made at Zhoukoudian, fire and stone tools at a site were generally taken as signs of *Homo sapiens* or Neander-thals. According to Dubois and von Koenigswald, no stone tools or signs of usage of fire were found in connection with *Pithecanthropus erectus* in Java. The Selenka expedition did report remnants of hearths at Trinil, but this information did not attain wide circulation.

So perhaps the original investigators of Zhoukoudian purposely held back from reporting stone tools and fire because they were aware such things might have confused the status of *Sinanthropus*. Doubters might have very well attributed the fire and tools to a being contemporary with, yet physically and culturally more advanced than *Sinanthropus,* thus removing *Sinanthropus* from his position as a new and important human ancestor.

As we shall see, that is what did happen once the tools and signs of fire became widely known. For example, Breuil said in 1932 about the relationship of *Sinanthropus* to the tools and signs of fire: "Several distinguished scientists have independently expressed to me the thought that a being so physically removed from Man. . . . was not capable of the works I have just described. In this case, the skeletal remains of *Sinanthropus* could be considered as simple hunting trophies, attributable, as were the traces of fire and industry, to a true Man, whose remains have not yet been found." But Breuil himself thought that *Sinanthropus* was the manufacturer of tools and maker of fire at Zhoukoudian.

Modern investigators have tended to confirm Breuil's views. *Sinanthropus* is usually pictured as an expert hunter, who killed animals with stone tools and cooked them on fires in the cave at Zhoukoudian.

A somewhat different view of *Sinanthropus* is provided by Lewis R. Binford and Chuan Kun Ho, anthropologists at the University of New Mexico. Concerning the ash deposits, they stated: "It would appear that at least some of them were originally huge guano accumulations inside the cave. In some cases, these massive organic deposits could have burned. . . . The assumption that man introduced and distributed the fire is unwarranted, as is the assumption that burned bones and other materials are there by virtue of man's cooking his meals."

Binford and Ho's theory that the ash deposits are composed mostly of bird droppings has not received unanimous support. But their assertions about the unreliability of the common picture of Beijing man, drawn from the presence of bones, ashes, and hominid remains at the site, are worthy of serious consideration.

The most that can be said of Beijing man, according to Binford and Ho, is that he was perhaps a scavenger who may or may not have used primitive stone tools to cut meat from carcasses left by carnivores in a large cave where organic materials sometimes burned for long periods. Or perhaps Beijing man was himself prey to the cave's carnivores, for it seems unlikely he would have voluntarily entered such a cave, even to scavenge.

SIGNS OF CANNIBALISM

On March 15, 1934, Davidson Black was found at his work desk, dead of a heart attack. He was clutching his reconstruction of the skull of *Sinanthropus* in his hand. Shortly after Black's death, Franz Weidenreich assumed leadership of the Cenozoic Research Laboratory and wrote a comprehensive series of reports on the Beijing man fossils. According to Weidenreich, the fossil remains of *Sinanthropus* individuals, particularly the skulls, suggested they had been the victims of cannibalism.

Most of the hominid bones discovered in the cave at Zhoukoudian were cranial fragments. Weidenreich particularly noted that the relatively complete skulls all lacked portions of the central part of the base. He observed that in modern Melanesian skulls "the same injuries occur as the effects of ceremonial cannibalism."

Besides the missing basal sections, Weidenreich also noted other signs that might possibly be attributed to the deliberate application of force. For example, some of the skulls showed impact marks of a type that "can only occur if the bone is still in a state of plasticity," indicating that "the injuries described must have been inflicted during life or soon after death." Some of the few long bones of *Sinanthropus* found at Zhoukoudian also displayed signs that to Weidenreich suggested human breakage, perhaps for obtaining marrow.

As to why mostly cranial fragments were found, Weidenreich believed that except for a few long bones, only heads were carried into the caves. He stated: "The strange selection of human bones . . . has been made by *Sinanthropus* himself. He hunted his own kin as he hunted other animals and treated all his victims in the same way."

Some modern authorities have suggested that Weidenreich was mistaken in his interpretation of the fossil remains of *Sinanthropus*. Binford and Ho pointed out that hominid skulls subjected to transport over river gravel are found with the basal section worn away. But the skulls recovered from Zhoukoudian were apparently not transported in this fashion.

Binford and Ho proposed that carnivores had brought the hominid bones into the caves. But Weidenreich wrote in 1935: "Transportation by . . . beasts of prey is impossible. . . . traces of biting and gnawing ought to have been visible on the human bones, which is not the case." Weidenreich felt that cannibalism among *Sinanthropus* individuals was the most likely explanation.

But Marcellin Boule, director of the Institute de Paleontologie Humaine in France, suggested another possibility—namely, that *Sinanthropus* had been hunted by a more intelligent type of hominid. Boule believed that the small cranial capacity of *Sinanthropus* implied that this hominid was not sufficiently intelligent to have made either fires or the stone and bone implements that were discovered in the cave.

If the remains of *Sinanthropus* were the trophies of a more intelligent hunter, who was that hunter and where were his remains? Boule pointed out that there are many caves in Europe that have abundant products of Paleolithic human industry, but the "proportion of deposits that have yielded the skulls or skeletons of the manufacturers of this industry is infinitesimal."

Therefore, the hypothesis that a more intelligent species of hominid hunted *Sinanthropus* is not ruled out simply because its fossil bones have not yet been found at Zhoukoudian. From our previous chapters, it may be recalled that there is evidence, from other parts of the world, of fully human skeletal remains from periods of equal and greater antiquity than that represented by Zhoukoudian. For example, the fully human skeletal remains found at Castenedolo in Italy are from the Pliocene period, over 2 million years ago.

THE FOSSILS DISAPPEAR

As we have previously mentioned, one reason that it may be difficult to resolve many of the questions surrounding Beijing man is that the original fossils are no longer available for study. By 1938, excavations at Zhoukoudian, under the direction of Weidenreich, were halted by guerilla warfare in the surrounding Western Hills. Later, with the Second World War well underway, Weidenreich left for the United States in April of 1941, carrying a set of casts of the Beijing man fossils.

In the summer of 1941, it is said, the original bones were packed in two footlockers and delivered to Colonel Ashurst of the U.S. Marine Embassy Guard in Beijing. In early December of 1941, the footlockers were reportedly placed on a train bound for the port of Chinwangtao, where they were to be loaded onto an American ship, the *President Harrison,* as part of the U.S. evacuation from China. But on December 7, the train was intercepted, and the fossils were never seen again. After World War II, the Chinese Communist government continued the excavations at Zhoukoudian, adding a few fossils to the prewar discoveries.

A CASE OF INTELLECTUAL DISHONESTY

In an article about Zhoukoudian that appeared in the June 1983 issue of *Scientific American,* two Chinese scientists, Wu Rukang and Lin Shenglong, presented misleading evidence for human evolution.

Wu and Lin made two claims: (1) The cranial capacity of *Sinanthropus* increased from the lowest level of the Zhoukoudian excavation (460,000 years old) to the highest level (230,000 years old), indicating that *Sinanthropus* evolved towards *Homo sapiens.* (2) The type and distribution of stone tools also implied that *Sinanthropus* evolved.

In support of their first claim, Wu and Lin analyzed the cranial capacities of the 6 relatively complete *Sinanthropus* skulls found at Zhoukoudian. Wu and Lin stated: "The measured cranial capacities are 915 cubic centimeters for the earliest skull, an average of 1075 cubic centimeters for four later skulls and 1140 cubic centimeters for the most recent one." From this set of relationships, Wu and Lin concluded: "It seems the brain size increased by more than 100 cubic centimeters during the occupation of the cave."

A chart in the *Scientific American* article showed the positions and sizes of the skulls found at Zhoukoudian Locality 1 (Table 10.1, Column A). But in their explanation of this chart, Wu and Lin neglected to state that the earliest skull, found at layer 10, belonged to a child, who according to Franz Weidenreich died at age 8 or 9 and according to Davidson Black died between ages 11 and 13.

Wu and Lin also neglected to mention that one of the skulls discovered in layers 8 and 9 (skull X) had a cranial capacity of 1,225 cc, which is 85 cc larger than the most recent skull (V), found in layer 3. When all the data is presented, (Table 10.1, column B) it is clear that there is no steady increase in cranial capacity from 460,000 to 230,000 years ago.

In addition to discussing an evolutionary increase in cranial capacity, Wu and Lin noted a trend toward smaller tools in the Zhoukoudian cave deposits. They also reported that the materials used to make the tools in the recent levels were superior to those used in the older levels. The recent levels featured more high-quality quartz, more flint, and less sandstone than the earlier levels.

But a change in the technological skill of a population does not imply that this population has evolved physiologically. For example, consider residents of Germany in 1400 and residents of Germany in 1990. The technological differences are awesome—jet planes and cars instead of horses; television and telephone instead of unaided vision and voice; tanks and missiles instead of swords and bows. Yet one would be in error if one concluded that the Germans of 1990 were physiologically more evolved than the Germans of 1400. Hence, contrary to the claim of Wu and Lin, the distribution of various kinds of stone tools does not imply that *Sinanthropus* evolved.

The report of Wu and Lin, especially their claim of increased cranial capacity in *Sinanthropus* during the Zhoukoudian cave occupation, shows that one should not uncritically accept all one reads about human evolution in scientific journals. It appears the scientific community is so committed to its evolutionary doctrine that any article purporting to demonstrate it can pass without much scrutiny.

DATING BY MORPHOLOGY

Although Zhoukoudian is the most famous paleoanthropological site in China, there are many others. These sites have yielded fossils representative of early *Homo erectus, Homo erectus,* Neanderthals, and early *Homo sapiens,* thus providing an apparent evolutionary sequence. But the way in which this progression has been constructed is open to question.

As we have seen in our discussion of human fossil remains discovered in China and elsewhere, it is in most cases not possible to date them with a very high degree of precision. Finds tend to occur within what we choose to call a

TABLE 10.1

**Evidence for Supposed Evolutionary Increase
in Sinanthropus Cranial Capacity at Zhoukoudian, China**

Years B.P.	Layer	A: Data Reported by Wu and Lin, 1983	B: Complete Data
230,000	1–2		
	3	1140 cc (V)	1140 cc (V)
290,000	4		
	5		
350,000	6		
	7		
420,000	8	1075 cc = average of 4 skulls	1225 cc (X), 1015 cc (XI), 1030 cc (XII), 1025 cc (II)
	9		
460,000	10	915 cc (III)	915 cc (III) child
700,000	11–13		

In *Scientific American* (June 1983), Wu Rukang and Lin Shenglong used the data in column A to suggest that *Sinanthropus* individuals evolved a larger cranial capacity during the 230,000 years they occupied the Zhoukoudian cave. But in their table Wu and Lin did not mention that the oldest skull (III) was that of a child, making it useless for comparison with the other skulls, which were those of adults. Furthermore, Wu and Lin gave an average for 4 skulls from layers 8 and 9 (II, X, XI, and XII), without mentioning that one of these skulls (X) had a cranial capacity of 1225 cc, larger than the most recent skull from layer 3. The complete data, shown in column B, reveals no evolutionary increase in cranial capacity. All of the data in the table was originally reported by Weidenreich, except for the cranial capacity of the skull found at layer 3. In 1934, Weidenreich reported the discovery of some pieces of this skull, which he later designated skull V. Then in 1966, Chinese paleontologists found other pieces of this same skull. The reconstruction of this skull and the cranial capacity measurement were carried out in 1966.

"possible date range," and this range may be quite broad, depending upon the dating methods that are used. Such methods include chemical, radiometric, and geomagnetic dating techniques, as well as analysis of site stratigraphy, faunal remains, tool types, and the morphology of the hominid remains. Furthermore, different scientists using the same methods often come up with different age ranges for particular hominid specimens. Unless one wants to uniformly consider the age judgement given most recently by a scientist as the correct one, one is compelled to take into consideration the entire range of proposed dates.

But here one can find oneself in difficulty. Imagine that a scientist reads several reports about two hominid specimens of different morphology. On the basis of stratigraphy and faunal comparisons, they are from roughly the same period. But this period stretches over several hundred thousand years. Repeated testing by different scientists using different paleomagnetic, chemical, and radiometric methods gives a wide spread of conflicting dates within this period. Some test results indicate one specimen is the older, some that the other is the older. Analyzing all the published dates for the two specimens, our investigator finds that the possible date ranges broadly overlap. In other words, by these methods it proves impossible to determine which of the two came first.

What is to be done? In some cases, as we shall show, scientists will decide, solely on the basis of their commitment to evolution, that the morphologically more apelike specimen should be moved to the early part of its possible date range, in order to remove it from the part of its possible date range that overlaps that of the morphologically more humanlike specimen. As part of the same procedure, the more humanlike specimen can be moved to the later, or more recent, part of its own possible date range. Thus the two specimens are temporally separated. But keep in mind the following: this sequencing operation is performed primarily on the basis of morphology, in order to preserve an evolutionary progression. It would look bad to have two forms, one generally considered ancestral to the other, existing contemporaneously.

Here is an example. Chang Kwang-chih, an anthropologist from Yale University, stated: "The faunal lists for Ma-pa, Ch'ang-yang, and Liu-chiang [hominid] finds offer no positive evidence for any precise dating. The former two fossils can be anywhere from the Middle to the Upper Pleistocene, as far as their associated fauna is concerned. . . . For a more precise placement of these three human fossils, one can only rely upon, at the present time, their own morphological features in comparison with other better-dated finds elsewhere in China." This may be called dating by morphology.

Jean S. Aigner stated in 1981: "In south China the faunas are apparently stable, making subdivision of the Middle Pleistocene difficult. Ordinarily the presence of an advanced hominid or relict form is the basis for determining later and earlier periods." This is a very clear exposition of the rationale for morphological dating. The presence of an advanced hominid is taken as an unmistakable sign of a later period.

In other words, if we find an apelike hominid in connection with a certain Middle Pleistocene fauna at one site and a more humanlike hominid in connection with the same Middle Pleistocene fauna at another site, then we must, according to this system, conclude that the site with the more humanlike hominid is of a later Middle Pleistocene date than the other. The Middle Pleistocene, it may be recalled, extends from 100,000 to 1 million years ago. It is taken for granted that the two sites in question could not possibly be contemporaneous.

With this maneuver completed, the two fossil hominids, now set apart from each other temporally, are then cited in textbooks as evidence of an evolutionary progression in the Middle Pleistocene! This is an intellectually dishonest procedure. The honest thing to do would be to admit that the evidence does not allow one to say with certainty that one hominid preceded the other and that it is possible they were contemporary. This would rule out using these particular hominids to construct a temporal evolutionary sequence. All one could honestly say is that both were found in the Middle Pleistocene. For all we know, the "more advanced" humanlike hominid may have preceded the "less advanced" apelike one. But by assuming that evolution is a fact, one can then "date" the hominids by their morphology and arrange the fossil evidence in a consistent manner.

Let us now consider a specific example of the date range problem. In 1985, Qiu Zhonglang reported that in 1971 and 1972 fossil teeth of *Homo sapiens* were found in the Yanhui cave near Tongzi, in Guizhou province, southern China. The Tongzi site contained a *Stegodon-Ailuropoda* fauna. *Stegodon* is a type of extinct elephant, and *Ailuropoda* is the giant panda. This *Stegodon-Ailuropoda* fauna is typical of southern China during the Middle Pleistocene.

The complete faunal list for the Tongzi site given by Han Defen and Xu Chunhua contains 24 kinds of mammals, all of which are also found in Middle (and Early) Pleistocene lists given by the same authors. But a great many of the genera and species listed are also known to have survived to the Late Pleistocene and the present.

The author of the report on the Tongzi discoveries stated: "The Yanhui Cave was the first site containing fossils of *Homo sapiens* discovered anywhere in the province. . . . The fauna suggests a Middle-Upper Pleistocene range, but the archaeological [human] evidence is consistent with an Upper [Late] Pleistocene age."

In other words, the presence of *Homo sapiens* fossils was the determining factor in assigning a Late Pleistocene age to the site. This is a clear example of dating by morphology. But according to the faunal evidence reported by Qiu, all that can really be said is that the age of the *Homo sapiens* fossils could be anywhere from Middle Pleistocene to Late Pleistocene.

There is, however, stratigraphic evidence suggesting a strictly Middle Pleistocene range. Qiu gave the following information: "The deposits in the cave contain seven layers. The human fossils, stone artifacts, burned bones, and mammalian fossils were all unearthed in the fourth layer, a stratum of greyish-yellow sand and gravel." This concentration in a single layer suggests that the human remains and the animal fossils, all of mammals found at Middle Pleistocene sites, are roughly contemporaneous. And yellow cave deposits in South China are generally thought to be Middle Pleistocene.

Our own analysis of the faunal list also suggests it is reasonable to narrow the age range to the Middle Pleistocene. *Stegodon,* present at Tongzi, is generally said to have existed from the Pliocene to the Middle Pleistocene. In a list of animals considered important for dating sites in South China, Aigner indicated that *Stegodon orientalis* survived only to the late Middle Pleistocene, although she did place a question mark after this entry.

A strictly Middle Pleistocene age for the Tongzi cave fauna is also supported by the presence of a species whose extinction by the end of the Middle Pleistocene is thought to be more definite. In her list of mammals considered important for dating sites in South China, Aigner included, in addition to *Stegodon orientalis,* other species found at Tongzi. Among them is *Megatapirus* (giant tapir), which Aigner said is confined to the Middle Pleistocene. The species found at Tongzi is listed by Chinese researchers as *Megatapirus augustus* Matthew et Granger. Aigner characterized *Megatapirus augustus* as a "large fossil form of the mid-Middle Pleistocene south China collections." We suggest that *Megatapirus augustus* limits the most recent age of the Tongzi faunal collection to the end of the Middle Pleistocene (Figure 10.1).

Another marker fossil listed by Aigner is *Crocuta crocuta* (the living hyena), which first appeared in China during the middle Middle Pleistocene. Since *Crocuta crocuta* is present at Tongzi, this limits the oldest age of the Tongzi fauna to the beginning of the middle Middle Pleistocene.

In summary, using *Megatapirus augustus* and *Crocuta crocuta* as marker fossils, we can conclude that the probable date range for the *Homo sapiens* fossils found at Tongzi extends from the beginning of the middle Middle Pleistocene to the end of the late Middle Pleistocene.

So Qiu, in effect, extended the date ranges of some mammalian species in the *Stegodon-Ailuropoda* fauna (such as *Megatapirus augustus*) from the Middle Pleistocene into the early Late Pleistocene in order to preserve an acceptable date for the *Homo sapiens* fossils. Qiu's evolutionary preconceptions apparently demanded this operation. Once it was carried out, the Tongzi *Homo sapiens,* placed safely in the Late Pleistocene, could then be introduced into a temporal

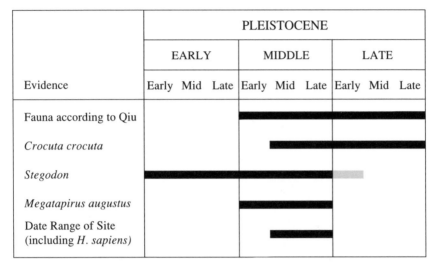

| | PLEISTOCENE | | |
| | EARLY | MIDDLE | LATE |
Evidence	Early Mid Late	Early Mid Late	Early Mid Late
Fauna according to Qiu			
Crocuta crocuta			
Stegodon			
Megatapirus augustus			
Date Range of Site (including *H. sapiens*)			

Figure 10.1. Age of *Homo sapiens* fossils at Tongzi site, South China. Qiu said the Tongzi mammalian fauna was Middle to Late Pleistocene, but used *Homo sapiens* fossils to date the site to the Late Pleistocene. But if we instead use the mammalian fauna to date the *Homo sapiens* fossils, we arrive at a different age for the site. *Stegodon* became extinct at the end of the Middle Pleistocene, possibly surviving into the early Late Pleistocene (grey part of bar) in some South China locales. *Megatapirus augustus* (giant tapir) definitely did not survive the Middle Pleistocene. The presence of *Stegodon* and especially *Megatapirus augustus* limit the most recent age for the Tongzi site to the end of the Middle Pleistocene. The presence of *Crocuta crocuta* (the living hyena), which first appears in the middle Middle Pleistocene, limits the oldest age for the Tongzi site to the beginning of the middle Middle Pleistocene. Therefore, the allowed range for the *Homo sapiens* fossils at Tongzi extends from the beginning of the middle Middle Pleistocene to the end of the late Middle Pleistocene.

evolutionary sequence and cited as proof of human evolution. If we place Tongzi *Homo sapiens* in the older part of its true faunal date range, in the middle Middle Pleistocene, he would be contemporary with Zhoukoudian *Homo erectus*. And that would not look very good in a textbook on fossil man in China.

We have carefully analyzed reports about several other Chinese sites, and we find that the same process of morphological dating has been used to temporally separate various kinds of hominids. At Lantian, a *Homo erectus* skull was found in 1964. It was more primitive than Zhoukoudian *Homo erectus*. Various authors, such as J. S. Aigner, have therefore placed it earlier than Zhoukoudian *Homo erectus*. But our own analysis of the faunal evidence, site stratigraphy, and paleomagnetic dating shows the date range for the Lantian *Homo erectus* skull overlaps that of Zhoukoudian *Homo erectus*. The same is true for a *Homo erectus* jaw found at Lantian.

We do not, however, insist that the Lantian *Homo erectus* skull is contemporaneous with *Homo erectus* of Zhoukoudian Locality 1. Following our standard procedure, we simply extend the probable date range of primitive Lantian *Homo erectus* to include the time period represented by the Zhoukoudian occupation.

So now we have overlapping possible date ranges in the middle Middle Pleistocene for the following hominids: (1) Lantian man, a primitive *Homo erectus*; (2) Beijing man, a more advanced *Homo erectus*; and (3) Tongzi man, described as *Homo sapiens*. We are not insisting that these beings actually coexisted. Perhaps they did, perhaps they did not. What we are insisting on is this—scientists should not propose that the hominids definitely did not coexist simply on the basis of their morphological diversity. Yet this is exactly what has happened. Scientists have arranged Chinese fossil hominids in a temporal evolutionary sequence primarily by their physical type. This methodology insures that no fossil evidence shall ever fall outside the realm of evolutionary expectations. By using morphological differences in the fossils of hominids to resolve contradictory faunal, stratigraphic, chemical, radiometric, and geomagnetic datings in harmony with a favored evolutionary sequence, paleoanthropologists have allowed their preconceptions to obscure other possibilities.

FURTHER DISCOVERIES IN CHINA

In 1956, peasants digging for fertilizer in a cave near Maba, in Guangdong province, southern China, found a skull that was apparently from a primitive human being. There seems to be general agreement that the Maba skull is *Homo sapiens* with some Neanderthaloid features.

It is easy to see that scientists, in accordance with their evolutionary expectations, would want to place the Maba specimen in the very latest Middle Pleistocene or early Late Pleistocene, after *Homo erectus*. Although Maba might be as recent as the early Late Pleistocene, the animal bones found there were from mammals that lived not only in the Late Pleistocene, but also in the Middle Pleistocene, and even the Early Pleistocene. The principal justification for fixing the date of the Maba cave in the very latest part of the late Middle Pleistocene or in the early Late Pleistocene seems to be the morphology of the hominid remains.

Updating our list, we now find overlapping date ranges in the middle Middle Pleistocene for: (1) primitive *Homo erectus* (Lantian); (2) *Homo erectus* (Zhoukoudian); (3) *Homo sapiens* (Tongzi); and (4) *Homo sapiens* with Neanderthaloid features (Maba).

The possibility that *Homo erectus* and more advanced hominids may have coexisted in China adds new fuel to the controversy about who was really responsible for the broken brain cases of Beijing man and the presence of advanced stone tools at Zhoukoudian Locality 1. Did several hominids, of various grades of advancement, really coexist in the middle Middle Pleistocene? We do not assert this categorically, but it is definitely within the range of possibilities suggested by the available data. In our study of the scientific literature, we have come upon no clear reason for ruling out coexistence other than the fact that the individuals are morphologically dissimilar.

Some will certainly claim that the fact of human evolution has been so conclusively established, beyond any reasonable doubt, that it is perfectly justifiable to engage in dating hominids by their morphology. But we believe this claim does not hold up under close scrutiny. As we have demonstrated in Chapters 2–7, abundant evidence contradicting current ideas about human evolution has been suppressed or forgotten. Furthermore, scientists have systematically overlooked shortcomings in the evidence that supposedly supports current evolutionary hypotheses.

If peasants digging for fertilizer in a Chinese cave had uncovered a fully human skull along with a distinctly Pliocene fauna, scientists would certainly have protested that no competent observers were present to conduct adequate stratigraphic studies. But since the Maba skull could be fitted into the standard evolutionary sequence, no one objected to its mode of discovery.

Even after one learns to recognize the highly questionable practice of morphological dating, one may be astonished to note how frequently it is used. In the field of human evolution research in China, it appears to be not the exception but the rule. The *Homo sapiens* maxilla (upper jaw) found by workers in 1956 at Longdong in Changyang county, Hubei Province, South China, has provided many authorities with a welcome opportunity for unabashed morphological dating.

The upper jaw, judged *Homo sapiens* with some primitive features, was found in association with the typical South China Middle Pleistocene fauna including *Ailuropoda* (panda) and *Stegodon* (extinct elephant). In 1962, Chang Kwang-chih of Yale University wrote: "This fauna is generally believed to be of Middle Pleistocene age, and the scientists working on the cave suggest a late Middle Pleistocene dating, for the morphology of the maxilla shows less primitive features than does that of *Sinanthropus*." It is clear that Chang's primary justification for assigning Changyang *Homo sapiens* a date later than Beijing *Homo erectus* was morphological.

In 1981, J. S. Aigner joined in with her statement: "A Middle Pleistocene age is suggested by some of the fauna with the presence of the hominid which is considered near *H. sapiens* indicating a dating late in that period."

That scientists could confront the faunal evidence at Changyang without even considering the possibility that *Homo sapiens* coexisted in China with

Homo erectus is amazing. In this regard, Sir Arthur Keith wrote in 1931: "It has so often happened in the past that the discovery of human remains in a deposit has influenced expert opinion as to its age; the tendency has been to interpret geological evidence so that it would not clash flagrantly with the theory of man's recent origin."

In 1958, workers found human fossils in the Liujiang cave in the Guangxi Zhuang Autonomous Region of South China. These included a skull, vertebrae, ribs, pelvic bones, and a right femur. These anatomically modern human remains were found along with a typical *Stegodon-Ailuropoda* fauna, giving a date range for the site of the entire Middle Pleistocene. But Chinese scientists assigned the human bones to the Late Pleistocene, primarily becaused of their advanced morphology.

The Dali site in Shaanxi province has yielded a skull classified as *Homo sapiens* with primitive features. The Dali fauna contains animals that are all typical of the Middle Pleistocene and earlier.

Some Chinese paleoanthropologists suggest a late Middle Pleistocene age for Dali. While this may account for the human skull, the associated fauna does not dictate such a date. Rather it suggests for Dali *Homo sapiens* a possible date range extending further back into the Middle Pleistocene, overlapping, once more, Beijing man at Zhoukoudian Locality 1.

We thus conclude that Beijing man *Homo erectus* at Zhoukoudian Locality 1 may very well have lived at the same time as a variety of hominids—early *Homo sapiens* (some with Neanderthaloid features), *Homo sapiens sapiens*, and primitive *Homo erectus* (Figure 10.2).

In attempting to sort out this Middle Pleistocene hominid logjam, scientists have repeatedly used the morphology of the hominid fossils to select desirable dates within the total possible faunal date ranges of the sites. In this way, they have been able to preserve an evolutionary progression of hominids. Remarkably, this artificially constructed sequence, designed to fit evolutionary expectations, is then cited as proof of the evolutionary hypothesis.

For example, as we have several times demonstrated, a *Homo sapiens* specimen with a possible date range extending from the middle Middle Pleistocene (contemporary with Beijing man) to the Late Pleistocene will be pushed toward the more recent end of the date range. One would be equally justified in selecting a middle Middle Pleistocene date within the possible date range, even though this conflicts with evolutionary expectations.

We conclude our review of fossil hominid discoveries in China with some cases of sites regarded as Early Pleistocene. At Yuanmou, in Yunnan province, southwest China, geologists found two hominid teeth (incisors). According to Chinese scientists, these were more primitive than those of Beijing man. The teeth are believed to have belonged to an ancestor of Beijing man, a very

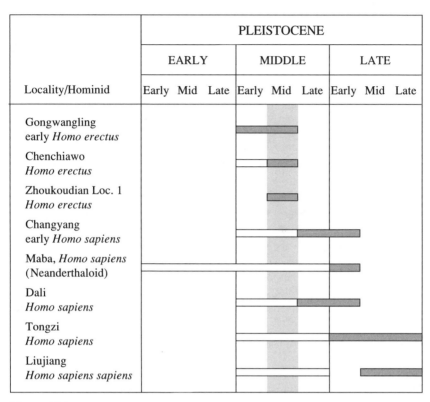

	PLEISTOCENE		
	EARLY	MIDDLE	LATE
Locality/Hominid	Early Mid Late	Early Mid Late	Early Mid Late
Gongwangling early *Homo erectus*			
Chenchiawo *Homo erectus*			
Zhoukoudian Loc. 1 *Homo erectus*			
Changyang early *Homo sapiens*			
Maba, *Homo sapiens* (Neanderthaloid)			
Dali *Homo sapiens*			
Tongzi *Homo sapiens*			
Liujiang *Homo sapiens sapiens*			

Figure 10.2. The probable date ranges of Chinese hominids, as determined by their accompanying mammalian faunas, are shown. Scientists have assigned dates to the hominids, within their probable date ranges, that conform to evolutionary expectations. These dates are represented by the darker portion of each bar. For example, although the faunal date range for the Maba site extends from the Early Pleistocene to the early Late Pleistocene, scientists have used the presence of a Neanderthaloid skull to fix the date for the site in the most recent part of its date range. At Liujiang, the human fossils were given a date completely outside the faunal date range. We call this phenomenon morphological dating. But putting aside evolutionary expectations, the faunal evidence indicates that it is possible that all of the hominids were contemporary with *Homo erectus* at Zhoukoudian Locality 1 in the middle Middle Pleistocene (shaded vertical bar).

primitive *Homo erectus,* descended from an Asian *Australopithecus.*

Stone tools—three scrapers, a stone core, a flake, and a point of quartz or quartzite—were later found at Yuanmou. Published drawings show the Yuanmou tools to be much like the European eoliths and the Oldowan industry of East Africa. Layers of cinders, containing mammalian fossils, were also found with the tools and hominid incisors.

The strata yielding the incisors gave a probable paleomagnetic date of 1.7 million years within a range of 1.6–1.8 million years. This date has been challenged, but leading Chinese scientists continue to accept it, pointing out that the mammal fossils are consistent with an Early Pleistocene age for the site.

There are, however, problems with an Early Pleistocene age for Yuanmou *Homo erectus*. *Homo erectus* is thought to have evolved from *Homo habilis* in Africa about 1.5 million years ago and migrated elsewhere about 1.0 million years ago. *Homo habilis* is not thought to have left Africa. Implicit in Jia's age estimate for the Yuanmou hominid is a separate origin for *Homo erectus* in China. Jia seems to require the presence in China about 2.0 million years ago of *Australopithecus* or *Homo habilis,* something forbidden by current theory.

In this regard, Lewis R. Binford and Nancy M. Stone stated in 1986: "It should be noted that many Chinese scholars are still wedded to the idea that man evolved in Asia. This view contributes to the willingness of many to uncritically accept very early dates for Chinese sites and to explore the possibility of stone tools being found in Pliocene deposits." One could also say that because Western scholars are wedded to the idea that humans evolved in Africa they uncritically reject very early dates for hominid fossils and artifacts around the world.

As previously mentioned, one need not suppose that either Africa or Asia was a center of evolution. There is, as shown in preceding chapters, voluminous evidence, much found by professional scientists, suggesting that humans of the modern type have lived on various continents, including South America, for tens of millions of years. And, during this same period, there is also evidence for various apelike creatures, some resembling humans more than others.

A question encountered in our discussions of anomalous cultural remains (Chapters 2–6) once more arises: why should one attribute the Early Pleistocene stone tools and signs of fire at Yuanmou to primitive *Homo erectus*?

The tools and signs of fire were not found close to the *Homo erectus* teeth. Furthermore, there is evidence from China itself and other parts of the world that *Homo sapiens* existed in the Early Pleistocene and earlier.

In 1960, Jia Lanpo investigated Early Pleistocene sand and gravel deposits at Xihoudu in northern Shanxi province. He found three stones with signs of percussion, and more artifacts turned up in 1961 and 1962. Because of Early Pleistocene faunal remains, the site was given an age of over a million years. Paleomagnetic dating yielded an age of 1.8 million years. Cut bones and signs of fire were also found at Xihoudu. Jia believed *Australopithecus* was responsible for the artifacts and fire. But *Australopithecus* is not currently regarded as a maker of fire. *Homo erectus,* the Neanderthals, and *Homo sapiens* are the only hominids now thought capable of this.

J. S. Aigner, as one might well imagine, expressed strong reservations about Jia's evidence: "Despite the strong support for Lower [Early] Pleistocene human activity in north China claimed for Hsihoutu [Xihoudu], I am reluctant to accept unequivocally the materials at this time. . . . if Hsihoutu is verified, then humans occupied the north of China some 1,000,000 years ago and utilized fire. This would call into question some of our current assumptions about both the course of human evolution and the adaptational capabilities of early hominids." If one could, however, become detached from current assumptions, interesting possibilities open up.

This ends our review of discoveries in China. We have seen that age determinations of fossil hominids have been distorted by "morphological dating." When these ages are adjusted to reflect reasonable faunal date ranges, the total evidence fails to exclusively support an evolutionary hypothesis. Rather, the evidence appears also consistent with the proposal that anatomically modern human beings have coexisted with a variety of humanlike creatures throughout the Pleistocene.

11

Living Ape-Men?

Reviewing the fossil hominids of China, we found signs that humans may have coexisted with more apelike hominids throughout the Pleistocene. This may be true even today. Over the past hundred or so years, researchers have accumulated substantial evidence that creatures resembling Neanderthals, *Homo erectus,* and the australopithecines even now roam wilderness areas of the world.

Professional scientists have (1) observed wildmen in natural surroundings, (2) observed live captured specimens, (3) observed dead specimens, and (4) collected physical evidence for wildmen, including hundreds of footprints. They have also interviewed nonscientist informants and investigated the vast amount of wildman lore contained in ancient literatures and traditions.

CRYPTOZOOLOGY

For some researchers, the study of creatures such as wildmen comes under the heading of a genuine branch of science called cryptozoology. Cryptozoology, a term coined by the French zoologist Bernard Heuvelmans, refers to the scientific investigation of species whose existence has been reported but not fully documented. The Greek word *kryptos* means "hidden," so cryptozoology literally means "the study of hidden animals." There exists an International Society of Cryptozoology, the board of directors of which includes professional biologists, zoologists, and paleontologists from universities and museums around the world. The purpose of the society, as stated in its journal *Cryptozoology,* is "the investigation, analysis, publication, and discussion of all matters related to animals of unexpected form or size, or unexpected occurrence in time or space." A typical issue of *Cryptozoology* usually contains one or more articles by scientists on the topic of wildmen.

Is it really possible that there could be an unknown species of hominid on this planet? Many will find this hard to believe for two reasons. They suppose that every inch of the earth has been quite thoroughly explored. And they also

215

suppose that scientists possess a complete inventory of the earth's living animal species. Both suppositions are incorrect.

First, even in countries such as the United States, there remain vast unpopulated and little-traveled areas. In particular, the northwestern United States still has large regions of densely forested, mountainous terrain, which, although mapped from the air, are rarely penetrated by humans on the ground.

Second, a surprising number of new species of animals are still being found each year—about 5,000 according to a conservative estimate. As might be suspected, the great majority of these, some 4,000, are insects. Yet Heuvelmans in 1983 noted: "Quite recently, in the mid 1970's, there were discovered each year, around 112 new species of fish, 18 new species of reptiles, about ten new species of amphibians, the same number of mammals, and 3 or 4 new species of birds."

EUROPEAN WILDMEN

Reports of wildmen go back a long time. Many art objects of the Greeks, Romans, Carthaginians, and Etruscans bear images of semi-human creatures. For example, in the Museum of Prehistory in Rome, there is an Etruscan silver bowl on which may be seen, among human hunters on horses, the figure of a large, ape-man-like creature. During the Middle Ages, wildmen continued to be depicted in European art and architecture. A page from *Queen Mary's Psalter,* composed in the fourteenth century, shows a very realistically depicted hairy wildman being attacked by a pack of dogs.

NORTHWESTERN NORTH AMERICA

For centuries, the Indians of the northwestern United States and western Canada have believed in the reality of wildmen, known by various names, such as Sasquatch. In 1792, the Spanish botanist-naturalist José Mariano Moziño, describing the Indians of Nootka Sound on Vancouver Island, Canada, stated: "I do not know what to say about Matlox, inhabitant of the mountainous district, of whom all have an unbelievable terror. They imagine his body as very monstrous, all covered with stiff black bristles; a head similar to a human one, but with much greater, sharper and stronger fangs than those of the bear; extremely long arms; and toes and fingers armed with long curved claws."

U.S. President Theodore Roosevelt included an intriguing wildman report in his 1906 book *The Wilderness Hunter*. The incident took place in the Bitterroot Mountains, between Idaho and Montana. Wildman reports still come out of this region.

According to Roosevelt, in the early to middle 1800s a trapper named Bauman and his partner were exploring a particularly wild and lonely pass. An unknown creature ravaged their camp several times—at night, when they could not see the large animal clearly, and in the day, when they were absent. One day, Bauman found his partner dead in the camp, apparently killed by the creature. The creature left footprints that were quite humanlike. And unlike a bear, which normally walks on all four legs, this creature walked on two legs.

Taken on its own, the Bauman story is not very impressive as evidence for the existence of wildmen in North America, but when considered along with the more substantive reports it acquires greater significance.

On July 4, 1884, the *Colonist,* a newspaper published in Victoria, British Columbia, carried a story about a strange creature captured near the town of Yale. The *Colonist* reported: "'Jacko,' as the creature has been called by his capturers, is something of the gorilla type, standing about four feet seven inches in height and weighing 127 pounds. He has long, black, strong hair and resembles a human being with one exception, his entire body, excepting his hands (or paws) and feet is covered with glossy hair about one inch long. His forearm is much longer than a man's forearm, and he possesses extraordinary strength."

That the creature was not a gorilla seems clear—its weight was too small. Some might suppose that Jacko was a chimpanzee. But this idea was apparently considered and rejected by persons who were familiar with Jacko. In 1961, zoologist Ivan Sanderson mentioned "a comment made in another paper shortly after the original story was published, and which asked . . . how anybody could suggest that this 'Jacko' could have been a chimpanzee that had escaped from a circus." Additional reports of creatures like Jacko came from the same region. For example, Alexander Caulfield Anderson, a surveyor for the Hudson Bay Company, reported that some hairy humanoid creatures had several times thrown rocks at his party as they surveyed a trade route in 1864.

In 1901, Mike King, a well-known lumberman, was working in an isolated region in northern Vancouver Island. As King came over a ridge, he spotted a large humanlike creature covered with reddish brown fur. On the bank of a creek, the creature was washing some roots and placing them in two orderly piles beside him. The creature then left, running like a human being. Footprints observed by King were distinctly human, except for the "phenomenally long and spreading toes."

In 1941, several members of the Chapman family encountered a wildman at Ruby Creek, British Columbia. On a sunny summer afternoon, Mrs. Chapman's oldest son alerted her to the presence of a large animal coming down out of the woods near their home. At first, she thought it was a large bear. But then, much to her horror, she saw that it was a gigantic man covered all over with yellow-brown hair. The hair was about 4 inches long. The creature moved directly towards the house, and Mrs. Chapman rounded up her three children and fled downstream to the village.

In October of 1955, Mr. William Roe, who had spent much of his life hunting wild animals and observing their habits, encountered a wildman. The incident took place near a little town called Tete Jaune Cache in British Columbia. One day, said Roe in a sworn statement, he climbed up Mica Mountain to an old deserted mine and saw, at a distance of about 75 yards, what he first took to be a bear. When the creature stepped out into a clearing, Roe realized that it was something different: "My first impression was of a huge man, about six feet tall, almost three feet wide, and probably weighing somewhere near three hundred pounds. It was covered from head to foot with dark brown silver-tipped hair. But as it came closer I saw by its breasts that it was female."

In 1967, in the Bluff Creek region of Northern California, Roger Patterson and Bob Gimlin managed to shoot a short color film of a female Sasquatch. They also made casts of her footprints, which were 14 inches long.

Several opinions have been expressed about the film. While some authorities have said it is an outright fake, others have said they think it provides good evidence in favor of the reality of the Sasquatch. Mixed opinions have also been put forward. Dr. D. W. Grieve, an anatomist specializing in human walking, studied the film and had this to say: "My subjective impressions have oscillated between total acceptance of the Sasquatch on the grounds that the film would be difficult to fake, to one of irrational rejection based on an emotional response to the possibility that the Sasquatch actually exists."

Anthropologist Myra Shackley of the University of Leicester observed that the majority view seems to be "that the film could be a hoax, but if so an incredibly clever one." But this explanation could be used to dismiss almost any kind of scientific evidence whatsoever. All one has to do is posit a sufficiently expert hoaxer. Therefore the hoax hypothesis should be applied only when there is actual evidence of hoaxing, as at Piltdown, for example. Ideally, one should be able to produce the hoaxer. Furthermore, even a demonstrated case of hoaxing cannot be used to dismiss entire categories of similar evidence.

As far as Sasquatch footprints are concerned, independent witnesses have examined and reported hundreds of sets, and of these more than 100 have been preserved in photographs and casts. Critics, however, assert that all these footprints have been faked. Undoubtedly, some footprints have been faked, a fact the staunchest supporters of the Sasquatch will readily admit. But could every single one of them be a hoax?

In 1973, John R. Napier, a respected British anatomist, stated that if all the prints are fakes "then we must be prepared to accept the existence of a conspiracy of Mafia-like ramifications with cells in practically every major township from San Francisco to Vancouver."

Napier declared that he found the prints he himself studied "biologically convincing." Napier wrote: "The evidence that I have examined persuades me that some of the tracks are real, and that they are manlike in form. . . . I am convinced that the Sasquatch exists."

Grover S. Krantz, an anthropologist at Washington State University, was initially skeptical of Sasquatch reports. In order to determine whether or not the creature really existed, Krantz studied in detail some prints found in 1970 in northeast Washington State. In reconstructing the skeletal structure of the foot from the print, he noted that the ankle was positioned more forward than in a human foot. Taking into consideration the reported height and weight of an adult Sasquatch, Krantz, using his knowledge of physical anthropology, calculated just how far forward the ankle would have to be set. Returning to the prints, he found that the position of the ankle exactly matched his theoretical calculations. "That's when I decided the thing is real," said Krantz. "There is no way a faker could have known how far forward to set that ankle. It took me a couple of months to work it out with the casts in hand, so you have to figure how much smarter a faker would've had to be."

Krantz and wildman expert John Green have written extensive reports on the North American footprint evidence. Typically the prints are 14 to 18 inches long and 5 to 9 inches wide, giving a surface roughly 3 to 4 times larger than that of an average human foot. Hence the popular name Bigfoot. Krantz estimated that to make typical Sasquatch prints a total weight of at least 700 pounds is required. Thus a 200-pound man would have to be carrying at least 500 pounds to make a good print.

But that is only the beginning. There are reports of series of prints extending from three-quarters of a mile up to several miles, in deserted regions far away from the nearest roads. The stride length of a Sasquatch varies from 4 to 6 feet (the stride length of an average man is about 3 feet). Try walking a mile with at least 500 pounds on your back and taking strides 5 feet long.

"A footprint machine, a kind of mechanical stamp, has been suggested," stated Napier, "but an apparatus capable of delivering a thrust of approximately 800 lb per square foot that can be manhandled over rough and mountainous country puts a strain on one's credulity." Some of the reported series of tracks were in fresh snow, enabling observers to verify that no other marks were made by some machine paralleling the prints or hovering over them. In some cases, the distance between the toes of the footprints varied from one print to the next in a single series of prints. This means that besides all the other problems facing a hoaxer, he would have had to incorporate moving parts into his artificial feet.

On June 10, 1982, Paul Freeman, a U.S. Forest Service patrolman tracking elk in the Walla Walla district of Washington State, observed a hairy biped around 8 feet tall, standing about 60 yards from him. After 30 seconds, the large animal walked away. Krantz studied casts of the creature's footprints and found dermal ridges, sweat pores, and other features in the proper places for large primate feet. Detailed skin impressions on the side walls of the prints indicated the presence of a flexible sole pad.

In the face of much good evidence, why do almost all anthropologists and zoologists remain silent about Sasquatch? Krantz observed, "They are scared for their reputations and their jobs." Napier similarly noted: "One of the problems, perhaps the greatest problem, in investigating Sasquatch sightings is the suspicion with which people who claim to have seen a Sasquatch are treated by their neighbours and employers. To admit such an experience is, in some areas, to risk personal reputation, social status and professional credibility." In particular, he told of "the case of a highly qualified oil company geologist who told his story but insisted that his name should not be mentioned for fear of dismissal by his company." In this regard, Roderick Sprague, an anthropologist from the University of Idaho, said of Krantz: "It is Krantz's willingness to openly investigate the unknown that has cost him the respect of many colleagues as well as timely academic promotion."

The majority of the Sasquatch reports come from the northwestern United States and British Columbia. "One is forced to conclude," said Napier, "that a man-like life-form of gigantic proportions is living at the present time in the wild areas of the north-western United States and British Columbia." There are also numerous reports from the eastern parts of the United States and Canada. "That such a creature should be alive and kicking in our midst, unrecognized and unclassifiable, is a profound blow to the credibility of modern anthropology," concluded Napier. It might also be said that it is a blow to the credibility of biology, zoology, and science in general.

CENTRAL AND SOUTH AMERICA

From southern Mexico's tropical forests come accounts of beings called the Sisimite. Wendell Skousen, a geologist, said the people of Cubulco in Baja Verapaz reported: "There live in the mountains very big, wild men, completely clothed in short, thick, brown, hairy fur, with no necks, small eyes, long arms and huge hands. They leave footprints twice the length of a man's." Several persons said that they had been chased down mountainsides by the Sisimite. Skousen thought the creature may have been a bear. However, upon questioning the natives carefully, he decided it was not. Similar creatures are reported in Guatemala, where, it has been said, they kidnap women and children.

People in Belize (formerly British Honduras) speak of semi-human creatures called Dwendis, which inhabit the jungles in the southern part of their country. The name Dwendi comes from the Spanish word *Duende*, meaning "goblin." Ivan Sanderson, who conducted research in Belize, wrote in 1961: "Dozens told me of having seen them, and these were mostly men of substance who had worked for responsible organizations like the Forestry Department and who had, in several cases, been schooled or trained either in Europe or the United States. One, a junior forestry officer born locally, described in great detail two of these little creatures that he had suddenly noticed quietly watching him on several occasions at the edge of the forestry reserve near the foot of the Maya Mountains. . . . These little folk were described as being between three foot six and four foot six, well proportioned but with very heavy shoulders and rather long arms, clothed in thick, tight, close brown hair looking like that of a short-coated dog; having very flat yellowish faces but head-hair no longer than the body hair except down the back of the neck and midback." The Dwendis appear to represent a species different from the large Sasquatch of the Pacific Northwest of North America.

From the Guianas region of South America come accounts of wildmen called Didis. Early explorers heard reports about them from the Indians, who said they were about five feet tall, walked erect, and were covered with thick black hair.

In 1931, Nelloc Beccari, an anthropologist from Italy, heard an account of the Didi from Mr. Haines, the Resident Magistrate in British Guiana. Heuvelmans gave this summary of what Haines related to Beccari: "In 1910 he was going through the forest along the Konawaruk, a tributary which joins the Essequibo just above its junction with the Potaro, when he suddenly came upon two strange creatures, which stood up on their hind feet when they saw him. They had human features but were entirely covered with reddish brown fur. . . . the two creatures retreated slowly and disappeared into the forest."

After giving many similar accounts in his book about wildmen, Sanderson stated: "The most significant single fact about these reports from Guiana is that never once has any local person—nor any person reporting what a local person says—so much as indicated that these creatures are just 'monkeys.' In all cases they have specified that they are tailless, erect, and have human attributes."

From the eastern slopes of the Andes in Ecuador come reports of the Shiru, a small fur-covered hominidlike creature, about 4 to 5 feet tall. In Brazil, people tell of the large apelike Mapinguary, which leaves giant humanlike footprints and is said to kill cattle.

YETI: WILDMEN OF THE HIMALAYAS

Writings of British officials residing in the Himalayan region of the Indian subcontinent during the nineteenth century contain sporadic references to sightings and footprints of wildmen called Yeti. The Yeti were first mentioned by B. H. Hodgson, who from 1820 to 1843 served as British resident at the Nepalese court. Hodgson reported that in the course of a journey through northern Nepal his bearers were frightened by the sight of a hairy, tailless, humanlike creature.

Many will suggest, on hearing a report like this (and hundreds have been recorded since Hodgson's time), that the Nepalese mistook an ordinary animal for a Yeti. The usual candidates for mistaken identity are bears and the langur monkey. But it is hard to imagine that lifelong residents of the Himalayas, intimately familiar with the wildlife, would have made such mistakes. Myra Shackley observed that Yeti are found in Nepalese and Tibetan religious paintings depicting hierarchies of living beings. "Here," said Shackley, "bears, apes, and langurs are depicted separate from the wildman, suggesting there is no confusion (at least in the minds of the artists) between these forms."

During the nineteenth century, at least one European reported personally seeing a captured animal that resembled a Yeti. A South African man told anthropologist Myra Shackley: "Many years ago in India, my late wife's mother told me how her mother had actually seen what might have been one of these creatures at Mussorie, in the Himalayan foothills. This semi-human was walking upright, but was obviously more animal than human with hair covering its whole body. It was reportedly caught up in the snows. . . . his captors had it in chains."

During the twentieth century, sightings by Europeans of wildmen and their footprints continued, increasing during the Himalayan mountain-climbing expeditions.

In November of 1951, Eric Shipton, while reconnoitering the approaches to Mt. Everest, found footprints on the Menlung glacier, near the border between Tibet and Nepal, at an elevation of 18,000 feet. Shipton followed the trail for a mile. A close-up photograph of one of the prints has proved convincing to many. The footprints were quite large. John R. Napier considered and rejected the possibility that the particular size and shape of the best Shipton footprint could have been caused by melting of the snow. In the end, Napier suggested that the Shipton footprint was the result of superimposed human feet, one shod and the other unshod. In general, Napier, who was fully convinced of the existence of the North American Sasquatch, was highly skeptical of the evidence for the Yeti. But, as we shall see later in this section, new evidence would cause Napier to become more inclined to accept the Himalayan wildmen.

In the course of his expeditions to the Himalaya Mountains in the 1950s and 1960s, Sir Edmund Hillary gave attention to evidence for the Yeti, including footprints in snow. He concluded that in every case the large footprints attributed to the Yeti had been produced by the merging of smaller tracks of known animals. To this Napier, himself a skeptic, replied: "No one with any experience would confuse a melted footprint with a fresh one. Not all the prints seen over the years by reputable observers can be explained away in these terms; there must be other explanations for footprints, including, of course, the possibility that they were made by an animal unknown to science."

In addition to Westerners, native informants also gave a continuous stream of reports on the Yeti. For example, in 1958 Tibetan villagers from Tharbaleh, near the Rongbuk glacier, came upon a drowned Yeti, said Myra Shackley in her book on wildmen. The villagers described the creature as being like a small man with a pointed head and covered with reddish-brown fur.

Some Buddhist monasteries claim to have physical remains of the Yeti. One category of such relics is Yeti scalps, but the ones studied by Western scientists are thought to have been made from the skins of known animals. In 1960, Sir Edmund Hillary mounted an expedition to collect and evaluate evidence for the Yeti and sent a Yeti scalp from the Khumjung monastery to the West for testing. The results indicated that the scalp had been manufactured from the skin of the serow, a goatlike Himalayan antelope. But some disagreed with this analysis. Shackley said they "pointed out that hairs from the scalp look distinctly monkey-like, and that it contains parasitic mites of a species different from that recovered from the serow."

In the 1950s, explorers sponsored by American businessman Tom Slick obtained samples from a mummified Yeti hand kept at Pangboche, Tibet. Laboratory tests were inconclusive, but Shackley said the hand "has some curiously anthropoid features."

In May of 1957, the *Kathmandu Commoner* carried a story about a Yeti head that had been kept for 25 years in the village of Chilunka, about 50 miles northeast of Kathmandu, Nepal.

In March of 1986, Anthony B. Wooldridge was making a solo run through the Himalayas of northernmost India on behalf of a small third world development organization. While proceeding along a forested snow-covered slope near Hemkund, he noticed fresh tracks and took photographs of them, including a close-up of a single print that resembled the one photographed by Eric Shipton in 1951.

Pressing onward, Wooldridge came to a recent avalanche and saw a shallow furrow, apparently caused by a large object sliding across the snow. At the end of the furrow, he saw more tracks, which led to a distant shrub, behind which stood "a large, erect shape perhaps up to 2 meters [about 6 feet] tall."

Wooldridge, realizing it might be a Yeti, moved to within 150 meters (about 500 feet) and took photos. "It was standing with its legs apart," he stated, "apparently looking down the slope, with its right shoulder turned towards me. The head was large and squarish, and the whole body appeared to be covered with dark hair." In Wooldridge's opinion, the creature was definitely not a monkey, bear, or ordinary human being.

Wooldridge observed the creature for 45 minutes but had to leave when the weather worsened. On the way back to his base, he took more photographs of the footprints, but by this time they had become distorted by melting.

On his return to England, Wooldridge showed his photographic evidence to scientists interested in the wildman question, including John Napier. At a distance of 150 meters, the creature appeared quite small on the 35 mm film, but enlargements did show something humanlike. Describing the reactions of those who saw his photos, Wooldridge stated: "John Napier, a primatologist and author of the 1973 book *Bigfoot: The Yeti and Sasquatch in Myth and Reality,* has reversed the skeptical position he had previously expressed, and now describes himself as a Yeti devotee. Myra Shackley, an archaeologist and author of the 1983 book *Wildmen: Yeti, Sasquatch and the Neanderthal Enigma,* has seen the full sequence of photographs, and believes that the whole experience is very consistent with other reports of Yeti sightings. Lord Hunt, leader of the successful 1953 Mount Everest Expedition, who has twice seen Yeti tracks himself, is similarly convinced."

THE ALMAS OF CENTRAL ASIA

The Sasquatch and the Yeti, from the descriptions available, are large and very apelike. But there is another wildman, the Almas, which seems smaller and more human. Reports of the Almas are concentrated in an area extending from Mongolia in the north, south through the Pamirs, and then westward into the Caucasus region. Similar reports come from Siberia and the far northeast parts of the Russian republic.

Early in the fifteenth century, Hans Schiltenberger was captured by the Turks and sent to the court of Tamerlane, who placed him in the retinue of a Mongol prince named Egidi. After returning to Europe in 1427, Schiltenberger wrote about his experiences, which included wildmen: "In the mountains themselves live wild people, who have nothing in common with other human beings. A pelt covers the entire body of these creatures. Only the hands and face are free of hair. They run around in the hills like animals and eat foliage and grass and whatever else they can find. The lord of the territory made Egidi a present of a couple of forest people, a man and a woman. They had been caught in the wilderness."

A drawing of an Almas is found in a nineteenth-century Mongol compendium of medicines derived from various plants and animals. Myra Shackley noted: "The book contains thousands of illustrations of various classes of animals (reptiles, mammals and amphibia), but not one single mythological animal such as are known from similar medieval European books. All the creatures are living and observable today. There seems no reason at all to suggest that the Almas did not exist also and illustrations seem to suggest that it was found among rocky habitats, in the mountains."

In 1937, Dordji Meiren, a member of the Mongolian Academy of Sciences, saw the skin of an Almas in a monastery in the Gobi desert. The lamas were using it as a carpet in some of their rituals.

In 1963, Ivan Ivlov, a Russian pediatrician, was traveling through the Altai mountains in the southern part of Mongolia. Ivlov saw several humanlike creatures standing on a mountain slope. They appeared to be a family group, composed of a male, female, and child. Ivlov observed the creatures through his binoculars from a distance of half a mile until they moved out of his field of vision. His Mongolian driver also saw them and said they were common in that area.

After his encounter with the Almas family, Ivlov interviewed many Mongolian children, believing they would be more candid than adults. The children provided many additional reports about the Almas. For example, one child told Ivlov that while he and some other children were swimming in a stream, he saw a male Almas carry a child Almas across it.

In 1980, a worker at an experimental agricultural station, operated by the Mongolian Academy of Sciences at Bulgan, encountered the dead body of a wildman: "I approached and saw a hairy corpse of a robust humanlike creature dried and half-buried by sand. . . . The dead thing was not a bear or ape and at the same time it was not a man like Mongol or Kazakh or Chinese and Russian."

The Pamir mountains, lying in a remote region where the borders of Tadzhikistan, China, Kashmir, and Afghanistan meet, have been the scene of many Almas sightings. In 1925, Mikhail Stephanovitch Topilski, a major-general in the Soviet army, led his unit in an assault on an anti-Soviet guerilla force hiding in a cave in the Pamirs. One of the surviving guerillas said that while in the cave he and his comrades were attacked by several apelike creatures. Topilski ordered the rubble of the cave searched, and the body of one such creature was found. Topilski reported: "At first glance I thought the body was that of an ape. It was covered with hair all over. But I knew there were no apes in the Pamirs. Also, the body itself looked very much like that of a man. We tried pulling the hair, to see if it was just a hide used for disguise, but found that it was the creature's own natural hair. We turned the body over several times on its back and its front, and measured it. Our doctor made a long and thorough inspection of the body, and it was clear that it was not a human being."

"The body," continued Topilski, "belonged to a male creature 165–170 cm [about 5 feet] tall, elderly or even old, judging by the greyish colour of the hair in several places. . . . The colour of the face was dark, and the creature had neither beard nor moustache. The temples were bald and the back of the head was covered by thick, matted hair. The dead creature lay with its eyes open and its teeth bared. The eyes were dark and the teeth were large and even and shaped like human teeth. The forehead was slanting and the eyebrows were very powerful. The protruding jawbones made the face resemble the Mongol type of face. The nose was flat, with a deeply sunk bridge. The ears were hairless and looked a little more pointed than a human being's with a longer lobe. The lower jaw was very massive. The creature had a very powerful chest and well developed muscles."

In 1957, Alexander G. Pronin, a hydrologist at the Geographical Research Institute of Leningrad University, participated in an expedition to the Pamirs, for the purpose of mapping glaciers. On August 2, 1957, while his team was investigating the Fedchenko glacier, Pronin hiked into the valley of the Balyandkiik River. Shackley stated: "At noon he noticed a figure standing on a rocky cliff about 500 yards above him and the same distance away. His first reaction was surprise, since this area was known to be uninhabited, and his second was that the creature was not human. It resembled a man but was very stooped. He watched the stocky figure move across the snow, keeping its feet wide apart, and he noted that its forearms were longer than a human's and it was covered with reddish grey hair." Pronin saw the creature again three days later, walking upright. Since this incident, there have been numerous wildman sightings in the Pamirs, and members of various expeditions have photographed and taken casts of footprints.

We shall now consider reports about the Almas from the Caucasus region. According to testimony from villagers of Tkhina, on the Mokvi River, a female Almas was captured there during the nineteenth century, in the forests of Mt. Zaadan. For three years, she was kept imprisoned, but then became domesticated and was allowed to live in a house. She was called Zana. Shackley stated: "Her skin was a greyish-black colour, covered with reddish hair, longer on her head than elsewhere. She was capable of inarticulate cries but never developed a language. She had a large face with big cheek bones, muzzle-like prognathous jaw and large eyebrows, big white teeth and a 'fierce expression.'" Eventually Zana, through sexual relations with a villager, had children. Some of Zana's grandchildren were seen by Boris Porshnev in 1964. In her account of Porshnev's investigations, Shackley noted: "The grandchildren, Chalikoua and Taia, had darkish skin of rather negroid appearance, with very prominent chewing muscles and extra strong jaws." Porshnev also interviewed villagers who as children had been present at Zana's funeral in the 1880s.

In the Caucasus region, the Almas is sometimes called Biaban-guli. In 1899, K. A. Satunin, a Russian zoologist, spotted a female Biaban-guli in the Talysh hills of the southern Caucasus. He stated that the creature had "fully human movements." The fact that Satunin was a well-known zoologist makes his report particularly significant.

In 1941, V. S. Karapetyan, a lieutenant colonel of the medical service of the

Soviet army, performed a direct physical examination of a living wildman captured in the Dagestan autonomous republic, just north of the Caucasus mountains. Karapetyan said: "I entered a shed with two members of the local authorities. . . . I can still see the creature as it stood before me, a male, naked and bare-footed. And it was doubtlessly a man, because its entire shape was human. The chest, back, and shoulders, however, were covered with shaggy hair of a dark brown colour. This fur of his was much like that of a bear, and 2 to 3 centimeters [1 inch] long. The fur was thinner and softer below the chest. His wrists were crude and sparsely covered with hair. The palms of his hands and soles of his feet were free of hair. But the hair on his head reached to his shoulders partly covering his forehead. The hair on his head, moreover, felt very rough to the hand. He had no beard or moustache, though his face was completely covered with a light growth of hair. The hair around his mouth was also short and sparse. The man stood absolutely straight with his arms hanging, and his height was above the average—about 180 cm [almost 5 feet 11 inches]. He stood before me like a giant, his mighty chest thrust forward. His fingers were thick, strong and exceptionally large. On the whole, he was considerably bigger than any of the local inhabitants. His eyes told me nothing. They were dull and empty—the eyes of an animal. And he seemed to me like an animal and nothing more." It is reports like this that have led scientists such as British anthropologist Myra Shackley to conclude that the Almas may represent surviving Neanderthals or perhaps even *Homo erectus*. What happened to the wildman of Dagestan? According to published accounts, he was shot by his Soviet military captors as they retreated before the advancing German army.

WILDMEN OF CHINA

"Chinese historical documents, and many city and town annals, contain abundant records of Wildman, which are given various names," states Zhou Guoxing of the Beijing Museum of Natural History. "Even today, in the area of Fang County, Hubei Province," says Zhou, "there are still legends about 'maoren' (hairy men) or 'wildmen.'" In 1922, a militiaman is said to have captured a wildman there, but there are no further records of this incident.

In 1940, Wang Zelin, a graduate of the biology department of Northwestern University in Chicago, was able to directly see a wildman shortly after it was shot to death by hunters. Wang was driving from Baoji, in Shanxi Province, to Tianshui, in Gansu Province, when he heard gunfire ahead of him. He got out of the car to satisfy his curiosity and saw a corpse. It was a female creature, six and a half feet tall and covered with a coat of thick greyish-red hair about one and a quarter inches long. The hair on its face was shorter. The cheek bones were prominent, and the lips jutted out. The hair on the head was about one foot long.

According to Wang, the creature looked like a reconstruction of the Chinese *Homo erectus.*

Ten years later, another scientist, Fun Jinquan, a geologist, saw some living wildmen. Zhou Guoxing stated: "With the help of local guides, he watched, at a safe distance, two local Wildmen in the mountain forest near Baoji County, Shanxi Province, in the spring of 1950. They were mother and son, the smaller one being 1.6 meters [5.25 feet] in height. Both looked human."

In 1957, a biology teacher in Zhejiang province obtained the hands and feet of a "manbear" killed by local peasants. Zhou Guoxing later examined them. Although he did not think they were from a wildman, he concluded that "they came from an unknown primate."

In 1961, workers building a road through the heavily forested Xishuang Banna region of Yunnan province in southernmost China reported killing a humanlike female primate. The creature was 1.2–1.3 meters (about 4 feet) tall and covered with hair. It walked upright, and according to the eyewitness reports, its hands, ears, and breasts were like those of a female human. The Chinese Academy of Sciences sent a team to investigate, but they were not able to obtain any physical evidence. Some suggested that the workers had come upon a gibbon. But Zhou Guoxing stated: "The present author recently visited a newsman who took part in that investigation. He stated that the animal which had been killed was not a gibbon, but an unknown animal of human shape."

In 1976, six cadres from the Shennongjia forestry region in Hubei province were driving at night down the highway near the village of Chunshuya, between Fangxian county and Shennongjia. On the way, they encountered a "strange tailless creature with reddish fur." Fortunately, it stood still long enough for five of the people to get out of the car and look at it from a distance of only a few feet, while the driver kept his headlights trained on it. The observers were certain that it was not a bear or any other creature with which they were familiar. They reported the incident in a telegram to the Chinese Academy of Sciences in Beijing.

Over the years, Academy officials had received many similar reports from the same region of Hubei province. So when they heard about this incident, they decided to thoroughly investigate the matter. A scientific expedition consisting of more than 100 members proceeded to Hubei province. They collected physical evidence, in the form of hair, footprints, and feces, and recorded sightings by the local inhabitants. Subsequent research has added to these results. Altogether, more than a thousand footprints have been found in Hubei province, some more than 19 inches long. Over 100 wildman hairs have been collected, the longest measuring 21 inches.

Some have sought to explain sightings of wildmen in the Shennongjia region of Hubei province as encounters with the rare golden monkey, which inhabits the same area. The golden monkey might very well account for reports of creatures glimpsed for a moment at a great distance. But consider the case of Pang Gensheng, a local commune leader, who was confronted in the forest by a wildman.

Pang, who stood face to face with the creature, at a distance of five feet for about an hour, said: "He was about seven feet tall, with shoulders wider than a man's, a sloping forehead, deep-set eyes and a bulbous nose with slightly upturned nostrils. He had sunken cheeks, ears like a man's but bigger, and round eyes, also bigger than a man's. His jaw jutted out and he had protruding lips. His front teeth were as broad as a horse's. His eyes were black. His hair was dark brown, more than a foot long and hung loosely over his shoulders. His whole face, except for the nose and ears, was covered with short hairs. His arms hung down to below his knees. He had big hands with fingers about six inches long and thumbs only slightly separated from the fingers. He didn't have a tail and the hair on his body was short. He had thick thighs, shorter than the lower part of his leg. He walked upright with his legs apart. His feet were each about 12 inches long and half that broad—broader in front and narrow behind, with splayed toes."

WILDMEN OF MALAYSIA AND INDONESIA

In 1969, John McKinnon, who journeyed to Borneo to observe orangutans, came across some humanlike footprints. McKinnon asked his Malay boatman what made them. "Without a moment's hesitation he replied 'Batutut,'"wrote McKinnon. Later, in Malaya, McKinnon saw some casts of footprints even bigger than those he had seen in Borneo, but he recognized them as definitely having been made by the same kind of creature. The Malayans called it Orangpendek (short fellow). According to Ivan Sanderson, these footprints differ from those of the anthropoid apes inhabiting the Indonesian forests (the gibbon, siamang, and orangutan). They are also distinct from those of the sun bear.

Early in the twentieth century, L. C. Westenek, a governor of Sumatra, received a written report about an encounter with a type of wildman called Sedapa. The overseer of an estate in the Barisan Mountains, along with some workers, observed the Sedapa from a distance of 15 yards. The overseer said he saw "a large creature, low on its feet, which ran like a man, and was about to cross my path; it was very hairy and it was not an orang-utan."

In a journal article about wildmen published in 1918, Westenek recorded a report from a Mr. Oostingh, who lived in Sumatra. Once while proceeding through the forest, he came upon a man sitting on a log and facing away from him. Oostingh stated: "I suddenly realised that his neck was oddly leathery and extremely filthy. 'That chap's got a very dirty and wrinkled neck!' I said to myself. . . . Then I saw that it was not a man."

"It was not an orang-utan," declared Oostingh. "I had seen one of these large apes a short time before." What was the creature if not an orangutan? Oostingh could not say for sure. As we have seen, some have suggested that wildmen may represent surviving representatives of the Neanderthals or *Homo erectus.*

If there is uncertainty about what kinds of hominids may be around today, how can we be so sure about what kinds of hominids may or may not have been around in the distant past?

Empiric investigation of the fossil record may not be a sure guide. As Bernard Heuvelmans stated in a letter (April 15, 1986) to our researcher Stephen Bernath: "Do not overestimate the importance of the fossil record. Fossilization is a very rare, exceptional phenomenon, and the fossil record cannot thus give us an exact image of life on earth during the past geological periods. The fossil record of primates is particularly poor because very intelligent and cautious animals can avoid more easily the very conditions of fossilization—such as sinking in mud or peat, for instance."

The empiric method undoubtedly has its limitations, and the fossil record is incomplete and imperfect. But when all the evidence, including that for very ancient humans and living ape-men, is objectively evaluated, the pattern that emerges is one of continuing coexistence rather than sequential evolution.

AFRICA

Native informants from several countries in the western part of the African continent, such as the Ivory Coast, have given accounts of a race of pygmylike creatures covered with reddish hair. Europeans have also encountered them.

Wildman reports also come from East Africa. Capt. William Hitchens reported in 1937: "Some years ago I was sent on an official lion-hunt in this area (the Ussure and Simibit forests on the western side of the Wembare plains) and, while waiting in a forest glade for a man-eater, I saw two small, brown, furry creatures come from dense forest on one side of the glade and disappear into the thickets on the other. They were like little men, about 4 feet high, walking upright, but clad in russet hair. The native hunter with me gazed in mingled fear and amazement. They were, he said, *agogwe,* the little furry men whom one does not see once in a lifetime." Were they just apes or monkeys? It does not seem that either Hitchens or the native hunter accompanying him would have been unable to recognize an ape or monkey. Many reports of the Agogwe emanate from Tanzania and Mozambique.

From the Congo region come reports of the Kakundakari and Kilomba. About 5.5 feet tall and covered with hair, they are said to walk upright like humans. Charles Cordier, a professional animal collector who worked for many zoos and museums, followed tracks of the Kakundakari in Zaire in the late 1950s and early 1960s. Once, said Cordier, a Kakundakari had become entangled in one of his bird snares. "It fell on its face," said Cordier, "turned over, sat up, took the noose off its feet, and walked away before the nearby African could do anything."

Reports of such creatures also come from southern Africa. Pascal Tassy, of the Laboratory of Vertebrate and Human Paleontology, wrote in 1983: "Philip V. Tobias, now on the Board of Directors of the International Society of Cryptozoology, once told Heuvelmans that one of his colleagues had set traps to capture living australopithecines." Tobias, from South Africa, is a recognized authority on *Australopithecus*.

According to standard views, the last australopithecines perished approximately 750,000 years ago, and *Homo erectus* died out around 200,000 years ago. The Neanderthals, it is said, vanished about 35,000 years ago, and since then fully modern humans alone have existed throughout the entire world. Yet many sightings of different kinds of wildmen in various parts of the world strongly challenge the standard view.

MAINSTREAM SCIENCE AND WILDMAN REPORTS

Despite all the evidence we have presented, most recognized authorities in anthropology and zoology decline to discuss the existence of wildmen. If they mention wildmen at all, they rarely present the really strong evidence for their existence, focusing instead on the reports least likely to challenge their disbelief.

Skeptical scientists say that no one has found any bones of wildmen; nor, they say, has anyone produced a single body, dead or alive. But hand and foot specimens of reputed wildmen, and even a head, have been collected. Competent persons report having examined bodies of wildmen. And there are also a number of accounts of capture. That none of this physical evidence has made its way into museums and other scientific institutions may be taken as a failure of the process for gathering and preserving evidence. The operation of what we call a knowledge filter tends to keep evidence tinged with disrepute outside official channels.

However, some scientists with solid reputations, such as Krantz, Napier, Shackley, Porshnev, and others, have found in the available evidence enough reason to conclude that wildmen do in fact exist, or, at least, that the question of their existence is worthy of serious study.

Myra Shackley wrote to our researcher Steve Bernath on December 4, 1984: "As you know, this whole question is highly topical, and there has been an awful lot of correspondence and publication flying around on the scene. Opinions vary, but I guess that the commonest would be that there is indeed sufficient evidence to suggest at least the possibility of the existence of various unclassified manlike creatures, but that in the present state of our knowledge it is impossible to comment on their significance in any more detail. The position is further complicated by misquotes, hoaxing, and lunatic fringe activities, but a surprising number of hardcore anthropologists seem to be of the opinion that the matter is very worthwhile investigating."

So there is some scientific recognition of the wildman evidence, but it seems to be largely a matter of privately expressed views, with little or no official recognition.

12

Always Something New Out of Africa

The controversies surrounding Java man and Beijing man, what to speak of Castenedolo man and the European eoliths, have long since subsided. As for the disputing scientists, most of them are in their graves, their bones on the way to disintegration or fossilization. But today Africa, the land of *Australopithecus* and *Homo habilis,* remains an active battlefield, with scientists skirmishing to establish their views on human origins.

RECK'S SKELETON

The first significant African discovery took place early in this century. In 1913, Professor Hans Reck, of Berlin University, conducted investigations at Olduvai Gorge in Tanzania, then German East Africa. While one of Reck's African collectors was searching for fossils, he saw a piece of bone sticking up from the earth. After removing the surface rubble, the collector saw parts of a complete and fully human skeleton embedded in the rock. He called Reck, who then had the skeleton taken out in a solid block of hard sediment. The human skeletal remains, including a complete skull (Figure 12.1), had to be chipped out with hammers and chisels. The skeleton was then transported to Berlin.

Reck identified a sequence of five beds at Olduvai Gorge. The skeleton was from the upper part of Bed II, which is now considered to be 1.15 million years old. At Reck's site, the overlying layers (Beds III, IV, and V) had been worn away by erosion. But Bed II was still covered by rubble

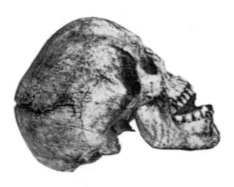

Figure 12.1. This skull is from a fully human skeleton found in 1913 by H. Reck at Olduvai Gorge, Tanzania.

233

from bright red Bed III and from Bed V (Figure 12.2). Perhaps as little as 50 years ago, the site would have been covered by Beds III and V, including a hard limestonelike layer of calcrete. Bed IV was apparently removed by erosion before the deposition of Bed V.

Reck, understanding the significance of his find, carefully considered the possibility that the human skeleton had arrived in Bed II through burial. Reck observed: "The wall of the grave would have a definite border, an edge that would show in profile a division from the undisturbed stone. The grave filling would show an abnormal structure and heterogeneous mixture of excavated materials, including easily recognizable pieces of calcrete. Neither of these signs were to be found despite the most attentive inspection. Rather the stone directly around the skeleton was not distinguishable from the neighboring stone in terms of color, hardness, thickness of layers, structure, or order."

Louis Leakey examined Reck's skeleton in Berlin, but he judged it more recent than Reck had claimed. In 1931, Leakey and Reck visited the site where the skeleton had been found. Leakey was won over to Reck's view that the anatomically modern human skeleton was the same age as Bed II.

In February of 1932, zoologists C. Forster Cooper of Cambridge and D.M.S. Watson of the University of London said the completeness of the skeleton found by Reck clearly indicated it was a recent burial.

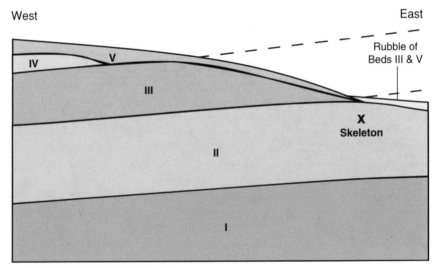

Figure 12.2. This section of the northern slope of Olduvai Gorge shows the location where H. Reck found a fully human skeleton in 1913 in upper Bed II. Bed II is 1.15–1.7 million years old.

Leakey agreed with Cooper and Watson that Reck's skeleton had arrived in its position in Bed II by burial, but he thought the burial had taken place during Bed II times.

In a letter to *Nature,* Leakey argued that no more than 50 years ago the reddish-yellow upper part of Bed II would have been covered by an intact layer of bright red Bed III. If the skeleton had been buried after the deposition of Bed II, there should have been a mixture of bright red and reddish-yellow sediments in the grave filling. "I was lucky enough personally to examine the skeleton at Munich while it was still intact in its original matrix," wrote Leakey, "and could detect no trace whatever of such admixture or disturbance."

Cooper and Watson were still not satisfied. In June 1932, they said in a letter to *Nature* that red pebbles from Bed III may have lost their color. This would explain why Reck and Leakey did not see the Bed III pebbles in the matrix surrounding the skeleton. A. T. Hopwood, however, disagreed that Bed III pebbles would have lost their bright red color. He pointed out that the top of Bed II, in which the skeleton was found, was also reddish and stated: "The reddish colour of the matrix is against the theory that any inclusions of Bed III would have been decolorised."

Despite the broadsides from Cooper and Watson, Reck and Leakey seemed to be holding their own. But in August 1932, P. G. H. Boswell, a geologist from the Imperial College in England, gave a perplexing report in the pages of *Nature.*

Professor T. Mollison had sent to Boswell from Munich a sample of what Mollison said was the matrix surrounding Reck's skeleton. Mollison, it may be noted, was not a completely neutral party. As early as 1929, he had expressed his belief that the skeleton was that of a Masai tribesman, buried in the not too distant past.

Boswell stated that the sample supplied by Mollison contained "(*a*) pea-sized bright red pebbles like those of Bed 3, and (*b*) chips of concretionary limestone indistinguishable from that of Bed 5." Boswell took all this to mean that the skeleton had been buried after the deposition of Bed V, which contains hard layers of steppe-lime, or calcrete.

The presence of the bright red Bed III pebbles and Bed V limestone chips in the sample sent by Mollison certainly calls for some explanation. Reck and Leakey had both carefully examined the matrix at different times over a period of 20 years. They did not report any mixture of Bed III materials or chips of limestonelike calcrete, even though they were specifically looking for such evidence. So it is remarkable that the presence of red pebbles and limestone chips should suddenly become apparent. It would appear that at least one of the participants in the discovery and the subsequent polemics was guilty of extremely careless observation—or cheating.

The debate about the age of Reck's skeleton became more complicated when Leakey brought new soil samples from Olduvai. Boswell and J. D. Solomon studied them at the Imperial College of Science and Technology. They reported their findings in the March 18, 1933 issue of *Nature,* in a letter signed also by Leakey, Reck, and Hopwood.

The letter contained this very intriguing statement: "Samples of Bed II, actually collected at the 'man site,' at the same level and in the immediate vicinity of the place where the skeleton was found consist of pure and wholly typical Bed II material, and differ very markedly from the samples of matrix of the skeleton which were supplied by Prof. Mollison from Munich." This suggests that the matrix sample originally supplied by Mollison to Boswell may not have been representative of the material closely surrounding Reck's skeleton.

But Reck and Leakey apparently concluded from the new observations that the matrix sample from Reck's skeleton was in fact some kind of grave filling, different from pure Bed II material. As far as we can tell, they offered no satisfactory explanation for their previous opinion that the skeleton had been found in pure, unmistakable Bed II materials.

Instead, both Reck and Leakey joined Boswell, Hopwood, and Solomon in concluding that "it seems highly probable that the skeleton was intrusive into Bed II and that the date of the intrusion is not earlier than the great unconformity which separates Bed V from the lower series."

It remains somewhat of a mystery why both Reck and Leakey changed their minds about a Bed II date for Reck's skeleton. Perhaps Reck was simply tired of fighting an old battle against odds that seemed more and more overwhelming. With the discovery of Beijing man and additional specimens of Java man, the scientific community had become more uniformly committed to the idea that a transitional ape-man was the only proper inhabitant of the Middle Pleistocene. An anatomically modern *Homo sapiens* skeleton in Bed II of Olduvai Gorge did not make sense except as a fairly recent burial.

Leakey, almost alone, remained very much opposed to the idea that Java man (*Pithecanthropus*) and Beijing man (*Sinanthropus*) were human ancestors. Furthermore, he had made additional discoveries in Kenya, at Kanam and Kanjera. The fossils he found there, in his opinion, provided indisputable evidence for *Homo sapiens* in the same period as *Pithecanthropus* and *Sinanthropus* (and Reck's skeleton). So perhaps he abandoned the fight over Reck's highly controversial skeleton in order to strengthen support for his own recent finds at Kanam and Kanjera.

There is substantial circumstantial evidence in support of this hypothesis. Leakey's statement abandoning his previous position on the antiquity of Reck's skeleton appeared in *Nature* on the same day that a committee met to pass judgement on the Kanam and Kanjera finds. Some of the most vocal opponents of Reck's skeleton, such as Boswell, Solomon, Cooper, Watson, and Mollison, would be sitting on that committee.

Although Reck and Leakey gave up their earlier opinion that Reck's skeleton was as old as Bed II, their revised opinion that the skeleton was buried into Bed II during Bed V times still gives a potentially anomalous age for the fully human skeleton. The base of Bed V is about 400,000 years old, according to current estimates. Today, however, most scientists believe that humans like ourselves first appeared about 100,000 years ago, as shown by the Border Cave discoveries in South Africa.

Stone tools characterized as "Aurignacian" were found in the lower levels of Bed V. Archeologists first used the term Aurignacian in connection with the finely made artifacts of Cro-Magnon man (*Homo sapiens sapiens*) found at Aurignac, France. According to standard opinion, tools of the Aurignacian type did not appear before 30,000 years ago. The tools lend support to the idea that anatomically modern humans, as represented by Reck's skeleton, were present in this part of Africa at least 400,000 years ago. Alternatively, one could attribute the tools to *Homo erectus*. But this would mean granting to *Homo erectus* toolmaking abilities substantially greater than scientists currently accept.

In 1935, in his book *The Stone Age Races of Kenya*, Leakey repeated his view that Reck's skeleton had been buried into Bed II from a land surface that existed during the formation of Bed V. But now he favored a time much later in that period. He thought that Reck's skeleton resembled skeletons found at Gamble's Cave, a site with an age of about 10,000 years. But from the standpoint of geology, all that could truthfully be said (granting the Bed V burial hypothesis) was that the skeleton could be anywhere from 400,000 to perhaps a few thousand years old.

Reiner Protsch later attempted to remedy this situation by dating Reck's skeleton itself, using the radiocarbon method. In 1974, he reported an age of 16,920 years. But there are several problems with this age determination.

First of all, it is not clear that the bone sample actually came from Reck's skeleton. The skull was considered too valuable to use for testing. And the rest of the skeleton had disappeared from a Munich museum during the Second World War. The museum director provided some small fragments of bone, which Protsch said were "most likely" part of the original skeleton.

From these fragments, Protsch was able to gather a sample of only 224 grams, about one third the normal size of a test sample. Although he obtained an age of 16,920 years for the human bone, he got very much different dates from other materials from the same site, some older and some younger.

Even if the sample actually belonged to Reck's skeleton, it could have been contaminated with recent carbon. This would have caused the sample to yield a falsely young age. By 1974, the remaining bone fragments from Reck's skeleton, if they in fact belonged to Reck's skeleton, had been lying around in a museum for over 60 years. During this time, bacteria and other microorganisms, all containing recent carbon, could have thoroughly contaminated the bone fragments. The bones also could have been contaminated with recent carbon when they were still in the ground. Furthermore, the bones had been soaked in an organic preservative (Sapon), which contained recent carbon.

Protsch did not describe what chemical treatment he used to eliminate recent carbon 14 contributed by the Sapon and other contaminants. Thus we have no way of knowing to what degree the contamination from these sources was eliminated.

The radiocarbon method is applied only to collagen, the protein found in bones. This protein must be extracted from the rest of the bone by an extremely rigorous purification process. Scientists then determine whether a sample's amino acids (the building blocks of proteins) correspond to those found in collagen. If they do not, this suggests that amino acids may have entered the bone from outside. These amino acids, being of a different age than the bone, could yield a falsely young radiocarbon date.

Ideally, one should date each amino acid separately. If any of the amino acids yield dates different from any of the others, this suggests the bone is contaminated and not suitable for carbon 14 dating.

Concerning the radiocarbon tests on Reck's skeleton reported by Protsch, the laboratories that performed them could not have dated each amino acid separately. This requires a dating technique (accelerator mass spectrometry) that was not in use in the early 1970s. Neither could these labs have been aware of the stringent protein purification techniques now deemed necessary. We can only conclude that the radiocarbon date Protsch gave for Reck's skeleton is unreliable. In particular, the date could very well be falsely young.

There are documented cases of bones from Olduvai Gorge giving falsely young radiocarbon dates. For example, a bone from the Upper Ndutu beds yielded an age of 3,340 years. The Upper Ndutu beds, part of Bed V, are from 32,000 to 60,000 years old. A date of 3,340 years would thus be too young by at least a factor of ten.

In his report, Protsch said about Reck's skeleton: "Theoretically, several facts speak against an early age of the hominid, such as its morphology." This suggests that the skeleton's modern morphology was one of the main reasons Protsch doubted it was as old as Bed II or even the base of Bed V.

In our discussion of China, we introduced the concept of a probable date range as the fairest age indicator for controversial discoveries. The available evidence suggests that Reck's skeleton should be assigned a probable date range extending from the late Late Pleistocene (10,000 years) to the late Early

Pleistocene (1.15 million years). There is much evidence that argues in favor of the original Bed II date proposed by Reck. Particularly strong is Reck's observation that the thin layers of Bed II sediment directly around the skeleton were undisturbed. Also arguing against later burial is the rocklike hardness of Bed II. Reports favoring a Bed V date seem to be founded upon purely theoretical objections, dubious testimony, inconclusive test results, and highly speculative geological reasoning. But, setting aside the questionable radiocarbon date, even these reports yield dates of up to 400,000 years for Reck's skeleton.

THE KANJERA SKULLS AND KANAM JAW

In 1932, Louis Leakey announced discoveries at Kanam and Kanjera, near Lake Victoria in western Kenya. The Kanam jaw and Kanjera skulls, he believed, provided good evidence of *Homo sapiens* in the Early and Middle Pleistocene.

When Leaky visited Kanjera in 1932 with Donald MacInnes, they found stone hand axes, a human femur, and fragments of five human skulls, designated Kanjera 1–5. The fossil-bearing beds at Kanjera are equivalent to Bed IV at Olduvai Gorge, which is from 400,000 to 700,000 years old. But the morphology of the Kanjera skull pieces is quite modern.

At Kanam, Leakey initially found teeth of *Mastodon* and a single tooth of *Deinotherium* (an extinct elephantlike mammal), as well as some crude stone implements. On March 29, 1932, Leakey's collector, Juma Gitau, brought him a second *Deinotherium* tooth. Leakey told Gitau to keep digging in the same spot. Working a few yards from Leakey, Gitau hacked out a block of travertine (a hard calcium carbonate deposit) and broke it open with a pick. He saw a tooth protruding from a piece of travertine and showed it to MacInnes, who identified the tooth as human. MacInnes summoned Leakey.

Upon chipping away the travertine surrounding Gitau's find, they saw the front part of a human lower jaw with two premolars. Leakey thought the jaw from the Early Pleistocene Kanam formation was much like that of *Homo sapiens,* and he announced its discovery in a letter to *Nature.* The Kanam beds are at least 2.0 million years old.

For Leakey, the Kanam and Kanjera fossils showed that a hominid close to the modern human type had existed at the time of Java man and Beijing man, or even earlier. If he was correct, Java man and Beijing man (now *Homo erectus*) could not be direct human ancestors, nor could Piltdown man with his apelike jaw.

In March of 1933, the human biology section of the Royal Anthropological Institute met to consider Leakey's discoveries at Kanam and Kanjera. Chaired by Sir Arthur Smith Woodward, 28 scientists issued reports on four categories of evidence: geological, paleontological, anatomical, and archeological. The geology committee concluded that the Kanjera and Kanam human fossils were as old as the beds in which they were found. The paleontology committee said the Kanam beds were Early Pleistocene, whereas the Kanjera beds were no more recent than Middle Pleistocene. The archeology committee noted the presence at both Kanam and Kanjera of stone tools in the same beds where the human fossils had been found. The anatomical committee said the Kanjera skulls exhibited "no characteristics inconsistent with the reference to the type *Homo sapiens.*" The same was true of the Kanjera femur. About the Kanam jaw, the anatomy experts said it was unusual in some respects. Yet they were "not able to point to any detail of the specimen that is incompatible with its inclusion in the type of the *Homo sapiens.*"

Shortly after the 1933 conference gave Leakey its vote of confidence, geologist Percy Boswell began to question the age of the Kanam and Kanjera fossils. Leakey, who had experienced Boswell's attacks on the age of Reck's skeleton, decided to bring Boswell to Africa, hoping this would resolve his doubts. But all did not go well.

Upon returning to England, Boswell submitted to *Nature* a negative report on Kanam and Kanjera: "Unfortunately, it has not proved possible to find the exact site of either discovery." Boswell found the geological conditions at the sites confused. He said that "the clayey beds found there had frequently suffered much disturbance by slumping." Boswell concluded that the "uncertain conditions of discovery. . . force me to place Kanam and Kanjera man in a 'suspense account.'"

Replying to Boswell's charges, Leakey said he had been able to show Boswell the locations where he had found his fossils. Leakey wrote: "At Kanjera I showed him the exact spot where the residual mound of deposits had stood which yielded the Kanjera No. 3 skull *in situ.* . . . the fact that I did show Prof. Boswell the site is proved by a small fragment of bone picked up there in 1935 which fits one of the 1932 pieces."

Regarding the location of the Kanam jaw, Leakey said: "We had originally taken a level section right across the Kanam West gullies, using a Zeiss-Watts level, and could therefore locate the position to within a very few feet—and, in fact, we did so."

Boswell suggested that even if the jaw was found in the Early Pleistocene formation at Kanam, it had entered somehow from above—by "slumping" of the strata or through a fissure. To this Leakey later replied: "I cannot accept this interpretation, for which there is no evidence. The state of preservation of the fossil is in every respect identical to that of the Lower [Early] Pleistocene fossils found with it." Leakey said that Boswell told him he would have been inclined to accept the Kanam jaw as genuine had it not possessed a humanlike chin structure.

Nevertheless, Boswell's views prevailed. But in 1968 Philip V. Tobias of South Africa said, "There there is a good prima facie case to re-open the question of Kanjera." And the Kanjera case was in fact reopened. Leakey's biographer Sonia Cole wrote: "In September 1969 Louis attended a conference in Paris sponsored by UNESCO on the theme of the origins of *Homo sapiens*. . . . the 300 or so delegates unanimously accepted that the Kanjera skulls were Middle Pleistocene."

Tobias said about the Kanam jaw: "Nothing that Boswell said really discredited or even weakened the claim of Leakey that the mandible belonged to the stratum in question."

Scientists have described the Kanam jaw, with its modern chin structure, in a multiplicity of ways. In 1932, a committee of English anatomists proclaimed that there was no reason the jaw should not be considered *Homo sapiens*. Sir Arthur Keith, a leading British anthropologist, also considered the Kanam jaw *Homo sapiens*. But in the 1940s Keith decided the jaw was most likely from an australopithecine. In 1962, Philip Tobias said the Kanam jaw most closely resembled a late Middle Pleistocene jaw from Rabat in Morocco, and Late Pleistocene jaws such as those from the Cave of Hearths in South Africa and Dire-Dawa in Ethiopia. According to Tobias, these jaws display neanderthaloid features.

In 1960, Louis Leakey, retreating from his earlier view that the Kanam jaw was *sapiens*-like, said it represented a female *Zinjanthropus*. Leakey had found *Zinjanthropus* in 1959, at Olduvai Gorge. He briefly promoted this apelike creature as the first toolmaker, and thus the first truly humanlike being. Shortly thereafter, fossils of *Homo habilis* were found at Olduvai. Leakey quickly demoted *Zinjanthropus* from his status as toolmaker, placing him among the robust australopithecines (*A. boisei*).

In the early 1970s, Leakey's son Richard, working at Lake Turkana, Kenya, discovered fossil jaws of *Homo habilis* that resembled the Kanam jaw. Since the Lake Turkana *Homo habilis* jaws were discovered with a fauna similar to that at Kanam, the elder Leakey changed his mind once more, suggesting that the Kanam jaw could be assigned to *Homo habilis*.

That over the years scientists have attributed the Kanam jaw to almost every known hominid (*Australopithecus, Australopithecus boisei, Homo habilis,* Neanderthal man, early *Homo sapiens*, and anatomically modern *Homo sapiens*) shows the difficulties involved in properly classifying hominid fossil remains.

Tobias's suggestion that the Kanam jaw came from a variety of early *Homo sapiens,* with neanderthaloid features, has won wide acceptance. Yet as can be

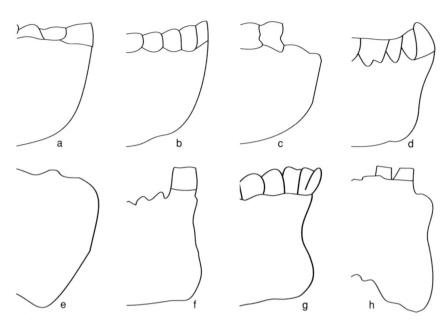

Figure 12.3 The outlines of the mandibles shown here (not to scale) were traced from published photographs, except for (a) and (g), which were traced from drawings. (a) *Australopithecus,* Omo, Ethiopia; (b) *Homo erectus,* Heidelberg (Mauer), Germany; (c) early *Homo sapiens,* Arago, France; (d) Neanderthal, Shanidar, Iraq; (e) *Homo sapiens rhodesiensis* ('neanderthaloid' according to P. V. Tobias), Cave of Hearths, South Africa; (f) *Homo sapiens sapiens,* Border Cave, South Africa; (g) *Homo sapiens sapiens,* modern South African native; (h) the Kanam mandible.

seen in Figure 12.3, which shows outlines of the Kanam mandible and other hominid mandibles, the contour of the Kanam mandible's chin region (h) is similar to that of the Border Cave specimen (f), recognized as *Homo sapiens sapiens,* and to that of a modern South African native (g). All three share two key features of the modern human chin, namely, an incurvation toward the top and a swelling outward at the base.

But even if one were to accept Tobias's view that the Kanam jaw was neanderthaloid, one would still not expect to discover Neanderthals in the Early Pleistocene, over 1.9 million years ago. Neanderthaloid hominids came into existence at most 400,000 years ago and persisted until about 30,000 or 40,000 years ago, according to most accounts.

To ascertain the age of the Kanam jaw and Kanjera skulls, K. P. Oakley of the British Museum performed fluorine, nitrogen, and uranium content tests.

Bones buried in the ground absorb fluorine. The Kanam jaw and the Kanjera skulls had about the same fluorine content as other bones from the Early and

Middle Pleistocene formations where they were found. These results are consistent with the hypothesis that the human bones at Kanam and Kanjera are as old as the faunal remains at those sites.

Nitrogen is a component of bone protein. Bones normally tend to lose nitrogen over time. Oakley found that a Kanjera 4 skull fragment showed just a trace of nitrogen (0.01 percent), while a Kanjera 3 skull fragment showed none. Neither of the two animal fossils tested showed any nitrogen. The presence of "measurable traces" of nitrogen in the Kanjera 4 skull fragment meant, said Oakley, that all the human fossils were "considerably younger" than the Kanjeran fauna.

But certain deposits, such as clay, preserve nitrogen, sometimes for millions of years. So perhaps the Kanjera 4 fragment was protected from complete nitrogen loss by clay. In any case, the Kanjera 3 fragment, like the animal samples, had no nitrogen. So it is possible that all the bones were of the same age.

As shown in Table 12.1, the uranium content values for the Kanjera human fossils (8–47 parts per million) overlapped the values for the Kanjeran fauna (26–216 parts per million). This could mean they were of the same age.

But the human bones averaged 22 parts per million while the mammalian fauna averaged 136 parts per million. To Oakley, the substantial difference between the averages meant that the human bones were "considerably younger" than the animal bones. Similar uranium content results were obtained at Kanam.

But Oakley himself pointed out that the uranium content of ground water can vary considerably from place to place. For example, Late Pleistocene animal bones from Kugata, near Kanam, have more uranium than the Early Pleistocene bones at Kanam.

TABLE 12.1

Uranium Content of Kanjera Hominid Fossils

Fossil Identification	Description of Fragment Tested	Uranium (eU_3O_8) Content (parts per million)
Kanjera 3	orbital fragment, *in situ*	15
	right parietal fragment, *in situ*	21
	cranial fragments from surface	16, 27, 27, 30, 42
	femoral fragment from surface	8, 14
Kanjera 4	frontal fragments from surface	11, 21, 35
Fauna	Kanjeran mammal fragments	26, 131, 146, 159, 216

Significantly, the uranium content values that Oakley reported in 1974 were apparently not the first he had obtained. In a paper published in 1958, Oakley said, immediately after discussing the uranium content testing of the Kanam jaw: "Applied to the Kanjera bones our tests did not show any discrepancy between the human skulls and the associated fauna." It would appear that Oakley was not satisfied with these early tests and later performed additional tests on the Kanjera bones, obtaining results that were more to his liking.

Our review of the chemical testing of the Kanam and Kanjera fossils leads us to the following conclusions. The fluorine and nitrogen content tests gave results consistent with the human bones being as old as their accompanying faunas. This interpretation can nevertheless be challenged. The uranium content test gave results consistent with the human bones being younger than their accompanying faunas. But here again, if one chooses to challenge this interpretation, one will find ample grounds to do so.

All in all, the results of chemical and radiometric tests do not eliminate the possibility that the Kanam and Kanjera human fossils are contemporary with their accompanying faunas. The Kanjera skulls, said to be anatomically modern, would thus be equivalent in age to Olduvai Bed IV, which is 400,000 to 700,000 years old. The taxonomic status of the Kanam jaw is uncertain. Recent workers hesitate to call it anatomically modern, although this designation cannot be ruled out completely. If it is as old as the Kanam fauna, which is older than Olduvai Gorge Bed I, then the Kanam mandible would be over 1.9 million years old.

THE BIRTH OF AUSTRALOPITHECUS

In 1924, Josephine Salmons noticed a fossil baboon skull sitting above the fireplace in a friend's home. Salmons, a student of anatomy at the University of the Witwatersrand in Johannesburg, South Africa, took the specimen to her professor, Dr. Raymond A. Dart.

The baboon skull given to Dart by Salmons was from a limestone quarry at Buxton, near a town called Taung, about 200 miles southwest of Johannesburg. Dart asked his friend Dr. R. B. Young, a geologist, to visit the quarry and see what else might be found. Young collected some fossil-bearing chunks and sent them to Dart.

Two crates of fossils arrived at Dart's home on the very day a friend's wedding was to be held there. Dart's wife pleaded with him to leave the fossils alone until after the wedding, but Dart opened the crates. In the second crate, Dart saw something that astonished him: "I found the virtually complete cast of the interior of a skull among them. This brain cast was as big as that of a large gorilla." Dart then found another piece of rock that appeared to contain the facial bones.

After the wedding guests departed, Dart began the arduous task of detaching the bones from their stony matrix. Without proper instruments, he used his wife's knitting needles to carefully chip away the stone. "What emerged," wrote Dart, "was a baby's face, an infant with a full set of milk teeth and its permanent molars just in the process of erupting. I doubt if there was any parent prouder of his offspring than I was of my Taung baby on that Christmas."

After freeing the bones, Dart reconstructed the skull (Figure 12.4). He characterized the Taung baby's brain as unexpectedly large, about 500 cubic centimeters. The average brain capacity of a large male adult gorilla is only about 600 cubic centimeters. Dart noted the absence of a brow ridge and thought that the teeth displayed some humanlike features.

Dart also noted that the foramen magnum, the opening for the spinal cord, was set toward the center of the base of the skull, as in human beings, rather than toward the rear, as in adult apes. Dart took this to indicate the creature had walked upright, which meant the Taung specimen was, in his eyes, clearly a human ancestor.

Dart sent a report to *Nature,* the prestigious British science journal. "The specimen," said Dart, "is of importance because it exhibits an extinct race of apes intermediate between living anthropoids and man." From the accompanying animal fossils, he estimated his find's age at 1 million years. He named his Taung baby *Australopithecus africanus*—the southern ape of Africa. *Australopithecus,* he believed, was ancestral to all other hominid forms.

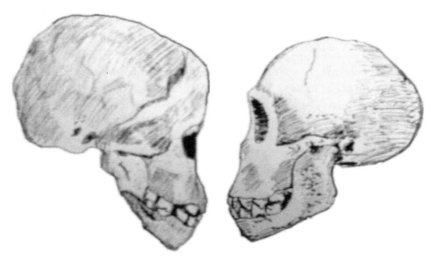

Figure 12.4. Left: The infant *Australopithecus* skull from a quarry near Taung, South Africa. Right: The skull of an immature gorilla,.

In England, Sir Arthur Keith and Sir Arthur Smith Woodward received the report from Dart with utmost caution. Keith thought *Australopithecus* belonged with the chimpanzees and gorillas.

Grafton Elliot Smith was even more critical. In May 1925, in a lecture delivered at University College, Smith stated: "It is unfortunate that Dart had no access to skulls of infant chimpanzees, gorillas, or orangs of an age corresponding to that of the Taung skull, for had such material been available he would have realized that the posture and poise of the head, the shape of the jaws, and many details of the nose, face, and cranium upon which he relied for proof of his contention that *Australopithecus* was nearly akin to man, were essentially identical with the conditions met in the infant gorilla and chimpanzee." Grafton Elliot Smith's critique remains valid even today. As we shall see, despite the enshrinement of *Australopithecus* as an ancestor of human beings, several scientists remain doubtful.

Dart was dismayed by the cool reception he received from the British scientific establishment. For many years, he remained silent and stopped hunting for fossils. British scientists, led by Sir Arthur Keith, maintained their opposition to Dart's *Australopithecus* throughout the 1930s. Piltdown man, believed to be similar in geological age to the Taung specimen, entered Keith's calculations. The skull of Piltdown man was like that of *Homo sapiens*. This fact argued against *Australopithecus,* with its apelike skull, being in the line of human ancestry.

When Dart retired from the world stage, his friend Dr. Robert Broom took up the battle to establish *Australopithecus* as a human ancestor. From the beginning, Broom displayed keen interest in Dart's discovery. Soon after the Taung baby made his appearance, Broom rushed to Dart's laboratory. Dart said "he strode over to the bench on which the skull reposed and dropped on his knees 'in adoration of our ancestor,' as he put it." British science, however, demanded an adult specimen of *Australopithecus* before it would kneel in adoration. Early in 1936, Broom vowed to find one.

On August 17, 1936, G. W. Barlow, the supervisor of the Sterkfontein limestone quarry, gave Broom a brain cast of an adult australopithecine. Broom later went to the spot where the brain cast had turned up and recovered several skull fragments. From these he reconstructed the skull, naming its owner *Plesianthropus transvaalensis.* The deposits in which the fossil was discovered are thought to be between 2.2 and 3.0 million years old.

More discoveries followed, including the lower part of a femur (TM 1513). In 1946, Broom and G. W. H. Schepers described this femur as essentially human. W. E. Le Gros Clark, initially skeptical of this description, later admitted that the femur "shows a resemblance to the femur of *Homo* which is so close as to amount to practical identity." This estimation was reconfirmed in

1981 by Christine Tardieu, who said the key diagnostic features of the Sterkfontein femur are "characteristic of modern Man." Since the TM 1513 femur was found by itself, it is not clear that it belongs to an australopithecine. It is possible, therefore, that it could belong to a more advanced hominid, perhaps one resembling anatomically modern humans.

On June 8, 1938, Barlow gave Broom a fragment of a palate with a single molar attached. When Broom asked from where it had come, Barlow was evasive. Some days later, Broom again visited Barlow and insisted that he reveal the source of the fossil.

Barlow told Broom that Gert Terblanche, a local schoolboy, had given the bone fragment to him. Broom obtained some teeth from Gert, and together they went to the nearby Kromdraai farm, where the boy had gotten the teeth. There Broom collected some skull fragments. After reconstructing the partial skull, Broom saw it was different from the Sterkfontein australopithecine. It had a larger jaw and bigger teeth. He called the new australopithecine creature *Paranthropus robustus*. The Kromdraai site is now considered to be approximately 1.0 to 1.2 million years old.

Broom also found at Kromdraai a fragment of humerus (the bone of the upper arm) and a fragment of ulna (one of the bones of the lower arm). Although he attributed them to the robust australopithecine called *Paranthropus,* he said: "Had they been found isolated probably every anatomist in the world would say that they were undoubtedly human." An analysis done by H. M. McHenry in 1972 puts the TM 1517 humerus from Kromdraai "within the human range." In McHenry's study, a robust australopithecine humerus from Koobi Fora, Kenya, fell outside the human range. So perhaps the TM 1517 humerus belonged to something other than a robust australopithecine. It is not impossible that the Kromdraai humerus and ulna, like the Sterkfontein femur, belonged to more advanced hominids, perhaps resembling anatomically modern humans.

World War II interrupted Broom's excavation work in South Africa. After the war, at Swartkrans, Robert Broom and J. T. Robinson found fossils of a robust australopithecine called *Paranthropus crassidens* (large-toothed near-man). This creature had large strong teeth and a bony crest on top of the skull. The crest served as the point of attachment for big jaw muscles.

Broom and Robinson also found the jaw of another kind of hominid in the Swartkrans cave. They attributed the jaw (SK 15), smaller and more humanlike than that of *Paranthropus crassidens,* to a new hominid called *Telanthropus capensis.* Member 1 at Swartkrans, where all of the *Paranthropus* bones were found, is now said to be 1.2 to 1.4 million years old. Member 2, where the SK 15 *Telanthropus* mandible was found, is said to be 300,000 to 500,000 years old. In 1961, Robinson reclassified the Swartkrans jaw as *Homo erectus.*

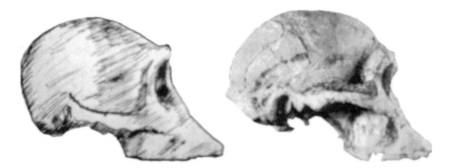

Figure 12.5. Left: The skull of a female chimpanzee. Right: The St 5 *Plesianthropus (Australopithecus) transvaalensis* skull discovered by Robert Broom at Sterkfontein, South Africa.

Broom and Robinson found another humanlike lower jaw at Swartkrans. This fragmentary mandible (SK 45) came from the main deposit containing the *Paranthropus* fossils. Broom and Robinson said in 1952: "In shape it is more easily matched or approached by many modern *Homo* jaws than by that of *Telanthropus*." Robinson later referred the SK 45 jaw to *Telanthropus* and then to *Homo erectus*. But there are reasons, admittedly not unclouded, to consider other possibilities.

In the postwar years, Broom also found another australopithecine skull (St 5) at Sterkfontein (Figure 12.5). Later he discovered further remains of an adult female australopithecine (St 14)—including parts of the pelvis, vertebral column, and legs. Their morphology, along with certain features of the Sterkfontein skulls, demonstrated, in Broom's opinion, that the australopithecines had walked erect.

In 1925, Raymond A. Dart investigated a tunnel at Makapansgat, South Africa. Noting the presence of blackened bones, Dart concluded hominids had used fire there. In 1945, Philip V. Tobias, then Dart's graduate student at the University of the Witwatersrand, found the skull of an extinct baboon in the cave deposits of Makapansgat and called it to Dart's attention. In 1947, Dart himself went back out into the field, after a lapse of two decades, to hunt for *Australopithecus* bones at Makapansgat.

At Makapansgat, Dart found australopithecine skull fragments and other bones, along with more signs of fire. Dart therefore called the creature who lived there *Australopithecus prometheus,* after the Titan who stole fire from the gods. Today, *Australopithecus prometheus* is classified, along with the Taung and Sterkfontein specimens, as *Australopithecus africanus,* distinct from the robust australopithecines of Kromdraai and Swartkrans.

Dart discovered 42 baboon skulls at Makapansgat, 27 of which had smashed fronts. Seven more showed blows on the left front side. From this evidence, Dart created a lurid portrait of *Australopithecus prometheus* as a killer ape-man, bashing in the heads of baboons with primitive bone tools and cooking their flesh over fires in the Makapansgat cave.

"Man's predecessors," said Dart, "differed from living apes in being confirmed killers; carnivorous creatures, that seized living quarries by violence, battered them to death, tore apart their broken bodies, dismembered them limb from limb, slaking their ravenous thirst with the hot blood of victims and greedily devouring their writhing flesh."

Today, however, paleoanthropologists characterize *Australopithecus* as merely a scavenger, not a hunter and maker of fire. Nevertheless, the new discoveries by Broom and Dart convinced influential scientists, especially in Great Britain, that *Australopithecus* was not just a variety of fossil ape but was a genuine human ancestor.

ZINJANTHROPUS

The next important discoveries were made by Louis Leakey and his second wife Mary. On July 17, 1959, Mary Leakey came across the shattered skull of a young male hominid in Bed I of Olduvai Gorge at site FLK. When the skull was pieced together, Louis and Mary Leakey saw that the creature had a saggital crest, a bony ridge running lengthwise along the top of the skull. In this respect, it was very much like *Australopithecus robustus*. Leakey nevertheless created a new species for this hominid, partly because its teeth were bigger than those of the South African *robustus* specimens. Leakey called the new find *Zinjanthropus boisei*. Zinj is a name for East Africa and *boisei* refers to Mr. Charles Boise, one of the Leakeys' early financial backers. Along with the skull, Leakey found stone tools, causing him to call *Zinjanthropus* the first stone toolmaker, and hence the first "true man."

Leakey became the first superstar that paleoanthropology had seen in a while. The National Geographic Society honored Leakey with funds, publication of lavishly illustrated articles, television specials, and worldwide speaking tours.

But despite an outpouring of publicity, the reign of *Zinjanthropus* was all too brief. Leakey's biographer, Sonia Cole, wrote: "Granted that Louis had to persuade the National Geographic Society that in Zinj he had a likely candidate for 'the first man' in order to ensure their continued support—but need he have stuck out his neck quite so far? Even a layman looking at the skull could not be fooled: Zinj, with his gorilla-like crest on the top of the cranium and his low brow, was quite obviously far more like the robust australopithecines of South Africa than he was like modern man—to whom, quite frankly, he bears no resemblance at all."

HOMO HABILIS

In 1960, about a year after the discovery of *Zinjanthropus*, Leakey's son Jonathan found the skull of another hominid (OH 7) nearby. In addition to the skull, the OH 7 individual included the bones of a hand. Also in 1960, the bones of a hominid foot (OH 8) were found. In succeeding years, more discoveries followed, mostly teeth and fragments of jaw and skull. The fossil individuals were given colorful nicknames: Johnny's Child, George, Cindy, and Twiggy. Some of the bones were found in the lower part of Bed II of Olduvai Gorge.

Philip Tobias, the South African anatomist, gave the OH 7 skull a capacity of 680 cc, far larger than *Zinjanthropus* at 530 cc, and larger even than the biggest australopithecine skull, at roughly 600 cc. It was, however, around 100 cc less than the smallest *Homo erectus*.

Louis Leakey decided he had now come upon the real toolmaker of the lower levels of Olduvai, the real first true human. His bigger brain confirmed his status. Leakey called the creature *Homo habilis,* which means "handy man."

After the discovery of *Homo habilis, Zinjanthropus* was demoted to *Australopithecus boisei,* a somewhat more robust variety of *Australopithecus*

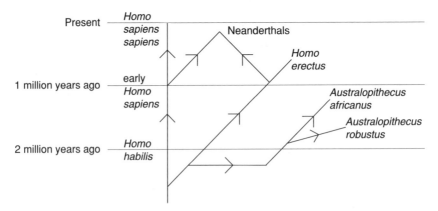

Figure 12.6. According to Louis Leakey, neither *Australopithecus* nor *Homo erectus* was ancestral to modern humans. The Neanderthals, said Leakey, were probably the result of crossbreeding between *Homo erectus* and *Homo sapiens*. Today, the details of human evolution remain a subject of active debate. But most paleoanthropologists favor a progression from one of the australopithecines to *Homo habilis, Homo erectus,* and early *Homo sapiens,*who gave rise to both Neanderthals and modern humans.

robustus. Both of these robust australopithecines had saggital crests, and are regarded not as human ancestors but as evolutionary offshoots that eventually became extinct.

The whole business of saggital crests complicates matters somewhat. Male gorillas and some male chimpanzees also have saggital crests, whereas the females of these species do not. Mary Leakey therefore said in 1971: "The possibility that *A. robustus* and *A. africanus* represent the male and female of a single species deserves serious consideration." If the possibility raised by Mary Leakey were found to be correct, this would mean that generations of experts have been wildly mistaken about the australopithecines.

With the discovery at Olduvai Gorge of *Homo habilis,* a creature contemporary with the early australopithecines but with a bigger brain, Louis Leakey believed he had excellent evidence supporting his view that *Australopithecus* was not in the direct line of human ancestry (Figure 12.6). The australopithecines would be merely a side branch. And because *Homo erectus* was thought to be a descendant of *Australopithecus, Homo erectus* would also be removed from the line of human ancestry.

But what about the Neanderthals? These, say some authorities, show clearly an evolutionary transition between *Homo erectus* and *Homo sapiens.* But Leakey had another explanation: "Is it not possible that they are all variants of the result of crossbreeding between *Homo sapiens* and *Homo erectus?*" One might object that such crossbreeding would have yielded hybrids that were unable to reproduce. But Leakey pointed out that American bison cross fertilely with ordinary cattle.

A TALE OF TWO HUMERI

In 1965, Bryan Patterson and W. W. Howells found a surprisingly modern-looking hominid humerus (upper arm bone) at Kanapoi, Kenya. In 1977, French workers found a similar humerus at Gombore, Ethiopia.

The Kanapoi humerus fragment, consisting of the intact lower (or distal) part of the bone, was found on the surface. But the deposit from which the bone apparently came was about 4.5 million years old.

Patterson and Howells found that the Kanapoi humerus was different from the humeri of gorillas, chimpanzees, and australopithecines but similar to those of humans. They noted that "there are individuals in our sample of man on whom measurements . . . of Kanapoi Hominoid I can be duplicated almost exactly."

Patterson and Howells would not have dreamed of suggesting that the Kanapoi humerus belonged to an anatomically modern human. Nevertheless, if an anatomically modern human had died at Kanapoi 4.0–4.5 million years ago, he or she might have left a humerus exactly like the one they found.

Further confirmation of the humanlike morphology of the Kanapoi humerus came from anthropologists Henry M. McHenry and Robert S. Corruccini of the University of California. They concluded that "the Kanapoi humerus is barely distinguishable from modern *Homo*" and "shows the early emergence of a *Homo*-like elbow in every subtle detail."

In a 1975 study, physical anthropologist C. E. Oxnard agreed with this analysis. He stated: "we can confirm clearly that the fossil from Kanapoi is very humanlike." This led Oxnard to suggest, as did Louis Leakey, that the australo-pithecines were not in the main line of human evolution. Keeping *Australopithecus* as a human ancestor would result in a very unlikely progression from the humanlike Kanapoi humerus, to the markedly less humanlike humerus of *Australopithecus,* and then to one more humanlike again.

The Gombore humerus, given an age of about 1.5 million years, was found along with crude stone tools. In 1981, Brigitte Senut said that the Gombore humerus "cannot be differentiated from a typical modern human." So now we seem to have two very ancient and humanlike humeri to add to our list of evidence challenging the currently accepted scenario of human evolution. These are the Kanapoi humerus at 4.0–4.5 million years in Kenya and the Gombore humerus at more than 1.5 million years in Ethiopia. They support the view that human beings of modern type have coexisted with other humanlike and apelike creatures for a very long time.

DISCOVERIES OF RICHARD LEAKEY

In 1972 Louis Leakey's son Richard found at Lake Turkana, Kenya, a shattered hominid skull. Richard's wife Meave, a zoologist, reconstructed the skull, which was designated ER 1470. Its cranial capacity was over 810 cc, bigger than the robust australopithecines. Richard Leakey initially hesitated to designate a species for the ER 1470 skull but eventually decided to call it *Homo habilis.*

The stratum yielding the skull lay below the KBS Tuff, a volcanic deposit with a potassium-argon age of 2.6 million years. The skull itself was given an age of 2.9 million years, as old as the oldest australopithecines. The KBS Tuff's age was later challenged, with critics favoring an age of less than 2 million years.

Some distance from where the ER 1470 skull had been found, but at the same level, John Harris, a paleontologist from the Kenya National Museum, discovered two quite humanlike femurs. Harris summoned Richard Leakey, who later reported that "these femurs are unlike those of *Australopithecus,* and astonishingly similar to those of modern man." Other workers found the femurs different from those of *Homo erectus.*

The first femur, with associated fragments of tibia and fibula, was designated ER 1481 and the other ER 1472. An additional fragment of femur was designated ER 1475. They were all attributed to *Homo habilis*.

But Leakey stated in a scientific journal that these leg bones "cannot be readily distinguished from *H. sapiens* if one considers the range of variation known for this species." In a *National Geographic* article, Leakey repeated this view, saying the leg bones were "almost indistinguishable from those of *Homo sapiens*." Other scientists agreed with Leakey's analysis. B. A. Wood, anatomist at the Charing Cross Hospital Medical School in London, stated that the femurs "belong to the 'modern human walking' locomotor group."

Although most scientists would never dream of it, one could consider attributing the Koobi Fora femurs to a hominid very much like modern *Homo sapiens,* living in Africa about 2 million years ago.

The ER 1472 and ER 1481 femurs show that distinctly anomalous discoveries are not confined to the nineteenth century. They have continued to occur with astonishing regularity up to the present day, right under our very noses, so to speak, although hardly anyone recognizes them for what they are. In Africa alone, we are building up quite a catalog: Reck's skeleton, the Kanam jaw, the Kanjera skulls, the Kanapoi humerus, the Gombore humerus, and now the Lake Turkana femurs. All have been either attributed to *Homo sapiens* or described as being very humanlike. Except for the Middle Pleistocene Kanjera skulls, all were discovered in Early Pleistocene or Pliocene contexts.

THE ER 813 TALUS

In 1974, B. A. Wood described a talus (ankle bone) found at Lake Turkana. It lay between the KBS Tuff and the overlying Koobi Fora Tuff. Wood compared the fossil talus, designated ER 813, with those of modern humans, gorillas, chimpanzees, and other arboreal primates. "The fossil aligned with the modern human tali," said Wood.

The humanlike ER 813 talus is 1.5 to 2.0 million years old, roughly contemporary with creatures designated as *Australopithecus robustus, Homo erectus,* and *Homo habilis.*

In a subsequent report, Wood said his tests confirmed "the similarity of KNM-ER 813 with modern human bones," showing it to be "not significantly different from the tali of modern bushmen." One could therefore consider the possibility that the KNM-ER 813 talus belonged to an anatomically modern human in the Early Pleistocene or Late Pliocene.

If the KNM-ER 813 talus really did belong to a creature very much like modern human beings, it fits, like the ER 1481 and ER 1472 femurs, into a continuum of such finds reaching back millions of years. This would eliminate *Australopithecus, Homo habilis,* and *Homo erectus* as human ancestors.

OH 62: WILL THE REAL HOMO HABILIS PLEASE STAND UP?

Artists, working from fossils and reports supplied by paleoanthropologists, have typically depicted *Homo habilis* as having an essentially humanlike body except for its apelike head (Figure 12.7).

This highly speculative portrait of *Homo habilis* persisted until 1987. In that year, Tim White and Don Johanson reported they had found at Olduvai Gorge the first *Homo habilis* individual (OH 62) with the bones of the body clearly associated with the skull. The skeletal remains showed the creature was only 3.5 feet tall and had relatively long arms. Drawings of the new *Homo habilis* (Figure 12.7) were decidedly more apelike than those of the past.

Johanson and his coworkers concluded it was likely that scientists had incorrectly attributed to *Homo habilis* many limb bones discovered prior to 1987.

The OH 62 find supports our suggestion that the ER 1481 and ER 1472 femurs from Koobi Fora, described as very much like those of modern *Homo sapiens,* might have belonged to anatomically modern humans living in Africa during the Late Pliocene. Some scientists attributed them to *Homo habilis.* But the new view of *Homo habilis* rules this out. Could the femurs perhaps belong to *Homo erectus?* G. E. Kennedy, for example, assigned the ER 1481 femur to *Homo erectus.* But E. Trinkhaus noted that key measurements of this bone, with one exception, are within the range of anatomically modern human femurs.

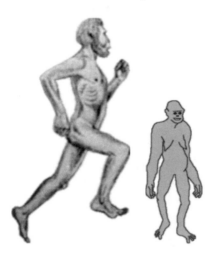

The discoverers of OH 62 had to grapple with the evolutionary link between the new, more apelike *Homo habilis* and *Homo erectus.* The two species are separated by only 200,000 or so years. But the *H. habilis-H. erectus* transition involves some rather extreme morphological changes, including a big change in size. Richard Leakey, applying normal human growth patterns, cal-

Figure 12.7. Left: This drawing shows *Homo habilis,* as generally depicted before 1987. Below the head, the anatomy is essentially human. Right: After OH 62 was found at Olduvai Gorge in 1987, a new picture of *Homo habilis* emerged, far smaller and more apelike than before.

culated that an adolescent *Homo erectus* discovered in 1984 (KNM-WT 15000) would have grown to over 6 feet tall as an adult. The adult OH 62, on the other hand, was only about 3.25 feet tall. Altogether, an evolutionary leap from small, apelike OH 62 to big, more humanlike KNM-WT 15000 in less than 200,000 years seems implausible.

Advocates of the much-debated punctuational model of evolution, however, can easily accept the transition. Unlike the traditional gradualists, punctuationalists assert that evolution proceeds by rapid episodes of change interrupted by long periods of stasis. Punctuationalism can, therefore, accommodate a variety of troublesome evolutionary anomalies, such as the *habilis* to *erectus* transition.

"The very small body size of the OH 62 individual," said its discoverers, "suggests that views of human evolution positing incremental body size increase through time may be rooted in gradualistic preconceptions rather than fact." But punctuational views may also be rooted in preconception rather than fact. The paleontological facts, considered in their entirety, suggest that various ape-man-like and humanlike beings, including some resembling modern humans, coexisted throughout the Pleistocene, and earlier.

It was not only new evidence such as OH 62 that challenged the long-accepted picture of *Homo habilis*. Previously discovered fossil evidence relating to *Homo habilis,* originally interpreted by some authorities as very human-like, was later characterized by others as quite apelike.

As mentioned earlier, a fairly complete foot skeleton, designated OH 8, was found in Bed I at Olduvai Gorge. Dated at 1.7 million years, the OH 8 foot was attributed to *Homo habilis.* In 1964, M. H. Day and J. R. Napier said the OH 8 foot very much resembled that of *Homo sapiens,* thus contributing to the overall humanlike picture of *Homo habilis.*

But O. J. Lewis, anatomist at St. Bartholomew's Hospital Medical College in London, demonstrated that the OH 8 foot was more like that of chimpanzees and gorillas. He considered the foot to be arboreal, adapted to life in trees. This poses a problem. It certainly does not serve the propaganda purposes of evolutionists to have the public visualizing a supposed human ancestor like *Homo habilis* climbing trees with an aboreally adapted foot rather than walking tall and brave across the African savannahs.

From Lewis's study of the OH 8 foot, one could conclude that *Homo habilis* was much more apelike than most scientists have tended to believe. The OH 62 discovery supports this view. Another possible conclusion: the OH 8 foot did not belong to *Homo habilis* but to an australopithecine. This view was favored by Lewis.

Over the years, different scientists have described the OH 8 foot skeleton as humanlike, apelike, intermediate between human and ape, distinct from both human and ape, and orangutanlike. This demonstrates once more an important characteristic of paleoanthropological evidence—it is often subject to multiple, contradictory interpretations. Partisan considerations often determine which view prevails at any given point in time.

The OH 7 hand was also found at Olduvai Gorge, as part of the type specimen of *Homo habilis.* In 1962, J. R. Napier described the hand as quite human in some of its features, especially the finger tips. As in the case of the OH 8 foot, subsequent studies showed the OH 7 hand to be very apelike, calling into question either its attribution to *Homo habilis* or the generally accepted humanlike picture of *Homo habilis,* which the original interpretation of the OH 7 hand helped create. The apelike character of the hand suggested to Randall L. Susman and Jack T. Stern that it was used in "in suspensory climbing behavior."

In others words, *Homo habilis,* or whatever creature owned the OH 7 hand, may have spent much of its time hanging by its arms from tree limbs. This apelike image differs from the very humanlike portrait of *Homo habilis* and other supposed human ancestors one usually encounters in Time-Life picture books and National Geographic Society television specials.

In light of the contradictory evidence connected with *Homo habilis,* some researchers have proposed that there was no justification for "creating" this species in the first place.

If the bones attributed to *Homo habilis* did not really belong to this species, then what did they represent? T. J. Robinson argued that *Homo habilis* had been mistakenly derived from a mixture of skeletal elements belonging to *Australopithecus africanus* and *Homo erectus.* Others have suggested that the *Homo habilis* bones are all australopithecine.

So in the end, we find that *Homo habilis* is about as substantial as a desert mirage, appearing now humanlike, now apelike, now real, now unreal, according to the tendency of the viewer. Taking the many conflicting views into consideration, we find it most likely that the *Homo habilis* material belongs to more than one species, including a small, apelike, arboreal australopithecine (OH 62 and some of the Olduvai specimens), a primitive species of *Homo* (ER 1470 skull), and anatomically modern humans (ER 1481 and ER 1472 femurs).

OXNARD'S CRITIQUE OF AUSTRALOPITHECUS

Homo habilis is not the only human ancestor to come under sustained criticism. According to most paleoanthropologists, *Australopithecus* was a direct human ancestor, with a very humanlike body. Advocates of this view have also asserted that *Australopithecus* walked erect, in a manner practically identical to modern human beings. But right from the very start, some researchers objected to this

Figure 12.8. Most scientists describe *Australopithecus* as an exclusively terrestrial biped, humanlike from the head down. But according to some studies by S. Zuckerman and C. E. Oxnard, *Australopithecus* was more apelike. Although capable of walking on the ground bipedally (left), *Australopithecus* was also "at home in the trees, capable of climbing, performing degrees of acrobatics [right] and perhaps of arm suspension." The unique functional morphology of *Australopithecus* led Zuckerman and Oxnard to doubt it is a human ancestor. Illustrations by Miles Tripplett.

depiction of *Australopithecus*. Influential English scientists, including Sir Arthur Keith, said that the *Australopithecus* was not a hominid but a variety of ape.

This negative view persisted until the early 1950s, when the combined effect of further *Australopithecus* finds and the fall of Piltdown man created a niche in mainstream paleoanthropological thought for a humanlike *Australopithecus*.

But even after *Australopithecus* won mainstream acceptance as a hominid and direct human ancestor, opposition continued. Louis Leakey held that *Australopithecus* was an early and very apelike offshoot from the main line of human evolution. Later, his son Richard Leakey took much the same stance.

In the early 1950s, Sir Solly Zuckerman published extensive biometric studies showing *Australopithecus* was not as humanlike as imagined by those who favored putting this creature in the lineage of *Homo sapiens*. From the late

1960s through the 1990s, Charles E. Oxnard, employing multivariate statistical analysis, renewed and amplified the line of attack begun by Zuckerman. According to Oxnard, "it is rather unlikely that any of the Australopithecines . . . can have any direct phylogenetic link with the genus *Homo.*"

Oxnard found the brain, teeth, and skull of *Australopithecus* to be quite like those of apes. The shoulder bone appeared to be adapted for suspending the body from the limbs of trees. The hand bones were curved like those of the orangutan. The pelvis appeared to be adapted for quadrupedal walking and acrobatic behavior. The same was true of the femur and ankle structure. "Pending further evidence," wrote Oxnard in 1975, "we are left with the vision of intermediately sized animals, at home in the trees, capable of climbing, performing degrees of acrobatics and perhaps arm suspension."

In 1973, Zuckerman and Oxnard presented a paper at a symposium of the Zoological Society of London in 1973. At the conclusion of the symposium, Zuckerman made some important remarks. He said: "Over the years I have been almost alone in challenging the conventional wisdom about the australopithecines—alone, that is to say, in conjunction with my colleagues in the school I built up in Birmingham—but I fear to little effect. The voice of higher authority had spoken, and its message in due course became incorporated in text books all over the world."

The situation has not changed since Zuckerman spoke in 1973. The voices of authority in paleoanthropology and the scientific community in general have managed to keep the humanlike view of *Australopithecus* intact. The extensive and well-documented evidence contradicting this favored view remains confined to the pages of professional journals, where it has little or no influence on the public in general, even the educated public.

Reviewing the decades-long controversy about the nature of *Australopithecus,* Oxnard wrote in 1984: "In the uproar, at the time, as to whether or not these creatures were near ape or human, the *opinion* that they were human won the day. This may well have resulted not only in the defeat of the contrary *opinion* but also in the burying of *that part of the evidence* upon which the contrary opinion was based. If this is so, it should be possible to unearth this *other part of the evidence.* This evidence may actually be more compatible with the new view; it may help open the possibility that these particular australopithecines are neither like African apes nor humans, and certainly not intermediate, but something markedly different from either."

Of course, this is exactly the point we have been making throughout this book. Evidence has been buried. We ourselves have uncovered considerable amounts of such buried evidence relating to the antiquity of the modern human type.

Summarizing his findings, Oxnard stated: "The various australopithecine fossils are usually quite different from both man and the African apes. . . . Viewed as a genus, they are a mosaic of features unique to themselves and features bearing some resemblance to those of the orang-utan." Considering the anatomical uniqueness of the australopithecines, Oxnard said: "If these estimates are true, then the possibility that any of the australopithecines is a direct part of human ancestry recedes."

Like Louis and Richard Leakey, Oxnard believed that the *Homo* line was far more ancient than the standard evolutionary scenario allows. In this connection, Oxnard called attention to some of the fossils we have previously discussed, such as the humanlike ER 813 talus, over 1.5 million years old, and the Kanapoi humerus, perhaps 4 or more million years old. From such evidence, Oxnard concluded that the genus *Homo* was 5 or more million years old. "The conventional notion of human evolution," said Oxnard, "must now be heavily modified or even rejected . . . new concepts must be explored."

LUCY IN THE SAND WITH DIATRIBES

Despite Oxnard's work, most scientists still adhere to the doctrine that *Australopithecus* is a direct human ancestor. One such scientist is Donald Johanson. Donald Johanson studied anthropology at the University of Chicago, under F. Clark Howell. As a young graduate student, eager to learn the romantic business of hominid fossil hunting, Johanson accompanied Howell to Africa, working at the Omo site in Ethiopia.

Johanson later returned to Africa, this time heading his own expedition to Hadar, in the Afar region of Ethiopia. One afternoon, he found the upper portion of a tibia, a long bone between the knee and the ankle. The bone was obviously from some kind of primate. Nearby, Johanson found a distal femur, the lower end of a thighbone. From the way the femur and tibia fit together, Johanson believed he had found the complete knee joint not of some ancient monkey but of a hominid, an ancestor of modern humans. The deposits yielding the fossils were over 3 million years old, making this one of the oldest hominid finds ever made.

In scientific publications that followed, Johanson reported that the Hadar knee (AL 129) was 4 million years old and belonged to a primitive australopithecine with a fully human bipedal gait.

During the next year's work, Alemayehu Asfaw, an Ethiopian working at the Hadar site with Johanson, found some fossil jaws. Classifying them proved difficult. Johanson asked Richard Leakey to come and have a look at them. Leakey took up the invitation and arrived accompanied by his mother Mary Leakey and wife Meave. Together with Johanson, they examined the jaws and judged them to be *Homo,* making them the oldest *Homo* fossils yet found.

On November 30, 1974, Donald Johanson and Tom Gray were searching Locality 162 at the Hadar site, collecting bits of mammalian bone. After some time, Gray was ready to call it quits and go back to the camp. Johanson, however, suggested they check out a nearby gully. Gray and Johanson did not find much.

But as they were about to leave, Johanson spotted a piece of arm bone lying exposed on the surface. As they looked around, they could see scattered on the surface other bones—apparently from the same hominid individual. Johanson and Gray started jumping and howling in the 110-degree heat, celebrating what was obviously an extremely significant find. That evening Johanson and his coworkers partied while a Beatles song, "Lucy in the Sky with Diamonds," blared repeatedly from the camp sound system. From the lyrics of that song, the female hominid received her name, Lucy.

By a combination of potassium-argon, fission track, and paleomagnetic dating methods, Johanson determined that Lucy was 3.5 million years old.

In 1975, Johanson was back at Hadar, this time with a *National Geographic* photographer, who recorded another important discovery. On the side of a hill, Johanson and his team found the fossil remains of 13 hominids, including males, females, and children. The group was called the First Family. They were the same geological age as Lucy, about 3.5 million years old.

With the First Family, the major discoveries at Hadar, which also included the Hadar knee, Alemayehu's jaws, and Lucy, were completed. We shall now examine how these fossils were interpreted and reinterpreted by various parties.

In classifying his finds, Johanson initially relied heavily upon the judgement of Richard and Mary Leakey that the Alemayehu jaws and First Family specimens were *Homo*. If Lucy and the AL 129 femur and tibia were australopithecine, as Johanson believed, then there were two kinds of hominids at Hadar.

Johanson was later influenced to change his mind about the number of species at Hadar. The person who convinced him to do so was Timothy D. White, a paleontologist who had worked at Lake Turkana with Richard Leakey. White also convinced Johanson that the Hadar hominid represented a new species. Johanson and White called it *Australopithecus afarensis,* after the Afar region of Ethiopia.

According to Johanson and White, *Australopithecus afarensis,* the oldest australopithecine ever discovered, gave rise to two lineages. The first led by way of *Australopithecus africanus* to the robust australopithecines. The second lineage led by way of *Homo habilis* to *Homo erectus* and thence to *Homo sapiens.*

A. AFARENSIS: OVERLY HUMANIZED?

Johanson said that *Australopithecus afarensis* individuals had "smallish, essentially human bodies." But several scientists have strongly disagreed with Johanson's picture of *Australopithecus afarensis.* These dissenters have painted a far more apelike portrait of Lucy and her relatives. In most cases, their views on Lucy parallel the earlier work of Oxnard, Zuckerman, and others on *Australopithecus.*

The Hadar fossils did not include a complete skull of an *A. afarensis* individual, but Tim White managed to pull together a partial reconstruction, using cranial fragments, pieces of upper and lower jaw, and some facial bones from several First Family individuals. According to Johanson, the reconstructed skull "looked very much like a small female gorilla." Here there was no dispute between Johanson and his critics. Both agreed that the *afarensis* head was apelike. As for the body of *A. afarensis,* Randall L. Susman, Jack T. Stern, Charles E. Oxnard, and others have found it very apelike, thus challenging Johanson's view that Lucy walked upright on the ground in human fashion. Lucy's shoulder blade was almost identical to that of an ape. The shoulder joint was turned upward, indicating that Lucy's arms were probably used for climbing in trees and perhaps suspending the body. The bones of the arm were like those of tree-climbing primates, and the spinal column featured points of attachment for very powerful shoulder and back muscles. The bones of the wrist and palm region of the hand were adapted for powerful grasping, as were the long, curved finger bones. The hip and leg bones were also adapted for climbing, and the foot had curved toes that would be useful in grasping branches of trees.

One can just imagine the effects of a painting or model of Lucy engaged in suspensory or other arboreal behavior. This would surely detract from her image as a creature well on the way to human status. Even if one believes Lucy could have evolved into a human being, one still has to admit that her anatomical features appear to have been misrepresented for propaganda purposes.

Before leaving the topic of *Australopithecus afarensis,* we note that Richard Leakey, Christine Tardieu, and many others have argued that the fossil material for this species actually included two or even three species.

Within the scientific community there is as yet no unanimous picture of what the australopithecines, including *A. afarensis,* were really like, both in terms of their morphology and their evolutionary relation with modern humans. Some see them as ancestors, while others, such as C. E. Oxnard, do not.

THE LAETOLI FOOTPRINTS

The Laetoli site is located in northern Tanzania, about 30 miles south of Olduvai Gorge. *Laetoli* is the Masai word for red lily. In 1979, members of an expedition led by Mary Leakey noticed some marks on the ground. They proved to be fossil footprints of animals. Among them were some that appeared to have been made by hominids. The prints had been impressed in layers of volcanic ash, which yielded a potassium-argon age of 3.6 to 3.8 million years.

National Geographic magazine featured an article by Mary Leakey titled "Footprints in the Ashes of Time." In her analysis of the prints, Leakey cited Louise Robbins, a footprint expert from the University of North Carolina, who said "they looked so human, so modern, to be found in tuffs so old."

Readers who have accompanied us this far in our intellectual journey will have little difficulty in recognizing the Laetoli footprints as potential evidence for the presence of anatomically modern human beings over 3.6 million years ago in

Africa. We were, however, somewhat astonished to encounter such a striking anomaly in the unexpected setting of the more recent annals of standard paleoanthropological research. What amazed us most was that scientists of world-wide reputation, the best in their profession, could look at these footprints, describe their humanlike features, and remain completely oblivious to the possibility that the creatures that made them might have been as humanlike as ourselves.

Their mental currents were running in the usual fixed channels. Mary Leakey wrote: "At least 3,600,000 years ago, in Pliocene times, what I believe to be man's direct ancestor walked fully upright with a bipedal, free-striding gait. . . . the form of his foot was exactly the same as ours."

Who was the ancestor? Taking Leakey's point of view, the Laetoli footprints would have been made by a nonaustralopithecine ancestor of *Homo habilis*. Taking the Johanson-White point of view, the Laetoli footprints would have been made by *Australopithecus afarensis*. In either case, the creature who made the prints would have had an apelike head and other primitive features.

But why not a creature with fully modern feet and fully modern body? There is nothing in the footprints that rules this out. Furthermore, we have compiled in this book quite a bit of fossil evidence, some of it from Africa, that is consistent with the presence of anatomically modern human beings in the Early Pleistocene and the Late Pliocene.

Are we perhaps exaggerating the humanlike features of the Laetoli foot-prints? Let us see what various researchers have said. Louise M. Robbins, who provided an initial evaluation of the Laetoli prints to Mary Leakey in 1979, later published a more detailed report. Several sets of tracks, identified by letters, were found at Laetoli. In examining the "G" trails, representing three individuals described by Mary Leakey as a possible family group, Robbins found that the prints "share many features that are characteristic of the human foot structure." She especially noted that the big toe pointed straight forward, as in humans, and not out to the side as in the apes. In apes, the big toe can be moved much like the human thumb. Robbins concluded that "the four functional regions—heel, arch, ball, and toes—of the hominids' feet imprinted the ash in a typically human manner" and that "the hominids walked across the ash surface in characteristic human bipedal fashion."

M. H. Day studied the prints using photogrammetric methods. Photogrammetry is the science of obtaining exact measurements through the use of photography. His study showed the prints had "close similarities with the anatomy of the feet of the modern human habitually unshod; arguably the normal human condition." Typically, Day concluded: "There is now no serious dispute as to the upright stance and bipedal gait of the australopithecines."

But what proof did he have that an australopithecine made the Laetoli footprints? There is no reason to rule out the possibility that some unknown creature, perhaps very much like modern *Homo sapiens,* was the cause of them.

R. H. Tuttle, a physical anthropologist, stated: "The shapes of the prints are indistinguishable from those of striding, habitually barefoot humans."

Tuttle concluded: "Strictly on the basis of the morphology of the G prints, their makers could be classified as *Homo* . . . because they are so similar to those of *Homo sapiens,* but their early date would probably deter many palaeoanthropologists from accepting this assignment. I suspect that if the prints were undated, or if they had been given younger dates, most experts would probably accept them as having been made by *Homo.*" Tuttle also stated: "They are like small barefoot *Homo sapiens.*"

Furthermore, Tuttle held that the *A. afarensis* foot could not have made the prints. As we have seen, the *A. afarensis* foot had long, curved toes, and Tuttle said it was hard to imagine them "fitting neatly into the footprints at Laetoli." The same would be true of any australopithecine foot.

Stern and Susman objected to this. Convinced that the apelike *A. afarensis* foot had made the Laetoli footprints, they proposed that the ancient hominids had walked across the volcanic ash with their long toes curled under their feet, as chimpanzees have sometimes been observed to do. Curled-under toes would explain why the *A. afarensis* footprints at Laetoli so much resembled those made by the relatively short-toed human foot.

Could an australopithecine walking with curled toes have made the human-like prints? Tuttle found this extremely unlikely. If the Laetoli hominid had long toes, then, said Tuttle, one would expect to find two patterns of toe impressions—long extended toes and short curled toes, with extra-deep knuckle marks. This was not the case, which meant the long-toed *afarensis* foot could not have made the prints.

Even Tim White, who believed *Australopithecus afarensis* made the footprints, stated: "The Stern and Susman (1983) model of toe curling 'as in the chimpanzee' predicts substantial variation in lateral toe lengths seen on the Laetoli prints. This prediction is not borne out by the fossil prints."

Directly challenging Johanson, White, Latimer, and Lovejoy, who asserted *Australopithecus afarensis* made the Laetoli prints, Tuttle said: "Because of digital curvature and elongation and other skeletal features that evidence arboreal habits . . . it is unlikely that *Australopithecus afarensis* from Hadar, Ethiopia, could make footprints like those at Laetoli." Such statements have provoked elaborate counterattacks from Johanson and his followers, who have continued to promote the idea that *A. afarensis* could have made the tracks.

Tim White, for example, published in 1987 a study of the Laetoli prints in which he disputed Tuttle's contention that their maker was a hominid more advanced than *A. afarensis.*

White asserted: "There is not a single shred of evidence among the 26 hominid individuals in the collection of over 5,000 vertebrate remains from Laetoli that would suggest the presence of a more advanced Pliocene hominid at this site." But, as we have seen in our review of African hominid fossils, there are in fact a few "shreds" of evidence for the presence of *sapiens*-like creatures in the Pliocene, some not far from Laetoli. Also, it is well known that human skeletal remains are quite rare, even at sites where there are other unmistakable signs of a human presence.

White predicted that "the Laetoli prints will eventually be shown to be subtly distinct from those left under analogous conditions by anatomically modern humans." But as far as anyone can see now, they are indistinguishable from those of modern humans. Even White himself once said: "Make no mistake about it. They are like modern human footprints. If one were left in the sand of a California beach today, and a four-year-old were asked what it was, he would instantly say that somebody had walked there. He wouldn't be able to tell it from a hundred other prints on the beach, nor would you. The external morphology is the same. There is a well-shaped modern heel with a strong arch and a good ball of the foot in front of it. The big toe is in a straight line. It doesn't stick out to the side like an ape toe."

And Tuttle noted: "in all discernible morphological features, the feet of the individuals that made the G trails are indistinguishable from those of modern humans."

BLACK SKULL, BLACK THOUGHTS

In 1985, Alan Walker of Johns Hopkins University discovered west of Lake Turkana a fossil hominid skull stained dark by minerals. Called the Black Skull, it raised questions about Donald Johanson's view of hominid evolution.

According to Johanson's original idea, *Australopithecus afarensis* gave rise to two lines of hominids. This arrangement can be visualized as a tree with two branches. The trunk is *Australopithecus afarensis*. On one branch is the *Homo* line, proceeding from *Homo habilis* to *Homo erectus* to *Homo sapiens*. On the second branch are the australopithecines arising from *Australopithecus afarensis*.

Johanson and White claimed that *Australopithecus afarensis* gave rise to *Australopithecus africanus*, which in turn gave rise to *Australopithecus robustus*. The trend was toward larger teeth and jaws, and a larger skull with a ridge of bone, the saggital crest, running lengthwise along the top. The saggital crest served as a point of attachment for the powerful jaw muscles of robust australopithecines. *Australopithecus robustus* then supposedly gave rise to the superrobust *Australopithecus boisei*, which manifested all the above-mentioned features in an extreme form. The Black Skull, designated KNM-WT 17000, was similar to *Australopithecus boisei*, but was 2.5 million years old—

older than the oldest robust australopithecines.

How did Johanson respond to the discovery of the *boisei*-like Black Skull? He admitted that the Black Skull complicated things, making it impossible to arrange *Australopithecus africanus, Australopithecus robustus,* and *Australopithecus boisei* in a single line of succession coming from *Australopithecus afarensis.* Johanson proposed four possible arrangements of these species, without suggesting which one was correct. There was, he said, not yet enough evidence to decide among them.

The uncertainty about the number of species at Hadar, combined with the confused relationships among the successor species (*Australopithecus africanus, Australopithecus robustus, Australopithecus boisei,* and *Homo habilis*), create problems for evolutionists. Pat Shipman said in 1986: "The best answer we can give right now is that we no longer have a very clear idea of who gave rise to whom."

In the midst of the new complexity, one question is especially important—the origin of the *Homo* line. Shipman told of seeing Bill Kimbel, an associate of Johanson, attempt to deal with the phylogenetic implications of the Black Skull. "At the end of a lecture on Australopithecine evolution, he erased all the tidy, alternative diagrams and stared at the blackboard for a moment. Then he turned to the class and threw up his hands," wrote Shipman. Kimbel eventually decided the *Homo* line came from *Australopithecus africanus.* Johanson and White continued to maintain that *Homo* came directly from *Australopithecus afarensis.*

After she considered various phylogenetic alternatives and found the evidence for all of them inconclusive, Shipman stated: "We could assert that we have no evidence whatsoever of where *Homo* arises from and remove all members of the genus *Australopithecus* from the hominid family. . . . I've such a visceral negative reaction to this idea that I suspect I am unable to evaluate it rationally. I was brought up on the notion that *Australopithecus* is a hominid." This is one of the more honest statements we have heard from a mainstream scientist involved in paleoanthropological research.

In the foregoing discussion, we have considered only the evidence that is generally accepted today by most scientists. Needless, to say, if we were to also consider the evidence for anatomically modern humans in very ancient times that would complicate the matter even further.

Having reviewed the history of African discoveries related to human evolution, we can make the following summary observations. (1) There is a significant amount of evidence from Africa suggesting that beings resembling anatomically modern humans were present in the Early Pleistocene and Pliocene. (2) The conventional image of *Australopithecus* as a very humanlike terrestrial biped appears to be false. (3) The status of *Australopithecus* and *Homo erectus* as human ancestors is questionable. (4) The status of *Homo habilis* as a distinct species is questionable. (5) Even confining ourselves to conventionally accepted evidence, the multiplicity of proposed evolutionary linkages among the hominids in Africa presents a very confusing picture. Combining these findings with those from the preceding chapters, we conclude that the total evidence, including fossil bones and artifacts, is most consistent with the view that anatomically modern humans have coexisted with other primates for tens of millions of years.

Summary of Anomalous Evidence
Related to Human Antiquity

Sites mentioned in this book are listed in order of the published minimum ages we find most likely or otherwise worthy of consideration. The following is a glossary of terms used in the table.

eoliths = naturally broken stone with one or more edges intentionally modified or worn by use.

paleoliths = stones purposely fashioned by chipping into a recognizable tool type.

neoliths = the most advanced stone tools and utensils.

human = identified by at least some workers as anatomically modern human.

incised, broken, carved, or scraped bones = purposely modified animal bones.

PART 1

Summary of Anomalous Evidence Related to Human Antiquity (General)

Period or Millions of Years	Site	Category	Reference	Pages
Precambrian				
2800	Ottosdalin, South Africa	grooved metallic sphere	Jimison 1982	120–22
>600	Dorchester, Mass.	metal vase	*Scientific Amer.,* June 5, 1852	106–7
Cambrian				
505–590	Antelope Spring, Utah	shoe print	Meister 1968	118–20

267

PART 1—*Continued*

Period or Millions of Years	Site	Category	Reference	Pages
Devonian				
360–408	Kingoodie Quarry, Scotland	iron nail in stone	Brewster 1844	105–6
Carboniferous				
320–360	Tweed, England	gold thread in stone	*Times* (London) June 22, 1844	106
312	Wilburton, Oklahoma	iron pot	Rusch 1971	114–15
286–360	Webster, Iowa	carved stone	*Daily News,* Omaha, Neb., April 2, 1897	114
286–320	Macoupin, Illinois	human skeleton	*The Geologist,* December 1862	150
286–320	Rockcastle County in Kentucky and other sites	humanlike footprints	Burroughs 1938	150–52
280–320	Wilburton, Oklahoma	silver object	Steiger 1979	117
260–320	Morrisonville, Illinois	gold chain	*Morrisonville Times,* June 11, 1891	113
260–320	Heavener, Oklahoma	block wall in coal	Steiger 1979	116–17
Triassic				
213–248	Nevada	shoe print	Ballou 1922	115–16
Jurassic				
150	Turkmenian Republic	human footprint	*Moscow News* 1983, no. 24	152
Cretaceous				
65–144	Saint-Jean de Livet, France	metal tubes in chalk	Corliss 1987a	117–18

PART 1—*Continued*

Period or Millions of Years	Site	Category	Reference	Pages
Eocene				
50–55	Clermont, France	eoliths, paleoliths	Breuil 1910	40–43
45–55	Laon, France	chalk ball, cut wood	Melleville 1862	107–9
38–55	Barton Cliff, England	carved stone	Fisher 1912	26
38–45	Delémont, Switzerland	human skeleton	de Mortillet 1883	149
Oligocene				
33–55	Boston Tunnel, Tuolumne Table Mt., Calif.	neolith, carved stone	Whitney 1880	106
33–55	Montezuma Tunnel, Tuolumne Table Mt., Calif.	neoliths	Whitney 1880	107–109
33–55	Tuolumne Table Mt., Calif.	human skeleton	Winslow 1873	145–47
26–54	Baraque Michel, Belgium	paleoliths	Rutot 1907	68
26–54	Bay Bonnet, Belgium	paleoliths	Rutot 1907	68
26–30	Boncelles, Belgium	paleoliths	Rutot 1907	68–70
Early Miocene				
20–25	Thenay, France	paleoliths	Bourgeois 1867	59–63

PART 1—*Continued*

Period or Millions of Years	Site	Category	Reference	Pages
Middle Miocene				
12–25	Santacrucian Formation, Argentina	paleoliths, signs of fire, cut bones, broken bones, burned bones	F. Ameghino 1912	77
12–19	Billy, France	incised bone	Laussedat 1863	15–16
12–19	Sansan, France	broken bones	Garrigou 1871	16–17
12–19	Pouancé, France	incised bone	Bourgeois 1867	21–22
12–19	Clermont, France	incised bone	Pomel and de Mortillet 1876	22–23
Late Miocene				
9–55	Tuolumne Table Mt., Calif.	Snell collection, neoliths, advanced paleoliths, human jaw	Whitney 1880	104–5 147
9–55	Valentine Mine, Tuolumne Table Mt., Calif.	neolith, human skull fragment	Whitney 1880	105 147
9–55	Stanislaus Co. Mine, Tuolumne Table Mt., Calif.	neolith	Whitney 1880	105–6
9–55	Sonora Tunnel, Tuolumne Table Mt., Calif.	stone bead	Whitney 1880	106

PART 1—*Continued*

Period or Millions of Years	Site	Category	Reference	Pages
9–55	Tuolumne Table Mt., Calif.	neolith (King pestle)	Becker 1891	109–10
9–10	Harital-yangar, India	eolith	Prasad 1982	51
>8.7	Placer County, Calif.	human bones	Whitney 1880	148
7–9	Aurillac, France	paleoliths	Verworn 1905	63–68
5–25	Midi de France, France	human skeleton	de Mortillet 1883	149
5–25	Tagus Valley, Portugal	paleoliths	Ribeiro 1872	55–58
5–25	Dardanelles, Turkey	carved bone, broken bones, flint flake	Calvert 1874	18–19
5–12	Yenang-yaung, Burma	paleoliths	Noetling 1894	72–73
5–12	Pikermi, Greece	broken bones	von Dücker 1872	17
5–12	Entrerrean Formation, Argentina	paleoliths, signs of fire, incised bones, broken bones, scraped bones, burned bones	F. Ameghino 1912	77
>5	Marshall Mine, San Andreas, Calif.	neoliths	Whitney 1880	100

PART 1—*Continued*

Period or Millions of Years	Site	Category	Reference	Pages
>5	Smilow Mine, San Andreas, Calif.	neoliths	Whitney 1880	100
>5	Bald Hill, Calif.	human skull (hoax?)	Whitney 1880	143–45
>5	Clay Hill, Calif.	partial human skeleton (recent?)	Whitney 1880	148–49
Pliocene				
4–7	Antwerp, Belgium	cut shells, paleoliths, incised bones, human toe prints	Freudenberg 1919	70–72
4–4.5	Kanapoi, Kenya	human humerus	Patterson and Howells 1967	251–52
3.6–3.8	Laetoli, Kenya	human footprints	M. Leakey 1979	261–64
3–5	Monte Hermoso, Argentina	paleolith, hearths, slag, burned bones, burned earth, human vertebra	F. Ameghino 1888	75–76 141–42
3–4	Castenedolo, Italy	partial human skeleton,	Ragazzoni 1880	134–40
		partial human skeletons (3),	Ragazzoni 1880	134–40
		human skeleton	Ragazzoni 1880	134–40
3–4	Savona, Italy	human skeleton	Issel 1867	140–41
2.5–55	Sub-Crag Detritus Beds, England	bone tools, sawed bone, eoliths, neolith	Moir 1917 Moir 1935 Moir 1929	23–24 24–25 34–40 84–85

PART 1—*Continued*

Period or Millions of Years	Site	Category	Reference	Pages
2.5–3.0	According to standard opinion, the oldest stone tools are about 2.5–3.0 million years old at most, and occur only in Africa. One would not expect to find stone tools outside of Africa more than 1 million years ago . . . when *Homo erectus* is thought to have migrated from his African homeland.			
2.2–3	Sterkfontein, South Africa	human femur	Tardieu 1981	246–47
2–4	Kent Plateau, England	eoliths, paleoliths	Prestwich 1889	30–34
2–4	Rosart, Belgium	paleoliths	Rutot 1907	68–70
2–3	Haritalyangar, India	eoliths	Sankhyan 1981	50–51
2–3	San Valentino, Italy	pierced bone	Ferretti 1876	22
2–3	Monte Aperto, Italy	incised bones, flint blades	Capellini 1876	19–21
2–3	Acquatra-versa, Italy	paleolith	Ponzi 1871	72
2–3	Janicule, Italy	paleoliths	Ponzi 1871	72
2–3	Miramar, Argentina	hearths, slag, burned earth	Hrdlicka 1912	76–77
2–3	Miramar, Argentina	paleoliths, neoliths	Roth *et al.* 1915, C. Ameghino 1914, Boman 1921	77–84
2–3	Miramar, Argentina	human jaw	Boman 1921	142–43
2.5	Hadar, Ethiopia	eoliths (attributed to *H. habilis*)	Johanson and Edey 1981	259–60
2–2.5	San Giovanni, Italy	incised bones	Ramorino 1865	15

PART 1—*Continued*

Period or Millions of Years	Site	Category	Reference	Pages
2–2.5	Red Crag, England	pierced teeth	Charlesworth 1873	17–18
2–2.5	Red Crag, England	carved shell	Stopes 1881	23
2–2.5	Foxhall, England	paleoliths, signs of fire, human jaw	Moir 1927 Collyer 1867	36–37 133–34
2	Soan Valley, Pakistan	eoliths	Bunney 1987	49–50
2	Nampa, Idaho	clay figurine	Wright 1912	110–113
2	According to most scientists, the first toolmaking hominid was *Homo habilis*, the earliest fossils of which are just over 2 million years old and confined to Africa.			
Early Pleistocene				
1.8	Diring Yurlakh, Siberia	eoliths	Daniloff and Kopf 1986	50
1.8	Xihoudu, China	paleoliths, cut bones, charred bones	Jia 1980	212–13
1.7–2	Olduvai, Tanzania	eoliths, paleoliths, bolas, bone tool (for leather work), stone circle (shelter base)	M. Leakey 1971 L. Leakey 1960	51–52 52–53 85–86 86 52–53
	All of the Olduvai material (above) is normally attributed to *Homo habilis,* but the bone leather-working tool, the shelter, and bolas suggest fully human capability.			
1.7–2	Kanam, Kenya	human jaw, eoliths	L. Leakey 1960	239–44

PART 1—*Continued*

Period or Millions of Years	Site	Category	Reference	Pages
1.7	Yuanmou, China	paleoliths	Jia 1980	210–12
	According to the dominant view, the first hominid to leave Africa was *Homo erectus*, who did so about 1 million years ago. So who made the Yuanmou tools (above)?			
1.5–2.5	Ulalinka, Siberia	eoliths	Okladinov and Ragozin 1984	50–51
1.5–1.8	Koobi Fora, Kenya	human talus	Wood 1974	253–54
1.5	Gombore, Ethiopia	human humerus, eoliths	Senut 1981b	251–52
1.2–3.5	Dewlish, England	trench in chalk	Fisher 1912	26
1.2–2.5	Val d'Arno, Italy	incised bones	de Mortillet 1883	15
1.2–2	St. Prest, France	incised bones, eoliths	Desnoyers 1863 de Mortillet 1883	11–13 11–13
1.15	Olduvai, Tanzania	human skeleton	Reck 1914a,b	233–39
1–2.5	Monte Hermoso, Argentina	eoliths	Hrdlicka 1912	76–77
1–1.9	Trinil, Java	human tooth	MacCurdy 1924a	159–60
1–1.8	Kromdraai, South Africa	human ulna, human humerus	Zuckerman 1954 McHenry 1973	247
1–1.5	Buenos Aires, Argentina	human skull	F. Ameghino 1909	131–32
1	According to most scientists, the first hominid to leave Africa was *Homo erectus*, who did so about 1 million years ago.			

PART 1—*Continued*

Period or Millions of Years	Site	Category	Reference	Pages
Middle Pleistocene				
.83	Trinil, Java	human femurs	Day and Molleson 1973	161–62
.83	Trinil, Java	broken bones, charcoal, hearths	Keith 1911	159
.4–1.75	Cromer Forest Bed, England	bone tools, incised bone, sawn wood, paleoliths	Moir 1927 \ \ Moir 1924	24 \ \ 25 \ 37
.4–.7	Kanjera, Kenya	human skull fragments, paleoliths	L. Leakey 1960	239–44
.4	Olduvai, Tanzania	advanced paleoliths (modern human type)	L. Leakey 1933	237
.33–.6	Ipswich, England	human skeleton	Keith 1928	129–30
.33	Galley Hill, England	human skeleton (burial?), paleoliths	Newton 1895	124–26
.33	Moulin Quignon, France	human jaw and paleoliths (forgeries?)	Keith 1928	126–28
.33	Clichy, France	partial human skeleton (hoax?)	Bertrand 1868	128–29
.3–.4	Terra Amata, France	shelters, hearths, bone tools, paleoliths, human footprint	de Lumley 1969	130–31

PART 1—*Continued*

Period or Millions of Years	Site	Category	Reference	Pages
	Terra Amata (above) is a typical European Middle Pleistocene site where stone tools and other artifacts are automatically attributed to *Homo erectus*. But anatomically modern humans could also be responsible for the artifacts.			
.25–.45	Vértesszöllös, Hungary	human skull fragment	Pilbeam 1972	163
.25	Hueyatlaco, Mexico	advanced paleoliths	Steen-McIntyre 1981	101–3
.25	Sandia Cave, New Mexico	advanced paleoliths	*Smithsonian Misc. Coll.* v. 99, n. 23	103–4
	The implements from Hueyatlaco and Sandia Cave (above) are of a type normally attributed only to *Homo sapiens sapiens* (maximum age 100,000 years in Africa).			
.2–.4	Lawn Ridge, Illinois	metal coin (oldest known coins 1000 B.C.)	Dubois 1871	109–10
.1–1	Tongzi, China	human teeth	Qiu 1985	205–8
.1–1	Liujiang, China	partial human skeleton	Han and Xu 1985	210
.1	Trenton, New Jersey	human femur, human skull fragments	Volk 1911	123–24
	The Trenton fossils (above), with an age of 107,000 years, predate the oldest recognized anatomically modern human fossils (about 100,000 years old, from South Africa).			
.1	According to many scientists, anatomically modern humans first appeared about 100,000 (.1 million) years ago in Africa.			

PART 1

Period or Millions of Years	Site	Category	Reference	Pages
Late Pleistocene				
.08–.125	Piltdown, England	human cranium	Dawson and Woodward 1913	177–90
.03–2	La Denise, France	human skull fragments	de Mortillet 1883	129
	La Denise and Piltdown fossils (above) are anomalous if they are over .1 million years old.			

The following Pleistocene discoveries are anomalous only for North and South America. According to most scientists, humans first entered North America not more than 12,000 (.012 million) years ago.

PART 2

Summary of Anomalous Evidence Related to Human Antiquity
(North and South America Only)

Period or Millions of Years	Site	Category	Reference	Pages
Middle Pleistocene				
.3–.75	Anza-Borrego Desert, Calif.	incised bones	Graham 1988	14–15
.28–.35	El Horno, Mexico	paleoliths	Steen-McIntyre 1981	91
.2–.5	Calico, Calif.	eoliths	Simpson 1986	46–47
.2–.3	Toca da Esperança, Brazil	eoliths	de Lumley *et al.* 1988	47–48
.12–.19	Black's Fork River, Wyoming	paleoliths	Renaud 1940	73–74
Late Pleistocene				
.08–.09	Texas Street, San Diego, Calif.	eoliths	Carter 1957	45–46
.08	Old Crow River, Canada	incised bones	Morlan 1986	13–14
.07	Timlin, New York	paleoliths	Raemish 1977	90
.06–.12	Sheguiandah, Canada	paleoliths	T. E. Lee 1972	87–90
>.05	Whiteside County, Illinois	copper ring	W. E. Dubois 1871	110
>.04	Santa Barbara Island, Calif.	hearth, eoliths, mammal bones	*Science News* 1977	45
.04	Lewisville, Texas	paleolith	Alexander 1978	90

PART 2—*Continued*

Period or Millions of Years	Site	Category	Reference	Pages
.03	El Cedral, Mexico	hearths, mammal bones	Lorenzo 1986	45
.03	Boq. do Sitio de P. Furada, Brazil	hearths, eoliths, painted rock	Guidon and Delibrias 1986	45

BIBLIOGRAPHY

Unless otherwise noted in the text, quotations from entries followed by (*) have been translated into English by us.

Aigner, J. S. (1978) Pleistocene faunal and cultural stations in south China. *In* Ikawa-Smith, F., ed. *Early Paleolithic in South and East Asia*. The Hague, Mouton, pp. 129–162.

Aigner, J. S. (1981) *Archaeological Remains in Pleistocene China*. Munich, C. H. Beck.

Aigner, J. S., and Laughton, W. S. (1973) The dating of Lantian man and his significance for analyzing trends in human evolution. *American Journal of Physical Anthropology, 39(1):* 97–110.

Alexander, H. L. (1978) The legalistic approach to early man studies. *In* Bryan, A. L., ed. *Early Man in America from a Circum-Pacific Perspective*. Edmonton, Archaeological Researches International, pp. 20–22.

Alsoszatai-Petheo, J. (1986) An alternative paradigm for the study of early man in the New World. *In* Bryan, A. L., ed. *New Evidence for the Pleistocene Peopling of the Americas*. Orono, Maine, Center for the Study of Early Man, pp. 15–26.

Ameghino, C. (1915) El femur de Miramar, *Anales del Museo nacional de historia natural de Buenos Aires, 26:* 433–450. (*)

Ameghino, F. (1908) Notas preliminares sobre el *Tetraprothomo argentinus*, un precursor del hombre del mioceno superior de Monte Hermoso. *Anales del Museo nacional de historia natural de Buenos Aires, 16:* 105–242. (*)

Ameghino, F. (1909) Le *Diprothomo platensis*, un précurseur de l'homme du pliocène inférieur de Buenos Aires. *Anales del Museo nacional de historia natural de Buenos Aires, 19:* 107–209. (*)

Ameghino, F. (1910a) *Vestigios industriales en el eoceno superior de Patagonia*. Report to Congreso cientifico internacional americano, Buenos Aires, July 10–25, 1910, 8 pp.

Ameghino, F. (1910b) *Vestigios industriales en la formation entrerriana (oligoceno superior ó mioceno el más inferior)*. Report to Congreso cientifico internacional americano, Buenos Aires, July 10–25, 1910, 8 pp.

Ameghino, F. (1911) Énumération chronologique et critique des notices sur les terres cuites et les scories anthropiques des terrains sédimentaires néogenes de l'Argentine parues jusqu'a la fin de l'année 1907. *Anales del Museo nacional de historia natural de Buenos Aires, 20:* 39–80. (*)

Ameghino, F. (1912) L'age des formations sedimentaires tertiaires de l'Argentine en relation avec l'antiquité de l'homme. *Anales del Museo nacional de historia natural de Buenos Aires, 22:* 45–75. (*)

Anderson, E. (1984) Who's who in the Pleistocene: a mammalian bestiary. *In* Martin, P. S., and Klein, R. G., eds. *Quaternary Extinctions*. Tucson, University of Arizona Press, pp. 40–90.

Ayres, W. O. (1882) The ancient man of Calaveras. *American Naturalist,*

25(2): 845–854.

Ballou, W. H. (1922) Mystery of the petrified 'shoe sole' 5,000,000 years old. *American Weekly* section of the *New York Sunday American,* October 8, p. 2.

Barker, H., Burleigh, R., and Meeks, N. (1971) British Museum natural radio-carbon measurements VII. *Radiocarbon, 13:* 157–188.

Barker, H., and Mackey, J. (1961) British Museum natural radiocarbon measurements III. *Radiocarbon, 3:* 39–45.

Barnes, A. S. (1939) The differences between natural and human flaking on prehistoric flint implements. *American Anthropologist, N. S. 41:* 99–112.

Bartstra, G. J. (1978) The age of the Djetis beds in east and central Java. *Antiquity 52:* 30–37.

Bateman, P. C., and Wahrhaftig, C. (1966) Geology of the Sierra Nevada. *Bulletin of the California Division of Mines and Geology, 190:* 107–172.

Bayanov, D. (1982) A note on folklore in hominology. *Cryptozoology, 1:* 46–48.

Beaumont, P. B., de Villiers, H., and Vogel, J. C. (1978) Modern man in sub-Saharan Africa prior to 49,000 years B.P.: a review and evaluation with particular reference to Border Cave. *South African Journal of Science, 74:* 409–419.

Becker, G. F. (1891) Antiquities from under Tuolumne Table Mountain in California. *Bulletin of the Geological Society of America, 2:* 189–200.

Bellucci, G. and Capellini, G. (1884) L'homme tertiaire en Italie. *Congrès International d'Anthropologie et d'Archéologie Préhistoriques, Lisbon 1880, Compte Rendu,* p. 138.

Bertrand, P. M. E. (1868) Crane et ossements trouves dans une carriere de l'avenue de Clichy. *Bulletins de la Societe d'Anthropologie de Paris (Series 2), 3:* 329–335. (*)

Binford, L. R. (1981) *Bones: Ancient Men and Modern Myths.* New York, Academic Press.

Binford, L. R., and Ho, C. K. (1985) Taphonomy at a distance: Zhoukoudian, 'the cave home of Beijing man?' *Current Anthropology, 26:* 413–430.

Binford, L. R., and Stone, N. M. (1986) The Chinese Paleolithic: an outsider's view. *Anthroquest:The Leakey Foundation News, 35:* 1, 14–21.

Birdsell, J. B. (1975) *Human Evolution,* 2nd edition. Chicago, Rand McNally.

Black, D. (1927) Further hominid remains of Lower Quaternary age from the Chou Kou Tien deposit. *Nature, 120:* 927–954.

Black, D. (1929) Preliminary notice of the discovery of an adult *Sinanthropus* skull at Chou Kou Tien. *Bulletin of the Geological Survey of China, 8:* 207–208.

Black, D. (1931) Evidence of the use of fire by *Sinanthropus. Bulletin of the Geological Survey of China, 11(2):* 107–108.

Black, D., Teilhard de Chardin, P., Yang, Z., and Pei, W. (1933) Fossil man in China. *Memoirs of the Geological Survey of China, A.11:* 1–158.

Boman, E. (1921) Los vestigios de industria humana encontrados en Miramar (Republica Argentina) y atribuidos a la época terciaria. *Revista Chilena de Historia y Geografia, 49(43):* 330–352. (*)

Boswell, P. G. H. (1932) The Oldoway human skeleton. *Nature, 130:* 237–238.
Boswell, P. G. H. (1935) Human remains from Kanam and Kanjera, Kenya Colony. *Nature, 135:* 371.
Boule, M. (1923) *Fossil Men: Elements of Human Paleontology.* Edinburgh, Oliver and Boyd.
Boule, M. (1937) Le Sinanthrope. *L'Anthropologie, 47:* 1–22.
Boule, M., and Vallois, H. V. (1957) *Fossil Men.* London, Thames and Hudson.
Bourgeois, L. (1872) Sur les silex considérés comme portant les marques d'un travail humain et découverts dans le terrain miocène de Thenay. *Congrès International d'Anthropologie et d'Archéologie Préhistoriques, Bruxelles 1872, Compte Rendu,* pp. 81–92. (*)
Bowden, M. (1977) *Ape-Men, Fact or Fallacy?* Bromley, Sovereign Publications.
Bower, Bruce (1988) Retooled ancestors. *Science News, 133:* 344–345.
Brain, C. K. (1978) Some aspects of the South African australopithecine sites and their bone accumulations. *In* Jolly, C. J., ed. *Early Hominids of Africa.* London, Duckworth, pp. 130–161.
Bräuer, G. (1984) A craniological approach to the origin of anatomically modern *Homo sapiens* in Africa, and implications for the appearance of modern Europeans. *In* Smith, F. H., and Spencer, F., eds. *The Origin of Modern Humans: A World Survey of the Fossil Evidence.* New York, Alan R. Liss, pp. 327–410.
Bray, W. (1986) Finding the earliest Americans. *Nature, 321:* 726.
Breuil, H. (1910) Sur la présence d'éolithes a la base de l'Éocene Parisien. *L'Anthropologie, 21:* 385–408. (*)
Breuil, H. (1922) Les industries pliocenes de la region d'Ipswich. *Revue anthropologique, 32:* 226–229. (*)
Breuil, H. (1932) Le feu et l'industrie de pierre et d'os dans le gisement du 'Sinanthropus' á Choukoutien. *L'Anthropologie, 42:* 1–17. (*)
Breuil, H. (1935) L'état actuel de nos connaissances sur les industries paléothiques de Choukoutien. *L'Anthropologie, 45:* 740–746. (*)
Breuil, H., and Lantier, R. (1965) *The Men of the Old Stone Age.* New York, St. Martin's.
Brewster, D. (1844) Queries and statements concerning a nail found imbedded in a block of sandstone obtained from Kingoodie (Mylnfield) Quarry, North Britain. *Report of the British Association for the Advancement of Science, Notices and Abstracts of Communications,* p. 51.
Broad, W., and Wade, N. (1982) *Betrayers of the Truth.* New York, Simon and Schuster.
Broom, R. (1950) *Finding the Missing Link.* London, Watts.
Broom, R., and Robinson, J. T. (1952) Swartkrans ape-man. *Transvaal Museum Memoir, 6.*
Broom, R., Robinson, J. T., and Schepers, G. W. H. (1950) Sterkfontein ape-man *Pleisanthropus. Transvaal Museum Memoir, 4.*
Broom, R., and Schepers, G. W. H. (1946) The South African fossil ape-men, the Australopithecinae. *Transvaal Museum Memoir, 2.*

Brown, F., Harris, J., Leakey, R., and Walker, A. (1985) Early *Homo erectus* skeleton from west Lake Turkana, Kenya. *Nature, 316:* 788–793.

Brush, S. G. (1974) Should the history of science be rated X? *Science, 183:* 1164–1172.

Bryan, A. L. (1978) An overview of paleo-American prehistory from a circum-Pacific perspective. *In* Bryan, A. L., ed. *Early Man in America from a Circum-Pacific Perspective.* Edmonton, Archaeological Researches International, pp. 306–327.

Bryan, A. L. (1979) A preliminary look at the evidence for a standardized stone tool technology at Calico. *Quarterly of the San Bernardino County Museum Association, 26(4):* 75–79.

Bryan, A. L. (1986) Paleoamerican prehistory as seen from South America. *In* Bryan, A. L., ed. *New Evidence for the Pleistocene Peopling of the Americas.* Orono, Maine, Center for the Study of Early Man, pp. 1–14.

Budiansky, S. (1987) New light on when man came down from the trees. *U.S. News & World Report,* June 1, pp. 10–11.

Budinger, Jr., F. E. (1983) The Calico early man site. *California Geology, 66(4):* 75–82.

Bunney, S. (1987) First migrants will travel back in time. *New Scientist, 114(1565):* 36.

Burkitt, M. C. (1956) *The Old Stone Age.* New York, New York University.

Burleigh, R. (1984) New World colonized in Holocene. *Nature, 312:* 399.

Burroughs, W. G. (1938) Human-like footprints, 250 million years old. *The Berea Alumnus.* Berea College, Kentucky. November, pp. 46–47.

Calvert, F. (1874) On the probable existence of man during the Miocene period. *Journal of the Royal Anthropological Institute, 3:* 127.

Capellini, G. (1877) Les traces de l'homme pliocène en Toscane. *Congrès International d'Anthropologie et d'Archéologie Préhistoriques, Budapest 1876, Compte Rendu.* Vol. 1, pp. 46–62. (*)

Carrington, A. (1963) *A Million Years Before Man.* London, Weidenfeld & Nicholson.

Cartailhac, E. (1879) L'homme tertiaire. *Matériaux pour l'Histoire de l'Homme, 2nd series, 11:* 433–439. (*)

Carter, G. F. (1957) *Pleistocene Man at San Diego.* Baltimore, Johns Hopkins.

Carter, G. F. (1979) The blade and core stage at Calico. *Quarterly of the San Bernardino County Museum Association, 26(4):* 81–89.

Carter, G. F. (1980) *Earlier Than You Think: A Personal View of Man in America.* College Station, Texas A & M University.

Chang, K. (1962) New evidence on fossil man in China. *Science, 136:* 749–759.

Chang, K. (1977) *The Archaeology of Ancient China.* 3rd edition. New Haven, Yale University.

Chang, K. (1986) *The Archaeology of Ancient China.* 4th edition. New Haven, Yale University.

Charlesworth, E. (1873) Objects in the Red Crag of Suffolk. *Journal of the Royal Anthropological Institute of Great Britain and Ireland, 2:* 91–94.

Chavaillon, J., Chavaillon, N., Coppens, Y., and Senut, B. (1977) Présence d'hominidé dans le site oldowayen de Gomboré I à Melka Kunturé, Éthiopie. *Comptes Rendus de l' Académie des Sciences, Series D, 285:* 961–963.

Choffat, P. (1884a) Excursion à Otta. *Congrès International d'Anthropologie et d'Archaéologie Préhistoriques, Lisbon 1880, Compte Rendu,* pp. 61–67. (*)

Choffat, P. (1884b) Conclusions de la commission chargée de l'examen des silex trouvés à Otta. Followed by discussion. *Congrès International d'Anthropologie et d'Archaéologie Préhistoriques, Lisbon 1880, Compte Rendu,* pp. 92–118. (*)

Clark, W. B. (1979) Fossil river beds of the Sierra Nevada. *California Geology, 32:* 143–149.

Cole, S. (1975) *Leakey's Luck, The Life of Louis Leakey.* London, Collins.

Coles, J. M. (1968) Ancient man in Europe. *In* Coles, J. M., and Simpson, D., eds. *Studies in Ancient Europe.* Bristol, Leicester University, pp. 17–43.

Cook, D. C., Buikstra, J. E., DeRousseau, C. J., and Johanson, D. C. (1983) Vertebral pathology in the Afar australopithecines. *American Journal of Physical Anthropology, 60:* 83–101.

Cooke, H. B. S. (1963) Pleistocene mammal faunas of Africa, with particular reference to Southern Africa. *In* Howell, F. C., and Boulière, F., eds. *African Ecology and Human Evolution.* Chicago, Aldine, pp. 78–84.

Cooke, H. B. S. (1976) Suidae from Plio-Pleistocene strata of the Rudolf Basin. *In* Coppens, Y., Howell, F. C., Isaac, G., and Leakey, R. E., eds. *Earliest Man and Environments in the Lake Rudolf Basin.* Chicago, University of Chicago, pp. 251–263.

Coon, C. S. (1969) *Origin of Races.* New York, Alfred Knopf.

Cooper, C. F., and Watson, D. M. S. (1932a) The Oldoway human skeleton. *Nature, 129:* 312–313.

Cooper, C. F., and Watson, D. M. S. (1932b) The Oldoway human skeleton. *Nature, 129:* 903.

Corliss, W. R. (1978) *Ancient Man: A Handbook of Puzzling Artifacts.* Glen Arm, Sourcebook Project.

Cousins, F. W. (1971) *Fossil Man.* Emsworth, A. E. Norris.

Creely, R. S. (1965) Geology of the Oroville quadrangle, California. *Bulletin of the California Division of Mines and Geology, 184.*

Cuenot, C. (1958) *Teilhard de Chardin.* London, Burns & Oates.

Daniloff, R., and Kopf, C. (1986) Digging up new theories of early man. *U.S. News & World Report,* September 1, pp. 62–63.

Dart, R. A. (1948) The Makapansgat proto-human *Australopithecus prometheus. American Journal of Physical Anthropology, New Series, 6:* 259–283.

Dart, R. A. (1957) The osteodontokeratic culture of *Australopithecus prometheus. Transvaal Museum Memoirs, 10:* 1–105.

Dart, R. A. (1959) *Adventures with the Missing Link.* New York, Viking Press.

Darwin, C. R. (1859) *The Origin of Species.* London, J. Murray.

Darwin, C. R. (1871) *The Descent of Man.* London, J. Murray.

Dawson, C., and Woodward, A. S. (1913) On the discovery of a Paleolithic human skull and mandible in a flint bearing gravel at Piltdown. *Quarterly Journal of the Geological Society, London, 69:* 117–151.

Dawson, C., and Woodward, A. S. (1914) Supplementary note on the discovery of a Palaeolithic human skull and mandible at Piltdown (Sussex). *Quarterly Journal of the Geological Society, London, 70:* 82–99.

Day, M. H. (1978) Functional interpretations of the morphology of postcranial remains of early African hominids. *In* Jolly, C. J., ed. *Early Hominids of Africa.* London, Duckworth, pp. 311–345.

Day, M. H. (1985) Hominid locomotion—from Taung to the Laetoli footprints. *In* Tobias, P. V., ed. *Hominid Evolution: Past, Present, and Future.* New York, Alan R. Liss, pp. 115–128.

Day, M. H. (1989) Fossil man: the hard evidence. *In* Durant, J. R., ed. *Human Origins.* Oxford, Clarendon, pp. 9–26.

Day, M. H., and Molleson, T. I. (1973) The Trinil femora. *Symposia of the Society for the Study of Human Biology, 2:* 127–154.

Day, M. H., and Napier, J. R. (1964) Hominid fossils from Bed I, Olduvai Gorge, Tanganyika: fossil foot bones. *Nature, 201:* 967–970.

Day, M. H., and Wood, B. A. (1968) Functional affinities of the Olduvai Hominid 8 talus. *Man, Second Series, 3:* 440–455.

De Lumley, H. (1969) A Palaeolithic camp at Nice. *Scientific American, 220(5):* 42–50.

De Lumley, H., de Lumley, M., Beltrao, M., Yokoyama, Y., Labeyrie, J., Delibrias, G., Falgueres, C., and Bischoff, J. L. (1988) Découverte d'outils taillés associés à des faunes du Pléistocene moyen dans la Toca da Esperança, État de Bahia, Brésil. *Comptes Rendus de l' Académie des Sciences, (Series II) 306:* 241–247. (*)

De Mortillet, G. (1883) *Le Préhistorique.* Paris, C. Reinwald. (*)

De Mortillet, G., and de Mortillet, A. (1881) *Musée Préhistorique.* Paris, C. Reinwald. (*)

De Quatrefages, A. (1884) *Hommes Fossiles et Hommes Sauvages.* Paris, B. Baillire. (*)

De Quatrefages, A. (1887) *Histoire Générale des Races Humaines.* Paris, A. Hennuyer. (*)

Deméré, T. A., and Cerutti, R. A. (1982) A Pliocene shark attack on a cetotheriid whale. *Journal of Paleontology, 56:* 1480–1482.

Deo Gratias, Rev. [D. Perrando] (1873) Sur l'homme tertiaire de Savone. *Congrès International d'Anthropologie et d'Archéologie Préhistoriques, Bologna 1871, Compte Rendu,* pp. 417–420. (*)

Deperet, C. (1926) Fouilles préhistoriques dans le gisement des Hommes fossiles de la Denise, près le Puy-en-Velay. *Comptes Rendus de l' Académie des Sciences, 182:* 358–361. (*)

Desmond, A. (1976) *The Hot-Blooded Dinosaurs.* New York, Dial.

Desnoyers, M. J. (1863) Response à des objections faites au sujet d'incisions constatées sur des ossements de Mammiferes fossiles des environs de Chartres. *Comptes Rendus de l' Académie des Sciences, 56:* 1199–1204. (*)

Diamond, J. (1987) The American blitzkrieg: a mammoth undertaking. *Discover,* June, pp. 82–88.

Dietrich, W. O. (1933) Zur Altersfrage der Olduwaylagerstätte. *Centralblatt für Mineralogie, Geologie und Paläontologie, Abteilung B, 5:* 299–303.

Dreimanis, A., and Goldthwait, R. P. (1973) Wisconsin glaciation in the Huron, Erie, and Ontario lobes. *Geological Society of America Memoir, 136:* 71–106.

Drury, C. M., ed. (1976) *Nine Years with the Spokane Indians: The Diary, 1838–1848, of Elkanah Walker.* Glendale, California, Arthur H. Clark.

Dubois, E. (1932) The distinct organization of *Pithecanthropus* of which the femur bears evidence now confirmed from other individuals of the described species. *Proceedings of the Koninklijke Nederlandse Akademie van Wetenschappen Amsterdam, 35:* 716–722.

Dubois, E. (1934) New evidence of the distinct organization of *Pithecanthropus. Proceedings of the Koninklijke Nederlandse Akademie van Wetenschappen Amsterdam, 37:* 139–145.

Dubois, E. (1935) The sixth (fifth new) femur of *Pithecanthropus erectus. Proceedings of the Koninklijke Nederlandse Akademie van Wetenschappen Amsterdam, 38:* 850–852.

Dubois, W. E. (1871) On a quasi coin reported found in a boring in Illinois. *Proceedings of the American Philosophical Society, 12(86):* 224–228.

Durham, J. W. (1967) The incompleteness of our knowledge of the fossil record. *Journal of Paleontology, 41:* 559–565.

Durrell, C. (1966) Tertiary and Quaternary geology of the northern Sierra Nevada. *Bulletin of the California Division of Mines and Geology, 190:* 185–197.

Eckhardt, R. B. (1972) Population genetics and human origins. *Scientific American, 226(1):* 94–103.

Edmunds,F. H. (1954) *British Regional Geology: The Wealden District.* London, Geological Survey.

Evans, P. (1971) Towards a Pleistocene time-scale. *In* Harland, W. B., *et al.,* eds. *The Phanerozoic time-scale, a supplement. Part 2.* Geological Society of London, Special Publication No. 5, pp. 123–356.

Feldesman, M. R. (1982a) Morphometric analysis of the distal humerus of some Cenozoic catarrhines; the late divergence hypothesis revisited. *American Journal of Physical Anthropology, 59:* 73–95.

Feldesman, M. R. (1982b) Morphometrics of the ulna of some cenozoic 'hominoids.' *American Journal of Physical Anthropology, 57:* 187.

Ferguson, W. W. (1983) An alternative interpretation of *Australopithecus afarensis* fossil material. *Primates, 25:* 397–409.

Ferguson, W. W. (1984). Revision of fossil hominid jaws from Plio/Pleistocene of Hadar, in Ethiopia including a new species of the genus *Homo* (Hominoidea:Homininae). *Primates, 25:* 519–529.

Fisher, A. (1988a) On the emergence of humanness. *Mosaic, 19(1):* 34–45.

Fisher, A. (1988b) The more things change. *Mosaic, 19(1):* 23–33.

Fisher, D. E. (1971) Excess rare gases in a subaerial basalt from Nigeria. *Nature, 232:* 60.

Fisher, O. (1905) On the occurrence of *Elephas meriodionalis* at Dewlish (Dorset). *Quarterly Journal of the Geological Society of London, 61:* 35–38.

Fisher, O. (1912) Some handiworks of early men of various ages. *The Geological Magazine, London, 9:* 218–222.

Fitch, F. J., and Miller, J. A. (1976) Conventional potassium-argon and argon-40/argon-39 dating of volcanic rocks from East Rudolf. *In* Coppens, Y., Howell, F. C., Isaac, G., and Leakey, R. E., eds. *Earliest Man and Environments in the Lake Rudolf Basin.* Chicago, University of Chicago, pp. 123–147.

Fix, W. R. (1984) *The Bone Peddlers.* New York, Macmillan.

Fleming, S. (1976) *Dating in Archaeology: A Guide to Scientific Techniques.* London, Dent.

Flint, R. F. (1971) *Glacial and Quaternary Geology.* New York, John Wiley.

Fosdick, R. D. (1952) *The Story of the Rockefeller Foundation.* New York, Harper.

Freudenberg, W. (1919) Die Entdeckung von menschlichen Fußspuren und Artefakten in den tertiären Gerölschichten und Muschelhaufen bei St. Gilles-Waes, westlich Antwerpen. *Praehistorische Zeitschrift, 11:* 1–56. (*)

Garrigou, F. (1873) Sur l'etude des os cassés que l'on trouve dans divers gisements paleontologiques de l'époque Quaternaire et de l'époque Tertiaire. *Congrès International d'Anthropologie et d'Archéologie Préhistoriques, Bologna 1871, Compte Rendu,* pp. 130–148. (*)

Garrigou, F., and Filhol, H. (1868) M. Garrigou prie l'Académie de vouloir bien ouvrir un pli cacheté, déposé au nom de M. Filhol fils et au sien, le 16 mai 1864. *Comptes Rendus de l'Académie des Sciences, 66:* 819–820. (*)

The Geologist, London (1862) Fossil man. *5:* 470.

Gomberg, D. N., and Latimer, B. (1984) Observations on the transverse tarsal joint of *A. afarensis* and some comments on the interpretation of behaviour from morphology (abstract). *American Journal of Physical Anthropology, 61:* 164.

Goodman, J. (1982) *American Genesis.* New York, Berkley Books.

Goodman, J. (1983) *The Genesis Mystery.* New York, Times Books.

Gould, R. A., Koster, D. A., and Sontz, A. H. L. (1971) The lithic assemblage of the Western Desert aborigines of Australia. *American Antiquity 36(2):* 149–169.

Gould, S. J., and Eldredge, N. (1977) Punctuated equilibria: the tempo and mode of evolution reconsidered. *Paleobiology, 3:* 115–151.

Gowlett, J. A. J. (1984) *Ascent to Civilization.* London, Collins.

Graham, D. (1988) Scientist sees an early mark of man. *San Diego Union,* October 31.

Green, J. (1978) *Sasquatch: The Apes Among Us.* Seattle, Hancock House.

Griffin, J. B. (1979) The origin and dispersion of American Indians in North America. *In* Laughlin, W. S., and Harper, A. B., eds. *The First Americans: Origins, Affinities, and Adaptations.* New York, Gustav Fischer, pp. 43–55.

Griffin, J. B. (1983) The Midlands. *In* Jennings, J. D., ed. *Ancient North Americans.* San Francisco, W. H. Freeman, pp. 243–302

Groves, C. P. (1989) *A Theory of Human and Primate Evolution.* Oxford, Clarendon.

Guidon, N., and Delibrias, G. (1986) Carbon-14 dates point to man in the Americas 32,000 years ago. *Nature, 321:* 769–771.

Guo, S., Zhou, S., Meng, W., Zhang, R., Shun, S., Hao, X., Liu S., Zhang, F., Hu, R., and Liu, J. (1980) The dating of Peking man by the fission track technique. *Kexue Tongbao 25(8):* 384.

Haeckel, E. (1905) *The Evolution of Man.* Vol. 1. New York, G. Putnam's Sons.

Han, D., and Xu, C. (1985) Pleistocene mammalian faunas of China. *In* Wu, R., and Olsen, J. W. eds., *Palaeoanthropology and Palaeolithic Archaeology of the People's Republic of China.* Orlando, Academic Press, pp. 267–289.

Harland, W. B., Cox, A. V., Llewellyn, P. G., Pickton, C. A. G., Smith, A. G., and Walters, R. (1982) *A Geologic Time Scale.* Cambridge, Cambridge University Press.

Harrison, E. R. (1928) *Harrison of Ightham.* London, Oxford University Press.

Harte, Bret (1912) *The Poetical Works of Bret Harte.* Boston, Houghton Mifflin.

Hassan, A. A., and Ortner, D. J. (1977) Inclusions in bone material as a source of error in radiocarbon dating. *Archaeometry, 19(2):* 131–135.

Haynes, C. V. (1973) The Calico site: artifacts or geofacts. *Science, 187:* 305–310.

Heizer, R. F., and Whipple, M. A. (1951) *The California Indians: A Source Book.* Berkeley, University of California Press.

Herbert, W. (1983) Lucy's family problems. *Science News, 124:* 8–11.

Heuvelmans, B. (1962) *On the Track of Unknown Animals.* London, Rupert Hart-Davis.

Heuvelmans, B. (1982) What is cryptozoology? *Cryptozoology, 1:* 1–12.

Heuvelmans, B. (1983) How many animal species remain to be discovered? *Cryptozoology, 2:* 1–24.

Hicks, C. S. (1933) Scientific centralisation in the British Empire. *Nature, 131:* 397.

Hill, O. (1945) Nittaewo, an unsolved problem of Ceylon. *Loris, 4:* 21–262.

Ho, T. Y., Marcus, L. F., and Berger, R. (1969) Radiocarbon dating of petroleum-impregnated bone from tar pits at Rancho La Brea, California. *Science, 164:* 1051–1052.

Holmes, W. H. (1899) Review of the evidence relating to auriferous gravel man in California. *Smithsonian Institution Annual Report 1898–1899,* pp. 419–472.

Holmes, W. H. (1919) Handbook of aboriginal American antiquities, Part I. *Smithsonian Institution, Bulletin 60..*

Hood, D. (1964) *Davidson Black.* Toronto, University of Toronto.

Hooijer, D. A. (1951) The age of *Pithecanthropus. American Journal of Physical Anthropology, 9:* 265–281.

Hooijer, D.A. (1956) The lower boundary of the Pleistocene in Java and the age of *Pithecanthropus. Quaternaria, 3:* 5–10.

Hopwood, A. T. (1932) The age of Oldoway man. *Man, 32:* 192–195.

Hough, J. L. (1958) *Geology of the Great Lakes.* Urbana, University of Illinois.

Howell, F. C. (1966) Observations on the earlier phases of the European Lower Paleolithic. *American Anthropologist, 68(2, part 2):* 89.

Howell, F. C. (1978) Hominidae. *In* Maglio, V. J., and Cooke, H. B. S., eds. *Evolution of African Mammals.* Cambridge, Harvard University.

Howells, W. W. (1977) Hominid fossils. *In* Howells, W. W., and Tsuchitani, P. J., eds. *Palaeoanthropology in the People's Republic of China.* Washington, D. C., National Academy of Sciences, pp. 66–77.

Hrdlicka, A. (1907) Skeletal remains suggesting or attributed to early man in North America. *Smithsonian Institution, Bureau of American Ethnology, Bulletin 33.*

Hurford, A. J., Gleadow, A. J. W., and Naeser, C. W. (1976) Fission-track dating of pumice from the KBS Tuff, East Rudolf, Kenya. *Nature, 263:* 738–740.

Huxley, T. H. (1911) *Man's Place in Nature.* London, Macmillan.

Huyghe, P. (1984) The search for Bigfoot. *Science Digest,* September, pp. 56–59, 94, 96.

Ingalls, A. G. (1940) The Carboniferous mystery. *Scientific American, 162:* 14.

Irving, W. N. (1971) Recent early man research in the north. *Arctic Anthropology, 8(2):* 68–82.

Irwin-Williams, C. (1978) Summary of archaeological evidence from the Valsequillo region, Puebla, Mexico. *In* Bowman, D. L., ed. *Cultural Continuity in Mesoamerica.* London, Mouton, pp. 7–22.

Irwin-Williams, C. (1981) Comments on geologic evidence for age of deposits at Hueyatlaco archaeological site, Valsequillo, Mexico. *Quaternary Research, 16:* 258.

Isaac, G. L. (1978) The archaeological evidence for the activities of early African hominids. *In* Jolly, C. J., ed. *Early Hominids of Africa.* London, Duckworth, pp. 219–254.

Issel, A. (1868) Résumé des recherches concernant l'ancienneté de l'homme en Ligurie. *Congrès International d'Anthropologie et d'Archéologie Préhistoriques, Paris 1867, Compte Rendu,* pp. 75–89. (*)

Issel, A. (1889) Cenni sulla giacitura dello scheletro umano recentmente scoperto nel pliocene di Castenedolo. *Bullettino di Paletnologia Italiana, 15:* 89–109. (*)

Jacob, K., Jacob, C., and Shrivastava, R. N. (1953) Spores and tracheids of vascular plants from the Vindhyan System, India: the advent of vascular plants. *Nature, 172:* 166–167.

Jacob, T. (1964) A new hominid skull cap from Pleistocene Sangiran. *Anthropologica, New Series, 6:* 97–104.

Jacob, T. (1966) The sixth skull cap of *Pithecanthropus erectus. American Journal of Physical Anthropology, 25:* 243–260.

Jacob, T. (1972) The absolute age of the Djetis beds at Modjokerto. *Antiquity 46:* 148.

Jacob, T. (1973) Palaeoanthropological discoveries in Indonesia with special reference to finds of the last two decades. *Journal of Human Evolution, 2:* 473–485.

Jacob, T., and Curtis, G. H. (1971) Preliminary potassium-argon dating of early man in Java. *Contribution of the University of California Archaeological*

Research Facility, 12: 50.

Jessup, M. K. (1973) *The Case for the UFO.* Garland, Texas, Varo Manufacturing Company.

Jia, L. (1975) *The Cave Home of Peking Man.* Beijing, Foreign Languages Press.

Jia, L. (1980) *Early Man in China.* Beijing, Foreign Languages Press.

Jia, L. (1985) China's earliest Palaeolithic assemblages. *In* Wu, R., and Olsen, J. W., eds. *Palaeoanthropology and Palaeolithic Archaeology of the People's Republic of China.* Orlando, Academic Press, pp. 135–145.

Jimison, S. (1982) Scientists baffled by space spheres. *Weekly World News,* July 27.

Johanson, D. C. (1976) Ethiopia yields first 'family' of man. *National Geographic, 150:* 790–811.

Johanson, D. C., and Coppens, Y. (1976) A preliminary anatomical description of the first Plio-pleistocene hominid discoveries in the Central Afar, Ethiopia. *American Journal of Physical Anthropology, 45:* 217–234.

Johanson, D. C., and Edey, M. A. (1981) *Lucy: The Beginnings of Humankind.* New York, Simon and Schuster.

Johanson, D. C., Masao, F. T., Eck, G. G., White, T. D., Walter, R. C., Kimbel, W. H., Asfaw, B., Manega, P., Ndessokia, P., and Suwa, G. (1987) New partial skeleton of *Homo habilis* from Olduvai Gorge, Tanzania. *Nature, 327:* 205–209.

Johanson, D. C., and Shreeve, J. (1989) *Lucy's Child.* New York, William Morrow.

Johanson, D. C., and White, T. D. (1979) A systematic assessment of the early African hominids. *Science, 203:* 321–330.

Jones, E. (1953) *The Life and Work of Freud.* Vol. 1. New York, Basic Books.

Josselyn, D. W. (1966) Announcing accepted American pebble tools: the Lively Complex of Alabama. *Anthropological Journal of Canada, 4(1):* 24–31.

Kahlke, H. (1961) On the complex *Stegodon-Ailuropoda* fauna of southern China and the chronological position of *Gigantopithecus blacki* von Koenigswald. *Vertebrata Palasiatica, 5(2):* 83–108.

Keith, A. (1928) *The Antiquity of Man.* Vol. 1. Philadelphia, J. B. Lippincott.

Keith, A. (1931) *New discoveries relating to the antiquity of man.* New York, W. W. Norton.

Keith, A. (1935) Review of *The Stone Age Races of Kenya,* by L. S. B. Leakey. *Nature, 135:* 163–164.

Kennedy, G. E. (1983) Femoral morphology in *Homo erectus. Journal of Human Evolution, 12:* 587–616.

Klaatsch, H. (1907) Review of *La question de l'homme tertiaire* by L. Mayet. *Zeitschrift für Ethnologie, 39:* 765–766. (*)

Klein, C. (1973) *Massif Armoricain et Bassin Parisien.* Strasbourg, Association des Publications près les Universités de Strasbourg. 2 vols.

Kourmisky, J., ed. (1977) *Illustrated Encyclopedia of Minerals and Rocks.* London, Octopus.

Krantz, G. S. (1975) An explanation for the diastema of Javan *erectus* skull IV. *In* Tuttle, R. H., ed. *Paleoanthropology: Morphology and Paleoecology.* The

Hague, Mouton, pp. 361–370.

Krantz, G. S. (1982) Review of Halpin, M., and Ames, M. M., eds. *Manlike Monsters on Trial: Early Records and Modern Evidence. Cryptozoology, 1:* 94–100.

Krantz, G. S. (1983) Anatomy and dermatoglyphics of three Sasquatch footprints. *Cryptozoology, 2:* 53–81.

Kurtén, B. (1968) *Pleistocene Mammals of Europe.* Chicago, Aldine.

Laing, S. (1893) *Problems of the Future.* London, Chapman and Hall.

Laing, S. (1894) *Human Origins.* London, Chapman and Hall.

Latimer, B., and Lovejoy, C. O. (1990a) Hallucial metatarsal joint in *Australopithecus afarensis. American Journal of Physical Anthropology, 82:* 125–133.

Latimer, B., and Lovejoy, C. O. (1990b) Metatarsophalangeal joint of *Australopithecus afarensis. American Journal of Physical Anthropology, 83:* 13–23.

Latimer, B., Ohman, J. C., and Lovejoy, C. O. (1987) Talocrural joint in African hominoids: implications for *Australopithecus afarensis. American Journal of Physical Anthropology, 74:* 155–175.

Laussedat, A. (1868) Sur une mâchoire de Rhinoceros portant des entailles profondes trouvée à Billy (Allier), dans les formations calcaires d'eau douce de la Limagne. *Comptes Rendus de l'Académie des Sciences, 66:* 752–754. (*)

Le Gros Clark, W. E., and Campbell, B. G. (1978) *The Fossil Evidence for Human Evolution.* Chicago, University of Chicago.

Leakey, L. S. B. (1928) The Oldoway skull. *Nature, 121:* 499–500.

Leakey, L. S. B. (1931) *The Stone Age Cultures of Kenya Colony.* Cambridge, Cambridge University.

Leakey, L. S. B. (1932a) The Oldoway human skeleton. *Nature, 129:* 721–722.

Leakey, L. S. B. (1932b) The Oldoway human skeleton. *Nature, 130:* 578.

Leakey, L. S. B. (1935) *The Stone Age Races of Kenya.* London, Oxford University Press.

Leakey, L. S. B. (1936) Fossil human remains from Kanam and Kanjera, Kenya colony. *Nature, 138:* 643.

Leakey, L. S. B. (1960a) Recent discoveries at Olduvai Gorge. *Nature, 188:* 1050–1052.

Leakey, L. S. B. (1960b) Finding the world's earliest man. *National Geographic, 118:* 420–435.

Leakey, L. S. B. (1960c) The origin of the genus *Homo. In* Tax, S., ed. *Evolution after Darwin.* Vol. II. Chicago, Chicago University.

Leakey, L. S. B. (1960d) *Adam's Ancestors,* 4th edition. New York, Harper & Row.

Leakey, L. S. B. (1968) Bone smashing by Late Miocene Hominidae. *Nature, 218:* 528–530.

Leakey, L. S. B. (1971) *Homo sapiens* in the Middle Pleistocene and the evidence of *Homo sapiens'* evolution. *In* Bordes, F., ed. *The Origin of Homo sapiens.* Paris, Unesco, pp. 25–28.

Leakey, L. S. B. (1972) *By the Evidence: Memoirs, 1932–1951.* New York, Harcourt Brace Jovanovich.

Leakey, L. S. B. (1979) Calico and early man. *Quarterly of the San Bernardino County Museum Association 26(4):* 91–95.

Leakey, L. S. B, Hopwood, A. T., and Reck, H. (1931) Age of the Oldoway bone beds, Tanganyika Territory. *Nature, 128:* 724.

Leakey, L. S. B., Reck, H., Boswell, P. G. H., Hopwood, A. T., and Solomon, J. D. (1933) The Oldoway human skeleton. *Nature, 131:* 397–398.

Leakey, L. S. B., Tobias, P. V., and Napier, J. R. (1964) A new species of the genus *Homo* from Olduvai Gorge. *Nature, 202:* 7–9.

Leakey, M. D. (1971) *Olduvai Gorge.* Vol. 3. *Excavations in Beds I and II, 1960–1963.* Cambridge, Cambridge University.

Leakey, M. D. (1978) Olduvai fossil hominids: their stratigraphic positions and locations. *In* Jolly, C. J., ed. *Early Hominids of Africa.* London, Duckworth, pp. 3–16.

Leakey, M. D. (1979) Footprints in the ashes of time. *National Geographic, 155:* 446–457.

Leakey, R. E. (1973a) Evidence for an advanced Plio-Pleistocene hominid from East Rudolf, Kenya. *Nature, 242:* 447–450.

Leakey, R. E. (1973b) Skull 1470. *National Geographic, 143:* 819–829.

Leakey, R. E. (1973c) Further evidence of Lower Pleistocene hominids from East Rudolf, North Kenya, 1972. *Nature, 242:* 170–173.

Leakey, R. E. (1984) *One Life.* Salem, New Hampshire, Salem House.

Leakey, R. E., and Lewin, R. (1977) *Origins.* New York, Dutton.

Leakey, R. E., and Lewin, R. (1978) *People of the Lake: Mankind and Its Beginnings.* Garden City, Anchor Press.

Lee, R. E. (1983) "For I have been a man, and that means to have been a fighter." *Anthropological Journal of Canada, 21:* 11–13.

Lee, T. E. (1964) Canada's national disgrace. *Anthropological Journal of Canada, 2(1):* 28–31.

Lee, T. E. (1966a) Untitled editorial note on the Sheguiandah site. *Anthropological Journal of Canada, 4(4):* 18–19.

Lee, T. E. (1966b) Untitled editorial note on the Sheguiandah site. *Anthropological Journal of Canada, 4(2):* 50.

Lee, T. E. (1968) The question of Indian origins, again. *Anthropological Journal of Canada, 6(4):* 22–32.

Lee, T. E. (1972) Sheguiandah in retrospect. *Anthropological Journal of Canada, 10(1):* 28–30.

Lee, T. E. (1977) Introduction to Carter, G. F., On the antiquity of man in America. *Anthropological Journal of Canada, 15(1):* 2–4.

Lee, T. E. (1981) A weasel in the woodpile. *Anthropological Journal of Canada, 19(2):* 18–19.

Lee, T. E. (1983) The antiquity of the Sheguiandah site. *Anthropological Journal of Canada, 21:* 46–73.

Legge, A. J. (1986) Seeds of discontent. *In* Gowlett, J. A. J., and Hedges, R. E. M., eds. *Archaeological Results from Accelerator Dating.* Oxford, Oxford University Committee for Archaeology, pp. 13–21.

Leriche, M. (1922) Les terrains tertiaires de la Belgique. *Congrès Géologique International (13e, Bruxelles), Livret-Guide des Excursions en Belgique, A4:* 1–46.

Lewis, O. J. (1980) The joints of the evolving foot, part III. *Journal of Anatomy, 131:* 275–298.

Li, P., Qian, F., Ma, X., Pu, Q., Xing, L., and Ju, S. (1976) A preliminary study of the age of Yuanmou man by paleomagnetic techniques. *Scientia Sinica, 6:* 579–591.

Li, R., and Lin, D. (1979) Geochemistry of amino acid of fossil bones from deposits of Peking man, Lantian man, and Yuanmou man in China. *Scientia Geologica Sinica, 1:* 56–61.

Liu, D., and Ding, M. (1983) Discussion on the age of Yuanmou man. *Acta Anthropologica Sinica, 2(1):* 40–48.

Lisowski, F. P., Albrecht, G. H., and Oxnard, C. E. (1974). The form of the talus in some higher primates: a multivariate study. *American Journal of Physical Anthropology, 41:* 191–216.

Lohest, M., Fourmarier, P., Hamal-Nandrin, J. , Fraipont, C., and Capitan, L. (1923) Les silex d'Ipswich: conclusions de l'enquéte de l'Institut International d'Anthropologie. *Revue Anthropologique, 33:* 44–67. (*)

Longin, R. (1971) New method of collagen extraction for radiocarbon dating. *Nature, 230:* 241–242.

Lorenzo, J. L. (1978) Early man research in the American hemisphere: appraisal and perspectives. *In* Bryan, A. L., ed. *Early Man in America From a Circum-Pacific Perspective.* Edmonton, Archaeological Researches International, pp. 1–9.

Lorenzo, J. L., and Mirambell, L. (1986) Preliminary report on archaeological and paleoenvironmental studies in the area of El Cedral, San Luis Potosi, Mexico 1977–1980. *In* Bryan, A. L., ed. *New Evidence for the Pleistocene Peopling of the Americas.* Orono, Maine, Center for the Study of Early Man, pp. 106–111.

Lovejoy, C. O. (1988) Evolution of human walking. *Scientific American, 259(5):* 118–125.

Lyell, Charles (1863) *Antiquity of Man.* London, John Murray.

Ma, X., Qian, F., Li, P., and Ju, S. (1978) Paleomagnetic dating of Lantian man. *Vertebrata PalAsiatica, 16(4):* 238–243.

MacCurdy, G. G. (1924a) *Human Origins: A Manual of Prehistory.* Vol. 3. *The Old Stone Age and the Dawn of Man and His Arts.* New York, D. Appleton.

MacCurdy, G. G. (1924b) What is an eolith? *Natural History, 24:* 656–658.

Macalister, R. A. S. (1921) *Textbook of European Archaeology.* Vol. 1. *Paleolithic Period.* Cambridge, Cambridge University.

Maglio, V. J. (1972) Vertebrate faunas and chronology of hominid-bearing sediments east of Lake Rudolf, Kenya. *Nature, 239:* 379–385.

Maglio, V. J. (1973) Origin and evolution of the Elephantidae. *American Philosophical Society Transactions, 63:* 1–149.

Malde, H. E., and Steen-McIntyre, V. (1981) Reply to comments by C. Irwin-Williams: archaeological site, Valsequillo, Mexico. *Quaternary Research, 16:* 418–421.

Mallery, A. H. (1951) *Lost America: The Story of Iron-Age Civilization Prior to Columbus.* Washington, D. C., Overlook.

Mammoth Trumpet (1984) Life in ice age Chile. *1(1):* 1.

Marks, P. (1953) Preliminary note on the discovery of a new jaw of *Meganthropus* von Koenigswald in the lower Middle Pleistocene of Sangiran, central Java. *Indonesian Journal of Natural Science, 109(1):* 26–33.

Marshall, L. G., Pascual, R., Curtis, G. H., and Drake, R. E. (1977) South American geochronology: radiometric time scale for Middle to Late Tertiary mammal-bearing horizons in Patagonia. *Science, 195:* 1325–1328.

Marshall, L. G., Webb, S. D., Sepkoski, Jr., J. J. and Raup, D. M. (1982) Mammalian evolution and the great American interchange. *Science, 215:* 1351–1357.

Marzke, M. W. (1983) Joint function and grips of the *Australopithecus afarensis* hand, with special reference to the region of the capitate. *Journal of Human Evolution, 12:* 197–211.

McHenry, H. M. (1972) Postcranial skeleton of Early Pleistocene hominids. Ph.D. thesis, Harvard University.

McHenry, H. M. (1973) Early hominid humerus from East Rudolf, Kenya. *Science, 180:* 739–741.

McHenry, H. M., and Corruccini, R. S. (1975) Distal humerus in hominoid evolution. *Folia Primatologica 23:* 227–244.

Meister, W. J. (1968) Discovery of trilobite fossils in shod footprint of human in "Trilobite Bed"—a Cambrian formation, Antelope Springs, Utah. *Creation Research Quarterly, 5(3):* 97–102.

Meldau, F. J. (1964) *Why We Believe in Creation, Not in Evolution.* Denver, Christian Victory.

Melleville, M. (1862a) Foreign intelligence. *The Geologist, 5:* 145–148.

Melleville, M. (1862b) Note sur un objet travaillé de main d'homme trouve dans les lignites du Laonnois. *Revue Archéologique, 5:* 181–186. (*)

Merriam, J. C. (1938) *The Published Papers of John Campbell Merriam.* Vol. IV. Washington, D. C., Carnegie Institution.

Michels, J. W. (1973) *Dating Methods in Archaeology.* New York, Seminar Press.

Millar, Ronald (1972) *The Piltdown Men.* London, Victor Gollancz.

Miller, M. E., and Caccioli, W. (1986) The results of the New World Explorers Society Himalayan Yeti Expedition. *Cryptozoology, 5:* 81–84.

Minshall, H. L. (1989) *Buchanan Canyon: Ancient Human Presence in the Americas.* San Marcos, Slawson Communications.

Moir, J. R. (1916) Pre-Boulder Clay man. *Nature, 98:* 109.

Moir, J. R. (1917a) A series of mineralized bone implements of a primitive type from below the base of the Red and Coralline Crags of Suffolk. *Proceedings of the Prehistoric Society of East Anglia, 2:* 116–131.

Moir, J. R. (1917b) A piece of humanly-shaped wood from the Cromer Forest Bed. *Man, 17:* 172–173.

Moir, J. R. (1919) A few notes on the sub-Crag flint implements. *Proceedings of the Prehistoric Society of East Anglia, 3:*158–161.

Moir, J. R. (1923) An early palaeolith from the glacial till at Sidestrand, Norfolk. *The Antiquaries Journal, 3:* 135–137.

Moir, J. R. (1924) Tertiary man in England. *Natural History, 24:* 637–654.

Moir, J. R. (1927) *The Antiquity of Man in East Anglia.* Cambridge, Cambridge University.

Moir, J. R. (1929) A remarkable object from beneath the Red Crag. *Man, 29:* 62–65.

Moir, J. R. (1935) The age of the pre-Crag flint implements. *Journal of the Royal Anthropological Institute, 65:* 343–364.

Mongait, A. (1959) *Archaeology in the U.S.S.R.* Moscow, Foreign Languages Publishing House.

Morlan, R. E. (1986) Pleistocene archaeology in Old Crow Basin: a critical reappraisal. *In* Bryan, A. L., ed. *New Evidence for the Pleistocene Peopling of the Americas.* Orono, Maine, Center for the Study of Early Man, pp. 27–48.

Moziño, J. M. (1970) *Noticias de Nutka: An Account of Nootka Sound in 1792.* Translated and edited by Iris Higbie Wilson. Seattle, University of Washington.

Napier, J. R. (1962) Fossil hand bones from Olduvai Gorge. *Nature, 196:* 400–411.

Napier, J. R. (1973) *Bigfoot: The Yeti and Sasquatch in Myth and Reality.* New York, Dutton.

Nelson, D. E., Vogel, J. S., Southon, J. R., and Brown, T. A. (1986) Accelerator radiocarbon dating at SFU. *Radiocarbon 28:* 215–222.

New York Times (1988) Fossil hands in S. African cave may upset ideas on evolution. May 6, p. A-12.

New York Times News Service (1990) 17-million-year-old leaf fossil yields strands of DNA. *San Diego Union,* April 12, p. A-2.

Newell, N. D. (1959) Symposium on fifty years of paleontology. Adequacy of the fossil record. *Journal of Paleontology, 33:* 488–499.

Newton, E. T. (1895) On a human skull and limb-bones found in the Paleolithic terrace-gravel at Galley Hill, Kent. *Quarterly Journal of the Geological Society of London, 51:* 505–26.

Nilsson, T. (1983) *The Pleistocene.* Dordrecht, D. Reidel.

Noetling, F. (1894) On the occurrence of chipped flints in the Upper Miocene of Burma. *Records of the Geological Survey of India, 27:* 101–103.

Norris, R. M. (1976) *Geology of California.* New York, John Wiley.

O'Connell, P. (1969) *Science of Today and the Problems of Genesis.* Hawthorne, Christian Book Club of America.

Oakley, K. P. (1954) Evidence of fire in South African cave deposits. *Nature, 174:* 261–262.

Oakley, K. P. (1956) Fire as a Paleolithic tool and weapon. *Proceedings of the Prehistoric Society, New Series, 21:* 36–48.

Oakley, K. P. (1957) The dating of the Broken Hill, Florisbad, and Saldanha skulls. *In* Clark, J. D., ed. *Third Pan-African Congress on Prehistory.* London, Chatto and Windus, pp. 76–79.

Oakley, K. P. (1958) Physical Anthropology in the British Museum. *In* Roberts, D. F., ed. *The Scope of Physical Anthropology and Its Place in Academic Studies.* New York, Wenner Gren Foundation for Anthropological Research, pp. 51–54.

Oakley, K. P. (1961) *Man the Toolmaker.* London, British Museum (Natural History).

Oakley, K. P. (1974) Revised dating of the Kanjera hominids. *Journal of Human Evolution, 3:* 257–258.

Oakley, K. P. (1975) A reconsideration of the date of the Kanam jaw. *Journal of Archeological Science, 2:* 151–152.

Oakley, K. P. (1980) Relative dating of the fossil hominids of Europe. *Bulletin of the British Museum (Natural History), Geology Series, 34(1):* 1–63.

Oakley, K. P., Campbell, B. G., and Molleson, T. I. (1975) *Catalogue of Fossil Hominids.* Part III. *Americas, Asia, Australasia.* London, British Museum.

Oakley, K. P., Campbell, B. G., and Molleson, T. I. (1977) *Catalogue of Fossil Hominids.* Part I. *Africa,* 2nd edition. London, British Museum.

Oakley, K. P., and Hoskins, C. R. (1950) New evidence on the antiquity of Piltdown man. *Nature, 165:* 379–382.

Oakley, K. P., and Montagu, M. F. A. (1949) A re-consideration of the Galley Hill skeleton. *Bulletin of the British Museum (Natural History), Geology, 1(2):* 25–46.

Obermaier, H. (1924) *Fossil Man in Spain.* New Haven, Yale University.

Ogden, J. G. (1977) The use and abuse of radiocarbon dating. *Annals of the New York Academy of Sciences, 288:* 167–173.

Okladinov, A. P., and Ragozin, L. A. (1984) The riddle of Ulalinka. *Soviet Anthropology and Archaeology,* Summer 1984, pp. 3–20.

Osborn, H. F. (1910) *The Age of Mammals.* New York, Macmillan.

Osborn, H. F. (1916) *Men of the Old Stone Age.* New York, Charles Scribner's Sons.

Osborn, H. F. (1921) The Pliocene man of Foxhall in East Anglia. *Natural History, 21:* 565–576.

Osborn, H. F. (1927) *Man Rises to Parnassus.* London, Oxford University.

Osborn, H. F. (1928) *Man Rises to Parnassus,* 2nd edition. Princeton, Princeton University.

Oxnard, C. E. (1968) A note on the fragmentary Sterkfontein scapula. *American*

Journal of Physical Anthropology, 28: 213–217.

Oxnard, C. E. (1972) Some African fossil foot bones: a note on the interpolation of fossils into a matrix of extant species. *American Journal of Physical Anthropology 37:* 3–12.

Oxnard, C. E. (1975a) *Uniqueness and Diversity in Human Evolution.* Chicago, University of Chicago.

Oxnard, C. E. (1975b) The place of the australopithecines in human evolution: grounds for doubt? *Nature, 258:* 389–395.

Oxnard, C. E. (1984) *The Order of Man.* New Haven, Yale University.

Patterson, B., and Howells, W. W. (1967) Hominid humeral fragment from Early Pleistocene of northwestern Kenya. *Science, 156:* 64–66.

Patterson, L. W. (1983) Criteria for determining the attributes of man-made lithics. *Journal of Field Archaeology, 10:* 297–307.

Patterson, L. W., Hoffman, L. V., Higginbotham, R. M., and Simpson, R. D. (1987) Analysis of lithic flakes at the Calico site, California. *Journal of Field Archaeology, 14:* 91–106.

Payen, L. (1982) Artifacts or geofacts: application of the Barnes test. *In* Taylor, R. E., and Berger, R., eds. *Peopling of the New World.* Los Altos, Ballena Press, pp. 193–201.

Pei, J. (1980) An application of thermoluminescence dating to the cultural layers of Peking man site. *Quaternaria Sinica, 5(1):* 87–95.

Pei, W. (1939) The upper cave industry of Choukoutien. *Palaeontologica Sinica, New Series D, 9:* 1–41.

Peterlongo, J. M. (1972) *Guides Géologiques Régionaux: Massif Central.* Paris, Masson et Cie.

Phenice, T. W. (1972) *Hominid Fossils: An Illustrated Key.* Dubuque, William C. Brown.

Pilbeam, D. (1972) *The Ascent of Man, An Introduction to Human Evolution.* New York, Macmillan.

Poirier, F. E. (1977) *Fossil Evidence: The Human Evolutionary Journey,* 2nd edition. St. Louis, C. V. Mosby.

Poirier, F. E., Hu, H., and Chen, C. (1983) The evidence for wildman in Hubei province, People's Republic of China. *Cryptozoology, 2:* 25–39.

Pomerol, C. (1982) *The Cenozoic Era.* Chichester, Ellis Horwood.

Pomerol, C. and Feurgeur, L. (1974) *Guides Géologiques Régionaux: Bassin de Paris.* Paris, Masson et Cie.

Ponzi, G. (1873) Les relations de l'homme préhistorique avec les phénomènes géologiques de l'Italie centrale. *Congrès International d'Anthropologie et d'Archéologie Préhistoriques, Bologna 1871, Compte Rendu,* pp. 49–72. (*)

Prasad, K. N. (1971) A note on the geology of the Bilaspur-Haritalyangar region. *Records of the Geological Survey of India, 96:* 72–81.

Prasad, K. N. (1982) Was *Ramapithecus* a tool-user. *Journal of Human Evolution, 11:* 101–104.

Prest, V. K. (1969) Retreat of Wisconsin and recent ice in North America.

Geological Survey of Canada, Map 1257A.

Prestwich, J. (1889) On the occurrence of Palaeolithic flint implements in the neighborhood of Ightham. *Quarterly Journal of the Geological Society of London, 45:* 270–297.

Prestwich, J. (1891) On the age, formation, and successive drift-stages of the Darent: with remarks on the Palaeolithic implements of the district and the origin of its chalk escarpment. *Quarterly Journal of the Geological Society of London, 47:* 126–163.

Prestwich, J. (1892) On the primitive character of the flint implements of the Chalk Plateau of Kent, with reference to the question of their glacial or pre-glacial age. *Journal of the Royal Anthropological Institute of Great Britain and Ireland, 21(3):* 246–262.

Prestwich, Sir John (1895) The greater antiquity of man. *Nineteenth Century, 37:* 617 ff.

Previette, K. (1953) Who went there? *Courier-Journal Magazine,* Louisville, Kentucky, May 24.

Prost, J. (1980) The origin of bipedalism. *American Journal of Physical Anthropology, 52:* 175–190.

Protsch, R. (1974) The age and stratigraphic position of Olduvai hominid I. *Journal of Human Evolution, 3:* 379–385.

Puner, H. W. (1947) *Freud: His Life and His Mind.* New York, Grosset and Dunlap.

Qiu, Z. (1985) The Middle Palaeolithic of China. *In* Wu, R., and Olsen, J. W., eds. *Palaeoanthropology and Palaeolithic Archaeology of the People's Republic of China.* Orlando, Academic Press, pp. 187–210.

Raemsch, B. E., and Vernon, W. W. (1977) Some Paleolithic tools from northeast North America. *Current Anthropology, 18:* 97–99.

Ragazzoni (1880) La collina di Castenedolo, solto il rapporto antropologico, geologico ed agronomico. *Commentari dell' Ateneo di Brescia,* April 4, pp. 120–128. (*)

Raup, D., and Stanley, S. (1971) *Principles of Paleontology.* San Francisco, W. H. Freeman.

Reck, H. (1914a) Erste vorläufige Mitteilungen über den Fund eines fossilen Menschenskeletts aus Zentral-afrika. *Sitzungsbericht der Gesellschaft der naturforschender Freunde Berlins, 3:* 81–95. (*)

Reck, H. (1914b) Zweite vorläufige Mitteilung ber fossile Tiere- und Menschenfunde aus Oldoway in Zentralafrika. *Sitzungsbericht der Gesellschaft der naturforschender Freunde Berlins, 7:* 305–318. (*)

Reck, H. (1926) Prähistorische Grab und Menschenfunde und ihre Beziehungen zur Pluvialzeit in Ostafrika. *Mitteilungen der Deutschen Schutzgebiete, 34:* 81–86. (*)

Reck, H. (1933) *Oldoway: Die Schlucht des Urmenschen.* Leipzig, F. A. Brockhaus.

Reeves, B., Pohl, J. M. D., and Smith, J. W. (1986) The Mission Ridge site and the Texas Street question. *In* Bryan, A. L., ed. *New Evidence for the Pleistocene*

Peopling of the Americas. Orono, Maine, Center for the Study of Early Man, pp. 65–80.

Ribeiro, C. (1873a) Sur des silex taillés, découverts dans les terrains miocène du Portugal. *Congrès International d'Anthropologie et d'Archéologie Préhistoriques, Bruxelles 1872, Compte Rendu*, pp. 95–100. (*)

Ribeiro, C. (1873b) Sur la position géologique des couches miocènes et pliocènes du Portugal qui contiennent des silex taillés. *Congrès International d'Anthropologie et d'Archéologie Préhistoriques, Bruxelles 1872, Compte Rendu*, pp. 100–104. (*)

Ribeiro, C. (1884) L'homme tertiaire en Portugal. *Congrès International d'Anthropologie et d'Archaéologie Préhistoriques, Lisbon 1880, Compte Rendu*, pp. 81–91. (*)

Rightmire, G. P. (1984) *Homo sapiens* in Sub-Saharan Africa. *In* Smith, F. H., and Spencer, F., eds. *The Origin of Modern Humans: A World Survey of the Fossil Evidence.* New York, Alan R. Liss, pp. 327–410.

Robbins, L. M. (1987) Hominid footprints from Site G. *In* Leakey, M. D., and Harris, J., eds. *Laetoli: A Pliocene Site in Northern Tanzania.* Oxford, Clarendon Press, pp. 497–502.

Romer, A. S. (1966) *Vertebrate Paleontology.* Chicago, University of Chicago.

Romero, A. A. (1918) El *Homo pampaeus. Anales de la Sociedad Cientifica Argentina, 85:* 5–48. (*)

Roosevelt, T. (1906) *The Wilderness Hunter.* Vol. 2. New York, Charles Scribner's Sons.

Roth, S., Schiller, W., Witte, L., Kantor, M., Torres, L. M., and Ameghino, C. (1915) Acta de los hechos más importantes del descubrimento de objetos, instrumentos y armas de piedra, realizado en las barrancas de la costa de Miramar, partido de General Alvarado, provincia de Buenos Aires. *Anales del Museo de historia natural de Buenos Aires, 26:* 417–431. (*)

Roujou, A. (1870) Silex taillé découvert en Auvergne dans le miocène supérieur. *Matériaux pour l'Histoire de l'Homme 2:* 93–96.

Rusch, Sr., W. H. (1971) Human footprints in rocks. *Creation Research Society Quarterly, 7:* 201–202.

Rutot, A. (1906) Eolithes et pseudoéolithes. *Société d'Anthropologie de Bruxelles. Bulletin et Memoires. Memoires 25(1).* (*)

Rutot, A. (1907) Un grave problem: une industrie humaine datant de l'époque oligocène. Comparison des outils avec ceux des Tasmaniens actuels. *Bulletin de la Société Belge de Géologie de Paléontologie et d'Hydrologie, 21:* 439–482. (*)

Sanderson, I. T. (1961) *Abominable Snowmen: Legend Come to Life.* Philadelphia, Chilton.

Sanford, J. T. (1971) Sheguiandah reviewed. *Anthropological Journal of Canada, 9(1):* 2–15.

Sanford, J. T. (1983) Geologic observations at the Sheguiandah site. *Anthropological Journal of Canada, 21:* 74–87.

Sankhyan, A. R. (1981) First evidence of early man from Haritalyangar area, Himalchal Pradesh. *Science and Culture, 47:* 358–359.

Sankhyan, A. R. (1983) The first record of Early Stone Age tools of man from Ghummarwin, Himalchal Pradesh. *Current Science, 52:* 126–127.

Sartono, S. (1964) On a new find of another *Pithecanthropus* skull: an announcement. *Bulletin of the Geological Survey of Indonesia, 1(1):* 2–5.

Sartono, S. (1967) An additional skull cap of a *Pithecanthropus. Journal of the Anthropological Society of Japan (Nippon), 75:* 83–93.

Sartono, S. (1972) Discovery of another hominid skull at Sangiran, central Java. *Current Anthropology, 13(2):* 124–126.

Sartono, S. (1974) Observations on a newly discovered jaw of *Pithecanthropus modjokertensis* from the Lower Pleistocene of Sangiran, central Java. *Proceedings of the Koninklijke Nederlandse Akadamie van Wetenschappen, Amsterdam, Series B, 77:* 26–31.

Savage, D. E., and Russell, D. E. (1983) *Mammalian Paleofaunas of the World.* Reading, Addison-Wesley.

Schlosser, M. (1911) Beitrage zur Kenntnis der oligozänen Landsäugetiere aus dem Fayum. *Beitrage zur Paläontologie und Geologie, 24:* 51–167.

Schmid, P. (1983) Eine Rekonstruktion des Skelettes von A.L. 288–1 (Hadar) und deren Konsequenzen. *Folia Primatologica, 40:* 283–306.

Schultz, A. H. (1930) The skeleton of the trunk and limbs of higher primates. *Human Biology, 2:* 303.

Schweinfurth, G. (1907) Über A. Rutots Entdeckung von Eolithen im belgischen Oligocän. *Zeitschrift für Ethnologie, 39:* 958–959.

Science News (1988) Bone marks: tools vs. teeth. *134:* 14.

Science News Letter (1938a) Geology and ethnology disagree about rock prints. *34:* 372.

Science News Letter (1938b) Human-like tracks in stone are riddle to scientists. *34:* 278–279.

Senut, B. (1979) Comparaison des hominidés de Gombore IB et de Kanapoi: deux pièces du genre *Homo? Bulletin et Mémoires de la Société d' Anthropologie de Paris, 6(13):* 111–117.

Senut, B. (1981a) Humeral outlines in some hominoid primates and in Plio-pleistocene hominids. *American Journal of Physical Anthropology, 56:* 275–283.

Senut, B. (1981b) Outlines of the distal humerus in hominoid primates: application to some Plio-Pleistocene hominids. *In* Chiarelli, A. B., and Corruccini, R. S., eds. *Primate Evolutionary Biology.* Berlin, Springer Verlag, pp. 81–92.

Sergi, G. (1884) L'uomo terziario in Lombardia *Archivio per L'Antropologia e la Etnologia, 14:* 304–318. (*)

Sergi, G. (1912) Intorno all'uomo pliocenico in Italia. *Rivista Di Antropologia (Rome), 17:* 199–216. (*)

Shackley, M. (1983) *Wildmen: Yeti, Sasquatch and the Neanderthal Enigma.* London, Thames and Hudson.

Shipman, P. (1986) Baffling limb on the family tree. *Discover, 7(9):* 87–93.

Simons, E. L. (1978) Diversity among the early hominids: a vertebrate palaeontologist's viewpoint. In Jolly, C. J., ed. *Early Hominids of Africa.* London, Duckworth, pp. 543–566.

Simons, E. L., and Ettel, P. C. (1970) *Gigantopithecus. Scientific American, 22:* 76–85.

Simpson, R. D., Patterson, L. W., and Singer, C. A. (1981) Early lithic technology of the Calico Mountains site, southern California. *Calico Mountains Archeological Site, Occasional Paper.* Presented at the 10th Congress of the International Union of Prehistoric and Protohistoric Sciences, Mexico City.

Simpson, R. D., Patterson, L. W., and Singer, C. A. (1986) Lithic technology of the Calico Mountains site, southern California. *In* Bryan, A. L., ed. *New Evidence for the Pleistocene Peopling of the Americas.* Orono, Maine, Center for the Study of Early Man, pp. 89–105.

Singh, P. (1974) *Neolithic Cultures of Western Asia.* New York, Seminar.

Sinclair, W. J. (1908) Recent investigations bearing on the question of the occurrence of Neocene man in the auriferous gravels of the Sierra Nevada. *University of California Publications in American Archaeology and Ethnology, 7(2):*107–131.

Slemmons, D. B. (1966) Cenozoic volcanism of the central Sierra Nevada, California. *Bulletin of the California Division of Mines and Geology, 190:* 199–208.

Smith, G. E. (1931) The discovery of primitive man in China. *Antiquity, 5:* 20–36.

Snelling, N. J. (1963) Age of the Roirama formation, British Guiana. *Nature, 198:* 1079–1080.

Sollas, W. J. (1911) *Ancient Hunters,* 1st edition. London, Macmillan.

Sollas, W. J. (1924) *Ancient Hunters,* 3rd edition, revised. London, Macmillan.

Southall, J. (1882) Pliocene man in America. *Journal of the Victoria Institute, 15:* 191–201.

Sparks, B. W., and West, R. G. (1972) *The Ice Age in Britain.* London, Methuen.

Spencer, F. (1984) The Neandertals and their evolutionary significance: a brief historical survey. *In* Smith, F. H., and Spencer, F., eds. *The Origin of Modern Humans: A World Survey of the Fossil Evidence.* New York, Alan R. Liss, pp. 1–49.

Sprague, R. (1986) Review of *The Sasquatch and Other Unknown Hominoids,* V. Markotic, ed. *Cryptozoology, 5:* 99–108.

Stafford, T. W., Jull, A. J. T., Brendel, K., Duhamel, R. C., and Donahue, D. (1987) Study of bone radiocarbon dating accuracy at the University of Arizona NSF Accelerator Facility for Radioisotope Analysis. *Radiocarbon, 29:* 24–44.

Stainforth, R. M. (1966) Occurrence of pollen and spores in the Roraima Formation of Venezuela and British Guiana. *Nature, 210:* 292–294.

Stanley, S. M. (1981) *The New Evolutionary Timetable.* New York, Basic Books.

Steen-McIntyre, V., Fryxell, R., and Malde, H. E. (1981) Geologic evidence for age of deposits at Hueyatlaco archaeological site, Valsequillo, Mexico.

Quaternary Research 16: 1–17.

Steiger, B. (1979) *Worlds Before Our Own.* New York, Berkley.

Stern, Jr., J. T., and Susman, R. L. (1983). The locomotor anatomy of *Australopithecus afarensis. American Journal of Physical Anthropology, 60:* 279–318.

Stokes, W. L. (1974) Geological specimen rejuvenates old controversy. *Dialogue, 8:* 138–141.

Stopes, H. (1881) Traces of man in the Crag. *British Association for the Advancement of Science, Report of the Fifty-first Meeting,* p. 700.

Stopes, M. C. (1912) The Red Crag portrait. *The Geological Magazine, 9:* 285–286.

Straus, Jr., W. L. (1929) Studies on the primate ilia. *American Journal of Anatomy, 43:* 403.

Stringer, C. B., Hublin, J. J., and Vandermeersch, B. (1984) The origin of anatomically modern humans in Western Europe. *In* Smith, F. H., and Spencer, F., eds. *The Origin of Modern Humans: A World Survey of the Fossil Evidence.* New York, Alan R. Liss, pp. 51–135.

Susman, R. L. (1979) Comparative and functional morphology of hominoid fingers. *American Journal of Physical Anthropology, 50:* 215–236.

Susman, R. L. (1988) Hand of *Paranthropus robustus* from Member I, Swartkrans: fossil evidence for tool behavior. *Science 240:* 781–783.

Susman, R. L., and Creel, N. (1979) Functional and morphological affinities of the subadult hand (O.H. 7) from Olduvai Gorge. *American Journal of Physical Anthropology, 51:* 311–332.

Susman, R. L., and Stern, Jr., J. T. (1979) Telemetered electromyography of the flexor digitorum profundus and flexor digitorum superficialis in *Pan troglodytes* and implications for interpretation of the O.H. 7 hand. *American Journal of Physical Anthropology, 50:* 565–574.

Susman, R. L., Stern, Jr., J. T., and Jungers, W. L. (1984) Arboreality and bipedality in the Hadar hominids. *Folia primatologica, 43:* 113–156.

Szabo, B. J., Malde, H. E., and Irwin-Williams, C. (1969) Dilemma posed by uranium-series dates on archaeologically significant bones from Valsequillo, Puebla, Mexico. *Earth and Planetary Science Letters, 6:* 237–244.

Tamers, M. A., and Pearson, F. J. (1965) Validity of radiocarbon dates on bone. *Nature, 208:* 1053–1055.

Tardieu, C. (1979) Analyse morpho-functionelle de l'articulation du genou chez les Primates. Application aux hominides fossiles. *Thesis, University of Pierre.*

Tardieu, C. (1981) Morpho-functional analysis of the articular surfaces of the knee-joint in primates. *In* Chiarelli, A. B., and Corrucini, R. S., eds. *Primate evolutionary biology.* Berlin, Springer Verlag, pp. 68–80.

Tassy, P. (1983) Review of *Les Bêtes Humaines d'Afrique,* by B. Heuvelmans. *Cryptozoology, 2:* 132–133.

Taylor, L. R., Compagno, L. J. V., and Struhsaker, P. J. (1983) Megamouth—a new species, genus, and family of lamnoid shark (*Megachasma pelagois,*family Megachasmidae) from the Hawaiian Islands. *Proceedings of the California Academy of Sciences, 43(8):* 87–110.

Taylor, R. E. (1987) *Radiocarbon Dating: An Archaeological Perspective.* Orlando, Academic Press.

Teilhard de Chardin, P. (1931) Le *Sinanthropus,* de Pekin. *L'Anthropologie, 41:* 1–11.

Teilhard de Chardin, P. (1965) *The Appearance of Man.* New York, Harper & Row.

Teilhard de Chardin, P., and Yang, Z. [Young, C. C.] (1929) Preliminary report on the Chou Kou Tien fossiliferous deposit. *Bulletin of the Geological Survey of China, 8:* 173–202.

Thorson, R. M., and Guthrie, R. D. (1984) River ice as a taphonomic agent: an alternative hypothesis for bone 'artifacts.' *Quaternary Research, 22:* 172–188.

Time-Life (1973) *Emergence of Man: The First Men.* New York, Time-Life Books.

Tobias, P. V. (1962) A re-examination of the Kanam mandible. *In* Mortelmans, G., and Nenquin, J., eds. *Actes du IVe Congres Panafricain de Prehistorie et de l'Etude du Quaternaire.* Tervuren, Belgium, Musee Royal de l'Afrique Centrale, pp. 341–360.

Tobias, P. V. (1968) Middle and early Upper Pleistocene members of the genus *Homo* in Africa. *In* Kurth, G., ed. *Evolution and Hominisation,* 2nd edition. Stuttgart, Gustav Fischer, pp. 176–194.

Tobias, P. V. (1971) Human skeletal remains from the Cave of Hearths, Makapansgat, northern Transvaal. *American Journal of Physical Anthropology, 34:* 335–368.

Tobias, P. V. (1978) The South African australopithecines in time and hominid phylogeny, with special reference to dating and affinities of the Taung skull. *In* Jolly, C. J., ed. *Early Hominids of Africa.* London, Duckworth, pp. 44–84.

Tobias, P. V. (1979) Calico Mountains and early man in North America. *Quarterly of the San Bernardino County Museum Association, 26(4):* 97–98.

Tobias, P. V. (1980). 'Australopithecus afarensis' and *A. africanus:* critique and an alternative hypothesis. *Paleontologica Africane, 23:* 1–17.

Traill, D. A. (1986a) Schliemann's acquisition of the Helios Metope and his psychiatric tendencies. *In* Calder, W. M., and Traill, D. A., eds. *Myth, Scandal, and History: The Heinrich Schliemann Controversy and a First Edition of the Mycenaean Diary.* Detroit, Wayne State University, pp. 48–80.

Traill, D. A. (1986b) Priam's treasure: Schliemann's plan to make duplicates for illicit purposes. *In* Calder, W. M., and Traill, D. A., eds. *Myth, Scandal, and History: The Heinrich Schliemann Controversy and a First Edition of the Mycenaean Diary.* Detroit, Wayne State University, pp. 110–121.

Trinkhaus, E. (1984) Does KNM-ER 1481A establish *Homo erectus* at 2.0 myr B.P.? *American Journal of Physical Anthropology, 64:* 137–139.

Tuttle, R. H., ed. (1975) *Paleoanthropology: Morphology and Paleoecology.* The

Hague, Mouton, pp. 361–370.

Tuttle, R. H. (1981) Evolution of hominid bipedalism and prehensile capabilities. *Philosophical Transactions of the Royal Society of London, B, 292:* 89–94.

Tuttle, R. H. (1985) Ape footprints and Laetoli impressions: a response to the SUNY claims. *In* Tobias, P. V., ed. *Hominid Evolution: Past, Present, and Future.* New York, Alan R. Liss, pp. 129–133.

Tuttle, R. H. (1987) Kinesiological inferences and evolutionary implications from Laetoli biped trails G-1, G-2/3, and A. *In* Leakey, M. D., and Harris, J. eds. *Laetoli: A Pliocene Site in Northern Tanzania.* Oxford, Clarendon Press, pp. 508–517.

Van Andel, T. H. (1981) Consider the incompleteness of the geological record. *Nature, 294:* 397–398.

Vasishat, R. N. (1985) *Antecedents of Early Man in Northwestern India.* New Delhi, Inter-India Publications.

Vere, F. (1959) *Lessons of Piltdown.* Emsworth, A. E. Norris.

Verworn, M. (1905) Die archaeolithische Cultur in den Hipparionschichten von Aurillac (Cantal). *Abhandlungen der königlichen Gesellschaft der Wissenschaften zu Göttingen. Mathematisch-Physikalische Klasse, Neue Folge, 4(4):* 3–60. (*)

Volk, E. (1911) The archaeology of the Delaware Valley. *Papers of the Peabody Museum of American Archaeology and Ethnology, Harvard University, 5.*

Von Dücker, Baron (1873) Sur la cassure artificelle d'ossements recueillis dans le terrain miocène de Pikermi. *Congrès International d'Anthropologie et d'Archéologie Préhistoriques, Bruxelles 1872, Compte Rendu,* pp. 104–107. (*)

Von Koenigswald, G. H. R. (1937) Ein Unterkieferfragment des *Pithecanthropus* aus den Trinilschichten Mitteljavas. *Proceedings of the Koninklijke Nederlandse Akadamie van Wetenschappen Amsterdam, 40:* 883–893.

Von Koenigswald, G. H. R. (1940a) Neue *Pithecanthropus* Funde 1936–1938. *Wetenschappelijke Mededeelingen Dienst Mijnbouw Nederlandse Oost-Indie, 28:* 1–223.

Von Koenigswald, G. H. R. (1940b), Preliminary note on new remains of *Pithecanthropus* from central Java. *Proceedings of the Third Congress of Prehistorians of the Far East, Singapore, 1938,* pp. 91–95.

Von Koenigswald, G. H. R. (1947) Search for early man. *Natural History, 56:* 8–15.

Von Koenigswald, G. H. R. (1949a) The discovery of early man in Java and Southern China. *In* W. W. Howells, ed. *Early Man in the Far East.* Detroit, American Association of Physical Anthropologists, pp. 83–98.

Von Koenigswald, G. H. R. (1949b), The fossil hominids of Java. *In* van Bemmelen, R. W., ed. *The Geology of Indonesia.* Vol. IA. The Hague, Government Printing Office, pp. 106–111.

Von Koenigswald, G. H. R. (1956) *Meeting Prehistoric Man.* London, Thames and Hudson.

Von Koenigswald, G. H. R. (1968a) Observations upon two *Pithecanthropus* mandibles from Sangiran, central Java. *Proceedings of the Koninklijke Nederlandse Akadamie van Wetenschappen Amsterdam, Series B, 71:* 99–107.

Von Koenigswald, G. H. R. (1968b) Das absolute Alter des *Pithecanthropus Erectus* Dubois. *In* Kurth, G., ed. *Evolution and Hominisation,* 2nd edition. Stuttgart, Gustav Fischer Verlag, pp. 195–203.

Von Koenigswald, G. H. R., and Weidenreich, F. (1939) The relationship between *Pithecanthropus* and *Sinanthropus. Nature, 144:* 926–929.

Wada, D. N. (1953) *The Geology of India,* 3rd edition. London, Macmillan.

Walker, A., Leakey, R. E., Harris, J. M., and Brown, F. H. (1986) 2.5-myr *Australopithecus boisei* from west of Lake Turkana, Kenya. *Nature, 322:* 517–522.

Wallace, A. R. (1869) *The Malay Archipelago.* New York, Dover.

Wallace, A. R. (1887) The antiquity of man in North America. *Nineteenth Century, 22:* 667–679.

Wallace, A. R. (1905) *My Life.* Vol. 2. London, Chapman & Hall.

Warren, S. H. (1920) A natural 'eolith' factory beneath the Thanet Sand. *Quarterly Journal of the Geological Society of London, 76:* 238–253.

Wayland, E. J. (1932) The Oldoway human skeleton. *Nature, 130:* 578.

Weaver, K. F. (1985) The search for our ancestors. *National Geographic, 168:* 560–624.

Weaver, W. (1967) *U. S. Philanthropic Foundations.*New York, Harper & Row.

Weidenreich, F. (1935) The *Sinanthropus* population of Choukoutien (Locality 1) with a preliminary report on new discoveries. *Bulletin of the Geological Survey of China, 14(4):* 427–468.

Weidenreich, F. (1941) The extremity bones of *Sinanthropus pekinensis. Palaeontologia Sinica,* New Series, D, *5:* 1–150.

Weidenreich, F. (1943) The skull of *Sinanthropus pekinensis. Palaeontologia Sinica,* New Series D, *10:* 1–484.

Weidenreich, F. (1945) Giant early man from Java and South China.*Anthropological Papers of the American Museum of Natural History, 40:* 1–134.

Weiner, J. S. (1955) *The Piltdown Forgery.* Oxford, Oxford University.

Weiner, J. S., Oakley, K. P., and Le Gros Clark, W. E. (1953) The solution of the Piltdown problem. *Bulletin, British Museum (Natural History), Geology, 2(3):* 141–146.

Weiner, J. S., Oakley, K. P., and Le Gros Clark, W. E. (1955) Further contributions to the solution of the Piltdown problem. *Bulletin, British Museum (Natural History), Geology, 2(6):* 228–288.

Weinert, H. (1934) *Homo sapiens* im Altpaläolithischen Diluvium? *Zeitschrift für Morphologie und Anthropologie. Erb-und Rassenbiologie,* Stuttgart, pp. 459–468.

Wendt, H. (1955) *In Search of Adam.* Boston, Houghton Mifflin.

Wendt, H. (1972) *From Ape to Adam.* Indianapolis, Bobbs-Merrill.

West, R. G. (1968) *Pleistocene Geology and Biology.* New York, John Wiley.

West, R. G. (1980) *The Pre-glacial Pleistocene of the Norfolk and Suffolk Coasts.* Cambridge, Cambridge University.

Wetzel, R. M., Dubos, R. E., Martin, R. L., and Myers, P. (1975) *Catagonus:* an 'extinct' peccary, alive in Paraguay. *Science, 189:* 379–380.

White, T. D., and Suwa, G. (1987) Hominid footprints at Laetoli: facts and interpretations. *American Journal of Physical Anthropology, 72:* 485–514.

Whitney, J. D. (1880) The auriferous gravels of the Sierra Nevada of California. *Harvard University, Museum of Comparative Zoology Memoir 6(1).*

Wilford, J. N. (1990) Mastermind of Piltdown hoax named. New York Times News Service story reprinted in *San Diego Union,* June 11, p. C-1.

Williams, S. (1986) Fantastic archaeology: alternate views of the past. *Epigraphic Society Occasional Papers, 15:* 41.

Willis, D. (1989) *The Hominid Gang.* New York, Viking.

Winchell, A. (1881) *Sparks from a Geologist's Hammer.* Chicago, S. C. Griggs.

Winslow, C. F. (1873) The President reads extracts from a letter from Dr. C. F. Winslow relating the discovery of human remains in Table Mountain, Cal. (Jan 1). *Proceedings of the Boston Society of Natural History, 15:* 257–259.

Witthoft, J. (1955) Texas Street artifacts, part I. *New World Antiquity, 2(9):* 132–134; part II, *2(12):* 179–184.

Wolpoff, M. H. (1980) *Paleoanthropology.* New York, Alfred A. Knopf.

Wood, B. A. (1974a) Evidence on the locomotor pattern of *Homo* from early Pleistocene of Kenya. *Nature, 251:* 135–136.

Wood, B. A. (1974b) Olduvai Bed I postcranial fossils: a reassessment. *Journal of Human Evolution, 3:* 373–378.

Wood, B. A. (1976) Remains attributable to *Homo* in the East Rudolf succession. *In* Coppens, Y., Howell, F. C., Isaacs, G. I., and Leakey, R. E., eds. *Earliest Man and Environments in the Lake Rudolf Basin.* Chicago, University of Chicago, pp. 490–506.

Wood, B. A. (1987) Who is the 'real' *Homo habilis? Nature, 327:* 187–188.

Woodmorappe, J. (1979) Radiometric geochronology reappraised. *Creation Research Quarterly, 16:* 102–129,147.

Woodward, A. S. (1917) Fourth note on the Piltdown gravel with evidence of a second skull of *Eoanthropus dawsoni. Quarterly Journal of the Geological Society of London, 73:* 1–8

Woodward, A. S. (1948) *The Earliest Englishman.* London, Watts.

Woodward, A. S., *et al.* (1933) Early man in East Africa. *Nature, 131:* 477–478.

Wooldridge, A. B. (1986) First photos of the Yeti: an encounter in North India. *Cryptozoology, 5:* 63–76.

Wright, G. F. (1912) *Origin and Antiquity of Man.* Oberlin, Bibliotheca Sacra.

Wu, R. (1965) Preliminary report on a skull of *Sinanthropus lantianensis* of Lantian, Shensi. *Scientia Sinica, 14(7):* 1032–1035.

Wu, R. (1966) The skull of Lantian man. *Current Anthropology, 7(1):* 83–86.

Wu, R. (1973) Lantian hominid. *Wenwu, Peking 6:* 41–44.

Wu, R., and Dong, X. (1985) *Homo erectus* in China. *In* Wu, R., and Olsen, J. W.,

eds. *Palaeoanthropology and Paleolithic Archaeology in the People's Republic of China*. Orlando, Academic Press, pp. 79–89.

Wu, R., and Lin, S. (1983) Peking man. *Scientific American, 248:* 86–94.

Wu, X., and Wang, L. (1985) Chronology in Chinese palaeoanthropology. *In*
Wu, R., and Olsen, J. W., eds. *Palaeoanthropology and Palaeolithic Archaeology in the People's Republic of China*. Orlando, Academic Press, pp. 29–
51.

Wu, X., and Wu, M. (1985) Early *Homo sapiens* in China. *In* Wu, R., and Olsen,
J. W., eds. *Palaeoanthropology and Palaeolithic Archaeology in the People's
Republic of China*. Orlando, Academic Press, pp. 91–106.

Wu, X., and Zhang, Z. (1985) Late Palaeolithic and Neolithic *Homo sapiens*. *In*
Wu, R., and Olsen, J. W., eds. *Palaeoanthropology and Palaeolithic Archaeology of the People's Republic of China*. Orlando, Academic Press, pp. 107–
134.

Yuan, Z., and Huang, W. (1979) 'Wild man' - fact or fiction? *China Reconstructs.*
July, pp. 56–59.

Zaguin, W. H. (1974) The palaeogeographic evolution of the Netherlands during
the Quaternary. *Geologie en Mijnbouw N.S. 53:* 369–385.

Zhang, S. (1985) The early Palaeolithic of China. *In* Wu, R., and Olsen, J. W., eds.
*Palaeoanthropology and Palaeolithic Archaeology in the People's Republic
of China*. Orlando, Academic Press, pp. 147–186.

Zhou, G. (1982) The status of wildman research in China. *Cryptozoology, 1:* 13–
23.

Zhou, M., Hu, C., and Lee, Y. (1965) Mammalian fossils associated with the
hominid skull cap of Lantian, Shensi. *Scientia Sinica, 14:* 1037–1048.

Zihlman, A. L. (1985) *Australopithecus afarensis:* two sexes or two species? *In*
Tobias, P. V., ed. *Hominid Evolution: Past, Present, and Future*. New York,
Alan R. Liss, pp. 213–220.

Zuckerman, S. (1954) Correlation of change in the evolution of higher primates.
In Huxley, J., Hardy, A. C., and Ford, E. B., eds. *Evolution as a Process*.
London, Allen and Unwin, pp. 300–352.

Zuckerman, S. (1973) Closing remarks to symposium. *The Concepts of Human
Evolution. Symposia of the Zoological Society of London, 33:* 449–453.

Zuckerman, S., Ashton, E. H., Flinn, R. M., Oxnard, C. E., and Spence, T. F. (1973)
Some locomotor features of the pelvic girdle in primates. *The Concepts of
Human Evolution. Symposia of the Zoological Society of London, 33:* 71–
165.

INDEX

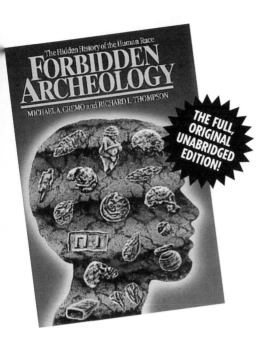

Book Order Form ———————————

☎ Telephone orders: Call 1-800-HIDDEN (1-800-443-3361).
Have your credit card ready.

✳ Fax orders: 559-337-2354

✉ Postal orders: Torchlight Publishing, P. O. Box 52,
Badger, CA 93603, USA

▲ **World Wide Web: www.torchlight.com**

Please send the following:

○ *Forbidden Archeology* — The full, unabridged original edition, 952 pages,
141 illustrations, 25 tables, hardback $44.95 (Canada $64.95)

○ *Forbidden Archeology's Impact: How a Controversial New Book Shocked
the Scientific Community and Became an Underground Classic* —
600 pages, hardback $35.00 (Canada $50.00)

○ *The Hidden History of the Human Race* — The abridged version of *Forbidden
Archeology,* 352 pages, 120 illustrations, softback $15.95 (Canada $22.95)

○ **Please send me your catalog and info on other books by Torchlight Publishing.**

Company_____

Name_____

Address_____

City _____ State_____ Zip_____

(I understand that I may return any books for a full refund—no questions asked.)

Payment:

○ Check / money order enclosed   ○ VISA   ○ MasterCard   ○ AmEx

Card number_____

Name on card_____ Exp. date_____

Signature_____

Shipping and handling (CA residents add 7% sales tax):

Forbidden Archeology and *Forbidden Archeology's Impact* — Book rate: USA $5.00 for
first book, $3.00 for each additional book. Canada: $6.00 for first book, $4.00 for each
additional book. Foreign countries: $7.00 for first book, $5.00 for each additional book.

The Hidden History of the Human Race — Book rate: USA $3.00 for first book, $2.00
for each additional book. Canada: $3.00 for first book, $2.00 for each additional book.
Foreign countries: $4.00 for first book, $3.00 for each additional book.

Surface shipping may take 3–4 weeks. Foreign orders please allow 6–8 weeks for delivery.

It's a Bunny-Eat-Bunny World

Also by Olga Litowinsky

FOR ADULTS

Writing and Publishing Books for
Children in the 1990s:
The Inside Story from the Editor's Desk

FOR YOUNG READERS

Boats for Bedtime

Bug Blast

The Dream Book

The High Voyage: The Last Crossing of
Christopher Columbus

The New York Kids Book

Oliver's High-Flying Adventure

The Pawloined Paper

Short Circuit

Walker & Company

New York

It's a
Bunny-Eat-Bunny
World

◆

A Writer's Guide to Surviving
and Thriving in Today's Competitive
Children's Book Market

◆

Olga Litowinsky

For Edward,

sempre a minha beira

First published in the United States of America
in 2001 by Walker Publishing Company, Inc.

Published simultaneously in Canada by
Fitzhenry and Whiteside, Markham, Ontario L3R 4T8

Library of Congress Cataloging-in-Publication Data

Litowinsky, Olga.
    It's a bunny-eat-bunny world : a writer's guide to
surviving and thriving in today's competitive
children's book market / Olga Litowinsky.
       p.   cm.
    Includes bibliographical references.
    ISBN 0-8027-8637-5 —
    ISBN 0-8027-7523-3 (pbk.)
    1. Children's literature—Authorship.   I. Title.

PN147.5 .L57   2001
808.06'8—dc21
                                        00-047317

Illustrations by Lonnie Sue Johnson

Book design by Jennifer Ann Daddio

Printed in the United States of America
2   4   6   8   10   9   7   5   3   1

Contents

Part I: Background

Part II: Foreground

Welcome to the

Rabbit Hole

✦

The word "impossible" is not in my dictionary
—Napoleon Bonaparte

A writer—let's call him Gus Casey—came up to me recently and said, "I've heard it's impossible for new writers to get a children's book published. Is that true?"

"It's more difficult than it used to be," I answered, "but it's not impossible."

Writers like Gus are worried and confused as we ease into the third millennium. Some even wonder whether the book itself will survive in the face of competition from electronic technology. History demonstrates it will, because in spite of the temptations of movies, television, video games, and computers, a place remains for Bound Orderly Organized Knowledge, otherwise known as the BOOK. In fact, more books for children are being published—and sold—than ever before. The demand for new books is high, and it is the writer who is the indispensable provider of information, enlightenment, and entertainment, or, as the media moguls say nowadays, "content."

However, to succeed in the dizzying Rabbit Hole world of children's book publishing, Gus will have to adjust to new ways. Much of what I wrote in my previous book, *Writing and Publishing Books for Children in the 1990s: The View from the Editor's Desk* (1992), remains relevant. For those who haven't read the first book, I repeat in this one the basic information about such matters as how to find a publisher and submit a manuscript.

Nonetheless, a great deal has changed since 1992, in the industry and in my own life. I was then an executive editor at Simon & Schuster. A few years later, with the advent of a new children's publisher, hired to engineer a major overhaul of the division, my job was eliminated. I decided to become a literary agent, which provided me with valuable insights into that field. And all along, I have been writing and trying to sell my own manuscripts, so I understand how writers feel about editors and publishers and reviewers, especially in these changing times.

To help writers understand how the children's market for books has changed, Part I: Background—the first four chapters— provides a brief history of children's publishing. In the beginning it was the invaluable and pioneering support of librarians and the growth of libraries that created the children's book industry. Everything we do today began with the librarians, and the library market remains the guiding inspiration for good children's books.

Important innovations during the past twenty-five years lead us to the present, where new ways coexist with the old. Recent developments include the rise of paperbacks and the mass market, which brought affordable books to more children; (2) the transformation of most of the former independent publishing firms into global media corporations; and (3) the rapid, widespread growth of chain and on-line bookstores.

Some readers may prefer to begin with Part II, Foreground. Chapters 5 through 9 provide material on how to write for children—taking into account genres and age levels. Chapters 10 to 15 are concerned with the business of publishing and deal with how to find a publisher, negotiate a contract, and market your work after publication.

Books are acquired and edited much as they always were. Writing for children remains a calling, a passion, a delight. And some writers have found that writing a successful children's book is as good as winning the lottery: sales and income have never been higher. As with Gus later in the book, it's my hope that you, the aspiring writer, will find your path to getting published successfully in this fast-changing world. The writer today must wear many hats, so hold on to all of them and jump right in!

ACKNOWLEDGMENTS

This book is based on my life after the age of six, when I learned to read. I've had a book nearby ever since. Most of my working life was spent in publishing, and I wish to express my appreciation to my first mentors, under whom I served my apprenticeship, Erik Wensberg of the Columbia University *Forum* and Carolyn Trager of Crowell-Collier Press. After that came the writers and colleagues I've worked with—a long list from A to Z—who also inspired and informed me.

Most recently, my former editor, Bebe Willoughby, sustained me through the writing of *It's a Bunny-Eat-Bunny World* with her comments and good sense, and I'm grateful to her, Edward Babun, Don Hinkle, and Carol Carrick for reading the early drafts of the manuscript and pointing out places for improvement. I also wish to thank all the people who spoke to me about the state of writing and publishing today and who are quoted in the book.

Finally, I am grateful to Marilyn Marlow, my agent, and to Soyung Pak and Emily Easton, my editors, for their patience and guidance while I was writing *It's a Bunny-Eat-Bunny World*. They are proof that publishing remains a noble endeavor.

PART I

◆

Background

1

The Bunny Also Rises

✦

THE BEGINNINGS OF CHILDREN'S
PUBLISHING IN AMERICA

When one door is shut, another opens.
—Miguel de Cervantes

Born during the Great Depression, I grew up in an immigrant family in Newark, New Jersey, and longed to be part of the small-town world shown in movies like *The Music Man* or performed in now-forgotten radio shows like *Henry Aldrich*. My mother loved the way Mrs. Aldrich called, at the beginning of each show, "Hen-RY! Henry AL-drich!" It wasn't too different from the way she called her children to come home from the streets where we roller-skated, played hide-and-seek, stickball, and marbles. Later, most of my generation moved to the suburbs in pursuit of the American dream as exemplified by a white frame house with a picket fence on Elm Street. No matter where they live, parents still call to their children the way Mrs. Aldrich and my mother called to theirs. Nonetheless, an era has ended.

Historians agree that people living in the twentieth century witnessed more changes than people in any other period of human history. When my father, who was born in 1887 in the Austro-Hungarian Empire, arrived in Newark in 1907, he saw horses everywhere, even pulling buses full of people. There were no radios or refrigerators, movies or vacuum cleaners, television or automatic washing machines. Only the rich had telephones. But he lived long enough to drive a car down superhighways while Sputnik beeped overhead. He observed more changes than he could have ever dreamed of—and so have we in our lifetimes.

One important change, which we take for granted, is that high culture became accessible to ordinary people through the expansion of a system of free public libraries that began at the end of the nineteenth century.

Books had arrived in the English colonies with the earliest settlers on the *Mayflower*, a number of men had private libraries in their houses, and university libraries served students. As early as 1731, Benjamin Franklin founded a public subscription (not free) library in Philadelphia, with similar institutions arising in Boston; Charleston, South Carolina; Newport, Rhode Island; and New York. These libraries already had some books appropriate for children on their shelves, including classics like *Aesops' Fables* (1484), *The Arabian Nights* (available in English by 1712), and *Mother Goose* (translated from the French around 1729). As time went

4

on, books like *Alice in Wonderland* (1865), *Little Women* (1868), and *The Adventures of Tom Sawyer* (1876) joined them.

However, most books for children written before the twentieth century were either religious like *Pilgrim's Progress* (1678) or didactic like *The Book of Courtesye* (1497). The latter book, from the great English printer William Caxton, described how a well-bred English child ought to behave. In addition, many of the books, such as *Robinson Crusoe* (1719–20), had originally been published for adults; although children read them, they skipped the dull and difficult parts, and special children's editions expurgated material deemed inappropriate for young readers.

The first publishers were either printers like Caxton or booksellers like John Newbery (1713–67), who was one of the first to publish books especially designed for children. (The Newbery Medal—for the best children's book of the year written by an American—is named after him. It is awarded by the American Library Association.)

British illustrators like Walter Crane, Kate Greenaway, and Randolph Caldecott emerged in the nineteenth century with their drawings of cheerful people, flowers, action scenes, and animals. Advances in printing made color drawings possible. (The Caldecott Medal—for the best illustrated book of the year— is named for Randolph Caldecott and bears a reproduction of a drawing by him. This medal is also awarded by the American Library Association. Its winner and the winner of the Newbery Medal are both chosen at the association's midwinter meeting.)

Still, with some exceptions, there was a quaintness and unreality in many of these books, which tended to portray childhood as a universally happy time and gave children sentimental tales about fairies and elves.

It is perhaps significant that 1900 saw the publication of *The Tale of Peter Rabbit,* the story of a mischievous bunny remarkably like a real child. This was the same year Sigmund Freud's *The Interpretation of Dreams* was published in Vienna, heralding a new century with exciting ideas in psychology, education, and child development.

The public library system continued to expand, and by 1900 more than nine thousand libraries could be found around the country in rural and urban areas. Some libraries began to open children's rooms, and elementary and secondary schools also started to establish their own libraries. By 1915, the American Library Association had set up a school library division. It was not long before a number of librarians and other women (it was mostly women) decided children needed more books to enrich their minds and imaginations, books that were not textbooks, books that were not religious, trendy, or commercial. Dedicated librarians convinced publishers that a market was waiting for new books written and illustrated especially for children. The first trade children's book, or juvenile, department was opened in 1921 by Louise Seaman at Macmillan. This marked the beginning of modern children's trade book publishing, which set the standards for the books still being published today.

A few male publishers, whose families owned the firms, put the children's book departments in offices at the back of their quarters and let the ladies publish all the books about bunny rabbits they desired. At other houses, children's books like Felix Salten's *Bambi* (1928) were published by the adult department. It soon became clear the "bunny books" were profitable, and juvenile departments opened at other firms.

Working in harmony with professional librarians like Anne Carroll Moore of the New York Public Library, the editors and librarians had high standards. Seaman of Macmillan, May Massee of Doubleday and Viking, and others wanted to publish literary, intelligent, and truthful books that would appeal to all children. They wanted the best artists to illustrate them. The librarians wanted the same things, and 95 percent of the juvenile books were sold to school and public libraries. Devoted to children's literature, the *Horn Book Magazine* began publication in Boston in 1921 with Bertha Mahoney as editor. And in 1929, the first children's book club, the Junior Literary Guild, began to send selected books to children all over the country.

In those days, most people in positions of power in the United States were white, Anglo-Saxon, Protestant, and upper middle-class. Since the librarians (and the publishers) were of similar background, the books they published were largely about and for middle-class children and their concerns. Many of the most highly regarded titles, such as *Wind in the Willows, The Story of Doctor Dolittle*, and *Winnie the Pooh*, came from England. In spite of their origin, these books transcended class boundaries. Of universal interest, with unforgettable characters, settings, and ideas, they appealed to all children, not only in the United States but around the world—which is what the best books do.

Talented people have long flocked to and from the United States to create new lives or to escape political troubles. Writers and artists like Wanda Gag from Czechoslovakia; Kate Seredy from Hungary; and Ludwig Bemelmans from Austria added a continental flavor to the predominantly Anglo-Saxon menu of books. William Pène du Bois's father was an American artist who moved to France, where Pène du Bois was educated. This was the golden age of children's books, which many say began in the United States in 1929 with the publication of a hopeful tale born on the eve of the Great Depression, *Millions of Cats* by Wanda Gag.

Kate Seredy, who had fallen on hard times in the 1970s, declared in a letter to her publisher that her books—and those of other juvenile writers—had kept the Viking Press afloat during the Depression. This was true, and Thomas Guinzburg, the owner of Viking, acknowledged it by sending her an advance on her royalties to help her.

To their amazement, publishers had found that juvenile books sold well even though jobs were scarce, people were standing in bread lines, and the banks were bankrupt. It was not only books. All forms of entertainment—especially the movies—did well as people looked for ways to forget their economic woes and the horrors of World War II. In the 1940s Walt Disney movies thrilled families with versions of favorite children's books and stories, such as *Pinocchio* by Carlo Collodi and *Ferdinand*, a pacifist tale about a bull, by Robert Lawson.

Commercial lines of books—the ancestors of today's mass

market titles—for children were also available. Literary quality took second place to action-packed, often garish, stories in the form of the dime novel or series books like the Horatio Alger stories with stereotyped characters and cliffhangers at the end of every chapter.

The most enduring and successful "fiction factory" was that of Edward Stratemeyer, who, as owner of what became known as the Stratemeyer Syndicate, published hundreds of books from Tom Swift to the Hardy Boys series under a variety of pseudonyms around the turn of the century and later. Howard R. Garis and his wife, Lillian, wrote most of the Tom Swift and Bobbsey Twins books—he could write a book every eight or ten days. Leslie McFarlane, who used the pseudonym Franklin W. Dixon, wrote most of the original Hardy Boys books.

When Stratemeyer's daughter, Harriet, protested that her father wasn't publishing books for girls, he said, "Girls don't read." Harriet proved him wrong by starting the Nancy Drew line of mysteries, which were written by Mildred Wirt Benson under the pseudonym Carolyn Keene. Benson said in a National Public Radio interview in 1993 that Nancy was perfect, a fantasy creation who never made a mistake or had any flaws. Nancy Drew is still going strong, as are other, newer lines of series books, mostly in paperback editions. The stock complaint now is that boys don't read!

As the century grew older, children had access to comic books (*Superman* was born in 1936), radio, movies, television, video games, and computers. When each new temptation to put down a book arose, so did dire predictions about the death of high-quality books for children. Yet juvenile publishing, though it has changed a great deal from the days of Louise Seaman, remains a strong and vital industry.

In the first half of the twentieth century, the editors at the major publishing houses founded a reading empire that is to be envied. As the editorial staffs grew, young women joined them straight from college, without becoming librarians first. The editors gave the youngest children picture books with first-rate artwork, in black and white and in color. Many of these are still on the shelves of libraries. Fiction for older children, including marvelous books of folk and fairy tales, opened up the world and gave readers an enviable vocabulary. Books satisfied curious children by providing accurate and up-to-date information about science, history, and other nonfiction topics. The first winner of the Newbery Award, in 1922, was *The Story of Mankind* by Hendrik van Loon, a writer born in the Netherlands. For the first time ever, thanks to the free public library system in the United States, nearly all children had access to books of poetry, humor, fantasy, and realistic fiction as well as up-to-date nonfiction written especially for them.

This trend continued to the end of the century. By the year 2001, no longer was the juvenile publishing field dominated by white middle-class women. Editors actively sought out writers from minority groups, and the 1970s saw a flowering of multicultural literature. Children's book writers and editors today come from many classes, races, religions, sexual preferences, and national backgrounds. Old taboos about sexual activity, street language, and controversial subject matter began to fade in the 1960s, though censorship and informed concern about what is appropriate for children remained alive.

However, the most serious threat to the continuation of the library-centered tradition was the discovery that children's books made money, or "Children's Books Mean Business," a slogan from the 1980s. Large corporations bought and absorbed small publishing houses; the family firms nearly became extinct. As Craig Virden, president and publisher of juvenile hardcovers and paperbacks at Bantam Doubleday Dell said ruefully in *Publishers Weekly*, "Forget quaint and old-fashioned children's book publishing. 'Bunny eat bunny' has become dog eat dog." The profits and prestige have improved, so men head many children's departments today and must answer to executives who hold M.B.A.s, not degrees in the liberal arts.

We all know about the many babies born since 1990, a peak year for births. Parents—and grandparents—eagerly buy books for children; schools emphasize reading. Yet, paradoxically, in the 1990s many writers began to wonder whether they had chosen the right career as publishing houses reduced their lists, cut back on staff, and shut the doors to unsolicited manuscripts. Some venerable houses even vanished.

In spite of the changes, this is an excellent time to be a writer for children if you cast off old ideas. A time of transition is never easy, but neither is it a disaster. It is a time to take up the challenge of new markets and new ways of doing things.

2

Multiplying Like, Well, Rabbits

✦

THE GROWTH OF PAPERBACK BOOKS
FOR CHILDREN

*I'd rather be a failure at something I enjoy
than be a success at something I hate.* —George Burns

It was summer, and I was eleven, walking past a candy store on Main Street. I glanced in the window and saw something new: a rack of thick paperback books. One book was titled *A Wonder Book for Boys and Girls*, and the other was *Tanglewood Tales for Girls and Boys*; both were by Nathaniel Hawthorne. I couldn't believe the phrase "for girls and boys" was on a book cover in a candy store! The books cost twenty-five cents each. I didn't know who Hawthorne was, but I knew I could afford to buy those books of Greek myths from the money I'd made collecting soda bottles for the deposit. It wasn't long before I owned the books and was reading them over and over. They were the first books I ever bought for myself.

Many Americans can remember a time when books—whether for adults or children—were almost exclusively published in expensive hardcover editions, available for sale only in some three thousand bookstores nationwide, most of them in cities. Books were treasured possessions in some families, status symbols in others. But many homes had no books at all, not even a Bible. At the time of the Great Depression, the only places to find good books to read were schools, libraries, and lending libraries, which were private "libraries" that rented books.

A few attempts had been made to introduce paperbound editions to American readers, but they had failed. Although he was not alone in wanting to change this state of affairs, Ian Ballantine was probably the most innovative, the most enthusiastic, and the most loved of a new breed that successfully brought paperback books into American life. As Irwyn Applebaum of what was then known as Bantam Doubleday Dell (now Random House) said at Ballantine's memorial service in 1995, "Ian was the Mad Hatter who hopped [sic] away [from the literary tea] and started up the wild, wonderful mass-market paperback party, invited everybody—absolutely everybody—to join in, and made it his lifelong mission to keep it roaring."

Around the same time that Ballantine began to import the English line of Penguin paperbacks into the United States, Pocket Books issued its first ten reprints of popular books, making it the

first modern American paperback publisher. Booksellers and readers greeted the two new lines, which complemented each other,
with enthusiasm, so much so that people began to call all paperbacks "pocket books."

In 1943 George Delacorte, founder of Dell Publishing, added
mysteries, westerns, and romances to his successful lines of magazines and comic books. Dell and the other magazine publishers
had unparalleled direct distribution into the magazine market:
about one hundred thousand candy stores, newsstands, drugstores,
general stores—outlets found in the smallest of towns and the
most far-flung places.

Ballantine was ready to fight it out with Pocket and Dell for
leadership in the American market. He had signed a distribution
contract with the Curtis Publishing Corporation, publishers of
two of the most popular magazines in the country, the *Ladies'
Home Journal* and the *Saturday Evening Post*. But Allen Lane, the
British publisher of Penguin, was aghast. He did not want Penguin
Books in outlets other than bookstores (a Penguin practice that
was true until recently), he disliked the idea of illustrated covers
(the original Penguins did not have art on the covers), and he was
afraid the line would lose its British character.

Ballantine left Penguin, which continued with a new staff.
Eventually the staff left, too, for reasons similar to Ballantine's,
and founded New American Library. As president of Bantam,
where he worked with Oscar Dystel, the cofounder, Ballantine
was able to prove that packaging was as important as distribution.
The first twenty books Ballantine published under the Bantam

imprint appeared in November 1945, with printings of 200,000 each. He designed a rack for paperbacks, then went one step farther and *gave* the rack to merchants to display Bantam Books.

Under Ballantine and Dystel, Bantam also developed a separate sales force that sold to independent trade bookstores (there were almost no chains then). This was the first time mass-market paperbacks were sold from trade bookstores. Even before the merger in 1998 with Random House, Bantam, combined with Doubleday and Dell, was the largest paperback publisher in the United States, followed by Pocket Books.

Successful as Bantam was, Ballantine was dissatisfied. Always the innovator, he proposed some startling new ideas to the board of directors. When they turned down the ideas, he left Bantam and founded Ballantine Books in 1952.

As the science-fiction writer Robert Silverberg has said, "Writers don't consider publishers a lovable life-form." But, he went on to say about Ballantine, "he made us prosperous . . . he spread joy as well as dollars among us." Ballantine understood that writers needed economic security while writing, which is why advances are offered: to give the writer the time to write. Ballantine offered writers big advances, $5,000 per book, which could support a family quite nicely in the 1950s. His most helpful idea for writers was to sign up the rights simultaneously for books in hardcover and paper, known as a hard/soft deal. This effectively doubled the writer's income, because he could collect the full royalty on the paperback instead of splitting the income from a mass-market paperback sale with his hardcover publisher.

Ballantine was far ahead of his time. It was not until 1966 that Dell set up a hardcover line, Delacorte Press, and signed "hard/soft deals" with major writers like James Jones and Irwin Shaw. Although more publishers offer hard/soft deals these days, it is still not the norm.

Where do paperback books for children fit into this story? The adult paperbacks are, in effect, the parents of the juvenile lines. It was natural, once adult paperbacks were developed and established, for the business practice to spill over into the juvenile world. The paperback revolution in children's books could begin.

In the 1960s, only a few of the principal hardcover publishers had trade paperback lines, adult and some juvenile. Trade paperbacks are usually facsimiles—with card stock covers—of the hardbound editions. Sometimes the trim and type sizes are different, but that's for technical reasons. Viking had the Seafarer line, Harper's had Trophy, and Penguin had Puffin. Trade paperbacks were sold primarily through bookstores and did not have the same distribution as mass-market paperbacks.

In 1965, encouraged by the high sales of comic books, Helen Meyer, president of Dell, believed its magazine distribution system could handle children's books as well. She was right. A year later, under George Nicholson, Dell began its Yearling line of children's books, with such titles as *Charlotte's Web* by E. B. White and *Johnny Tremain*, a Newbery Medal book, by Esther Forbes. Dell had already launched the Laurel-Leaf imprint, which specialized in young adult titles.

Yearling Books were what is known as digest-sized trade paperbacks as far as quality went (except for the paper), but since they were sold by the paperback sales force, not the trade reps, they were considered mass market. Yearling Books never penetrated the mass market the way adult paperbacks did, but they did find their way into those bookstores that didn't have a bias against children's books or paperback books as many upscale stores did. The same was true for Laurel-Leaf, which were rack-sized editions and looked like adult books.

Dell and other mass-market paperback houses like Pocket Books and Avon Books managed to get juvenile paperbacks into more places than traditional hardcover sales strategies could. Hardcover houses with trade paper lines were happy to sell reprint rights to mass-market lines, splitting the advances and royalties with authors.

In the 1970s, publishers (and the rest of the country) were in deep financial trouble. Inflation was endemic because of the OPEC oil embargo, the end of the Vietnam War, and the many costly social programs of the Johnson administration. Taxpayers tightened local purses, salaries were frozen, yet prices kept going up. Juvenile book publishers had to take a different course, find new markets, if they were to survive. The fare served at the literary teas in the schools and libraries—which now made up about 65 percent of the market—simply was no longer substantial enough to keep publishers and writers healthy. Publishers took some cues from the hardcover mass-market houses like Random House and began to offer novelty books, such as pop-ups, to the stores.

In the 1970s, the chain bookstores like Waldenbooks and

Brentano's in the malls, unlike the independent store on Main Street, offered anonymity to children, who were clutching their own money, whether from allowances or jobs. The salespeople did not hover, nor did they know their young customers, who were free to buy what they liked, not what their parents dictated. The children and teenagers bought books like *Are You There, God? It's Me, Margaret* by Judy Blume and S. E. Hinton's *The Outsiders*.

Ron Buehl, who had replaced George Nicholson at Dell, seemed to have a bottomless checkbook in the early 1970s, and he astutely paid the highest advances at the time for paperback rights. Shock waves reverberated around the industry when word came that Dell had paid William Morrow and Company $1 million for the license to reprint eighteen titles by Beverly Cleary for seven years. Hardcover houses were grateful for the infusion of cash, but they began to lose some of their best-selling writers, who discovered how lucrative it was to close a hard/soft deal with a publisher that had its own mass-market paperback line. A book would be published in hardcover by Delacorte, for example, then in paperback by Yearling or Laurel-Leaf.

The 1970s also saw the rise of book producers, or packagers, like Cloverdale Press (founded by Dan and Jeff Weiss). Packagers had been around for a long time, but Cloverdale specialized in young adult paperback series—the hottest market at the time. Cloverdale astonished traditional publishers by creating Sweet Dreams, a romance series, which became number one on B. Dalton's best-seller list in 1982. The 1970s had seen the heyday of the problem novel, but in the 1980s these were not the books the kids in the malls wanted to read. Romance novels from Cloverdale and other packagers caused the demise of trade hi/lo books (high interest/low reading level) for reluctant readers, a genre that still survives in the school market. Nonfiction for teenagers had never sold well in paperback; it, too, died after ailing since the 1970s. Sales of literary novels and historical fiction in paper began to slacken. The mood of the country had become conservative and escapist. Juvenile paperbacks were well on the way to holding a fabulous mass-market feast of their own in the 1980s, especially since other companies like Pocket Books, Avon, New American Library, and Scholastic helped to feed the growing chain store markets with series that sold millions of copies.

By the 1990s, movie and TV tie-ins proliferated, with such successes as the *Teen-Age Mutant Ninja Turtles*, which went from a Saturday morning TV show to paperback, and Goosebumps, which went from a series of books by R. L. Stine to TV and the movies and racks in the supermarkets. Series came and went on TV and in the bookstores. Juvenile paperbacks were no longer simply inexpensive reprints of high-quality hardcover books. They had become the principal moneymakers for the corporations that now owned almost all of juvenile publishing. Some writers made more money than they had ever dreamed of. It was backbreaking to write book after book, as Ann M. Martin did to keep her successful Baby-Sitters Club series going, but the financial return was mind-boggling. Many writers longed to create a best-selling paperback series, but only a few were smash successes, like the Animorphs books by Katherine Applegate, which appeared at the end of the 1990s. Like all bonanzas, the rise of paperbacks in the bookstores was a mixed blessing, as we shall see later.

3

Mr. McGregor Buys a Suit

✦

JUVENILE PUBLISHING BECOMES
BIG BUSINESS

The future has a way of arriving unannounced.
—*George Will*

Most firms were privately held and paternalistic when I started my publishing career in the 1960s; that is, they were owned by families like the Doubledays and the Scribners, who did not open their accounts to public scrutiny, because the firms were not on the stock exchange. The owners worked on the premises, knew the staff personally, and often came by to visit the various departments. At the old Viking Press, one such owner, Thomas Guinzburg, would send champagne to the juvenile department whenever something needed to be celebrated, such as winning a major award. The atmosphere was professional, the feeling collegial.

Anyone can become a publisher, which used to mean "owner."

The pattern is that a man, like Henry Holt, or a woman, like Mary Roberts Rinehart, would begin a publishing house and use his or her name. Later they might merge and pick up another partner, like Winston. In spite of the hyphens or ampersands, the firms were still private and "family" owned, passing down from founder to heirs. A few major corporations are still privately held, but that is the exception.

Bennett Cerf and Donald Klopfer made publishing history in 1925 when they bought the Modern Library, hardcover reprints of classics, from Boni & Liveright, one of the most distinguished literary houses at that time. Two years later Cerf and Klopfer established Random House. In 1960 Cerf became the first of the publishers to go cosmodemonic (as per Henry Miller, who coined the name Cosmodemonic for the firm where he worked as a young man), with his purchase of Knopf (including Vintage Paperbacks), Beginner Books, I. W. Singer, then Pantheon. RCA bought it all in 1966 and sold it to S. I. Newhouse and Donald Newhouse in 1980. But that's history, because eighteen years later Random House was sold to the same people who own Bantam Doubleday Dell, the Bertlesmann Corporation based in Germany.

Meanwhile, the 1960s saw other significant mergers take place. The Macmillan Company was absorbed into a large corporation: Crowell Collier Macmillan. New antitrust laws permitted the joining of many different companies into one corporation, or conglomerate, as long as the companies were in related industries.

Employees of the old Macmillan (publishers of *Gone with the Wind* and *The Collected Poems of W. B. Yeats* and *A Snowy Day* by Ezra Jack Keats) went into shock when they were forced to move from their fusty, historic offices in Greenwich Village into a new (and air-conditioned) office building at Fifty-third Street and Third Avenue in New York. Employees felt they were working inside a giant machine, and the spirit of rebellion was in the air. It was the 1960s, after all.

Collier's magazine and encyclopedia had disappeared by then, but the name was preserved in the Collier line of trade paperbacks and in a new juvenile line called Crowell-Collier Press, dedicated to publishing curriculum-related nonfiction for school and public libraries, or the "institutional market." President Lyndon B. Johnson's Great Society plans included Title II, a government program, which made $100 million available for creating or improving school libraries. Schools that had never had a library could start one with federal help, and existing libraries could buy new books. Always an important market, libraries became even more influential and demanded nonfiction especially. The usual print run for a Crowell-Collier Press book was 15,000. Many new and established writers and illustrators did books for this growing market. Susan Jeffers, for example, illustrated one of her first books for Crowell-Collier Press. Ben Bova and Jan Slepian also wrote for the line.

At that time, the Macmillan trade juvenile department was headed by Susan Carr Hirschmann, who had served her publishing apprenticeship under the great editor at Harper's, Ursula Nordstrom. Crowell-Collier Press and Macmillan juvenile had different editorial staffs and goals, but they shared many of the design, pro-duction, and marketing facilities, and both lines prospered.

Like a surreal technological garden, Third Avenue was grow-ing high rises, because the old elevated railway, the El, had re-cently been torn down, bringing light, air, and relative quiet back to the broad street. As time went on, to save money on rent, more publishers moved east of Madison Avenue, with Dell and Dial the farthest, on Second Avenue near the United Nations. Young edi-tors often worked at one house, then went to another to further their careers, and finally ended up at a third, where they stayed for the rest of their lives. It seemed that everyone knew everyone else and that the houses where one worked were like so many alma maters. One observed certain mores, such as not raiding authors edited by acquaintances. *Raiding* meant "stealing," and it was frowned upon as much as actual theft was.

No major trend happens overnight. What happened to the "gentleman's (or lady's) profession" of publishing happened to other corporations much earlier primarily because publishing was never a Big Money business like steel, banking, or the movies. "Children's books stay straight," the illustrator Donald Carrick said in the 1960s, "because there's no money in it." Gertrude P. Schafer, the managing editor with whom I worked at Viking, put it another way: "It's a nickel-and-dime business," she told me, by which she meant every nickel counted. Salaries were low, but that was the price one paid for what economists call high "psychic in-come"—deriving pleasure in one's work.

In the 1970s, though, children's publishing felt the pinch.

After the Vietnam War ended, Title II dried up, and we were in the midst of "stagflation": low economic growth accompanied by high prices. The prices of everything, including paper, skyrocketed; the words *cash flow* came into common parlance, because the cash was hardly flowing at all; interest rates were too high; salaries were frozen by President Richard M. Nixon's economic policies. The small, private publishers were in serious financial trouble.

Media corporations bought and sold publishers like herring. CBS bought Little, Brown and later sold it to Time-Warner; Gulf + Western bought Simon & Schuster, then sold it to Paramount. The publishing executives touted an exciting concept dubbed *synergy*. It would be more profitable, they said, to publish the books that would become blockbuster movies, and thereby save money since the same firm—albeit a different division— would already own the performance rights. Foreign publishers also began to buy American publishers. Penguin (English) bought Viking, Holtzbrinck (German) bought Holt, and Collins (English) bought Harper's.

For the most part, children's books, still in the back rooms, remained a cottage industry under the corporate roof, and the editor in chief was still the boss of her or his department. She approved the purchases of manuscripts she and her editors discovered, and she supervised the work of the library promotion department. She selected the art to go on the catalog cover, for example, and decided which book should get a poster. The library promotion department carried out her wishes.

We in the children's book field had always thought that our

work was important and profitable enough, and we suffered through all the jokes about bunny rabbit books. The prestige was in the front office with the "grown-ups," but freedom and happiness was in the back, exactly as Beatrix Potter's Tom Kitten had discovered when he was banned from his mother's tea party. Whenever a famous writer or an occasional celebrity was in the building, the news hit the grapevine. Like children during their parents' cocktail party, we'd sneak peeks at Mary Hemingway or William Saroyan or Willie Mays or Saul Bellow or Nadine Gordimer. But in the back room, we got to *talk* to people like Don Freeman and Robert Burch and Joan Aiken and Ossie Davis. They were at the children's table with us, and we were delighted to be in their company.

Publishing is labor-intensive. Acquiring, editing, designing, producing, marketing a number of new books every year require that each one be handled by many people during the process between submission of a manuscript and selling a finished book. It is not the same as producing, say, cans of soda, which are identical, year after year. As the 1970s trudged on, book paper got flimsier, the full cloth binding just about disappeared, and raises were nonexistent. Although sales to the paperback reprint houses saved many a hardcover children's line, writers began to find that their success was being measured first by whether the rights were sold and second by how many copies "went out the door."

After Ronald Reagan was elected president in 1980, the antitrust and tax laws were rewritten. Any company could pretty much buy any other, whether it was in a related industry or not.

Underpaid workers who had felt secure began to find they were "redundant." The buzzword among the M.B.A.s was *productivity*, which meant "downsizing" and being "lean and mean." This thinking affected all industries, not only publishing.

After years of editors and sales reps telling booksellers that children's books could be profitable, the penny dropped. Booksellers who hadn't paid attention before heard the message: "Children's Books Mean Business." At annual meetings of the American Booksellers Association in the mid-1980s, owners and salespeople heard about the quantities of children's books being sold, especially backlist books. At almost the same moment, Collins Publishers bought the venerable house of Harper's and renamed it HarperCollins; the Australian publishing magnate Rupert Murdoch owns about a third of the stock.

Children's publishers had always made most of their profits from the backlists. The *frontlist* is the current group of books published by a house. The *backlist* contains all the books published in previous seasons to which the publisher still holds the rights. "Plant costs" (such as the cost of setting type or making color plates) had been paid for, and second, third, and twenty-ninth printings were cheaper than first printings. All the traditional houses had important backlists, but Harper's may have had the most impressive of all. This is a bit fanciful, of course, but I believe that when the new HarperCollins management people saw how the Harper juvenile backlist brought in money, they realized that children's books indeed meant business. Harper's "cash cows" like *Charlotte's Web* and Laura Ingalls Wilder's Little House books—a mere sample of the feast—sped into and out of stores and libraries. "Publish more books," the M.B.A.s said! "This is a piece of cake."

And that spelled the end of traditional hardcover publishing as it had been in so many houses. Business majors who had no feeling for the liberal arts began to tell editors in chief what to publish. One lost her job, she told me, because the executives said she didn't publish enough best-sellers! The library promotion department became the library marketing department, and then simply "marketing." Gradually, the people who knew and loved books, including editors, lost power to people who probably would have been just as happy selling underwear.

Meanwhile, one publishing company after another began to merge (or be submerged) at a dizzying rate. In its March 17, 1997, issue, the *Nation* published a chart of the "octopoly," the eight major corporations that made up what the magazine called "The Media Nation." It seemed even more certain that all the major publishers would eventually be joined into the Cosmodemonic Media Corp. We are not far from that day, since at this writing only five major trade publishers from the *Nation* list remain, with most of the traditional juvenile imprints under their control.

This has had serious repercussions for the writers of children's books since many imprints either have been moved to new homes or have vanished entirely. Imprints are individual publishing departments within a larger company. Many were once publishing houses themselves. In 1994 Simon & Schuster bought Macmillan, including the juvenile books, which had fallen on hard times after the mysterious death of Robert Maxwell, the British tycoon who owned it. It seemed that Macmillan had no sooner bought a number of private publishing companies (Atheneum, Bradbury Press, Scribners, Margaret McElderry Books) when they were sold and ended up as part of Simon & Schuster or were closed down, as in the case of Bradbury, the Scribner juvenile department, and the Atheneum adult trade department. The loss of an imprint is a loss of a market for manuscripts.

Paramount owned Simon & Schuster, but in 1995 Viacom purchased Paramount. By the year 2000, Viacom had achieved its announced intention to sell all of its publishing businesses other than the Consumer Group (which had briefly been called Paramount Publishing), which publishes trade books, many of them best-sellers. Viacom is on the way to becoming, said Sumner M. Redstone, chairman of the board and chief executive officer, in a letter to stockholders, "*the* preeminent software-driven entertainment company in the world." Given that Viacom owns, in part or wholly, Blockbuster, MTV, Nickelodeon, Paramount Pictures, UPN, and Paramount Parks (among other entities), selling off its educational, reference, and professional book groups would enable Viacom to step "ahead boldly into a new era as a focused entertainment company." It also meant that several markets for nonfiction books shrank or vanished, including the Silver Burdett school library line.

When the Viking Penguin Putnam merger occurred in 1997, Cobblehill Press and Lodestar, at the Viking-Penguin group, "disappeared." In 1998, as already mentioned, the Bertlesmann Corporation bought Random House to add to its earlier acquisitions of Bantam, Doubleday, and Dell. Not much later, in 1999, HarperCollins bought the Hearst Group, a privately held company, which included Morrow Junior Books; Lothrop, Lee, and Shepard; Greenwillow Books; and Avon Books. The Harper children's book department moved to 1350 Avenue of the Americas, and the Morrow adult departments moved to the Harper Fifth Avenue office.

Writers found it mind-boggling to keep track of all the changes as publishers moved their offices, got rid of existing staff and hired new people, and had confusing policies about manuscript submissions. At some houses, each imprint has its own readers; at others, readers evaluate manuscripts for several departments.

The results of the consolidations have had other consequences for writers, agents, and publishing staff. The saddest is that imprints vanish, as with Bradbury Press, the original publisher of Judy Blume's *Are You There, God? It's Me, Margaret*. (Ironically, two former Macmillan employees, Richard Jackson and Bob Verrone, had founded Bradbury in the 1960s to escape corporate life!) All the nonfiction institution-oriented imprints at Simon & Schuster and Macmillan—Julian Messner, Dillon Press, Crestwood, Silver Burdett trade—became part of Macmillan Reference and were later sold to Pearson, which owned the Viking Penguin complex. All the imprints were later disbanded, contracts canceled, and backlists destroyed, meaning a significant loss of income to writers.

The principal difference between a cosmodemonic corporation and a small firm is that the big companies want huge profits in a hurry to please their stockholders. Andre Schiffrin, publisher of the New Press, noted in the *Nation* that after-tax profits of about 4 to 5 percent contented the owners of small trade houses. By contrast, the cosmodemonic firms are looking for profits of from 12 to 15 percent. They need new blockbuster books, including children's books, every year! The independent firms, which are in business for the long haul, can afford to be patient and will support and publish many books by a writer until she becomes established. Cosmodemonic will give you one or two chances to make it as a profitable writer. If you don't, you are dropped.

If an editor at a private firm (or at an old-style imprint at some major corporations) feels sure you'll make it eventually, you'll have the chance to write more books for that company. If your books are well received, you will become better known as you write more. Slowly (if not surely), your reputation will grow, and so will your sales. This is how it used to be done almost everywhere. A writer could survive by writing one book a year, every year, and by the time ten had been published, he could probably afford to live on the income from his royalties and become a full-time writer. This is rarely so now. Back when Ian Ballantine paid writers advances of $5,000, children's book writers were getting advances of $750 to $1,500 per book. Some best-selling juvenile writers may do extremely well today, but most of the rest are earning between $1,500 and $10,000 a book.

Although this sounds grim, it is not the whole story. We may never return to the way things were once done, but writers will continue to get their books published, and we may be in the midst of a new era as exciting as that of the past, when anyone could start a publishing company and prosper. It is still possible. It is happening now.

4

What's Up, Doc?

✦

THE CHANGING MARKETPLACE

Teaching kids to count is fine, but teaching them what counts is best. —Bob Talbert

The mergers and restructuring of the 1980s and 1990s shrank the literary, library-oriented, juvenile hardcover market. With the vanishing of so many imprints, it became harder for writers to get their work published at a traditional house. On the other hand, the bookstore market was hopping, especially with mass-market children's books. One reason: We are in the midst of a baby boom louder than the one after World War II.

Businesses pay serious attention to demographics, and writers, too, must be aware of how the young population is "aging" and tailor their books appropriately. If you live in a small town or suburb, you already know of the need for new or expanded schools. The wedge of readers born since around 1990 is determining which markets publishers are most eager to reach. A U.S. Department of

Background

Education statistical projection predicts that the total enrollment of children from kindergarten to the twelfth grade will be 54.2 million students by 2003, which is more than the 51.3 million students in 1971 during the post-World War II baby boom. About 38 million will be in kindergarten through the eighth grade, and about 16 million in secondary school. That is a lot of children and teenagers! They will need a lot of books—*new* books!

A high proportion of these children have parents who are college educated and upwardly mobile. Composed of all races and ethnic backgrounds, this group of parents has high expectations for its children. Knowing that reading is important for material success, parents begin to read to their children as soon as they're born, if not before. They want their children to attend the best schools—often private or parochial—and do well on tests. The grandparents of these children feel the same way. In a survey commissioned by the American Association of Retired Persons, published in the spring of 2000, 60 percent of the grandparents surveyed listed books as their first choice of gifts for their grandchildren; only 38 percent bought toys. These middle-class parents and grandparents, as well as aunts, uncles, and other relations, all buy children's books, beginning with board books for the cradle set, picture books for the slightly older children, and then paperback fiction and some hardcover nonfiction.

So even though publishing has become more competitive, it has a large and diverse market to serve, which is good for writers. More books are being published. On the other hand, the big numbers are not in the traditional hardcover trade books (except for some picture books) for a number of reasons, one of which is that most parents and many booksellers are in the dark about children's literature, especially contemporary books. Sales are highest in mass market, which includes not only paperbacks but the "low end" (inexpensive books) of hardcover publishing. Dr. Seuss and Richard Scarry were among the wealthiest of writers for children.

After children's publishers bragged to American booksellers that "children's books mean business," and the publishing executives saw it was true, bookstores began to take children's books seriously—but only in the categories they felt they could sell. And there's the rub. There's little room for eccentricity of taste or titles that don't sell in large numbers. While many of the clerks in the adult departments are first-rate, many in the children's book area are not educated about their stock.

The independent bookstore still survives in a form not too different from that shown in old movies and television programs. The owners of independent stores are just that: independent. They decide what to stock, depending on their knowledge of the local market. They read books and are known for their ability to recommend, or "hand sell," titles they admire. More than a few times, they have been instrumental in propelling books to the best-seller lists.

Tempting and cheaper though it may be to order books from on-line sources or to sip coffee and then buy your book at a major chain bookstore, if you are a writer, your best friend may be the struggling owner of your local bookstore—especially if it's a children's-only shop. Make friends with the staff and buy books there. Otherwise, the independent bookstore may one day exist only in the fantasies of book lovers, and it will be even harder to get into print.

The major bookstore chains like Barnes & Noble, the largest chain, and Borders, the second largest, have come to dominate the bookselling scene, dwarfing even the old chains like Doubleday, Brentano's, and B. Dalton. Venerable and respected stores all over the United States have closed their doors for good or been submerged; Waldenbooks, for example, is now part of Borders.

It is frightening to contemplate the carnage that can occur when a major chain comes on the scene, even in a place as densely populated with bookstores as Manhattan. The chains offer discounts, thousands of books and related merchandise, special programs, comfortable places to sit and read, and cafés. Store after store—many of them legendary and successful, once beloved by readers and writers—has been forced out of business because it could not compete with the high-volume chain stores.

This trend affects publishers and writers alike. The publishers strive to produce books the national chains will buy. If the buyers for these chains, known as national accounts, turn down an individual title or declare lack of interest in a category, the book is in trouble. In March 1998, the American Booksellers Association (ABA) filed an antitrust lawsuit in the U.S. District Court for the Northern District of California against Barnes & Noble and Borders. The suit on behalf of the ABA and more than twenty independent bookstores alleges that these large national chain stores are using their clout with publishers to obtain secret and illegal deals and preferential treatment such as deep discounts not available to the independent booksellers. One of the plaintiffs, Clark Kepler, owner of Kepler's Books & Magazines in Menlo Park, California, said: "This fight is about preserving what America is able to read. A network of healthy independent bookstores spurs publishers to produce a diversity of literature and to take risks with authors who are of less commercial but greater critical appeal."

Who doesn't like the convenience of buying books online? I wonder how many people are browsing at a local bookstore, then buying from Amazon.com, which claims an inventory of 2.5 million titles? Books Online from Bertelsmann offers books in major languages with discounts competitive with Amazon.com and Barnes & Noble on-line, which stocks 350,000 titles. Bertelsmann also operates Boulevard Online, an electronic bookstore based in Germany.

Not to be outdone, many independent stores have set up Web sites of their own; it's just as easy to order from down the street as from other on-line sources. And when it made its debut in the fall of 2000, the American Booksellers Association Book Sense (www.BookSense.com) marketing program featured a database of more than 2 million titles, which can be ordered on-line, offered by independent bookstores.

Another major influence on book sales remains the giant book wholesalers, such as Baker and Taylor and Ingram, which order copies in advance of publication and hold them ready to ship to libraries and bookstores at a moment's notice. If the rate of movement (ROM) of a title is energetic, the wholesaler will keep ordering stock. On the other hand, if the ROM is lethargic, the wholesaler will not order more copies, and the ROM will slow down and even stop.

Publishers, national accounts, and wholesalers monitor the ROMs of all titles. A best-seller might fly out of the warehouses and stores at the rate of 10,000 copies a week. Or 800 copies of a new children's novel may be ordered by a wholesaler, and then, if sales are not brisk, never reordered. At some publishers, a ROM under, say, 250 hardcover copies a month guarantees the book will be declared "out of stock" (OS) as soon as the supply is exhausted.

"Out of stock" is not the same as "out of print" (OP), though it can seem that way to the writer and even the bookseller. I learned about this when my sister-in-law, Jackie, went to a local small-town bookstore in 1981 to buy a copy of *The New York Kids Book*, which had been published by Doubleday in the fall of 1979. Unlike most books for children, this one had been reviewed by the *New York Times*, *New York* magazine, and other media, including newspapers and TV. Along with seven other writers, I'd been a contributing editor to this book and knew it intimately, to say the least. Jackie told me the clerk had looked it up "on the computer" and discovered it was "out of print." I called our editor at Doubleday, and she assured me copies were in the Doubleday warehouse. But the *wholesaler* had not reordered after the initial copies had sold out, and the bookstore computer told the owner the book was out of stock—at the wholesaler! Jackie was able to buy a copy directly from Doubleday, but, regrettably, that was not enough of a market to keep the book *in print* for long.

The good news for writers of children's books is that the major chains have large, well-stocked, and inviting children's book departments. Decorated with colorful art showing favorite characters from children's books, the areas are designed so that as soon as customers get close they will see the merchandise (dolls and the like) that goes with certain titles. Unfortunately, the emphasis on toys contributes to the feeling that the department is for the youngest of children. Nannies and babies in strollers find it's a comfortable place to meet other nannies and babies, especially in inclement weather.

Past the area dedicated to the youngest readers is shelf after shelf of paperback fiction, including classics and all the Newbery Medal books in print. The series readers, many of whom like to buy by number instead of title, will find the latest additions for their collections. Dotted around the area are dumps, or cardboard display units, featuring the most popular current series, seasonal promotions, movie and TV tie-ins, new series, or a variety of titles of other books of special interest. Bookstores also stock some nonfiction. The likeliest to be found have catchy titles and lavish illustrations. It seems as if all young needs can be satisfied here, except for new hardcover fiction for young readers, which traditionally has sold poorly in bookstores.

If a teenager sets foot in this department, he might find the paperback books for his age group in a corner, embarrassingly close to the nonfiction adult titles relating to breast-feeding and other aspects of child rearing. This is policy at some chains, and the staff is not free to change it. A good independent bookseller is sensitive to her clientele and segregates the books for small children; books for teen readers are in a rack strategically placed next to the novels in the *adult* section of the store.

If the major chains dominate the bookstore world, how can you, the writer, increase the chances of having your book sold at a chain? People unversed in the children's book field think creating a doll or other toy to accompany a book is a great idea. Well, yes it is, but it is illegal for someone to create a doll based on an existing character in a book without permission, or a license, from the owner. Characters are considered intellectual property, and their use is regulated through licensing.

Before the 1980s, only the most famous of juvenile trade book characters—Raggedy Ann and Andy, Corduroy, Madeline, Pippi Longstocking—had dolls developed in their likenesses. The rule was—and remains—that "merchandise" will sell to the public only when a character is already well established and popular, which was the case with mass-market characters like Snoopy and Mickey Mouse but not with trade book characters, even the most beloved. The number of people who recognized these characters was too small, it was believed.

A glance at the shelves at the bookstore demonstrates how this policy has changed. Publishers dived into their backlists and, sometimes with the help of outside book producers, found all kinds of ingenious ways to present merchandise featuring what are known as "licensed characters" to accompany certain books. Clifford the Big Red Dog, the Wild Thing (from Maurice Sendak's book *Where the Wild Things Are*), and many others are on the shelves now. But the old rule remains: The books must already be well known before their characters will be licensed.

On occasion, a toy may become so popular that a book or series of books (mass market) will be developed for it—like Barbie, who even has her own magazine. But it took Barbie a long time to reach printed form. For a good part of her life, she was just a toy! Therefore, if you have an idea for a toy and think it lends itself to books, think again. Publishers are conservative. They need to be sure the toy, the licensed character, is indeed popular before they will invest in books to accompany it. As always, they want to sell books, not toys; the manuscript comes first. If someone is willing to publish the book, the next step may come in regard to the toy. Keep in mind that publishers do not manufacture the toys themselves; they or the creators license the rights to others.

Near the merchandise books are a fair number of board, or concept, books for the youngest of children, babies and toddlers. Since these books are usually conceived in-house or by packagers, this is not a recommended path for a writer unless the writer is also an illustrator or knows an experienced, professional children's book artist who can carry out the idea. It is possible to "package" a simple eight-page book, offering text and art together. Since every possible concept has been done already—from counting to colors—the creator must supply a fresh and unique execution of old ideas, usually in a set of four books. Rosemary Wells did this brilliantly in her Max books, for example.

Novelty books, such as pop-ups, have also become favorites in bookstores. These require elaborate, *working* dummies, or mock-ups, for presenting to publishers. If you are able to do this yourself or to pay something like $10,000 to a paper engineer for a *professional* presentation, you can then send or take the material around yourself. Another possibility is to show your work to packagers, who have the resources to develop your ideas in return for a share of the proceeds.

If you are determined to do board or novelty books, be persistent and learn from your failures. Meeting editors, art directors, and packagers will give you exposure, and you may one day be invited to develop an idea for a publisher or packager. The American Book Producers Association, listed in the appendix, can help you find out which packagers specialize in concept and novelty books. Publishing people have traditionally been helpful. Once you have a list of editors, you'll find it will grow quickly through referrals.

The young writer who was mentioned in the preface, Gus, isn't sure he can succeed in the new world of publishing, by which he means support himself as a full-time writer. The chances are about the same as always. Writing for a living remains a risky undertaking. Few juvenile writers have ever earned enough to quit their day jobs.

It's no coincidence that so many published writers for children were married women, who had husbands to support them, or men who had wives who worked outside the home to supplement the family income. They could write a book a year for the library market and eventually break through to a comfortable living, sometimes surpassing their spouses' incomes. But if writers like

Gus have only one income from a day job and wish to support themselves solely by writing, they will have to hustle to find other work as freelance writers. Fortunately, the children's book field has grown, and opportunities for freelancers exist in new sorts of ventures.

The strong interest in children's books at all the bookstores—chain and independent—is great news for juvenile writers. People love children's books, and they are now available to more readers than ever. According to one bookseller, the Harry Potter books by J. K. Rowling have taught buyers about the wealth of reading material available only in hardcover, and her store is now stocking more hardcover fiction.

If this means a new trend will be established, let us give thanks to J. K. Rowling. As she knows, finding your book on sale in bookstores is a great boost to your career and to your determination to succeed as a writer.

PART II

◆

Foreground

5

Hop to It!

◆

*If a window of opportunity appears, don't pull down
the shade. —Tom Peters*

My friend Gus, the writer, was scratching his head. "On the one hand," he said to me, "the market has contracted. Then you say more opportunities exist than ever. Which is it?"

"Both statements are true," I answered. "Many of the traditional imprints no longer exist. On the other hand, adjustments have been made to counter the effects of the mergers among the cosmodemonic firms."

I went on to remind Gus that the children's book market has always been diverse and stratified. Today, it is more diverse than ever, which is good news for writers. Some publishers continue in the venerable traditions of the library-oriented market. Others aim at schools, bookstores, or even toy stores. Therefore, many children's book markets exist, and what is wrong for one may well be perfect for another.

Literary editors have had to learn to coexist with the business-minded executives and their new procedures. Other editors have been lucky enough to found imprints at kinder, gentler publishers of the old school. Some have established publishing companies of their own or gone into book producing. Many editors are working freelance for packagers or as consultants. Most important, though, for the writer is the rise of new publishers all over the country.

Understanding the different markets is a major step toward success as a writer for children. As a literary agent and a former editor, I've received thousands of manuscripts to consider for publication. Many looked as if they might be publishable, and they were read and either accepted or declined. (Editors never reject manuscripts; they decline them.) However, many submissions were clearly not right from the start; they were sent back unread in the enclosed SASE (self-addressed stamped envelope) or thrown away if no SASE had been enclosed. This was often not a reflection on the quality of the work but on the writer's failure to understand what a trade children's book was.

Traditional hardcover children's books, like Maurice Sendak's picture book *Where the Wild Things Are* and E. B. White's novel *Charlotte's Web*, are trade juveniles. One definition of a trade book is "a book sold in bookstores." Publishers like Viking; Harper-Collins; Farrar, Straus, & Giroux; and Little, Brown are in the trade book business.

As you've seen in the previous chapters, the primary destination for a trade juvenile (fiction or nonfiction) was not a book-store but a school or public library (the institutional market). Thirty years ago, few hardcover trade books for children were sold in bookstores—about 95 percent went to libraries. It's been estimated that today only 50 percent of trade juveniles go to libraries.

Therefore, during the last twenty-five years juvenile trade houses began to publish books that would have a greater appeal in bookstores, books that would entice parents and other book buyers. Unlike librarians, booksellers were often not knowledgeable about juvenile literature. They knew that bright covers, a "gift" look, or a trendy topic like dinosaurs, attracted customers. And juvenile publishing changed drastically as editors strove to acquire "mainstream" books that would be best-sellers, much as had happened in the world of adult publishing earlier. As one former editor said when asked to define *mainstream*:

> *I'll try not to be too cynical. My understanding of what makes a book "mainstream" is that it has the following attributes: The title and cover illustration clearly convey the content; i.e., you don't have to open the book to know what it's about. It has an easily grasped "handle" or "hook"—bedtime, Halloween, mother love, etc. It is written or illustrated by a famous author or illustrator. It has a strong appeal to adults, either by virtue of its art (nostalgic, "edgy," self-referential, sentimental), or the concept is similar to an already existing successful title. It is inexpensive (except for the "famous illustrator" book, which can be very expensive).*

The first such best-selling commercial juvenile books from trade houses were novelty books like expensive, high-quality pop-ups, which began to appear in the 1970s, and which sold in the tens of thousands. Although libraries bought fewer copies of pop-ups because they were likely to be damaged by their young patrons, bookstore sales more than made up for the lower library sales.

Meanwhile another category—paperback editions of hard-cover books—had already made its appearance in the trade and was also helping the bottom line. The main outlet for children's paperbacks was also bookstores, which carried both mass-market and trade editions.

Although there is a difference in trim size and physical quality, the distinction between mass market and trade simply refers to *how* books are distributed. Mass-market channels include newsstands, drugstores, supermarkets, and so on. Mass-market paperbacks are distributed much as magazines are because the first paperbacks in the United States were published and distributed by magazine publishers. Mass-market paperbacks were primarily for adults, though children's paperbacks began to filter in as the demand grew.

Trade paperbacks come directly from trade publishers like HarperCollins, whose Trophy line is printed on good-quality paper instead of high-acid spruce pulp and is a bit more expensive. The mass-market paperbacks from Avon, Bantam, Dell, and Pocket Books are usually sold into stores by one set of publishers' representatives, the trade paperbacks from HarperCollins and other publishers by another. Although the consumer rarely notices the difference, the distinction is important for the writer who wants to understand the market and calculate his estimated income, because the royalty percentages are different.

There is another kind of mass-market book. Sometimes in hardcover, sometimes in paper, the books have low prices and come from Random House, Simon & Schuster, Grosset and Dunlap, and other houses. These books include the original hardcover Nancy Drew and Hardy Boys titles, the Dr. Seuss books, the Little Simon line, the Berenstain Bears, and many other titles. The low prices and bright, commercial art have long caught book buyers' eyes in discount stores, gift shops, some bookstores, shopping mall department stores, and even toy stores.

Other titles are "tie-ins," based on licensed characters from TV shows or movies and can have many incarnations. One set of books featuring a licensed character might be in the supermarket, another in the video store, a different one available only through mail order, yet another one through a book club, and so on. Packagers are usually involved in producing tie-in editions. This is an enormous, if ephemeral, market.

To add to the mix, children are growing up with their own TVs, Walkmans, and computers, and publishers are providing them with multimedia products such as audiotapes and CD-ROMs. As young as its readership, the electronic market was expected to grow fast and wild. Sales of books on CD-ROM have been disappointing, however, and publishers have grown conservative in this area.

It's also still too early to tell how E-books, or books self-published on-line, will fare, but this does not mean that new growth won't occur later on, so writers should be aware of the possibilities of electronic publishing. For the moment, the bookstores are still selling books published in the traditional way, and will be doing so for some time to come.

Added to the commercial and library markets mentioned above is the educational market, which is expanding to keep up with the school population and changes in educational trends. After the optimistic introduction of "whole language" in the 1980s, the pendulum has swung back to "phonics." Tons of textbooks were dumped and other tons bought to take their places. Although sales to schools of trade books have recently declined, Jennifer Brown, children's Forecasts editor of *Publishers Weekly*, noted that sales are still strong because teachers discovered trade books stimulated interest in reading.

To find out more about publishers, you can consult the *Literary Market Place*, which is a weighty annual list of publishers and ancillary enterprises. In addition to names and addresses of publishers (including small presses) in the United States and Canada, the *LMP* contains brief descriptions of publishers and lists the names of editors. One section is devoted to attorneys specializing in intellectual property, another to agents. A separate list is organized by names of people in all these areas, yet another by names of publishers' imprints. The *LMP* also contains a list broken down into categories such as educational and religious publishers. The best place to consult this book is at a library, where it's usually behind the reference desk. Bookstores may also have a copy you can look at, and it's available on-line (at www.bowker.com). Since the *LMP* is so bulky, ephemeral, and expensive, it's not a wise purchase for most writers, but it's invaluable for research.

The most helpful resources for writers of children's books are the Children's Book Council, the Society of Children's Book Writers & Illustrators, the Institute for Children's Literature, and *Publishers Weekly* (see sidebar). Other magazines like *The Writer* and *Writer's Digest* can be useful from time to time since they periodically carry news from the children's book world. The *Children's Book Market*, published annually, is also an excellent reference.

Fortunately, with the advent of Web sites, it's never been easier to do research. However, on-line research is no substitute for going to bookstores and libraries and holding books in your hand. This literal "hands-on" approach, which includes reading the books, is the most satisfying way of getting to know the children's book world.

The marketplace for children's books is like a long corridor. As you walk along it, one door slips shut, another is half-closed or half-open, and another opens wide, welcoming writers. The following chapters will discuss the various markets for manuscripts in greater detail. However, this book is neither the last word nor the most detailed about editors' wants. Since editors leave their jobs and publishing houses move and undergo internal changes, it's important to keep up with the latest news. The sources mentioned in this chapter will endeavor to keep you up-to-date. Nevertheless, before sending in your manuscript, you should telephone the publishing house to be sure the editor you want is still working there and is still accepting unsolicited manuscripts, and to verify the address.

After all, change, like fashion, will not stop. The writer must continue to meet the new challenges of an industry in perpetual transition. However, you may be sure that one thing will remain the same: Writing for children is valuable, enjoyable, and rewarding.

✦ Surfing the Web ✦

For a moderate charge, you can obtain a list of publishers from the **Children's Book Council (CBC)** in New York, or get the list free from its Web site (www.cbcbooks.org). The list, which is frequently updated, contains the names of the major publishers, their editorial and marketing staffs, along with addresses, telephone numbers, and submission policies.

The CBC Web site also provides direct links to most of the member-publishers' Web sites. This is an excellent way to see what is being published at the various houses. The CBC is funded by a group of publishers, and the board of directors consists of editors and other publishing staff. The CBC also maintains a library, open to visitors by appointment, which contains all the books published by the member-publishers during the past three years. The CBC list is indispensable, but note that it does not contain information about every publisher in the United States, only member-publishers.

The Society of Children's Book Writers & Illustrators (SCBWI) offers published and unpublished writers and illustrators memberships in the organization, which has its home office in California; there are also regional divisions and a Web site. Members receive the instructive SCBWI bimonthly newsletter, the *Bulletin,* with articles and current market information. The SCBWI also provides inexpensive lists of magazine, religious, and educational publishers and other materials of value. Joining the SCBWI is highly recommended. Through its regional network you can become acquainted with writers in your area, and other writers are always an excellent source of news. The Web site address, which provides membership information, is www.scbwi.org.

The Institute for Children's Literature in West Redding, Connecticut, is a correspondence school for writers. You do not need to be a student at the school to subscribe to its informative monthly newsletter, the *Children's Writer.* The newsletter is divided into two parts: One carries articles on editors, publishers, trends, and more; the other is the *Marketplace,* which gives specific information on magazine and book markets, including new and small publishers, educational and religious as well as trade. The Web site is www.childrenswriter.com.

To get a quick overview of publishers and forthcoming titles, look into **Publishers Weekly,** a magazine you can find on the Web or at your local library. Twice a year, the spring and fall announcement issues are replete with ads for children's books. A study of the ads and annotated announcements of new books will give you an idea of what publishers are doing *now*. The Web site is www.publishersweekly.com.

6

Quick Like a Bunny

♦

TIPS FOR WRITING PICTURE BOOKS

Happiness makes up in height for what it lacks in length.
—Robert Frost

When most people say they want to write a "children's book," they usually mean a "picture book." The picture book is the star of the children's book world. It is a showcase for the illustrator, who may win the coveted Caldecott Medal if her art is spectacular. However, without a text, the artist has nothing to illustrate, so editors are always looking for texts. If you wish to write a picture book, my advice is to do it, but keep in mind that the market is tight; it is harder than ever to place a picture book. You can make it easier if you write one in keeping with the times we live in.

Many adults have no understanding of this genre. They think of children's book writers, illustrators, and editors as milquetoasts who babble on about bunny rabbits. Even worse, so do some neophyte writers and illustrators, who bombard editors with picture books written in sing-song verse about animals with alliterative names like Harry Hare and Bitsy Bunny, poorly illustrated by themselves or an "artist friend." If you have written a book that begins something like, "One day Peter Pigeon (Harriet Hippo, Sally Seal, Walter Wolf) decided to . . ." put it aside and begin work on a new one. Do not use alliterative names. You'll notice that Beatrix Potter used names like Jemima Puddleduck and Jeremy Fisher—names that subtly conveyed the characters' species and even personalities. It was Walt Disney and other cartoonists of the 1930s and 1940s who used alliterative names like Mickey Mouse, Donald Duck, and Bugs Bunny. Although these characters are successful and beloved, they are not book characters but come from comic books and cartoon features and lack the literary stature of such book characters as Kenneth Grahame's Mr. Toad and Lewis Carroll's March Hare. In short, don't be *condescending*. Respect the reader, no matter what age he is.

Most beginning writers think nothing is easier to write than a children's book, and if the result is as follows, they are correct. Consider this typical manuscript:

Imogene Ibex woke up in her bed.
"It's a beautiful day," she said.
Out of her bed she hopped.
Without making a single stop.
Her mom was in the kitchen
But she was itchin'
To go out and play
On such a sunny day.

With art, this text could fill up to three book pages, but so far Imogene hasn't done anything except hop! (Do ibexes hop?) This manuscript is typical of many that come to editors and agents, destined to be returned immediately. It contains predictable flaws such as the forced meter in the lines "without making a single stop" and "to go out and play / on such a sunny day." Words are stuffed into the line simply to fill it up with the right number of syllables. When the writer can't find a rhyme, she comes close, rhyming *stop* with *hopped* and *kitchen* with *itchin'*, which, of course, is cheatin'. As for "her mom," watch out for inappropriate colloquialisms.

Can it be that people who send in manuscripts like this have read no contemporary children's books? Was their most recent encounter with children's verse Clement Clarke Moore's beloved 1823 poem, "A Visit from St. Nicholas"? In meter, rhyme scheme, and strong narrative line ("'Twas the night before Christmas, and all through the house, not a creature was stirring, not even a mouse"), it was in tune with popular culture a hundred years ago.

Of course, not all verse should be damned. Verse in the hands of Mother Goose, Ludwig Bemelmans, or Dr. Seuss can be delightful, and children love rhyme and strong meter, or rhythm, as we know from our own experience. Rhyme and meter are still found in modern songs, especially in the world of rap, which Bill Martin Jr. and John Archambault used to advantage in *Chicka-Chicka Boom-Boom*, illustrated by Lois Ehlert.

Like a poem, a picture book is short, tells a story, and captures an emotional moment. It shows a love of language and has memorable imagery. But it also reflects the literary era in which we live, which is why editors say they don't want to publish books in verse. By *verse*, they mean sing-song verses like those in "A Visit from St. Nicholas," which they regard as old-fashioned.

Some editors have gone so far as to shy away from even the best of verses because they don't trust their own judgment. In short, because of this prejudice, you might as well put away your rhymed story for now. (I have a rollicking one about a frog and cat in my drawer.) To be fair, most rhymed stories I've seen have been dreadfully amateurish, which only reinforces the prejudice.

Something comes over people when they sit down to write a children's book, as if they've had a personality change. Many beginning writers think it's de rigueur to tell a story about animals to children. Perhaps their past encounters with children's books surface, and the writing becomes automatic, an echo of some half-formed idea developed in childhood. I'll leave the reason to the psychoanalysts and will confess that my first children's book was based on a newspaper story about a pigeon, which had caught its foot in a clam on the beach.

Beatrix Potter, a sheltered middle-class English gentlewoman, was the mother of today's picture-book animal story. Using animals as stand-ins for people, Potter provided charming, accessible stories to generations of children and their parents. And numerous artists from Don Freeman to Marc Brown have published books with talking animals. Potter was a trailblazer and a genius.

She is, as they say, a hard act to follow. Unfortunately, too many writers saw only that Potter used animals with names and clothing. They failed to see that she was never guilty of being SCAD. The acronym stands for:

1. sentimental
2. condescending
3. anthropomorphic
4. didactic

Memorize these words. They are the cardinal sins of picture-book manuscripts, and they'll be discussed further in this chapter. If your manuscript is guilty of even one of the SCAD sins, your work will likely not even be read to the end. For example, baby talk is condescending and will get a knee-jerk negative response every time.

Nearly all children's picture books deal with homely details, but the very best deal with universal themes as well. Peter Rabbit may have suffered through a life-and-death struggle (universal theme) because he disobeyed his mother (universal theme), but he also had a great time scoffing up the forbidden goodies (universal theme) in Mr. McGregor's garden. Unfortunately, too many writers have imitated the superficial aspects of Potter's work and failed to understand the psychological brilliance underlying it. All her animals are memorable characters, complex in their ways. They are never sentimental, though they are charming, appealing, and lovable. (Note that the best trade editors never use the words *cute* or *adorable* to describe a character.)

The next most important rule in writing for children is that *the protagonist must solve the problem*. Peter Rabbit managed to escape by wriggling under the fence. But in my first picture-book story, a passerby liberated the pigeon's foot from the clam. Although my pigeon, like Peter, had the guts to explore, he did not, like Peter, solve the problem of being trapped. He was a passive hero. As an editor told me, "Thousands of books have been written about individuals wanting to be someone else. Yours has to be different and delightful." It wasn't. It was derivative and dull in spite of its universal theme. Be careful: "Universal" can easily become hackneyed.

Therefore, if you choose to write about animals, imagine that they are people, with quirks and flaws. Choose your animals carefully, matching them to type—without stereotyping or using clichés. Consider all the attributes of a particular animal, not just one. Although technically speaking, your manuscript will be anthropomorphic, if you succeed with your story, it will transcend that classification.

For example, my story would have been different if I had spent some time observing pigeons. I've since learned that a pigeon is patient. It prefers walking to flying. It is always looking for something to eat. It will peck anything on the ground in its search for food. Any one of these characteristics would be enough to inspire a story more original than the one I'd written.

Do they perhaps explain why my pigeon ended up with a clam on its foot? Peck, *slam!*

The writer of the story about Imogene Ibex confessed she didn't know much about ibexes. Since an ibex is so leggy, I have trouble imagining one sleeping in a bed. Still, being leggy, Imogene must be a good runner and kicker, and that's what the writer should have emphasized. I can imagine a book about a chase and a clever use of the art of kicking, not a domestic tale beginning in a kitchen.

Readers can suspend disbelief enough to accept aardvarks, cats, dogs, bears, monkeys, and mice as using their forepaws like hands. An ibex or other large, hoofed animal with "hands" seems too awkward and unnatural to be convincing. Readers will not suspend disbelief, and the editor will decline the manuscript on the ground of anthropomorphism.

What exactly is anthropomorphism? The dictionary says it's endowing animals or machines or even structures with human attributes. When I was a child, *The Little Engine that Could* and *Little Toot the Tugboat* were popular successes featuring "humanized" machines. Today we have the adventures of Budgie the helicopter and the Flying Toaster. (Anthropomorphic? Yes. Best-sellers? Yes. Good books? No. Whoever said children had good taste?)

Even though they are anthropomorphic, animal characters can enjoy adventures denied to children and real animals, and writers and illustrators want to take literary advantage of this freedom. Children can easily cross the invisible line between person and animal or thing. However, if, as a writer or illustrator, you want to cross the barrier between human and nonhuman, you must make the reader suspend disbelief as you would with a fantasy. In general, while stories about talking animals are still being published, stories about talking molecules, buildings, and machinery are not, unless they're written by a celebrity. In other words, sometimes anthropomorphism works, and sometimes it doesn't. Book editors hate cloying anthropomorphism as much as they hate rhyme!

One way to avoid anthropomorphism is to write about children instead of animals. *Blueberries for Sal* by Robert McCloskey is a good example of a realistic picture book that draws a parallel between animal children and human children without being anthropomorphic. Many other writers from Taro Yashima to Tomie de Paola featured children in their stories.

Once you've selected your characters, you must write a story. A series of incidents like the ones in the manuscript about Imogene Ibex is not a story. As Humpty Dumpty told Alice when she was in Wonderland, a story has a beginning, a middle, and an end. (How did Lewis Carroll make us believe an egg could talk?) For example, Peter Rabbit's mother tells him not to go into Mr. McGregor's garden. Peter disobeys. Mr. McGregor chases him and almost nabs him. That is a story. The fact that he and the reader also learn a lesson about the dangers of disobedience is incidental. Heavy-handed stories teaching lessons are *didactic,* and no one likes them, especially children and editors.

If Peter had simply gone for a walk, found Mr. McGregor's garden, and then described everything he saw, we would not be reading about his adventures today. The entry-level reader at the publishing house suspects that's what Imogene Ibex is going to do, and he's already unfolding the self-addressed, stamped envelope the author included. The manuscript will not make it to an editor's desk for a second reading.

Always begin your story in media res—in the middle of the action—instead of with a word like *decided* or with a character's waking up, which only delays the moment of action. Ask yourself where the story begins, and begin it there. For example, "Imogene thought she was alone at the river. Then she saw the lion."

Keep on writing after that. Don't worry about length or anything else until you get to the end of your story. Then ask yourself: Is it a story? What is the conflict? From whose point of view is it told? Are the characters distinct and realistic? Use your word-processing program to count the words. If you have over a thousand, begin to cut out the dead spots. Keep in mind that the future illustrations save you the trouble of describing the characters and setting at length. Delete all unnecessary description.

Once the story satisfies you, cut it apart and tape the sentences in a blank dummy. (You can make a thirty-two-page dummy by folding eight pieces of paper in half.) You are now crafting your story to fit into a format of approximately twenty-six pages, or thirteen double spreads. Most picture books are thirty-two pages long because that is how many pages one large press sheet, known as a signature, can hold. From one to six pages might be front and back matter, which are explained in Chapter 13. See how the story breaks according to the potential illustrations. Are there enough scene changes? Something different and interesting for the illustrator (and reader) must be on each spread. Are the words distributed evenly throughout the dummy, or do some pages run too full and others look too skimpy? Make the appropriate adjustments. Writing a picture book is hard. The writer conveys her ideas in words placed on blank pieces of paper. Not a word, not an action can be superfluous. You must be original, the story must be complete enough to be understood without illustrations, and you must capture the reader's emotions. (If you are an illustrator, you have an advantage, because you can draw what you mean and submit an illustrated dummy.)

If you're a writer and not an artist as well, type your brief text on white bond, double spaced and with paragraphs, and submit it to editors at publishing houses. Do not get an artist friend to illustrate it. Do not illustrate it yourself, not even with stick figures. It has to stand on its own as a story that can be read aloud by a parent, teacher, or librarian. Once you're famous, you'll be able to break these rules, but don't waste your time now.

Many writers have rewritten well-known folk- and fairy tales and had some success. This is not recommended today because editors and illustrators usually do the retelling themselves or hire someone to do it, and most of the popular tales such as "Cinderella" and "Little Red Riding Hood" have been told and retold ad infinitum.

However, with the emphasis on multiculturalism and new immigrant groups in schools, the market for tales from certain cultures—African, Asian, Latin American—expanded, and a demand remains. If you find a remarkable tale that is virtually unknown, it might be worth your while to retell it. Be sure to acknowledge the copyright and find out whether rights are available if you are working from a translation. At Delacorte Press years ago, an illustrator wanted to illustrate a piece by a dead French poet. Jim Bruce, the editor, was enthusiastic. A former professor of French, he helped the artist translate the poem. The artist began his drawings, the book was announced in the catalog—and then it turned out the poet's widow, who was the executor of his estate, refused to grant permission. She didn't think her husband would have wanted the poem published for children! The project was abandoned.

Folk- and fairy tales are a good way for illustrators to break into the picture-book market. Jan Brett retold and accurately illustrated *The Mitten*, a Ukrainian folktale, with great success, and John Scieszka took the folktale format even farther with *The True Story of the Three Little Pigs*. Don't be afraid to be innovative.

If you're an artist who has illustrated either an original story or a folktale, send in a tight dummy and color photocopies of a few pieces of finished art. (Do not send original art until the editor requests it.) A tight dummy is a mock-up of the book with the text pasted in and sketches that are almost finished for each page or spread. Do not do finished art for the entire book. The art director will provide you with specifications after you've signed the contract. Before you can proceed, you'll need to know the trim size, whether the art bleeds or butts, the best media for printing purposes, gutter margin, and many other technical details.

If you've illustrated a friend's story, put the art away for now. Your friend should submit the story on its own, without any art. A neophyte cannot expect to ride into publishing on the coattails of a friend's story. Editors and art directors resent it when authors choose an artist. It remains their prerogative, and, though it is hard to accept, you are hurting your friend's chances if your art is sent in with her story. Editors and art directors review the work of many artists before they select one who meets their needs. They often choose an illustrator whose work is well known and has market value, which is to the writer's (and publisher's) long-term advantage.

If you wish to illustrate children's books, you must make the rounds to art directors with your portfolio or find an artist's agent. Art directors are always interested in seeing illustrations of children and animals in black and white and in color. Your first assignment may well be novels, and a strong black-and-white style will help you get started.

When you write a picture book, try to keep the manuscript to a maximum of four pages, fewer than a thousand words. Long picture books exist, but short ones stand a better chance. The most common criticism you'll hear from the sales reps in publishing houses is "too many words." It's hard to believe that a thirty-two-page book can have too many words, but reps believe consumers want to be able to read the book in a few moments and then buy it on impulse, the way they would a T-shirt.

Once you've written a story that has been accepted for publication, it no longer belongs to you but to the world. The illustrator will open up your story in ways you could never have imagined. Her job is not to reproduce your mind-pictures but to create the world your words evoked for her. The result may delight you or dismay you, but the words are still yours.

Picture books have come a long way since *The Tale of Peter Rabbit* appeared. Writers and artists like Chris van Allsburg, David Macaulay, and David Wiesner have taken the picture book in exciting directions. Before you write or illustrate, go to the bookstore and see what's new.

Having made the journey myself from the pitiful pigeon story to two picture books that were accepted for publication, I have learned that writing a picture book is a joy in itself. Both times the subject moved me, and I therefore lovingly labored to do the best I could with the words. If you don't feel love for the story, put it away. If you do feel the love, you will be compelled to rewrite the story until, as Goldilocks said, it is "just right."

7

How Does the
Garden Grow?

◆

WRITING FICTION

There are no shortcuts to any place worth going.
— Beverly Sills

Miss Lillian Davis, the librarian, sat at her big front desk in the center of the Belmar Public Library. No expense had been spared when the one-room library had been built. It stood on a grassy knoll on an acre of land in an affluent residential district in the center of town. Light streamed in through shining Palladian windows.

Timidly, but aware I had the right to do so, I asked Miss Davis for a library card. In turn, she asked me for my name and address. A few moments later, Miss Davis stamped the date on a piece of cardboard and handed it to me. She asked me, "How old are you?"

"Eleven." What a strange question, I thought.

"Go to the left."

I looked wistfully at the loaded bookshelves on the right. "That's the adult section," Miss Davis said. "You can go there when you're in high school."

The idea that children should read certain books at certain ages persists in the juvenile book world. Libraries still have children's departments, though children are no longer drawn and quartered for wandering into the adult section. The "level" issue vexes people not familiar with the children's book market, and if you wish to write for children, you must understand the differences between *age level*, *grade level*, *reading level*, and *interest level*. It seems more complicated than it is. (And it's more complicated than it seems.) Librarians and booksellers need to know the age levels or the grade levels of books, because adults will come in and ask for a book "appropriate for an eight-year-old" or "right for a third grader." Therefore, publishers provide age and grade levels in their catalogs and age levels on the books themselves, usually in easily deciphered codes (e.g., 008012) on the jacket flap, sometimes on the copyright page.

Age and grade levels acknowledge that children of the same age may read at different levels of proficiency. Some second graders can read at a fifth-grade level; some fifth graders can read only at a second-grade level—which is why a range is provided.

Editors are the ones who decide what the age and grade levels are, and when the editors were former librarians, they were well equipped to judge. Most other editors guess by the seat of their pants. They feel confident in their choices because they are based on their own reading experience, the difficulty of the texts, and the subject matter. Since age and grade levels usually span three or four years, educated guesses have a good chance of hitting the right number. The difference between a book suitable for ages nine to thirteen and one for ages ten to fourteen is a subtle measure of a speck of maturity. Publishers usually inflate age levels because they believe children will "read up"—that is, read books older than prescribed—but will not "read down"—that is, read books meant for younger children. A number of publishers send manuscripts to reading laboratories to get "scientific" reading levels. Some methods are based on the writer's choices from a list of approved words; others count syllables and words and calculate the ratio. Computer programs also purport to give accurate reading levels.

However, it's not only reading proficiency that determines an age level; interest level is important as well. The only way to be sure of the interest level is to be the person reading the book. When I was ten, I found *Little Women* to be difficult and tedious. At twelve, I thought it the best book I ever read. As an adult, I couldn't finish reading it. The book doesn't change, but the reader does.

Why is it important for the writer to realize that the reading level of a book depends on the reader? As Emerson said, "'Tis the good reader makes a good book." A good reader will struggle through a difficult text. Good readers read books more than once, gleaning something different each time, depending on one's interests at a given moment. The best writers write about what they know and infuse it with their passions. That is the secret of writing for the ages, not magic formulas about age levels.

Therefore, keep in mind that trade publishers' reading levels are only guidelines; they should not be followed slavishly. In 1947, Harper's advertised *Goodnight Moon* by Margaret Wise Brown as suitable for ages three to six. This did not mean that a three-year-old was expected to read it. It meant that the interest level made it suitable to be read *to* a three-year-old. Today, *Goodnight Moon* is read to babies, and children older than six love it too. It brings back pleasant memories of babyhood and validates their sense of having graduated into the "young reader" group. The babies aren't smarter than babies fifty years ago, but the parents are aware that some books can be for children of all ages. Savvy parents also know that children will ask for books to be read over and over, so they are careful to bring home only books that can pass the multiple-reading test—in other words, books they themselves like.

Trade books, including picture books, fit into a long literary tradition. They are supposed to stretch the mind, enrich the reader, inform as well as entertain. They are a counterweight to all the watered-down and overedited texts used in schools. Trade books provide children with the values missing from commercial entertainment such as movies. They also assume children have minds and can use dictionaries. Most novels for teenagers no longer carry age levels, but age levels remain on books for younger readers to guide those who need them, whether parent or bookseller.

Publishers strive to publish books that librarians and booksellers can categorize. On the other hand, some of these categories are becoming extinct or changing, and new ones are appearing. In general, books meant to be read *by* the youngest of children are short, with short sentences and short words. These may be picture books, storybooks, easy readers, or simple books with chapters. One category that almost disappeared is the storybook, which is a long story told in a picture-book format. But the classic storybooks like the Babar books and the Madeline titles are still with us. And not too long ago, readers over seven began to discover the delights of long picture books, such as the Caldecott Medal winner *Snowflake Bentley* by Jacqueline Briggs Martin, illustrated by Mary Azarian.

Like everything else, childhood has been accelerated. Eight-year-olds in jeans, T-shirts, and running shoes don't want to be seen with picture books or storybooks (though they might sneak peeks at them in private). "They're for babies!" they say. They want "real books" with chapters. What they call a chapter book has become a new and thriving genre, broken into categories. In the last two decades, more fiction for first- and second-grade readers has been published than ever before.

Beverly Horowitz is vice president, deputy publisher, and editor in chief at Random House Children's Publishers. Horowitz told me she considers the words *chapter books* to be an educational term, one used in classrooms to indicate that children have reached a certain reading level. It's a child's term, also, she says, a sign that he or she is ready to read a text longer than that in a primer, which may have only one or two words a page.

According to Michelle Poploff, vice president, editorial director of children's paperbacks at Bantam Doubleday Dell (Random House), *chapter book* can also be an "umbrella term." Dell was the original publisher of Patricia Reilly Giff's The Kids of the Polk Street School books, one of the first trade series especially written for second-grade readers. Dell expanded the Yearling line to include chapter books for children between the ages of six and ten. Manuscripts run from about twenty-five to sixty manuscript pages (shorter ones are for younger readers) and usually have black-and-white drawings on most of the pages. As I said earlier about picture books, the protagonists in all juvenile fiction must be active and solve their own problems. Adult characters are welcome, but they must not interfere in the child's story line.

Books for older readers, the "middle-grade," are usually illustrated with six to ten black-and-white drawings and run from 96 to 192 pages. (Teachers sometimes require that students read a book over 100 pages long for a book report. Given the technology of book publishing, many books run only 96 pages—that is, a quantity divisible by 32—so your book may not make it to the book report stage. On the other hand, many children prefer short books.)

When I first entered the children's publishing field, manuscripts for children between the ages of eight and twelve were often declined because they were "episodic"; that is, consisting of loosely connected episodes, each a chapter long, with a minimal plot, about the same characters. In spite of the success of Robert McCloskey's *Homer Price*, few episodic books (although they were not called by that name) were published, with the exception of Joan Aiken's Arabel stories and *Pippi Longstocking* by Astrid Lindgren.

Editors today don't seem to have the same prejudices, and the episodic book has made a comeback. (It was popular in the sixteenth and seventeenth centuries in Europe.) Middle-grade children adore episodic books, because they can read one chapter and put the book down—satisfied—knowing they can pick it up again tomorrow for another story. Sometimes the episodes add up to a plot, and the characters may change and develop over time, but these are not requirements. The stories could continue indefinitely, the way situation comedies do on television. Some contemporary examples of episodic books include *Tales of the Wayside School* by Louis Sachar, *Brooklyn Doesn't Rhyme* by Joan W. Blos, and *The Watsons Go to Birmingham—1963* by Christopher Paul Curtis. These books are just right for children who've graduated from second-grade chapter books but are not ready for older novels. This is also a good place for humorous manuscripts.

The middle-age novel wins the prize, literally, among books for older children: the Newbery Medal. Most of the award-winning books are suitable for ages ten to fourteen. Newbery novels usually address themselves to serious issues such as war, racism, or an individual's struggle for justice. Once a writer has won a Newbery, his or her career is established. Every school and public library will buy a copy, a paperback edition will be issued, and bookstores will carry the book in hardcover at first, in paperback later.

Editors, reviewers, and writers agree that the sine qua non in all literary novels for middle-grade and teen readers is that as the protagonists act in the story, they grow and change.

Also, because of their length, children's novels can usually support only one point of view; that is, the action is seen through the eyes of one character only. The books have coherent plots constructed around a strong conflict, and each action has a purpose.

Here are two examples of writing for different ages. The story is about a brother and sister, Adam and Eve. Note that the reading level is lower for Adam's point of view than for Eve's. His has shorter sentences and words, hers longer, which is natural, because she is older than he is.

Adam dashed into the kitchen. He was in front of his sister, Eve. She tripped over his foot.

"Ouch!" he yelled. He hopped on one foot. He held the toes on the other. He bet they were broken.

"What a dweeb," Eve said. "Wear your shoes. Then your feet won't get hurt."

"Your feet are too big. That's why you trip all the time,"
Adam said. He put his foot on the floor. It hurt. But he could
walk. I'll get even, he thought. He limped out of the kitchen.
"Mommy, Eve broke my foot."

Here's the same incident from Eve's point of view.

"Watch out!" Eve yelled. She tried to catch her balance. Her
dweeby little brother, Adam, had stopped short when they both
ran into the kitchen, and she felt his toes grind under her foot.

She grit her teeth when he yelled, "Ouch!"

"It's your fault," she said. "Mom told you to wear your
shoes."

Adam was hopping around on one foot, cradling the other.
"You broke my toes, you broke my toes," he chanted.

Eve knew he was faking. She probably had hurt him, but he
was making too much of it.

"Mommy," he yelled. "Eve broke my foot." He ran out of
the kitchen.

"I don't need this," Eve said to herself.

Whichever point of view you choose, you can see that the
book immediately sets up certain tensions, such as the sibling relationship and the suspense of discovering how the mother will
handle this situation. The single point of view forces you to focus
on the main character and how he or she acts.

A third benefit is that a single point of view *shows* emotions

via crisp dialogue or action rather than through *telling* in artificially long passages of explanatory dialogue. "Telling" how people
feel is what leads to condescension and didacticism. Good writing
for children encourages them to figure out what is happening, and
believe me, they can do so.

Most important, the single child's point of view will relegate
adults to the sidelines because the reader will be observing them
through a child's eyes. Adults should never—well almost never—
be the central characters in a book for children.

However, as I said in chapter 6, *the most important rule of
children's books is that the hero has to have a conflict, a problem that
he or she solves*. From what we've seen so far, Adam and Eve have
no problems except with each other, and those aren't serious;
indeed, their rivalry is somewhat trite, but with imagination
and skill it can underlie an important plot. Add one or more
subplots involving friends, family, or others, and you will add
richness to the texture of the novel. The conflict is the source of
the plot.

The classic literary conflicts are:

1. hero against another person
2. hero against society
3. hero against nature
4. hero against self.

Literary novels are character driven, not plot driven; therefore, before beginning to write, you must know the main charac-

ter physically and emotionally. The plot will grow from the character and his personality and how he chooses to deal with the conflict. A useful exercise is to list everything about a character—from what he eats for breakfast to the name of his favorite movie. Name your character; live with him; imagine how he would act in various situations. He is not cardboard; he is a living person.

The most complex characters probably exist in what were once called young adult novels. Librarians, editors, and writers are never satisfied with the definition of a young adult novel, meant for teenage readers. The readers themselves prefer to be called teens, and their books, books for teens. "Young adult novel" used to mean a book written for adults—like *Lord of the Flies* by William Golding or *The Old Man and the Sea* by Ernest Hemingway—that was also suitable for teenagers. It was a book with literary merit, no swear words or explicit scenes involving sexual activity, and on a topic of interest to young people. Life has changed a great deal since that definition held sway. This is one reason librarians cannot agree on an acceptable definition and why novels for twelve- to sixteen-year-olds are often shelved with adult novels.

A teen novel can be one of three types. All should have protagonists who are at least twelve years old. The first type treats subject matter of interest to students in middle school or junior high through high school. A novel, say, about camping—with jokes about falling in the lake and playing tricks on the opposite sex at the next camp—is fine for readers under twelve. At twelve and older, most teenagers would rather read about finding a way to date the kids of the opposite sex at the other camp. Again, it all depends on the age development of the readers. Some are ready for no more than a conversation or maybe a kiss; others may want sexual relations under the stars.

Originally published as young adult novels, some of Paula Danziger's titles, like *The Cat Ate My Gymsuit*, are now considered to be at the low end of the age group. Danziger's books are written simply and appeal to readers from about the fourth grade up. They deal with family problems, social problems, and a touch of romance, only a touch, and are humorous.

The second category would be the novel about teenage concerns like Richard Peck's or P. J. Petersen's books or mysteries like those by Lois Duncan and Joan Lowery Nixon, where the protagonists are teenagers. These books may be found in the junior high libraries because they contain little or no swearing or explicit sex.

The third category might be labeled for "mature" readers and be said to be "edgy." Like Robert Cormier's *Fade* or Francesca Lia Block's *Weetzie Bat*, the books may have street language, sex, or violence treated in a responsible, not exploitative, way. Or the mature teen novel may have little or no sex or violence at all but simply be a thoughtful novel for gifted teenagers and adults, like *Catcher in the Rye* by J. D. Salinger. Considered to be the grandfather of the young adult novel, *Catcher in the Rye* was originally published as an adult book in 1951. We can see how times have changed since then. In the last twenty or thirty years, a number of people who tried to sell books with teenage characters could not find homes for them in the adult divisions of publishing houses. They were happily welcomed by many children's departments.

No matter which of the above genres you choose to write, fiction demands that you know who your characters are, have a general idea of what they are going to do, and how the book will end. You may wonder whether you should outline the plot. For the beginning novelist (and certainly for the writer of nonfiction), an outline is invaluable.

What you need to work on after you have an idea of your plot, theme, and characters is choosing the main action of each chapter. I once began a novel with a long description of the town where the action takes place. Later, this ended up in my reference pile, along with the character questionnaires, not in the book. *Descriptions and explanations are not action.* In other words, some important event must occur in each chapter, so your first step might be to list ten or twelve such events. Also, be sure to set up the time frame: Is the action to take place in one day, one season, one year? Sometimes a chronology or time line helps in mapping out the chapters.

In general, the first four or five chapters serve to introduce the characters and set up the conflicts. By chapter 5, a major event should have taken place. The rest of the book is about resolving the events—with a major turning point coming toward the end—and a satisfactory denouement, tying the loose ends together in a conclusion.

At the same time, each chapter is advancing the plot. Don't play games with the reader. Characters may have secrets from one another, but the reader should be aware of what the protagonist is thinking. You have to plant and foreshadow and establish events throughout, which is easier to do once you're sure of where you're going. You cannot, for example, in the final chapter, say: "He pulled out a treasure map and showed it to his friends. 'Let's dig there,' he said." The reader should have known this map existed from early on and should have had some idea of its contents. You cannot spring a surprise like this on unsuspecting readers at the last minute.

Work in descriptions of people and locations as you go along, and sprinkle in subtle clues to the characters' personalities. Dig into your reference pile to make sure that your geography is consistent, your characters' names are the same—in other words, Eve stays Eve and does not become Eva. Consider the themes of the book, and create events to highlight them.

A common problem with many first novels is poor staging. The characters seem to be floating in outer space, not set firmly in a definable area such as a kitchen, garden, football field, and so on. The writer must help the reader see what the writer is seeing in her mind's eye. You don't need much, a detail or two will suffice, as in this passage:

*They went through the gate of the cemetery, up a path beneath
trees centuries old. Eve's feet crunched the fallen leaves on the
path. From time to time she glanced at the tombstones and
monuments as she passed them by.*
    "What's that?" Adam cried.

And then there's the opposite flaw. Cataloging each trivial
movement, each item, obsessively. Learn how to condense the
information and provide only the essentials. Do not write, for
example:

*Eve looked at Adam. He was standing ten feet away from her on
the path. He was pointing at something. She couldn't see what it
was. She walked up to him. As she walked, she read the names
on the tombstones aloud to give herself courage.*
    "Abbott, Nestor, Baciagalupo, Partridge . . ."

This is not the time for Eve to drag her feet. "Eve ran up to
Adam and looked where he was pointing" will do the job.
    Unfortunately, until the writer of serious novels for young people wins the Newbery, his career may languish in the shadows of
the land called Midlist, novels by writers who are not well known
or who have not had a "blockbuster" best-seller. Bookstores still
carry almost no juvenile fiction in hardcover because it does not
sell well enough. The few you see will be prizewinners or by popular authors. Libraries with reduced budgets may not be able to afford novels by little-known writers. It used to be that when a

midlist book went into paperback, the writer could hope for decent sales, but that's no longer true, for reasons to be discussed later. Nonetheless, it's important to persevere in spite of the obstacles, because the road to fame still begins with the midlist, novels by writers yet to be discovered.

Hone your writing skills. Chapter 9 contains more writing tips and will help you edit your work. It remains true that the more you write, the better you get, and the more you *can* write. The field is always wide-open for books that are funny or serious, timely or historical. One bookseller recently lamented the lack of books about prehistory! Will she be heard in New York? Will prehistory be the next trend? Who can tell? Don't worry about trends. Write your book and worry about publishing it later.

A few years ago, I traveled to Chincoteague in Virginia to see the annual pony swim described in Marguerite Henry's classic, *Misty of Chincoteague*. I felt as if I were on a pilgrimage. While there, I bought and reread the book, which was on sale in one of the few souvenir stores. In the newspaper, I read about Misty's great-granddaughter, who had just foaled at the age of twenty-three. People lined up after the pony swim to watch the movie, presented at no charge in the local theater. About seventy thousand other people—mostly families with "middle-aged" children—attended the pony swim, an event that has changed little since 1947, when the book was published. The pony swim is not a "media event," and Chincoteague is not a garish theme park out to gouge the tourist; it is a community with pride in its heritage.

This experience validated my own feelings about the beauty and value of the best children's books. I know that somewhere in a library a child is running her fingers along the spines, looking for a book to read. Maybe she'll find yours, and maybe the delight of reading it will remain in her memory for a lifetime.

8

Bunnies in the Money

✦

SHOULD YOU WRITE A SERIES?

Miracles happen to those who believe in them.
—*Bernard Berenson*

Almost every writer has dreamed of creating a successful paperback series. Notable best-selling series like Choose Your
Own Adventure and the Baby-Sitters Club were published in the
1980s, and by the 1990s, others, like Goosebumps and the Animorphs books, became blockbuster properties. Publishers were
crying out for more, and writers were eager to gain fame and fortune this way. It turned out to be easier to marry royalty.

First, all the successful series above have an easily grasped
hook or identity. Second, a series has to be on a topic that appeals to children or teenagers. Third, it has to be fresh and
unique. Writers and editors have been racking their brains for
years to come up with concepts for series. The same ideas have
been batted back and forth across conference tables at paperback

publishing houses as well as among writers. Mention a topic, any topic—it's been done or thought of. Yet you and I know that come next season, some series will hit the charts with an idea so simple that we will berate ourselves for not having thought of it ourselves.

If there are no new ideas, there are new ways of executing them, and the challenge for the writer is to find that new way, a way that is in tune with the third millennium. As Jean Feiwel, publisher and editor in chief at Scholastic, told me, "Tried-and-true themes to which an author has given her own spin can be highly successful, but she better be current in her language and details." The best place to look for those themes, language, and details is at home or wherever there are children. If I were to tell you what's hot with kids right now, it would be out-of-date before this book could get published. During a visit in 1998 to an elementary school, I mentioned that I'd been to the former Soviet Union. The children asked me, "When?" I answered, "1990." They began to laugh. "What's so funny?" One child answered, "That's when we were born." Lordy, lordy, it's bad enough to reach forty, but to be passé after such a short time in an adult life is sobering, indeed.

So forget about what worked in 1985 or even 1995. As Feiwel also said: "Do not follow what is being published with your own version of the concept. It's been done, and we don't need another one. We need something different." Think about 2005 or even later, then write down the concept and series title. After that, she suggests, prepare a series proposal, two or three pages long, in which you name and describe the characters and give plot summaries for *twelve* books. As Feiwel said: "The idea must have the potential for continuity, for many different kinds of stories featuring the same characters and concepts. This was true of the Baby-Sitters Club, but we learned to our regret that it was not true for the Sleepover Club—how many sleepovers can you have?"

If you are a successful writer with a track record, you can probably get away with writing and submitting a few chapters of the first book in the series. If you are an unknown, you should write a complete book. However, contrary to what you might expect, my advice is that an unknown writer should send in the complete book only, not the series proposal. If an editor expresses interest in the book and makes an offer, *then* tell her you want to write a sequel or a series.

Here are two examples of how two different writers managed to create series. One is by a writer with several published books behind her, Gibbs Davis, and one by a former neophyte, Betsy Duffey. Davis is the author of the series White House Ghosthunters. This is what she told me about how the series evolved:

I had recently visited the White House and learned that over two hundred kids had once lived there. Sparking my imagination with the old "what if" exercise so useful to writers, I imagined, What if the daughter of the president of the United States were a budding detective and solved mysteries in the famous house?

I drew up a proposal and wrote some sample chapters, and my agent sent the material out. Eventually, Jill Parsons at Pocket Books offered a contract.

Soon after, over lunch with Jill, she told me how much she liked my proposal, but, she said, the concept needed to be stronger. That's when I mentioned that during my research I had discovered the White House was the most haunted house in the country. Jill's eyes lit up as she took the concept one step farther. "What if the ghosts of past presidents and first ladies secretly help our young sleuth?" We looked at each other and knew that was it!

I then took the important step of testing the new concept with children and adults with this sentence: "The daughter of the president of the United States (her mother) solves mysteries in the White House with help from the ghosts of past presidents and first ladies." The children responded to the fantasy of living in the White House, while adults loved the entertaining blend of mystery and history.

Every series has to have appealing characters, but it's vital to find a concept that has legs, that can go the distance from book to book. I knew White House Ghosthunters would provide an unending supply of interesting characters and dramatic situations.

The evolution of Betsy Duffey's series about George and his dog, Lucky, took a different course. *A Boy in the Doghouse* was first published in hardcover at Simon & Schuster, illustrated by Leslie

Morrill. As the editor, I felt that Duffey's title had two words in it, *boy* and *dog*[house], with an immediate appeal to readers, so perennially popular it's hard to write about them without being trite. However, *doghouse* indicated amusing troubles—and that was also appealing. The book was exceptionally well written, it had a funny twist, and it was informative on the subject of training a puppy. It had the spark. It couldn't miss, and it didn't. Reviews were excellent, and so were sales in both hardcover and paperback. The success of *A Boy in the Doghouse* led to Duffey's being asked to write more books and to create a series, with each book having the dog's name, Lucky, in the title. Again, stories about a boy and his dog are infinite. Duffy has since gone on to create several other successful series.

As a new agent, I took on a few writers who presented complete proposals and finished novels to kick off a series, which I sent around to various publishers; I was unable to sell their work, even though the editor in me thought the concepts were strong. One was a girls' sports series; the other was about a rock band in a New York City high school. Editors said things like "We already have books about girls and sports on our list," and "Books set in New York don't sell." To be honest, the novels were not well written and needed a great deal of editorial work. I'd had the mistaken notion that editors would be willing to work with these writers if they felt the concepts were strong. I'm quite sure the weak writing was at least half the cause of the books' being declined.

Because of these and other experiences, I would encourage beginning writers to build up a track record by writing one good book at a time, as Duffey did. If the book takes off, your editor may ask you to do either a companion novel (literary jargon for a sequel) or a series.

Once you are, like Davis, known to librarians, reviewers, and readers—and have an agent—selling a series will be a little easier. Writers may be surprised at how modest an advance may be for a new series. Publisher and writer both are investing in the future success of the books, and publishers are cautious. Your editor and publisher are taking a chance on something new because they have had time to get to know you and your capabilities.

Sometimes it seems that anyone can predict which book will be a best-seller, that it's like a disease, presenting signs that would cause it to erupt. I was incredulous when I overheard Peter Ritner, editor in chief of adult trade at Macmillan in the 1960s, say, "No one can tell which book will be a best-seller." I've learned he was right.

No matter how clever and timely your idea may be, the chances are that you will not be the only one writing on that subject—and many others that simultaneously reach the attention of writers. The trick is to put your own imagination to work on the idea. New twists on ideas are always welcome. We live together in the same society and are exposed to many of the same influences. Therefore, coincidences happen. A successful TV series for adults might inspire a writer to undertake a juvenile version. Every two years we watch the Olympics on TV. Naturally, that's a series topic many writers consider. Another way to write a book the stores will want is to write something trendy, but timing is everything. You almost have to be able to foretell the future and know what will be all the rage two or three years before it happens.

Let's say you decide to develop a series called Gopher Broke. You write one book and a proposal, send it out, and you find an editor who adores it! Once it's clear that gophers are hot, every paperback house will be sure to want gopher books, but it'll be too late, because your gopher books were out there first and are selling like hot dogs at Coney Island. By the time the imitators get into the stores, the craze may be over. If the genre is strong enough, as with horror or mysteries, one or two imitators may survive as well. This can happen. It has happened!

People have also won the lottery. Sure, it's fun to think up concepts and catchy titles, but it's also hard work and extremely speculative to develop the books themselves. If truth were told, series publishing is part inspiration, part guesswork, part talent, great marketing, and tons of luck.

Although editors will deny it, series ideas have been stolen, which is another reason not to offer series proposals indiscriminately. One young writer told me she'd written a series with characters that had unusual names. It was turned down by a publisher, but shortly thereafter, the same publisher launched a series with only a slightly different concept. One of the books had a character with the same name doing the same thing as in her series. Was the idea stolen? I have no idea. I prefer to think an editor subconsciously absorbed the idea and then suggested it to another writer. As for the characters' having the same unusual name, that could have been a coincidence.

In another case, a young writer had an idea for a series, and the publisher was gung ho. A contract was almost in the offing, when the editor decided to decline the series. A season or two later, a famous writer came out with the same series idea from the same publisher. The young writer cried, "Foul!" but the affair was hushed up; even the writer's agent told him to forget what had happened.

A number of cases such as this have occurred in the adult world and have drawn attention from the media. Some writers have won their cases; others have not. A young adult book I edited by a well-known juvenile and adult writer became a blockbuster movie for all ages with no acknowledgment of the original source. The writer was told he couldn't prove his book had inspired the movie, and the case never even made it to court.

Old codes of ethics and honor have disappeared as some aggressive and eager editors take on the habits of Hollywood and network TV. If you value your idea, keep it to yourself and a few trusted friends. If your idea pops up in an article or review in *Publishers Weekly* before you've even begun your book, you'll know that it was the result of a coincidence, not loose lips.

Although they are of a different nature, nonfiction series are popular with some trade publishers and educational publishers whose work is aimed mainly at the school library market. One way to learn about these publishers is to peruse their catalogs. If a series on a particular topic has many different authors, you can write to the editor and suggest doing a new book; some series are open-ended. Or you might suggest an entire new series on your own. Publishers find it easier to market series, a group of related books, to the library market. So think big. Again, be warned that all the good ideas have been taken—except for the new one from you. Publishers already have series on countries, social problems, women's biographies, science, math, history; whatever is taught in schools or featured in the news.

The good news about nonfiction series is that often the writer need not write the whole book before receiving a contract. An outline, three complete chapters, and perhaps a statement about why a book on this topic is needed will suffice. If you are writing about the life of girls in ancient Egypt and you know ancient Egypt is studied in third grade, be sure to mention this. It will help the editor position the book. Three chapters are enough to tell the editor whether you can write. She may trust you to finish the rest according to your outline. Nonfiction writers are usually asked to supply the illustrations for the book. It would be premature for you to submit actual photos and artwork, but you should consider the value of presenting photocopies of the art you will furnish from photographic sources.

If you prefer to try a single title, you can send it to some of the trade publishers who do nonfiction. Some nonfiction writers worth emulating are Penny Colman, Russell Freedman, and James Giblin. All three write well and do impeccable research on a variety of topics from women doing defense work in World War II to Abraham Lincoln to chimney sweeps, subjects they clearly love.

These writers—and others—have written many award-winning nonfiction books that appeal to young people and sell well in bookstores and to libraries.

It's always a good idea to talk to teachers and school librarians about which subjects are studied in different grades and what may be needed to help fill out a reading list. Some subjects, like health and social studies, are studied in nearly every grade, but the level of information varies according to age. The youngest children are introduced to the idea that tobacco is a drug, for example, but older children learn more about other drugs and their effects.

You may also be able to find freelance writing work on a series with a packager, or book producer. Both trade and educational publishers buy books that packagers have developed. Packagers have long existed to create books for publishers, but the 1970s and 1980s saw many new companies such as Cloverdale Press, Dan Weiss Associates, Mega-Books, and Parachute Press come into existence.

Not only do packagers create series, they work on material commissioned by the owners of licensed material. Have you noticed the increase in TV programs for young people, especially (though not exclusively) on Nickelodeon, the Disney Channel, and PBS? Many writers are supporting themselves by writing tie-ins on a work-for-hire or royalty basis for book packagers and publishers. TV series have spawned quite a few lines of books, with *Sesame Street* and *Barney* heading the list for the toddler set. Other TV and book series, like *Wishbone* and *Malcolm in the Middle*, are being directed to older viewers and readers. Pokemon is probably the first computer game to become a hot series of books. But what's hot today will be cold by the time you read this book. The mass-media world moves fast.

Movie studios like Disney and DreamWorks each produce at least one major movie a year, which gets the full tie-in licensing treatment, from toys at Burger King to bed linens and books. The largesse from a major motion picture is spread around to many different suppliers and vendors.

How is such a massive effort coordinated? It begins two to three years before the release date of the movie, when the studio has already prepared a set of guidelines for distribution to interested parties. The guidelines contain artwork and strict rules on how to present the various characters so that they look alike no matter who produces the final product. The book rights are often shared among the different publishers, who bid on them. Random House may buy the mass-market hardcover picture-book rights, Avon the paperback tie-in license, Grolier a mail-order book-club deal. No matter how the tie-in market works, writers are wanted, but it's not always clear who the publishers and packagers of the various titles are.

How do you find out? If you live at the End of the World and have no access to any of the publications mentioned in chapter 5, you can write to the publishers of the series books. The publisher's name and address are always on the copyright page. If you see a line like "Produced by Felix Press, Inc.," it means Felix Press (not a real firm) was the book producer. You can find that address either through the American Book Producers Association in

New York City, the SCBWI *Guide to Book Packagers/Producers*, or in *Literary Market Place*. You could also try the national telephone directory assistance services, which may be able to help. If none of these gets results, write to Felix Press in care of the juvenile editorial department at the publisher and ask that your letter be forwarded.

If you consult the SCBWI *Bulletin* or the *Children's Writer* regularly, you'll have an edge. These publications provide information on who is looking for what and where they are located. Because they always need dependable writers, many packagers look at unsolicited material. It's also not a bad idea to read the entertainment trade publications like *Variety* to find out about possible assignments based on a future film or TV project. For the writer, by the time something is featured in a *consumer* publication like *People*, it's too late. The best way to find out about freelance projects is to join a writers' group and network with other writers and the editors, many of them freelance, who work for packagers.

Writing on demand can pay well, with advances ranging from about $1,000 to $10,000 per book, depending on the series. Usually the work is done for a flat fee or on a "for hire" basis, and no royalty is paid. Your byline may or may not be used. (The Nancy Drew series, for example, has the pen name Carolyn Keene on all the titles.) Finally, the writer must relinquish all rights to his written material and may be asked to sign a document promising to keep all the information he's been given confidential.

Writing series books based on licensed characters is different from writing trade books. Series editors are pressed for deadlines and rarely have time to praise the writers, who must adhere to the writing criteria of the series. Perhaps the hardest part is the time constraint. More than once, the writer may have submitted the manuscript in time, but the publisher hadn't read it for months— and then asked the writer for a complete revision a week before the manuscript was due to the printer. The book has been announced; it must be published on time. Without your permission, sections are slashed or rewritten; the book may even be given to another writer for a rewrite. Writers must be extraordinarily resilient and professional to withstand such treatment.

On the other hand, the writer may take great pleasure in telling her family and friends that she wrote a book based on a TV show everyone has heard of, and that it's available in nearly all bookstores. Her prestige will shoot up among the people who never paid attention to her literary work. The writer will also have learned a great deal about her craft from her demanding editor. Writing a mass-market paperback series for a packager can be an excellent way to become a better writer. And it may be a way for a writer to develop the network and track record she needs to propose a series idea of her own.

Here is a heartening story to keep in mind, about a writer who had written a number of series for various publishers, with none being a success. She then proposed a new series to Scholastic. Feiwel, who asks only that she be given "something I haven't seen before," was enthusiastic. But though she and her staff at Scholastic had faith in the idea, they suggested a change in the name. They then coordinated all the elements necessary to promote a series, creating a package that had good timing, sequence of titles, and publicity. At first booksellers were reluctant to take on the series, because the author did not have a stellar track record. Scholastic insisted. The rest is history, as they say. Katherine Applegate's series, originally called Changelings, became a hit called Animorphs. The trail of unsuccessful series gave Applegate the writing experience to follow through with her successful one. As the Ukrainian proverb has it, "Winter snow brings spring flowers."

9

Inside the Fence

✦

HOW TO EDIT YOUR OWN WORK

To see what is in front of one's nose requires a constant struggle. —George Orwell

By now Gus had come to understand how the publishing field has changed in recent years. He'd also written a novel and wanted to send out the manuscript right away.

"Hold on," I told him. "Submitting your book hot off the computer is a mistake."

"But I finished it. I want to get it out of the house. I know an editor will buy it as soon as she reads it."

"Right," I answered, fingers crossed.

Writers will improve their chances if they wait a day or even a week or more until their excitement abates, allowing passions to cool. Go over your manuscript with an objective eye, a pencil in your hand. A manuscript with too many errors will annoy editors and make them doubt your abilities. And it wouldn't hurt, since we all have blind spots, to ask a friend to mark misspellings, typo-graphical errors, and faulty punctuation. Even a computer spelling program cannot distinguish between *its* and *it's*.

In the following excerpt from "An Owed to the Spelling Checker," circulated on the Internet, Dave Burnham wrote:

I have a spelling checker.
It came with my PC.
It plane lee marks four my revue
Miss steaks aye can knot sea.

Eye ran this poem threw it,
Your sure reel glad two no.
Its vary polished in it's weigh,
My checker tolled me sew.

It's also a good idea for writers to read their texts aloud, es-pecially picture books. Since parents, teachers, librarians, and other adults read books aloud to children, the way the text sounds is important. Reading to children is also a good idea; they are honest critics. You'll quickly learn from them where the manuscript falters and dead spots lurk in your text, as well as what makes the audience laugh or sigh. Many writers submit manuscripts saying they've tried it out on children, who adored it. However, *never, ever, tell this to an editor!* It's quite possible that the child simply enjoyed sitting in your lap and would have tolerated a software manual. Children can have the worst taste in the world, and, as Dr. Seuss discovered, you can make them laugh with the most obvious of jokes, such as funny-sounding names. Laughter is infectious, and once one child in a group begins to giggle, the rest will too. They also tend to fidget during the serious parts. Take this as a sign that your text may be too wordy or over their heads, and revise accordingly.

Zena Sutherland, the noted literary critic, once scolded the committee members discussing potential award-winning books at a meeting of the American Library Association and forbade them to say "I liked it" or "I didn't like it." She was right to do so. Like or dislike is not the issue. Literary criticism includes evaluating books with an eye to effective characterization, plausibility, universality of theme, motivation. Also, different people, including children, have different tastes, and a book that bores one child may delight another.

The editorial problems listed here are by no means complete, but this is a good place to begin your own critique of your manuscript.

1. *Effective writing depends on showing through action, dialogue, or detail.* Don't think that children need everything spelled out, because it leaves little for the reader to imagine. For example, picture two children alone in a graveyard at night.

> *"Did you hear something?" asked Adam.*
> *"No," said Eve. She stumbled.*
> *"What's that?" Adam asked.*
> *"Only an open grave."*

What should you write next? Should you say, "Adam was frightened"? Or have him say, "I want to go home"? The first is telling, the second is showing. (It's also clear from these four sentences that Eve is in charge and unafraid.)

Let the showing do the work; don't tell the reader what to think or feel. If you wrote your manuscript on a word processor, use the Find command to search for every use of *felt*. Then examine each sentence: Are you telling instead of showing? You may have more work to do, after all.

2. *Does each scene and incident in the book advance the plot or develop the characterization?* Are you certain you're not just filling up space on the page, because you didn't know what else to say? Be sure you're not going off on tangents enthralling to you but meaningless to your reader, who would rather you dealt with your characters and plot. In the heat of composition, everything seems relevant to the book, and the temptation to throw it all in is great, especially for writers using word processors. Hard-hearted as you may be, it's a rare writer who cuts all the beloved irrelevancies and tangents; a good editor might do the rest, provided you've not so bored her that she refuses to finish reading your book.

3. *None of the characters in your book should be perfect*, that is, as one-dimensional as Nancy Drew, who *is* perfect. In formula fiction (which many paperback series are), characters are fantasies, because that's what the readers want: a princess, a prince, and a rival, or a good twin and an evil twin, or space explorers who never

get killed. But literature shows that people are complex, with plots growing out of their faults as well as their virtues. Take a hard look at each of your characters. Each one should have good traits and flaws. The more human your characters, the more memorable they'll be. Take an especially hard look at old people, small children, and villains. They are the easiest to stereotype, to the point where they become ludicrous caricatures.

◆ Character Description ◆

This is a useful exercise to help you define your characters, especially the main ones. Just for fun, imagine your protagonist is Peter Rabbit as you read the exercise.

- What is his (her, understood) name? Sex? Age?
- Where does he live?
- Are his parents married or single or widowed or divorced?
- Does he have siblings and other important relatives?
- Who are his friends?
- Who are the people he dislikes or who dislike him?
- What is his personal life like? Hobbies, interests, pets?
- What is his favorite color?
- What does he eat for breakfast? Who prepares it?
- What does he want?
- What is the conflict or obstacle to getting it?
- Where is the suspense in the plot?

> When you use the exercise for your characters, you may
> not be able to fill in the blanks immediately, but as you write,
> the other information will come forth from your unconscious.

4. Dialogue shows character, and *each character should sound like himself*, but be on the alert for the kinds of caricatures you still see on TV. Few grandmothers today wear iron gray hair in a bun, granny glasses, and long aprons and use phrases like "Land's sake, young man. You are a caution." Grandmothers, mothers, aunts, teachers, and librarians use contemporary expressions, and many wear jeans and T-shirts.

The following passage from Todd Strasser's novel, *How I Changed My Life*, demonstrates how he handled dialogue by different persons. These are the reactions from strangers in a pizza parlor to Bo's new hairdo when her friend Bobby asks:

"*Doesn't she look great? . . . Would you believe she's terrified that the kids at school are going to laugh at her?*"

"*No way. She looks gorgeous,*" *said one of the countermen.*

"*What do you care what other people think?*" *asked one of the big-hair girls.*

"*They're just jealous, honey,*" *said one of the overweight grandmothers. . . .*

"*If anyone laughs at you, smash 'em in the face,*" *said one of the twelve-year-old Marlboro smokers.*

It's only fair to mention that Strasser spent several years writ-ing for TV, where he learned how to refine the writing of dialogue. If editors say you have trouble with dialogue, consider taking a playwriting course and keep your ears open to how the people around you speak. Note the use here of *overweight* instead of *fat*. Bo, the narrator, is being euphemistic, and there's more about eu-phemism later in this chapter.

5. *Avoid long descriptions of people and places.* Many writers get carried away and describe everything a character is wearing. Sometimes this is done to fill up the pages. Other times, writers think it's necessary for the reader to know exactly what everyone looks like. Again, trust the reader to fill in the blanks, and cut back on the adjectives. When a telemarketer calls you, don't you immediately imagine from the voice alone what he or she looks like? I do that as soon as a character speaks in a book. Note how succinctly Strasser describes his characters above.

Appearance should be mentioned briefly and only if it mat-ters; that is, if it's a clue to character or has some other function in the story, such as showing how the character plans to impress someone of the opposite sex.

> *Eve couldn't decide how to do her nails. Blue to show she was*
> *with it? Red to show she was sexy? Green to show she was*
> *daring? She studied her hands. No matter how she tried, she*
> *couldn't help biting her nails to the quick. She reached for the*
> *bottle of clear polish. Would it look strange if she wore white*
> *gloves all night? she wondered. Maybe she'd start a trend.*

Whatever you do, please don't have the character look in the mirror so that we can find out what she looks like. This worked in *Snow White and the Seven Dwarfs*, but that was in 1815.

Similarly, do not describe the landscape or the interiors of rooms in fine detail. Set the scene as briefly as you can without neglecting "the details that give a book its richness," according to Joan Aiken. Use details that count, adding color, texture, life— and, above all, meaning. Evoke the atmosphere of a room with a few phrases such as "velvet curtains" or "shoes piled on every surface." For example, in *The Pawloined Paper*, when I wanted to *show* how vain yet insecure a villain was, I decorated his room with portraits of himself.

6. "*Omit needless words*," advised William Strunk in 1935. This is still excellent advice. One of the first things to look for is *periphrasis*, taking the long way to say something. For example, some writers still worry about repeating nouns, including proper nouns, and will try to use other words in their place. Help your readers keep the characters straight by using their names or a pronoun instead of descriptions.

> "*I want to go home,*" *Adam said.*
> "*Don't be silly,*" *Eve said. "It's just a hole in the ground.*"
> *The boy began to cry.*

Boy? What boy? Oh, Adam. *That* boy. . . . Two words instead of one.

It also drives me crazy when a writer keeps reminding me of a person's job, even though we know his name.

Eve's mother's friend, Bob, was a waiter at the Pizza Grill, where they were eating. "Hi," said Bob when he came over to their table. He was handsome, Eve thought while he was being introduced to them. The waiter took their orders and went to the kitchen.

The waiter? Right, Bob.

It's so easy to write, "There is . . . ," but be warned and avoid those two words, especially in fiction. Highlight "there is" (and "there are," "there was," "there were") whenever they appear, and rephrase the statement if you can. The usage is correct, but the effect is dullness. With all its faults, advertising has perfected vivid, active writing, and I can't recall any ad that used a variation of "there is."

Also insidious is the creep of verbal clutter like extra wire coat hangers. In a mistaken attempt at emphasis, the following words automatically flow out of our fingers as we write: *just, really, very, all,* and *now.* Erase them. Put back only the ones you really need—I mean, you need. See?

Suddenly, quickly, and other such adverbs, especially at the beginning of a sentence, fail to convey speed because they slow down the reader, interfering with his getting to the all important verb. ("Suddenly, she fell into the open grave.") It seems that a transitional adverb is required, but that's because the sentence is not strong enough. Consider: "Eve stumbled. 'Yeow!' she screamed. She fell into the open grave." (Whoops! Delete *open*; not required because self-evident).

It's not nice to hate, but the word *somehow* makes me see red. What does it mean? If it means you have no idea ("Somehow I'll get even"), it's all right. But if you do know either intuitively or because you have good reasons for knowing, let the reader in on the secret. Don't write, "Somehow, Eve got out of the grave"; tell us how she did it. Watch out, too, for *something*, and *thing*, which are also vague. If the right word doesn't come to mind while you're writing, put in a vague one, but find a substitute when you revise!

Steer clear, too, of meaningless vogue words like *incredible, amazing, awesome, tremendous,* which, like *colossal, awful, gigantic,* and *huge,* have lost their force through being overused. Save powerful words for the right occasion, such as a volcanic explosion or the birth of octuplets.

7. *Learn the verbs of speech.* Nothing looks so amateurish as the sort of dialogue attribution found in many mass-market books. People sigh, joke, and lie, smile, remind, and breathe sentences. These are not legitimate verbs of speech. Do not write: "'Your nails look great,' she smiled." It should be: "'Your nails look great.' She smiled." (If you find yourself using *smiled* often, you are relying on it to convey emotion. Go back and work on your dialogue. The same is true for *nodded*.)

Whispered, mumbled, and *bellowed* are verbs of speech, but they should be used sparingly, only when the occasion demands it. One of the worst offenders is *hissed*—which is a verb of speech but should not be used when there are no s's in the sentence!

Effective dialogue does not require adverbs after the verbs of speech because the dialogue conveys the emotion. Writers of mass-market romances and series are usually telling their readers what to think, so they tack adverbs on after illegitimate verbs of speech like this: "'I'll never see him again,' she sighed longingly." To be honest, many mainstream writers get away with prose like this in the hardcover market, too.

The current trend is to keep attribution simple, using words like *said* and *answered* but not *replied*, because it is too formal and sounds dated. Write dialogue so that the reader knows who is speaking without your having to attribute the words. This works best, of course, when only two people are speaking.

You can also avoid direct attribution by having the character act and speak in the same passage, as in "Goldilocks sat down. 'This chair is too high.' She got up and sat in Mama Bear's chair."

8. *Avoid the passive voice* whenever possible. Although it's correct, the passive voice results in flat writing because it's impossible to see an invisible agent, which is why it's so often used—or, to use the active voice, why bureaucrats use it so often. A simple example: "Make sure your name is spelled correctly." If it isn't, no one is responsible, because we don't know who did it! (That's the government for you!) In the following example, which sentence is more vivid: "The land was settled by farmers" or "Farmers moved in and settled on the land"?

9. *Does your book have a voice?* As an editor and agent, I've seen many unsolicited manuscripts that fell into what I called a gray middle, like overcooked vegetables without salt. The characters and plot were promising, but the writing style was undistinguished. All the words were in the correct places, but the manuscript lacked a voice, a style.

In books for young adults, the voice is often that of the narrator. Richard Peck has said his first-person narrators always sound older and more intelligent than the intended readers. The reader thinks she's older and wiser than she is, and doesn't want to read a story told by someone who's still wet behind the ears. Peck strikes the balance between contemporaneity versus formality with consummate skill and thought.

You are who you sound like, as George Bernard Shaw demonstrated in *Pygmalion*. Take a look at the early work of the greatest writers: It, too, lacked style. Your voice will arrive after experience and practice, just as it did when you discovered your own style of dressing.

10. *Collect and savor verbs.* Good writers love verbs the way good cooks love herbs. Flat writing is the result of using tired verbs, along with all the faults listed above. To avoid monotony, to convey different kinds of action, to move your work along, you need verbs, especially for simple, everyday actions. You should own a copy of *Webster's New Dictionary of Synonyms*, which, unlike a thesaurus, gives the sources of usages and discriminates among synonyms. Each page is a revelation.

Also, use verbs, not participles, when trying to convey separate, *consecutive* actions. For example, "Adam ran to the edge of the grave, lay down on the grass, and stared at Eve" is better than "Running to the edge of the grave, Adam lay down on the grass and stared at Eve." (He can't run, lie down, and stare at the same time, but lazy writers defy logic.) Participles should be used only with *simultaneous* actions: "Looking up at Adam, Eve shouted, 'Get me out of here!'"

11. *Pay attention to the little words like prepositions*, the correct use of which can be one of the most vexing points in English usage. The writer should know when to use *in* and when *into*, when *on to* and when *onto*. He does not have his characters "enter into" a room or go "outside of" the house, because *into* and *of* are redundant. Words like *incorporate* and *exit* carry the preposition within, the joey in a kangaroo's pouch, as it were, so there's no need to "incorporate into" or "exit out of." You do need the *of*, however, after *couple*, as in "a couple of grapes." In New York City, people stand "on line," but elsewhere, they stand "in line" and go "on-line" when they use the Internet. Observing the fine distinctions, such as using "compare with" instead of "compare to" will strengthen your command of the craft of writing.

Because of space constraints, journalism has done its share to cause language to become sloppy. As it becomes more clipped, so does thought.

12. *Watch your usage.* Pernicious influences attack the English language from all sides: advertising, business, street slang, pretentiousness. In the 1950s, when Winston cigarettes were advertised as "tasting good, like a cigarette should," thoughtful people were

more dismayed at the flagrant bad grammar than at tobacco.

Soon thereafter the third edition of the Merriam-Webster unabridged dictionary was published, causing even more alarm. The editors of this influential dictionary produced the first waves on the shore of permissiveness, or loosening of standards, which came to characterize the last part of the twentieth century. Unlike its predecessor, the still revered second edition, the third edition did not *prescribe*, or differentiate between what was "the preferred usage among educated people," but *described*, that is, recorded "common usage." Students, teachers, journalists, and readers became confused. They could no longer look up a word and find out whether it was preferred usage or substandard. It was not "all right," for example, when I was a copy editor to spell the word *alright*. It now is, according to Webster, since so many people spell it that way.

Because they wanted students to read, writers, reviewers, and editors relaxed their standards a generation ago to make literature "more relevant," something readers could "relate to." By the 1970s, the trend was to allow the first-person narrator to sound like a young person, complete with slang and grammatical errors. As an editor, I wanted the characters to sound convincing, yet I hated to perpetuate grammatical barbarisms, even though it seemed to be worth it, because the readership of young adult novels increased in schools as students saw themselves reflected on the pages.

13. *Respect other cultures.* When the dominant class in publishing was white and Protestant, unflattering stereotypes rou-

tinely appeared in books, including children's books. I enjoyed reading *The Five Chinese Brothers* and *Little Black Sambo* when I was a child and did not realize how racist the books were. The wonderful stories were not meant to be racist, but the illustrations were, and both have since been reissued with new art. Ask the person whose sex, nationality, religion, or race is being depicted whether the portrait is true or gratuitously offensive. Outsiders are often unwittingly insensitive to the feelings of certain groups.

We use *African-American*, although *black* is still accepted, and the use of *people of color* is widespread. The word *Oriental* is no longer acceptable usage for the Arab, Chinese, Japanese, Korean, Pakistani, Philippine, Vietnamese, and East Indian peoples; *Asian* is preferred since *oriental* is a Eurocentric compass direction and implies that Asians are east of London, once the capital of the British Empire.

The picture is not so clear when dealing with Native Americans, who call one another *Indians* and regard *Native American* as having been coined by guilt-struck white people. All persons of whatever race born in North, Central, or South America are *native Americans*. It is better to honor the Indians by using tribal names, like Sioux or Wampanoag or Maya, when possible.

With the dissolution of the Soviet Union and its control over other European countries, national designations have changed. People are no longer Czechoslovakian but either Czech or Slovak. Bosnians are no longer Yugoslavs; the only Yugoslavs left are Serbs and Montenegrins. It is no longer *the* Ukraine, but Ukraine. Be sure your sources are up-to-date.

14. *Write for the long term,* because your book may be in print for years and too much slang will make it seem dated. Do you remember that by the time the first President George Bush used the word *nerd* in the 1980s, young people scoffed at him? "Nobody says that anymore!" (Well, *adults* still do, but it has a specific meaning related to rich scientists.) Children have new words all the time. Use the wrong word, and your credibility as a writer for contemporary children is lost. Remember, too, that many of your readers do not recall the time when Bush was president.

Some slang has passed into the language and become almost legitimate, but when you're trying to be current, you can't know whether the latest slang will stick around, so it's best to avoid it. Lively modern writing does not depend on slang. It depends on how you use the English language.

The same idea holds true for current events, from movies to music to election campaigns. Ten or fifteen years down the line, a new generation of young people may be reading your book, and if they find it dated, it will not stay in print. If you must use a real name, when referring to contemporary culture, find one you believe will be around for a long time. Fortunately, with reruns and the rise of the VCR, classic movies and TV shows like *Babe* and the *X Files* will be enjoyed for years. But few teenagers care who Madonna or Michael Jackson are. Time moves fast in these mass-media days, so be selective.

15. *Think twice before you use a brand name* in your book, and be sure you use it correctly, because you might end up in court. For example, it's Xerox copy, not a Xerox, and it's Levi's jeans, not

simply Levis. Coke, Kleenex, Windbreaker, Polaroid, Windsurfer, Corn Flakes, Frisbee, Roller Blades, Dumpster are all trademark names and must be capitalized. If the proprietor of a good allows a lowercased product name to be used without challenging it, he can lose the trademark, which is what happened with products like kerosene. Some manufacturers are even insisting the trademark symbol (™) be used with the name, but publishers have resisted this trend. They and readers do not want to see books littered with little letters all over the pages.

Brand names are realistic, to be sure. On the other hand, books are one of the last places without ads or commercials.

16. *Eschew euphemisms.* It's not nice to call a person a fat slob; it's no more polite to call him an overweight slob. *Fat* is not an insult; it is an adjective, pejorative today, but complimentary yesterday, as in "the fat of the land," meaning prosperity. However, since Hollywood and the fashion industry have decreed that being fat is unacceptable, Bo, the narrator in Strasser's book quoted earlier, is being euphemistic, if not coy, when she describes "the grandmothers" with a medical diagnosis instead of her own opinion. She could have used another descriptive word like *dumpy* or *voluptuous*—but since she didn't use the f-word, we sense her discomfort regarding fat women. (She is fat herself, by the way.) Notice, too, that she doesn't say *old* or *middle-aged*. It would be too impolite, she thinks, too unpleasant, even though they are fat and middle-aged women. (This says more about society than it does about the women.) Bo's choice of words reflects her character, but a third-person narrator should write in standard English.

Foreground

Does it matter? Yes, because as George Orwell and others have pointed out, euphemisms reflect attitudes of society. In his essay "Politics and the English Language," Orwell writes: "[The English language] becomes ugly and inaccurate because our thoughts are foolish, but the slovenliness of our language makes it easier for us to have foolish thoughts. . . . Bad habits spread by imitation."

New euphemisms turn up every day, as in the use of *home* instead of *house* in the real estate business. My sixth-grade teacher, Miss Griggs, told us that "home is where the heart is," whereas a house is only a building. Realtors, obviously, are selling fantasies of happy homes, and it seems everyone is selling a fantasy of some sort. Do not let yourself be seduced by euphemisms. You owe it to your readers because you are, after all, their teacher. The writer of serious books is an observer of humanity, a thinker, a critic.

You'll find many good books on writing at the library or bookstore, including books on usage. Most writers swear by *The Elements of Style* by William Strunk, Jr.; it's full of good advice not only from Strunk but also from E. B. White. Most copy editors and proofreaders refer to *Words into Type* or *The Chicago Manual of Style* for matters of punctuation and grammar. Writers should keep these books at the ready, to understand why copy editors, who strive for consistency and accuracy, have made changes in the manuscript.

The search for the right word, the nuances of punctuation, the ability to connote with language as well as to denote are as important as knowing what kind of flour to use when baking bread, how long to knead, how long to let the dough rise. We're used to seeing perfect loaves in the bakery. But like writers, bakers have created their share of misshapen loaves. Learn from your mistakes and go on to do your best. A book should be like a loaf of bread, tender, tasty, and nutritious under a crackling crust, something we can chew on with satisfaction.

10

Secrets from the
Carrot Patch

◆

HOW TO SUBMIT A MANUSCRIPT

A friend is a lot of things, but a critic he isn't.
—Berm Williams

"Don't you need an agent to get published?" Gus asked me. He was depressed. His novel had been returned—again. "Nobody is reading unsolicited manuscripts any longer."

"True and false," I told Gus. "Many houses no longer read unsolicited manuscripts except for those submitted by agents."

"How do I get an agent?" he asked next.

"The best way," I said, "is to sell a book to an editor."

"Very funny. You mean once it's sold, an agent will want me. Catch-22. I can't sell a book without an agent."

"False. You can still sell a manuscript over the transom."

As I told Gus, some editors, even at the most cosmodemonic houses, welcome unsolicited material, which, figuratively speaking, comes in "over the transom," a phrase coined in the days when offices had transoms, small windows above the doors. Hopeful writers would toss manuscripts through open transoms, and editors would read them. Although transoms have virtually disappeared, many publishers still handle unsolicited manuscripts (or "slush" or the "discovery pile") the traditional way. After all, the most cosmodemonic publishing house in the world could not exist were it not for the writers. Grace Clarke, the former vice president and editor in chief at the Simon & Schuster Children's Book Division, once said to me: "The writers hold the apex of an inverted pyramid in their hands. Without writers, no one in the pyramid would have a job." Reading slush is one way to find new writers.

Every day, someone from the mail room drops off stacks of manuscripts in editors' in boxes. If the editor is not accepting unsolicited manuscripts, the envelope may be returned unopened or with a form letter stating the policy. A better way to find out who does not welcome unsolicited manuscripts is to check the sources mentioned in chapter 5. The listings state which houses will read unsolicited manuscripts, and the publications keep writers up-to-date on editors who are seeking material.

Receptive editors usually have assistants who open each submission and read the cover letter and a few pages or the whole manuscript. This is called the first reading. The pile of submissions goes down quickly, because by now the assistants are fairly sure that those who write notes on stationery with pictures of puppies and kittens or those saying "my grandchildren loved the story" or those who have the word *writer* after their names are amateurs. Not always, but most of the time. The assistant will decline those manuscripts by returning them to the writers with a form letter saying something like "Thank you, but your work isn't right for our list." New writers are puzzled by this phrase and may wonder how to make the manuscript right for the list. Be bemused no longer. Phrases such as this are simply a polite way for editors to say, "We do not want your manuscript." It means nothing else. A few manuscripts will get a second reading, either from the assistant, who may write a report recommending it, or from the editor herself.

Let's assume Gus found out through networking (the best way) that Annabelle Jones, who recently joined Upstart Books, where she has her own imprint, Annabelle Jones Books, has put out a call for fiction. Annabelle used to be an executive editor at Floe, Iceberg, and Glacier, but she was fired during the restructuring after FIG merged with Newton Books and became part of Cookie Cutter Publishing Empire.

Gus sent off his novel, titled *Five by the Sea,* to Annabelle. From what he'd told me, Gus's novel sounded as if it had a chance. It was not an amateurish picture book about Octavia Octopus who fell in love with Otto Otter or a cell that wanted to be fertilized.

In spite of all his pessimistic feelings about publishing, the first week or so Gus found himself fantasizing once again about the fate of his work, as so many writers have done before and will do forever. Annabelle would begin to read his manuscript the day she received it, Gus thought, counting on his fingers. Enchanted and impressed, she'd spend the rest of the day turning the pages. "Splendid!" she'd cry at last. "This is perfect for my new list." She would telephone him before the week was out and send a contract and check a few days after that.

Instead, Gus waited. He checked the mail every day. Weeks went by, then months, then years. Surely she's had time to read it by *now*, Gus thought as he combed his beard. (He'd vowed not to shave till he sold a book, and by now he had to wrap his beard around his waist.) One snowy day, as he was contemplating applying for a job as a sidewalk Santa, he received *Five by the Sea* with a polite form letter saying it wasn't right for the Upstart list. In despair, he burned the manuscript, shaved off his beard, and took a job on an oil rig off the Alaskan coast.

Well, that's all fantasy, of course. Gus knew better than to wait so long for one editor to read his manuscript! Gus had been writing for a while, and he'd already made the classic mistakes and learned from them. He'd been to writers' conferences, had his work critiqued professionally, and a few editors had praised his writing. He'd sold two stories to a children's magazine, but so far, he hadn't sold a book.

He'd abided by the ground rules. He'd printed out his manuscript on 8 1/2-by-11-inch white bond in double-spaced Courier font, 12 point, which looks like a typewriter face and is what editors are used to reading. He could have typed the manuscript on a typewriter, but he no longer used one since word processing was so much easier. He could also have used another font, like Garamond or Times Roman, both of which are easy to read, but he certainly would not have used all italics or boldface or anything elaborate, which most editors would regard as amateurish looking. Some writers try to impress editors with fancy typesetting, but this can backfire, because type is supposed to be "invisible," not a distraction from the words on the page.

Gus then sat down, and again on plain white bond, this time with his name, address, telephone number, and date at the top, wrote a cover letter to Annabelle Jones. He mentioned in his letter that he was glad to see that she had her own imprint. As if he were writing an autobiography for a jacket flap, he told her a bit about himself, such as where he'd been educated, what kind of work he was doing—teaching is relevant to writing—and mentioned the two stories he'd published.

He also mentioned that he was sending the manuscript to two other editors. "Anyone who doesn't multiple-submit is crazy," declared Susan Hirschmann, publisher of Greenwillow Books and senior vice president of HarperCollins Children's Books, at a writers' conference. Given the long turnaround time, writers no longer can afford the luxury of sending a manuscript to one editor at a time. Most editors understand this, though not so long ago, they resented multiple submissions. Some editors still will not read multiple submissions, and it is so stated in the lists of publishers mentioned earlier. Each writer has to decide for himself which course to follow.

Gus had discovered it wasn't a good idea for him to send a manuscript to more than three editors at a time. For one, it was

✦ The Cover Letter ✦

This is the letter Gus sent accompanying his manuscript. One need not include a cover letter with a manuscript, but it's wise to do so. Here is your chance to introduce yourself, supply some credentials, and to pitch the manuscript. A manuscript without a cover letter is like a sandwich with no bread: It may be tasty, but something is missing.

GUS CASEY

P.O. BOX 236

WEST ARLINGTON, VT 05252

(802) 555-9906

March 1, 2001

Ms. Annabelle Jones

Annabelle Jones Books

Upstart Books

123 Fourth Avenue

New York, NY 10005

Dear Annabelle Jones:

Having heard you speak at several writers' conferences, for a long time I've wanted to send you my work for consideration but until recently did not have anything worth your attention.

I'm pleased now, however, to enclose my manuscript, *Five by the Sea*, a novel of 160 pages about five mother-less young people left on their own in a summer cottage after their father mysteriously disappeared. Can they sur-vive until they find out what has happened to their father?

I teach English at Hudson Community College in Ver-mont and have studied writing with James Purdy. This is my first full-length book, though I have had two stories for children published in *JellyBean* magazine.

I hope all is going well for you at your new imprint. I look forward to hearing from you.

Sincerely,

Gus Casey

P.S. I have also sent *Five by the Sea* to two other publish-ers. If either one accepts the novel, I will let you know immediately.

Enc. SASE

hard to keep track of many multiple submissions. More important, an editor would occasionally make perceptive comments about the manuscript when she returned it, and in those cases he'd revise the manuscript accordingly before sending it out again.

Sometimes, however, the comments showed a lack of understanding of what he was trying to achieve. He ignored those. It wasn't always easy for him to be sure whether an editor wanted to see the manuscript again, but he'd learned the hard way that unless she specifically asked to see it, it was pointless to send it back. Editors frequently offered comments, even when they weren't interested in buying a particular manuscript; it was an editorial reflex to be helpful.

Gus knew his work would have to sell itself, but he hoped that by showing he knew who Annabelle Jones was and by giving himself a personality, it would help his submission stand out from the rest. He also knew that obvious form letters, indicating the writer had blanketed the city, were also a bad idea.

One day, at Simon & Schuster, I was standing with another editor by the mailboxes outside our office doors. We both picked up envelopes addressed to us by name. They looked identical. We opened them together. Inside each envelope was a form letter addressed to "the editor" and a manuscript. We then peeked at a third editor's mailbox. She had the same envelope in hers. This is the wrong way to handle a multiple submission. The manuscript should go to only one editor at a publishing house at a time. Do I have to say that all three of us declined this particular manuscript?

Appearance counts. Gus had heard that a manuscript which looked gray and dog-eared, as if it had been making the rounds for years, silently doomed itself to rejection. He put the letter and his clean, freshly printed manuscript in a box to protect them and slipped the box into a Priority Mail envelope (available free from the U.S. Post Office), along with an SASE (self-addressed stamped envelope). He then prepared similar submissions to the other two editors. Priority Mail costs the same as first class for manuscripts weighing a pound or more. He could have used the special manuscript rate, but sometimes those packages are delayed in delivery. It's expensive to be a writer, printing out fresh copies of your work or having them photocopied. The postage is high, too, but this is part of the cost of doing business.

Gus noted the date on his calendar. He knew editorial staffs were underpaid and overworked, and silence meant nothing either way about the fate of his book. After two months had gone by, he was going to write to the publishers he hadn't heard from. He picked up the bulky envelopes and headed for the car. Because the packages weighed over a pound, by law he couldn't put them in the corner mailbox. He'd drop them off at the post office before heading for his job at the community college. At the rate he was going, it would be a long time before he could afford to quit. Meanwhile, he would think about a new book to write, the best way to spend his time while waiting.

Two months went by. One copy of *Five by the Sea* had come back from Editor No. 2 within thirty days with a form letter. He'd sent it to a fourth editor and made a note reminding himself to write her in two months. He wrote to Annabelle Jones and Editor No. 3 to remind them that he was waiting to hear what they thought. He desperately wanted to telephone them, but he resisted the temptation. "After all," he asked himself, "how do I know they even got my manuscript?"

Gus wished more publishers would send acknowledgment notes. He could have sent the manuscripts by certified mail, return receipt requested, but he thought that service was too expensive. He'd sent postcards in the past, asking that receipt be acknowledged, but that didn't always work. Many editors didn't open the envelopes until they were ready to read the enclosures. He comforted himself with the thought that none of his manuscripts had been lost in the mail yet. Once he'd misaddressed one, but the post office had bounced it back to him and he'd sent it out again, with the correct address this time.

His patience was rewarded. A few days later, Annabelle's assistant, Joanna, called him to say that Annabelle would like more time to consider his work. He graciously assented. He heard nothing from the third editor.

A month later, Gus wrote to him again. Gus didn't withdraw the manuscript from Editor No. 3, but he made a mental note to break the rules and call Editor No. 3 the following week. By this time, he didn't have much hope, so he sent another copy of his novel to a fifth editor and made a note to write to that one in two months if he hadn't heard anything.

The following week he called Editor No. 3 at FIG-Newton, where Annabelle used to work. It took a while to press all the buttons and be routed toward Editor No. 3. At last he got his voice mail. Gus left his message, name, and number. Voice mail! Oh, no.

From previous experience, he was sure he'd never hear from Editor No. 3. He didn't have Editor No. 3's direct line number, and he hated the thought of calling him again and pounding his way through all those buttons. Besides, many editors kept their voice mail on permanently, and Gus knew he'd never get through to them. Nor would they return his calls. He could drop Editor No. 3 a note and ask for a return of his manuscript, which is what his writer friends advised. Instead, he decided to play the same game as Editor No. 3: incommunicado. He scratched FIG-Newton off his list. A slim chance remained that someday, Editor No. 3 would find *Five by the Sea* under his bed and decide to buy it. Gus shook his head. No time for more fantasies.

He dropped a follow-up note to Editor No. 4 and one to Annabelle Jones; he still hadn't heard from her in spite of her assistant Joanna's promise over a month earlier.

Why not? Let's admit that some editors are lazy, arrogant, and unprofessional. Period. As for the others, they are swamped. Many no longer have secretaries, but assistants, who are perpetually busy doing editorial work the editors don't have time for. Assistants don't answer editors' telephones as they did in the old days; most editors place and answer their calls by themselves. When they're busy or have visitors or are on the telephone, they have to turn on voice mail. It's often easier to leave it on until they're ready to deal with calls.

More important, in addition to the disappearance of juvenile imprints like Scribners, Cobblehill, and Lothrop, editorial staffs have been cut at the cosmodemonic corporate publishing houses while the output of books per editor has increased. Some editors handle as many as fifty books a year, or one a week. Half that many is still a heavy load and not unusual. According to an article in the *New York Times* (June 29, 1998), "The work force of publishing professionals in New York, who are largely editors, has declined by 16 percent . . . according to data from the Federal Equal Employment Opportunity Commission . . . but the number of books published in the United States has surged."

Since so many top publishing executives, most of whom are not serious readers themselves, believe anyone can be an editor, editing has a low priority. But few people other than an editor know how to give the specific advice that can help a writer revise his work. An editor is like a doctor who can diagnose symptoms and prescribe a treatment when a patient complains of pain. Seasoned editors in their prime were the first to go at many of the houses. Eager but inexperienced younger people have taken their place—or no one has—and writers and their books are suffering.

Once upon a time, the editor and her immediate supervisor made the decision about whether to buy a book—except in cases where major sums of money (say, over $25,000)—were involved. Nowadays, as Jimmy Durante used to say, "Everybody wants to get into the act." In addition to the acquiring editor and editorial director, those attending the editorial meeting to discuss the purchase of books include the art director (who will present her ideas for an illustrator), the subsidiary rights director, the marketing director, the publicity director, the sales director, the financial people, and a few more middle-management staff members.

At the juvenile division of one cosmodemonic house, for example, the editorial meetings consist of more than thirty people who had—allegedly—read the manuscript under consideration and will decide whether to buy it. Before one of these meetings, the editorial director urges the editor to be "passionate" about the book under consideration. The editor, who is bookish and somewhat shy, has been overruled and undercut so often, she finds it hard to warm up to anything except hot fudge sundaes. Her quiet presentation fails to impress those attending. The art director and some of the other staff members are restless; they'd rather be back in their offices meeting the deadlines on the books already under contract. Trapped at the table, they watch in amused horror as the sales manager says the proposed book stinks and sticks his finger down his throat. Then the marketing director says books on that subject don't sell. Finally, the president of the division (the one with an M.B.A.) says the book is "a downer" and nobody will read it. (That means he didn't read past the first chapter.) Obviously, everyone's tired by now, and nobody wants to buy anything. The thirty experts decline the manuscript. Besides, it's time for lunch.

Aware of scenes like this, Jane Yolen, the writer and editor, wrote me the following:

I am an eternal optimist about my writing, always sure that a better word, a bigger plot twist, the perfect character is about to appear. And it always does. About publishing I have no such feeling. I expect the worst, am never surprised when it comes, and only modestly surprised when something even remotely nice happens.

Gus, however, was still optimistic about getting published. He was sure that if he persisted, he'd find an editor who admired his work. He wished he had an agent. It was tiresome keeping track of all the submissions and writing the follow-up letters. But it was early yet, he told himself. Who knew what tomorrow might bring?

11

Bunnies to the Rescue

◆

DEALING WITH AGENTS, EDITORIAL CONSULTANTS, AND EDITORS

Champions keep playing till they get it right.
—Billie Jean King

G us knew which agent he wanted, Julia Saunders. He'd heard her speak at a writers' conference and liked her style and what she said. After the conference, he'd asked her if she'd represent him, but Julia had said she could take on only writers whose books had been published or those who'd sold a book and wanted an agent to negotiate the contract. She'd given him her card, and he was waiting for that sale so he could call her.

Wouldn't it be easier for Gus if Julia took him on? Of course. Meanwhile, who is paying Julia's salary? She is, and her income depends on selling books to publishers and taking her 15 percent commission. Although she has a respectable stable of writers whom she represents, she has to work hard for them and for her income. Of course Gus was tired of submitting his own work to so many editors and keeping track. But Julia has about twenty clients, twenty times as much confusion to contend with, and her income is only slightly higher than Gus's.

When she'd first started her agency—she'd worked in publishing many years but had been let go during a restructuring—she actively sought clients. Unfortunately, she found out that 90 percent of the manuscripts she received were like those she'd seen as a slush reader when she was younger. As Sheldon Fogelman, a lawyer and literary agent, had remarked at a writers' conference, because so many publishers had closed their doors to unsolicited manuscripts, the agents are now the ones who get the slush.

Especially vexing, Julia found, were the submissions that consisted of one picture book, the first the writer had ever written. Sometimes the hopeful writers would say they'd already submitted the manuscripts to many editors but had no luck. That's why they wanted an agent: They were confident she could place the book because of her "connections." Julia tried to maintain her professionalism when she sent the material back. (She did not return manuscripts or artwork when no SASE was enclosed.) Whether the book goes to the publisher from a writer or an agent, it still has to be publishable. An agent is not a trickster, able to transform slush into silk. Julia could not afford to take on people who had written only one (unsold) book and already exposed it to all the potential buyers.

Further, as Grace Morgan, a literary agent, once told me, the condition of many of the submissions she receives is distressing.

They often are downright messy (to be kind), full of typing errors. She also wondered why some writers, when submitting proposals, send her three nonconsecutive chapters of a manuscript. "There's no point in sending unrelated chapters," she said, "even if they are the best chapters a writer has. Writers should send the first three so I can get an idea of what they're writing about." Like all agents, Julia and Grace want serious writers, writers whom they could help build careers.

It isn't that agents don't want to encourage new writers. They know from bitter experience that even the books they admire will not pass muster with editors if they are flawed. Many editors today are looking for outstanding books that are publishable upon sub-mission. Editors of the old school still enjoy working with writers to improve their work, but many do this only for writers whose books they've published before, not for new writers. Most other editors either do not have time or do not know how to edit!

As for agents, they simply don't have the time to edit manu-scripts, read the revisions, and then send them out. Nor can rep-utable agents charge editing, or reading, fees without being criticized for the practice. Some agents charge fees for reading or editing, but it's wise for writers to avoid them unless they come highly recommended. On occasion, Julia had paid people to read for her, but she couldn't afford to keep that up. Anyway, agents are supposed to *sell* manuscripts, not edit them. She'd begun referring hopeful writers to freelance editorial consultants, or book doctors.

Many writers benefit from going to workshops where they re-ceive advice from published writers and working editors, but because of time constraints and other considerations, this advice is often too general or too brief. Some writers are fortunate enough to live near a college that offers first-rate courses in writing for children. For years, writers have sought out Margaret "Bunny" Gable at the New School in New York City and profited from her thoughtful critiques of their work and from class reaction to it. (I could name a few published writers who took work already under contract to Bunny's class before they submitted it to their editors!)

For those without an appropriate school nearby, the Institute for Children's Literature (ICL) offers a correspondence course for children's writers. Each writer works with the same teacher during the course, and this close attention can result in great strides being made, especially by new writers. The teachers at ICL are usually writers themselves or former editors.

It is also possible to join or form a juvenile writers' group, where other aspiring writers offer support and suggestions. These groups vary in their usefulness. For one thing, too-kind friends hesitate to say anything negative. Blunt friends who openly declare their distaste for a manuscript crush the feelings of insecure writers. And writers themselves are not always aware of market trends and will encourage work that doesn't have a hope of being sold. Where else is a writer to turn for an objective judgment of his work?

If you're sick, you go to a doctor, who prescribes a course of treatment. If your manuscript is ailing, you can take it to a book doctor. The best way to find a good book doctor is the same as finding a good agent. Ask your friends or knowledgeable people whether they know of a reputable editorial consultant. Writers' magazines carry ads and are another source of names, but the quality of the people is impossible to judge that way. Still, if no other opportunity presents itself, you can answer those ads, being sure to stick to those who specify they have had editorial experience with juvenile books. Most editorial consultants will send you material about themselves and their fees. As you read their material, you can discover how clearly the book doctors themselves write. Is there more hyperbole than information? Do they give you a reasonable time frame for editing your work? How professional do they seem from the presentation? Do they provide reputable credentials? What do they promise to do for you? If they promise publication, be wary! Unfortunately, some editorial consultants, like some agents, are confidence men and women, promising much, relieving you of your money, and delivering nothing.

Since you are hiring your own editor, you have the right to telephone and ask questions. Again, this will give you an idea of whom you are dealing with. Editing falls into two types. The first is "structural," devoted to the "big picture," examining the strengths and weaknesses of plot, theme, characterization, pacing. Once the structure is solid, an editor might go through the manuscript again and "line edit," which is a fine-tuning, paying attention sentence by sentence to details—such as effective dialogue—with a combination of editing and rewriting. (Copyediting is yet another type of editorial procedure. However, it is done by the publisher *after* a book is under contract. A copy editor checks facts, consistency of spelling, capitalization, and punctuation, and marks up a manuscript for the printer, and her work should not be confused with line editing, though copy editors often line edit as well.)

Fees for structural and line editing vary with the book doctors, and estimates might range from $50 to $500, or possibly more, depending on the amount of work required. If, after discussing the fee with the book doctor, you regard it as too high, you can withdraw your manuscript. If the fee is satisfactory, you will likely have to pay in advance.

What should a critique consist of? The book doctor may ask the following questions: Are the characters believable and true to life? What is the conflict in the book? Does the book have a clear point of view? Does the book tell a compelling story, one that is not predictable? Do we learn something from each scene? Which scenes should be cut? A thoughtful critique will point out such problems as a faltering plotline, weak motivation, and poorly developed characters—all of which prevent a book from getting published.

As an agent, I've referred many new writers to book doctors, and the result was usually something like this: "Although the editor's comments were painful and disconcerting, he did an outstanding job of pointing out the areas that required revision and of providing suggestions for improvement. In short, his comments left me with definite insight into my writing."

Although a book doctor will suggest what might be done to strengthen a manuscript, upon reflection, a writer might come up with a different solution. According to Pamela D. Pollack, a former editor in the Simon & Schuster Children's Book Division and now the owner of an independent editorial service called Book Doctors, Ink: "The important thing is to find out where and why a story isn't working, and to do something about it. Whether or not a book doctor's advice leads to publication, it is enormously helpful to have such information. One lasting benefit is that you can apply what you have learned to other projects and use it to aid your development as a writer."

Having your own book doctor is like having your own piano teacher if you're an aspiring pianist. Even some published writers have used book doctors before sending their manuscripts to their regular editors. They want the material to be as close to perfect as possible. They are also prepared to have an editor ask them for yet another revision because different editors focus on different aspects of manuscripts, just as readers vary in their reactions.

Gus had faith in his work. He promised himself he'd follow up with Annabelle and Editor No. 4 the next day. And maybe, if Annabelle said she was returning his manuscript, he'd consult a book doctor instead of sending *Five by the Sea* to Editor No. 6.

Gus didn't have to call Annabelle. When the telephone rang the next morning, he was almost out the door on his way to work. After a moment of indecision, he picked up the receiver. It was Annabelle Jones of Upstart Books. He managed to say hello and then listened to her talk about how much she loved *Five by the Sea*. She wasn't ready to offer a contract yet, she went on, because the book had problems. Would he be willing to revise the manuscript and send it in once more?

Gus liked the sound of Annabelle's voice, but he didn't know what to say next, other than "Of course I'd be willing to take another stab at the manuscript." Then he asked, "Does this mean you want to buy the book?" He waited anxiously for her answer.

"I can't be sure now," Annabelle said. "We'd rather wait till we see the revised manuscript. We want to be certain you can make the necessary changes before we offer a contract."

Gus shook his head, then said, "I understand." But he didn't. He wondered why she was reluctant to make him an offer. He remembered hearing from experienced writer friends that editors used to buy books first, then ask for revisions.

Fortunately for Gus, Annabelle said she was returning the manuscript with an editorial letter. She didn't want to go into detail on the telephone, she said, but she wanted him to know again how much she admired his work.

Gus wanted to ask Annabelle specific questions about the manuscript, but he'd been warned by writer friends that it was a bad idea to ask for comments on the telephone. If an editor criticizes, say, the motivation of a character, the writer will reflexively defend his work and an argument could break out. Or he might find himself being so overeager that he agrees to make the change and later finds he doesn't want to. Being of the old school, Annabelle herself prefers to keep the author-editor relationship pigeonholed. The telephone is for good news, small talk, and making lunch dates.

Editorial suggestions belong in writing, she believes, especially if they are extensive. A letter spells matters out, page by page, with specifics. It becomes a record for both the editor and the writer. Often a writer needs time to absorb the news about a requested change. He can put a letter aside until he is ready to deal with it. Friends of Gus complained about getting editorial suggestions over the phone, revising the manuscript, and then being told by the forgetful editor that the changes were unnecessary! Other writers become so anxious they can remember nothing from the phone call and have to call back. Others scribble down notes so quickly they can't read them later.

On the other hand, after Gus hung up, he stared at the phone wondering what was wrong with his novel. He also wondered if he'd made a mistake, agreeing to revise without a contract. He shrugged. What choice did he have? He could withdraw the manuscript and send it elsewhere, but he'd already done that without success. At least Annabelle had mentioned the word *contract*, although it was not a sure thing. He considered informing the editors who still had not responded to his submission that Annabelle was interested in the novel. But why should he withdraw the manuscript from them? Suppose one of them made an offer ahead of Annabelle? He decided to let events take their course.

By the time he received Annabelle's letter and the edited manuscript a month later, Gus was ready to rewrite the entire book. He'd still had no word from Editors No. 3 and No. 5, and Editor No. 4 had declined the manuscript with a form letter. Gus imagined all the flaws Annabelle had found and held innumerable arguments in his head with her.

And then he read her letter. It was eight pages long, and she'd made a number of suggestions. More than anything else, she wanted him to reconsider the ages of some of the young people. Gus wasn't sure he wanted to change the ages, so he put down the letter and picked up the manuscript itself. Annabelle hadn't written much, but now and then she'd scrawled notes like "wonderful!" or "needs development" or "please clarify" in the margins. And "cut?" In spite of himself, Gus found he was caught up in her suggestions, and he began to pencil in some of the simple changes as he read and made most of the suggested deletions. Considering what he'd been thinking before he got the package, most of her suggestions would be a breeze to make, and he even wondered whether she had a valid point about changing the ages of the protagonists.

This story has a happy ending. Gus changed the ages and made the other revisions and sent in the manuscript. A month later, Annabelle called to say she wanted to buy it. She made a modest offer with a standard, she said, 10 percent royalty. This time Gus was ready. He told her to discuss the amount of the advance and the other terms of the contract with his new agent, Julia Saunders.

Before he'd begun revising, he'd been in touch with Julia and told her Annabelle was seriously interested in the novel. Julia had commiserated with him about the delay in getting a firm offer, but she said asking for revisions in advance of the contract is common practice if an editor has not previously worked with a writer. "The main thing," Julia had said, "is that she likes your book enough to want to work on it. She wants to present the best manuscript she can to the publication board so that she'll get approval to buy it—and that means you have to revise it first." Julia had agreed to handle the negotiations for him when Annabelle made an offer.

The time had come. Julia congratulated him on the offer and agreed to speak to Annabelle on his behalf. She also told Gus she was sending him a copy of her agency agreement. After being a happy creator, Gus had now become a businessman. During the next several days, he read over Julia's agency agreement and showed it to a few writer friends. They told him it was standard, similar in most respects to those they had. Some writers had no agreements with their agents, but they'd been writing for a long time, when a handshake sealed a deal. "It's not a ladies and gentlemen's business any longer," one writer said. "It's a businessman's business. Nobody trusts anybody, and putting terms in writing protects everybody."

Julia's agency agreement spelled out how long it would remain in effect, in this case until terminated by either party upon ninety days' written notice to the other. The ninety days would allow for pending submissions and other matters to be dealt with. The agreement went on to spell out that Julia would represent *all* Gus's books—no matter who sold them, writer or agent—but not his short stories, articles, or poetry unless agreed to otherwise. She would also control all subsidiary rights of books placed with a publisher either before or *after* termination of the agency agreement. She also promised not to sell any such rights without his agreement. Many writers don't realize that the rights do not automatically revert to the author if the author and agent agree to separate; the agent is still entitled to income from books she has represented.

Julia's compensation would be 15 percent for the sale of domestic or dramatic rights and 20 percent for the placement of foreign rights. The rate was higher for the latter because she had to employ subagents in foreign countries, and the higher rate covered their shares. She also expected to be reimbursed for certain expenses—such as for photocopying manuscripts and extra postage—none of which would be incurred without his permission. Unlike the established agents in big firms, Julia had no backlist of commissions to help her with office expenses.

In return, Julia would review Gus's manuscripts and assist in preparing them for submission. She would also negotiate and review all book contracts, collect and render payments in a timely fashion—usually within sixty days—and examine royalty statements. Gus had no objections, and he signed the agreement and returned it to Julia.

A few days later, Julia called Gus to tell him about the contract with Upstart Books, which she had just finished negotiating. "Annabelle would not agree to a larger advance," Julia said, "but she had agreed to an escalated royalty." She went on to explain that if *Five by the Sea* sold over 15,000 hardcover copies, the royalty would go up from 10 percent to 12-1/2 percent. Annabelle had also agreed to give Gus twenty-five free copies of his book instead of the standard ten. "Since this is your first book," Julia said, "I wasn't able to get much more for you, but you'll see the contract in a few weeks and can judge for yourself.

If there's anything you take exception to, please give me a call and we'll discuss it."

The rules may have changed, Gus realized, but the game wasn't over. He was getting his book published! It was time for some champagne. Tomorrow he would write to the editors who still had not returned his manuscript, informing them of the sale and asking that the manuscripts be returned to him in the SASEs. What a good feeling that was! He headed for the refrigerator and the bottle of champagne that had been in there since Annabelle's letter had arrived.

12

Splitting Hares

✦

CONTRACTS, COPYRIGHT, AND
WRITERS' RIGHTS

You must do the things you think you cannot do.
—Eleanor Roosevelt

Once you have an agreement with an editor, the amount of time it takes to receive a contract depends on the publishing house and the amount of bureaucracy entailed. At some houses, before an editor can get a contract for an author, she must fill out a form specifying the advance, royalty rate, number of book pages, quantity to be printed, cost of artwork, and so forth, and send it to the production department for an estimate of how much it will cost to manufacture the book. Then a business manager will take that figure and do a "profit-and-loss" analysis. (The names of these steps may differ from house to house, but the aim is the same: to find out whether it is financially feasible to publish the book.)

If the numbers work out, the editor will then fill out another form, a contract request, and give it to the editorial director for approval. If all goes well, the editorial director will then ask the publisher or president of the firm to approve the request. Finally, a month or so later (depending on whether all the principals are available), the request will reach the contracts department, where it will wait its turn to be typed. It then goes back to the editor for checking. Sometimes the typed contract circulates once again to the editorial director and publisher. One editor told me that contracts at her firm go through over thirty steps before the check due on signing is mailed, and the process takes about three months.

Luckily, being a small house, Upstart sped Gus's contract through the efficient contracts department in only a month. From there, it went to Julia, who reviewed it, negotiated a few changes, returned it to Upstart for revising, and then got it back. This time she sent four copies to Gus for his signature. Why four copies? One is for the contracts department, one for the editorial files, one for the agent, and one for the author.

Gus sat at his desk and went over the papers, clause by clause—there were forty. He stopped for a minute when he read that all monies were due and payable to Julia Saunders Literary Agency. Then he realized Julia would take out her commission and pass on the rest to him as per their agreement. This was a part of the writing game he knew little about. He had to trust Julia, but for the future, he was going to do some research on his own about contracts. He continued reading, using a ruler to keep his place as he perused the fine print.

Most of the fine print in a publisher's contract is what is called "boiler plate." It consists of standard legal protections for the publisher and spells out various percentages, amounts of money for various items, and a number of nonmonetary clauses. One such is the warranty clause, where the writer "warrants," or guarantees, that the book contains no "recipe, formula, or instruction" that may harm the user; this is especially important in books for children. Another clause asks the writer to warrant that the book contains no obscenity. Julia had told him about this one. She'd said definitions of obscenity differ so dramatically, it's best to ask that this clause be deleted. Gus saw it was crossed out on all four copies.

Gus read every word of the contract. He also had to warrant that he would not invade the privacy of a third person or state anything libelous about him. Defamation in writing is called libel; in speech it's termed slander. Because written material is often used in a spoken medium like TV, the term *defamation* is heard more often. Another reason not to use brand names, Gus thought. If he made a disparaging statement about a real product, it might result in a lawsuit.

He paused at the permissions clause. He had to pay the fees in advance of publication for material requiring permission, such as songs and poetry. He called Julia. "In advance?" he cried. "Sorry," she said, "but publishers no longer will lay out the money and deduct it from your royalties. You have to pay for everything up front. Also, when the book is published," she continued, "you can order copies at your author's discount, but you'll have to pay on delivery. Publishers are afraid they won't collect." Gus hung up the phone. He saw that even with an agent, he couldn't fight all the battles. Maybe later, when he was rich and famous. If he ever got there! At this rate, every move he made cost him money!

Under the copyright law, he knew that as a writer he owned his creation, or intellectual property. Written material copyrighted before 1978, when the current law was put into effect, was protected by copyright for twenty-eight years, with the right of renewal for another twenty-eight, for a total of a maximum of fifty-six years. The 1978 law extended the renewal term to forty-seven years, for a total of seventy-five years. More recently, in 1998, Congress voted to extend the copyright term another twenty years. Along with authors and songwriters, corporations like Disney fought to protect characters like Mickey Mouse, which was scheduled to enter the public domain in 2000. Therefore, in general, works published more than ninety-five years ago may be in the public domain; that is, they are no longer protected by copyright unless the author has been dead for fewer than seventy years. In Gus's case, his work will be protected for ninety-five years after his death.

Gus is entitled to payment for any reuse of his work. Julia had negotiated these rights, granting some to Upstart and retaining others for herself to sell. Gus decided at last that the following clauses concerned him most.

Upstart Books had bought North American English-language rights to the novel. That meant Julia was free to sell rights to the book in the rest of the world. These are known as territorial rights.

After 1992, many of the cosmodemonic publishers began to insist on buying *world* English-language rights. Foreigners owned so many American publishers that the business had become global, multinational. It made sense for a German, British, or Australian owner to have the world English-language rights to a property, and it would offer more money for them. It was more profitable for an "American" publisher to sell the books in the rest of the English-speaking world than to sell rights to a British publisher, which would then be entitled to sell English-language books in the European Economic Community because of an agreement made allowing this in 1992. Being a small, privately held publisher, Upstart worked in the traditional way. Using subagents she employed in various countries, Julia would try to sell British (English-language) and other foreign (translation) rights, and Gus would keep a larger percentage of the money received on those sales.

Gus sped over that part. He wasn't interested in global politics. Then he found what he wanted: the advance. There it was: Upstart agreed to pay $4,000 in advance of publication. The advance was split so that half would be paid on signing of the contract and the other half on delivery of an acceptable manuscript. Gus wondered about that and made a note to ask Julia for clarification. He'd already delivered a manuscript Annabelle had thought was publishable. Didn't that make it acceptable?

Gus studied the royalty schedule next: He was to receive 10 percent of the cover price of his book. He knew his $4,000 advance would come out of the royalties, so the publisher had to bring in $40,000 in retail sales before he was entitled to receive any more money. He did some quick arithmetic. If his book sold for $15.00, he would receive $1.50 per copy; the publisher would then have to sell 2,667 copies before the advance was "earned out" and he would receive more money. This deal, he knew, was preferable to receiving a percentage of the "amount received" by the publisher. The amount received is often based on half the cover price, because of discounts to various buyers. Buried in the contract were other royalty amounts based on different kinds of sales, such as export sales, special sales, book club sales, and so on.

Julia was aware of those, but most were boiler plate items she didn't regard as important enough to dispute. She had tried to rework the "book fair" special-sales clause, where the amount the author received was based on a small percentage of the amount received by the publisher. A writer could see 25,000 copies of his book sold to a book fair enterprise and then receive only a little over $1,000 himself. Annabelle had refused to change the clause because publishers rarely make much money on these deals either. Julia told Gus she had no way of getting more money for him in this case.

An important part of the juvenile market, book fair sales—and other special sales—are made with the understanding that the books are not returnable. It is a cash sale, so to speak, and favorable reduced royalty terms are extended to firms like Scholastic and Troll, among others, which run book fairs on a national level. The firms buy large quantities and put their own prices on their editions' covers. Local book fairs also discount the cover prices of books, but the royalty may not change. Book fairs are usually held in schools, where books, mostly paperbacks, are sold to the children themselves at bargain prices. This system works to everyone's advantage, it is said, because the children can afford to buy their own books, and it's a way for an author to begin building word-of-mouth publicity. Gus wondered why the author has to pay for this kind of publicity, then suppressed the thought. He continued reading.

Julia and Annabelle had worked out how income from the various subsidiary rights would be divided between the publisher and the author. Subsidiary rights include the following: *British publication*, in English, including the EEC; *foreign-language translations*; *trade paperback*; *mass-market paperback*; *first serial*, publication in magazines and newspapers (before the book is published); *second serial*, publication in periodicals (after the book is published); *textbook*; *large print*; *anthologies*; *book club*; *performance* (motion pictures, plays, TV, radio, etc.); *computer software*; *electronic*; and "all other rights not specifically mentioned."

The income from sales of subsidiary rights is divided between the publisher and the author, and the "splits" vary. Unlike most of the cosmodemonic publishers, Upstart Books does not have its own mass-market paperback line, so the subsidiary rights manager will try to sell those rights to one of the houses that does. Upstart will divide the income with Gus, who will get 60 percent of the amount. If one of the cosmodemonic houses had bought *Five by the Sea*, it would have offered a "hard/soft deal," meaning it would have paid a higher advance to get the rights to the mass-market paperback. Gus would also have kept all the royalty income because he would not be sharing it with Upstart or another publisher.

As it turned out, that would be the case with the trade paperback edition. Upstart could publish *Five by the Sea* as a trade paperback and pay Gus a 7 percent royalty. Gus wondered about that 7 percent. He called Julia and asked for an explanation. "You mean," Gus said, "that by changing the quality of the cardboard used for the cover, Upstart gets away with paying me a 7 percent royalty? The inside is exactly the same as the hardcover edition." Julia agreed that the trade paper royalty was low, but publishers' margins on paperbacks are also low, because the retail price is less while it still costs a substantial amount for paper, printing, and binding; less money is made per book. Perhaps at a future date she might get him 8 percent, but 7 percent was a good rate these days, Julia said. Many publishers were paying only 6 percent. One editor she knew had refused to go up to 8 on another contract, saying it was "giving up the store."

Gus found himself getting more bewildered as he read through the contract. He found the reversion-of-rights clause, which he'd heard was important. If his book went out of print, and another publisher wanted to reissue it, he had to have the rights returned to him by the original publisher before he could publish the book elsewhere. Some publishers will not revert rights if any edition is in print anywhere. Gus saw that Upstart had modified this clause so that it referred only to English-language rights. He also noted that a typewritten addition said Upstart had up to three years to sell the various rights; after that, they reverted to him. Gus was glad he had an agent, but he vowed to read up on contracts and pay closer attention at writers' conferences to the contract negotiation seminars. Someday his contracts would be even more complicated and the advances larger (he hoped). He wanted to be prepared for that.

What should a writer do who has no agent? Some writers seek out their family attorneys, but this isn't always a good idea because publishing law is a specialty that's not completely understood by people who practice other forms of law. Still, a writer may feel more comfortable having a lawyer's advice, as she would before signing any contract. For a fee, attorneys who deal in publishing law will read and negotiate a contract for a writer. Some professional groups like the National Writers Union (NWU), and the American Society of Journalists and Authors (ASJA) offer contract training sessions. The Society of Children's Book Writers and Illustrators has an informative brochure about contracts, and a number of books on the subject are available. A writer can also ask colleagues for their recommendations, keeping in mind that since she is dealing with a reputable, established publisher, the firm is not out to cheat her, legally speaking. Naturally, the publisher wants the best deal possible, and so does the author. But the author also needs publishing credits, so this is not the time to be striking a blow for writers' rights, except, perhaps, in the following cases.

For the last decade or so, publishers have included one or more clauses relating to electronic rights in contracts. This is a complex and controversial issue. (Keep in mind that dramatic or *perfor-*

mance rights for movies and TV are included separately in the list of subsidiary rights and do not constitute "electronic rights" as used here.)

As publishers grew bigger, many formed their own divisions to handle audio (tape recordings) and computer disk versions of the material under contract. This, obviously, is a growing and lucrative field. Because of mergers and acquisitions, the cosmodemonic houses include divisions that can exploit the rights acquired in the editorial departments. They call this "synergy," and as a phenomenon it has had varying degrees of success within the corporations.

An "electronic version" means any method of copying a work (or a portion of it)—whether as a recording, for storage in a database, retrieval, broadcast, or any other transmission—that uses an electronic, electromagnetic, analog, or digital signal. This includes, but is not limited to, magnetic tape, floppy disks, laser disks, integrated circuit chips, CD-ROM, and methods not yet devised! In short, your book might end up on a CD-ROM. Bill Gates's book, *The Road Ahead,* came with a CD-ROM tucked into it, for example. That CD-ROM was probably an exercise of the electronic rights granted to the publisher—which Bill Gates, being heavily invested in the software business, is eager to see happen more often.

Since so much entertainment is stored electronically on tape, disk, and CD-ROM, electronic rights can be a gold mine for the proprietor, and writers and agents must defend their right to negotiate electronic rights. Several years ago, Random House, for example, declared that electronic rights are not negotiable; they must remain with the publisher. As a consequence, a number of writers, including Julia Child and Jacques Pepin, left Random House. Other publishers either split the rights fifty-fifty or say they will "negotiate them in good faith" when the time comes to sell those rights. If a publisher insists on retaining electronic rights, the latter is probably the best way to proceed for now. Even better is for the author or agent to retain the rights, though most authors do not know where or how to sell those rights to their best advantage.

The right to photocopy a work is not included in most book publishing contracts, but the ease and low cost of photocopying and scanning led to professional concern about this particular electronic right. First, writers learned that their work was often illegally copied for use in classrooms and other public places. Then, as periodicals went on-line, writers discovered their works were made accessible to viewers on the Internet through various providers. The NWU, ASJA, the Authors Guild, and other writers' organizations immediately cried "Foul!" Through the united efforts of these organizations and literary agencies, the copyright law was enforced so that photocopiers would pay fees for the right to make copies of written works for corporations, schools, universities, and others. The Authors Registry was formed to handle the licensing and bookkeeping for nearly every important writers' group and almost one hundred literary agencies, whose members and clients total more than fifty thousand. The Registry collects and pays out the accumulated amounts for photocopy and electronic use. For the first time, writers are seeing income from the photocopying of their material.

The struggle for equity in regard to on-line electronic rights has also had success. The president of the NWU, Jonathan Tasini, and six other writers sued the *New York Times* and others because the *Times* would not pay freelance writers fees for the use of their articles in its on-line version of the paper. Tasini and the other writers lost the case in 1998, but it was appealed, and in September 1999, the Second Court of Appeals reversed the federal district court decision—to the joy of all writers, and especially to those who write for magazines and newspapers. The new ruling stated that the reuse of freelance work on databases (such as Nexis) and CD-ROMs without the author's express permission constitutes copyright infringement. Also, both parties must sign a contract granting permission for additional uses of material. However, that is not the end of the story. The *New York Times* has since taken the case to the U.S. Supreme Court for a final opinion.

Writers are fortunate that their agents and organizations are fighting for an equitable distribution of monies. Electronic publishing is such a new area that it's safe to say many don't understand it yet. It is all the more important for writers to band together in organizations that will look out for them and to remain current by reading newsletters, newspapers, and other professional material. The ASJA has a free on-line service called Contracts Watch (www.asja.org), which keeps a running document on electronic and other rights. In one article, Alexandra Cantor Owens, executive director of ASJA, pointed out, for example, that Bantam Books was changing its standard offer for a *Star Trek* TV tie-in novel from advance-plus-royalties to flat fee. This led to protests by writers and writers' organizations. Such battles go on all the time, and writers must remain vigilant or else they will become simply vendors and not creators of valuable and original intellectual property.

The writer or artist remains the creator, the source, of material that publishers and filmmakers desperately desire. Intellectual properties are among the major exports of the United States. Consider how much income Shakespeare's works still generate—and he's been dead for centuries! It's unfortunate that his heirs do not benefit from this, but the fact that intellectual property comes into the public domain eventually enriches readers (and publishers) while it impoverishes the heirs.

In future struggles, writers' organizations and literary agents will be on the side of the authors, and it's in the interest of all writers to support them. It is also in the long-term interest of publishers, Owens said, because "when talented, skillful, authoritative, professional writers encounter deteriorating work conditions and diminished career prospects, they move on. . . . Chasing away the most reliable providers of content is a dumb way to grow a business that relies on content."

So, writer, be aware!

13

The Tail End

✦

YOUR PART IN THE
PRODUCTION PROCESS

*True ease in writing
comes from art, not chance,
As those move easiest
who have learned to dance. —Alexander Pope*

After the contract for *Five by the Sea* had been signed, Gus did one more revision for Annabelle and received the second half of his advance, which was due on the delivery of an acceptable manuscript. This is a time-honored practice, where the publisher delays payment until the editor is satisfied the author has made all the required revisions. Gus had read that *acceptable* can be an ambiguous term, but, in essence, it means that the editor judges the manuscript to be satisfactory.

Meanwhile, Gus had begun to work on another book, a biography of E. B. White, the author of *Charlotte's Web* and other books for children and adults. Before starting to work, he had gone to the library and checked *Children's Books in Print,* which lists books by title, author, and subject. He checked the library database and found no listing of a juvenile book on White. Nor had he seen any mention of one in any of the publishers' catalogs he'd read on the Internet. It seemed the field was clear, so after he'd done his research, he'd written a summary, an outline, and three chapters and turned them over to his agent, Julia Saunders. As a courtesy, Julia had already offered the book to Annabelle, who had declined it since her firm did little or no nonfiction. Gus wanted to keep up his writing momentum, but he wasn't sure whether he should finish the E. B. White biography before it was sold or work on a new novel.

Gus had faith in the E. B. White idea, and he wanted to continue with his research and writing while he was still enthusiastic. When (not if) the book was sold, he thought, he'd be that much farther ahead with it. He'd already asked Annabelle if Upstart would be interested in a new novel, but she'd said Upstart couldn't take on another book from him until they'd seen how the first one sold.

Gus was puzzled. Wasn't he supposed to be "building a career"? He telephoned Julia and asked her advice. "Publishers are reluctant to take risks on unknown or little-known writers these days," she said. "Put aside the E. B. White manuscript and work on a new novel. I can only sell finished novels," she told him. "Meanwhile, the White proposal is in shape for submitting, so we should send it out now."

Gus took a long walk and pondered the advice he'd received. He wanted to write and get published. He'd had one book accepted by a publisher who didn't seem eager to have a second one from him. His agent had told him to write that second book anyway. Although she was sending the nonfiction book out, she wasn't all that excited about it. Was he supposed to spend the next year writing a book that no one might want?

Julia's advice was consistent with that from agent George Nicholson, who told me that the best way for a new writer to build a career is to set limits on what he wants to publish.

Hopeful writers send me samples of all their work, from picture books to encyclopedic nonfiction works. I tell them to concentrate on one genre and become so good at it that I can place their work with a publisher. Once they've become established, they can work in other genres.

I have given up sending out picture books for writers and suggest they do it themselves. The market is tight, and marketing picture books is too time-consuming for me with my small staff. I will negotiate any sales, of course, because it's my job to protect the writer and get her a good contract.

It's also probably a good idea for a writer to have more than one publisher, but each publisher should focus on one kind of book. For a prolific writer, it would be ideal to have one house to do picture books, another nonfiction, and a third for fiction exclusively.

The writer must write whether her books sell or not. She

must also take responsibility for her career, because as an agent I can only recommend an action, not enforce it.

At Upstart Books, meanwhile, it was time to put the *Five by the Sea* manuscript into production. Like most writers, Gus was unaware of what happens at a publishing house after it deems a manuscript acceptable. The wheels have begun rolling, and people are getting into gear to work on the manuscript and see it through a long, unwieldy process that takes about nine months for the finished book to be produced.

Although it's true that most houses request manuscripts on disk, some hardcover houses still follow the traditional practice of working directly from hard copy—or, as it still is called, a manuscript. The writer should check his contract to see exactly what the publisher expects. Most houses want a disk and a manuscript. A word count for the entire book printed on the title page can be useful, and a character count for each chapter will be even more useful, but it's not necessary for the writer to furnish this information.

After Gus turned in his third revision, Annabelle read it, lead pencil in hand. She made a few comments here and there, corrected some spelling, and asked a few questions, which Gus could answer later on in the publishing process. She was pleased with the manuscript. Gus was a good writer, and she was glad to have him on her list.

The steps that follow are essentially the same for all kinds of books. Picture books have an added step in that the art is proofed, and the color proofs corrected, during the production process. Writers do not get involved in this stage, but some top-selling illustrators may be invited to watch the book on press and make color adjustments.

While the book was fresh in her memory, Annabelle drafted selling copy. She had learned this was the best time to write the copy that would be the basis for all the written material about the book which would appear during its lifetime, in the publisher's catalog, on jacket flaps, in fact sheets to be distributed to other departments, and possibly in ads—if there were any. Sometimes lazy reviewers reprinted the flap copy, hoping to pass it off as a review. Annabelle smiled. That was so good for the book when it happened!

Using the present tense and keeping proper names to a minimum, she finished summarizing the plot. Then she considered her final paragraph. Publishers used the same adjectives over and over, and she tried not to use the same ones twice on the same list. She remembered the time, years ago, when someone had proposed taping up a sheet of paper so editors and assistants could declare dibs on the adjectives they'd used in the current season's copy; no one else would be allowed to use an adjective on the list. *Moving* was always good, as was *poignant*. Maybe *touching*? She reached for her dictionary of synonyms, perused the entries (*pathetic*? no! *affecting*? too vague), and settled on *moving*.

Since *Five by the Sea* is a young adult, or teen, novel, for readers over twelve, it will not have interior art. Had it been a middle-grade book, the art director might have suggested possible illustrators to do six or eight black-and-white drawings and the jacket. After a brief conference with Annabelle, one would have been selected. Illustrators often receive a portion of the royalties, usually 1 or 2 percent. This is negotiated at the time the book is signed up, and authors receive lower royalties as a consequence.

Annabelle instructed Joanna, her assistant, to transmit *Five by the Sea* to production, and in a note gave Joanna the information she would need for the transmittal form. This included an estimate of how many pages the book would run; the trim size (the size of the page); the kind of binding; the quantity to be printed and bound; the publication date; and other details. She also summarized the plot in two sentences and suggested how the book should look—she wanted it to have a serious and contemporary appearance, which matched the text.

She asked Joanna to write copy about the author, based on the biographical questionnaire Gus had returned with the contract several months earlier. Joanna had kept a copy of the questionnaire on file and sent the original, along with the photo of himself Gus had provided, to the publicity department. Staff members would refer to it when writing biographical copy for their own purposes.

Joanna got to work on *Five by the Sea*. Luckily, all concerned were satisfied with this title. Otherwise, production would be held up until a final title was chosen because the front matter could not be prepared or a jacket assigned to an artist. Joanna found the biographical questionnaire and wrote Gus's bio. Since this was Gus's first book, she emphasized his hometown, his education, and where he lived now. These are selling points for the book; publishers hope sentiment will cause booksellers to order books based on where the author might have friends or colleagues interested in buying his book.

Joanna then retyped Annabelle's draft of the copy into the proper format for the jacket, which included the price, the ISBN number (see below), age and grade codes, the publisher's name and address, and the line required by law, "Printed in the U.S.A." She gave it to Annabelle for perusal, along with the bio. If Annabelle was satisfied, the flap copy would go to the editorial director for her approval.

Joanna went on to prepare the front matter for the book, which included a half title, title page, copyright, and dedication. When the author has titled the chapters, a contents page is also included, which Joanna would prepare if the author had neglected to do it. Front matter for a nonfiction book may be more elaborate. All editors and designers refer to the *Chicago Manual*, *Words into Type*, or *Bookmaking* when they have questions about the order in which the various components should appear.

In general, the first page is the half title: the title of the book— no subtitle, no author, no publisher. Years ago, booksellers would stack unbound books in their shops and identify them by the half titles, which also protected the insides of the books from being damaged. Customers would take the books elsewhere for binding.

Page 2 is usually a blank or it may be an "ad card" (a list of other books by the same author in chronological order). If it contains an illustration or map, it is called a frontispiece.

Facing the second page is the title page, which carries the *official* title (and subtitle, if there is one) of the book, the names of the author and illustrator, and the name and location of the publisher.

The copyright page comes next, on the reverse, or verso, of the title page. The book contract specifies the name in which the book will be copyrighted, and writers must make sure it's specified properly when they review their contracts. In addition to the copyright notice and a statement "reserving all rights," the copyright page carries the full address of the publisher, a line indicating the edition, and the Library of Congress Cataloging in Publication (CIP) notice. The CIP is prepared at the Library of Congress and is the official catalog card used in the Library of Congress and at many other libraries. The Dewey decimal system number is also on the card.

The ISBN, or International Standard Book Number, appears on the copyright page as well. This is the order number, which was assigned to the book when the contract was final. The first digit is usually 0, which stands for "English language"; the next three or four indicate the publisher; the next group is the number of the book itself; and the last is a checking number. The title and copyright pages are like an identity card; each book must have one for legal protection as well as identification.

Sometimes the name of the book designer appears on the copyright page—often the only person other than the author and illustrator who takes credit for her work. Editors of hardcover books remain anonymous by tradition, as do all the other people who have made the book possible. Were a list of credits to be published in the book, it would not be so long as those on movies from Hollywood, but it would be substantial—especially if it included the delivery person from the local coffee shop.

If there's enough room, the dedication will appear on the first right-hand page after the copyright notice. Again, "Everybody wants to get into the act," but this time it's the writers who sometimes go overboard on the dedication page, remembering every person they've ever known, perhaps afraid they'll never have a chance to dedicate a book to someone again! Books come from a clerical and aristocratic tradition, where restraint is favored, and that applies to the dedication.

If the book has chapter titles, a table of contents, which should be prepared by the writer, comes on the next right-hand page. Sometimes a writer will want to open his book with a quotation, or epigraph. It goes on a right-hand page after the dedication, if space permits, with the contents page afterward.

A second half title or a part title may appear before the text proper begins. Part titles are necessary when a book is broken into parts; for example, "Part One: The Family Together." If there's no part title, a second half title can be inserted if the designer needs to fill a page. Designers choose a typeface and calculate the size, number of lines per page, and so on to ensure that all the pages will be utilized, leaving no blanks, or pages without type, at the front or back of the book.

In a nonfiction book, there may be other matter, such as a preface, foreword, author's note, or introduction. A preface is often an aside on the text itself, perhaps discussing research methods or giving thanks to people who helped with the book. This is the place to thank people, instead of on the dedication page. Or a brief acknowledgments page can be inserted. Both of these elements may come before the contents page; if they do they should not be listed in the contents. A foreword is an essay written by someone other than the author, perhaps to lend credibility to the book or to elucidate it in some way. An introduction is by the author and is an integral part of the text.

The front matter is sometimes numbered with Roman numerals, which are usually not printed in novels, though they can be seen in textbooks. If there's a part title, the two pages before the first text page are Arabic number 1 and Arabic number 2, because by tradition a part title and verso are considered part of the text. In some books, the counting begins with Arabic numerals in the front matter, so that the first page of text might carry a folio (page number) reading 7 or 9.

The term *back matter* applies primarily to nonfiction, and the contents page might list the following as part of the back matter: appendix, glossary, source notes, bibliography, and, last of all, the index, because it is not prepared until the page proof stage of the production process.

The short biography of the author and illustrator at the end of the book is not considered an integral part of the book—the author did not write it; the editor did. It carries no page number and is not listed in the contents.

After Annabelle and the editorial director approved the flap copy and bio, Joanna retyped the bio, this time with the heading "About the Author." She placed it at the end of the manuscript, with a blank piece of paper behind it for protection. Manuscripts take a beating as they make their way through the production process. Many people handle them, and the last page, if not shielded, gets dirty and torn. Joanna added the author's photo and photo credit to the bundle and gave it to Annabelle for a last look. All the necessary pieces were in place. Annabelle and Joanna triumphantly passed on the manuscript and a duplicate copy to the next person who would handle it, the managing editor.

If there is one person who knows everything in an editorial department, it is the managing editor. Although the duties vary at each publishing house, usually the managing editor is in charge of trafficking the manuscript; that is, she makes sure the manuscript and the ancillary parts are complete and then sends it on to the different departments that will work on it, in this case the copy-editing and design departments. The managing editor keeps track of the schedule and deadlines and makes sure each person does his part on time. Once a week she chairs a production meeting, where editors, assistants, art director, designers, copy editors, and others convene to discuss the schedules for the various books.

While the original manuscript is being copyedited, a designer will begin her work with the duplicate.

The chief of copyediting decided to send *Five by the Sea* to a freelance copy editor, Allen Gale. Allen works at home, where he has a small but thorough collection of reference books. He refers to them often while working on the manuscript and flap copy. Allen is a graduate of a well-known university, where he majored in Latin, of all things. He loves facts and is a storehouse of information. He had once astounded everyone at a meeting where a rebus book was discussed. *"Rebus,"* he'd said, "is the ablative plural of the Latin *res,* or 'thing.'" Allen had taught for a while, but teaching didn't suit him because he preferred to work alone. Copyediting makes use of his education and knowledge, and he feels part of a noble tradition. He's also a crackerjack speller. As he works, he keeps an alphabetical list of proper names and unusual spellings on a separate piece of paper called a style sheet, which will later go to the proofreader for his reference. Allen will also rewrite ungrammatical passages, correct misspellings, and revise punctuation so it conforms to house style.

English grammar and spelling keep changing, but the style should be uniform in a given book. Therefore, each publisher has a list of house rules, and the copy editor ensures that the book conforms to it. For example, some houses prefer the serial comma—the comma before *and* in a list of items, as in: "baseball, bat, and glove"—and others don't use it. Years ago, "closed" punctuation was favored; today an "open" style is preferred, with fewer punctuation marks, especially after short adverbial phrases at the beginnings of sentences. A house rule may dictate that commas be inserted only if the phrase is longer than five words—or eight.

Spellings can be tricky as well, especially of ordinary words, which is why copy editors use the latest edition of the dictionary. Not so long ago *backseat* and *backyard* were each two words; the spelling checker on my word processor says *backseat* is still two words, but Webster's tenth edition says it's one, as is *backyard*. Would anyone but a copy editor notice that in Leo Tolstoy's *War and Peace* (translated by Constance Garnett) *cannonball* is sometimes one word, sometimes two? They didn't have style sheets in those days, but custom today dictates that inconsistent spelling, typographical errors, and misspellings that may distract the reader must not pass uncorrected.

Copy editors are also supposed to doubt all facts in a book and to check each one. Sometimes the simplest, most obvious errors occur, as when I copyedited a picture book that mentioned "President Stonewall Jackson" and left it that way. It is not a good idea to cut costs by having the person who copyedited a book proofread it; errors are perpetuated. Luckily, one of the sales reps caught the gaffe while the book was still in proofs, and the error was fixed. The author had made the mistake, and the editor and copy editor hadn't noticed because it *seemed* correct; type lends legitimacy. Much more serious is the error that makes its way into a finished book—and then into a review. Some reviewers pay more attention to errors than to content and will effectively kill a book with too many errors in it.

✦ Frequently Used Proofreader's Marks ✦

Editors, copy editors, and proofreaders use the following marks to indicate changes to be made in a manuscript or proof. Changes in a manuscript are written directly in the body of the text, while the proofreader's written changes go in the margins of the proofs, with marks placed in the text to indicate where the changes are to be made. Editors use pencil—not pen—because nobody's perfect, and the other people use different colors to indicate which person suggested the changes. Authors should also use pencil.

OK/⟨?⟩	Query to author; i.e., is this change all right with you?
stet	Leave the material as written (dots placed under words show which material is meant)
ℓ/	Delete (a letter, word, phrase, sentence)
Cap	a, set as capital letter(s)
lc	X, set as lowercase letter(s)
⟨Feb.⟩	Word (or number) should be spelled out
#	Add space (either between words or lines)
∧	Insert a word, phrase, letter, etc., here
ital	Set underlined material in italic type
rom	Set circled material in ⟨roman⟩ type
⊙	Set a period
⌃	Set a comma

$\frac{1}{M}$	Set a one-em dash (the width of the letter M)
$\frac{1}{N}$	Set a one-en dash (half the width of a one-em dash, used to indicate a range of numbers or dates, as in 1863$\frac{1}{N}$1901)
=	Set a hyphen, as in jewel-like
¶	Begin a new paragraph here
run in	Run text together without a paragraph break

A more complete list of marks can be found in most dictionaries.

As he works, Allen uses proofreader's marks on the manuscript because it is the language publishers and printers use to convey instructions precisely. It's easy enough to learn, and writers should teach themselves the basic marks so they'll understand the changes made in their copyedited manuscripts. Allen writes directly in the body of the text when he makes his corrections in brown pencil and puts his queries on colored slips of paper attached to the manuscript.

When Allen completed his work on *Five by the Sea*, he sent the manuscript back to the chief of copyediting, who forwarded it to Annabelle. She reviewed it a final time and asked Joanna to send it to the author. Gus was given two weeks to answer Annabelle's final editorial queries as well as the copy editor's. Annabelle had asked him to use a colored pencil (not brown) and to strike through (not erase) any changes he didn't agree with, and to answer editorial queries on the colored slips of paper, which he should not tear off. He didn't have to agree to every suggestion. *The book is, ultimately, the author's work, and he has the final word, even when he's wrong.* This is known as poetic license. One bestselling writer wanted the sun to set in the Atlantic Ocean east of Long Island, and no argument would persuade her to change it.

According to *Dear Genius: The Letters of Ursula Nordstrom,* collected and edited by Leonard S. Marcus, Nordstrom handled a change she wanted to make in the galleys for *The Sign on Rosie's Door* (1960) by writing to Maurice Sendak:

> *I had an idea about that one line "Everybody shook their heads yes"—which was the one that we left even though it wasn't grammatical. I tried to call you . . . to ask would it be OK with you if we changed it to "Everybody nodded." That means everybody shook their heads yes but it will protect you and your book and your ever-loving cotton-picking publishers from being ostracised by the English teachers of this here great and gorgeous country with its locked-in goodness. Well, since I couldn't get you on the phone I made this slight change but if it sends you screaming out into the street we can go back to the other.*

Nordstrom was in a hurry to get those galleys back to the production department because the book was on a schedule and all deadlines had to be met. Each deadline involves many people: The compositor has scheduled a time to set the type for the book, and far off in the distance, the bookbinder is waiting. Some houses do composition on their own computers in the production department, but schedules are still important. After Gus returned the copyedited manuscript, it would take a few more weeks before he saw the next stage of production, galley proofs.

Meanwhile, in the art department, the art director, who assigns books to freelance illustrators and supervises the design staff, had given the duplicate manuscript to a book designer for a *cast off*, or *character count*. The average children's novel of 160 pages may contain over a quarter of a million characters. (A character is each letter, numeral, space, or punctuation mark in the manuscript.) The designer chose an appropriate typeface and size to fill the number of pages Annabelle had asked for.

In some houses, the display type for the title page and chapter headings will not be selected until after the jacket art is in. Ideally, the display type on the jacket, which complements the artwork, is used inside the book as well for a uniform, custom appearance. Other houses work more quickly and don't care whether the jacket type and title page type are the same.

To make sure that the book will look attractive, the designer may ask the compositor, the person who sets the type, to provide sample layouts showing how the chapter openings and text pages will look in the chosen typeface. Annabelle and the designer studied the layouts and sample pages to be sure the size of the type and the number of lines per page were right for the age of the reader. The younger the reader, for example, the larger the type and the fewer lines of type per page. The book was running long. Annabelle and the designer discussed the possibility of subtracting two pages from the front matter by printing the dedication on the copyright page. The alternative was to add more pages to the book (which would make it more expensive because of the extra paper) or use smaller type or less "leading" (the spaces between the lines).

When Annabelle was satisfied with the layouts, the designer marked up the copyedited manuscript with the type specifications. These specifications include such details as how much space should be left between the top of the page and the first line of each chapter ("sinkage"), how wide the margins and gutters (the center margin between the pages) should be, where the folios should be placed, the style of the running heads (or feet) on each page, and much more. (Running heads appear at the top of the pages, usually with the author's name or part title on the left-hand page and the book title or the chapter title on the right; when they are at the bottoms of pages, they are called running feet.) Printer's jargon is colorful and steeped in tradition. *Widows*, for example, are partial lines of type at the top of a page, and good bookmakers frown on them. *Orphans* are single words at the bottom of the page. Type can be adjusted to kill the widows and orphans.

Finally, the manuscript was ready for the production department to take charge. These are the people who select the printer and purchase the paper for all the books. An enormous amount of material flows through their department as they traffic manuscripts and all stages of proofs back and forth between compositors, printers, binders, and the editorial and design staff. If Gus's book went into a second printing, they would handle that too.

Five by the Sea went to the compositor at last. A few weeks later, the galleys arrived. (Technically speaking, these were not true galley proofs, which are long sheets of paper, not yet broken into pages. With computer typesetting, it's possible for the compositor to supply proofs broken into pages. These are called first pass by some, galleys by traditionalists.) The proofs were distributed to staff members, including Annabelle. She sent a set to Gus and asked him to return it in two weeks. She reminded him that this was the last chance he'd have to see his book in type before it was printed. He was allowed 10 percent of the composition cost as an allowance to pay for any further corrections; if he exceeded that amount, he'd be charged.

Gus didn't know exactly how many corrections he was allowed, but he was more concerned with publishing a good book than with money. Still, he worked carefully and kept the changes to a minimum. He was surprised at how authoritative his words looked now that they were in type. It also struck him that he'd read the book so often, it seemed boring. Was it any good? he wondered.

Meanwhile, the copyediting chief had sent the master, or main, set to a freelance proofreader, who would read it while comparing it to the original manuscript. Proofreaders mark each correction as either a printer's error, PE, or an editorial alteration,

EA, when the change is the result of a lapse in the editing or copyediting.

The proofread galleys went back to Annabelle, who had Joanna transfer Gus's changes to the master set, marking each one as an author alteration, or AA. Later, the printer would count up the AAs, and if Gus had exceeded his allowance, the amount would be deducted on his first royalty statement.

Over the next months, Annabelle and Joanna would be checking three more stages of proof: second pass (formerly called page proof); repros (reproduction proof, printed on coated paper so it can be photographed); and blues, or blueprints, made from the film to be used to print the book.

The blues come from the printer and are folded into book pages. This is the first time anyone has seen how the finished book will look as a unit. This step is especially important for illustrated books, since artwork or photographs and captions are in place along with the display type for the chapter headings. The house proofreader checks the blues not only for PEs but to see that all the pages are there and in the right order.

The blues go back to the printer. He exposes the film to a flexible metal sheet, which is treated with chemicals and placed on cylinders within the press. The entire book is printed quickly on immense sheets of paper. They go to the bookbinder by truck, where they are folded and gathered into signatures, or groups of pages, and then trimmed. The pages are sewn together and glued into cases, or bindings, which are usually made of thick cardboard covered with cloth and paper. (Paperbacks are not sewn but only glued into stiff paper covers.) Each book then gets dressed in a new jacket, which is folded and put on the books by hand.

The jacket had arrived at the bookbinder by a different route from the rest of the book, but work on it had begun months ago, at about the same time as the manuscript for *Five by the Sea* went into production. The jacket has its own schedule because it is printed at a different place from the text. Annabelle needed the jacket proofs for the sales conferences, and the deadlines were tight. (In the paperback world, cover proofs are needed at least six months before the books are shipped from the warehouse.)

Gus, of course, had no idea of the activity that had been going on at the publishing house during these months. His proposal for the E. B. White book was still making the rounds, and he'd been working on the second novel as Julia had advised him to do. He was thrilled when Annabelle at last sent him a copy of the finished book, and he sat down to examine it. Good jacket, intelligent flap copy, flattering photo of himself. He began to read the book. "Not bad, not bad at all," he said.

In her office, Annabelle opened a copy of *Five by the Sea* and stood it on a bookshelf next to the other titles on the current list.

"Terrific jacket," Joanna said.

Annabelle nodded and went back to her desk and picked up a manuscript. "This one is ready for production. Would you do the transmittal?" She handed the manuscript to Joanna.

"This business is never boring, is it?" Joanna said.

"Each book, each writer, each journey to publication is different," said Annabelle. "When we start publishing books as if they were as interchangeable as potato chips, then the game will be over." She sat down. "Meanwhile, we're lucky to be publishing children's books the old-fashioned way. With hard work and love."

14

Bunny Goes to Market

◆

PUBLICITY AND PROMOTION

Courage is very important. Like a muscle, it is strengthened by use. —Ruth Gordon

Gus was not aware of all the marketing that had taken place well before he held the finished copy of his book. As you may remember, Annabelle, his editor, had written selling copy for the catalog months earlier, when she'd transmitted *Five by the Sea* to production. Versions of this copy were used on the jacket flap and on the fact, or tip, sheets, which would be given to the sales reps when the book was discussed at the sales conferences in the months ahead.

After the selling copy had been written, work began on the jacket for the book. The dust jacket (for hardcovers) or cover (for paperbacks) is not the writer's responsibility but the publisher's. The publisher can put whatever it likes on the jacket or cover, be-cause a jacket not only protects the book but is an advertisement for it, thus part of the marketing program. The artwork lends value to the book and is often copyrighted separately from the text. According to a 1998 survey cosponsored by *Publishers Weekly* and BookExpo America, fifty-seven out of one hundred teenage book buyers said the book jacket is the single greatest influence on their choice of a book.

Once all the manuscripts were in production, Annabelle and the other editors, the art director, assistants, and designers attended a meeting to discuss the jackets for the current list. Before the meeting, Joanna, Annabelle's assistant, had gone through yet another duplicate copy of Gus's manuscript to look for scenes that might be illustrated. Her criteria included showing the principal characters in action that reflected the theme and spirit of the book. She and Annabelle discussed the six possibilities for *Five by the Sea* and chose three to present to the art director.

Hardcover editors favor jackets that reflect the theme of a book, while paperback editors want high action and emotion appealing to readers' fantasies. For example, the hardcover jacket art for *The Night Swimmers* by Betsy Byars showed a pensive young girl, with two boys (her brothers) and a swimming pool in the distance behind her, and, on the verso, a seated man playing a guitar. Painted by Troy Howell, it suited the book perfectly. The book was about a motherless girl whose insouciant country singer father had put her in charge of her younger brothers, who were causing difficulties too serious for her to handle. The swimming pool belonged to the man next door. When the jacket was shown to the reps at the presales conference, they screamed,

"Downer!" "Change it!" In those days, editors prevailed over sales and marketing people, so the jacket remained as it was. The editors were therefore doubly pleased when the book with the downer jacket won the American Book Award in 1981. When the paperback came out, the cover emphasized cheerful children at a swimming pool. That cover was also a fair, if incomplete, representation of the story, but it emphasized good times over sad times, in the mistaken belief that children don't like to read sad books. Howell's interior art was preserved, but, obviously, the cover no longer matched his style. This often happens because the paperback world demands covers with an instant appeal for the mass-market rack.

At the jacket meeting where Gus's book was discussed, editors and the art director talked over ideas and selected the scenes to feature. After the meeting, Joanna typed up a jacket request for *Five by the Sea,* including copyedited copy for the title, author, ISBN, et cetera, and then provided a duplicate manuscript for the jacket artist to read. She described the desired scenes in detail and highlighted the manuscript pages to which the artist would need to refer. Some artists read the manuscripts, and some don't. Some prefer to choose their own scenes, and some prefer to work from prescribed ones. Practices differ at different houses, but however the jacket art is done, it will be Annabelle's responsibility to approve the art and Joanna's job to check the sketches to be sure all the details are correct. Sometimes a sketch will be sent to the author; often it is not. Usually, the first the author sees of the jacket for his book is the proof.

A writer may dislike the jacket art for his book because it doesn't match his mental image of the scene and characters. But an artist is hired to do an artistic interpretation that will entice a reader to pick up the book. If Gus, an unknown writer, hates the art, there's not much he or his agent can do about it. Long ago, at Crowell-Collier Press, when I was fussing over the type layout on a jacket proof and asked that it be changed, Janet Schulman, the vice president, asked, "Will it sell one more copy of the book if we spend the money to make that change?" I had to agree the change was not worth the cost. In the years to come, I kept that question in mind and asked it of myself—and others—for the rest of my career.

However, if a serious *editorial* error has occurred, the writer should insist it be corrected. Once, for example, the jacket flap for a novel said that the protagonist was seeing a *psychiatrist*. The author telephoned immediately to say no, the protagonist was seeing a *psychologist*. That was a relatively simple error to correct because it involved setting only a few lines of type and correcting the black plate. (Jackets are printed in four colors, and each color has its own "plate," which, when combined with the other three—red, yellow, and blue—gives the illusion of full color.)

Another time an author had described the protagonist as having short, curly red hair, but the artist had painted her with long, curly black hair. The author insisted on having the art changed. The artist, however, refused to correct the hairstyle unless the publisher paid him to hire another model. (He also said the girl looked better with long hair!) The publisher, who had to pay for making four new color plates, said it could not absorb the cost of a model as well. The artist finally agreed to paint over the black with red, so that the heroine ended up with rusty long hair. The author was so angry she wrote an article, which appeared in a writers' magazine, complaining that the publisher had not been sensitive to her book. In truth, the editorial department had supported her wish, but it was the production department, art director, and artist who'd dug in their heels because of the cost.

I never felt the same about that writer afterward because she saw me as her foe, not her ally. Yes, it was a stupid mistake on the artist's part. No one likes such mistakes, but sometimes the inevitable has to be accepted with grace. For the long term, authors and editors must strive to preserve a harmonious relationship, even though they will often disagree. Editors do their best to accommodate writers, but circumstances often make it impossible to satisfy everyone. Fortunately, Gus was happy with the jacket on his book.

Another factor influencing a purchase is the title. Imagine a reader walking into a bookstore or library where she sees hundreds and thousands of books. How does she select one? An attractive jacket may catch her eye, and she'll pick up the book and read the flap copy. If that intrigues her, she may read a page or two and decide the book is right for her to buy or take out of the library.

In other cases, the first thing she sees may be the spine, with only the title and author's name. Author recognition is important, because if a reader enjoyed a book by a particular writer, she's likely to want to read other books by him. If the writer is unknown, the title may invite a potential reader to pick up a particular book. I remember being fascinated as a child by a book title I pronounced "nerby," wondering what it meant. I took down the book and read a few pages, then put it back on the shelf. The title was actually *Nearby*, and the book itself didn't interest me.

Writing in the *Boston Globe*, Diane White suggested the best-seller of all best-sellers in the year 2000 would be *Golf Your Way to Fat-Free Fitness the Feng Shui Way with Harry Potter's Cat*. This would be a good crossover title, working in the juvenile as well as the adult market. The standard industry joke used to be that the most commercial title would include the words *doctor*, *dog*, and *Lincoln*. As far as I know, no one has ever written *Abraham Lincoln's Doctor's Dog*, although George Edward Stanley's *The Dog That Collected Baseball Cards* is in the right tradition. Two of my favorite children's titles are *The Celery Stalks at Midnight* and *The Girl of the Limberlost*, both of which, like "nerby," piqued my curiosity.

Not too long ago, it became trendy to put grades in titles, following the success of Judy Blume's *Tales of a Fourth-Grade Nothing*. Booksellers found it easy to sell books to aunts and uncles who wanted books for children in particular grades. Like all trends, this one faded, too, when so many "grade" books crowded the shelves that readers got bored.

When the title lacks spark and the author is unknown, the jacket illustration is triply important as a selling tool. Ideally, a book should have a memorable illustration that will appeal to everybody—sales reps, librarians, reviewers, booksellers, parents, and (let us not forget), the young prospective readers—which is not so easy to do as it sounds. Also ideally, the book should always be displayed face out so that this marvelous jacket is visible to all. Writers (and some editors) have been known to go into bookstores and libraries and shamelessly rearrange the shelves so that certain titles are face out instead of spine out. (Just don't get caught!)

The jacket proof for Gus's book was ready by the time the sales conference began, about four months before publication day. Most houses have presales conferences, where key staff members get a preview of the upcoming lists in all the divisions of the company. Sometimes a jacket meets with stiff resistance here and is changed before the actual sales conference. Once long ago, at Viking, an adult sports book for women showed a woman in a T-shirt, but only between her neck and waist. The women sales reps objected, and the male art director shook his head. "I thought it was a great concept," he said. A new jacket was ready for the sales conference six weeks later.

At the large companies, the sales conference lasts about a week and is often held at an out-of-town resort so the reps and head office staff can relax. Smaller companies will hold their conferences either at the home office or at a local hotel. The atmosphere is casual but businesslike. All the reps attend and listen to the editors present the new lists.

Months earlier, Annabelle and Joanna had written the tip sheet, full of information about Gus and his book. Accompanied by full-color photos of the jackets, the tip sheets for all the new books had been collected in a massive loose-leaf notebook that was handed out to each sales rep as part of the sales kit. Bound galleys of the books and color proofs of picture books were also in the sales kit, along with the publisher's catalog and other promotional material.

When it was her turn to speak at the conference, Annabelle enthusiastically presented the books she was responsible for. The reps made notes on their tip sheets while she spoke, keeping one eye on slides of the jackets, which were projected on a screen in front of the audience. This was the first time most of the reps had heard of Gus's book.

The marketing people then explained the marketing plans for all the books. At some publishers, these plans include ads, author tours, posters, bookmarks, and other giveaways. Children's publishers have small advertising and promotion budgets, so most new books get only a mention in list ads in the professional media. Later, at dinner, the reps and editors discussed the books and got to know one another.

As soon as the conference was over, the reps would go to their sales territories all over the United States and Canada, where they'd call on wholesalers and individual bookstores. A rep has only a short time to present a long list of books to each prospective buyer, and the stores do not buy every book on a publisher's list. By the time the rep gets around to the children's books, the buyer may limit herself to picture books and the occasional hardcover novel by a best-selling writer. Those stores that have separate children's buyers will be more adventurous. The wholesalers take copies of almost everything, since they supply libraries as well as stores.

In the last ten years, publishers have had to give special attention to the buyers for the superstore chains like Barnes & Noble and Borders, who place big orders when they like a book and no order at all when they don't. The chain stores are especially important to the success of picture books and "merchandise" books—those that come with a doll or game or are watered-down texts of classics such as the Little House books. They buy hardcover novels only by Newbery Medal winners and a handful of best-selling juvenile writers.

As publication day approached, like most new writers, Gus was surprised to find out how little promotional help Upstart was giving his book. When he asked his editor, Annabelle Jones, about the advertising budget, she laughed. "Budget? There's no advertising budget." She explained that after his book appeared in the catalog and in a few list ads (buried among two dozen other titles) in professional media, that was it for print advertising, except for reviews. Upstart was generous with review copies; it sent 500 copies of each book to reviewers and library systems around the country. That was in addition to the select list of influential reviewers who'd received preliminary bound galleys well before publication date. Some publishers send only selected titles to the majority of reviewers, promoting the books they think will sell the best; therefore many books never even get to the reviewer's desk. (This is apparently a cost-cutting measure.) The only way for a writer to know whether his book went to a specific reviewer is to ask the marketing department.

Leonard Marcus, a contributing editor and book reviewer for

Parenting magazine, told me that some writers personally send him their books for review, which he regards as a waste of time and money. He reads all the publishers' catalogs—especially from small presses—and will request a book that interests him if the publisher has failed to send it to him. More often than not, he's already received a copy from the publisher, so nothing is gained for the writer. If a writer tells Marcus how wonderful the book is, that doesn't help, because as a reviewer he makes up his own mind. "That's my job," he said.

There's a difference between making someone a victim of a bad review and being honest about whether the writer achieved his purpose. The reviewer is charged with the responsibility of giving his reasons for his opinions. In that way the reviewer can be judged by the reader, which makes it fair. Nothing gives me more pleasure than to discover a new writer or illustrator and to call attention to his work.

The reviews Annabelle and Joanna sent Gus were favorable for the most part. Some media, like *Horn Book* and *Booklist*, review only books they recommend, preferring not to run unfavorable reviews. Some review almost every book published, and one reviewer of Gus's book was especially cruel. Gus wanted to write to the reviewer, but Julia, his agent, dissuaded him. "You'll only alienate that reviewer if you complain," she said. "Let it go." Gus let it go, but he never forgot the nasty words of that review.

Then Gus received a pleasant surprise that (almost) made up for the nasty review. The Upstart publicity department had sent *Five by the Sea* to award committees all over the country, most especially to the state library or reading associations that award state prizes. Groups in Iowa, Utah, Tennessee, and other states draw up master lists of books for the children in their states to read and vote on. *Five by the Sea* was selected for the Texas master list, as a potential winner of the Bluebonnet Award. Not only was this a boost to Gus's ego, but it meant substantial sales, since every school library in Texas had to buy the book for the children to read.

The marketing department also sent *Five by the Sea* to many other groups for consideration. Some of the best-known accolades a book can receive are the ones from the American Library Association such as the Newbery Medal, the Caldecott Medal, a Notable Book Award, or Best Book for Young Adults award. Others include the Coretta Scott King Award, the National Book Award, the *Boston Globe-Horn Book* Award, the SCBWI Golden Kite Award, the Christopher Award, a *New York Times* Ten Best-Illustrated Children's Books Award, and to be included on the *School Library Journal*'s "Best Books" list. The New York Public Library recommends books in its annual Books for the Teen-Age selection and 100 Books for Reading and Sharing list. The National Council of Social Studies and the National Council of Teachers of English also single out books for awards. Each award lends prestige to a book and puts its title out in front of prospective buyers, especially school and public libraries.

After reviews, the most important promotion a book can receive is to be featured at one of the many professional conferences held in the United States and other countries. The most important of these for a juvenile writer is the American Library Association (ALA), which holds a working meeting in January (midwinter) and a mammoth annual conference at the end of June, where as many as fifteen thousand people may attend. The American Booksellers' BookExpo America (BEA) holds its meeting for booksellers around Memorial Day. Other important conferences are held during the year by such groups as the International Reading Association (IRA), which holds meetings in the United States and abroad in May and also has state meetings for teachers; the National Council of Teachers of English (NCTE) in November; and state meetings of local library associations, such as, in April, the Texas Library Association (TLA) and, in September, the New England Library Association (NELA). The Children's Book Fair in Bologna, Italy, in April presents an opportunity to sell rights to foreign publishers, as does the autumn Frankfurt Book Fair in Germany, where the foreign rights to American books are sold to foreign publishers.

Whether it's a book fair held in Europe or a BEA, ALA, or a state library association conference, publishers set up booths. Books are on display, and representatives from the publishers stand and talk with potential buyers, showing off the wares. A potential buyer may come up and ask for a certain type of book, and the publisher's rep will show him what she has.

Held at convention centers in cities like Atlanta, Chicago,

Dallas, Los Angeles, New Orleans, New York, Philadelphia, San Francisco, or Washington, the ALA conferences feature aisles full of booths of books and library equipment, from computers to furniture. The exhibition floor is open to the public for a moderate charge. If a writer can attend an ALA conference, he will find it of immense interest and value.

Librarians representing major library systems and small ones dutifully go from booth to booth, examining the new books on display. Publishers provide tons of giveaways having to do with the new books, from author biographies and bookmarks to posters and shopping bags—and sometimes free paperbacks and advance copies of new hardcover titles. Authors and illustrators stand or sit behind tables to autograph their new books, which are available for purchase at a discount. In some cases the lines have hundreds of people; in others, the publishers' representatives invite passersby to meet the signer, especially when the signer is a virtually unknown author.

A great deal of entertaining takes place, especially of authors and illustrators with the members of the various award-giving committees of the ALA, such as the Newbery, Caldecott, Notable Book, and the Young Adult Services Division committees. This gives publishers and librarians (many of whom head state or municipal library systems) a chance to talk about books and authors in relaxed surroundings.

Although it is smaller, the midwinter ALA conference is as important as the summer one. Throughout the year, committee members have been reading and discussing the new books. At the conferences, they get together to go over the lists and make preliminary nominations for the prizes. But it's at midwinter that final decisions are reached and editors told the results. The editors of prizewinning books race for the telephones to call their authors or illustrators with the news, sometimes at four in the morning.

Winning any award makes the publisher and the author happy. It will also influence sales by bringing the book to the attention of people, which may be the first step to a bigger award for another book by that author later. The Newbery and Caldecott Medals are formally presented at a gala dinner during the summer ALA conference.

Even without winning an award, a writer may begin to get invitations to speak at schools or before library groups or other writers. As time goes on, her fame grows, and she can begin to ask for fees ranging from as little as $50 to $1,000 or more. Many writers have enhanced their careers substantially—and their incomes—by going on the road.

Another joy for the writer is to receive mail, especially from children. Some receive so much mail, they need a secretary to handle it. Others ask publicity departments to send back a form letter, especially to children who are writing and asking for information for a book report. The most common questions children ask are: "How much money do you make?" and "How long did it take you to write the book?" Have your answers ready. It's a great honor to receive a personal letter from a child.

Unfortunately, a number of self-styled moral guardians are also liable to write regarding material they consider offensive, material ranging from the use of street language to "controversial" subject matter, usually dealing with sex or religion. In addition, during the last thirty years or so, hundreds of local, state, and national groups descended on schools and libraries nationwide, demanding that certain books be banned.

It is easy to forget that literature *should* show the truth about people and life. Let us not forget what Leo Tolstoy said: "If a country has a great writer—this is like having another government." Artists have a valuable, unique vision of reality that is often at odds with community standards. If your book is attacked, get in touch with your editor. She will lend you moral support and suggest ways you can get help from various organizations, including the Committee on Intellectual Freedom of the ALA and the National Coalition against Censorship. As a writer, you *must* get involved in protecting your First Amendment rights, or we will all lose them. If the case against your book is made public, you're ahead of the game, because most people are against self-appointed censors. And you won't be alone. Every September the ALA holds its "Banned Book Week," when books for adults and children that have been censored are displayed in libraries around the country. It's worth taking a look at the display and trying to figure out why a particular book was banned.

Gus didn't want his book to get the kind of attention a banned book gets. On the other hand, he did want it to get *some* attention. He brought up the matter the next time he attended his writers' group. The members agreed that publisher publicity was virtually useless, other than in getting reviews. "You've got to do it yourself," one writer said, and she gave him some tips. Others joined in, and before he knew it, Gus had a marketing plan, which will be described in the next chapter.

15

Who Needs a Rabbit's Foot?

◆

WHAT YOU CAN DO TO MARKET YOUR BOOK

Mañana is often the busiest day of the week.
—Spanish proverb

It's not so easy for Peter Rabbit to get into Mr. McGregor's garden any longer, as we've seen. While Peter stares at his foot, wondering what to do, remember the adage "You make your own luck." It's never too early to start thinking about what you can do to promote your book. The word *publish* derives from *publicare*, "to make public," and having a manuscript accepted for publication is only part of the endeavor; it is vitally important to tell the world the book exists.

While you were still writing, you should have been composing a list of individuals, media contacts, and key personnel at organizations who might have a special interest in reading your book, especially if it's nonfiction or fiction dealing with a topic that would be of interest to them. Don't overlook neighborhood "throwaway" papers and even newspapers in places you mentioned in your book. The publisher will send your book for review to the standard media such as *Booklist*, the *School Library Journal*, *Horn Book*, the *New York Times*, and other major newspapers. You can help the publisher by finding media that are less well known.

Around the time you sign the contract, your editor will send you a printed form to fill out. This is the publisher's biographical questionnaire. If you did not get one, ask your editor to send a copy. This is probably the most important part of your marketing plan, and you can fill in some of the answers even before you finish your manuscript and arrange to have your picture taken.

✦ The Biographical Questionnaire ✦

Your publisher will send you a biographical questionnaire similar to the one that Upstart Books sends to its authors (see below). Make a photocopy of the questionnaire from your publisher, fill in what corresponds to Section A below, and return it with your contract or soon thereafter. This is the information that will appear on the jacket flap or tip sheet. (By the way, you don't have to supply the year of your birth if you'd rather not.) Tell your editor that you will send in Section B later.

During the next few months, research the information you will need for Section B. The publicity department will not look up names, addresses, and telephone numbers for you! This research is time-consuming, but it will ensure that news of your book—or copies of the book—will get to people who can help you promote it. When you are finished, fill in Section B and send it to your editor for forwarding to the publicity department.

Upstart Books: Biographical Questionnaire

SECTION A

Author's Name: Date:

Title of Book:

Home address and phone:

Business address and phone:

Date and place of birth: citizenship:

Schools attended/degrees (with dates):

Titles of previous books (including publishers and publication dates):

Honors and awards received:

Besides writing or illustrating, what other work have you done or are you doing now?

Other places you have lived or traveled:

Your interests, activities, hobbies, pets:

Describe your book, mentioning points to emphasize in promotion.

Let us know about books that are comparable or competitive with yours.

Who is the audience for this book?

How did you come to write this book? An anecdote about the process of writing it might be used in promotion.

SECTION B

Please list prominent people (scholars, reviewers, well-known professionals) who might be helpful in promoting your book. Please indicate with an asterisk those you know personally and include addresses.

Please provide names and addresses of organizations or associations of which you are a member or which you feel will have a special interest in your book.

Copies of your book will be sent to children's book review media and to periodicals that will reach readers interested in your subject. Please list professional periodicals, college papers, alumni magazines, special-interest media, and local newspapers that should also receive information on your book, with address and name of contact person if possible.

Please list localities where you are known and where local publicity might be arranged.

Please provide names and addresses of your local bookstores (please mark with an asterisk those where you are known personally).

Please list names and addresses of local libraries and librarians.

Are you available for radio, TV, or press interviews if the opportunity arises (yes/no)?

Will you speak to audiences of children (yes/no)? Adults (yes/no)? Large groups (yes/no)? Small groups (yes/no)?

If you have speaking engagements planned for the next six months, please list them, mentioning date, place, and contact.

You don't need a formal studio photograph, but you should always provide your publisher with a photo showing you as you would like to be perceived. Ask friends with good cameras to take lots of pictures of you. You don't have to go so far as some adult novelists do and dress in costumes that match the books! The effect of the pose you select should be relaxed and personal, yet dignified. The photo I sent my publisher when *Boats for Bedtime* was published had boats in the background, for example. On the other hand, try to avoid showing a blackboard or classroom behind you, unless you want young readers to see you as a teacher. When you send the photograph to your publisher, include the photographer's name as a credit. The photograph may or may not appear on the finished book; picture books almost never have author or illustrator photos. Your publisher needs to have a good photograph to give to various people along the publicity trail.

Important people—including writers, of course—may provide advance praise for your book. When you submit your final manuscript, you should give likely names *and addresses* to your editor, who will send out a manuscript early on in the publishing process for comments that can be used in catalog copy, ads, and on jacket proofs.

Although marketing plays an important role in the publishing process, many marketing departments are low on staff, especially for the grunt work. Someone has to type all those labels, insert books into padded bags, and see they get mailed to library acquisition departments and reviewers. One library promotion manager I knew told me she did all this work herself because she did not have an assistant. This is not unusual. Therefore, the marketing people can give the writer only limited help. Whatever a writer can do to aid the marketing department will be considered and done if possible, beginning with sending your book out to the right people.

Every writer needs a printed biography. Gus found out that most publishers provide biographical brochures only for their "A" authors—the ones whose books they've been publishing the longest or are the best selling. Now that the questionnaire had helped him organize his personal information, he wrote his autobiography. Pretending he was the publicist and using the third person he wrote: "As one of five children, Gus Casey has long wanted to write about the dynamics of a large family." It felt strange at first to write about himself, but it became easier and even enjoyable as he wrote about his favorite subject.

Writers can pick up complimentary author bios at conferences and use them as prototypes or can ask their publisher to send samples from its files. Everyone enjoys reading why a person wrote a particular book, so be sure to include that story in your bio. If you or a friend are proficient with desktop publishing, print out this bio with a photograph of yourself. At the least, do a "quick and dirty" bio—a photocopy on colored paper of your typed version. It will come in handy. If you have a Web site, be sure to include the address on the bio. If you are uncomfortable about supplying your home address and telephone number to strangers, have all your mail sent to your publisher or agent for forwarding to you. As for providing your E-mail address, that's up to you.

When you have either bound galleys (which many publishers use as review copies), a jacket proof—ask your editor if you can have extra copies—the printed catalog, or folded and gathered sheets of a picture book, you can visit your local bookstores and libraries to show them the material and introduce yourself. At that time you can drop off one of your bios or just a photocopy of the page featuring your book in the catalog. If this is your first book, don't expect an invitation to sign books at the store. You are not yet a draw. You might nevertheless offer to sign copies of your book later for the store to have on hand. Many bookstores have special bins for autographed copies.

Libraries also welcome authors who offer to sign copies already on the shelves. If you plan to travel to another part of the country, mention it to the publicist. It may be possible for her to arrange school or library visits at your destination. Even if she doesn't, it's exhilarating to drop into a library or bookstore in a far-off city and find your books there. Take the time to chat with the staff, who will usually be delighted to meet you.

Another possibility is to arrange an "event," which librarians, store owners, or event managers would support, once the book is published. (It is pointless to tout your book to the public before bookstores have copies; the public has a short memory.) You could, for example, suggest reading your picture book aloud during a story hour and give away autographed bios as souvenirs. People love freebies. One writer went to the expense of printing bookmarks she had designed. The bookmark contained an illustration, some text, and information about where her book might be obtained. If you are an illustrator, you could draw pictures and present them—or copies—to the audience. If your book is nonfiction, you could do a short talk on the subject and invite questions and answers from the audience.

At bookstores, the idea is to sell your books, so a pile of them should be handily displayed with a store employee to help the buyers. Don't be disappointed if the books don't fly out the store or the number of people requesting your autograph is small. That is to be expected. Remain gracious and friendly, without holding up the line (if there is one). Open the book to the title page and ask to whom the book should be inscribed; then add a greeting, your signature, and date. Look up, smile, and make eye contact. A few seconds of closeness means a great deal to your readers.

It is not good form for a writer to sell her own books; that is, handle the money. If necessary, press a friend into service for you. It's part of the image. A writer also should not carry her books or boxes of them where people can see her. Consider yourself a presence, a personage, not a cashier or messenger!

Always maintain a healthy supply of your books in the trunk of your car or in an extra suitcase. It doesn't hurt to create a couple of small posters, each featuring a jacket proof and your name, in case your sponsor forgets to provide a suitable announcement. One poster should be for the tabletop where you will be signing or standing. The other is for tacking up (with low-tack tape or push-pins, which you also have in your suitcase).

One morning long ago, as I walked up Madison Avenue from the subway to my office at the Viking Press, I spotted a book on display in the window of a custom tailor. Curious, I took a closer look. That was the first time I saw the children's classic, *A Day No Pigs Would Die* by Robert Newton Peck. At that time Peck was working in advertising and was probably a customer of that tailor. How many other people walking up Madison Avenue—the heart of advertising country—saw Peck's book? If you know of any local merchants who'd be happy to have your book on display, don't hesitate to offer them an autographed copy for that purpose. They are not to sell the book—after all, bookstores don't sell clothes— but simply to show it off for a few months, after which it is their property. I carry a copy of my latest book on the dashboard of my car to be seen wherever I go. Publicity is precious!

See whether your publisher will agree to printing an order form or flyer for your book—or do it yourself with the publisher's approval. You can distribute these among your acquaintances and set them out at writers' conferences so that people will have an easy time of getting your book directly from your publisher. The piece of paper will later remind them of your book, and they'll have all the necessary ordering information, including the correct title and spelling of your name.

Family members expect free copies from you, so it may not be a bad idea to let them have an order form, too. You must let them know, gracefully, that you have to pay for the books once your supply of author's copies is gone. Depending on your relationships with different family members, you can also express the hope that they will get a copy of the book from their local bookstore.

A dear friend of mine in Virginia bought a copy of *Boats for Bedtime* through her children's bookstore. The owner had not known about the book. She ordered a dozen or so and displayed them face out. Later, she told my friend that the book was selling well, especially to people looking for books for boys. There is nothing like the personal touch.

Dozens of writers have supplemented their incomes with school visits and other presentations. In addition to your author bio, print up a brochure about your availability for school visits. Sometimes the invitation to speak comes via your publisher, but you can seek out opportunities yourself as well. Stay on good terms with your publisher's publicity department. For example, be sure to notify the staff six weeks in advance of a speaking engagement you have set up so that they may inform local media and book-stores of your appearance and to ensure books will be available for you to sign. Even so, books may not arrive in time, so in an emer-gency—only—you can use the supply you bring with you. Ac-cording to some contracts, you are not supposed to sell your own books, especially at a discount. But what is a writer to do when, for whatever reason, the books don't arrive? It's better to be prepared for this contingency than to sit and moan.

If you've not spoken in public before, learn how to. The more public speaking you do, the easier it gets. Practice on friends and family, then approach local schools and libraries and offer to speak or read your work. While you are learning, the experience is worth more than a speaker's fee. It should not be long, however, before you begin to charge for travel expenses and finally, for speaking. In my own experience, speaking at a nearby school takes at least three days out of my work life. The first is the day I prepare my program. The second is the day of the speech. The third day is re-covery. Consider this when you set your fees, which should be on a sliding scale from, say, $100 to $3,000 if you are famous. Your writer friends or the publicity associate at your publisher will help you set a fee schedule. Many schools have funds to pay for speak-ers, and it's only just that you be paid.

Finally, a great number of writers have their own Web sites.

You can hire someone to design and build one for you, or you can try your hand at creating your own, using software you can buy. The Web site should provide some information about you and perhaps some samples from your book. While your book is in print, be sure to mention your publisher and its marketing department as the source for services such as review copies and public appearances. This is what they do best, and you may find that trying to handle this on your own will be overwhelming. So that a potential buyer can order the book directly, include the name and address of your publisher, its toll-free order number, the ISBN, and price.

Before your book is out of print (OP) and rights have reverted to you, your publisher will give you the opportunity to buy up surplus copies at a generous discount. Once the book is officially OP, you can advertise and sell your book through your Web site. You will be responsible for warehousing, bookkeeping, shipping, and handling. Some companies on-line offer to handle OP books for authors for a commission.

To my delight, when I visited Powell's bookstore in Portland, Oregon, copies of my OP books were listed on the store computer. Powell's, and other stores, buy used books and shelve them cheek-by-jowl with virgin copies, so the buyer often has a choice of editions.

As long as your book is available to purchasers, keep looking for opportunities to present it. How many times have I watched a breaking news event and known of a book I'd edited that would be relevant. If you're the author of such a book, send it immediately, with a letter, to a newspaper, magazine, or other possible source that would welcome it. You might even manage to get a speaking engagement if you show such initiative. It doesn't matter whether you make money from these efforts. You are building a career, and keeping your name and your work, even if it's out of print, in front of the public is vital.

The great American poet Emily Dickinson (1830–86) once wrote, "There is no frigate like a book / To take us lands away. . . . [it is a] chariot that bears a human soul." But of her two thousand poems, only two were published in her lifetime. Today, in this information age, any writer can see her work published in some form. It is through publication that our human souls will sail on to readers today and to future generations. Books make thoughts, feelings, and stories permanent. They are small and can travel anywhere. They are one of the miracles of humanity, for only people can write and read books. They are also essential to a civilized, advanced society. Tyrants and reactionaries attack books and ideas before they attack people—a society "without a head," as the writer Edward Fenton once said, is easy to subjugate.

Over 3 billion books are printed each year in the United States, and almost four thousand titles are juvenile books. Therefore, if you want to write—and publish—books for children, the opportunities are there, and the rewards can be enormous. Many firms still operate with grace and culture, so you will be treated well if you are lucky. Research the market, do your networking, and present your work as professionally as possible.

A number of children's book publishers have come into existence since 1995 to publish the books the cosmodemonic firms won't touch. This number will increase. Just as fast-food restaurants did not cause the demise of family-owned restaurants, the cosmodemonic publishers will never be the only game in town. Small firms can make enough money to survive. The big firms are top-heavy, especially in the high-priced executive suites, where big salaries do not guarantee success for anyone for long. Innovative, successful books are coming from the smallest publishers, imprints, and packagers. Keep up with your research and target the new houses for your work.

It's easy to feel depressed or cynical about the children's market today, but if, like Gus, you want to write for children—and have talent—you will get your work published because there are still editors and houses who want good books that will sell reasonably well. Greed hasn't won, not by a long shot.

A while ago, I attended a program in the library at a local school. On the shelves I saw many old friends, books I'd edited, artwork I'd chosen, copy I'd written. It was a good feeling. And then I heard a dozen children give reports based on books they'd read. That was an even better feeling.

Writing is a lonely, painful, frustrating occupation. It may or may not earn you enough money to live on. Yet we persist because human beings are creative animals who want to transmit ideas. As George Frideric Handel said after the first London performance of *Messiah* in 1743, "I should be sorry . . . if I have only succeeded in entertaining them; I wished to make them better."

APPENDIX

Important Addresses

American Book Producers Association
160 Fifth Avenue
New York, NY 10010
www.abpaonline.org

The Children's Book Council
12 West Thirty-seventh Street, 2nd floor
New York, NY 10018
www.cbcbooks.org

Committee on Intellectual Freedom
American Library Association
50 East Huron Street
Chicago, IL 60611
www.ala.org/alaorg/oif/if/brochure.html

Institute of Children's Literature
93 Long Ridge Road
West Redding, CT 06896-0812
www.childrenswriter.com

National Coalition Against Censorship
275 Seventh Avenue
New York, NY 10001
www.ncac.org

National Writers Union
National Office
13 University Place
New York, NY 10003
www.nwu.org

Society of Children's Book Writers & Illustrators
8271 Beverly Boulevard
Los Angeles, CA 90048
www.scbwi.org

PUBLICATIONS

Booklist
50 East Huron Street
Chicago, IL 60611
www.ala.org/booklist/index.html

Appendix: Important Addresses

The Horn Book
14 Beacon Street
Boston, MA 02108
www.hbook.com

Publishers Weekly
245 West Seventeenth Street
New York, NY 10011
www.publishersweekly.com

School Library Journal
245 West Seventeenth Street
New York, NY 10011
www.slj.com

The Writer
120 Boylston Street
Boston, MA 02116
www.channel1.com/the writer

Writer's Digest
1507 Dana Avenue
Cincinnati, OH 45207
www.writersdigest.com

SUGGESTIONS FOR
FURTHER READING

The following list is by no means a complete one, but it will serve as an introduction to literature, publishing, and writing for children. Many of the titles below have their own lists of suggested books.

Aldiss, Brian W., with David Wingrove. *Trillion Year Spree: The History of Science Fiction.* New York: Atheneum, 1986; Avon Books, 1988.

Applebaum, Judith. *How to Get Happily Published.* New York: Harper Perennial, 1998.

Applebaum, Judith, and Florence Janovic. *The Writer's Workbook: A Full and Friendly Guide to Boosting Your Book's Sales.* Wainscott, N.Y.: Pushcart Press, 1991.

Benét, William Rose, et al., eds. *Benét's Reader's Encyclopedia.* 3d ed. New York: Harper & Row, 1987.

Burack, Sylvia K., ed. *The Writer's Handbook.* Boston: The Writer, 1999.

Cart, Michael. *From Romance to Realism: Fifty Years of Growth and Change in Young Adult Literature.* New York: HarperCollins, 1996.

The Chicago Manual of Style: For Writers, Editors, and Publishers. Chicago: University of Chicago Press, 1993.

Cooke, Alistair, ed. *The Vintage Mencken*. New York: Vintage Books, 1956.

Crawford, Tad. *Business and Legal Forms for Authors and Self-Publishers*. New York: Allworth Press, 2000.

Fowler, H. W. *A Dictionary of Modern English Usage*. New York: Oxford University Press, 1983.

Gilman, Mary Louise. *One Word, Two Words, Hyphenated?* National Court Reporter Association, 1998.

Goldberg, Natalie. *Writing Down the Bones: Freeing the Writer Within*. Boston: Shambala Publications, 1986.

Healy, Jane M. *Endangered Minds: Why Our Children Don't Think*. New York: Simon & Schuster, 1990.

Jenkinson, Edward B. *Censors in the Classroom: The Mind Benders*. Carbondale and Edwardsville, Ill.: Southern Illinois University Press, 1979.

Lamott, Anne. *Bird by Bird: Some Instructions on Writing and Life*. New York: Pantheon Books, 1994; Doubleday Anchor Books, 1995.

McCrum, Robert, William Cran, and Robert MacNeil. *The Story of English*. New York: Viking Penguin, 1986.

Marcus, Leonard S., ed. *Dear Genius: The Letters of Ursula Nordstrom*. New York: HarperCollins, 1998.

Merriam-Webster's Collegiate Dictionary. Springfield, Mass.: Merriam-Webster, 1998.

Opie, Robert, Iona Opie, and Brian Alderson. *The Treasures of Childhood: Books, Toys, and Games from the Opie Collection*. New York: Arcade, 1989.

Orwell, George. *A Collection of Essays*. Garden City, N.Y.: Doubleday, 1954.

Phillips, Kathleen C. *How to Write A Story*. New York: Franklin Watts, 1995.

Polking, Kirk, et al., eds. *Writer's Encyclopedia*. Cincinnati: Writer's Digest Books, 1996.

Postman, Neil. *The Disappearance of Childhood*. New York: Dell, 1982.

Raab, Susan Salzman. *An Author's Guide to Children's Book Promotion*. Chappaqua, N.Y.: Raab Associates, 1999.

Seuling, Barbara. *How to Write a Children's Book and Get It Published*. New York: Scribner's, 1991.

Shulevitz, Uri. *Writing with Pictures: How to Write and Illustrate Children's Books*. New York: Watson-Guptill, 1985.

Silvey, Anita, ed. *Children's Books and Their Creators*. Boston: Houghton Mifflin, 1995.

Strunk, William, Jr. *The Elements of Style*. New York: Macmillan, 1959.

Townsend, John Rowe. *Written for Children: An Outline of English-language Children's Literature*. New York: Lippincott, 1983.

Webster's Dictionary of English Usage. Springfield, Mass.: Merriam-Webster, 1993.

Webster's New Dictionary of Synonyms: A Dictionary of Discriminated Synonyms with Antonyms and Analogous and Contrasted Words. Springfield, Mass.: Merriam-Webster, 1994.

INDEX

Index

Index

Index

Index

Index

Index